TRUTH FOR TODAY
COMMENTARY

EDDIE CLOER, D.MIN.

GENERAL EDITOR

TRUTH FOR TODAY
COMMENTARY

AN EXEGESIS & APPLICATION OF THE HOLY SCRIPTURES

THE LIFE OF CHRIST, 1
A SUPPLEMENT

DAVID L. ROPER

RESOURCE □
PUBLICATIONS
2205 S. Benton
Searcy, AR 72143

Truth for Today Commentary
The Life of Christ, 1
Copyright © 2003 by Resource Publications
2205 S. Benton, Searcy, AR 72143

2nd printing, 2010

ISBN: 978-0-945441-45-8

CONTENTS

APPLICATION

Editor's Preface

This volume is Part 1 of a two-part study of the life of Christ, "a supplement" to the series of commentaries on the Holy Scriptures that will eventually cover every book in God's divine revelation to us. This special study of Christ's life is not intended to replace thorough commentaries on Matthew, Mark, Luke, and John that are scheduled to be released later. Its purpose is to provide a continuous treatment of our Lord's life so that one can study straight through His life without much interruption.

The author of this study of the sacred life of Christ does not intend for his comments to be regarded as infallible; he knows that he is subject to mistakes, as is everyone else. Consequently, we must admit at the start that perfection is beyond our reach. "The Life of Christ" is not perfect, and no such study ever will be. In writing a harmony of the Gospels, the author only wishes to share with others the fruits of his lifelong study of the Scriptures. We hope that this sharing will aid and encourage the reader in his or her pursuit of the knowledge of God as revealed in the inspired Scriptures.

I have known David Roper for many years. He has proven himself to be one of God's finest servants. Many have read and reread his studies of Acts and Revelation, the first volumes of the commentary series, and have found them to be faithful studies of those books. We believe that this study of the life of Jesus will bring anyone who reads it to a better understanding of why Jesus came to the earth, what He did while here, and the blessings His life brought.

So far as we know, scholars of the church have not printed a harmony of the Gospels since the days of J. W. McGarvey. Although we would not call this treatment of the life of Jesus a true harmony of the Gospels, it does have that flavor and will be very helpful in understanding His earthly life and ministry. We can leave to future generations no finer legacy than presentations on every deed and speech of the life of our Lord, resulting from our faithful scholarship and responsible handling of the Scriptures.

The churches of Christ have never completed a multi-authored commentary series on the entire Bible. Surely, the time for producing such a set is here. A project of this magnitude requires many faithful laborers, much time, and great persistence. Let us join together, as brothers and sisters bought by Christ's blood, and work together until the task is completed.

May we all, through a diligent study of God's Word, walk in God's will for us and for the world.

EDDIE CLOER
General Editor

ABBREVIATIONS

OLD TESTAMENT

Genesis	Gen.	Ecclesiastes	Eccles.
Exodus	Ex.	Song of Solomon	Song
Leviticus	Lev.	Isaiah	Is.
Numbers	Num.	Jeremiah	Jer.
Deuteronomy	Deut.	Lamentations	Lam.
Joshua	Josh.	Ezekiel	Ezek.
Judges	Judg.	Daniel	Dan.
Ruth	Ruth	Hosea	Hos.
1 Samuel	1 Sam.	Joel	Joel
2 Samuel	2 Sam.	Amos	Amos
1 Kings	1 Kings	Obadiah	Obad.
2 Kings	2 Kings	Jonah	Jon.
1 Chronicles	1 Chron.	Micah	Mic.
2 Chronicles	2 Chron.	Nahum	Nahum
Ezra	Ezra	Habakkuk	Hab.
Nehemiah	Neh.	Zephaniah	Zeph.
Esther	Esther	Haggai	Hag.
Job	Job	Zechariah	Zech.
Psalms	Ps.	Malachi	Mal.
Proverbs	Prov.		

NEW TESTAMENT

Matthew	Mt.	1 Timothy	1 Tim.
Mark	Mk.	2 Timothy	2 Tim.
Luke	Lk.	Titus	Tit.
John	Jn.	Philemon	Philem.
Acts	Acts	Hebrews	Heb.
Romans	Rom.	James	Jas.
1 Corinthians	1 Cor.	1 Peter	1 Pet.
2 Corinthians	2 Cor.	2 Peter	2 Pet.
Galatians	Gal.	1 John	1 Jn.
Ephesians	Eph.	2 John	2 Jn.
Philippians	Phil.	3 John	3 Jn.
Colossians	Col.	Jude	Jude
1 Thessalonians	1 Thess.	Revelation	Rev.
2 Thessalonians	2 Thess.		

AB   Amplified Bible

ASV   American Standard Version

KJV   King James Version

LB   Living Bible

NASB   New American Standard Bible

NCV   New Century Version

NIV   New International Version

NLT   New Living Translation

RSV   Revised Standard Version

INTRODUCTION

THE FOUR GOSPEL ACCOUNTS

We are beginning a study of the life of Jesus Christ as told in the first four books of the New Testament, each of which is named after its author:

Matthew—a former tax collector and an apostle of Jesus.

Mark—the John Mark of the Book of Acts, a young preacher of the apostolic age.

Luke—Dr. Luke, who accompanied Paul on several of his missionary journeys, including the trip to Rome.

John—a former fisherman and the "beloved" apostle.

This study, as a kind of harmony of the Gospels, brings together the four accounts of His life into one story. Later, thorough commentaries will be issued on the Books of Matthew, Mark, Luke, and John individually.

Four Accounts of One Story

The Books of Matthew, Mark, Luke, and John are often called "the four Gospels," but actually they are *four accounts* of the one gospel. The term "Gospels" has been used to refer to the first four books of the New Testament since the second or third century.

The first three books are generally called "the synoptic

1

Gospels." "Synoptic" combines a Greek word for "together" with a word meaning "to see or view." "Synoptic" thus means "to view together." The first three books are designated "the synoptic Gospels" because they present similar views of Jesus. All of them were probably written before the destruction of Jerusalem in A.D. 70.

The Book of John is sometimes called "the autoptic [self-view] Gospel" because it takes a somewhat different approach than the other three. The word "autoptic" can also convey the idea of an eyewitness. John's account was probably written later than the first three, in the A.D. 90s.

Why Four Accounts?

Why did God give us four books that cover the same period of time and the same story? In the Scriptures, other periods of time are covered by more than one book (many events in 1 Sam. through 2 Kings are also reported in 1 and 2 Chron.), but to have four accounts of the same story is unusual.

In the early history of the church, men speculated as to why there were four accounts. One guess was that "four is the [symbolic] number of man." We do not know why God decided on this specific number, but the fact that He inspired multiple accounts indicates several truths:

(1) Four accounts show *how important* the story of Jesus is.

(2) Four accounts impress the need to *authenticate* the story of Jesus. Moses said that "on the evidence of *two or three* witnesses a matter shall be confirmed" (Deut. 19:15b; emphasis added). *Four* witnesses is even better.

(3) Four accounts reveal *the multifaceted nature* of Jesus. One writer could probably never do Him justice.

In the National Gallery in London there are three representations on a single canvas of Charles I. In one his head is turned to the right; in another, to the left; and in the center we find the full-face view. This is the story of this production. Van Dyck painted them for Bernini, the Roman sculptor, that he might by their help make a bust of the king. By combining the impressions so received,

Bernini would be better able to produce a "speaking" likeness. One view would not have been enough.

It may be true that the Gospels were intended to serve the very purpose of these portraits. Each presents a different aspect of our Lord's life on earth. Together we have the complete picture. He was a King, but He was the Perfect Servant, too. He was the Son of Man, but we must not forget He was the Son of God.[1]

Comparing the Four Accounts

All of the four accounts have the same basic purpose—to reveal Jesus—but each was written from a slightly different point of view, apparently appealing to a somewhat different audience. For an example of tailoring an account for different audiences, see the three accounts of the conversion of Paul in the Book of Acts: In Acts 9 the account was written for Luke's readers; in Acts 22 it was part of Paul's defense before Jews in Jerusalem; in Acts 26 it was part of Paul's sermon in Caesarea which was primarily directed to King Agrippa. Simon Kistemaker made this comment on the last two of these accounts: "From that same incident [his conversion], [Paul] wisely chose different words and emphasized different aspects in his effort to bring the gospel to each party. . . ."[2]

Regarding the four Gospel Accounts, Matthew was apparently writing primarily for the *Jews*. He quoted over one hundred Old Testament passages and used terms familiar to the Jews, such as "son of David" (Mt. 1:1). He presented Jesus as a King who came to set up His kingdom; the word "kingdom" appears fifty-five times in the book. He put special emphasis on Jesus as the Messiah and wrote of His teachings, His kingdom, and His authority.

Unlike Matthew, Mark seems to have written for a non-Jewish audience. He eliminated matters of little interest to Gentiles, such

[1]Henrietta C. Mears, *What the Bible Is All About* (Glendale, Calif.: Gospel Light Publications, 1966), 348.

[2]Simon Kistemaker, *New Testament Commentary: Exposition of the Acts of the Apostles* (Grand Rapids, Mich.: Baker Book House, 1990), 899.

as genealogies. When He mentioned Jewish tradition, He usually added an explanation. Many writers think that Mark was addressing a *Roman* audience; he sometimes used Latin phrases in stories where the other writers used Greek phrases. According to Clement of Alexandria (c. A.D. 150–215), Mark received a request from Christians at Rome to record the life of Christ as he had heard it from Peter.[3] Mark seems to have been more concerned with what Jesus *did* than with what He *taught*. He presented Jesus as a Servant, One who helped others (Mk. 10:45). He emphasized the miracles of Jesus because, in them, the Lord's love and care for people can be seen.

Like Mark, Luke apparently wrote for a non-Jewish audience. However, while Mark's account seems directed to the action-oriented Roman, Luke's account appears to have been written for the intellectual, the student. Many conclude that Luke had a *Greek* audience in mind. His account presents Jesus as "the Son of Man" (Lk. 19:10) and puts special emphasis on His perfect humanity.

John's account, which was probably written near the end of the first century, has its own special emphasis. Erroneous concepts had arisen regarding the nature of Jesus, causing confusion among *believers*. John presented Jesus as "the Son of God" (Jn. 20:31) and stressed His deity.

We could say that Matthew has special appeal today for the Bible student and Mark has special appeal for the average person, including businessmen, while Luke appeals especially to scholars, thinkers, idealists, and truth-seekers. On the other hand, John has been called "the universal Gospel," appealing to all people for all time.

Further, we could say that Matthew's purpose is to present Jesus as the *promised* Savior; Mark, the *powerful* Savior; Luke, the *perfect* Savior; and John, the *personal* Savior. As we make these distinctions, however, we must not lose sight of the fact that the ultimate purpose of each book is the same: *to bring all men to a saving knowledge of Jesus!*

---

[3]Clement *Fragments* 4.

What the Four Accounts Cover

The term "biography" is sometimes applied to the Gospel Accounts; but in the strict sense of the word, these four books are not biographies. Rather, they are "didactic narratives." ("Didactic" comes from a Greek word and basically means "teaching.") Here are a few reasons why the accounts cannot be classified as true biographies:

(1) They made no attempt to cover all of Jesus' life. The first thirty years are almost a blank, while over one-third of the text in the four accounts is concerned with a single event (Jesus' death). We have no record of any event in Jesus' life between ages twelve and thirty.

(2) Although the accounts basically use a chronological approach—birth, childhood, baptism, ministry, death, and resurrection—chronology was not always important to the writers. They often grouped together events to emphasize certain truths.

(3) None of the writers described the physical appearance of Jesus. What biographer ever failed to do that?

Since the four books are didactic narratives not overly concerned with chronology, it is not easy to fit the four accounts together into a single narrative (a "harmony"). However, there can be value in the attempt.

The synoptic accounts present basically the same material, while John's account mainly presents additional material. Even when covering the same time period, John presents different information than Matthew, Mark, and Luke. John's account omits the birth of Jesus, Jesus' baptism and temptation, the Sermon on the Mount, all the parables, the Transfiguration, the institution of the Lord's Supper, and the agony in Gethsemane—all of which are covered in the synoptic Gospels.

Other than the death, burial, and resurrection of Jesus, only a few events are mentioned in all four accounts. When all four books tell of an event, that is worth noting; that event must have special significance.

Variations in the Four Accounts

When one begins to fashion a harmony of the gospel, it is soon apparent that variations exist between accounts of the same event. How can these variations be explained? As noted earlier, in the Book of Acts Luke gave three accounts of the conversion of Saul (Acts 9; 22; 26). John Stott commented on this: "Our study of how a single author (Luke) tells the same story differently will help us understand how the three synoptic evangelists (Matthew, Mark and Luke) could also tell their same stories differently."[4]

In most cases, one account simply supplements another account. Consider the story of the anointing of Jesus at Bethany. In Matthew's account (Mt. 26:6–13), Jesus was in Bethany at the home of Simon the leper when an unnamed woman came with a container of precious perfume and anointed Jesus, which resulted in Jesus' disciples expressing their disapproval. Mark's account (Mk. 14:3–9) is much the same, but some details are added: The perfume was pure nard, the woman broke the container, and the perfume was worth three hundred denarii. ("Denarii" is the plural form of "denarius," which was equivalent to one day's wages for the common laborer.) John's account (Jn. 12:1–8) gives other details, including these: Jesus was at a banquet held in His honor; Martha was serving the meal; Lazarus was also a guest of honor; the woman who anointed Jesus was Mary, sister of Martha; and the one who started the criticism was Judas Iscariot. These details are obviously not contradictory, but rather are supplementary.

It has been noted that when witnesses give supplementary details, this does not discredit their testimony but rather establishes their veracity. Dr. Henry Van Dyke said,

> If four witnesses should appear before a judge to give an account of a certain event, and each should tell exactly the same story in the same words, the judge would probably conclude, not that their testimony was exceptionally valuable, but that the only event which was certain beyond a doubt was that they had agreed to tell the same story. But

---

[4]John R. W. Stott, *The Message of Acts: The Spirit, the Church & the World*, The Bible Speaks Today Series, ed. John R. W. Stott (Downers Grove, Ill.: Inter-Varsity Press, 1990), 380.

if each man had told what he had seen, as he had seen it, then the evidence would be credible. And when we read the four Gospels, is not that exactly what we find? The four men tell the same story each in his own way.[5]

In some cases, however, the details are not simply supplementary; instead, they are different. The order of events may not be the same, different personnel may be mentioned, or numbers may vary. For instance, note the story of Jesus healing one or more blind men near Jericho. In Matthew's account (Mt. 20:29–34), Jesus was *leaving* Jericho and *two* men were healed. In Luke's account (Lk. 18:35–43), Jesus was *approaching* Jericho and only *one* blind man is mentioned. In Mark's account (Mk. 10:46–52), only *one* blind man is healed (Bartimaeus). How do we explain differences such as these? Here are some possibilities:

(1) Some variations in details exist because of differences in the writers' emphases. In the above example, Luke put the spotlight on only one blind man, but that does not eliminate the possibility that two blind men were present and were healed.

(2) Differences in details may exist because the writers were recording similar events, but not the same event. F. LaGard Smith noted,

Sometimes it is . . . difficult to judge whether two very similar events actually occurred twice or whether there was only one such event which was recorded in a somewhat different context by a different writer. Examples of this problem are the cleansing of the temple and the laments over Jerusalem.[6]

(3) Contradictions may seem to exist when we do not possess all the facts of the case. Regarding the above example, it has been suggested that there was the old site of Jericho and the new city of Jericho. Therefore, the incident could have taken place as

---

[5]Quoted in Mears, 345.

[6]F. LaGard Smith, *The Narrated Bible in Chronological Order* (Eugene, Oreg.: Harvest House Publishers, 1984), 1351.

Jesus *left* one and *entered* the other. Those who assert that contradictions exist are admitting a lack of knowledge.

(4) Contradictions may seem to exist because we do not understand something about the original text. For years, skeptics claimed that a contradiction existed in the Old Testament regarding a payment that was made: One account referred to the payment as a certain amount while another account gave a different figure. Later, archaeologists discovered that two systems of appraising the value of precious metals existed at that time; probably one writer referred to one system of appraisal while the other referred to the second. From time to time, archaeology sheds new light on the text.

As we proceed through the story of Jesus, some of the more publicized "differences" between the accounts will be noted and possible ways to reconcile the variations will be suggested.

Similarities in the Four Accounts

For those who believe in the inspiration of the Scriptures (2 Tim. 3:16, 17), it is the *variations* in the Gospel Accounts that cause concern. However, many scholars are concerned about the *similarities* between the Gospel Accounts—especially Matthew, Mark, and Luke. These men refer to "the synoptic problem" and debate at length why the three books are so similar: why the writers sometimes used similar or even identical language. They struggle with questions such as these: "Did one writer copy from another writer?"; "Did the writers copy from a common source?"

The perplexity of these learned men is needless. Such similarities would be the natural result of all of the books being inspired by a common Author, the Holy Spirit. As in Old Testament times, "men moved by the Holy Spirit spoke from God" (2 Pet. 1:21). If one has faith in the inspiration of the Scriptures, the common Authorship of all four books forever solves the so-called "synoptic problem."

Throughout this commentary, it will be assumed that the Holy Spirit inspired Matthew, Mark, Luke, and John to write what they did. Sometimes this will be stated; sometimes it will not. Whenever the remark is made that one of the gospel writers "said" this or that, it is to be understood that he said it *by inspiration.*

The Four Accounts Can Be Trusted

Matthew's, Mark's, Luke's, and John's accounts of the life of Jesus have been considered part of the inspired New Testament since the early days of the church—and *only* these four accounts have been included.

> Except for a few fragmentary statements [found in other books in the New Testament], the authentic records of [Jesus'] life are contained only in the four Gospels of Matthew, Mark, Luke, and John, which have been regarded as canonical by the Christian church from the earliest period of its history. Although there were numerous other Gospels which purported to recount facts concerning His life that are not recorded in the famous four, the apocryphal Gospels, as they are called, are generally of later date and of doubtful reliability. They contain little information that is not a duplication of what the canonical Gospels impart and much of what they add is obviously fanciful and legendary. Furthermore, they often betray by their language that they were written to bolster the views of some particular sect. . . .[7]

As we begin our study of the life of Christ, it is important for us to realize that we can *depend* on the four accounts God gave us.

> One of the greatest American lawyers of the past was Simon Greenleaf, who wrote one of the most important works on the law of evidence ever to appear in the English language. His book, *A Treatise on the Law of Evidence,* was unsurpassed on the subject for nearly one hundred years. It ran through sixteen editions. When he was a

---

[7]Merrill C. Tenney, *New Testament Survey* (Grand Rapids, Mich.: Wm. B. Eerdmans Publishing Co., 1961), 131.

mature lawyer at the age of sixty-three, just seven years before his death, Simon Greenleaf published a volume in which he examined the testimony of the four evangelists to Jesus Christ. He used the same laws of evidence employed in courts of justice in the civilized world. He said: "Our profession leads us to explore the mazes of falsehood, to detect its artifices, to pierce its thickest veils, to follow and expose its sophistries, to compare the statements of different witnesses with severity, to discover truth and separate it from error." In this book, which ran to 543 pages, Simon Greenleaf came to the conclusion that the Gospels are absolutely trustworthy and that the four evangelists could not possibly have lied about Jesus Christ, for their testimony rings true.[8]

Matthew, Mark, Luke, and John are exactly what they claim to be: true accounts of the greatest life ever lived! You can trust your life—and your eternity—to these books. Paul put it this way: "It is a trustworthy statement, deserving full acceptance, that Christ Jesus came into the world to save sinners" (1 Tim. 1:15a).

THE WORLD INTO WHICH CHRIST CAME

Early readers of the Gospel Accounts were familiar with the world into which Jesus came, but most of us are not. Regarding the land of Palestine in Christ's day, B. S. Dean observed that "the natural scenery is the same as when Abraham first pitched his tent at Shechem," but "all else is changed."[9] The period during which most of the changes occurred were the years between the Old Testament and the New Testament record.

The Period Between the Testaments

Changes from Old Testament times included the following: The synagogue had become a key feature of the religious scene. Sects, such as the Pharisees and the Sadducees, exerted

---

[8]John Phillips, *Exploring the Scriptures* (London: Victory Press, 1965), 189–90.
[9]B. S. Dean, "Introduction," *Truth for Today* (March 1992): 6.

great influence. The country was ruled by Rome. How did such changes come about?

When the Old Testament closed, many Jews had recently returned to Canaan[10] from the Babylonian Captivity and were under Persian rule. The last Old Testament historical book written was Nehemiah; the last Old Testament prophetic book was Malachi. The Jews were looking for God's Messiah and the messenger who would prepare the way for Him. Malachi had written,

> "Behold, I am going to send My messenger, and he will clear the way before Me. And the Lord, whom you seek, will suddenly come to His temple; and the messenger of the covenant, in whom you delight, behold, He is coming," says the Lord of hosts (Mal. 3:1; see also 4:5, 6).

Silence

Between Malachi and the events in the Gospel Accounts, there were approximately four hundred years of prophetic silence. The last Old Testament Scripture was written around 430–425 B.C. The first New Testament events—those related to the birth of John the Baptizer—took place about 5 B.C. This makes an interval of a little over four hundred years. During that time between the Testaments, God did not send special inspired messengers. The Israelites were guided by the written Law and Prophets (Mt. 11:13; Lk. 16:16; see also Lk. 24:44).

Why did God allow this interlude of several centuries before sending His Son? F. LaGard Smith suggested several possibilities:[11] (1) Perhaps God desired to dramatize the most important event in the history of mankind. By the time Jesus finally came, anticipation was at an extremely high level. (2) Perhaps God wanted to make the fulfillment of the Messianic prophecies more impressive. The long interval would ensure that

---

[10]Other Jews did not return but stayed in the lands where they had been scattered. They were known as "the Dispersion" (Jn. 7:35; see Jas. 1:1).

[11]Three of Smith's possibilities were selected and adapted (Smith, 1338–39).

11

the fulfillment was not contrived. (3) Perhaps God was waiting until the religious and political situation was exactly right for the Messiah's mission. Paul wrote, "But when the fullness of the time came, God sent forth His Son" (Gal. 4:4a). The NLT has "But when the right time came, God sent His Son."

Sources

The fact that the period between the Testaments was a time of prophetic silence does not mean that we know nothing of the years that shaped Jesus' world. We have several sources of information.

(1) *Apocryphal Writings.* "The Apocrypha" is the name given to the fourteen books contained in some Bibles between the Old and New Testaments. The word "apocrypha" means "hidden." These books were not considered inspired by the Jews. They were not included in the Old Testament "canon" (the collection of Old Testament books considered inspired). They were not considered inspired by Jesus and His apostles. Jesus and His apostles quoted often from the Old Testament, but they did not quote from the Apocrypha. Several of the volumes reflect the superstitious beliefs of the Persians and other pagan people. Nevertheless, the books as a whole give some insight into the history and customs of the Jews. First Maccabees is especially helpful; it contains the history of the Jewish people in Judea between 175 and 132 B.C.

(2) *Writings of Josephus.* Josephus was a Jewish historian, born about A.D. 37. He survived the siege and destruction of Jerusalem by Titus and wrote two important works: *The Antiquities of the Jews* (a history of his people from creation) and *The Jewish Wars* (an account of the Jews from 170 B.C. to his time). Josephus also wrote two works of lesser importance to us, *Against Apion* and *Autobiography.* Some of Josephus' "facts" have been questioned, but his writings remain a major source of information.

(3) *Miscellaneous Greek and Roman witnesses.* Mention will be made of some of these sources.

(4) *Archaeological findings.* Discoveries in Palestine and other places sometimes throw light on the history and lifestyle of the Jews.

(5) *The Scriptures.* Some information about this time period can be gleaned from the Gospel Accounts themselves.

Four Empires

During the four hundred or so years between the Testaments, God was moving in the affairs of men, working out His purposes. The political framework of those years was outlined in Daniel 2, in a dream of Nebuchadnezzar, king of Babylon.

> . . . there was a single great statue . . . which was large and of extraordinary splendor, . . . and its appearance was awesome. The head of that statue was made of fine gold, its breast and its arms of silver, its belly and its thighs of bronze, its legs of iron, its feet partly of iron and partly of clay (Dan. 2:31–33).

Daniel told King Nebuchadnezzar that he (as ruler over the kingdom of Babylon) was represented by the head of gold (Dan. 2:37, 38). Then the prophet said,

> After you there will arise another kingdom inferior to you, then another third kingdom of bronze, which will rule over all the earth. Then there will be a fourth kingdom as strong as iron; inasmuch as iron crushes and shatters all things, so, like iron that breaks in pieces, it will crush and break all these in pieces (Dan. 2:39, 40).

We know from the Scriptures and history that the four kingdoms of Daniel 2 were (1) the Babylonian Empire, (2) the Medo-Persian Empire, (3) the Grecian Empire, and (4) the Roman Empire. The prophetic dream also contained other details, such as the inherent weakness of the Roman Empire. For us, the most important aspect of the prophecy is the promise that God would set up His kingdom (Dan. 2:44)—a promise fulfilled when the church was established.

Before the Old Testament was complete, the first empire (Babylon) had fallen and the second (Medo-Persia) had come to power (see Dan. 5:28, 30, 31; 6:8, 12, 15, 28; 8:20; 10:1; 11:1; Ezra 1:1–4; Esther 1:19). Our concern, then, is with events during the second, third, and fourth kingdoms.

The Medo-Persian Period (539—333 B.C.)

The Medes and Persians combined forces to conquer the world, so the Medo-Persian Period can be thought of as the time when the Medo-Persian Empire was at the height of its power. On the other hand, Persia predominated, so reference is often made to the Persian Empire or to Persian rule. The dates of the different periods vary by a few years as given by different authorities. They are limited to the rule over Palestine only.

When the Old Testament came to a close, the Persians controlled Canaan. This was basically a period of tolerance toward the Jews. The Persians allowed the Jewish nation to be ruled by the high priest—subject to a neighboring Persian governor.

During this period, tension grew between the returning Jews and the mixed-race inhabitants of Canaan (see Ezra 4:4; Neh. 4:1–8). These inhabitants had largely settled north of Judah in the area known as Samaria (see Ezra 4:10, 17; Neh. 4:2); they became known as "Samaritans." Second Kings 17:24–33 tells how the Samaritans merged the worship of Jehovah with the worship of pagan deities. Verse 33 says, "They feared the Lord and served their own gods. . . ." When Jesus came, the Samaritans occupied the center of the country (Jn. 4:3, 4). The strained relationship between Jews and Samaritans provided the background for a number of events in Jesus' life (Lk. 10:33; 17:16; Jn. 4:9).

The Grecian Period (333–165 B.C.)

The Grecian Period is also known as "The Macedonian Period," since Alexander the Great was from Macedonia. Daniel 8:21 uses the word "Greece," which is the term that will be used in this study.

(1) *Alexander the Great (333–323 B.C.).* In 336 B.C., twenty-year-old Alexander the Great assumed command of the army of Greece. Within a few years, he conquered the world. During his conquests, he annihilated the city of Tyre, fulfilling the prophecy

against that city in Ezekiel 26 and 28. Because of his influence, Greek culture spread across the world. He established a city on the Nile, Alexandria, to be a center of Greek influence. Of special significance to Christians is the fact that Greek became the universal language. The New Testament is written in *koine* (common) Greek, the Greek spoken by the common man in that day, as opposed to classical Greek.

Alexander took control of Jerusalem about 333 B.C. The writings of Josephus tell how the high priest welcomed the conqueror outside the walls of the city. Alexander gave special privileges to the Jews. He used them as colonists, persuading them to settle in far-flung areas of his empire.

During this period, the scribes made their appearance as a distinct class among the Jews. We will say more about the scribes later.

Alexander's death in 323 B.C. was followed by a twenty-year struggle for power. Ultimately, his kingdom was divided into four territories: Greece, Asia, Egypt, and Syria. This division of Alexander the Great's kingdom into four parts was prophesied in Daniel 8:8, 21, 22. The two that interest us are Egypt and Syria. The Ptolemies took control of Egypt, and the Seleucids ruled over Syria. The name "Ptolemies" was derived from the name of the general who gained control of Egypt: Ptolemy. The name "Seleucids" comes from the name of the general who gained control of Syria: Seleucus.

(2) *The Ptolemies (323–198 B.C.).* Situated between Egypt and Syria, Palestine was trapped in the struggle between the two powers. When Egyptian armies marched to Syria, they would capture Palestine on their way north. When Syrian armies moved south toward Egypt, they tried to seize Palestine either coming or going.

Over the next hundred years, the Jews were occasionally under the control of Syria, but most of the time they were subject to Egypt. Ptolemy I captured Jerusalem and took a number of Jews to help colonize Alexandria. He gave them full citizenship and encouraged Jewish scholarship.

The time of the Ptolemies' rule was basically a peaceful period for the Jewish people. A significant achievement was the translation of the Septuagint in Egypt. Ptolemy II commissioned a Greek translation of the Hebrew Scriptures for the great library of Alexandria. This translation was completed around 285 B.C. According to tradition, it was produced by seventy Jewish scholars—hence the name "Septuagint," which means "seventy." Many Old Testament quotations by New Testament writers and speakers are from the Septuagint.

The struggle between Egypt and Syria continued throughout this period. Finally, around 198 B.C., Palestine came under Syrian domination.

(3) *The Seleucids (198–165 B.C.).* To facilitate their rule of the land, the Seleucids divided Palestine into five provinces: Judea, Samaria, Galilee, Perea, and Trachonitis. We will say more about these and other divisions later.

The period of Syrian rule was the darkest in the history of Judaism. The principal villain was Antiochus IV, also known as Antiochus Epiphanes. F. LaGard Smith labeled him "one of the cruelest men ever to hold public office."[12] It is generally agreed that several prophecies in Daniel relate to the tyrannical reign of Antiochus Epiphanes (e.g., Dan. 8:9–11). Epiphanes (175–165 B.C.) hated the Jewish people and tried to make Greeks of them. He erected a temple to Jupiter in Jerusalem and tried to stamp out the Jewish religion. He closed the temple, made circumcision illegal, and promised death to any who practiced Judaism. He sold thousands of Jews into slavery and killed thousands more. He took treasures from the temple and sacrificed a sow on the altar. Then he put the ashes in water and sprinkled "sow water" throughout the temple. Since the pig was an unclean animal to the Jews (Lev. 11:3, 7), these actions desecrated the holy structure.

The Period of Independence (165–63 B.C.)

The atrocities of Antiochus Epiphanes motivated a Jewish insurrection led by an aged priest named Mattathias. Mattathias had five bold and warlike sons, one of whom—Judas—became the leader of the revolt. Judas was known as "Judas the Hammer." "Maccabee" is the Greek word for "hammer," so this is

---

[12]Smith, 1346.

sometimes called the Maccabean period of Jewish history. It is also known as the Asmonean (or Hasmonean) period (derived from the name of Hashmon, an ancestor of Mattathias). Judas Maccabeus re-conquered Jerusalem in 165 B.C. The temple was purified and rededicated to Jehovah. This was the origin of the Feast of the Dedication (see Jn. 10:22).

War with Syria continued from 163 to 143 B.C. Finally, the Jews won their independence. A Jewish dynasty under John Hyrcanus was established in 135 B.C.

During this period, Jewish sects arose, including the Pharisees and the Sadducees. Also during this period, the office of the high priest became more a political position than a religious one. High priests were appointed by whoever was in power. Moses had decreed that the high priest must be a descendant of Aaron (see Ex. 29:9; Num. 25:10–13), usually the oldest son. Apparently, Moses' instructions were forgotten or ignored.

The closing years of this period were years of civil strife. Different members of John Hyrcanus' descendants were rivals for the throne. There were plots, counterplots, and political assassinations. Finally, one party in the dispute appealed to a rising power—Rome—for support. Seeking Rome's involvement in this Jewish dispute was like chickens inviting a fox into the hen house to arbitrate their differences. It was not long before the Jews lost their independence.

The Roman Period (63 B.C.—A.D. 70)

Jerusalem was conquered by Pompey the Great in 63 B.C. At this time, Rome was ruled by a Triumvirate which included Pompey and Julius Caesar. Ultimately, Julius Caesar took control. The Roman rulers during the lifetime of Jesus were Augustus (Octavius) Caesar (27 B.C.—A.D. 14) (Lk. 2:1) and Tiberius Caesar (A.D. 14–37) (Lk. 3:1).

Palestine was put under rulers responsible to Rome. Initially, Antipater was made ruler of Judea. He was succeeded by his son Herod the Great, who was king of Judea 37–3 B.C. (Lk. 1:5). Herod had a genius for governing, but his vices exceeded his governing skills. He aroused the hatred of the Jews by introducing chariot races and other Greek customs into Jerusalem. In an attempt to regain their favor, he started rebuilding the temple (see Jn. 2:20), which had been basically destroyed by Epiphanes. This Herod is infamous as the king who killed the babies in an attempt to destroy Jesus (Mt. 2:1–18).

When Herod the Great died (Mt. 2:19), the country was placed in the hands of a tetrarchy ("rule of four"): (1) A son of Herod named Archelaus was put over Judea and Samaria (Mt. 2:22). He was removed from office in A.D. 6 and was replaced by a series of governors. (Pilate was the sixth governor [Lk. 3:1].) (2) Another son, Herod Antipas (sometimes called simply "Herod" and sometimes distinguished as "Herod the tetrarch" in the New Testament), was made tetrarch of Galilee and Perea (Lk. 3:1; see Mt. 14:1). He is the best known of the Herods since he ruled during the personal ministry of Jesus. (3) A third son, Philip, was "tetrarch of the region of Ituraea and Trachonitis" (Lk. 3:1; see Mt. 14:3)—an area sometimes called the Bashan District. "Bashan" is often mentioned in the Old Testament (Josh. 22:7; 1 Chron. 6:71; Is. 33:9), but not in the New Testament. The area around Ituraea and Trachonitis roughly corresponds to the ancient nation of Bashan. (4) A fourth area, called Abilene, was given to Lysanias (Lk. 3:1), who was not a Herod. Abilene was not part of the area that had been ruled by Herod the Great.

The Romans gave the Jews a number of concessions. They were exempt from military duty. They could not be called to court on a Sabbath day. They were allowed to issue copper coins with inscriptions only and no image. Coins did circulate with the image of Caesar (Mt. 22:20), but Jews did not have to handle the "accursed coins" except to pay their taxes to Rome. Roman soldiers were forbidden to carry banners with images in their land.

Of greatest significance to Christians is how the Roman period prepared the way for Christ. Catalysts included the establishment of the *Pax Romana* (the Roman peace), the spread of a universal language (Greek), and the building of massive networks of roads which permitted empire-wide transportation and communication.

The Land of Palestine

In the Old Testament, the land where Jesus was later born

was called "Canaan" (Gen. 12:5; Ex. 6:4; Josh. 14:1). By New Testament times, it was known as "Palestine"—although that name is not found in the New Testament. The name "Palestine" is found once in the KJV in the Old Testament, in Joel 3:4. The NASB translates the word there "Philistia."

The name "Palestine" was derived from the Philistines, a people who lived on the southern coast of Canaan (see Zeph. 2:5). The Maccabees fought against the Philistines, but the Philistines are not mentioned by name in the New Testament. Some think that they were absorbed into the Jewish nation.

A good Bible map helps to visualize the movements of Jesus (see "Palestine During the Life of Christ" in the appendix). The Gospel Accounts record around 150 events in the life of Christ; a hundred or so of these are tied with specific geographic locations.

A popular way of speaking of the length of the land of Palestine was "from Dan to Beersheba" (Judg. 20:1; see 1 Sam. 3:20; 1 Kings 4:25). From Dan in the north to Beersheba in the south was a distance of about 150 miles. The land covered between 10,000 and 12,000 square miles.[13] By way of comparison, forty of the fifty US states are larger than this.

Three provinces were prominent in the life of Christ, all of them west of the Jordan River. (1) *Judea*. The province of Judea was dominated by the Jews. Judeans were proud of their orthodoxy. Jesus frequently visited Judea—especially during feast days. (2) *Samaria*. Samaria was occupied by the half-breed people known as "Samaritans." Jesus sometimes passed through Samaria on His way north or south. (3) *Galilee*. Galilee had a mixture of Jews and Gentiles (see Mt. 4:15). It was looked upon as a backward area by Judeans. Jesus spent most of His life in Galilee.

Other areas are also significant in the life of Christ. On several occasions, Jesus crossed the Sea of Galilee to its eastern shore, which is often designated as "The Bashan District." The southern part of this area was called "Decapolis," which literally means "ten cities" (Mt. 4:25; Mk. 5:20; 7:31). There were more than ten

---

[13]John D. Davis, "Palestine," *A Dictionary of the Bible*, 4th ed. (Grand Rapids, Mich.: Baker Book House, 1956), 562.

cities in the area, but apparently ten of them were considered predominant.

Near the end of Jesus' ministry, He made a number of withdrawals from Galilee. One of these was west into the region of Tyre and Sidon, cities in the country of Phoenicia (Mt. 15:21). He also made several withdrawals to the east side of the Jordan. According to Josephus, this area was designated as "Perea," but the phrase used in the Gospel Accounts is "beyond the Jordan" (Mt. 4:25; 19:1; Mk. 10:1; Jn. 10:40).

Other Changes

The closing days of the Old Testament and the years between the Testaments also affected the Jewish world in other ways.

Changes in Designation

By the end of the Old Testament, God's people were already known as "Jews" (Ezra 4:12; 5:1). This name was derived from the southern kingdom of Judah: Most who returned from the Babylonian Captivity were descendants of people from that area (and from the tribe of Judah). By New Testament times, "Jews" was the primary designation used for these people (Mt. 2:2; Jn. 1:19).

They were still occasionally called "Israelites" (see Jn. 1:47; 2 Cor. 11:22), indicating that they were descendants of Israel. They were also sometimes labeled "Hebrews" (Acts 6:1; 2 Cor. 11:22) because of their traditional language.

Changes in Language

After the return from the Babylonian Captivity, Aramaic gradually replaced Hebrew as the common language of the Jews. Aramaic, the language of Syria, was similar to Hebrew—as Italian is similar to Latin. Jewish boys still learned Hebrew in school—as Italian schoolboys study Latin.

The universal language in Jesus' day was Greek, while the official language of the Roman government was Latin. When Jesus was nailed to the cross, the sign over His head was written in three languages: Hebrew, Latin, and Greek (Jn. 19:20).

Changes in Occupation

Before the Captivity, the Jews had been primarily farmers

and herdsmen. Separated from their property during the Captivity, they discovered that they possessed trading skills. By the time of Jesus, Jewish businessmen were scattered all over the world.

Changes in Worship

The *temple* in Jerusalem was still important to the Jews. The temple that had been built by Zerubbabel after the return from the Babylonian Captivity had largely been destroyed by Epiphanes. Herod the Great had begun rebuilding the temple (see Jn. 2:20) about sixteen years before Jesus' birth; that project was still in process during Jesus' ministry. It was not completed until the late A.D. 60s, shortly before it was destroyed in A.D. 70 by the Roman army. (Some even believe that construction was still not completed at the time of its destruction.)

The faithful who lived in Palestine traveled to Jerusalem several times a year for the feasts (see "The Feasts of the Jews" in the appendix). All these feasts are mentioned in the New Testament with the exception of the Feast of Trumpets and the Feast of Purim. Pious Jews in other lands also made the arduous journey to Jerusalem from time to time (Acts 2:5–11).

By the time of Christ, however, the *synagogue* was the heart of religious life among the Jews. The synagogue is not mentioned in the Old Testament but is prominent in the New (Mt. 12:9; 13:54). The synagogue probably originated while the Jews were in captivity and unable to go to Jerusalem on the prescribed feast days. It only took ten Jewish men to organize a synagogue. The word "synagogue" actually referred to the people rather than to a building. Nevertheless, the word is often used in the New Testament to refer to the building in which the people met (Lk. 7:5). There were hundreds of synagogues in Jerusalem and around the world. The Sabbath services in the synagogue were simple—consisting of songs, prayers, and the reading and study of the Scriptures. Attached to most synagogues were schools which Jewish boys in the area were required to attend.

Changes in Religious Leadership

In the Old Testament, the *priests* were the recognized religious leaders. Their work was supplemented by an occasional prophet sent by God. As we study the life of Christ, we will still encounter priests and their Levite assistants (Lk. 10:31, 32) and the high priest (John 18:15). Of special significance will be the fact that, during Jesus' ministry, in effect, Judaism had *two* high priests (see Lk. 3:2). The high priest Annas had been removed from the high priesthood by the Roman governor, but he had enough influence to have his son-in-law Caiaphas (Jn. 18:13) appointed (Mt. 26:3, 57; Jn. 11:49; 18:24). In the eyes of most Jews, Annas remained the true high priest (see Acts 4:6).

In addition to the priests, other leadership had emerged by New Testament times. First were the *rabbis* (Mt. 23:7, 8), who were the teachers in the synagogues and in the synagogue schools. "Rabbi" (רַבִּי) is a transliterated Hebrew word meaning "my master." It can also mean "my teacher" (see Jn. 20:16; "rabboni" is a variation of "rabbi"). Jesus was called "Rabbi" by His disciples as a sign of respect (Mt. 26:25; Mk. 9:5; Jn. 3:2). Rabbis had largely replaced the priests as the religious authorities. For some, rabbinic interpretations of the Law had the same weight as the Law itself. These interpretations were eventually gathered into a volume known as the *Talmud*.

Next were the *scribes* (Mt. 2:4; 5:20; 7:29; 9:3). The Greek word translated "scribe" (γραμματεύς, *grammateus*) literally means "writer." Originally, scribes had the responsibility of recording important events. In 2 Samuel 8:17 the word translated "secretary" in the NASB is the word for "scribe." By New Testament times, the scribes were responsible for making copies of the Old Testament. They were known as authorities on the Law and were sometimes called "lawyers" (Lk. 7:30; 11:45, 46, 52). The KJV also occasionally uses the word "doctor" to refer to teachers of the Law (Lk. 2:46; 5:17). They were not specialists in civil law, but in religious law. Many of the scribes were Pharisees.

Then there was the *Sanhedrin*. The Sanhedrin was the Jewish "Supreme Court." "Sanhedrin" is a transliteration of the Greek word (συνέδριον, *sunedrion*). The KJV and NASB translate it as "Council," while the NIV renders it "Sanhedrin" (Mt. 26:59; Mk. 15:43; Lk. 22:66). The Sanhedrin first appeared in history about 200 B.C. as the body responsible for regulating the internal affairs of the Jewish nation. Traditionally, the Sanhedrin had seventy members—plus the high priest, who served as president. A majority of the members were Sadducees, but there was a powerful Pharisaic minority.

It was important to all of the influential Jews mentioned above to maintain the status quo and their positions of authority. They thus became Jesus' greatest foes.

The Rise of Sectarianism

The subject of Jewish sects in Jesus' day is significant enough to merit a separate section. Most of these sects were as motivated by politics and culture as they were by religion.

The Pharisees

"Pharisee" is from a Hebrew verb meaning "to separate" (פְּרוּשִׁים, *perushim*). Some think that this sect originated when pressure was exerted during the time of Seleucid domination for Jews to accept Greek culture. Originally, Pharisees blended patriotism with religious devotion. By the time of Jesus, they had deteriorated into a sect of self-righteousness and formalism (Mt. 23:1–36). They were small in number, but they were popular with the people and thus had considerable influence. For all practical purposes, they considered the uninspired "traditions of the elders" (Mk. 7:3) as binding as the Law itself. When Jesus disregarded these traditions (Mt. 15:1–14), the Pharisees became His bitterest enemies.

The Sadducees

The name "Sadducee" may have been derived from Zadok, the first of the high-priestly line under Solomon (1 Kings 1:32, 34, 38, 45; see Ezek. 40:46; 44:15). Every high priest from the time of Herod the Great to the fall of Jerusalem was a Sadducee. This was a wealthy, aristocratic group, many of whom were priests. Some believe that the Sadducees originated about the same time as the Pharisees. They *did* accept Greek ways. Because of their willingness to cooperate with whoever was in power, they became a political force. Because of their acceptance of Greek philosophy, they rejected the concepts of resurrection and life after death (Mk. 12:18; Acts 23:6–8). They came to hate Jesus because He threatened their authority.

Other Sects

Other sects are also mentioned in the Gospel Accounts. One was the Herodians (Mt. 22:16; Mk. 3:6; 12:13; see Mk. 8:15), a politically active group dedicated to placing a Herod on the throne over all Palestine.

The Zealots were a band of Jewish rebels dedicated to overcoming Rome with the sword. One from this group, Simon, became an apostle (Mt. 10:4; Mk. 3:18; Lk. 6:15).

We know from secular history that another religious group existed: the Essenes. This was a body of religious extremists who had separated themselves from society. (They may have originated within the sect of the Pharisees.) Some think that the Qumran community (the source of the famed "Dead Sea scrolls") was associated with the Essenes. Although the name "Essenes" does not appear in the Bible, an oft-heard claim is that John the Baptizer was either an Essene or else derived his doctrine and practices from the Essenes. There is no evidence to confirm this claim and much to disprove it. The New Testament teaches that John was sent from God with God's message (Jn. 1:6; Lk. 3:2). Further, a comparison of the doctrines and practices of the Essenes with those of John reveals many differences.

Messianic Expectations

As mentioned earlier, the Jews were eagerly looking for God's Messiah. "Messiah" is from a Hebrew word (מָשִׁיחַ, *mashiach*) meaning "anointed [one]." The Greek equivalent is "Christ" (Χριστός, *Christos*; Jn. 1:41). Anointing was used in the appointment of priests (Ex. 28:41; 29:7) and others; but when a Jew heard the term "God's anointed," he thought of a *king* (see 1 Sam. 10:1; 24:6; Ps. 2:2, 6).

By the time Jesus finally came, anticipation regarding the coming of the Messiah was at an extremely high level. This can be seen in the excitement of Simeon and Anna, who welcomed the baby Jesus in the temple (Lk. 2:25–38). Simeon had been looking for "the Lord's Christ" (Lk. 2:26). Anna talked about Jesus "to all those who were looking for the redemption of Jerusalem" (Lk. 2:38). When John the Baptizer began his work, "the people were in a state of expectation and all were wondering in their hearts about John, as to whether he was the Christ" (Lk. 3:15). Even the Samaritans believed that "Messiah is coming (He who is called Christ)" (Jn. 4:25). Joseph of Arimathea was described as one "who was waiting for the kingdom of God" (Lk. 23:51). The longing of the people in general can be seen in the attempt to crown Jesus as king (Jn. 6:15) and in the excitement during the Triumphal Entry into Jerusalem (Jn. 12:13).

The coming of the Messiah was evidently a popular subject of discussion. Details of His life were known: He would be a descendant of David (Mt. 22:42); He would be born in Bethlehem (Mt. 2:5, 6; Jn. 7:42). Tied in with the discussion concerning the Messiah was speculation concerning His forerunner (see Jn. 1:21; Mt. 16:14). False Messiahs had apparently arisen, fanning the hopes of the people. Jesus told His disciples that this would happen after His departure (Mt. 24:5, 23, 24), and most scholars believe it had also happened before His birth. Acts 5:36, 37 may tell of two pretenders.

With all this anticipation, the words of John may be hard to understand: "He [Jesus] came to His own, and those who were His own did not receive Him" (Jn. 1:11). The rejection of Jesus by Jews in general and by Jewish leaders in particular is a prominent theme in the New Testament (Mt. 21:42; Mk. 12:10; Lk. 17:25; Acts 4:11; 1 Pet. 2:4, 7). Why was Jesus not accepted as the long-awaited Messiah?

Basically, Jesus was rejected because He did not fit the Jews' preconceived concept of the Messiah. The Old Testament taught that the Messiah was to be a God-sent King (Is. 9:6, 7) from the royal line of David (Ps. 89:3, 4). The Old Testament *also* taught that the Messiah was to be a *suffering* Servant (Ps. 22:1–21; Is. 53:1–12), but prophecies of this nature were largely ignored. It was clear in the minds of the Jewish people that they needed a strong political and military leader to defeat the Romans and re-establish the kingdom of Israel as it had been in the days of David and Solomon. A Christ who said, "My kingdom is not of this world" (Jn. 18:36a) would not do. Jesus was a "round peg" that did not fit the "square hole" that His people had conceived for the Messiah.

Regarding the world into which Jesus came, let us conclude by noticing the prophecy that the Messiah would grow up "like a root out of parched ground" (Is. 53:2). God had prepared for His coming (Gal. 4:4), but the hearts of the people were still like parched, dry earth. From this inhospitable environment, Christ would come. Nevertheless, the religion of Jesus would ultimately grow and spread throughout the world.

OUTLINE FOR VOLUME 1

I. **THE PERIOD OF CHRIST'S LIFE PRIOR TO HIS MINISTRY.**
   A. Luke's preface and dedication (Lk. 1:1–4).
   B. John's introduction (Jn. 1:1–18).
   C. The genealogies of Jesus (Mt. 1:1–17; Lk. 3:23–38).
      1. Matthew's genealogy (Mt. 1:1–17).
      2. Luke's genealogy (Lk. 3:23–38).
   D. The announcements (Lk. 1:5–38).
      1. The angel's announcement to Zacharias regarding the birth of John the Baptizer (Lk. 1:5–25).
      2. The angel's announcement to Mary regarding the birth of Jesus (Lk. 1:26–38).
   E. The visit of Mary (the expectant mother of Jesus) to Elizabeth (the expectant mother of John the Baptizer) (Lk. 1:39–56).
   F. The birth and early life of John the Baptizer (Lk. 1:57–80).
   G. The announcement to Joseph regarding the coming of Jesus (Mt. 1:18–25).
   H. The birth of Jesus (Lk. 2:1–7).
   I. The birth of Jesus proclaimed to the shepherds (Lk. 2:8–20).
   J. The circumcision and naming of Jesus; the temple service (Lk. 2:21–39).
   K. Jesus visited by eastern magi ("wise men") (Mt. 2:1–12).
   L. The flight into Egypt and the slaughter of baby boys

in Bethlehem (Mt. 2:13–18).
M. The child Jesus brought from Egypt to Nazareth (Mt. 2:19–23; see Lk. 2:39b).
N. Jesus living at Nazareth; a visit to Jerusalem when He was twelve (Lk. 2:40–52).

II. THE BEGINNING OF THE MINISTRY OF JOHN THE BAPTIZER.
A. John's ministry (Mt. 3:1–6; Mk. 1:1–6; Lk. 3:1–6).
B. John's message (Mt. 3:7–12; Mk. 1:7, 8; Lk. 3:7–18).

III. THE BEGINNING OF THE MINISTRY OF JESUS.
A. Jesus baptized by John in the Jordan River (Mt. 3:13–17; Mk. 1:9–11; Lk. 3:21, 22; Jn. 1:31–34).
B. Jesus tempted in the wilderness (Mt. 4:1–11; Mk. 1:12, 13; Lk. 4:1–13).
C. John's testimony concerning Jesus (Jn. 1:19–34).
D. Jesus' first disciples (in Judea) (Jn. 1:35–51).
E. Jesus' first miracle (at Cana in Galilee) (Jn. 2:1–11).
F. Jesus' first residence at Capernaum (in Galilee) (Jn. 2:12).

IV. FROM THE FIRST PASSOVER TO THE SECOND.
A. The first Passover of Jesus' ministry (Jn. 2:13—3:21).
   1. Cleansing the temple (Jn. 2:13–25).
   2. Teaching Nicodemus (Jn. 3:1–21).
B. The first ministry in Judea (and further testimony by John) (Jn. 3:22–36).
C. The shift from Judea to Galilee (Mt. 4:12; Mk. 1:14; Lk. 3:19, 20; Jn. 4:1–45).
   1. Reasons for the move to Galilee (Mt. 4:1, 2; Mk. 1:14; Lk. 3:19, 20; Jn. 4:1–3).
   2. The incident in Samaria (Jn. 4:4–42).
   3. Arrival in Galilee (Lk. 4:14; Jn. 4:43–45).
D. A general account of Jesus' teaching in Galilee (Mt. 4:17; Mk. 1:14, 15; Lk. 4:14, 15).
E. The second miracle at Cana (Jn. 4:46–54).
F. The shift to Capernaum in Galilee (Mt. 4:13–16).

G. The call of four fishermen (Mt. 4:18–22; Mk. 1:16–20; Lk. 5:1–11).

H. In Capernaum: healing a demoniac in the synagogue (Mk. 1:21–28; Lk. 4:31–37).

I. In Capernaum: healing Peter's mother-in-law and others (Mt. 8:14–17; Mk. 1:29–34; Lk. 4:38–41).

J. In Galilee: Jesus' first teaching and healing tour (Mt. 4:23–25; Mk. 1:35–39; Lk. 4:42–44).

K. In Galilee: healing a leper—and resultant excitement (Mt. 8:2–4; Mk. 1:40–45; Lk. 5:12–16).

L. Back at Capernaum: healing a paralytic (Mt. 9:2–8; Mk. 2:1–12; Lk. 5:17–26).

M. Near Capernaum: the call of Matthew (Mt. 9:9; Mk. 2:13, 14; Lk. 5:27, 28).

V. FROM THE SECOND PASSOVER TO THE THIRD.

A. Jesus healed a crippled man on the Sabbath and defended the act (Jn. 5:1–47).

B. Jesus defended His disciples who plucked grain on the Sabbath (Mt. 12:1–8; Mk. 2:23–28; Lk. 6:1–5).

C. Jesus defended healing a withered hand on the Sabbath (Mt. 12:9–14; Mk. 3:1–6; Lk. 6:6–11).

D. Jesus healed multitudes beside the Sea of Galilee (Mt. 12:15–21; Mk. 3:7–12).

E. After prayer, Jesus selected twelve apostles (Mt. 10:2–4; Mk. 3:13–19; Lk. 6:12–16).

F. The Sermon on the Mount (Mt. 5:1—7:29; Lk. 6:17–49).

   1. Introductory statements (Mt. 5:1, 2; Lk. 6:17–20).

   2. The Beatitudes: promises to the Messiah's subjects (Mt. 5:3–12; Lk. 6:20–26).

   3. Influence (and responsibilities) of the Messiah's subjects (Mt. 5:13–16).

   4. The relationship of Messianic teaching to the Old Testament and to man-made traditions concerning Old Testament teaching (Mt. 5:17–48; Lk. 6:27–30, 32–36).

   5. Religious acts to be from the heart, not for show

(Mt. 6:1–18).
6. The security of heavenly treasures contrasted with earthly anxieties (Mt. 6:19–34).
7. Teaching on judging (Mt. 7:1–6; Lk. 6:37–42).
8. Teaching on prayer (Mt. 7:7–11).
9. The Golden Rule (Mt. 7:12; Lk. 6:31).
10. The two ways—and false prophets (Mt. 7:13–23; Lk. 6:43–45).
11. Conclusion and application (the two builders) (Mt. 7:24–29; Lk. 6:46–49).
G. A centurion's servant healed (Mt. 8:1, 5–13; Lk. 7:1–10).
H. A widow's son raised (Lk. 7:11–17).
I. John the Baptizer answered (Mt. 11:2–30; Lk. 7:18–35).
J. Jesus' feet anointed (Lk. 7:36–50).
K. Second Galilean tour (Lk. 8:1–3).
L. Blasphemous accusations (Mt. 12:22–37; Mk. 3:20–30; Lk. 11:14–23).
M. Sign-seekers (Mt. 12:38–45; Lk. 11:16, 24–26, 29–36).
N. Jesus' family (Mt. 12:46–50; Mk. 3:31–35; Lk. 8:19–21; 11:27, 28).
O. The first great group of parables (Mt. 13:1–53; Mk. 4:1–34; Lk. 8:4–18).
1. The occasion and setting (Mt. 13:1–3; Mk. 4:1, 2; Lk. 8:4).
2. The parable of the sower—and explanation (Mt. 13:3–23; Mk. 4:3–25; Lk. 8:5–18).
3. The parable of silent growth (Mk. 4:26–29).
4. The parable of the tares—and explanation (Mt. 13:24–30, 36–43).
5. The parables of the mustard seed and the leaven (Mt. 13:31–35; Mk. 4:30–34).
6. The parables of the treasure and the pearl (Mt. 13:44–46).
7. The parable of the dragnet (Mt. 13:47–53).
P. Stilling the storm (Mt. 8:18, 23–27; Mk. 4:35–41; Lk. 8:22–25).
Q. Healing two demoniacs (Mt. 8:28–34; 9:1; Mk. 5:1–21;

Lk. 8:26–40).

R. Eating with sinners (and a discourse on fasting) (Mt. 9:10–17; Mk. 2:15–22; Lk. 5:29–39).

S. Raising Jairus' daughter (and healing an invalid) (Mt. 9:18–26; Mk. 5:22–43; Lk. 8:41–56).

T. Healing blind men and a demoniac (and being criticized) (Mt. 9:27–34).

U. Visiting Nazareth (and being rejected) (Mt. 13:54–58; Mk. 6:1–6a; Lk. 4:16–30).

V. Jesus' third tour of Galilee (and instructions to the Twelve) (Mt. 9:35–38; 10:1–42; 11:1; Mk. 6:6b–13; Lk. 9:1–6).

W. Herod's interest in Jesus (and account of the death of John the Baptizer) (Mt. 14:1–12a; Mk. 6:14–29; Lk. 9:7–9).

X. Jesus' withdrawal from Herod's territory (and return) (Mt. 14:12b–36; Mk. 6:30–56; Lk. 9:10–17; Jn. 6:1–21a).
  1. Return of the Twelve and retirement to the east coast of the Sea of Galilee (Mt. 14:12b, 13; Mk. 6:30–32; Lk. 9:10; Jn. 6:1).
  2. Feeding five thousand men (Mt. 14:13–21; Mk. 6:33–44; Lk. 9:11–17; Jn. 6:2–14).
  3. Walking on the water (Mt. 14:22–36; Mk. 6:45–56; Jn. 6:15–21a).

Y. Jesus' discourse on the Bread of Life (and Peter's confession) (Jn. 6:21b–71).

VI. FROM THE THIRD PASSOVER UNTIL JESUS' ARRIVAL AT BETHANY.

A. The third Passover (see Jn. 6:4; 7:11).

B. Reproached for disregarding tradition (Mt. 15:1–20; Mk. 7:1–23).

C. Withdrawal from Herod's territory (Mt. 15:21; Mk. 7:24).

D. Healing of the daughter of a Phoenician (or Canaanite) woman (Mt. 15:21–28; Mk. 7:24–30).

E. Avoiding Herod's territory (Mt. 15:29; Mk. 7:31).

F. Healing of many, including a deaf man (Mt. 15:30, 31;

Mk. 7:32–37).
G. Feeding four thousand men (Mt. 15:32–39; Mk. 8:1–9).
H. Another withdrawal from Herod's territory (Mt. 15:39—17:23; Mk. 8:10—9:32; Lk. 9:18–45).
  1. In Galilee: another attack by Jesus' enemies—followed by another withdrawal (Mt. 15:39—16:12; Mk. 8:10–21).
  2. In Bethsaida: a blind man healed (Mk. 8:22–26).
  3. Near Caesarea Philippi: the good confession (Mt. 16:13–20; Mk. 8:27–30; Lk. 9:18–21).
  4. Near Caesarea Philippi: Jesus' death foretold (Mt. 16:21–28; Mk. 8:31–38; Lk. 9:22–27).
  5. Near Caesarea Philippi (on Mount Hermon?): the Transfiguration (Mt. 17:1–13; Mk. 9:2–13; Lk. 9:28–36).
  6. Healing a demon-possessed boy (Mt. 17:14–21; Mk. 9:14–29; Lk. 9:37–43).
  7. Returning to Galilee (Jesus' death again foretold) (Mt. 17:22, 23; Mk. 9:30–32; Lk. 9:43–45).
I. Question about the temple tax (Mt. 17:24–27).
J. Teaching on the necessity of childlikeness (Mt. 18:1–14; Mk. 9:33–50; Lk. 9:46–50).
K. Final teaching in Galilee: problems between brethren (Mt. 18:15–35).

PART I

THE PERIOD OF CHRIST'S LIFE PRIOR TO HIS MINISTRY

Includes a Harmony of

Mt. 1:1—2:23

Lk. 1:1—2:52; 3:23–38

Jn. 1:1–18

LUKE'S PREFACE AND DEDICATION
(LK. 1:1–4)

¹Inasmuch as many have undertaken to compile an account of the things accomplished among us, ²just as they were handed down to us by those who from the beginning were eyewitnesses and servants of the word, ³it seemed fitting for me as well, having investigated everything carefully from the beginning, to write it out for you in consecutive order, most excellent Theophilus; ⁴so that you may know the exact truth about the things you have been taught.

In Luke's introduction to his Gospel Account, he wrote, "...it seemed fitting for me . . . to write it [the life of Christ] out for you . . . so that you may know the exact truth about the things you have been taught" (Lk. 1:3, 4). A basic purpose of his presentation of Christ's life was to help Theophilus know "the exact truth" about Jesus.

Here are highlights from his introduction: **Inasmuch as many have undertaken to compile an account of the things accomplished among us.** Evidently, there was a basic body of beliefs about Jesus that was common to all the church.

...just as they were handed down to us by those who from the beginning were eyewitnesses and servants of the word. The words "eyewitnesses and servants" probably refer primarily to the apostles (see Acts 1:21, 22), but they indicate the solidarity of the body of beliefs.

...it seemed fitting for me as well, having investigated everything carefully. This may indicate that some who wrote accounts of the life of Christ did *not* investigate everything carefully. Matthew, Mark, and John would be excluded from this statement. Several early uninspired manuscripts—which purport to be accounts of the life of Jesus—are in existence today, but they are filled with nonsense.

…from the beginning. Apparently, Luke had contact with the "eyewitnesses" early in the history of the church.

…to write it out for you in consecutive order. This may indicate that Luke made a more deliberate attempt than the other gospel writers to produce a chronological account of Christ's life. However, not even Luke's account is chronological throughout. The term "consecutive order," therefore, probably refers to the writing of an *orderly* account—a logical, thought-out version.

…most excellent Theophilus. "Most excellent" was an address of respect to an official. "Theophilus" is a Greek name meaning "lover of God." It could refer to all who love God, but probably refers to a specific person. Perhaps this individual was Luke's patron and financed the publication of the book. "Publication" refers to having copies of the letter made and distributed.

…so that you may know the exact truth about the things you have been taught. Some think that the phrase "the things you have been taught" refers to formal instruction. At any rate, the words again stress the existence of a common body of belief in the early church.

Luke might be thought of as Christianity's first formal "critic." He did not simply accept the various accounts that were circulating. Rather, he thoroughly checked the facts. Thus what he wrote was "exact." He seemed to invite his readers to check his account, for he constantly gave historical information that could be verified (see Lk. 1:5; 2:1, 2; 3:1; 13:1, 2). Archaeological discoveries confirm that Luke was an accurate historian, giving great weight to his account of the life of Christ and his account of the early church.

JOHN'S INTRODUCTION
(JN. 1:1–18)

[1]In the beginning was the Word, and the Word was with God, and the Word was God. [2]He was in the beginning with

God. [3]All things came into being through Him, and apart from Him nothing came into being that has come into being. [4]In Him was life, and the life was the Light of men. [5]The Light shines in the darkness, and the darkness did not comprehend it.

[6]There came a man sent from God, whose name was John. [7]He came as a witness, to testify about the Light, so that all might believe through him. [8]He was not the Light, but he came to testify about the Light.

[9]There was the true Light which, coming into the world, enlightens every man. [10]He was in the world, and the world was made through Him, and the world did not know Him. [11]He came to His own, and those who were His own did not receive Him. [12]But as many as received Him, to them He gave the right to become children of God, even to those who believe in His name, [13]who were born, not of blood nor of the will of the flesh nor of the will of man, but of God.

[14]And the Word became flesh, and dwelt among us, and we saw His glory, glory as of the only begotten from the Father, full of grace and truth. [15]John testified about Him and cried out, saying, "This was He of whom I said, 'He who comes after me has a higher rank than I, for He existed before me.'" [16]For of His fullness we have all received, and grace upon grace. [17]For the Law was given through Moses; grace and truth were realized through Jesus Christ. [18]No one has seen God at any time; the only begotten God who is in the bosom of the Father, He has explained Him.

A study of the life of Christ generally starts with His birth in Bethlehem. John wanted his readers to know that Jesus existed long before that event. He even existed before the creation of the world—because He is, in fact, God: **In the beginning was the Word, and the Word was with God, and the Word was God** (Jn. 1:1).

Jesus is one of three divine Personalities who comprise what the KJV calls the "Godhead" (Acts 17:29; Rom. 1:20; Col. 2:9). The three are listed in Matthew 28:19: the Father, the Son, and the Holy Spirit. The fact that Jesus is God is not an easy concept to grasp. The word "God" is generally used in referring to God, the Father. We must also remember that Jesus is God, the Son.

When we think of Jesus, we usually think of Him as always having the name "Jesus" or being designated as "Christ." However, when the angel spoke to Joseph about Mary bearing a Son, he said, "You *shall* call His name Jesus" (Mt. 1:21; emphasis added). Regarding the designation "Christ" ("anointed one"), Jesus was anointed by God with the Spirit (Lk. 4:18; Acts 10:38) at His baptism (Mt. 3:13–17). What was Jesus' name *before* His earthly ministry?

John said that Jesus was the *logos*—"the Word"—prior to His earthly existence. *Logos* (λόγος) is the Greek word translated "Word" in John 1:1, 14. It is the word from which we get "logic." It is also used in combination with other words to mean "study of," as in "bio*logy*" (the study of life). The apostle John also used *logos* in other writings to refer to Jesus (see 1 Jn. 1:1; Rev. 1:2; 19:13). He was the only New Testament writer to use this term to refer to Christ.

Christ came to this earth as the Word of God personified. In 1:18 John wrote, **No one has seen God at any time; the only begotten God who is in the bosom of the Father, He has explained Him.** Jesus, by His teaching and by His Person, "explained" God. He told Philip, ". . . He who has seen Me has seen the Father . . ." (Jn. 14:9).

The most thought-provoking part of John's introduction is verse 14: **And the Word became flesh, and dwelt among us. . . .** We call this "the Incarnation" (from the Latin *incarnāre*, meaning "to make [as] flesh"). The KJV often uses the word "carnal" to mean "fleshly" (Rom. 7:14). The classic biblical statement regarding the Incarnation is Philippians 2:5–8. While all the mysteries of the Incarnation can never be understood, by faith we accept the great truth that "the Word became flesh." The author of the Book of Hebrews wrote,

> . . . He had to be made like His brethren in all things, so that He might become a merciful and faithful high priest. . . . For since He Himself was tempted in that which He has suffered, He is able to come to the aid of those who are tempted (Heb. 2:17, 18).

John had more to say in his introduction. (1) Jesus is the Light (the source of enlightenment) (Jn. 1:4, 5, 9; see also vv. 16–18; 3:19 –21). (2) The forerunner of Jesus bore witness to the Light (Jn. 1:6–8, 15). (3) A world in darkness rejected the Light (Jn. 1:5, 10, 11). (4) A few did accept the Light through faith and spiritual birth (Jn. 1:12, 13). However, we have focused on the reality of Christ's preexistence.

THE GENEALOGIES OF JESUS
(MT. 1:1–17; LK. 3:23–38)

Matthew's Genealogy (Mt. 1:1–17)

[1]The record of the genealogy of Jesus the Messiah, the son of David, the son of Abraham:
[2]Abraham was the father of Isaac, Isaac the father of Jacob, and Jacob the father of Judah and his brothers. [3]Judah was the father of Perez and Zerah by Tamar, Perez was the father of Hezron, and Hezron the father of Ram. [4]Ram was the father of Amminadab, Amminadab the father of Nahshon, and Nahshon the father of Salmon. [5]Salmon was the father of Boaz by Rahab, Boaz was the father of Obed by Ruth, and Obed the father of Jesse. [6]Jesse was the father of David the king.

David was the father of Solomon by Bathsheba who had been the wife of Uriah. [7]Solomon was the father of Rehoboam, Rehoboam the father of Abijah, and Abijah the father of Asa. [8]Asa was the father of Jehoshaphat, Jehoshaphat the father of Joram, and Joram the father of Uzziah. [9]Uzziah was the father of Jotham, Jotham the father of Ahaz, and Ahaz the father of Hezekiah. [10]Hezekiah was the father of Manasseh, Manasseh the father of Amon, and Amon the father of Josiah. [11]Josiah became the father of Jeconiah and his brothers, at the time of the deportation to Babylon.

[12]After the deportation to Babylon: Jeconiah became the father of Shealtiel, and Shealtiel the father of Zerubbabel. [13]Zerubbabel was the father of Abihud, Abihud the father of Eliakim, and Eliakim the father of Azor. [14]Azor was the father of Zadok, Zadok the father of Achim, and Achim the father of

Eliud. **¹⁵Eliud was the father of Eleazar, Eleazar the father of Matthan, and Matthan the father of Jacob. ¹⁶Jacob was the father of Joseph the husband of Mary, by whom Jesus was born, who is called the Messiah.**

¹⁷So all the generations from Abraham to David are fourteen generations; from David to the deportation to Babylon, fourteen generations; and from the deportation to Babylon to the Messiah, fourteen generations.

The Book of Matthew has no formal preface as do the Books of Luke and John. Rather, Matthew immediately stressed that Jesus was the Messiah for whom the Jews had been looking. He began, **The record of the genealogy of Jesus the Messiah, the son of David, the son of Abraham** (Mt. 1:1). Ken Gire said, "As a frontispiece to his gospel, Matthew placed a family tree. The tree is rooted in Israel's greatest patriarch, Abraham, and in its greatest king, David."[1] According to Old Testament prophecies, the Messiah was to be a descendant of Abraham (Gen. 22:18; see Gal. 3:16) and also of David (see 2 Sam. 7:16; Jn. 7:42).

Matthew thus started the family tree with Abraham (Mt. 1:2), moved through David (Mt. 1:6, 7), and continued on to Jesus (Mt. 1:16). His list is divided into three parts—(1) from Abraham to David, (2) from David to the deportation, and (3) from the deportation to Jesus—each with fourteen names (Mt. 1:17). The name of David is included in the fourteen names in the first division and is also included as one of the fourteen names in the second division. This double use of David's name probably acknowledges his considerable contribution to the fulfillment of God's purposes.

When Matthew's list is compared with Old Testament genealogies, it will be seen that several names are left out. For instance, Matthew 1:8 says that "to Joram [was born] Uzziah," but Uzziah was actually the great-great-grandson of Joram (see 2 Kings 8:25; 13:1; 14:1, 21). We are not sure why these specific individuals are not mentioned. They were evil, but so were some who are listed. Keep in mind two facts: (1) Jews

---

[1]Ken Gire, *Moments with the Savior* (Grand Rapids, Mich.: Zondervan Publishing House, 1998), 18.

were concerned about showing lineage, not in listing every individual in that lineage; and (2) Jews liked "neat" listings.

Matthew 1:1–17 may seem to be just a dull list of names until we take the time to look up the names in the Old Testament. F. LaGard Smith said,

> Matthew's genealogy contains several happy surprises. Back in Jesus' early roots are not only such notable righteous men as Abraham and David, but also several who stand out in history as being particularly unrighteous, including wicked King Manasseh. Not only are there Jews, as would be expected, but also Gentiles, including a Canaanite and a Moabite, whose respective countrymen have been notorious enemies of God's people. Also somewhat surprising, in view of their social status at this time, is the listing of women as well as men. Furthermore, at least two of the women are known best for sins which they had committed.[2]

Some of those included in the list were great individuals, some were not so great, and some (to be painfully honest) were despicable. As Gire observed, "the Savior's family tree had its share of blight and barrenness, of bent twigs and broken branches."[3] If we ever needed proof that God can accomplish His purposes in spite of mankind's weakness (and even stubbornness), it is generously supplied in Matthew's genealogy.

Luke's Genealogy (Lk. 3:23–38)

[23]**When He began His ministry, Jesus Himself was about thirty years of age, being, as was supposed, the son of Joseph, the son of Eli, [24]the son of Matthat, the son of Levi, the son of Melchi, the son of Jannai, the son of Joseph, [25]the son of Mattathias, the son of Amos, the son of Nahum, the son of**

---

[2]F. LaGard Smith, *The Narrated Bible in Chronological Order* (Eugene, Oreg.: Harvest House Publishers, 1984), 1353.
[3]Gire, 19.

Hesli, the son of Naggai, [26]the son of Maath, the son of Mattathias, the son of Semein, the son of Josech, the son of Joda, [27]the son of Joanan, the son of Rhesa, the son of Zerubbabel, the son of Shealtiel, the son of Neri, [28]the son of Melchi, the son of Addi, the son of Cosam, the son of Elmadam, the son of Er, [29]the son of Joshua, the son of Eliezer, the son of Jorim, the son of Matthat, the son of Levi, [30]the son of Simeon, the son of Judah, the son of Joseph, the son of Jonam, the son of Eliakim, [31]the son of Melea, the son of Menna, the son of Mattatha, the son of Nathan, the son of David, [32]the son of Jesse, the son of Obed, the son of Boaz, the son of Salmon, the son of Nahshon, [33]the son of Amminadab, the son of Admin, the son of Ram, the son of Hezron, the son of Perez, the son of Judah, [34]the son of Jacob, the son of Isaac, the son of Abraham, the son of Terah, the son of Nahor, [35]the son of Serug, the son of Reu, the son of Peleg, the son of Heber, the son of Shelah, [36]the son of Cainan, the son of Arphaxad, the son of Shem, the son of Noah, the son of Lamech, [37]the son of Methuselah, the son of Enoch, the son of Jared, the son of Mahalaleel, the son of Cainan, [38]the son of Enosh, the son of Seth, the son of Adam, the son of God.

Luke also gives a genealogy, but it is not found at the beginning of the book. It is found in chapter 3 and has a different purpose than Matthew's list. Matthew's genealogy begins with Abraham (Mt. 1:1, 2) and shows Jesus' kinship with the Jews. The earthly part of Luke's genealogy ends with Adam (Lk. 3:38) and shows Jesus' kinship with all people.

Matthew's and Luke's accounts of Jesus' genealogy are strikingly different. Both show that Jesus was a descendant of Abraham (Mt. 1:2; Lk. 3:34) and David (Mt. 1:6; Lk. 3:31), but most of the other names in the two lists are different. One exception to this statement might be Zerubbabel (Mt. 1:12; Lk. 3:27), although some do not believe that the Zerubbabels in the two lists are the same man.

Various suggestions have been given regarding the differences. The simplest—and probably the best—is that Matthew gives the *legal* line of Jesus through *Joseph* while Luke gives the *fleshly* line of Jesus through *Mary*. Jesus was Joseph's *legal* son but not his *fleshly* son. Jesus' only Father was God. These two ways of looking at Jesus' lineage are sometimes distinguished as the *legal* line (through Joseph) and the *regal* (royal) line (through Mary).

This conclusion is found in Christian writings as far back as Eusebius (c. A.D. 260–340). The view correlates with the emphasis of Matthew on the birth of Christ from the viewpoint of Joseph (Mt. 1:18–25; 2:13–15, 19–23) and Luke's emphasis on the birth of Jesus from Mary's viewpoint (Lk. 1:26–56; 2:1–20 [note 2:19]). It also meshes with Matthew's Jewish emphasis and Luke's Greek emphasis.

The primary difficulty with this view is that Mary is not mentioned in Luke's genealogy. The reason for this may be that, as a rule, Jews did not include women in genealogies. Women might be mentioned incidentally (Mt. 1:3, 5), but the lines of descent were through men. Notice, however, that the text implies that Jesus was not the actual son of Joseph (**being, as was supposed, the son of Joseph**), indicating that Luke was not giving Jesus' line through Joseph. If not through Joseph, through whom? The simplest answer is that Luke was giving Jesus' line through Mary. The phrase "being, as supposed, the son of Joseph" should probably be thought of as parenthetical, with the words **son of Eli** referring to Jesus, not Joseph. (Some translations have "Eli" while others have "Heli." These are two ways of spelling the same name.) A. T. Robertson wrote, "Jesus would thus be Heli's grandson, an allowable meaning of 'son.'"[4]

"Son" could indicate "descended from" (see Mt. 1:1). Another possible meaning of "son" in the Bible is "son-in-law." Some speculate that Eli had only daughters, which meant that a "son-in-law" could inherit as a son (see Num. 27:1–11; 36:1–13).

Matthew thus stressed that Jesus was a legal descendant of David, while Luke stressed that Jesus was a fleshly descendant of David. Matthew traced the line through David's son King Solo-

---

[4]A. T. Robertson, *A Harmony of the Gospels for Students of the Life of Christ* (New York: Harper & Row, 1950), 261.

mon, while Luke gave the lineage through David's son Nathan (2 Sam. 5:14). The diagram "Jesus' Lineage from David" in the appendix illustrates the two lines. Also refer to "Jesus' Lineage" in the appendix. If the Zerubbabel in the two lists of genealogy is the same man, the lists could converge in the middle and then separate again.

The two genealogies given in the Gospels leave no doubt that the prophecy of 2 Samuel 7:16 was fulfilled.

THE ANNOUNCEMENTS (LK. 1:5–38)
The Book of Luke has the fullest account of the events imme-diately preceding the arrival of the Christ. Luke followed his introduction with two announcements.

The Angel's Announcement to Zacharias Regarding The Birth of John the Baptizer (Lk. 1:5–25)

⁵**In the days of Herod, king of Judea, there was a priest named Zacharias, of the division of Abijah; and he had a wife from the daughters of Aaron, and her name was Elizabeth. ⁶They were both righteous in the sight of God, walking blame-lessly in all the commandments and requirements of the Lord. ⁷But they had no child, because Elizabeth was barren, and they were both advanced in years.**

⁸**Now it happened that while he was performing his priestly service before God in the appointed order of his division, ⁹according to the custom of the priestly office, he was chosen by lot to enter the temple of the Lord and burn incense. ¹⁰And the whole multitude of the people were in prayer outside at the hour of the incense offering. ¹¹And an angel of the Lord appeared to him, standing to the right of the altar of incense. ¹²Zacharias was troubled when he saw the angel, and fear gripped him. ¹³But the angel said to him, "Do not be afraid, Zacharias, for your petition has been heard, and your wife Elizabeth will bear you a son, and you will give him the name John. ¹⁴You will have joy and gladness, and many will rejoice at his birth. ¹⁵For he will be great in the sight of the Lord; and he will drink no wine or liquor,**

and he will be filled with the Holy Spirit while yet in his mother's womb. [16]And he will turn many of the sons of Israel back to the Lord their God. [17]It is he who will go as a forerunner before Him in the spirit and power of Elijah, to turn the hearts of the fathers back to the children, and the disobedient to the attitude of the righteous, so as to make ready a people prepared for the Lord."

[18]Zacharias said to the angel, "How will I know this for certain? For I am an old man and my wife is advanced in years." [19]The angel answered and said to him, "I am Gabriel, who stands in the presence of God, and I have been sent to speak to you and to bring you this good news. [20]And behold, you shall be silent and unable to speak until the day when these things take place, because you did not believe my words, which will be fulfilled in their proper time."

[21]The people were waiting for Zacharias, and were wondering at his delay in the temple. [22]But when he came out, he was unable to speak to them; and they realized that he had seen a vision in the temple; and he kept making signs to them, and remained mute. [23]When the days of his priestly service were ended, he went back home.

[24]After these days Elizabeth his wife became pregnant, and she kept herself in seclusion for five months, saying, [25]"This is the way the Lord has dealt with me in the days when He looked with favor upon me, to take away my disgrace among men."

Zacharias lived in the hill country southwest of Jerusalem. According to Moses' instructions, to be a priest, one had to be a descendant of the original high priest, Aaron (Ex. 28:1). Zacharias' wife, **Elizabeth**, was also a descendant of Aaron. Both were upright, godly individuals. Only one thing marred their lives: They had grown old without having children (Lk. 1:7).

The priests had been divided into twenty-four divisions, or orders (1 Chron. 24:1–19). Zacharias was of the division of Abijah (Lk. 1:5; see 1 Chron. 24:10). The orders took turns ministering in the temple, a week at a time. Each week, lots were cast regarding temple duties (Lk. 1:9). The most coveted task was offering incense on the altar that stood before the curtain that hid the Most Holy Place. This was the closest an ordinary priest could come to that hallowed spot. It was an honor that might come once in a lifetime.

As the story begins, it was Zacharias' week to serve in the temple—and he had the privilege of offering incense. As he walked into the holy place, he must have been thinking what a special day it was. It was to be even more special than he could have anticipated—for an angel of the Lord named **Gabriel** appeared to him. In the Bible, only two angels are named: Gabriel (Lk. 1:19, 26; see Dan. 8:16; 9:21) and Michael (Jude 9; Rev. 12:7; see Dan. 10:13, 21; 12:1). The word **angel** is a transliteration of the Greek word ἄγγελος (*aggelos*) which literally means "messenger."

God's messenger told the old priest that he and Elizabeth would have a son (Lk. 1:13). This son, who was to be named John, would come **in the spirit and power of Elijah** as the forerunner of the Messiah (Lk. 1:17). Gabriel quoted from Malachi 4:5, 6, a prophecy of that forerunner. In the angel's announcement, he mentioned that John would **drink no wine or liquor** (Lk. 1:15; compare with Num. 6:2, 3). Apparently, John was to be a Nazirite from birth. Others who were Nazirites from birth were Samson (Judg. 13:3–7) and Samuel (1 Sam. 1:11).

The priest found the angel's words hard to believe (Lk. 1:18, 20). As a sign—and a punishment for his unbelief—Zacharias was rendered incapable of speech (Lk. 1:20).

After he completed his week of service, Zacharias returned home (Lk. 1:23). His wife soon became pregnant as the angel had predicted (Lk. 1:24). The priest needed to learn that "with God nothing shall be impossible" (Lk. 1:37; KJV).

The Angel's Announcement to Mary Regarding The Birth of Jesus (Lk. 1:26–38)

²⁶**Now in the sixth month the angel Gabriel was sent from God to a city in Galilee called Nazareth, ²⁷to a virgin engaged to a man whose name was Joseph, of the descendants of David; and the virgin's name was Mary. ²⁸And coming in, he said to**

her, "Greetings, favored one! The Lord is with you." [29]But she was very perplexed at this statement, and kept pondering what kind of salutation this was. [30]The angel said to her, "Do not be afraid, Mary; for you have found favor with God. [31]And behold, you will conceive in your womb and bear a son, and you shall name Him Jesus. [32]He will be great and will be called the Son of the Most High; and the Lord God will give Him the throne of His father David; [33]and He will reign over the house of Jacob forever, and His kingdom will have no end." [34]Mary said to the angel, "How can this be, since I am a virgin?" [35]The angel answered and said to her, "The Holy Spirit will come upon you, and the power of the Most High will overshadow you; and for that reason the holy Child shall be called the Son of God. [36]And behold, even your relative Elizabeth has also conceived a son in her old age; and she who was called barren is now in her sixth month. [37]For nothing will be impossible with God." [38]And Mary said, "Behold, the bondslave of the Lord; may it be done to me according to your word." And the angel departed from her.

The first announcement had been made in the most sacred city in Palestine; the second was made in one of the most despised (Jn. 1:46).

When Elizabeth was about six months pregnant (Lk. 1:26, 36), Gabriel appeared to a young woman in **Nazareth,** a small insignificant village in Galilee. The first-century Jewish historian Josephus mentioned 204 cities and towns in Galilee but made no reference to Nazareth.[5] The *Talmud* listed sixty-three Galilean towns, but not Nazareth. The young woman in Nazareth was **a virgin engaged to a man whose name was Joseph, . . . and the virgin's name was Mary** (Lk. 1:27). Assuming that Mary became pregnant shortly after Gabriel's announcement to her, this would make John the Baptizer about six months older than Jesus.

---

[5]J. W. McGarvey and Philip Y. Pendleton, *The Fourfold Gospel or A Harmony of the Four Gospels* (Cincinnati: Standard Publishing Co., 1914), 14.

The Greek word μνηστεύω (*mnesteuo*), translated **engaged,** referred to a more binding arrangement than the engagements with which many of us are familiar. Jewish marriages had two stages: first a commitment ceremony (called "the betrothal" [Mt. 1:18]) and then, sometime later, the actual marriage service. As a rule, the marriage ceremony was about a year after the betrothal ceremony. The first ceremony legally bound the groom and the bride even though the marriage had not been consummated. Mary was legally bound to Joseph even though they were not yet officially married (see Deut. 22:23). This passage explains Joseph's predicament when he learned that Mary was pregnant (Mt. 1:18, 19).

The angel told Mary, **"And behold, you will conceive in your womb and bear a son, and you shall name Him Jesus"** (Lk. 1:31). "Jesus" is the Greek form of the Hebrew name "Joshua," the shortened form of a name meaning "Jehovah saves" or "Jehovah is salvation." It was a fairly common name in those days. Read Acts 13:6 and note that "Bar-Jesus" means "son of Jesus." "Jesus" is still a common name in some cultures. Nevertheless, it was chosen for Mary's Son because of its appropriateness (see Mt. 1:21).

Unlike Zacharias, Mary had no difficulty in believing that what the angel promised *would* happen (Lk. 1:45). She did have a question concerning *how* it would happen:

> **Mary said to the angel, "How can this be, since I am a virgin?" The angel answered and said to her, "The Holy Spirit will come upon you, and the power of the Most High will overshadow you; and for that reason the holy child shall be called the Son of God"** (Lk. 1:34, 35).

The usual Greek word for "virgin" (παρθένος, *parthenos*) was used in Luke 1:27. In verse 34, Mary literally said, "Since I know no man" (see the KJV). The text leaves no doubt that Mary was a virgin when the angel appeared to her.

The biblical doctrine of the virgin birth is beyond our capacity to comprehend fully, but we accept it by faith. Some teach that whether or not one believes in the virgin birth is unimportant. John Franklin Carter listed some reasons why this doctrine is vital to our faith:[6]

(1) Since the New Testament teaches the virgin birth of Jesus, denying the virgin birth involves a denial of the inspiration of the Scriptures.

(2) Since the virgin birth was an indispensable part of "God becoming flesh," denying the virgin birth destroys Jesus' essential deity.

(3) Since the virgin birth is tied with Jesus' being God, denying the virgin birth denies the efficacy of Jesus' death. How could the death of one mortal atone for the sins of all other mortals?

(4) Since the virgin birth was the first of the miracles in Jesus' life, denying the virgin birth renders one incapable of accepting the other miracles—including the Resurrection. Unbelief is both the root and the fruit of denying the virgin birth.

APPLICATION:
WHY GOD CHOSE MARY (LK. 1; 2)

In the passage on "the worthy woman," it is noted, "Her children rise up and bless her" (Prov. 31:28a). The KJV expresses the thought this way: "Her children arise up, and call her blessed."

Mothers are special. In a *Peanuts* comic strip, Charlie Brown said, "Everyone needs someone to love them, trust them, care for them, support them, laugh and cry with them." Lucy responded, "That's a lot of people." Then Snoopy added, "Or *one* wonderful mother." Of all who have believed in me and supported me, at the top of the list are two mothers: my own mother and the mother of my three girls. Most of us could rise up and call our mothers blessed.

In Luke 1 we are encouraged to call someone else's mother blessed. In verse 42 Elizabeth said to a mother-to-be: "Blessed are you among women." That was a Hebrew expression meaning, "You are the most blessed among women." In verse 48 the

---

[6]John Franklin Carter, *A Layman's Harmony of the Gospels* (Nashville: Broadman Press, 1961), 41, 42.

woman addressed replied, "For behold, from this time on all generations will count me blessed." Not only would her children call her blessed, but all people would acknowledge that she had been blessed of God. The passage speaks of Mary, the mother of Jesus.

All mothers are blessed, but Mary was especially blessed. Of all the Jewish women living at that time, God chose her to be the mother of His Son. As we consider this fact, we ask, "Why? What was special about Mary?"

God was not under compulsion to choose her. Nothing in the Word indicates that Mary was so good and perfect that God was forced to choose her. Rather, we are told that God chose her as an expression of His grace. The angel greeted Mary with the words "Greetings, favored one!" (Lk. 1:28). "Favored" is translated from χαριτόω (charitoo), a form of χάρις (charis), the Greek word for "grace"—and the word "grace" speaks of "unmerited favor." Nevertheless, Mary must have had certain special qualities to be chosen by God. Therefore, we again ask, "What were those qualities?" We will survey her life to discover "Why God Chose Mary."

Turn first to Luke 1:26. This verse begins, "Now in the sixth month. . . ." This was the sixth month of the pregnancy of Elizabeth, the mother of John the Baptizer. "Now in the sixth month the angel Gabriel was sent from God to a city in Galilee called Nazareth." Nazareth was a small village located fifteen miles west of the western tip of the Sea of Galilee and twenty-two miles from the Mediterranean, on one of the southernmost slopes of the Lebanon mountain ranges.

The angel was sent "to a virgin engaged to a man whose name was Joseph, of the descendants of David" (Lk. 1:27a). Joseph was a descendant of David the king, but the royal line had fallen on hard times. Joseph was a poor carpenter (Mt. 13:55) living in Nazareth (Lk. 2:4). One way we know that Joseph and Mary were poor is that they offered a sacrifice that the poor were allowed to make (compare Lk. 2:24 with Lev. 12:6–8). J. W. McGarvey was surely right when he wrote, "Knowing the greatness of the child, Joseph and Mary would never have used the lesser sacrifice if they could have afforded the regular and more costly one."[7] Jesus' lifestyle (Mt. 8:20) also suggests a humble beginning.

The name of the virgin to whom the angel was sent was Mary (Lk. 1:27b). "Mary" is the Greek form of the Hebrew name "Miriam" (meaning "bitter"). Like Joseph, she apparently came from an unpretentious family. She also was a descendant of King David.

Our text emphasizes that the Christ was a descendant of David (Lk. 1:32, 69). God told David that the Messiah would "come forth from" him (2 Sam. 7:12). Literally, God said that the Messiah would "proceed out of [David's] bowels" (see the KJV). The NIV has "will come from your own body." Since Jesus was not a fleshly descendant of David through Joseph, He had to be a fleshly descendant through Mary to fulfill this promise.

Mary was engaged—or betrothed—to Joseph (Mt. 1:18). In that day, most betrothals occurred very early in a young woman's life, so Mary may have been a teenager when Gabriel appeared to her. On the other hand, Joseph may have been an older man. Joseph is never mentioned during the personal ministry of Jesus, suggesting the possibility that he died before Jesus was thirty.

When it comes to fulfilling God's purposes, surroundings and circumstances are not that important. God can use anyone in any place. The passage also implies that one does not have to wait until he is old and wrinkled to be used by God. God's angel came to a young girl, probably still in her teens, to enlist her help in fulfilling the divine plan.

She Was Not Afraid to Use Her Mind

The angel said to Mary, "Greetings, favored one! The Lord is with you" (Lk. 1:28). Mary was "very perplexed" by the angel's statement (Lk. 1:29a). Most people in the Bible were troubled when confronted by a heavenly visitor. Instead of panicking, however, she pondered "what kind of salutation this was" (Lk. 1:29b).

Mary was a person who used her mind. Later we are told that she pondered over the events surrounding the birth of Jesus

---

[7]McGarvey and Pendleton, 34.

(Lk. 2:19). She was not afraid to use the mind that God had given her.

She Was a Godly Woman

"The angel said to her, 'Do not be afraid, Mary; for you have found favor with God'" (Lk. 1:30). No one finds favor with God without being basically good. We can think of Mary as honest and religious, with high moral standards—a person of integrity.

She Believed in God—And His Power

The angel continued:

> And behold, you will conceive in your womb and bear a son, and you shall name Him Jesus [which means "Jehovah saves"]. He will be great and will be called the Son of the Most High; and the Lord God will give Him the throne of His father David; and He will reign over the house of Jacob forever, and His kingdom will have no end (Lk. 1:31–33).

Jesus' kingdom is the church (Mt. 16:18, 19). Our Lord sat down on David's throne and began to reign over His kingdom when He ascended to the right hand of God (Acts 2:25–36). The angel's words anticipated all this.

Young Mary's concern, however, was not about what would happen thirty-plus years in the future. The words ringing in her ears were "you will conceive in your womb and bear a son." She said to the angel, "How can this be, since I am a virgin?" (Lk. 1:34).

At first glance, this sounds similar to Zacharias' response of unbelief which resulted in nine months of being unable to speak (Lk. 1:18, 20)—but Mary's question was not *whether* this would be, but *how* it would be. It is stressed in our text that she *believed* the angel (Lk. 1:45).

The angel answered her question of "how." He said, "The Holy Spirit will come upon you, and the power of the Most High will overshadow you; and for that reason the holy Child shall be called the Son of God" (Lk. 1:35). The Greek word ἐπισκιάζω (*episkiazo*), translated "overshadow," was used in the Septuagint (the Greek translation of the Old Testament) to speak of the presence of God filling the tabernacle (see Ex. 40:35).

Mary had not asked for a sign, but the angel gave her one: "And behold, even your relative [cousin, KJV] Elizabeth has also conceived a son in her old age; and she who was called barren is now in her sixth month" (Lk. 1:36). He added, "For nothing will be impossible with God" (Lk. 1:37). The Greek text literally has "because every word will not be impossible with God." The ASV thus renders the verse "For no word from God shall be void of power." This is what Mary was asked to believe—and she did (Lk. 1:45). This is also what we must believe if we are to meet the challenges of life.

She Had a Humble Spirit

Mary answered, "Behold, the bondslave of the Lord; may it be done to me according to your word" (Lk. 1:38a). If there is a single verse that makes clear why God chose Mary, this is it. First, notice the phrase "the bondslave of the Lord." The Greek word δοῦλος (*doulos*), translated "bondslave," is the feminine form of the word for "slave." Female slaves were the lowliest, often the most despised and mistreated, of slaves. Mary later sang, "He has had regard for the humble state of His bondslave" (Lk. 1:48).

She Was Submissive to the Will of God

Look at the second part of Lk. 1:38: "May it be done to me according to your word." Consider all the implications of this statement. (Remember that Mary was a thinking person; she went into this with her eyes open.) She was a young woman, engaged to be married, who would suddenly be pregnant. Her husband-to-be was sure to protest, "It's not mine!"

It is hard for us to realize how precarious her situation would be in a small town like Nazareth. Imagine the looks, the stares, the whispers, the gossip, and the vicious comments Some think that the implication of John 8:41 is "We were not born of fornication—but *you* were." She could even lose her life, for the Law said that an engaged woman who committed fornication was to be stoned to death (Deut. 22:23, 24; see also

Lev. 20:10; Ezek. 16:38; Jn. 8:5). Of all the sins punishable by death in the Old Testament, the sin of fornication was difficult for a woman to deny when the act made her pregnant. Finding two or three witnesses against her (Deut. 17:6; 19:15) would be no problem; the first two or three people who walked past Mary in the sixth or seventh month of her pregnancy would serve the purpose.

Mary was surely aware of all the repercussions. Nevertheless, she told the angel, "Be it done to me according to your word." In other words, "If that's the way God wants it, that is the way it will be." She was submissive to the will of God. *That* is the kind of person God can use—whether mother, father, son, or daughter.

After "the angel departed from her" (Lk. 1:38b), "Mary arose and went in a hurry to the hill country" (Lk. 1:39) to see her relative Elizabeth. Elizabeth was probably one of the few people who would believe what had happened to her.

When Elizabeth saw Mary, she "was filled with the Holy Spirit" (Lk. 1:41b) and "cried out with a loud voice" (Lk. 1:42a): "Blessed are you among women, and blessed is the fruit of your womb! And how has it happened to me, that the mother of my Lord would come to me?" (Lk. 1:42b, 43).

She Knew the Scriptures

Mary responded with a magnificent song of praise that begins in verse 46 and continues through verse 55. Ernest Hauser wrote that this short, exultant poem "is one of the literary gems of the New Testament."[8] In these ten verses, we have most of the recorded words of the mother of Jesus.

Mary's words remind us of the song of Hannah in 1 Samuel 2:1–10. Mary's song contains three main themes: (1) what God had done for her (Lk. 1:46–49), (2) what God had done for all people—He had helped the helpless, the humble, and the hungry (Lk. 1:50–53), and (3) what God had done for Israel (Lk. 1:54, 55). The last was proof that God always keeps His Word.

---

[8]Ernest O. Hauser, "Mary, Mother of Christ," *Reader's Digest* (December 1971): 170.

As we consider what Mary said, we are impressed with the fact that she knew the Scriptures. I am not discounting the possibility that Mary was "filled with the Holy Spirit" as Elizabeth was (Lk. 1:41) and as Zacharias later was (Lk. 1:67). Nevertheless, I believe that Mary's words indicate a personal knowledge of the Word. Twelve Old Testament passages are reflected in her words of praise. This fact was remarkable in a day when only boys were allowed to attend the synagogue schools.

We must quicken our pace through the life of Mary. Luke 2 tells the story of the birth of Jesus and the coming of the shepherds. Verse 19 says that "Mary treasured all these things, pondering them in her heart."

She Was Brave and Courageous

About forty days after Jesus' birth, Mary and Joseph took the baby to the temple in Jerusalem to offer a sacrifice (see Lev. 12:2–4, 6–8). There a man named Simeon took Jesus in his arms and spoke of all that the Child would accomplish (Lk. 2:25–35). His inspired words included this ominous warning to Mary: "And a sword will pierce even your own soul" (Lk. 2:35a).

Consider the task that awaited Mary. It was not easy for my wife and me to rear three daughters. Mary had at least *seven* children (by Joseph; see Mk. 6:3)—and the oldest of them was the Son of God. We cannot even imagine the stress of being responsible for rearing God's own Son. Now, on top of this, Simeon told her that, in the end, a sword would pierce her soul. Heartache was ahead.

Only a brave woman could have faced—and met—those challenges. Mary had shown her courage by being willing to accept the consequences of being an unwed mother in a day when such was almost unheard of. She continued to show her courage by accepting the consequences of being the mother of our Lord.

This truth may help explain why God chose a poor, unknown young woman from an obscure, even despised, town rather than a pampered darling in a royal court. God needed someone who was strong and resilient. We might say God needed someone who was *tough*.

We never read about Joseph during the time of Jesus' personal ministry; we read only of Mary and her children. Many think that this indicates that Joseph was older than Mary and died before Jesus began His public work. The fact that Jesus committed the care of His mother to John (Jn. 19:26, 27) also indicates that Joseph was no longer living. There is a strong possibility that Mary had to do much of the rearing of her seven or more children by herself. As the firstborn, Jesus would have assumed some of the responsibility when His father died. Nevertheless, the burden on Mary as the surviving parent would have been great.

She Was Willing to Accept Responsibility

Mary's toughness ties in with another characteristic she had, a characteristic lacking in many: She was willing to accept responsibility. We could use the story of Jesus at the age of twelve to illustrate this (Lk. 2:41–51). When Joseph and Mary did not know where Jesus was, they searched Jerusalem diligently for Him. After all, God had given them the responsibility to care for Him. Unfortunately, some today are unwilling to accept responsibility—in their personal lives, in their marriages, and in their families.

She Expressed Confidence in Her Son

We jump eighteen years to the time when Jesus began His public ministry. Early in that ministry, Mary and her Son were at a wedding feast in Cana. When they ran out of wine, Mary said to Jesus, "They have no wine" (Jn. 2:3). Then she said to the servants, "Whatever He says to you, do it" (Jn. 2:5). She believed her Son could take care of the situation.

She displayed a characteristic every parent needs: She had confidence in her child, and she expressed that confidence. One of the greatest gifts my mother gave me was the constant reinforcement of the thought "you can do it."

She Was Concerned About the Welfare of Others

One of the few times we read of Mary during the next three-plus years is when she seemed concerned that Jesus was not getting enough to eat (Mk. 3:20, 21). She and her other children came to bring Him home (Mk. 3:31–35). The incident does not flatter Mary and her family; they obviously had not fully grasped who Jesus was and what His mission was. Nevertheless, it shows that Mary cared about her Son.

She Was Faithful to Her Task to the End

At that point in the narrative we lose sight of Mary—until the cross. John recorded this poignant scene:

> . . . But standing by the cross of Jesus were His mother, and His mother's sister, Mary the wife of Clopas, and Mary Magdalene. When Jesus then saw His mother, and the disciple whom He loved [probably John] standing nearby, He said to His mother, "Woman, behold, your son!" Then He said to the disciple, "Behold, your mother!" . . . (Jn. 19:25–27).

Can you see Mary standing there, looking up at her Son on the cross? Can you see the tears coursing down her cheeks? Can you see her cradling her arms as she recalled holding His tiny form? Years ago I memorized a poem that captured this moment:

> I heard two women weeping
> As down the hill they came;
> And one was like a broken rose,
> And one was like a flame.
> One said, "Men shall rue this deed
> Their evil hands have done";
> The other said only through her tears,
> "My Son, my Son, my Son."[9]

On a hill called Golgotha, Mary at last understood the words spoken years before: "And a sword will pierce even your own soul" (Lk. 2:35a).

One last scene remains: After the death, burial, and resurrection of Jesus, the disciples waited in Jerusalem for the coming

---

[9]Author unknown.

of the Spirit and the ushering in of the kingdom / church. Luke recorded that there with the disciples were Mary and Jesus' brothers (Acts 1:14). The brothers had come to faith; Mary's faith had blossomed into understanding.

There we must leave Mary. One uninspired tradition says that she died in Jerusalem; another says that she moved to Ephesus with John and died there. We do not know what happened to her. God let us know that she was part of the exciting early days of the church, and with that He drew the curtain on the story of the mother of our Lord.

Conclusion

Why did God choose Mary? Several characteristics were suggested that surely helped Mary to meet the almost-impossible task that God gave her:

- She was not afraid to use her mind.
- She was a godly woman.
- She believed in God—and His power.
- She had a humble spirit.
- She was submissive to the will of God.
- She knew the Scriptures.
- She was brave and courageous.
- She was willing to accept responsibility.
- She expressed confidence in her Son.
- She was concerned about the welfare of others.
- She was faithful to her task to the end.

These characteristics will help anyone to succeed in the tasks of life. More important, they will qualify anyone to be used by God in His service.

THE VISIT OF MARY (THE EXPECTANT MOTHER OF JESUS) TO ELIZABETH (THE EXPECTANT MOTHER OF JOHN THE BAPTIZER) (LK. 1:39–56)

39Now at this time Mary arose and went in a hurry to the

hill country, to a city of Judah, ⁴⁰and entered the house of Zacharias and greeted Elizabeth.

Gabriel mentioned that God had also visited a relative of Mary's named Elizabeth, and that this relative was pregnant. Shortly after the angel's appearance, Mary traveled seventy or eighty miles south to the city where Zacharias and Elizabeth lived (Lk. 1:39, 40). Perhaps she thought that her cousin was the one person who could understand and appreciate what was happening to her.

Elizabeth Praised Mary (Lk. 1:41–45)

⁴¹When Elizabeth heard Mary's greeting, the baby leaped in her womb; and Elizabeth was filled with the Holy Spirit. ⁴²And she cried out with a loud voice and said, "Blessed are you among women, and blessed is the fruit of your womb! ⁴³And how has it happened to me, that the mother of my Lord would come to me? ⁴⁴For behold, when the sound of your greeting reached my ears, the baby leaped in my womb for joy. ⁴⁵And blessed is she who believed that there would be a fulfillment of what had been spoken to her by the Lord."

Think of the reunion that must have taken place—two women, one elderly and one still a girl, both touched by the hand of God. When Elizabeth saw Mary, she burst into inspired praise for Mary: **"Blessed are you among women, and blessed is the fruit of your womb!"** (Lk. 1:42).

Mary Praised God (Lk. 1:46–55)

⁴⁶And Mary said:
"My soul exalts the Lord,
⁴⁷And my spirit has rejoiced in God my Savior.
⁴⁸For He has had regard for the humble state of His bond-slave;
For behold, from this time on all generations will count me blessed.

[49]For the Mighty One has done great things for me;
And holy is His name.
[50]And His mercy is upon generation after generation
Toward those who fear Him.
[51]He has done mighty deeds with His arm;
He has scattered those who were proud in the thoughts of
    their heart.
[52]He has brought down rulers from their thrones,
And has exalted those who were humble.
[53]He has filled the hungry with good things;
And sent away the rich empty-handed.
[54]He has given help to Israel His servant,
In remembrance of His mercy,
[55]As He spoke to our fathers,
To Abraham and his descendants forever."

Mary responded with praise for the Lord. She spoke of great things God had done in the past, anticipating great things God would do in the future. Mary's words are sometimes called the *Magnificat*—a Latin term for the first word of her hymn to the Lord, which means "magnifying."

Mary stayed in Judea for three months—to the end of Elizabeth's pregnancy (Lk. 1:56). Then she returned home to Nazareth. Apparently, she left shortly before the birth of John. Perhaps she did not want to answer questions regarding her own pregnancy when Elizabeth's relatives arrived for the birth. (They would have been Mary's relatives also.)

THE BIRTH AND EARLY LIFE
OF JOHN THE BAPTIZER (LK. 1:57–80)

John's Birth (Lk. 1:57–79)

[57]Now the time had come for Elizabeth to give birth, and she gave birth to a son. [58]Her neighbors and her relatives heard that the Lord had displayed His great mercy toward her; and they were rejoicing with her.

[59]And it happened that on the eighth day they came to cir-

cumcise the child, and they were going to call him Zacharias, after his father. ⁶⁰But his mother answered and said, "No indeed; but he shall be called John." ⁶¹And they said to her, "There is no one among your relatives who is called by that name." ⁶²And they made signs to his father, as to what he wanted him called. ⁶³And he asked for a tablet and wrote as follows, "His name is John." And they were all astonished. ⁶⁴And at once his mouth was opened and his tongue loosed, and he began to speak in praise of God. ⁶⁵Fear came on all those living around them; and all these matters were being talked about in all the hill country of Judea. ⁶⁶All who heard them kept them in mind, saying, "What then will this child turn out to be?" For the hand of the Lord was certainly with him.

⁶⁷And his father Zacharias was filled with the Holy Spirit, and prophesied, saying:
⁶⁸"Blessed be the Lord God of Israel,
For He has visited us and accomplished redemption for
    His people,
⁶⁹And has raised up a horn of salvation for us
In the house of David His servant—
⁷⁰As He spoke by the mouth of His holy prophets from of
    old—
⁷¹Salvation from our enemies,
And from the hand of all who hate us;
⁷²To show mercy toward our fathers,
And to remember His holy covenant,
⁷³The oath which He swore to Abraham our father,
⁷⁴To grant us that we, being rescued from the hand of our
    enemies,
Might serve Him without fear,
⁷⁵In holiness and righteousness before Him all our days.
⁷⁶And you, child, will be called the prophet of the Most
    High;
For you will go on before the Lord to prepare His ways;
⁷⁷To give to His people the knowledge of salvation
By the forgiveness of their sins,
⁷⁸Because of the tender mercy of our God,
With which the Sunrise from on high will visit us,

⁷⁹**To shine upon those who sit in darkness and the shadow
   of death,
To guide our feet into the way of peace."**

When Zacharias and Elizabeth's baby was born, neighbors
and relatives gathered to rejoice with them.

According to Jewish law, baby boys were to be circumcised
on the eighth day (Lev. 12:3). At the circumcision ceremony of
the new baby, the family suggested that he be named **Zacharias**
after his father, but Elizabeth (who had evidently been told the
angel's words) said, **"No indeed; but he shall be called John"**
(Lk. 1:60). They appealed to Zacharias, but he confirmed Elizabeth's choice of names. **And at once his mouth was opened
and his tongue loosed, and he began to speak in praise of God**
(Lk. 1:64).

Luke 1:68–79 gives the old priest's inspired words. Verses 68
through 75 are praise for God for His promises to His people,
while verses 76 through 79 are directed to his son. He told little
John, **"And you, child, will be called the prophet of the Most
High; for you will go on before the Lord to prepare His ways"**
(Lk. 1:76). Like the angel, Zacharias quoted from the prophet
Malachi concerning the coming of the forerunner of the Mes-
siah.

John's Early Life (Lk. 1:80)

⁸⁰**And the child continued to grow and to become strong
in spirit, and he lived in the deserts until the day of his public appearance to Israel.**

Luke 1:80 gives a thumbnail sketch of the first thirty or so
years of John's life. The **deserts** were the sparsely settled area of
Judea just west of the Dead Sea.

Angels had appeared to humans. People had been inspired
by God's Spirit to speak. Four hundred years of silence had been
broken. "The fullness of the time" (Gal. 4:4) had come. The Messiah was coming!

THE ANNOUNCEMENT TO JOSEPH REGARDING THE COMING OF JESUS (MT. 1:18–25)

[18]Now the birth of Jesus Christ was as follows: when His mother Mary had been betrothed to Joseph, before they came together she was found to be with child by the Holy Spirit. [19]And Joseph her husband, being a righteous man and not wanting to disgrace her, planned to send her away secretly. [20]But when he had considered this, behold, an angel of the Lord appeared to him in a dream, saying, "Joseph, son of David, do not be afraid to take Mary as your wife; for the Child who has been conceived in her is of the Holy Spirit. [21]She will bear a Son; and you shall call His name Jesus, for He will save His people from their sins." [22]Now all this took place to fulfill what was spoken by the Lord through the prophet: [23]"Behold, the virgin shall be with child and shall bear a son, and they shall call His name Immanuel," which translated means, "God with us." [24]And Joseph awoke from his sleep and did as the angel of the Lord commanded him, and took Mary as his wife, [25]but kept her a virgin until she gave birth to a Son; and he called His name Jesus.

Isaiah prophesied the coming of the Messiah with these words: "For a child will be born to us, a son will be given to us; and the government will rest on His shoulders; and His name will be called Wonderful Counselor, Mighty God, Eternal Father, Prince of Peace" (Is. 9:6).

The Jews were looking for a man of war to lead them to victory; God would send a helpless baby to bring them back to Him. Men wanted a ruler on an earthly throne; God would give them a child in a feeding trough. It was not man's way, but it was God's way.

When Mary walked into Nazareth, returning from her three months with Elizabeth, it must have been obvious to everyone that she was pregnant. Gossip probably spread quickly.

Joseph must have been devastated. He struggled with what action he should take. A betrothal was sacred and legally binding, even though the wedding ceremony had not taken place and the marriage had not been consummated. Joseph had three options:

(1) He could ignore Mary's condition and proceed with the marriage. He apparently did not consider this possibility. As a righteous man (Mt. 1:19), he probably believed that it would be wrong for him to condone what seemed to be obvious immorality. We do not know whether or not Mary shared with him the news of her heavenly visit; but if she did, he probably found it hard to believe.

(2) He could have Mary stoned to death as one unfaithful to her betrothal vows (Deut. 22:23, 24). Joseph rejected this option. He was righteous, but also compassionate. His love for Mary probably still burned in his heart.

(3) He could divorce her. The Law made provision for a man to give his wife "a certificate of divorce" if he "found some indecency in her" (Deut. 24:1). Joseph decided on this action as the least of three evils. He would put Mary away as quickly and quietly as possible to save her further embarrassment. As a rule, the writing of divorcement was delivered in the presence of two or more witnesses. If the man desired, the ceremony could be very public and humiliating for the wife. Joseph wanted to avoid this: **. . . not wanting to disgrace her,** [he] **planned to send her away secretly** (Mt. 1:19). His decision no doubt filled him with sorrow. Among other considerations, once he handed the certificate to Mary, she could be lost to him forever (Deut. 24:2–4).

God delivered Joseph from his dilemma by sending an angel. (A major emphasis in Matthew 1 is how God arranged matters so that Isaiah's promise of a Child might be fulfilled.) The angel told the carpenter,

> **. . . Joseph, son of David, do not be afraid to take Mary as your wife; for the Child who has been conceived in her is of the Holy Spirit. She will bear a Son; and you shall call His name Jesus, for He will save His people from their sins** (Mt. 1:20, 21).

Joseph must have had mixed emotions. He would have been

happy to know that his beloved Mary had not been unfaithful, and he would have been thrilled at the announcement of the Messiah. He must have realized, however, that now both he and Mary would be targets for the snickers and snide remarks of the crude and unfeeling. Nevertheless, he did not hesitate. He **awoke . . . and did as the angel of the Lord commanded him, and took Mary as his wife, but kept her a virgin until she gave birth to a Son** (Mt. 1:24, 25a). The natural and normal way of interpreting the preceding words is that *after* Mary "gave birth to a Son," Joseph and Mary had the normal sex life of a married couple.

Matthew, who wanted to establish that Jesus was the promised Messiah, inserted an inspired observation:

> **Now all this took place to fulfill what was spoken by the Lord through the prophet: "Behold, the virgin shall be with child and shall bear a Son, and they shall call His name Immanuel [or Emmanuel]," which translated means, "God with us"** (Mt. 1:22, 23).

J. W. McGarvey's comment on "Immanuel" is worth repeating: "Nature shows God above us; the Law shows God against us; but the Gospel shows God with us, and for us."[10]

THE BIRTH OF JESUS (LK. 2:1–7)

[1]Now in those days a decree went out from Caesar Augustus, that a census be taken of all the inhabited earth. [2]This was the first census taken while Quirinius was governor of Syria. [3]And everyone was on his way to register for the census, each to his own city. [4]Joseph also went up from Galilee, from the city of Nazareth, to Judea, to the city of David which is called Bethlehem, because he was of the house and family of David, [5]in order to register along with Mary, who was engaged to him, and was with child. [6]While they were there, the days were completed for her to give birth. [7]And she gave birth to her firstborn

---

[10]McGarvey and Pendleton, 26.

TRUTH FOR TODAY COMMENTARY

son; and she wrapped Him in cloths, and laid Him in a manger, because there was no room for them in the inn.

Joseph and Mary's love for each other, plus their confidence in God's promises, enabled them to survive any innuendoes and insults that slithered their way. As Mary reached her ninth month, their anticipation must have grown daily. A problem existed, however, that they were apparently unaware of: The Messiah was to be born in Bethlehem (Mic. 5:2), and they lived in Nazareth.

Earlier, God had used an angel to further His cause. In this situation, He used the most unlikely of prospects: the emperor of Rome. **Now in those days a decree went out from Caesar Augustus, that a census be taken of all the inhabited earth** (Lk. 2:1). This census was probably for the purpose of broadening Rome's tax base.

Everyone in the Roman Empire was required to return to his ancestral city. Joseph, who was a descendant of King David, had to make the trip to the town of David's birth, **Bethlehem**, a village five miles south of Jerusalem. Bethlehem is mentioned several times in the Old Testament (Gen. 48:7; Ruth 1:22), but it is primarily known for being the home of David (1 Sam. 16:1; 17:12; 20:6).

The Scriptures imply that Joseph would not have made the trip to Bethlehem if Rome had not insisted, further implying that God did not tell Joseph and Mary that the baby needed to be born in Bethlehem. The law probably did not require Mary to go. Why, then, did she go? Probably, she did not wish to be parted from Joseph when her baby was born.

Joseph also went up from Galilee, from the city of Nazareth, to Judea, to the city of David which is called Bethlehem, because he was of the house and family of David, in order to register along with Mary, who was engaged to him, and was with child (Lk. 2:4, 5).

The grueling trip from Nazareth to Bethlehem is left to our imagination, along with the couple's disappointment when there was no room for them in the inn. We are not even told how they ended up sleeping with the livestock. We are simply told of the baby's birth. The most momentous event in history is relayed in an economy of words:

> While they were [in Bethlehem], the days were completed for her to give birth. And she gave birth to her first-born son; and she wrapped Him in cloths, and laid Him in a manger, because there was no room for them in the inn (Lk. 2:6, 7).

The birth of Jesus was no more momentous than His death and resurrection. The "momentous event" was God's becoming flesh *so that* He might pay the price for our sins. The term "first-born" can be used in a variety of ways (Heb. 1:6); but in the context of Luke 2, the natural and normal meaning of the term "first-born" in verse 7 indicates that Mary had other children.

THE BIRTH OF JESUS PROCLAIMED TO THE SHEPHERDS (LK. 2:8–20)

[8]In the same region there were some shepherds staying out in the fields and keeping watch over their flock by night. [9]And an angel of the Lord suddenly stood before them, and the glory of the Lord shone around them; and they were terribly frightened. [10]But the angel said to them, "Do not be afraid; for behold, I bring you good news of great joy which will be for all the people; [11]for today in the city of David there has been born for you a Savior, who is Christ the Lord. [12]This will be a sign for you: you will find a baby wrapped in cloths and lying in a manger." [13]And suddenly there appeared with the angel a multitude of the heavenly host praising God and saying,

[14]"Glory to God in the highest,
And on earth peace among men with whom He is pleased."

[15]When the angels had gone away from them into heaven, the shepherds began saying to one another, "Let us go straight

to Bethlehem then, and see this thing that has happened which the Lord has made known to us." ¹⁶So they came in a hurry and found their way to Mary and Joseph, and the baby as He lay in the manger. ¹⁷When they had seen this, they made known the statement which had been told them about this Child. ¹⁸And all who heard it wondered at the things which were told them by the shepherds. ¹⁹But Mary treasured all these things, pondering them in her heart. ²⁰The shepherds went back, glorifying and praising God for all that they had heard and seen, just as had been told them.

The wail of a newborn would have gone largely unnoticed in the babble of a town overflowing with visitors, but God did not let the moment go by unpublicized. The divine announcement was not made, however, to the town leaders or even to the officials in the synagogue. It was made to a group of shepherds **keeping watch over their flock by night** (Lk. 2:8).

The story of the appearance of the angel to the shepherds is one of the best-known in the world. The angel's words have been repeated again and again:

> **Do not be afraid; for behold, I bring you good news of great joy which will be for all the people; for today in the city of David there has been born for you a Savior, who is Christ the Lord. This will be a sign for you: you will find a baby wrapped in cloths and lying in a manger** (Lk. 2:10–12).

The shepherds probably had to check many feeding troughs before they found one with a baby in it. Once they had found the Baby, they told everyone they met (Lk. 2:17, 18). They have been called "the first evangelists," the first ones to share the good news. Notice verse 19: **But Mary treasured all these things, pondering them in her heart.** This verse, along with the last part of Luke 2:51, has caused many to conclude that Mary must have later shared her thoughts with Luke.

THE CIRCUMCISION AND NAMING OF JESUS; THE TEMPLE SERVICE (LK. 2:21–39)

[21]And when eight days had passed, before His circumcision, His name was then called Jesus, the name given by the angel before He was conceived in the womb.

[22]And when the days for their purification according to the law of Moses were completed, they brought Him up to Jerusalem to present Him to the Lord [23](as it is written in the Law of the Lord, "Every firstborn male that opens the womb shall be called holy to the Lord"), [24]and to offer a sacrifice according to what was said in the Law of the Lord, "A pair of turtledoves or two young pigeons."

[25]And there was a man in Jerusalem whose name was Simeon; and this man was righteous and devout, looking for the consolation of Israel; and the Holy Spirit was upon him. [26]And it had been revealed to him by the Holy Spirit that he would not see death before he had seen the Lord's Christ. [27]And he came in the Spirit into the temple; and when the parents brought in the child Jesus, to carry out for Him the custom of the Law, [28]then he took Him into his arms, and blessed God, and said,

[29]"Now Lord, You are releasing Your bond-servant to depart
   in peace,
According to Your word;
[30]For my eyes have seen Your salvation,
[31]Which You have prepared in the presence of all peoples,
[32]A Light of revelation to the Gentiles,
And the glory of Your people Israel."

[33]And His father and mother were amazed at the things which were being said about Him. [34]And Simeon blessed them and said to Mary His mother, "Behold, this Child is appointed for the fall and rise of many in Israel, and for a sign to be opposed— [35]and a sword will pierce even your own soul—to the end that thoughts from many hearts may be revealed."

[36]And there was a prophetess, Anna the daughter of Phanuel, of the tribe of Asher. She was advanced in years and had lived with her husband seven years after her marriage, [37]and

then as a widow to the age of eighty-four. She never left the temple, serving night and day with fastings and prayers. ³⁸At that very moment she came up and began giving thanks to God, and continued to speak of Him to all those who were looking for the redemption of Jerusalem.

³⁹When they had performed everything according to the Law of the Lord, they returned to Galilee, to their own city of Nazareth.

Some think that the birth of Jesus marked the end of the Old Testament Era, but the Bible teaches that Christ was "born under the Law" (Gal. 4:4). The New Testament teaches that the *death* of Jesus on the cross marked the close of the Old Testament period (Col. 2:14) and the beginning of the New Testament period (Heb. 9:16, 17). He was a Jewish child born to a Jewish mother and subject to Jewish regulations. When Christ was eight days old, He was circumcised as the Law prescribed (Lev. 12:3). At that time, He was given the name **Jesus**, as the angel had instructed (Lk. 1:31; Mt. 1:21).

The Law also gave Joseph and Mary other responsibilities. A first-born son had to be redeemed with money, in recognition of the deliverance of the Israelites' first-born children during the tenth plague in Egypt (Ex. 13:2, 10–14; 34:19, 20; Num. 3:40–51; 18:15, 16). Also, forty days after the birth of a son, a Jewish mother was to go to the temple for a ceremony of purification, which included a sacrifice (Lev. 12:2–8). Joseph and Mary offered the sacrifice that the poor were allowed to make. The presentation of Jesus in the temple and the purification of Mary were evidently made at the same time.

Most of those in the temple would not have noticed Joseph and his little family, but two individuals were excited to see them. First was Simeon, a God-fearing and devout old man who had been told by God that he would not die until he had seen the Messiah. His exuberant words upon seeing Jesus revealed the fact that Jesus would bring salvation to the Gentiles as well as to the Jews (Lk. 2:31, 32). Simeon's words also included the statement about the sword that would pierce Mary's soul (Lk. 2:35).

Second was Anna, an eighty-four-year-old prophetess. A

prophet was an inspired speaker for the Lord. A prophetess was a female prophet. Even during days of inspiration, prophetesses were uncommon. In the Old Testament, Deborah was a prophetess (Judg. 4:4). When Anna saw Jesus, she **began giving thanks to God, and continued to speak of Him to all those who were looking for the redemption of Jerusalem** (Lk. 2:38).

When they had performed everything according to the Law of the Lord (Lk. 2:39a), they returned to Bethlehem (see Mt. 2:8, 9). The end of Luke 2:39 says, **They returned to Galilee, to their own city of Nazareth.** This could refer to a trip back to Nazareth to get their belongings and Joseph's tools, after which they came back to Bethlehem. Perhaps such a trip was made, but Luke's words in 2:39 probably refer to their later return to Nazareth to make that city their home. Luke apparently compressed his story at this point, leaving out the visit of the magi and the trip to Egypt. (When Luke later gave the sequel to Saul's conversion [Acts 9:19–26], he left out the fact that Saul spent some time in Arabia [Gal. 1:17].) It was not the purpose of the writers of the Scriptures to give every detail.

Evidently, Joseph and Mary had decided that Bethlehem, the city of David (Lk. 2:4, 11), was the right place to rear the son of David (Mt. 1:1; Lk. 1:32). They had found a house in which to live (Mt. 2:11), and Joseph had probably begun plying his trade as a carpenter.

JESUS VISITED BY EASTERN MAGI ("WISE MEN") (MT. 2:1–12)

[1]**Now after Jesus was born in Bethlehem of Judea in the days of Herod the king, magi from the east arrived in Jerusalem, saying,** [2]**"Where is He who has been born King of the Jews? For we saw His star in the east and have come to worship Him."** [3]**When Herod the king heard this, he was troubled, and all Jerusalem with him.** [4]**Gathering together all the chief priests and scribes of the people, he inquired of them where the Messiah was to be born.** [5]**They said to him, "In Bethlehem of Judea; for this is what has been written by the prophet:**

[6]**'And you, Bethlehem, land of Judah,**

Are by no means least among the leaders of Judah;
For out of you shall come forth a Ruler
Who will shepherd My people Israel.'"
⁷Then Herod secretly called the magi and determined
from them the exact time the star appeared. ⁸And he sent
them to Bethlehem and said, "Go and search carefully for
the Child; and when you have found Him, report to me,
that I too may come and worship Him." ⁹After hearing the
king, they went their way; and the star, which they had seen
in the east, went on before them until it came and stood
over the place where the Child was. ¹⁰When they saw the star,
they rejoiced exceedingly with great joy. ¹¹After coming into
the house they saw the Child with Mary His mother; and they
fell to the ground and worshiped Him. Then, opening their
treasures, they presented to Him gifts of gold, frankincense,
and myrrh. ¹²And having been warned by God in a dream not
to return to Herod, the magi left for their own country by
another way.

Simeon had indicated that Jesus would not only be the Jews'
Messiah, but also the Gentiles'. Proof of this came soon—in the
persons of dignitaries from the East: **Now after Jesus was born
in Bethlehem of Judea . . . magi from the east arrived . . .** (Mt. 2:1).
"Magi" is a transliteration of the Greek text (μάγοι); it is the word
from which we get "magicians." Magi were seekers after knowledge, although their knowledge was a mixture of science and
superstition. A margin note in one edition of the NASB has "a
caste of wise men specializing in astrology, medicine, and natural
science." They were not kings, but they often served as advisors
to kings. The "wise men" of Esther 1:13 and Daniel 2:12 would
have been in the same category as the magi of Matthew 2. Some
magi had become charlatans and opposers of the truth. (The
same basic Greek word is found in Acts 8:9 and 13:6, 8.) However, the magi of Matthew 2:1 were honest searchers after truth.
In some way, God had convinced them that if they followed a
certain star, they would find the Messiah.

The star first led them to Jerusalem. They probably expected
the city to be bursting with the news of the birth of a King.

Instead, they heard only the everyday chatter of a major commercial center.

They began asking, **"Where is He who has been born King of the Jews?"** (Mt. 2:2a). Word of their inquiries reached the ear of King Herod. The king asked the Jewish religious leaders where the Messiah was to be born. Without hesitation, they said, **"Bethlehem"** (Mt. 2:5, 6). Herod shared that information with the magi and made them promise that, when they found the Child, they would tell him. **"I too** [will] **come and worship Him,"** he lied (Mt. 2:8).

Jesus did not later become a King; He was *born* a King. This phrase would have filled Herod with dread. Herod was not born a king; he had been appointed one by the Romans. Further, he had no scriptural right to the throne in Palestine, not being of the lineage of David. He would have considered anyone *"born* King of the Jews" a major threat to his reign.

As the magi headed south from Jerusalem, the star reappeared and led them **until it came and stood over the place where the Child was** (Mt. 2:9b). They rejoiced, and then, **coming into the house they saw the Child with Mary His mother; and they fell to the ground and worshiped Him. Then, opening their treasures, they presented to Him gifts of gold, frankincense, and myrrh** (Mt. 2:10, 11). Everyone is familiar with "gold." "Frankincense" was a costly white resin or gum obtained from a certain tree. It was burned by the rich to fill their homes with fragrance. "Myrrh" was produced almost in the same way as frankincense; it also had a pleasant aroma but was primarily used in embalming the dead.

Their mission completed, the magi started home. **And having been warned by God in a dream not to return to Herod, the magi left for their own country by another way** (Mt. 2:12).

APPLICATION:
SEEKING THE SAVIOR (MT. 2:1–13)

People seek many things in life: fame, fortune, happiness. However, to borrow words from Jesus, "only one thing is necessary" (Lk. 10:42a): seeking the Lord. Paul told his listeners on Mars' Hill that the Lord has given "to all people life and breath and all things . . . that they would seek God" (Acts 17:25–27a). David prayed, "O God, You are my God; I shall seek You earnestly . . ." (Ps. 63:1). Moses encouraged the Israelites to "seek the Lord your God"; and he assured them, "You will find Him if you search for Him with all your heart and all your soul" (Deut. 4:29).

In Matthew 2:1–13 we encounter a group of men who sought the Lord "with all their heart and soul" (2 Chron. 15:12). I almost said *"three* men who sought the Lord" because the number "three" is invariably used when they are mentioned. You have probably guessed that I am referring to the wise men who came to worship the child Jesus in Bethlehem.

This study is simple: The wise men sought Jesus, that they found Jesus, that they worshiped Jesus, and that their lives were blessed as a result. I also want to suggest that we need to follow their example. Since this is a well-known story, I will not spend much time on the familiar details—but I will ask this question: "Are we as wise as they?"

They Sought Jesus (Mt. 2:1–9, 11, 13)

The Magi

We need to look at those who sought Jesus. So many traditions have shrouded the wise men that the original visitors of Matthew 2 have become obscured.

The men are called "magi." "Magi" is the word from which we get "magic" and "magician." In those days, magi were noted for their knowledge and perception—thus we often use the phrase "wise men." By today's standards, their knowledge was defective, being a mixture of science and superstition. Nevertheless, they had a reputation for wisdom and often served as advisors to kings.

It is popularly thought that there were three of these magi—probably because three gifts are later mentioned (Mt. 2:11)—but three gifts could be given by few or by many. The word "magi" is plural, so we know that there were at least two, but there could have been a dozen or more.

The magi came "from the east," but we are not told their country of origin. Some scholars believe that they came from Arabia because of the gifts they brought. Persia might be a better guess, because magi flourished there. Frankly, we do not know where they started their journey. To the east of Palestine were Arabia, Persia, Babylonia, the whole Mesopotamian region, India, and other lands.

One detail regarding the men seems obvious: They were Gentiles. They did not say "our King," but rather "King of the Jews." When the baby Jesus was taken to the temple, old Simeon said that He would be "a light of revelation to the Gentiles" (Lk. 2:32; see Is. 42:1, 6; 49:6, 22; Mt. 12:18–21). The story of the wise men underlines the universal implications of Christ's birth. Jesus was not simply to be the Savior of Israel; He was to be "the Savior of the world" (Jn. 4:42).

There is much that we do not know about these men, but we know their most significant characteristic: They were persistent searchers for the "King of the Jews." Their true wisdom lay not in their decades of study or in their understanding of the natural world, but in their grasp of what is truly important. Whether or not a person is highly intelligent or well educated, if he is diligently seeking the "King of kings, and the Lord of lords" (Rev. 19:16), he is wise.

The Mission

Why did the magi make the long, hard trip to Palestine? Did they come as merchants, peddling their wares? No. Did they come as tourists, desiring to swim in the Mediterranean Sea or float on the Dead Sea? No. Did they come as ambassadors to establish a favorable relationship with King Herod? No. When they arrived in Jerusalem, they asked, "Where is He who has been born King of the Jews?" (Mt. 2:2a). They came to Palestine for one purpose: to find the Messiah.

Precisely *why* did they want to find Him? They said, "We . . . have come to *worship* Him" (Mt. 2:2b; emphasis added). He was not just the "King of the Jews"; He was also their King. They had traveled hundreds or thousands of miles in order to bow before Him.

If we would be as wise as these men, we need to learn that no sacrifice is too great in our search for Jesus. God "has blessed us with every spiritual blessing in the heavenly places *in Christ"* (Eph. 1:3; emphasis added). Those blessings are found nowhere else. God is still looking for honest souls who will make seeking the Lord the driving motivation of their lives. He continues to be "a rewarder of those who seek Him" (Heb. 11:6).

The Method

When we understand something about the magi and their mission, we may wonder, How could they possibly fulfill that mission? They were Gentiles. How could they even learn about the King of the Jews? Once they learned of Him, how would they know how to find Him?

Some speculate that they learned about the Christ from their Jewish neighbors. This is possible. By that time, Jews were scattered all over the world. In foreign lands, they not only plied their trades, but they also shared their faith.

Regarding the question of how the wise men knew how to find Jesus, the only clue is found in the words "we saw His star in the east." Some believe that the star was a natural phenomenon. One of the pseudo-sciences pursued by magi was astrology. The Old Testament mocks astrology (Is. 47:13–15; Dan. 1:20; 2:27; 4:7; 5:7, 8) and forbids God's people to get involved in it (Jer. 10:1, 2). Nevertheless, many are convinced that it was the magi's interest in astrology that brought them to Palestine. Pages are filled with speculation about the precise heavenly configuration that prompted the magi to travel west. Speculation includes planetary conjunctions, novas, and comets. None of these fit the textual description of the star or its action.

After sifting through all the guesses regarding how the wise men learned about the Messiah and how they decided that they should follow a certain star, my conclusion is the same reached by J. W. McGarvey many years ago. McGarvey listed all the possible influences on the wise men and concluded, "But all this put together can not account for the visit of the magi. They were guided directly by God, and nothing else may have even influenced them."[11]

---

[11]McGarvey and Pendleton, 42.

Understand that, although the Old Testament focuses on God's dealings with the Jews, God did not totally ignore the non-Jewish world. We know little about how God worked with the Gentiles, because the purpose of the Old Testament is to tell how God prepared one nation (the Israelites) through whom His Son would come. Nevertheless, from time to time, the Old Testament gives glimpses of the Lord's concern for the Jews' Gentile neighbors. For instance, God sent Jonah to Nineveh, a Gentile city (Jon. 1:1, 2). God even used a non-Jew named Balaam to proclaim a vivid Messianic utterance: "A star shall come forth from Jacob, a scepter shall rise from Israel" (Num. 24:17). The story of the wise men seems to be another example of God's interest in the Gentiles.

All we can say with certainty is that *some way* God made sure that the magi knew of the birth of Jesus, and *somehow* He informed them how they could find the Messiah. Later, God spoke to the wise men in a dream (Mt. 2:12). Perhaps the Lord used a similar method in conveying the initial information about the King of the Jews.

If proof is needed that God was guiding the Eastern sages, the star itself furnishes that proof. No natural celestial body moves as the magi's star did: No star moves from north to south or stops and "[stands] over" an earthly location (Mt. 2:9).

We can make application to those who would seek the Lord today. First of all, God is as interested in our finding the Savior as He was in having the wise men find the little King. If we are willing to search for the Savior, He will help us find Him (not miraculously, but providentially).

To find Jesus, however, we must be willing to *accept God's guidance.* "A man's way is not in himself, nor is it in a man who walks to direct his steps" (Jer. 10:23). Reason is important (Is. 1:18), but it cannot take the place of revelation. "'For My thoughts are not your thoughts, nor are your ways My ways,' declares the Lord. 'For as the heavens are higher than the earth, so are My ways higher than your ways and My thoughts than your thoughts'" (Is. 55:8, 9).

Once we accept God's guidance, we must be ready to *follow it—at once.* After God conveyed His message to the magi (however He did it), they did not hesitate. Off they went, on a journey involving hundreds of miles and years of exhaustive travel.

One other needed quality should be mentioned. In order to follow God's guidance, we must *remain humble*. When the wise men left their homes, they did not know their ultimate destination; they only knew they had to follow the star. When they reached Jerusalem, they did not know where to go next. Fortunately, they were not too proud to ask for directions. (Some of us men have a reputation for being unwilling to ask for directions when we are traveling to an unfamiliar place.) Humility is essential to seeking the Lord. Among the many passages on the need to be humble in order to please God are James 4:6 and 1 Peter 5:5.

God revealed the most important instructions of their journey through His Scriptures. The star led them only as far as Jerusalem. They still needed information from the Word. When Herod heard of the magi's inquiries, he called the Jewish leaders together and "inquired of them where the Messiah was to be born" (Mt. 2:4). They replied,

> In Bethlehem of Judea [as opposed to Bethlehem in Palestine]; for this is what has been written by the prophet: "And you, Bethlehem, land of Judah, are by no means least among the leaders of Judah; for out of you shall come forth a Ruler who will shepherd My people Israel" (Mt. 2:5, 6).

To find the answer to the king's question, the Jewish leaders had to go to the Scriptures—to Micah 5:2. The scribes and the priests also added a phrase from 2 Samuel 5:2.

We can learn something of God outside the Bible. He is active in this world. He sends the sunshine and the rain (Mt. 5:45). "The heavens declare the glory of God; and the firmament showeth his handiwork" (Ps. 19:1; KJV). To some extent, "His invisible attributes, His eternal power and divine nature" can be understood through His creation (Rom. 1:20). Nevertheless, if we would seek and find Him, ultimately we must (underline "must" in your mind) come to *the Word*. Speaking of the Scriptures, Jesus said, "In them you have eternal life; it is these that testify about Me" (Jn. 5:39).

James thus wrote, "In humility receive the word implanted, which is able to save your souls" (Jas. 1:21). Paul said that only "the sacred writings . . . are able to give you the wisdom that leads to salvation through faith which is in Christ Jesus" (2 Tim. 3:15). God will not give us a star in the heavens to guide us, but He has given us heavenly illumination to guide us—in His Book. The psalmist described the Word as "a lamp to my feet and a light to my path" (Ps. 119:105).

If we would be as wise as the magi, we must be willing to study God's Word and to do what it says. The New Testament reveals the path that we must follow on our way to the Lord. We must believe in Jesus (Jn. 3:16); we must repent of our sins (Lk. 13:3); we must confess our faith in Jesus (Mt. 10:32); we must be baptized (immersed in water) (Mk. 16:16; Acts 2:38). The Bible tells us that our baptism puts us "into Christ" (Rom. 6:3; Gal. 3:27)—and being with Christ is our goal. Our eternal home with Him is our desired destination.

They Found Jesus (Mt. 2:7–11)

The magi found Jesus. It is always thrilling to find what we are seeking, whether it is an unknown destination or just some keys that we have misplaced. Luke 15 tells of the joy experienced by a shepherd and by a woman who sought that which was lost and found it. There is, however, no thrill to compare with finding the Savior.

Years before Christ was born, David had told his son Solomon, "If you seek Him, He will let you find Him" (1 Chron. 28:9). Because the magi sought Jesus in the right way with the right attitude, God made sure that they found Him.

As soon as the wise men were told where the Messiah was to be born, they headed south from Jerusalem (Mt. 2:7–9a). As they started the five miles to Bethlehem, the star reappeared. "When they saw the star, they rejoiced exceedingly with great joy" (Mt. 2:10). They knew they were on the right track. The star "went on before them until it came and stood over the place where the

Child was" (Mt. 2:9). At last, "coming into the house they saw the Child with Mary His mother" (Mt. 2:11a).

Imagine the joy they experienced when they found the One whom they had sought for so long. Years ago, people shouted "Eureka!" when they made a discovery. (*Eureka* is a Greek word meaning "I have found [it]!") We do not know what the magi shouted—or if they said anything at all—as they looked at that Child in Mary's arms. We can be confident, however, that their minds were not on the difficulties of their journey or on any sacrifice they had made. Rather, their hearts were surely filled with joy at the successful completion of their quest.

When anyone seeks the Lord in the right way with the right attitude, God will also help that person to find Him. Then, when he is baptized into Christ, he will be able to say, as Philip did, "[I] have found Him of whom Moses in the Law and also the Prophets wrote—Jesus of Nazareth, the son of Joseph" (Jn. 1:45). Like the wise men, he can rejoice—"with joy inexpressible and full of glory" (1 Pet. 1:8).

They Worshiped Jesus (Mt. 2:2, 11)

Having found Jesus, the magi worshiped Him. They did not seek the King of the Jews so they could boast that they had solved a divine puzzle. They had announced that they had come to Palestine "to *worship* Him" (Mt. 2:2; emphasis added). Indeed, when they saw Him, "they fell to the ground and worshiped Him" (Mt. 2:11b). They gave Him the adoration He deserved as King of kings (Rev. 19:16).

They did more than just bow before Him, however. "Opening their treasures, they presented to Him gifts of gold, frankincense, and myrrh" (Mt. 2:11c). Some see symbolic significance in these gifts: Gold was a gift fit for a king. As the name indicates, frank*incense* was used as incense; it was a gift fit for a priest. Myrrh was used in preparing a body for burial; it was a gift fit for a Savior, a Savior who had to die for our sins. Jesus was all of these—King, Priest, and Savior. The gifts were appropriate; but they were probably chosen simply because, though they were valuable, they took up little space and could be transported on the long journey. The true significance of the gifts lies not in what they were but in what they represented. They were an expression of the wise men's desire to do homage to their King. True worship and giving cannot be separated. The Old Testament had its sacrifices, and the New Testament has its free-will offerings on the first day of each week (1 Cor. 16:1, 2; 2 Cor. 9:7).

Have you no gold, frankincense, or myrrh to lay before the Lord? Then give Him the best you have. First, give yourself (2 Cor. 8:5; see Rom. 12:1, 2); then, give that which is yours; and always, give Him your best. David would not offer to the Lord that which cost him nothing (2 Sam. 24:24).

When the magi found Jesus, they worshiped Him and gave Him gifts. Are we as wise as they?

Conclusion (Mt. 2:10, 12)

There is much we do not know about the magi. We know little about them before they arrived in Jerusalem. We know nothing about them after they returned to their own country. They appear on the pages of the Bible for one memorable scene and then vanish. One fact we know, however: Their lives were blessed as a result of seeking the Lord. Remember verse 10: "When they saw the star, they rejoiced exceedingly with great joy." The original text, translated literally, says that "they rejoiced with joy." The writer used a Hebrew expression indicating that they were *filled* with joy. That alone would be sufficient to let us know how happy the wise men were, but the text then adds the words "great" and "exceedingly." The magi were deliriously happy that they had found the Lord. As they left that humble home in Bethlehem, like the shepherds before them (Lk. 2:17, 18), they must have told all they met about the little King they had seen.

The passage we have been studying contrasts the attitudes of three groups regarding Jesus: There were the wise men, who sought Christ in order to worship Him. There was Herod, who sought Jesus in order to kill Him. There were the Jewish leaders, who put forth no effort to find Jesus even though He was only a few miles away. These three categories of people are still with us today: There are those who resent and oppose Jesus because they see Him as a threat to their self-centered lives. There are great masses of people who are oblivious to Jesus and how He could bless their lives. Thank God, however, there are still the few who seek Him.

THE FLIGHT INTO EGYPT
AND THE SLAUGHTER OF BABY BOYS
IN BETHLEHEM (MT. 2:13–18)

¹³Now when they had gone, behold, an angel of the Lord appeared to Joseph in a dream and said, "Get up! Take the Child and His mother and flee to Egypt, and remain there until I tell you; for Herod is going to search for the Child to destroy Him." ¹⁴So Joseph got up and took the Child and His mother while it was still night, and left for Egypt. ¹⁵He remained there until the death of Herod. This was to fulfill what had been spoken by the Lord through the prophet: "Out of Egypt I called My Son." ¹⁶Then when Herod saw that he had been tricked by the magi, he became very enraged, and sent and slew all the male children who were in Bethlehem and all its vicinity, from two years old and under, according to the time which he had determined from the magi. ¹⁷Then what had been spoken through Jeremiah the prophet was fulfilled:
¹⁸"A voice was heard in Ramah,
Weeping and great mourning,
Rachel weeping for her children;
And she refused to be comforted,
Because they were no more."

Anticipating Herod's reaction, the Lord sent an angel to tell Joseph to take his family into Egypt. Matthew emphasized that the trip resulted in the fulfillment of an Old Testament Scripture (Mt. 2:15). Once more, Joseph did not hesitate. One hundred miles would have taken the family to the border of Egypt. Another hundred miles along the rough trail through Sinai would have brought them to the Nile. They would have found fellow countrymen there, for many Jews had settled in Alexandria and elsewhere in Egypt.

We do not know how long Joseph, Mary, and Jesus stayed in Egypt. It could have been many months. What did they live on while they were there? Perhaps Joseph found some work as a carpenter—but do not forget the gifts of gold, frankincense, and myrrh. This time God had used foreign emissaries to serve His purpose.

Herod was furious when the magi did not return to him with the desired information. In an insane effort to eradicate all possible rivals to his throne, he had all baby boys in the area of Bethlehem killed, **from two years old and under, according to the time which he had determined from the magi** (Mt. 2:16). In the US, we consider a child "two years old" after he has lived twenty-four months. The Jews considered a child "two years old" after twelve months of life. This same type of reckoning is used in many countries of the world today. (A newborn is in his first year of life; when he celebrates the first anniversary of his birth, he enters his second year; and so forth.) Verse 16 implies that the star had first appeared twelve months or so earlier. Some believe that the star had appeared around six months earlier and that Herod doubled the figure "to be on the safe side." Jesus was probably somewhere between six months and twelve months old when the magi arrived in Palestine.

Bethlehem was not a large town, so the number of babies killed would have been relatively small (estimates range between twelve and fifty). Nevertheless, Herod's heartless act broke hundreds of hearts. Matthew compared the tragedy with the mourning over the fall of Jerusalem (Mt. 2:17, 18).

Some ask, "Why didn't God protect those babies as He protected Jesus?" Remember that God made men free moral agents. He thus allowed Herod to be Herod. However, we can be sure that God will overrule the actions of men when those actions would ultimately defeat His purposes. The death of Bethlehem's children would not negate His plan for the salvation of the world; the death of Jesus would. Even as we mourn the death of the innocents, let us celebrate the deliverance of Immanuel.

It has been said that Herod "thrust his sword into the nest but the bird was flown."[12]

THE CHILD JESUS BROUGHT FROM EGYPT TO NAZARETH (MT. 2:19–23; SEE LK. 2:39b)

Matthew 2:19–23

[19]**But when Herod died, behold, an angel of the Lord appeared in a dream to Joseph in Egypt, and said,** [20]**"Get up, take the Child and His mother, and go into the land of Israel; for those who sought the Child's life are dead."** [21]**So Joseph got up, took the Child and His mother, and came into the land of Israel.** [22]**But when he heard that Archelaus was reigning over Judea in place of his father Herod, he was afraid to go there. Then after being warned by God in a dream, he left for the regions of Galilee,** [23]**and came and lived in a city called Nazareth. This was to fulfill what was spoken through the prophets: "He shall be called a Nazarene."**

After Herod died, an angel came to Joseph, saying, **"Get up, take the Child and His mother, and go into the land of Israel; for those who sought the Child's life are dead"** (Mt. 2:20). Apparently, Joseph intended to return to Bethlehem until he learned that Herod's son Archelaus was ruling in Judea (Mt. 2:22). Archelaus had a reputation for being as cruel as his father.

They therefore avoided Judea (Mt. 2:22) and traveled north to their hometown of Nazareth in Galilee. More than a year had passed since they had left to go to Bethlehem; now they returned (Mt. 2:23; see Lk. 2:39b). The return to Nazareth was also part of God's plan (Mt. 2:23).

JESUS LIVING AT NAZARETH; A VISIT TO JERUSALEM WHEN HE WAS TWELVE (LK. 2:40–52)

[40]**The Child continued to grow and become strong, increas-**

---

[12]Author unknown. Quoted by B. S. Dean, "The Birth and Infancy," *Truth for Today* (March 1992): 10.

ing in wisdom; and the grace of God was upon Him.

[41]Now His parents went to Jerusalem every year at the Feast of the Passover. [42]And when He became twelve, they went up there according to the custom of the Feast; [43]and as they were returning, after spending the full number of days, the boy Jesus stayed behind in Jerusalem. But His parents were unaware of it, [44]but supposed Him to be in the caravan, and went a day's journey; and they began looking for Him among their relatives and acquaintances. [45]When they did not find Him, they returned to Jerusalem looking for Him. [46]Then, after three days they found Him in the temple, sitting in the midst of the teachers, both listening to them and asking them questions. [47]And all who heard Him were amazed at His understanding and His answers. [48]When they saw Him, they were astonished; and His mother said to Him, "Son, why have You treated us this way? Behold, Your father and I have been anxiously looking for You." [49]And He said to them, "Why is it that you were looking for Me? Did you not know that I had to be in My Father's house?" [50]But they did not understand the statement which He had made to them. [51]And He went down with them and came to Nazareth, and He continued in subjection to them; and His mother treasured all these things in her heart.

[52]And Jesus kept increasing in wisdom and stature, and in favor with God and men.

Jesus was fully God, but He was also fully man. Thus He grew as all boys grow—or, at least, as all boys should grow: **The Child continued to grow and become strong, increasing in wisdom; and the grace of God was upon Him** (Lk. 2:40; compare Lk. 1:80 and 1 Sam. 2:26).

Evidently, it was God's will for Jesus to experience what all of us experience (Heb. 4:15) as we develop from childhood to adulthood. Jesus not only "emptied Himself" by becoming human (Phil. 2:6, 7), but apparently He also emptied Himself of some of His divine prerogatives such as omniscience (see Mk. 13:32).

At this point in the story of Jesus, it becomes obvious that the purpose of the writers of the Gospel Accounts was not to compose a biography of Christ. Only Luke recorded anything of the next twenty-eight or so years, and he shared only a few notes about Jesus' growth, plus the details of a single incident.

We would like to know about Jesus' first words, His first steps, His early days in a humble home in Nazareth, His reaction when other children were born into that household. God, however, thought it enough for us to know that Jesus grew in much the same way as we had to grow.

Luke pulled back the curtain on Jesus' formative years only once—when He was twelve years old. Age twelve was a significant milestone in the life of a Jewish boy. He started to learn a trade; he was called "a son of the Law"; he began to sit with the men in the synagogue. When Jesus was twelve, Joseph and Mary took Him to the most sacred of the three major feasts: the Passover.

As Joseph and Mary were returning home, they missed Jesus. Panic-stricken, they hurried back to Jerusalem and began searching for Him.

> **Then, after three days they found Him in the temple, sitting in the midst of the teachers, both listening to them and asking them questions. And all who heard Him were amazed at His understanding and His answers** (Lk. 2:46, 47).

Do not misinterpret this scene. Jesus had not taken over the class; He was not teaching the teachers. It was a typical religious class of those days, with both teachers and students asking and answering questions. The amazement centered in the fact that a twelve-year-old had so much interest in spiritual realities and such an unusual grasp of spiritual principles.

Mary's outburst when they found Jesus was a typical motherly response—relieved and at the same time aggravated: . . . **His mother said to Him, "Son, why have You treated us this way? Behold, Your father and I have been anxiously looking for You"** (Lk. 2:48). Jesus seems to have been genuinely puzzled: **"Why is it that you were looking for Me? Did you not know that I had to be in My Father's house?"** (Lk. 2:49).

These are the first recorded words of Jesus. The words in the original text literally mean "I must be in the things of My Father," but what "things" are not specified. The KJV has "my Father's business." Hugo McCord's translation has "my Father's affairs."[13] Regardless of the translation, even at the age of twelve, Jesus obviously already had a sense of His divine mission.

Did this insight come on Jesus suddenly, like a flash of lightning; or did it come gradually, like the dawning of a new day? Did Jesus have a full comprehension of His mission at age twelve or only a partial understanding? We cannot answer these questions with certainty, but we can say that twelve-year-old Jesus was on His way to becoming the Man He would be.

In light of Jesus' grasp of His divine status, the next verse is amazing: **And He went down with them and came to Nazareth, and He continued in subjection to them . . .** (Lk. 2:51). If any child could ever be justified in disobeying His parents, it would have been Jesus—but He knew that obedience to parents is not optional (Ex. 20:12; see Eph. 6:1–3). Note: When people traveled to Jerusalem, it is always stated that people went "up to Jerusalem." When they returned home, it is always stated that they went "down." This is because Jerusalem was situated on the highest spot in the country. This may be one reason David had chosen the city centuries before to be his capital.

After the trip to Jerusalem, the curtain is drawn again, obscuring the next eighteen or so years of Jesus' life. The Scriptures give a few hints about those years. Jesus grew up in a large household, having at least two sisters and four brothers (Mt. 13:55, 56; Mk. 6:3). His younger brothers may have resented Him; at least in the beginning of His ministry, they did not believe in His divine origin (Jn. 7:5). He learned the carpenter's trade from Joseph (Mt. 13:55; Mk. 6:3). Jesus' use of the word "Abba" (Mk. 14:36)—an affectionate term meaning "father"—may indicate that He had a cordial relationship with Joseph. When Joseph died, Jesus, as the oldest, would have had to take over the pri-

---

[13]Hugo McCord, *McCord's New Testament Translation of the Everlasting Gospel* (Henderson, Tenn.: Freed-Hardeman University, 1988).

mary support of the family. Jesus learned the Scriptures, perhaps in a synagogue school and certainly in synagogue services. He was regular in attendance at the synagogue (Lk. 4:16). Jesus quoted from a high percentage of the books in the Old Testament. The emphasis on Jesus' growth suggests that He learned the Scriptures in the same way that we learn the Scriptures: through reading, memorization, and contemplation. The statement made later about Jesus' lack of education (Jn. 7:15 simply referred to the fact that He had not studied at the rabbinical schools. Today we would say, "He didn't have a college degree." We could add to this list of observations and speculations about Jesus' young manhood, but all that the Scriptures say about those years is found in Luke 2:52: **And Jesus kept increasing in wisdom and stature, and in favor with God and men**.

Jesus' development was fourfold (as ours should be): He grew mentally ("in wisdom"), physically (in "stature"), socially ("in favor with . . . men"), and spiritually ("in favor with God"). His growth was not easy (as ours is not). The word translated "kept increasing" is a compound Greek word (προέκοπτεν, *proekopten*) that combines the word for "cut" with the preposition meaning "toward." It literally means "to cut forward a way."[14] One illustration is an explorer cutting his way through heavy brush in order to make progress.

Isaiah promised that a Child would be born (Is. 9:6). That promise was fulfilled, as the Child was born and then protected and prepared by God. At each juncture of the story, God was firmly in control.

This has been a review of the first thirty years of Jesus' life. Some wonder why God took thirty years to prepare Jesus—why Jesus did not begin His ministry earlier. B. S. Dean said, "The world's sorest need is character; and no years of preparation are wasted that produce such manhood as came forth from the

---

[14]W. E. Vine, *The Expanded Vine's Expository Dictionary of New Testament Words*, ed. John R. Kohlenberger III with James A. Swanson (Minneapolis: Bethany House Publishers, 1984), 25.

obscurity of Nazareth."[15] Jesus was as much "about His Father's business" in the quiet years of preparation as He later was in the bustle of His public ministry. Preparation is necessary for any great task.

---

[15]B. S. Dean, "The Period of Preparation," *Truth for Today* (March 1992): 12.

PART II

THE BEGINNING OF THE MINISTRY OF JOHN THE BAPTIZER

Includes a Harmony of

Mt. 3:1–12

Mk. 1:1–8

Lk. 3:1–18

When John the Baptizer "came, preaching in the wilderness of Judea," the heart of his message was "Repent, for the kingdom of heaven is at hand" (Mt. 3:1, 2). It is difficult for us to comprehend how exciting these words would have been to his listeners. The Messianic Era was "at hand." It would not be long until the Messiah Himself would appear.

JOHN'S MINISTRY
(MT. 3:1–6; MK. 1:1–6; LK. 3:1–6)

Matthew 3:1–6

¹Now in those days John the Baptist came, preaching in the wilderness of Judea, saying, ²"Repent, for the kingdom of heaven is at hand." ³For this is the one referred to by Isaiah the prophet when he said,

"The voice of one crying in the wilderness,
'Make ready the way of the Lord,
Make His paths straight!'"

⁴Now John himself had a garment of camel's hair and a leather belt around his waist; and his food was locusts and wild honey. ⁵Then Jerusalem was going out to him, and all Judea and all the district around the Jordan; ⁶and they were being baptized by him in the Jordan River, as they confessed their sins.

Mark 1:1–6

¹The beginning of the gospel of Jesus Christ, the Son of God. ²As it is written in Isaiah the prophet:

"Behold, I send My messenger ahead of You,
Who will prepare Your way;
³The voice of one crying in the wilderness,
'Make ready the way of the Lord,

Make His paths straight.'"
⁴John the Baptist appeared in the wilderness preaching a baptism of repentance for the forgiveness of sins. ⁵And all the
country of Judea was going out to him, and all the people of
Jerusalem; and they were being baptized by him in the Jordan River, confessing their sins. ⁶John was clothed with camel's hair and wore a leather belt around his waist, and his diet
was locusts and wild honey.

Luke 3:1–6
¹Now in the fifteenth year of the reign of Tiberius Caesar, when Pontius Pilate was governor of Judea, and Herod
was tetrarch of Galilee, and his brother Philip was tetrarch of
the region of Ituraea and Trachonitis, and Lysanias was tetrarch of Abilene, ²in the high priesthood of Annas and Caiaphas, the word of God came to John, the son of Zacharias, in
the wilderness. ³And he came into all the district around the
Jordan, preaching a baptism of repentance for the forgiveness
of sins; ⁴as it is written in the book of the words of Isaiah the
prophet,
"The voice of one crying in the wilderness,
'Make ready the way of the Lord,
Make His paths straight.
⁵Every ravine will be filled,
And every mountain and hill will be brought low;
The crooked will become straight,
And the rough roads smooth;
⁶And all flesh will see the salvation of God.'"

The prophets had foretold that one would come before the
Messiah to prepare the way for Him (Is. 40:3–5; Mal. 3:1; 4:5, 6).
Zacharias, the priest, had been told that his son, John, was to be
that forerunner (Lk. 1:17). In Luke's account of John's ministry,
he quoted from Isaiah, who had compared the work that John
would have to do to that of a road builder:

Make ready the way of the Lord,
Make His paths straight.

Every ravine will be filled,
And every mountain and hill will be brought low;
The crooked will become straight,
And the rough roads smooth
(Lk. 3:4, 5; see Is. 40:3, 4).

In those days, when a king traveled in rough terrain, often a road crew went before him, preparing a smooth pathway. That imagery was used by the prophet. Of course, in the case of John's task, it was not gullies in the earth that need to be filled, but ravines of ignorance. It was not hills of rock that had to be lowered, but mountains of pride. Crooked concepts regarding the Messiah needed to be straightened by the teaching of truth.

As a whole, the Jewish people had a misunderstanding of the Messiah and His work. They thought He would be an earthly king who would vanquish their enemies and restore their nation to its past glory. John had the challenge of introducing the idea that the Messiah's kingdom would be a *spiritual* realm with *spiritual* requirements.

The importance of John's work cannot be overemphasized. Mark called it **the beginning of the gospel** (Mk. 1:1). In the Book of Acts, the formal beginning of Jesus' ministry is said to date from the baptism of John (Acts 1:21, 22; see 10:37, 38).

When we last saw John, he was "in the deserts" (Lk. 1:80). In that barren region, he lived an austere life. He wore rough clothing (Mt. 3:4; see 2 Kings 1:8); he ate locusts and wild honey (Mt. 3:4).

At last, **the word of God came** to him (Lk. 3:2)—the signal for him to start his preaching. Luke underlined the importance of John's ministry by using five political leaders and two religious leaders to fix the date of its inauguration (Lk. 3:1, 3).

A key word in John's preaching was **repent** (Mt. 3:2). The word "repent" means "a change of mind, resulting in a change of life." Those unwilling to repent would have to face God's wrath (Mt. 3:7, 10; Lk. 3:9). The kingdom was not for those with a certain blood line, but for those with a certain moral character (Mt. 3:8, 9; Lk. 3:8).

JOHN'S MESSAGE
(MT. 3:7–12; MK. 1:7, 8; LK. 3:7–18)

Matthew 3:7–12

⁷But when he saw many of the Pharisees and Sadducees coming for baptism, he said to them, "You brood of vipers, who warned you to flee from the wrath to come? ⁸Therefore bear fruit in keeping with repentance; ⁹and do not suppose that you can say to yourselves, 'We have Abraham for our father'; for I say to you that from these stones God is able to raise up children to Abraham. ¹⁰The axe is already laid at the root of the trees; therefore every tree that does not bear good fruit is cut down and thrown into the fire.

¹¹"As for me, I baptize you with water for repentance, but He who is coming after me is mightier than I, and I am not fit to remove His sandals; He will baptize you with the Holy Spirit and fire. ¹²His winnowing fork is in His hand, and He will thoroughly clear His threshing floor; and He will gather His wheat into the barn, but He will burn up the chaff with unquenchable fire."

Mark 1:7, 8

⁷And he was preaching, and saying, "After me One is coming who is mightier than I, and I am not fit to stoop down and untie the thong of His sandals. ⁸I baptized you with water; but He will baptize you with the Holy Spirit."

Luke 3:7–18

⁷So he began saying to the crowds who were going out to be baptized by him, "You brood of vipers, who warned you to flee from the wrath to come? ⁸Therefore bear fruits in keeping with repentance, and do not begin to say to yourselves, 'We have Abraham for our father,' for I say to you that from these stones God is able to raise up children to Abraham. ⁹Indeed the axe is already laid at the root of the trees; so every tree that does not bear good fruit is cut down and thrown into the fire."

¹⁰And the crowds were questioning him, saying, "Then

what shall we do?" ¹¹And he would answer and say to them,
"The man who has two tunics is to share with him who has
none; and he who has food is to do likewise." ¹²And some
tax collectors also came to be baptized, and they said to him,
"Teacher, what shall we do?" ¹³And he said to them, "Collect
no more than what you have been ordered to." ¹⁴Some soldiers
were questioning him, saying, "And what about us, what shall
we do?" And he said to them, "Do not take money from anyone by force, or accuse anyone falsely, and be content with
your wages."

¹⁵Now while the people were in a state of expectation and
all were wondering in their hearts about John, as to whether
he was the Christ, ¹⁶John answered and said to them all, "As
for me, I baptize you with water; but One is coming who is
mightier than I, and I am not fit to untie the thong of His sandals; He will baptize you with the Holy Spirit and fire. ¹⁷His
winnowing fork is in His hand to thoroughly clear His threshing floor, and to gather the wheat into His barn; but He will
burn up the chaff with unquenchable fire."

¹⁸So with many other exhortations he preached the gospel
to the people.

Regarding the need for change, John dealt not in generalities,
but in specifics in his preaching. He told people to **bear fruit in
keeping with repentance** (Mt. 3:8; see Lk. 3:8). He gave explicit
examples. He told the selfish masses to share (Lk. 3:11), the public officials to be honest (Lk. 3:13), and those with authority not
to misuse their power (Lk. 3:14). He called on all people to confess their sins (Mk. 1:5). He labeled those unwilling to do so a
brood of vipers (Mt. 3:7). The expression some would use today
is "snakes in the grass."

In spite of his audacity—or perhaps because of it—John
attracted a sizeable following. "And all the country of Judea was
going out to him, and all the people of Jerusalem; and they were
being baptized by him in the Jordan River, confessing their sins"
(Mk. 1:5; see Mt. 3:5, 6).

Baptism was an indispensable part of John's ministry. Some
try to find precedent for John's baptism in Jewish ceremo-

nial washings, but John's baptism was unique. The differences between John's baptism and the ceremonial washings are many, including a difference in purpose and a difference in administration. John became known as "the Baptist" (Mt. 3:1), because that was his distinctive vocation. If many others had been administering the same kind of baptism, as is sometimes claimed, John would never have been given such an identifying title.

"Baptist" is from βαπτιστής (*baptistes*), a transliterated Greek word. An ending (-*tes*) indicating a distinguishing characteristic was added to the Greek word for "baptize," βαπτίζω (*baptizo*). This ending is roughly comparable to the "tor" in "actor" and "doctor." "Baptist" literally means "one who baptizes." A word that expresses this concept is "Baptizer." This term is being used in our study to refer to John.

John baptized people in the Jordan River. He apparently moved up and down the river to make his message available to everyone. Luke 3:3 says, "And he came into all the district around the Jordan." The LB paraphrase has "Then John went from place to place on both sides of the Jordan River." We are told several of the areas where he baptized (Jn. 1:28; 3:23).

John's baptism was an immersion. The word "baptize" is a transliterated Greek word that means "to dip, immerse."[1] We could know that John's baptism was an immersion even if we did not know the meaning of the Greek word. John 3:23 stresses that "John also was baptizing in Aenon . . . , because there was much water there." Sprinkling does not require "much water," but immersion does. After John baptized Jesus, Christ came "up out of the water" (Mk. 1:10; see Mt. 3:16). That which keeps those who practice sprinkling out of the water today would have kept John out of the river if he had merely been sprinkling water on people.

John's baptism was called "a baptism of repentance for the forgiveness of sins" (Mk. 1:4; Lk. 3:3). It was called "a baptism of repentance" because it was an expression of repentance. It was "for the forgiveness of sins." John not only convicted men of sin, but he also gave them hope concerning forgiveness of those sins. His baptism anticipated Christ's death for the sins of mankind. Great Commission baptism could be called "a baptism of faith" because it is an expression of our faith. Those submitting to Great Commission baptism confess their faith in Jesus (Acts 8:35–38; Rom. 10:9, 10), while candidates for John's baptism were "confessing their sins" (Mk. 1:5; see Mt. 3:6).

John's basic purpose was to prepare people's hearts and lives for the Messiah (see Jn. 3:28). He told the crowds, **"He who is coming after me is mightier than I, and I am not fit to remove His sandals"** (Mt. 3:11; see Jn. 1:27, 30). Removing sandals was the work of a servant. John was saying, in effect, "I am not worthy to be His slave."

He made a contrast between his work and that of the Christ: **"As for me, I baptize you with water for repentance . . . ; He will baptize you with the Holy Spirit and fire"** (Mt. 3:11). The context shows that the baptism with the Holy Spirit and the baptism with fire are not the same baptism. John was speaking to a mixed group—the receptive and the unreceptive (Mt. 3:5–7). Mark, who did not mention the unreceptive, spoke only of the baptism with the Holy Spirit (Mk. 1:8). John also spoke only of the baptism with the Holy Spirit (Jn. 1:33). On the other hand, Luke, like Matthew, pictured an audience of the receptive and unreceptive (Lk. 3:7) and thus spoke of both the baptism with the Holy Spirit and baptism with fire (Lk. 3:16).

The baptism of the Holy Spirit came on the apostles on the first Pentecost after the death, burial, and resurrection of Christ (Acts 1:5, 8; 2:1–4). They were immersed in the power of the Spirit. On the other hand, the baptism of fire refers to the immersion of the ungodly in fire on the Day of Judgment (Mt. 3:12).

PART III
THE BEGINNING OF CHRIST'S MINISTRY

Includes a Harmony of

Mt. 3:13—4:11

Mk. 1:9–13

Lk. 3:21, 22; 4:1–13

Jn. 1:19—2:12

JESUS BAPTIZED BY JOHN
IN THE JORDAN RIVER
(MT. 3:13–17; MK. 1:9–11; LK. 3:21, 22; JN. 1:31–34)

Matthew 3:13–17

¹³Then Jesus arrived from Galilee at the Jordan coming to John, to be baptized by him. ¹⁴But John tried to prevent Him, saying, "I have need to be baptized by You, and do You come to me?" ¹⁵But Jesus answering said to him, "Permit it at this time; for in this way it is fitting for us to fulfill all righteousness." Then he permitted Him. ¹⁶After being baptized, Jesus came up immediately from the water; and behold, the heavens were opened, and he saw the Spirit of God descending as a dove and lighting on Him, ¹⁷and behold, a voice out of the heavens said, "This is My beloved Son, in whom I am well-pleased."

Mark 1:9–11

⁹In those days Jesus came from Nazareth in Galilee and was baptized by John in the Jordan. ¹⁰Immediately coming up out of the water, He saw the heavens opening, and the Spirit like a dove descending upon Him; ¹¹and a voice came out of the heavens: "You are My beloved Son, in You I am well-pleased."

Luke 3:21, 22

²¹Now when all the people were baptized, Jesus was also baptized, and while He was praying, heaven was opened, ²²and the Holy Spirit descended upon Him in bodily form like a dove, and a voice came out of heaven, "You are My beloved Son, in You I am well-pleased."

John 1:31–34

³¹"I did not recognize Him, but so that He might be manifested to Israel, I came baptizing in water." ³²John testified saying, "I have seen the Spirit descending as a dove out of heaven, and He remained upon Him. ³³I did not recognize Him, but He who sent me to baptize in water said to me, 'He upon whom you see the Spirit descending and remaining upon Him, this is the One who baptizes in the Holy Spirit.' ³⁴I myself have seen, and have testified that this is the Son of God."

At the height of John's popularity and the height of anticipation regarding the Messiah, Jesus came to him to be baptized. Christ was then "about thirty years of age" (Lk. 3:23).

We do not know if John had seen Jesus before. As previously noted, their mothers were relatives and friends. It is possible, perhaps even probable, that John and Jesus had met—maybe during the feast days in Jerusalem. Whether or not they had met, somehow John knew that Jesus was unlike the others waiting to be baptized. John's baptism was a baptism of repentance, and Jesus had no sins of which to repent. John's baptism was for the forgiveness of sins, and Jesus had none to be forgiven. At first John refused to baptize Christ: **"I have need to be baptized by You, and do You come to me?"** (Mt. 3:14).

Since, unlike us, Jesus had no sin, why *was* He baptized? Christ Himself answered that question. **"Permit it at this time,"** He said to John, **"for in this way it is fitting for us to fulfill all righteousness"** (Mt. 3:15). The psalmist said that all the commandments of God are righteousness (Ps. 119:172). The baptism of John was "from heaven" (see Mt. 21:25), and those who refused John's baptism "rejected God's purpose for themselves" (Lk. 7:30). Jesus was dedicated to staying in the center of the will of God—and He understood that John's baptism was part of that will. Therefore, there was no question in His mind concerning what He should do: He should be baptized—so He was. It would be wonderful if everyone had such a positive attitude toward baptism today.

John finally agreed to baptize Jesus. As He was baptized, Christ was praying (Lk. 3:21). The Book of Luke informs us that

Jesus prayed at crucial moments in His life (see Lk. 6:12, 13; 9:28, 29; 22:44, 45; 23:33, 34, 46). While Christ was praying, John saw and heard something wonderful:

> **After being baptized, Jesus came up immediately from the water;[1] and behold, the heavens were opened, and he saw the Spirit of God descending as a dove and lighting on Him, and behold, a voice out of the heavens said, "This is My beloved Son, in whom I am well-pleased"** (Mt. 3:16, 17).

The inspired writers did not say that the Holy Spirit was a dove, but rather that He descended as a dove would descend at the time of Jesus' baptism. With the words **"This is My beloved Son, in whom I am well-pleased,"** God put His stamp of approval on Jesus' thirty or so years of preparation, and thus He equipped Him for His ministry (see Lk. 4:18; Acts 10:38).

(This is a good text to use in discussing the three Persons in the Godhead, for at that moment, three Persons were in three locations, each doing something different. There is much about the Three-in-One aspect of God that we do not understand, but we accept it by faith because the Bible teaches it.)

Prior to this event, John may have suspected that Jesus was the Messiah, but he did not *know* it. The Lord had told him how he would recognize the Messiah: **He upon whom you see the Spirit descending and remaining upon Him, this is the One who baptizes in the Holy Spirit** (Jn. 1:33). John's joy must have known no bounds when he saw the Spirit coming from heaven. God had been true to His Word. The Christ had come.

JESUS TEMPTED IN THE WILDERNESS
(MT. 4:1–11; MK. 1:12, 13; LK. 4:1–13)

Matthew 4:1–11
[1]Then Jesus was led up by the Spirit into the wilderness to

---

[1]See pages 97 through 99 for an explanation of the baptism that John administered.

be tempted by the devil. [2]And after He had fasted forty days and forty nights, He then became hungry. [3]And the tempter came and said to Him, "If You are the Son of God, command that these stones become bread." [4]But He answered and said, "It is written, 'Man shall not live on bread alone, but on every word that proceeds out of the mouth of God.'"

[5]Then the devil took Him into the holy city and had Him stand on the pinnacle of the temple, [6]and said to Him, "If You are the Son of God, throw Yourself down; for it is written,

'He will command His angels concerning You';
and
'On their hands they will bear You up,
So that You will not strike Your foot against a stone.'"
[7]Jesus said to him, "On the other hand, it is written, 'You shall not put the Lord your God to the test.'"

[8]Again, the devil took Him to a very high mountain and showed Him all the kingdoms of the world and their glory; [9]and he said to Him, "All these things I will give You, if You fall down and worship me." [10]Then Jesus said to him, "Go, Satan! For it is written, 'You shall worship the Lord your God, and serve Him only.'" [11]Then the devil left Him; and behold, angels came and began to minister to Him.

Mark 1:12, 13

[12]Immediately the Spirit impelled Him to go out into the wilderness. [13]And He was in the wilderness forty days being tempted by Satan; and He was with the wild beasts, and the angels were ministering to Him.

Luke 4:1–13

[1]Jesus, full of the Holy Spirit, returned from the Jordan and was led around by the Spirit in the wilderness [2]for forty days, being tempted by the devil. And He ate nothing during those days, and when they had ended, He became hungry. [3]And the devil said to Him, "If You are the Son of God, tell this stone to become bread." [4]And Jesus answered him, "It is written, 'Man shall not live on bread alone.'"

⁵And he led Him up and showed Him all the kingdoms of the world in a moment of time. ⁶And the devil said to Him, "I will give You all this domain and its glory; for it has been handed over to me, and I give it to whomever I wish. ⁷Therefore if You worship before me, it shall all be Yours." ⁸Jesus answered him, "It is written, 'You shall worship the Lord your God and serve Him only.'"

⁹And he led Him to Jerusalem and had Him stand on the pinnacle of the temple, and said to Him, "If You are the Son of God, throw Yourself down from here; ¹⁰for it is written,

'He will command His angels concerning You to guard You,'

¹¹and,

'On their hands they will bear You up,

So that You will not strike Your foot against a stone.'"

¹²And Jesus answered and said to him, "It is said, 'You shall not put the Lord your God to the test.'"

¹³When the devil had finished every temptation, he left Him until an opportune time.

Immediately following the description of Jesus' baptism, we have the account of His temptation. Baptism does not mean the cessation of temptation. When we are baptized, Satan does not lessen his attacks but, rather, intensifies them. The fact that we have been baptized *does* mean that we now have God's help in meeting those temptations (1 Cor. 10:13; Heb. 13:5).

As Christ was about to begin His public ministry, He met the foe.[2] Evil appeared before Him in all its tremendous strength and naked horror. Never had such an attack occurred before, and never would such an attack occur again. While we can never fully understand God's purposes, the word "temptation" may give us a clue. The Greek word πειράζω (*peirazo*), translated "tempt," can also be translated "test." From Satan's viewpoint, Jesus' sojourn in the wilderness was a time of *temptation*—as the devil tried to induce Christ to sin. (He only had to make Him sin

---

[2]Some of the thoughts included came from G. Campbell Morgan, *The Crises of the Christ* (New York: Fleming H. Revell Co., 1936), 162–99.

once to destroy His mission.) From God's standpoint, however, the forty days was a season of *testing*—a time of proving Jesus' true worth and character.

Three aspects of the Temptation need to be highlighted by way of background:

(1) The *place*: The setting was "the wilderness." A solitary place cut off from human sympathy was selected as the battlefield. We are not told where this wilderness was. It may have been the wilderness of Judea, where John had been prepared and where he did much of his work (Mt. 3:1, 3; 11:7; Lk. 1:80; 3:1, 2). Mark 1:13 tells us that Jesus' only companions were **wild beasts**. Here superficial trappings were stripped away and the essence of temptation remained. It has been said that Adam turned a garden into a wilderness by sinning, but Jesus turned a wilderness into a garden by resisting sin.

(2) The *opponents*: First, there was Jesus, fresh from His baptism, an occasion when God had acknowledged Him as His Son. He had come forth from the water ready to begin His personal ministry. Then, there was the devil. In the wilderness experience, Jesus came face to face with the prince of the air, the god of this world, the leader of the hosts of darkness (2 Cor. 4:4; Eph. 2:2; 6:12).

(3) The *significance*: This confrontation was not an accident; it did not "just happen." Matthew 4:1 says, **Then Jesus was *led up by the Spirit* into the wilderness to be tempted by the devil.** (Emphasis added.) A divine plan was being worked out. Perhaps nothing shows this more clearly than the fact that the devil had to come out into the open for this contest. This is not the way Satan likes to fight. He prefers to work behind the scenes, through some agent. However, he was forced to meet Jesus face to face so that God's purposes might be accomplished.

During the Temptation, when the devil was forced into the open, his methods and goals were laid bare. As we study Jesus' three temptations, we can see the subtlety of Satan. He had been deceiving people for thousands of years. The expertise gained by millennia of experience was focused on Christ.

A great benefit of studying the Temptation is the opportunity to analyze each temptation: *why* it was wrong and how Christ countered it. Some think that Satan's suggestions were wrong simply because of their source, so they spend no more time considering them. It would save us a lot of thought if the devil came to us wearing a red suit, with horns and a pointed tail. We could then respond to his temptation, "That's wrong because it comes from Satan." Unfortunately, he can come to us as "an angel of light" (2 Cor. 11:14). If we do not understand *why* a specific temptation is wrong, he can easily deceive us.

Matthew gives the temptations in one order and Luke in another. Many commentators think that Matthew's order is more likely the chronological order. The exact sequence is not a matter of great importance. They basically correspond to the three avenues of temptation listed in 1 John 2:16: "the lust of the flesh [turning stones into bread to satisfy hunger] and the lust of the eyes [viewing the glory of the kingdoms of the world] and the boastful pride of life [astonishing the crowd by jumping safely from the temple]."

The First Temptation (Mt. 4:1–4)

The first temptation Satan set before Christ was a physical test. . . . **He had fasted forty days and forty nights, [and] He then became hungry. And the tempter came . . .** (Mt. 4:2, 3). Satan's objective in the first temptation was to test Christ's loyalty to God. He challenged Jesus: **"If You are the Son of God, command that these stones become bread"** (Mt. 4:3b). Forty days before, the Voice from heaven had said, "This is My beloved Son, in whom I am well-pleased" (Mt. 3:17). Now, the devil said, in effect, "If the Voice spoke the truth—if You really are God's Son—why are You hungry? What is the use of position without privilege?" Satan implied that Jesus could fulfill two aims by turning the desert rocks into bread: He could satisfy a legitimate need (His hunger), and, at the same time, He could prove His Sonship.

Christ saw through Satan's strategy. **But He answered and said, "It is written"** (Mt. 4:4a). Jesus' weapon against temptation was God's Word. The psalmist had said, "Your word I have treasured in my heart, that I may not sin against You" (Ps. 119:11). One of the best safeguards against succumbing to temptation is to fill your heart with the Word.

The appropriate text to counter this temptation came from Deuteronomy 8:3. Jesus quoted, **"Man shall not live on bread alone, but on every word that proceeds out of the mouth of God"** (Mt. 4:4b). First, mark the word "man": *"Man* shall not live on bread alone. . . ." The forty days in the wilderness were not primarily a test of Jesus' deity, but rather a test of His manhood. His purpose was not to prove that He was God, but to demonstrate that He was perfect Man living in perfect accord with God's revealed will.

Next, notice the contrast between the words "bread" and "every word that proceeds out of the mouth of God." Jesus could choose bread, or He could choose the will of God. It was evidently God's will that, on this occasion, He should be hungry—so He would remain squarely within the circle of that will.

Jesus had met the first temptation.

The Second Temptation (Mt. 4:5–7)

The second temptation was a spiritual test.

Satan does not give up easily. For the next temptation, he carefully selected the location. He carried Christ to **the holy city**, Jerusalem (Mt. 4:5a), a place precious to Jews—and to Jesus (Ps. 48:2; 137:5; Mt. 23:37). Then he took Him to the temple, the most revered site in that city. Finally, he took Him to the most prominent point of that structure. The text says that he **had Him stand on the pinnacle of the temple** (Mt. 4:5b). The temple did not have an architectural feature that we call a pinnacle, so this probably means that the devil took Jesus to the highest spot of the temple, which would have been on the south wing. From here one could look down on the temple complex and survey the city spread out in the distance. It was a magnificent and strategic position.

Standing beside Jesus on that lofty perch, Satan said to Him, **"If You are the Son of God, throw Yourself down; for it is written, 'He will command His angels concerning You'; and 'On their hands they will bear You up, so that You will not strike Your foot against a stone'"** (Mt. 4:6).

The devil was testing Christ's trust in God. In other words, he was saying, "You trust in God, do You? Let's see *how much* You trust in God. Do You trust Him enough to throw Yourself from this pinnacle?" He told Jesus, in effect, "You quoted a Scripture. I know some Scripture myself. Listen. . . ." He quoted Psalm 91:11, 12. Psalm 91 is a psalm of implicit trust in the Lord. The first verse says, "He who dwells in the shelter of the Most High will abide in the shadow of the Almighty."

This was (and is) a subtle temptation. It suggests that trust most perfectly expresses itself in attempting the unusual—in undertaking that which is heroic, daring, or even dangerous.

The devil had attempted to wield "the sword of the Spirit" (Eph. 6:17), but Jesus showed Himself the better swordsman. **Jesus said to him, "On the other hand, it is written"** (Mt. 4:7a). In other words, "Satan, you have quoted a passage of Scripture, but no single text exhausts what the Word says about a given subject. It is necessary to take *all* that the Bible says on that subject." Much error has resulted from isolating Scriptures and failing to consider other passages that deal with the same topic.

Jesus then quoted from Deuteronomy 6:16: **"You shall not put the Lord your God to the test"** (Mt. 4:7b). Do not misunderstand Christ's reply. He did not refer to Himself as God and say, "It is wrong to put *Me* to the test." (We must keep in mind that He was meeting these temptations in His perfect manhood, not His Godhood.) Rather, He said that it would be wrong for Him to put His *Father* to the test.

Satan said that jumping off the temple would show that Jesus *trusted* God; Jesus said that it would rather indicate that He was *testing* God. In fact, it would show that He did *not* trust God. If we have total trust in an individual, we see no need to test him or her. It is only when our confidence in a person wavers that the necessity for testing comes to mind.

Trust in God is expressed in our reliance on Him to help us face whatever life may bring. It is *not* expressed in artificial tests that we set for Him to meet.

Once again, Jesus showed Himself a Man driven by one principle: He was resolved to stay within the will of God. He had met the second temptation.

The Third Temptation (Mt. 4:8–10)

The third temptation was the most crucial, for it was a test of Jesus' mission—or, more accurately, a test of Jesus' resolve to carry through on His mission regardless of the cost. Having failed to destroy the Servant, Satan would try to destroy His service.

This temptation was the boldest and most audacious of all. In the first two temptations, Jesus had stripped the devil of his devious disguises and had revealed the true motives of evil. In the third temptation, Satan himself abandoned all masquerade and ceased to utilize secondary devices. He deliberately, directly, and defiantly asked for the homage of Christ.

Again, the devil took Him to a very high mountain and showed Him all the kingdoms of the world and their glory (Mt. 4:8). The traditional place for this temptation is Mount Tabor (see the map "Palestine During the Life of Christ" in the appendix), but the Scriptures do not tell what mountain it was. Try to imagine the glory of all the kingdoms of the world, all the empires present and past: the great Roman Empire, Greece, Persia, Babylonia, Assyria, Egypt, the kingdom of David and Solomon—not to mention such kingdoms as Bithynia and Syria, plus all the kingdoms in unexplored lands. All of this flashed before the eyes of Jesus.

Then Satan said, **"All these things I will give You, if You fall down and worship me"** (Mt. 4:9). The implication is that all this was the devil's to give (see Lk. 4:6)—and Jesus did not deny it. If the offer had not been genuine, there would have been no temptation. Some believe that the temptation here involved a lie: "Satan promised what he could not deliver." Such a temptation might have worked with us—but surely not with Jesus, who had an intimate knowledge of the spirit of the world. In the days of Jesus, it was as it is today: Satan held sway over the kingdoms of the world. They had submitted to his urgings; they were obedient to his commands; they had been led captive by his will. Jesus later called him "the ruler of this world" (Jn. 12:31). Paul used a similar expression in 2 Corinthians 4:4. (It should be understood that God has the *ultimate* control and that He has *allowed* Satan any power that he possesses. God limits the devil's activities.)

The devil was suggesting that Christ could obtain *almost* the same end without suffering and death. He held out a shortcut to a divine destination. It would have been much simpler to bow the knee than to die.

The temptation may have meant more to Jesus than Satan in the deepest reaches of his subtlety could possibly comprehend. To understand the terribleness of what awaited Christ, picture Him in the Garden of Gethsemane, sweat streaming down His face, as He poured out His heart to His Father: "My Father, if it is possible, let this cup pass from Me" (Mt. 26:39). See Him on the cross, crying out, "My God, My God, why have You forsaken Me?" (Mt. 27:46). Do not doubt that this was a genuine temptation.

In passing, observe Satan's estimation of Christ. He thought Jesus to be worth more than all the kingdoms he had gained. Some do not believe that the death of Jesus can suffice for all, but the devil understood His real value.

In Jesus' answer to the devil, for the first time He spoke in the language of His own authority. This authority had been created by the victories won in the previous attacks.

Christ first gave the Tempter a sharp command: **"Go, Satan!"** (Mt. 4:10a). Then Jesus again wielded the sword of the Spirit, quoting from Deuteronomy 6:13: **"For it is written, 'You shall worship the Lord your God, and serve Him only'"** (Mt. 4:10b). Christ's words laid bare the subtle nature of this temptation. The devil had, in effect, said, "Worship me and I will make *You* master of the kingdoms." Christ pointed out that *worship* and *servitude* cannot be separated. He could not worship Satan without becoming his servant. Satan might make Him a puppet ruler of the kingdoms of the world, but in reality He would have gained nothing. Satan would still retain control.

Again, Jesus stayed firmly within the will of His Father. He was ready to go to the cross to establish His kingdom.

Christ's answer showed that the rewards of God are infinitely better than those of Satan. Satan can make those rewards *look* good—as evidenced by the visual display of the glory of the kingdoms of the world. Luke's account of the Temptation has a revealing detail: The devil showed Jesus the empires **in a moment of time** (Lk. 4:5). Any longer than that would have shown the kingdoms to be worth little or nothing. Their glory was the glory of tinsel, not gold. As John said, "The world is passing away, and also its lusts" (1 Jn. 2:17a).

After Jesus' rebuke and answer, the devil was silent—proof of his defeat. Matthew 4:11 says, **Then the devil left Him; and behold, angels came and began to minister to Him.** Years ago, T. B. Larimore preached on the Temptation. His account was so vivid that when he said "the devil left Him," the audience let out a collective sigh.

Luke's account adds that **when the devil had finished every temptation, he left Him** *until* **an opportune time** (Lk. 4:13; emphasis added). As our studies continue, we shall see how Satan continued to try to tempt Christ: The crowds tried to crown Him as an earthly King (Jn. 6:15); people constantly asked Him for signs (Lk. 11:29); one of His own disciples even tried to discourage Him from going to the cross (Mt. 16:21–23). Nevertheless, from this time on, Jesus spoke to the devil and his agents as Master to servants. He had won the victory.

Christ came forth from the wilderness prepared for His ministry. Luke 4:14a tells us that "Jesus returned to Galilee in the power of the Spirit." He also came forth from His temptation prepared for His crucifixion. He remained the sinless Son of God, the "lamb unblemished and spotless" (1 Pet. 1:19).

The story of the Temptation emphasizes that to prepare for temptation, we need to learn, even memorize, God's Word. It also demonstrates the truth of James 4:7b: "Resist the devil and he will flee from you." One of the most precious messages is that, when we undergo temptation, Jesus understands and sympathizes. Christ did not endure the thousands of specific temptations to which we are subjected, but He did meet every *type* of temptation that we do. The three temptations are *representative* of all the enticements that we have to meet. The writer of the Book of Hebrews said,

> For we do not have a high priest who cannot sympathize with our weaknesses, but One who has been tempted

in all things as we are, yet without sin. Therefore let us draw near with confidence to the throne of grace, so that we may receive mercy and find grace to help in time of need (Heb. 4:15, 16).

With God's help, we, too, can be victors over Satan.

JOHN'S TESTIMONY CONCERNING JESUS (JN. 1:19–34)

[19]This is the testimony of John, when the Jews sent to him priests and Levites from Jerusalem to ask him, "Who are you?" [20]And he confessed and did not deny, but confessed, "I am not the Christ." [21]They asked him, "What then? Are you Elijah?" And he said, "I am not." "Are you the Prophet?" And he answered, "No." [22]Then they said to him, "Who are you, so that we may give an answer to those who sent us? What do you say about yourself?" [23]He said, "I am a voice of one crying in the wilderness, 'Make straight the way of the Lord,' as Isaiah the prophet said."

[24]Now they had been sent from the Pharisees. [25]They asked him, and said to him, "Why then are you baptizing, if you are not the Christ, nor Elijah, nor the Prophet?" [26]John answered them saying, "I baptize in water, but among you stands One whom you do not know. [27]It is He who comes after me, the thong of whose sandal I am not worthy to untie." [28]These things took place in Bethany beyond the Jordan, where John was baptizing.

[29]The next day he saw Jesus coming to him and said, "Behold, the Lamb of God who takes away the sin of the world! [30]This is He on behalf of whom I said, 'After me comes a Man who has a higher rank than I, for He existed before me.' [31]I did not recognize Him, but so that He might be manifested to Israel, I came baptizing in water." [32]John testified saying, "I have seen the Spirit descending as a dove out of heaven, and He remained upon Him. [33]I did not recognize Him, but He who sent me to baptize in water said to me, 'He upon whom you see the Spirit descending and remaining

**upon Him, this is the One who baptizes in the Holy Spirit.'
³⁴I myself have seen, and have testified that this is the Son
of God."**

After the Temptation, Jesus returned to the area where John
was preaching (Jn. 1:26, 29).

Apparently, the popularity of John had disturbed the religious
leaders in Jerusalem. The Pharisees (Jn. 1:24) thus sent priests and
Levites to question the prophet. They wanted to know if he was
the Messiah (the Christ), Elijah, or **the Prophet.** John emphati-
cally answered, **"No"** (Jn. 1:19–21).

The use of the term "the Prophet," in addition to the phrase
the Christ, illustrates the confusion of the Jewish religious leaders. Some of the Messianic prophecies did not fit their preconceived ideas, so they decided that those passages referred to One
that Moses said would be a prophet like himself (Deut. 18:15).
Moses' words referred to the coming Messiah (fulfilled in Jesus
[Acts 3:20, 22]), but Jewish teachers had devised a separate shad-
owy personality known as "the Prophet."

John's emphatic statement that he was not Elijah (Jn. 1:21)
is somewhat puzzling at first. After all, he told his questioners
that he was the forerunner of the Messiah and quoted Isaiah 40:3.
The prophecy of Isaiah 40:3 is tied with Malachi 3:1 (Mk. 1:2, 3),
which tells of the one coming before the Messiah, whom Malachi called "Elijah the prophet" (Mal. 4:5). John *was* the "Elijah"
foretold by Malachi. Jesus Himself later confirmed that that was
the case. He said, "John himself is Elijah who was to come" (Mt.
11:14; see 17:10–13).

Why, then, did John deny being Elijah? The Jews thought that
the *original* Elijah would return. Many Jews today are still looking for the return of the original Elijah. John was denying that he
was Elijah in the flesh. He came *"in the spirit and power* of Elijah"
(Lk. 1:17; emphasis added), but he was not literally Elijah.

The day after John confronted the Jerusalem committee, he
had his first opportunity to call public attention to Jesus as the
Messiah. . . . **he saw Jesus coming to him and said, "Behold,
the Lamb of God who takes away the sin of the world!"** (Jn.
1:29).

John did not introduce Jesus as "the military conqueror who will defeat our enemies," but as "the Lamb of God who takes away the sin of the world!" Jesus came to teach a better way of life; He came to give us an example of how we should live; but, first and foremost, He came to die for our sins (see Lk. 19:10). Lambs were not noted for teaching. Their relationship with sin was in giving their lives on the altar. Jesus is our Passover lamb (1 Cor. 5:7), the "lamb unblemished and spotless" (1 Pet. 1:19).

Then John explained how he knew Jesus was the Messiah (Jn. 1:31–33). He concluded, **"I myself have seen, and have testified that this is the Son of God"** (Jn. 1:34).

For all practical purposes, John's work was done, even though he would continue to teach and baptize for a few months more.[3] He had faithfully fulfilled God's mission for him. No man can do more. Everything was now ready for Jesus' work.

JESUS' FIRST DISCIPLES (IN JUDEA) (JN. 1:35–51)

[35]**Again the next day John was standing with two of his disciples,** [36]**and he looked at Jesus as He walked, and said, "Behold, the Lamb of God!"** [37]**The two disciples heard him speak, and they followed Jesus.** [38]**And Jesus turned and saw them following, and said to them, "What do you seek?" They said to Him, "Rabbi (which translated means Teacher), where are You staying?"** [39]**He said to them, "Come, and you will see." So they came and saw where He was staying; and they stayed with Him that day, for it was about the tenth hour.** [40]**One of the two who heard John speak and followed Him, was Andrew, Simon Peter's brother.** [41]**He found first his own brother Simon and said to him, "We have found the Messiah" (which translated means Christ).** [42]**He brought him to Jesus. Jesus looked at him and said, "You are Simon the son of John; you shall be called Cephas" (which is translated Peter).**

---

[3]The study "'A Voice Crying in the Wilderness': The Ministry of John," included on pages 436 through 445, contains the biblical accounts of the death of John the Baptizer.

⁴³The next day He purposed to go into Galilee, and He found Philip. And Jesus said to him, "Follow Me." ⁴⁴Now Philip was from Bethsaida, of the city of Andrew and Peter. ⁴⁵Philip found Nathanael and said to him, "We have found Him of whom Moses in the Law and also the Prophets wrote—Jesus of Nazareth, the son of Joseph." ⁴⁶Nathanael said to him, "Can any good thing come out of Nazareth?" Philip said to him, "Come and see." ⁴⁷Jesus saw Nathanael coming to Him, and said of him, "Behold, an Israelite indeed, in whom there is no deceit!" ⁴⁸Nathanael said to Him, "How do You know me?" Jesus answered and said to him, "Before Philip called you, when you were under the fig tree, I saw you." ⁴⁹Nathanael answered Him, "Rabbi, You are the Son of God; You are the King of Israel." ⁵⁰Jesus answered and said to him, "Because I said to you that I saw you under the fig tree, do you believe? You will see greater things than these." ⁵¹And He said to him, "Truly, truly, I say to you, you will see the heavens opened and the angels of God ascending and descending on the Son of Man."

The early days in Christ's ministry have been called "the period of obscurity." The synoptic writers began their reports of Jesus' public work with a later period which focuses on His success in Galilee. The apostle John wanted us to know about the earlier, less spectacular days.

We noted John the Baptizer's first testimony about Jesus in John 1:29: "Behold, the Lamb of God who takes away the sin of the world!" The following day, John was with two of his disciples. One was Andrew, Simon Peter's brother (Jn. 1:40). The other was probably John, the author of the fourth account. There are various reasons for believing that this was John: (1) The details that follow are such as would be given by an eyewitness; (2) it was John's practice to withhold his name; (3) if this was not John, he gave no account of his call to discipleship. For some reason, John was reluctant to name himself. On seven other occasions, he withheld his name (Jn. 13:23; 19:26, 35; 20:2–8; 21:7, 20, 24).

As Jesus walked by, the preacher again said, **"Behold, the Lamb of God!"** (Jn. 1:36). His two disciples followed Christ and spent the day with Him (Jn. 1:37–39). The text gives the time: **the tenth hour** (Jn. 1:39). Assuming that the unnamed disciple was John himself, the occasion was so memorable that he remembered the exact time. If he used the Jewish reckoning of time, this would have been about 4:00 p.m. The Jews reckoned time from sundown to sunrise and from sunrise to sundown. If he used Roman reckoning, it was 10:00 a.m. Since the Gospel of John was written long after the destruction of Jerusalem, and since John later used Roman time, most writers think that this is the time intended.

After several hours with Jesus, Andrew found his brother Simon and brought him to Christ (Jn. 1:40–42). One of Andrew's talents was to bring others to Jesus (see Jn. 6:8, 9; 12:20–22). Andrew's words to Simon are worth noting: **"We have found the Messiah" (which translated means Christ)** (Jn. 1:41). Jesus' first disciples recognized Him for who He was (see also Jn. 1:45, 49). As we shall see, they did not understand *all* the implications of the terms they used—but, at least, they realized that He was the fulfillment of the Old Testament promises concerning the Messiah.

When Jesus met Simon, He told him that he would be called "Cephas" or "Peter." The first name is Aramaic, and the second is Greek; both mean "rock." Jesus saw the possibilities in this man, even as He sees the potential in all of us.

The next day, as Jesus prepared to return to Galilee, He called Philip, who was probably also a disciple of the Baptizer. Christ's call to discipleship then and now is **"Follow Me"** (Jn. 1:43). Philip immediately found a friend named Nathanael and brought him to Jesus (Jn. 1:45, 46).

Christ astounded Nathanael by revealing details of his character and his life (Jn. 1:47–49). Jesus told him, **"You will see greater things than these"** (Jn. 1:50). Jesus' cryptic statement about **the angels of God ascending and descending on the Son of Man** (Jn. 1:51) is probably based on the Old Testament story of Jacob's ladder (Gen. 28:12). Through His death, burial, and resurrection, Jesus would become God's "ladder" for men to reach heaven. We are not sure who Nathanael was, but it is thought that he may have been the same as Bartholomew, one of Jesus' twelve apostles. There are various reasons for this conclusion. Among them is the fact that the rest of Jesus' first disciples were later chosen as His apostles, and, as J. W. McGarvey pointed out, "None are so highly commended as Nathanael."[4]

Thus Jesus gained His first small band of disciples (see Jn. 2:2). Five disciples are specifically mentioned in John 1:35–51: four named and one unnamed, who was probably the author of the book. Some think that the context indicates that John also found his brother James. If so, the number of disciples was at least six as Jesus headed north.

Note: The Greek word μαθητής (*mathetes*), translated **disciple**, basically means "learner." It referred to one who followed another in order to learn from him. Jesus would have all of us to be His disciples. Jesus often spoke of the challenge of discipleship (Lk. 14:26, 27, 33; Jn. 15:8). After the church was established, the most common term for members of the church was "disciples" (Acts 6:1, 2, 7; 9:1).

JESUS' FIRST MIRACLE
(AT CANA IN GALILEE)
(JN. 2:1–11)

[1]On the third day there was a wedding in Cana of Galilee, and the mother of Jesus was there; [2]and both Jesus and His disciples were invited to the wedding. [3]When the wine ran out, the mother of Jesus said to Him, "They have no wine." [4]And Jesus said to her, "Woman, what does that have to do with us? My hour has not yet come." [5]His mother said to the servants, "Whatever He says to you, do it." [6]Now there were six stone waterpots set there for the Jewish custom of purification, containing twenty or thirty gallons each. [7]Jesus said to them, "Fill the waterpots with water." So they filled them up to the brim. [8]And He said to them, "Draw some out now and take it to the headwaiter." So they took it to him. [9]When the

[4]J. W. McGarvey and Philip Y. Pendleton, *The Fourfold Gospel or A Harmony of the Four Gospels* (Cincinnati: Standard Publishing Co., 1914), 111.

headwaiter tasted the water which had become wine, and did not know where it came from (but the servants who had drawn the water knew), the headwaiter called the bridegroom, ¹⁰and said to him, "Every man serves the good wine first, and when the people have drunk freely, then he serves the poorer wine; but you have kept the good wine until now." ¹¹This beginning of His signs Jesus did in Cana of Galilee, and manifested His glory, and His disciples believed in Him.

Jesus and His disciples headed north to Galilee. On the third day, they reached Cana of Galilee (see the map "Palestine During the Life of Christ" in the appendix). This village, not far from Nazareth, was Nathanael's hometown (Jn. 21:2). They had come to attend a wedding (Jn. 2:1, 2). Jesus involved Himself in the lives of those He came to save.

Jesus' mother, Mary, was also present (Jn. 2:1). Subsequent events indicate that she was helping to serve at the wedding feast (see Jn. 2:3, 5). Perhaps a relative or a friend was getting married.

In the midst of the celebration, the refreshments ran out. Maybe more people than expected were present. At any rate, it was a potentially embarrassing situation. Mary came to her Son and said, **"They have no wine"** (Jn. 2:3). What she expected Him to do, we do not know; for He had previously performed no miracles (Jn. 2:11). However, she had probably been depending on Him for several years and thought He could do *something*.

Jesus' answer is significant: **"Woman, what does that have to do with us? My hour has not yet come"** (Jn. 2:4). In that society, to call one's mother "woman" was not insulting. (The term would later be used with tenderness [Jn. 19:26].) Nevertheless, Christ's words were a mild reprimand. Ernest Hauser wrote that this was one of three rebukes meant to "steel Mary for the recognition that Jesus, though her son, does not 'belong' to her." Hauser added that Christ's statement here "serves notice that, henceforth, his earthly bonds have to be loosened."[5]

---

[5]Ernest O. Hauser, "Mary, Mother of Christ," *Reader's Digest* (December 1971): 171.

Mary was not deterred. She told the servants, **"Whatever He says to you, do it"** (Jn. 2:5). Jesus apparently decided that this use of His miraculous powers would not be inconsistent with one of their purposes (to do good) and would not hasten His "hour" (the time of His death) as long as only the servants knew about it. He then performed the well-known miracle of turning water to wine (Jn. 2:6–10).

Controversy has raged over whether or not this incident proves that Jesus endorsed the use of alcoholic beverages. One side emphasizes the word "wine" and the remark recorded in verse 10. The other side has noted that Jesus made between 120 and 180 gallons of wine. There were six stone waterpots for the purpose of ceremonial washing (see Mk. 7:3). The Greek text says that these held two or three *metretas* (μετρητὰς) each and that they were filled to the brim (Jn. 2:7). In today's terms, this would be about twenty or thirty gallons (or 75 to 115 liters) in each pot. If the wine had significant alcoholic content (it is sometimes noted that the common drink of the land was one part wine to six parts water), He would have been encouraging drunkenness—which is condemned throughout the Bible (Prov. 20:1; Gal. 5:21). This is not, however, the passage to settle this question. The oft-quoted words of verse 10 would be true whether the wine had alcoholic content or not. Further, the Greek word translated "wine" (οἶνος, *oinos*) is the general word for wine and was even used in the Old Testament (in the Septuagint) to refer to the juice still in the grape (Is. 65:8).

Such disputation misses the point of the passage: Quietly, almost unnoticed, in an obscure little village, Jesus had begun to flex His spiritual muscles. He had performed His first miracle.

Today we use the word "miracle" in an offhand way to refer to anything that is remarkable. The Bible uses the word in a special sense to refer to a supernatural act. Jesus had surely done much that was *remarkable* in His first thirty years of life, but this was the first time He used His *supernatural* powers. Since we live in the natural world, it is beyond our ability to explain the supernatural. By faith, we accept what the Bible says on the subject.

John did not miss the significance of the event. He used his favorite word for a miracle: **sign** (Jn. 2:11a). What Jesus did was a sign that He really was from God. John noted that Christ had **manifested His glory** (Jn. 2:11a). This was a foretaste of the mighty works He would do. Further, as a result of this first sign, **His disciples believed in Him** (Jn. 2:11b). Their faith in Jesus as the Messiah was deepened.

JESUS' FIRST RESIDENCE AT CAPERNAUM (IN GALILEE) (JN. 2:12)

¹²**After this He went down to Capernaum, He and His mother and His brothers and His disciples; and they stayed there a few days.**

From Cana, Jesus traveled north and east. **After this He went down to Capernaum, He and His mother and His brothers and His disciples; and they stayed there a few days** (Jn. 2:12). Capernaum was a busy commercial city on the Sea of Galilee. It was not far from Bethsaida, the hometown of Peter and Andrew (Jn. 1:44), though, apparently, Peter and Andrew later moved to Capernaum (Mk. 1:21, 29). (See the map "Palestine During the Life of Christ" in the appendix.) Capernaum was not far from a major east-west highway that crossed Palestine. Later it would become Jesus' center of operations (Mt. 4:13).

PART IV

CHRIST'S MINISTRY FROM THE FIRST PASSOVER TO THE SECOND

Includes a Harmony of

Mt. 4:12–25; 8:2–4, 14–17; 9:1–9

Mk. 1:14—2:14

Lk. 3:19, 20; 4:14, 15, 31–44; 5:1–28

Jn. 2:13—4:54

THE FIRST PASSOVER OF JESUS' MINISTRY
(JN. 2:13—3:21)

Jesus cut short His initial visit to Capernaum to attend the Passover feast. The Passover feast commemorated God's "passing over" the Israelites in Egypt who had the blood of a lamb on their door posts (Ex. 12:1–28). No doubt, Jesus had attended this feast since He was twelve (Lk. 2:41, 42), but this was the first Passover of His public ministry. This was also Jesus' first public appearance since His ministry began. It began in a dramatic fashion, with His first cleansing of the temple.

Cleansing the Temple (Jn. 2:13–25)

[13]The Passover of the Jews was near, and Jesus went up to Jerusalem. [14]And He found in the temple those who were selling oxen and sheep and doves, and the money changers seated at their tables. [15]And He made a scourge of cords, and drove them all out of the temple, with the sheep and the oxen; and He poured out the coins of the money changers and overturned their tables; [16]and to those who were selling the doves He said, "Take these things away; stop making My Father's house a place of business." [17]His disciples remembered that it was written, "Zeal for Your house will consume me." [18]The Jews then said to Him, "What sign do You show us as your authority for doing these things?" [19]Jesus answered them, "Destroy this temple, and in three days I will raise it up." [20]The Jews then said, "It took forty-six years to build this temple, and will You raise it up in three days?" [21]But He was speaking of the temple of His body. [22]So when He was raised from the dead, His disciples remembered that He said this; and they believed the Scripture and the word which Jesus had spoken.

²³Now when He was in Jerusalem at the Passover, during the feast, many believed in His name, observing His signs which He was doing. ²⁴But Jesus, on His part, was not entrusting Himself to them, for He knew all men, ²⁵and because He did not need anyone to testify concerning man, for He Himself knew what was in man.

Temple commerce had resulted from the coming of Jews from all over the world for the major Jewish feast days (see Acts 2:5, 9–11a). Each Jew was required to pay a yearly temple tax of half a shekel. Jewish authorities based this on Exodus 30:13, even though there is no indication that this was to be a permanent requirement. Temple authorities would not allow this tax to be paid with foreign coins, so moneychangers were needed. Again, each Jew was to make certain animal sacrifices during the feast days. Most who came from other lands could not bring animals with them, so they had to purchase them after they arrived. Thus originated the selling of livestock in the temple. These enterprises may have originated as a service to world-travelers, but they had deteriorated into a money-making scheme controlled by the priests. The transactions were evidently carried on in the Court of the Gentiles. There are two Greek words for **temple**. One (ναός, *naos*) referred to the sacred part of the temple. The other (ἱερόν, *hieron*) referred to the temple complex as a whole, including the Court of the Gentiles. The latter word is used here.

The first public act of Jesus made a statement concerning His zeal for God's house and God's will. As He drove out the merchandisers, He said, **"Stop making My Father's house a place of business"** (Jn. 2:16b). Later, on a similar occasion, He would say, "It is written, 'My house shall be called a house of prayer'; but you are making it a robbers' den" (Mt. 21:13).

Jesus' first public act also made a statement regarding His God-endorsed authority (Mt. 3:17; see 7:29). Upset, the temple authorities challenged that authority. The NLT renders John 2:18, "'What right do you have to do these things?' the Jewish leaders demanded. 'If you have this authority from God, show us a miraculous sign to prove it.'"

For those willing to see and believe, Jesus would give many signs during His ministry (see Jn. 2:23), but the most significant miracle would be His resurrection (Rom. 1:4). He thus answered, **"Destroy this temple [Gk.: ναόν], and in three days I will raise it up"** (Jn. 2:19). **He was speaking of the temple of His body** (Jn. 2:21), but His foes misunderstood Him (Jn. 2:20), thinking only of the edifice of marble and gold that surrounded them. This statement of Jesus made an impression on them. Their misinterpretation of the prediction was brought up at Christ's trial (Mk. 14:58) and at His crucifixion (Mt. 27:40).

While Jesus was in Jerusalem, He did His first public miracles (Jn. 2:23). We are not told the nature of those miracles, but they would have included healing the sick (Mt. 4:23). (There is no indication that, at this time, Jesus was casting out demons. The first recorded account of this is found in Mark 1:23–28 and Luke 4:33–37. The astonishment on that occasion may indicate that casting out demons was a new manifestation of Jesus' power.) The group of believers began to grow (Jn. 2:23), but Jesus knew their faith was tenuous (Jn. 2:24, 25). The LB paraphrases verse 25, "No one needed to tell him how changeable human nature is!"

Teaching Nicodemus (Jn. 3:1–21)

¹**Now there was a man of the Pharisees, named Nicodemus, a ruler of the Jews;** ²**this man came to Jesus by night and said to Him, "Rabbi, we know that You have come from God as a teacher; for no one can do these signs that You do unless God is with him."** ³**Jesus answered and said to him, "Truly, truly, I say to you, unless one is born again he cannot see the kingdom of God."**

⁴**Nicodemus said to Him, "How can a man be born when he is old? He cannot enter a second time into his mother's womb and be born, can he?"** ⁵**Jesus answered, "Truly, truly, I say to you, unless one is born of water and the Spirit he cannot enter into the kingdom of God.** ⁶**That which is born of the flesh is flesh, and that which is born of the Spirit is spirit.** ⁷**Do not be amazed that I said to you, 'You must be born again.'** ⁸**The wind blows where it wishes and you hear the sound of it, but do not**

know where it comes from and where it is going; so is every-one who is born of the Spirit."

⁹Nicodemus said to Him, "How can these things be?" ¹⁰Jesus answered and said to him, "Are you the teacher of Israel and do not understand these things? ¹¹Truly, truly, I say to you, we speak of what we know and testify of what we have seen, and you do not accept our testimony. ¹²If I told you earthly things and you do not believe, how will you believe if I tell you heavenly things? ¹³No one has ascended into heaven, but He who descended from heaven: the Son of Man. ¹⁴As Moses lifted up the serpent in the wilderness, even so must the Son of Man be lifted up; ¹⁵so that whoever believes will in Him have eternal life.

¹⁶"For God so loved the world, that He gave His only begotten Son, that whoever believes in Him shall not perish, but have eternal life. ¹⁷For God did not send the Son into the world to judge the world, but that the world might be saved through Him. ¹⁸He who believes in Him is not judged; he who does not believe has been judged already, because he has not believed in the name of the only begotten Son of God. ¹⁹This is the judgment, that the Light has come into the world, and men loved the darkness rather than the Light, for their deeds were evil. ²⁰For everyone who does evil hates the Light, and does not come to the Light for fear that his deeds will be exposed. ²¹But he who practices the truth comes to the Light, so that his deeds may be manifested as having been wrought in God."

While Jesus was in Jerusalem, **a ruler of the Jews** (i.e., a member of the Sanhedrin; see Jn. 7:45–52) named Nicodemus came to see Him one night (Jn. 3:1, 2). The fact that Nicodemus **came ... by night** may have some significance (Jn. 19:39). Perhaps it indicates some nervousness on his part. On the other hand, this may simply be the only time that Jesus and Nicodemus could get together. He was one of those who had been impressed with Jesus' miracles (Jn. 2:23). He said, **"Rabbi** [an honorary title of respect], **we know that You have come from God as a teacher; for no one can do these signs that**

You do unless God is with him" (Jn. 3:2).

Jesus, who could read men's thoughts (Jn. 2:24, 25), knew why Nicodemus had come. The Jewish leader evidently had questions about the Messianic kingdom. He also had the common Jewish misconceptions of the kingdom. Thus Christ answered, **"Truly, truly, I say to you, unless one is born again he cannot see the kingdom of God"** (Jn. 3:3). The KJV has "Verily, verily." "Truly" and "verily" are translations of the Greek word for "amen," ἀμήν (*amen*), which can mean "this is (so)." The repetition of the word is an emphatic way of stressing "What I am about to say is *true.*"

The figure of being born again is a striking one and expresses the dramatic change that must characterize anyone who would be Jesus' disciple. Christ's purpose, however, was not to outline the conditions of discipleship. After the church was established, no one was ever told to "be born again" to become a Christian. Instead, honest inquirers were told to believe, repent, and be baptized (Acts 2:37, 38; 22:16). Peter later pointed out to Christians that, when they obeyed these commands, they *were* "born again" (see 1 Pet. 1:22, 23).

The conditions of becoming a Christian are *implied* in Jesus' words on the new birth. Faith is mentioned several times (Jn. 3:15, 16). Through the years, most have agreed that being "born of water" (Jn. 3:5) is a reference to baptism. Nevertheless, Jesus' emphasis was not on these conditions, but on the nature of the kingdom.

Jesus' purpose was to emphasize that the Messianic kingdom was not an earthly kingdom entered by an earthly birth (as the kingdom of Israel had been). Rather, it was a heavenly kingdom entered by a heavenly rebirth (or change of character). It was not a kingdom marked by the marching of human armies, but one characterized by the working of God's Spirit (Jn. 3:6–8). Jesus' illustration of the wind uses a play on words. The Greek word for "wind" is the same as the Greek word for "Spirit": πνεῦμα (*pneuma*). We cannot see the wind, but we can see the effect of its presence. Even so with the work of the Spirit. These were new concepts to Nicodemus, and he found them difficult to understand (Jn. 3:4, 10).

Jesus' basic message is followed by an extended section typical of John's account. The Book of John is noted for its reflective segments. Whether these words are a continuation of Jesus' discussion with Nicodemus or whether they are John's inspired comments, we do not know. The simplest approach is to take them as Jesus' words, and that is the way the NASB takes them. Either way, they contain a wealth of thought-provoking truths— including the fact that Jesus would be **lifted up** (on the cross) (Jn. 3:14) and the necessity of believing that Jesus is the Christ (the Messiah) (Jn. 3:15, 16, 18).

Included in the discourse is the most familiar passage in the Scriptures: John 3:16, the so-called "golden text of the Bible." It does not contain all we need to know about salvation (as some claim), but it *is* a beautiful and powerful statement concerning God's love for us.

THE FIRST MINISTRY IN JUDEA
(AND FURTHER TESTIMONY BY JOHN)
(JN. 3:22–36)

[22]After these things Jesus and His disciples came into the land of Judea, and there He was spending time with them and baptizing. [23]John also was baptizing in Aenon near Salim, because there was much water there; and people were coming and were being baptized— [24]for John had not yet been thrown into prison.

[25]Therefore there arose a discussion on the part of John's disciples with a Jew about purification. [26]And they came to John and said to him, "Rabbi, He who was with you beyond the Jordan, to whom you have testified, behold, He is baptizing and all are coming to Him." [27]John answered and said, "A man can receive nothing unless it has been given him from heaven. [28]You yourselves are my witnesses that I said, 'I am not the Christ,' but, 'I have been sent ahead of Him.' [29]He who has the bride is the bridegroom; but the friend of the bridegroom, who stands and hears him, rejoices greatly because of the bridegroom's voice. So this joy of mine has been made full.

³⁰He must increase, but I must decrease.

³¹"He who comes from above is above all, he who is of the earth is from the earth and speaks of the earth. He who comes from heaven is above all. ³²What He has seen and heard, of that He testifies; and no one receives His testimony. ³³He who has received His testimony has set his seal to this, that God is true. ³⁴For He whom God has sent speaks the words of God; for He gives the Spirit without measure. ³⁵The Father loves the Son and has given all things into His hand. ³⁶He who believes in the Son has eternal life; but he who does not obey the Son will not see life, but the wrath of God abides on him."

After the feast in Jerusalem, Jesus and His disciples moved into the Judean countryside to preach and teach. Estimates of the time of this ministry vary between three and eight months. We are given two bits of information concerning this period. First, Christ **was spending time** with His disciples; He was teaching them and allowing them to get to know Him. Second, He was **baptizing** (Jn. 3:22) as His forerunner had done. This baptism was apparently a continuation of John's baptism and was, therefore, also a preparatory baptism.

Jesus' ministry in Judea was evidently successful, for John's disciples complained, **"Behold, He is baptizing and all are coming to Him"** (Jn. 3:26). The next chapter states that "Jesus was making and baptizing more disciples than John (although Jesus Himself was not baptizing, but His disciples were)" (Jn. 4:1, 2).

Jesus' success was welcomed by the Baptizer, but not by the disciples who had remained with him. They were filled with jealousy (Jn. 3:26). Battles have been lost because of jealousy between generals. Jealousy is a constant threat to the harmony of the work of the Lord.

The complaints of John's disciples prompted him to testify again concerning who Jesus was (Jn. 3:27–35). The Baptizer emphasized the importance of believing in Jesus as the Messiah: **"He who believes in the Son has eternal life; but he who does not obey the Son will not see life, but the wrath of God**

abides on him" (Jn. 3:36). The concepts of believing and obeying are used interchangeably. The KJV has the word "believeth" twice in the verse, but two different words are used in the better Greek manuscripts. The faith that saves is an obedient faith (Jas. 2:20; see Rom. 1:5; 16:26).

As John once more defined his own role (Jn. 3:28, 29), he spoke one of the most noble sentiments in the Scriptures: **"He must increase, but I must decrease"** (Jn. 3:30). There will come a time when we must step down and let others take our places. Hard feelings would be avoided if each of us could say gracefully, without animosity, "He (or she) must increase, but I must decrease."

APPLICATION:
"GOD SO LOVED THE WORLD" (JN. 3:16)

In John 3:14–17, we have the most popular text in the Bible—that "golden" verse, John 3:16: "For God so loved the world, that He gave His only begotten Son, that whoever believes in Him shall not perish, but have eternal life." This verse is one of the greatest in the Bible for at least two reasons: (1) It touches on the entire scope of God's plan. Martin Luther, the renowned sixteenth-century Reformation leader, called it "the Bible in miniature." (2) It is filled with superlatives: supreme words suggesting the most wonderful themes known to man.

"For *God*": The Greatest Being

Even as the world, man, and all good things began with God, so does our text: "For *God* so loved the world. . . ."

Here is the greatest Being. Our minds cannot conceive of anything greater than God. A noted early American statesman said that the most important thought that had ever entered his mind was God and his individual responsibility to Him.[1]

Speaking of God, Paul wrote that He "is able to do far more abundantly beyond all that we ask or think . . ." (Eph. 3:20). We

---

[1]Daniel Webster, quoted in Frank S. Mead, comp. and ed., *12,000 Religious Quotations* (Grand Rapids, Mich.: Baker Book House, 1989), 189.

cannot think of anything that God cannot do. God is so great that in order to comprehend Him fully, we would have to be His equal. We would have to be gods ourselves.

"So Loved" : The Greatest Trait

It is said of the Greatest Being, "For God *so loved* the world . . . . " Love is the greatest trait in the world: "But now faith, hope, love, abide these three; but the greatest of these is love" (1 Cor. 13:13). Our text further declares that God had the greatest degree of this greatest trait: "For God *so* loved the world . . . ."

Ephesians 3:17–19 announces that God's love has dimensions: ". . . that you . . . may be able to comprehend . . . what is the *breadth* and *length* and *height* and *depth*, and to know the love of Christ which surpasses knowledge. . . ." (Emphasis added.) What is the "length" of God's love? Our text tells us: "God so loved the world, that He gave His only begotten Son. . . ." God's love went all the way.

"The World": The Greatest Company

To whom did God extend the greatest trait? "For God so loved *the world*, that He gave. . . . ": the world—the greatest company of which our minds can conceive—all who have lived, who are now living, and who will live before this earth is destroyed. However, it was not just the greatest company that our minds can imagine, but also the most undeserving company: a sinful world, a disobedient world, a world in darkness. God looked down at this ungodly world and loved it. God looked down at *us* and loved *us*.

Once a missionary from Africa was speaking to a group of small boys. He said, "I want to tell you about the gospel we preach in Africa. Would all the *good* boys present hold up their hands?" Not a hand went up. He smiled and said, "Then I have the same message for you that we have for those in Africa: God loves naughty boys."

That may not sound right, but it is the truth. "But God demonstrates His own love toward us, in that while we were yet sinners, Christ died for us" (Rom. 5:8).

"That He *Gave*": The Greatest Act

What did the Greatest Being do for the greatest company because He possessed the greatest trait? "God so loved the world, that He *gave*...." Three acts bring us closer to the Divine: giving, forgiving, and thanksgiving—and the root of them all is *giving*, the greatest act.

"*His Only Begotten Son*": The Greatest Gift

God showed the greatness of His love by *what* He gave: "God so loved the world, that He gave *His only begotten Son*," the greatest gift. Many gifts have been given. Wealthy men have been known to give large sums of money to worthy causes— sometimes incredibly large amounts—but no gift can compare with this gift.

Consider what God gave: (1) He gave His Son. Think of a loving, obedient, dutiful son. How heart-rending it would be to give up such a son. (2) God did not just give His Son, but He gave His "only begotten" Son—a Son in His likeness and His image with the stamp of Divinity on His brow. Think of giving up an *only* Son. (3) God did not just give His only Son, but He gave His only Son for a *sacrifice*. Jesus would die a terrible and shameful death for people who did not deserve it. God would have to give up His Son even as that Son's tears were ripping at His heart.

Here is a gift so great that we cannot begin to comprehend it. Paul said, "Thanks be to God for His indescribable gift!" (2 Cor. 9:15). The KJV has "Thanks be unto God for his unspeakable gift." Some things in the world we cannot comprehend, but we at least can speak of them—the population of the world or the national debt, for example—but God's gift is so incomprehensible that we cannot even speak of it with precision. "Love so amazing, so divine, demands my soul, my life, my all."[2]

---

[2]Isaac Watts, "When I Survey the Wondrous Cross," *Songs of Faith and Praise,* comp. and ed. Alton H. Howard (West Monroe, La.: Howard Publishing Co., 1994).

"That *Whoever*": The Greatest Opportunity

Having talked about God and Christ, we come at last to ourselves in the text: "For God so loved the world, that He gave His only begotten Son, that *whoever* believes in Him shall not perish, but have eternal life." The word "whoever" proclaims the greatest opportunity in the world. The provisions of God's love are for all (Lk. 2:10; Mt. 28:19; Acts 10:34, 35; 17:30; 2 Pet. 3:9). Jesus told His disciples, "Go into *all* the world and preach the gospel to *all* creation" (Mk. 16:15; emphasis added).

The word "whoever" should be meaningful to us as individuals. Phillips Brooks, a noted nineteenth-century preacher, said that he appreciated the way John 3:16 reads: God might have said "that Americans who believe in Him should not perish, but have eternal life"—but there are Latin Americans, South Americans, North Americans, and so on. God might have said "that Brooks might have everlasting life"—but there are many people named Brooks. God might even have said "that if Phillips Brooks believes, he will be saved"—but it is possible that there is more than one Phillips Brooks; again doubt could have existed. "How thankful I am," said Phillips Brooks, "that God said 'whoever,' for I know *that* applies to me!" Everyone of us can read this verse and know that *we* can be saved.

Understand, however, that the word "whoever" places the responsibility on *us*. The world is made up of "whoever will's" and "whoever won'ts." Each of us decides whether or not we will take advantage of the glorious opportunity (Rev. 22:17). Each of us determines his or her own eternal destiny.

"*Believes*": The Greatest Foundation

What must we do to take advantage of the greatest opportunity? Our text says, "that whoever *believes* in Him shall not perish, but have eternal life." Belief is the greatest foundation. On it rests all that we do to become Christians and all we do as Christians. "And without faith it is impossible to please Him, for he who comes to God must believe that He is and that He is a rewarder of those who seek Him" (Heb. 11:6).

It should be stressed that the word "believes" in John 3:16 is not mere mental assent. The AB translates the verse like this: "For God so greatly loved and dearly prized the world that He [even] gave up His only begotten (unique) Son, so that whoever believes in (*trusts in, clings to, relies on*) Him shall not perish . . . *but* have eternal (everlasting) life." (Emphasis added.)

True belief includes obedience to the will of God (see Jas. 2:20). Paul wrote, "For in Christ Jesus neither circumcision nor uncircumcision means anything, but faith working through love" (Gal. 5:6; emphasis added). Building on the foundation of faith and motivated by love, one will repent of his sins (Lk. 13:3), confess his faith before men (Mt. 10:32), and be buried in baptism for the remission of sins (Acts 2:38).

"In *Him*": The Greatest Attraction

What will produce such faith? What will move us to obedience? ". . . that whoever believes in *Him* shall not perish." Jesus makes salvation possible. He is the greatest attraction of the ages. He said, "And I, if I am lifted up from the earth, will draw all men to Myself" (Jn. 12:32). Our faith is not in some man, some doctrine, or some religious system. Our faith is in Christ, who died for our sins.

"Shall Not *Perish*": The Greatest Tragedy

If we have this faith, what will be the result? ". . . whoever believes in Him shall not *perish*...." Our obedient faith will prevent the greatest tragedy that can befall a man.

Many tragedies occur in this life. A barn burns, destroying all of a farmer's equipment and goods, and he says, "I am ruined." A home is lost in a flood, with all of a family's earthly possessions, and they weep, "We are ruined." The husband and father of a large family dies, and the family cries with broken heart, "We are ruined." Someone loses his health, and he, too, thinks, "I am ruined." However, as bad as the tragedies of life are, a man is never ruined until he is lost eternally. *Then* he "will pay the penalty of eternal destruction, away from the presence of the Lord and from the glory of His power" (2 Thess. 1:9; see Mt. 25:46; Rev. 20:10). That is what the word "perish" means.

"But": The Greatest Difference

We can be glad that the text does not end with the word "perish." It continues, ". . . that whoever believes in Him shall not perish, but have eternal life." "But" is a little word that makes the greatest difference in the world. In this text, on one side we have the word "perish," and on the other we have the phrase "eternal life." In between the two, making the difference, we have the little adversative conjunction "but."

"Have *Eternal Life*": The Greatest Promise

The passage closes with this promise: ". . . that whoever believes in Him shall not perish, but have *eternal life*." Here is the greatest promise: the promise of an eternity with God (see Mk. 10:30; Gal. 6:8; 1 Tim. 6:12; Tit. 1:2) in a place where "He will wipe away every tear from their eyes; and there will no longer be any death; there will no longer be any mourning, or crying, or pain; the first things have passed away" (Rev. 21:4). This is God's promise to us if we will trust and obey.

Conclusion

Here is the heart of the gospel story in a single verse:

"God"—the Greatest Being.
"So loved"—the greatest trait.
"The world"—the greatest company.
"That He gave"—the greatest act.
"His only begotten Son"—the greatest gift.
"That whoever"—the greatest opportunity.
"Believes"—the greatest foundation.
"In Him"—the greatest attraction.
"Shall not perish"—the greatest tragedy.
"But"—the greatest difference.
"Have eternal life"—the greatest promise.

THE SHIFT FROM JUDEA TO GALILEE
(MT. 4:12; MK. 1:14; LK. 3:19, 20; JN. 4:1–45)

The scene shifts north to Galilee. The synoptic accounts focus on "The Great Galilean Ministry," which lasted about a year and

139

one-half. In the verses under discussion, we will see some pre-liminary matters regarding that ministry.

Reasons for the Move to Galilee
(Mt. 4:12; Mk. 1:14; Lk. 3:19, 20; Jn. 4:1–3)

Matthew 4:12
¹²Now when Jesus heard that John had been taken into cus-tody, He withdrew into Galilee.

Mark 1:14
¹⁴Now after John had been taken into custody, Jesus came into Galilee, preaching the gospel of God.

Luke 3:19, 20
¹⁹But when Herod the tetrarch was reprimanded by him because of Herodias, his brother's wife, and because of all the wicked things which Herod had done, ²⁰Herod also added this to them all: he locked John up in prison.

John 4:1–3
¹Therefore when the Lord knew that the Pharisees had heard that Jesus was making and baptizing more disciples than John ²(although Jesus Himself was not baptizing, but His disci-ples were), ³He left Judea and went away again into Galilee.

Jesus and His disciples had been enjoying success in Judea—teaching and baptizing even more than John the Baptizer (Jn. 3:22, 26; 4:1). At the height of this success, Christ decided that it was time to leave Judea and go back to Galilee. Two factors contrib-uted to the move at this particular time.

Matthew and Mark gave one reason for the decision. Mat-thew 4:12 says, **"Now when Jesus heard that John had been taken into custody** [by Herod; see Mt. 14:1–12; Mk. 6:14–29], **He withdrew into Galilee"** (see Mk. 1:14). Herod, the tetrarch, was living with Herodias, a niece and his brother Philip's wife. The fearless Baptizer had told Herod, "It is not lawful for you to have her" (Mt. 14:4). This had infuriated Herodias, who had pressured Herod to have John arrested (Mk. 6:17–19). The ruler had **locked John up in prison** (Lk. 3:20).

When we read that Jesus withdrew into Galilee after John was imprisoned, it looks as though He was trying to get away from Herod, knowing that the tetrarch also desired to put Him in prison. In fact, Christ was heading into part of Herod's tetrarchy (see Lk. 23:6, 7). Why, then, did John's imprisonment prompt Jesus to go to Galilee? Jesus may have been hurrying north to encourage John's disciples in that area, to keep them from scattering. Most think that Aenon in John 3:23 was north of Judea.

John added another reason why Christ thought it advisable to leave Judea: **Therefore when the Lord knew that the Pharisees had heard that Jesus was making and baptizing more disciples than John, . . . He left Judea . . .** (Jn. 4:1–3). Jesus wanted to avoid direct confrontation with the Pharisees—at least for a while—so He left the province where their influence was the strongest. Having spent about a year in Judea, Jesus and His disciples **went away again into Galilee** (Jn. 4:3).

The Incident in Samaria (Jn. 4:4–42)

⁴**And He had to pass through Samaria. ⁵So He came to a city of Samaria called Sychar, near the parcel of ground that Jacob gave to his son Joseph; ⁶and Jacob's well was there. So Jesus, being wearied from His journey, was sitting thus by the well. It was about the sixth hour.**

⁷**There came a woman of Samaria to draw water. Jesus said to her, "Give Me a drink." ⁸For His disciples had gone away into the city to buy food. ⁹Therefore the Samaritan woman said to Him, "How is it that You, being a Jew, ask me for a drink since I am a Samaritan woman?" (For Jews have no dealings with Samaritans.) ¹⁰Jesus answered and said to her, "If you knew the gift of God, and who it is who says to you, 'Give Me a drink,' you would have asked Him, and He would have given you living water." ¹¹She said to Him, "Sir, You have nothing to draw with and the well is deep; where then do You get that living water? ¹²You are not greater than our father Jacob, are You,**

who gave us the well, and drank of it himself and his sons and his cattle?" ¹³Jesus answered and said to her, "Everyone who drinks of this water will thirst again; ¹⁴but whoever drinks of the water that I will give him shall never thirst; but the water that I will give him will become in him a well of water springing up to eternal life."

¹⁵The woman said to Him, "Sir, give me this water, so I will not be thirsty nor come all the way here to draw." ¹⁶He said to her, "Go, call your husband and come here." ¹⁷The woman answered and said, "I have no husband." Jesus said to her, "You have correctly said, 'I have no husband'; ¹⁸for you have had five husbands, and the one whom you now have is not your husband; this you have said truly." ¹⁹The woman said to Him, "Sir, I perceive that You are a prophet. ²⁰Our fathers worshiped in this mountain, and you people say that in Jerusalem is the place where men ought to worship." ²¹Jesus said to her, "Woman, believe Me, an hour is coming when neither in this mountain nor in Jerusalem will you worship the Father. ²²You worship what you do not know; we worship what we know, for salvation is from the Jews. ²³But an hour is coming, and now is, when the true worshipers will worship the Father in spirit and truth; for such people the Father seeks to be His worshipers. ²⁴God is spirit, and those who worship Him must worship in spirit and truth." ²⁵The woman said to Him, "I know that Messiah is coming (He who is called Christ); when that One comes, He will declare all things to us." ²⁶Jesus said to her, "I who speak to you am He."

²⁷At this point His disciples came, and they were amazed that He had been speaking with a woman, yet no one said, "What do You seek?" or, "Why do You speak with her?" ²⁸So the woman left her waterpot, and went into the city and said to the men, ²⁹"Come, see a man who told me all the things that I have done; this is not the Christ, is it?" ³⁰They went out of the city, and were coming to Him.

³¹Meanwhile the disciples were urging Him, saying, "Rabbi, eat." ³²But He said to them, "I have food to eat that you do not know about." ³³So the disciples were saying to one another, "No one brought Him anything to eat, did he?" ³⁴Jesus said

to them, "My food is to do the will of Him who sent Me and to accomplish His work. [35]Do you not say, 'There are yet four months, and then comes the harvest'? Behold, I say to you, lift up your eyes and look on the fields, that they are white for harvest. [36]Already he who reaps is receiving wages and is gathering fruit for life eternal; so that he who sows and he who reaps may rejoice together. [37]For in this case the saying is true, 'One sows and another reaps.' [38]I sent you to reap that for which you have not labored; others have labored and you have entered into their labor."

[39]From that city many of the Samaritans believed in Him because of the word of the woman who testified, "He told me all the things that I have done." [40]So when the Samaritans came to Jesus, they were asking Him to stay with them; and He stayed there two days. [41]Many more believed because of His word; [42]and they were saying to the woman, "It is no longer because of what you said that we believe, for we have heard for ourselves and know that this One is indeed the Savior of the world."

The most direct route from Judea to Galilee was through the province of Samaria, but most Jews, because of their dislike for the Samaritans, took a circuitous route from Judea to Galilee. They traveled east, crossed the Jordan, and then followed the eastern bank of the river until they could cross into Galilee. Jesus, though, traveled straight north through Samaria.

John wrote that Christ *had* **to pass through Samaria** (Jn. 4:4; emphasis added). Maybe He "had to" because He was in hurry. He could save about three days' travel time going the direct route. However, the fact that He stopped in Samaria for several days (Jn. 4:40) makes this improbable. It is more likely that He "had to" in order to make contact with the Samaritans. Where the Jews saw a despised mongrel race, Jesus saw a field **white for harvest** (Jn. 4:35).

In the heart of Samaria, Jesus met a woman at a well, and one of the most remarkable interchanges of Christ's ministry ensued. Jesus' conversation with the woman has been studied as a model of how to bring the irreligious to faith: how He made contact with her, how He aroused her interest, how He corrected error, how He led her to new truths, how He convicted her of sin, and especially how He developed faith in her heart.

As a result of this one contact, Christ had the opportunity to teach an entire town. **Many . . . believed because of His word** (Jn. 4:41).

Arrival in Galilee (Lk. 4:14; Jn. 4:43–45)

Luke 4:14
[14]And Jesus returned to Galilee in the power of the Spirit, and news about Him spread through all the surrounding district.

John 4:43–45
[43]After the two days He went forth from there into Galilee. [44]For Jesus Himself testified that a prophet has no honor in his own country. [45]So when He came to Galilee, the Galileans received Him, having seen all the things that He did in Jerusalem at the feast; for they themselves also went to the feast.

After several days with the Samaritans, Jesus and the disciples resumed their journey, traveling northward through the valley of Esdraelon. At last they reached the hills of southern Galilee. Christ would do His greatest work in this province.

Since Jerusalem and Judea were the heart of Judaism at that time, why did Jesus concentrate His efforts in Galilee? Here are three possible factors: (1) Jesus had grown up in Galilee, so it was the region with which He was most familiar; (2) Galilee was the more populous area; and (3) as a rule, Galileans were more receptive than Judeans, being less enamored with religious traditions. All of the apostles except Judas were Galileans.

News of Jesus' ministry in Judea preceded Him. John 4:45 says, **So when He came to Galilee, the Galileans received Him, having seen all the things that He did in Jerusalem at the feast . . .** (see Jn. 2:23). John inserted a strange note in 4:44: **For Jesus Himself testified that a prophet has no honor in his own country.** This could be part of the explanation of why Jesus left Judea.

Everywhere else in the Gospel Accounts, however, Galilee is presented as Jesus' "own country." Perhaps, then, this is a parenthetical thought indicating that He knew that His warm welcome in Galilee would not last. (See Mt. 13:57; Mk. 6:4; Lk. 4:24.)

A GENERAL ACCOUNT OF JESUS' TEACHING IN GALILEE (MT. 4:17; MK. 1:14, 15; LK. 4:14, 15)

Matthew 4:17
     [17]From that time Jesus began to preach and say, "Repent, for the kingdom of heaven is at hand."

Mark 1:14, 15
     [14]Now after John had been taken into custody, Jesus came into Galilee, preaching the gospel of God, [15]and saying, "The time is fulfilled, and the kingdom of God is at hand; repent and believe in the gospel."

Luke 4:14, 15
     [14]And Jesus returned to Galilee in the power of the Spirit, and news about Him spread through all the surrounding district. [15]And He began teaching in their synagogues and was praised by all.

Jesus began to preach as He had in Judea. Mark recorded that **Jesus came into Galilee, preaching the gospel of God, and saying, "The time is fulfilled, and the kingdom of God is at hand; repent and believe in the gospel"** (Mk. 1:14b, 15; see Mt. 4:17). The order to "repent and believe" is somewhat unusual. Generally, people first come to believe in Jesus, which causes them to repent of their sins. However, Jesus was preaching to Jews who already had a basic faith in God and some knowledge of the Scriptures. They first needed to repent of their failure to keep God's law. Then they needed to learn of the Messiah (Christ) and come to believe in Him.

Luke wrote, **He began teaching in their synagogues and**

was praised by all (Lk. 4:15). As a rule, synagogues had formal meetings twice on the Sabbath, once on Monday, and once on Thursday. Mondays and Thursdays were "market days" in many towns, assuring a good crowd. Synagogues could also be opened for informal meetings at other times. These circumstances provided excellent opportunities for Jesus to teach. It was an auspicious beginning.

THE SECOND MIRACLE AT CANA
(JN. 4:46–54)

⁴⁶**Therefore He came again to Cana of Galilee where He had made the water wine. And there was a royal official whose son was sick at Capernaum. ⁴⁷When he heard that Jesus had come out of Judea into Galilee, he went to Him and was imploring Him to come down and heal his son; for he was at the point of death. ⁴⁸So Jesus said to him, "Unless you people see signs and wonders, you simply will not believe." ⁴⁹The royal official said to Him, "Sir, come down before my child dies." ⁵⁰Jesus said to him, "Go; your son lives." The man believed the word that Jesus spoke to him and started off. ⁵¹As he was now going down, his slaves met him, saying that his son was living. ⁵²So he inquired of them the hour when he began to get better. Then they said to him, "Yesterday at the seventh hour the fever left him." ⁵³So the father knew that it was at that hour in which Jesus said to him, "Your son lives"; and he himself believed and his whole household. ⁵⁴This is again a second sign that Jesus performed when He had come out of Judea into Galilee.**

Jesus began to perform miracles in Galilee as He had in Judea. Luke 4:14a says that "Jesus returned to Galilee in the power of the Spirit." This refers to His exercising "the power of the Spirit" by doing miracles. The first miracle after Jesus' return took place at Cana. As the phrase **second sign** in John 4:54 indicates, there had been a previous miracle in Galilee. The first was turning water to wine (Jn. 2:11), and this was the second. Of course, Jesus had done other signs/miracles while in Judea (Jn. 2:23; 3:2).

For some reason, Jesus made another visit to the place **where He had made the water wine** (Jn. 4:46). Perhaps Nathanael, who was from there (Jn. 21:2), had invited Him to his home. In nearby Capernaum, **a royal official** (literally, "king's man," who was probably an officer in Herod's court) had a son **at the point of death** (Jn. 4:46, 47). Learning that Jesus was in Cana, he hurried to ask Him to heal his son.

Jesus' initial response to the official is rather unusual: **"Unless you people see signs and wonders, you simply will not believe"** (Jn. 4:48). This was not a personal rebuke but an indictment of mankind in general (the word "you" is plural in the Greek). Perhaps Jesus was contrasting the Galileans with the Samaritans, who believed "because of His word" (Jn. 4:41) without the need for miracles. Perhaps the words were intended to test the man's faith. At any rate, the words did not deter the official, who *did* believe in Jesus. Christ told him, **"Go; your son lives"** (Jn. 4:50). The man started home. When he arrived, he learned that his son had recovered at the exact time that Jesus said that he would live (Jn. 4:50–53a). Deeply impressed, the nobleman **himself believed and his whole household** (Jn. 4:53b). The royal official presents a commendable example of a man sharing his faith with his household.

This is one of four known healings that Jesus performed from a distance, including the healing of the centurion's servant in Matthew 8:5–13 and Luke 7:1–10; the healing of the Syrophoenician woman's daughter in Matthew 15:22–28 and Mark 7:25–30; and the healing of the ten lepers in Luke 17:11–37.

News of these miracles "spread through all the surrounding district" (Lk. 4:14b). The name of Jesus was on every tongue.

THE SHIFT TO CAPERNAUM IN GALILEE (MT. 4:13–16)

[13]And leaving Nazareth, He came and settled in Capernaum, which is by the sea, in the region of Zebulun and Naphtali. [14]This was to fulfill what was spoken through Isaiah the prophet:
[15]"The land of Zebulun and the land of Naphtali,

> By the way of the sea, beyond the Jordan, Galilee of the
> Gentiles—
> [16]The people who were sitting in darkness saw a great
> Light,
> And those who were sitting in the land and shadow of
> death,
> Upon them a Light dawned."

One of Jesus' first acts in Galilee was to establish Capernaum as His base of operations. Jesus had earlier visited Capernaum (see Jn. 2:12). Matthew wrote that Jesus "withdrew into Galilee; **and leaving Nazareth, He came and settled in Capernaum, which is by the sea**" (Mt. 4:12b, 13a). Capernaum was located **in the region of Zebulun and Naphtali** (Mt. 4:13b), the general area allotted to those two tribes when the Israelites entered Canaan (Josh. 19). Matthew informed his readers that Jesus' move fulfilled part of a familiar Messianic prophecy (Mt. 4:14–16; see Is. 9:1, 2).

Jesus never owned a home in Capernaum (Mt. 8:20), but some of His disciples did (Mk. 1:21, 29). From this time on, during His Galilean ministry, Christ would never be gone long from Capernaum. He would leave from that city on tours, and then He would return there (see Mk. 1:21, 29, 38, 39; 2:1).

Most harmonies insert Luke 4:16–30 at this point, to explain why Jesus made the switch from Nazareth to Capernaum. It is not included here for two reasons: First, the passage refers to what had been "done at Capernaum" (Lk. 4:23), but at this point in our harmony, nothing had been done at Capernaum. Second, the extreme nature of the rejection seems to fit better the latter part of Jesus' ministry in Galilee.

THE CALL OF FOUR FISHERMEN
(MT. 4:18–22; MK. 1:16–20; LK. 5:1–11)

Matthew 4:18–22
[18]**Now as Jesus was walking by the Sea of Galilee, He saw two brothers, Simon who was called Peter, and Andrew his brother, casting a net into the sea; for they were fishermen.**

[19]And He said to them, "Follow Me, and I will make you fishers of men." [20]Immediately they left their nets and followed Him. [21]Going on from there He saw two other brothers, James the son of Zebedee, and John his brother, in the boat with Zebedee their father, mending their nets; and He called them. [22]Immediately they left the boat and their father, and followed Him.

Mark 1:16–20

[16]As He was going along by the Sea of Galilee, He saw Simon and Andrew, the brother of Simon, casting a net in the sea; for they were fishermen. [17]And Jesus said to them, "Follow Me, and I will make you become fishers of men." [18]Immediately they left their nets and followed Him. [19]Going on a little farther, He saw James the son of Zebedee, and John his brother, who were also in the boat mending the nets. [20]Immediately He called them; and they left their father Zebedee in the boat with the hired servants, and went away to follow Him.

Luke 5:1–11

[1]Now it happened that while the crowd was pressing around Him and listening to the word of God, He was standing by the lake of Gennesaret; [2]and He saw two boats lying at the edge of the lake; but the fishermen had gotten out of them and were washing their nets. [3]And He got into one of the boats, which was Simon's, and asked him to put out a little way from the land. And He sat down and began teaching the people from the boat. [4]When He had finished speaking, He said to Simon, "Put out into the deep water and let down your nets for a catch." [5]Simon answered and said, "Master, we worked hard all night and caught nothing, but I will do as You say and let down the nets." [6]When they had done this, they enclosed a great quantity of fish, and their nets began to break; [7]so they signaled to their partners in the other boat for them to come and help them. And they came and filled both of the boats, so that they began to sink. [8]But when Simon Peter saw that, he fell down at Jesus' feet, saying, "Go away from

me Lord, for I am a sinful man, O Lord!" [9]For amazement had seized him and all his companions because of the catch of fish which they had taken; [10]and so also were James and John, sons of Zebedee, who were partners with Simon. And Jesus said to Simon, "Do not fear, from now on you will be catching men." [11]When they had brought their boats to land, they left everything and followed Him.

Almost everything was in place for Jesus to begin an aggressive campaign in Galilee. He needed one more component: full-time disciples. Matthew 4, Mark 1, and Luke 5 tell of the call of four fishermen: Peter, James, John, and Andrew. This was the second call for most or all of these men, for they had been Jesus' disciples during His Judean ministry. John 1:40, 41 specifically mentions Andrew and Peter. Earlier it was noted that the unnamed disciple (Jn. 1:37, 40) was probably John. We also observed that the wording of the text may suggest that John found his brother James in the same way Andrew found his brother Peter.

There were three stages in Jesus' call to discipleship. Stage one was an invitation to follow Him and learn from Him. This call did not necessarily involve the forsaking of family and job—as illustrated by the fishermen who had returned to their former occupation. During His ministry, Jesus had many part-time workers. He once sent out seventy disciples to preach (Lk. 10:1–20).

The second stage was full-time discipleship. Those who responded to this call would travel and live with Jesus. The number of these disciples was considerably smaller. The call of the four men in the above texts is in this second category.

The third stage would be reached when Jesus chose twelve of His disciples to be apostles. We will study about that momentous event later. For now, we want to concentrate on the call of four fishermen to be Jesus' constant companions.

All three synoptic Gospel Accounts tell of this call. The three passages demonstrate the difficulty involved in putting together a harmony. Matthew and Mark tell of four men who were called, while Luke mentions only three. If we were to read only Matthew's and Mark's accounts, we would not know that anyone else was present. Luke, however, recorded that Jesus was preaching to a crowd, and he related the miracle of the great catch of fish.

Because of the differences, some conclude that Luke tells of a different occasion than do Matthew and Mark. Several details, however, indicate that this is the same incident. First, all three accounts mention the same place—the Sea of Galilee (Mt. 4:18; Mk. 1:16). Luke has **the lake of Gennesaret** (Lk. 5:1), but this is just another name for the Sea of Galilee. Second, they all mention three of the same people—Peter, James, and John (Mt. 4:18, 21; Mk. 1:16, 19; Lk. 5:3, 10). Matthew and Mark also tell of a fourth man, Andrew. Luke does not specifically mention Andrew, but Peter had someone else in the boat with him who was not James or John (Lk. 5:6, 7, 10). Andrew, his brother, worked with him as a fisherman (Mt. 4:18). Third, they all record the same activity—cleaning/repairing nets (Mt. 4:21; Mk. 1:19; Lk. 5:2). Fourth, they refer to the same call—to be fishers of men (Mt. 4:19; Mk. 1:17; Lk. 5:10); and fifth, they all recount the same response—leaving and following Him (Mt. 4:20, 22; Mk. 1:18, 20; Lk. 5:11).

If these do refer to the same occasion, how can the accounts be reconciled? When there are differences in the accounts, it is sufficient to know that the differences *can* be reconciled—even if we do not know exactly how. In this particular instance, the accounts might be reconciled by the following scenario.

When Jesus and His disciples returned to Galilee, four of the disciples—Peter, James, John, and Andrew—returned to their occupation, fishing on the Sea of Galilee. One morning, very early, Jesus went walking on the shore near where the men usually fished. After a fruitless night, James and John had already given up and were cleaning and repairing their nets on the shore. More stubborn than the others, Peter kept trying; but, finally, even he had to admit defeat. He and Andrew returned to shore.

In the meantime, word had spread that Jesus was there. A crowd had gathered. Jesus began to preach to them. When the people pressed in on Him, He got into Peter's boat and had him row the vessel a short distance into the lake. He completed His sermon from this unusual "pulpit."

This was followed by an unusual miracle: a remarkable catch of fish that astonished the fishermen and caused Peter to fall to his knees. Jesus thus prepared the hearts of the fishermen to respond to His call. Matthew recorded the call and their response: **And He said to them, "Follow Me, and I will make you fishers of men." Immediately they left their nets and followed Him** (Mt. 4:19, 20; see 4:21, 22; Mk. 1:17–20). Luke's account is basically the same, quoting Jesus' call and describing the response with these words: **". . . from now on you will be catching men." When they had brought their boats to land, they left everything and followed Him** (Lk. 5:10, 11).

In this way, Jesus called the first men to permanent and uninterrupted discipleship. This event had far-reaching consequences. Not only would Jesus now have companionship day and night, but these four would also be one-third of the group of twelve selected as apostles. Further, three of the four would become Jesus' special "inner circle" (Mk. 5:37; 9:2; 14:33). Everything was ready for Jesus' Galilean ministry.

APPLICATION:
THE CALL TO DISCIPLESHIP (LK. 5:1–11)

One of the most commonly used terms in the Bible for a follower of Jesus is "disciple" (Mt. 5:1; 8:21, 23; 9:19; Acts 6:1, 2, 7; 9:1). "Disciple" is a translation of the Greek word μαθητής (*mathetes*) that means "learner." In the fullest sense, a disciple was one who followed a teacher (Mt. 16:24), learned from the teacher (Mt. 11:29), and then followed the dictates of that teacher (Jn. 8:31). A close teacher/disciple relationship existed. A true disciple became like his teacher (Mt. 10:25a).

Our text is Luke 5:1–11, which tells of the occasion when Jesus called Peter and his friends. During the study, we will discover some of the requirements of discipleship.

We Must Learn Something (Lk. 5:1–3)

If we would be disciples of Jesus, we must learn something.

We must be willing to be instructed by the Lord. Some have a know-it-all attitude and say, "No one can teach *me* anything." Until we are ready to listen and learn, we cannot be Christ's disciples.

As the story begins, Jesus was preaching by the Sea of Galilee. Nearby was Peter, beside his fishing boat, cleaning his nets. He and his partners had fished all night, but all they had to show for it were sore muscles and dirty nets. Imagine Peter, his head cocked to one side, listening to Jesus as his fingers deftly removed the weeds and mud from the knotted squares of the net. This was not the fisherman's first encounter with Jesus. He had traveled with Christ in Judea. However, after returning to the province of Galilee, he had gone back to his former occupation.

As Jesus preached, the crowd continued to grow. Eager listeners crowded in on Christ, forcing Him closer and closer to the lake until the water lapped at His sandals. He made His way to Peter's boat, stepped in, and asked the fisherman to push the boat out into the lake. There, from His makeshift pulpit in the bow, Jesus continued His discourse.

What was Peter doing as he sat in the center of the boat, keeping it steady? He was listening. Listening to what? Our text says that Jesus was preaching "the word of God" (Lk. 5:1). We cannot be disciples of the Lord without being students of the Word. Jesus said, "Take My yoke upon you and *learn* from Me, for I am gentle and humble in heart, and you will find rest for your souls" (Mt. 11:29; emphasis added). Some who claim to be disciples remain ignorant of the Bible year after year—but we cannot be His disciples unless we are serious students of His truths as found in the written Word.

We Must Understand Something (Lk. 5:3–8)

At last, Jesus closed His sermon. He was finished with the crowd, but not with Peter. Peter had much potential but also had much to learn. It was time for his next lesson. Jesus, ever the unorthodox teacher, did the unexpected. He commanded Peter, "Put out into the deep water and let down your nets for a catch" (Lk. 5:4).

Peter knew what every good fisherman on the Sea of Galilee knew. The time to fish was at night, when the fish came up to feed—not in the daytime. The place to fish was in the shallow water—not in the deep. Further, his effort should be exerted when there were fish to be caught—not after trying for ten or so hours without success, *not* when he had stayed awake all night and was exhausted.

As an experienced, hard-working, successful fisherman, it would have been natural for Peter to feel at least a touch of resentment at having a carpenter (Mk. 6:3) tell him how to fish. (I confess to feeling some resentment when people who have never preached tell me how it ought to be done.) Peter's response may indicate this: "Master, we worked hard all night and caught nothing . . ." (Lk. 5:5a).

Notice, however, the word that followed: "but." ". . . *but* I will do as You say and let down the nets" (Lk. 5:5). I like the word used by the KJV: "nevertheless." In other words, "We fished all night with no success . . . *nevertheless* . . . if *You* tell me to try again, I will. It may go against everything I have learned in more than a decade of fishing, but I will do what *You* tell me to do."

How could Peter have such an attitude? The answer is found in the title with which he addressed Jesus: "Master." In the original text, this is not the usual word for "master" or "lord." This special word, ἐπιστάτης (*epistates*), used only by Luke, is a designation applied only to Jesus (Lk. 8:24, 45; 9:33, 49; 17:13). It is from ἐφίστημι (*ephistemi*), a compound Greek word that combines the word ἵστημι (*histemi*) for "stand" with the word ἐπί (*epi*) for "over." It refers to "one who stands over"—one who has total authority over another. Whether or not Peter agreed with Jesus' command was unimportant. Jesus was the Master, and he was the slave; he was ready to obey.

If we would be Jesus' disciples, we must understand that He is the *Master*. We do not instruct the Master; He instructs us. We do not tell Him what we will and will not do; He tells us what we must do. "Master" is a strong word. Masters do not give suggestions; masters do not give advice; masters give *commands*—commands that are to be obeyed without question.

Peter perhaps felt foolish as he took the boat out to the deep water. He was probably a bit embarrassed as he tossed out his nets. He may have heard laughter from other fishermen on the shore. *Nevertheless,* he did what the Master said.

How did the Lord reward this obedience? It was not long until Peter felt a tug on the ropes. He and his helpers began to pull up the nets, which were filled with fish. Fish swarmed inside the nets, their tails slapping at the water. As the men strained to pull the nets into the boat, the twined squares began to snap. Frantically, they signaled to their partners on the shore to come and help them.

James and John came to help in their fishing boat. Soon both boats were full of flopping, slippery fish—so full that the boats were in danger of sinking. These were not the ten- to fifteen-foot rowboats familiar to some of us. These were the twenty- to thirty-foot professional fishing boats used on the Sea of Galilee. The seasoned fishermen had never seen such a catch.

This must have been quite a revelation to Peter and the other fishermen. Even when the topic is catching fish, our Lord knows what He is talking about.

Most of the time, the commands of the Lord make sense to us, but there is no guarantee that will always be the case. The question is not "Is this reasonable to me?" The question is "Is this what Christ has asked me to do?" If so, let us respond like Peter: "I will do as You say." If we obey, in the end we will find that the Lord's way is right.

If we would be Jesus' disciples, we must be convinced that He is Master of everything—and we must act on that belief.

We Must Acknowledge Something (Lk. 5:8–10a)

Peter had seen Jesus perform some impressive miracles. He had seen Him turn water into wine (Jn. 2:1–11). He had seen Him heal a nobleman's son (Jn. 4:46–54). He had been present to see Christ do many other signs and wonders (see Jn. 2:23; 3:2), but none of the other miracles affected him as this one did. This one involved Peter's occupation; it addressed the very way he lived. It caused him to see that Jesus is Lord of *everything*.

As Peter saw Jesus in a new light, he also saw himself in a new light. He was suddenly overwhelmed by his shortcomings.

"He fell down at Jesus' feet"—down into the mound of flopping fish—and said, "Go away from me Lord, for I am a sinful man, O Lord!" (Lk. 5:8). He responded as people have always responded when suddenly confronted with the power and glory of God (Gen. 18:27; Job 42:4; Is. 6:5).

If we would be Jesus' disciples, we must acknowledge two truths. First, we must acknowledge that *He* is everything. Peter addressed Jesus as he confessed his sinfulness: He called Him "Lord." Paul said that, to be saved, we must confess with the mouth that Jesus is Lord (Rom. 10:9). Second, as we acknowledge that He is everything, we acknowledge that *we* are nothing. We must admit our need for Him.

A man "full of himself" has no room for the Lord. Jesus cannot use those who say, "Lord, look how good I am. Look how smart I am, how talented, how successful. I hope You appreciate how much I can accomplish." Christ can only use those who fall at His feet, acknowledging their weaknesses and their dependency on Him. To borrow the words of another, we must be ready to say, "God be merciful to me a sinner" (Lk. 18:13b; KJV).

We Must Change Something (Lk. 5:10b)

When Peter saw the gulf separating him and Jesus, he said, "Go away from me" (Lk. 5:8). Fortunately, Jesus did not comply with his request. Rather, Jesus brought Peter closer with a special challenge. "And Jesus said to Simon, 'Do not fear, from now on you will be catching men'" (Lk. 5:10b). The word "catching" is in the present tense, indicating continuous action. This was not to be a one-time adventure, but a lifelong occupation. Further, the Greek word ζωγρέω (*zogreo*), translated "catching," literally means "to catch alive." They would bring men to Jesus, who "gives life to the world" (Jn. 6:33). Matthew records the call like this: "Follow Me, and I will make you fishers of men" (Mt. 4:19; see Mk. 1:17).

The challenge to Peter was to refocus his life. To this point, he had concentrated on fishing for fish, now his life would center on fishing for men.

Jesus calls farmers to sow the seed of the kingdom (the Word;

Lk. 8:11). Jesus calls merchants to tell men of the "pearl of great value" (the gospel; Mt. 13:46). Jesus calls carpenters to add to His house (the church; see Mt. 16:18; 1 Tim. 3:15; KJV). Jesus calls physicians to work with the Great Physician in the healing of souls (Jn. 12:40). Whatever our interests in life, if we would be Jesus' disciples, we must refocus *our* lives. When we change the center of our lives, there will be a change in emphases and priorities.

We Must Give Up Something (Lk. 5:11)

Peter and his friends had traveled with Jesus before. Now Jesus was calling them to a new level of discipleship: to follow Him full time. To do this, they would have to leave their boats, nets, and fish. They would have to forsake much that had been important to them. They would have to abandon a steady income and financial security.

According to every indication, the men had a fishing business of respectable proportions. We have already seen that the partners had more than one fishing boat. James and John hired servants (Mk. 1:20). The mother of James and John was one of the women who later financially supported Jesus and His disciples (Mt. 27:55, 56; Lk. 8:3). John was known to the high priest (Jn. 18:15); he and his family probably had business dealings with the religious official. Now that highly profitable business was to be left behind.

It was asking a lot, but evidently the men did not think that it was asking too much. We read in verse 11, "When they had brought their boats to land, they left everything and followed Him." Mark tells us that Peter and his brother Andrew "immediately . . . left their nets and followed Him" (Mk. 1:18), and that James and John "left their father Zebedee in the boat with the hired servants, and went away to follow Him" (Mk. 1:20).

Some have protested, "But the Lord surely doesn't require that of every disciple." In Luke 14 Jesus told a group of would-be followers, "So then, none of you can be My disciple who does not give up all his own possessions" (Lk. 14:33). Having worked with several preacher-training schools, I have known many men who gave up lucrative businesses and high-paying jobs—men who sold all they had in order to attend school to learn how to teach and preach God's Word.

Protestors also ask, "But what about those of us who do not plan to be full-time preachers?" You still must be willing to "give up something": You need to give up anything that stands between you and wholehearted service to the Lord. In Matthew 16:24 Jesus emphasized, "If anyone wishes to come after Me, *he must deny himself*, and take up his cross and follow me." (Emphasis added.)

We must also be willing to trust the Lord to take care of us, no matter what. As Peter, Andrew, James, and John followed Jesus away from the Sea of Galilee, they were trusting Him to supply their needs just as He had supplied the catch of fish. Sometimes we do not trust the Lord as we should. I have known men to say, "If I gave up the way I did business before I became a Christian, I could never make a living. My family would starve." Jesus has promised that if we put Him and His way first, we will have the necessities of life (Mt. 6:33). Paul wrote, "And my God will supply all your needs according to His riches in glory in Christ Jesus" (Phil. 4:19).

Once, Peter said to Jesus, "Behold, we have left everything and followed You" (Mk. 10:28). Jesus then gave him this assurance:

> Truly I say to you, there is no one who has left house or brothers or sisters or mother or father or children or farms, for My sake and for the gospel's sake, but that he will receive a hundred times as much now in the present age, houses and brothers and sisters and mothers and children and farms, along with persecutions; and in the age to come, eternal life (Mk. 10:29, 30).

No matter what we give up to be disciples of Christ, we can never out-give the Lord.

We Must Do Something (Lk. 5:11)

We need to mention one last requirement to be Jesus' disciple. This obvious requirement is implicit in the word "disciple," and we have already seen it in the text—but it must be mentioned:

We must *do* something. Specifically, we must *follow* Him. Our text says that Peter and the others "left everything and *followed* Him" (Lk. 5:11; emphasis added). Matthew and Mark stress that the four men left their boats and nets "and *followed* Him" (Mt. 4:20, 22; Mk. 1:18, 20; emphasis added). Jesus said, "If anyone wishes to come after Me, he must . . . take up his cross and *follow* Me" (Mt. 16:24; emphasis added).

Following Jesus was not easy for Peter and the others. The disciples experienced exhaustion, animosity, and eventually death for following Jesus. Nevertheless, they had made a commitment. They followed Christ wherever He wanted them to go.

Conclusion

We have seen several requirements for discipleship.

We must learn something: We must be students of the Word.

We must understand something: We must understand that Jesus is the Master of our lives.

We must acknowledge something: We must admit our own inadequacies and our dependence on Christ.

We must change something: We must change the focus of our lives. We must live to glorify the Lord and to bring others to Him.

We must give up something: We must be willing to give up anything that would keep us from wholehearted service, and be ready to trust the Lord.

We must do something: We must be ready to follow Him wherever He wants us to go.

IN CAPERNAUM: HEALING A DEMONIAC IN THE SYNAGOGUE (MK. 1:21–28; LK. 4:31–37)

Mark 1:21–28

²¹**They went into Capernaum; and immediately on the Sabbath He entered the synagogue and began to teach. ²²They were amazed at His teaching; for He was teaching them as one hav-**

ing authority, and not as the scribes. [23]Just then there was a man in their synagogue with an unclean spirit; and he cried out, [24]saying, "What business do we have with each other, Jesus of Nazareth? Have You come to destroy us? I know who You are—the Holy One of God!" [25]And Jesus rebuked him, saying, "Be quiet, and come out of him!" [26]Throwing him into convulsions, the unclean spirit cried out with a loud voice and came out of him. [27]They were all amazed, so that they debated among themselves, saying, "What is this? A new teaching with authority! He commands even the unclean spirits, and they obey Him." [28]Immediately the news about Him spread everywhere into all the surrounding district of Galilee.

Luke 4:31–37

[31]And He came down to Capernaum, a city of Galilee, and He was teaching them on the Sabbath; [32]and they were amazed at His teaching, for His message was with authority. [33]In the synagogue there was a man possessed by the spirit of an unclean demon, and he cried out with a loud voice, [34]"Let us alone! What business do we have with each other, Jesus of Nazareth? Have You come to destroy us? I know who You are—the Holy One of God!" [35]But Jesus rebuked him, saying, "Be quiet and come out of him!" And when the demon had thrown him down in the midst of the people, he came out of him without doing him any harm. [36]And amazement came upon them all, and they began talking with one another saying, "What is this message? For with authority and power He commands the unclean spirits and they come out." [37]And the report about Him was spreading into every locality in the surrounding district.

These passages cover Jesus' first tour of Galilee, plus some events in Capernaum before and after the tour. The incidents help to put the "great" in "The Great Galilean Ministry."

A key word in these texts and those that follow is "authority." When Jesus spoke in the synagogue in Capernaum, the people **were amazed at His teaching; for He was teaching them as one having *authority*, and not as the scribes** (Mk. 1:22; emphasis added). Jesus astonished those present not only by His teaching, but also by His actions. When He cast out a demon, **amazement came upon them all, and they began talking with one another saying, "What is this message? For with *authority* and power He commands the unclean spirits and they come out"** (Lk. 4:36; emphasis added).

Jesus' remarkable demonstrations of authority set Him on a collision course with Jewish religious leaders. As He later prepared to heal a paralyzed man, He made the shocking claim that "the Son of Man [speaking of Himself] has *authority* [power, KJV] on earth to forgive sins" (Mt. 9:6; emphasis added). When the paralytic walked, the crowd was "awestruck, and glorified God, who had given such *authority* to men" (Mt. 9:8; emphasis added).

When Jesus was ready to begin His ministry in Galilee, He found a ready audience in the synagogues, which were located in almost every town (see Lk. 4:15). In the synagogues, after the Scriptures were read, the one in charge of the service, called the synagogue "official" or the "ruler of the synagogue" (Mk. 5:36, 38; Lk. 8:41; 13:14), could call on anyone present (anyone he deemed qualified) to comment on the passage.

On the Sabbath after Jesus called the four fishermen, He and His disciples attended the service at the synagogue in Capernaum. At the appropriate time, Christ was allowed to speak. As already noted, those who heard Him "were amazed at His teaching; for He was teaching them as one having authority, and not as the scribes" (Mk. 1:22). The scribes did not speak on their own authority. Instead, they quoted endless authorities who had spoken on the subject. The LB paraphrase says, "The congregation was surprised . . . because he spoke as an authority, and didn't try to prove his points by quoting others—quite unlike what they were used to hearing."

Synagogue services were normally characterized by a basic decorum, but while Jesus was speaking, the stillness was shattered by a shout:

Just then there was a man in their synagogue with an unclean spirit; and he cried out, saying, "What business

do we have with each other, Jesus of Nazareth? Have
You come to destroy us? I know who You are—the Holy
One of God!" (Mk. 1:23, 24).

Luke tells us that the **unclean spirit** was a demon (Lk. 4:33,
35). "Demon" is a transliteration of the Greek word δαιμόνιον
(*daimonion*). The KJV translates the plural form of *daimonion*
as "devils," which is confusing since there is only one devil
(διάβολος, *diabolos*), Satan. Demons are evil supernatural beings—
Satan's subordinates (Mt. 12:22–29 refers to Satan as "the ruler
of the demons"), dedicated to carrying out his will. In New Testament times, demons could possess individuals against their
will. Liberal scholars deny the demon possession of Christ's
day, saying that physical illnesses were attributed to evil spirits by superstitious people. However, Dr. Luke made a distinction between those with physical illnesses and "those afflicted
with unclean spirits," or those possessed by demons. The other
writers of the Gospel Accounts made the same distinction. J. W.
McGarvey wrote, "It would be impossible to regard demon possession as a mere disease without doing violence to the language
used in every instance of the expulsion of a demon."[3] The phenomenon of demon possession gave Jesus additional opportunity to demonstrate His power and to show His compassion. In
Mark 1 and Luke 4, we have the accounts of the first recorded
incident when Jesus cast out a demon.

When the demon interrupted Him, Christ rebuked the
unclean spirit. The demon flew into a rage, throwing his host to
the floor, twisting his body with convulsions, and making him
cry out. Finally, though, the spirit **came out of him without doing
him any harm** (Lk. 4:35). The LB paraphrase has "without hurting him any further."

Those present were astonished, and **immediately the news
about Him spread everywhere into all the surrounding district
of Galilee** (Mk. 1:28).

---

[3]J. W. McGarvey and Philip Y. Pendleton, *The Fourfold Gospel or A Harmony
of the Four Gospels* (Cincinnati: Standard Publishing Co., 1914), 198.

IN CAPERNAUM: HEALING PETER'S
MOTHER-IN-LAW AND OTHERS
(MT. 8:14–17; MK. 1:29–34; LK. 4:38–41)

Matthew 8:14–17

[14]When Jesus came into Peter's home, He saw his mother-in-law lying sick in bed with a fever. [15]He touched her hand, and the fever left her; and she got up and waited on Him. [16]When evening came, they brought to Him many who were demon-possessed; and He cast out the spirits with a word, and healed all who were ill. [17]This was to fulfill what was spoken through Isaiah the prophet: "He Himself took our infirmities and carried away our diseases."

Mark 1:29–34

[29]And immediately after they came out of the synagogue, they came into the house of Simon and Andrew, with James and John. [30]Now Simon's mother-in-law was lying sick with a fever; and immediately they spoke to Jesus about her. [31]And He came to her and raised her up, taking her by the hand, and the fever left her, and she waited on them.

[32]When evening came, after the sun had set, they began bringing to Him all who were ill and those who were demon-possessed. [33]And the whole city had gathered at the door. [34]And He healed many who were ill with various diseases, and cast out many demons; and He was not permitting the demons to speak, because they knew who He was.

Luke 4:38–41

[38]Then He got up and left the synagogue, and entered Simon's home. Now Simon's mother-in-law was suffering from a high fever, and they asked Him to help her. [39]And standing over her, He rebuked the fever, and it left her; and she immediately got up and waited on them.

[40]While the sun was setting, all those who had any who were sick with various diseases brought them to Him; and laying His hands on each one of them, He was healing them. [41]Demons

also were coming out of many, shouting, "You are the Son of God!" But rebuking them, He would not allow them to speak, because they knew Him to be the Christ.

After the synagogue service, Jesus and His four disciples went to the home of Peter and Andrew (Mk. 1:29). There they found Peter's mother-in-law sick in bed with a high fever. Jesus took her by the hand, lifted her up, and the fever left her. **She immediately got up and waited on them** (Lk. 4:39). The LB paraphrase has "she got up and prepared a meal for them!" Note at this point that contrary to the human dogma that refers to Peter as "the first pope," he was married for many years (1 Cor. 9:5).

In the meantime, word had spread concerning what had happened in the synagogue. Thus, after sundown, **all those who had any who were sick with various diseases brought them to Him; and laying His hands on each one of them, He was healing them** (Lk. 4:40). The people may have waited until after sundown because the Sabbath ended at sundown and they did not want to violate the prohibition about carrying a burden on the Sabbath (see Jer. 17:22). Jesus also cast out unclean spirits. **Demons also were coming out of many, shouting, "You are the Son of God!" But rebuking them, He would not allow them to speak, because they knew Him to be the Christ** (Lk. 4:41; see 4:34; Mk. 1:24).

Somehow demons knew who Christ was (see Jas. 2:19). The demon in the synagogue had referred to Jesus as "the Holy One of God." These demons called Him "the Son of God." This slogan was recently seen on a sweatshirt: "Five out of five demons agree: Jesus is the Son of God!" It is sad that demons acknowledge Jesus' deity while many human beings refuse to do so.

Why did Jesus not allow the unclean spirits to tell who He was? He probably had many reasons. It was too soon to proclaim openly that He was the Christ. Also, it was inappropriate for the forces of evil to be chief witnesses as to who He was. Perhaps a predominant reason was that He did not want it to appear that He was aligned with demons in any way. Later, He would be accused of casting out demons by the power of Beelzebul (also spelled Beelzebub)—that is, the devil (Mt. 12:24).

IN GALILEE: JESUS' FIRST TEACHING AND HEALING TOUR
(MT. 4:23–25; MK. 1:35–39; LK. 4:42–44)

Matthew 4:23–25
²³Jesus was going throughout all Galilee, teaching in their synagogues and proclaiming the gospel of the kingdom, and healing every kind of disease and every kind of sickness among the people.

²⁴The news about Him spread throughout all Syria; and they brought to Him all who were ill, those suffering with various diseases and pains, demoniacs, epileptics, paralytics; and He healed them. ²⁵Large crowds followed Him from Galilee and the Decapolis and Jerusalem and Judea and from beyond the Jordan.

Mark 1:35–39
³⁵In the early morning, while it was still dark, Jesus got up, left the house, and went away to a secluded place, and was praying there. ³⁶Simon and his companions searched for Him; ³⁷they found Him, and said to Him, "Everyone is looking for You." ³⁸He said to them, "Let us go somewhere else to the towns nearby, so that I may preach there also; for that is what I came for." ³⁹And He went into their synagogues throughout all Galilee, preaching and casting out the demons.

Luke 4:42–44
⁴²When day came, Jesus left and went to a secluded place; and the crowds were searching for Him, and came to Him and tried to keep Him from going away from them. ⁴³But He said to them, "I must preach the kingdom of God to the other cities also, for I was sent for this purpose."
⁴⁴So He kept on preaching in the synagogues of Judea.

Early the next morning, Jesus went outside Capernaum to

a secluded place to pray (Mk. 1:35). Though He was divine, He needed to be alone with His Father. We have a similar need.

His disciples sought Him out and said, **"Everyone is looking for You"** (Mk. 1:37). They were excited that Jesus had been such a success in Capernaum, but Jesus' vision was greater than one city. He outlined His plan to preach to every town in Galilee (Mk. 1:38). By this time, a crowd from Capernaum had found Him. They urged Him to stay, but His decision was made (Lk. 4:42, 43). He and His disciples left on their first tour of Galilee.

At its longest and widest points, the province of Galilee was about sixty-three miles by thirty-three miles. It encompassed several hundred towns. The tour must have taken several months. Matthew's abbreviated report on the success of the trip is given in Matthew 4:23–25.

Though Matthew speaks of Jesus' tour **throughout all Galilee**, Luke 4:44 says, **He kept on preaching in the synagogues of Judea.** In this verse, "Judea" evidently does not refer to the province of Judea, but to the entire country of Palestine. A margin note in the NASB explains "Judea" as "the country of the Jews (including Galilee); some mss. [manuscripts] read *Galilee*."

IN GALILEE: HEALING A LEPER—
AND RESULTANT EXCITEMENT
(MT. 8:2–4; MK. 1:40–45; LK. 5:12–16)

Matthew 8:2–4
²**And a leper came to Him and bowed down before Him, and said, "Lord, if You are willing, You can make me clean." ³Jesus stretched out His hand and touched him, saying, "I am willing; be cleansed." And immediately his leprosy was cleansed. ⁴And Jesus said to him, "See that you tell no one; but go, show yourself to the priest and present the offering that Moses commanded, as a testimony to them."**

Mark 1:40–45
⁴⁰**And a leper came to Jesus, beseeching Him and falling**

on his knees before Him, and saying, "If You are willing, You can make me clean." [41]Moved with compassion, Jesus stretched out His hand and touched him, and said to him, "I am willing; be cleansed." [42]Immediately the leprosy left him and he was cleansed. [43]And He sternly warned him and immediately sent him away, [44]and He said to him, "See that you say nothing to anyone; but go, show yourself to the priest and offer for your cleansing what Moses commanded, as a testimony to them." [45]But he went out and began to proclaim it freely and to spread the news around, to such an extent that Jesus could no longer publicly enter a city, but stayed out in unpopulated areas; and they were coming to Him from everywhere.

Luke 5:12–16

[12]While He was in one of the cities, behold, there was a man covered with leprosy; and when he saw Jesus, he fell on his face and implored Him, saying, "Lord, if You are willing, You can make me clean." [13]And He stretched out His hand and touched him, saying, "I am willing; be cleansed." And immediately the leprosy left him. [14]And He ordered him to tell no one, "But go and show yourself to the priest and make an offering for your cleansing, just as Moses commanded, as a testimony to them." [15]But the news about Him was spreading even farther, and large crowds were gathering to hear Him and to be healed of their sicknesses. [16]But Jesus Himself would often slip away to the wilderness and pray.

One miracle on the preaching tour in Galilee is recorded in detail: the healing of a leper. Leprosy was one of the most dreaded diseases of ancient times, if not the most dreaded. The term apparently encompassed a variety of ailments that affected the skin and nerves, in addition to what we call leprosy today ("Hansen's disease"). Some of the symptoms of Bible leprosy do not fit the symptoms of what we commonly call leprosy today. In Bible times, even houses could have "leprosy" (see Lev. 14:34, 35). McGarvey discussed two of the principal diseases thought to be called leprosy in Bible times, psoriasis and elephantiasis.[4] Lepers were supposed to isolate themselves and avoid contact with the rest of the population (Lev. 13:45, 46).

As Jesus traveled in Galilee, a leper came to Him. The man was **covered with leprosy** (Lk. 5:12). The Greek text has "full of leprosy" (see the KJV). He was in the advanced stages of the disease: His skin would already be sloughing off; he was probably missing some of his extremities—fingers, toes, the tip of his nose, the top of his ears. The leper fell on his knees before Christ, and began to beg Him, **"If You are willing, You can make me clean"** (Mk. 1:40). **Moved with compassion, Jesus stretched out His hand and touched him, and said to him, "I am willing; be cleansed." Immediately the leprosy left him and he was cleansed** (Mk. 1:41, 42).

Since Jesus was "born under the Law" (Gal. 4:4), He kept the law of Moses and encouraged others to do the same. The Law required healed lepers to make a trip to the temple in Jerusalem for ritual cleansings and priestly inspections (Lev. 14:2–32). Jesus thus commanded the man, **"Show yourself to the priest and offer for your cleansing what Moses commanded, as a testimony to them"** (Mk. 1:44b).

Christ also **sternly warned him . . . , "See that you say nothing to anyone"** (Mk. 1:43, 44a). Nonetheless, the excited man **went out and began to proclaim it freely and to spread the news around** (Mk. 1:45a).

Jesus was not using reverse psychology. Such would be contrary to the nature of Jesus; He would not stoop to manipulating people. Christ was serious in the charge He gave the leper. He had told the disciples that He needed to preach to other towns and cities in Galilee (Mk. 1:38; Lk. 4:43)—but, as a result of the publicity of the healed leper, **Jesus could no longer publicly enter a city, but stayed out in unpopulated areas** (Mk. 1:45b).

Wherever He went, people sought Him out and **were coming to Him from everywhere** (Mk. 1:45c). The first tour was an unqualified success.

---

[4]Ibid., 176–78.

BACK AT CAPERNAUM:
HEALING A PARALYTIC
(MT. 9:2–8; MK. 2:1–12; LK. 5:17–26)

Matthew 9:2–8

²And they brought to Him a paralytic lying on a bed. See-ing their faith, Jesus said to the paralytic, "Take courage, son; your sins are forgiven." ³And some of the scribes said to them-selves, "This fellow blasphemes." ⁴And Jesus knowing their thoughts said, "Why are you thinking evil in your hearts? ⁵Which is easier, to say, 'Your sins are forgiven,' or to say, 'Get up, and walk'? ⁶But so that you may know that the Son of Man has authority on earth to forgive sins"—then He said to the paralytic, "Get up, pick up your bed and go home." ⁷And he got up and went home. ⁸But when the crowds saw this, they were awestruck, and glorified God, who had given such author-ity to men.

Mark 2:1–12

¹When He had come back to Capernaum several days after-ward, it was heard that He was at home. ²And many were gathered together, so that there was no longer room, not even near the door; and He was speaking the word to them. ³And they came, bringing to Him a paralytic, carried by four men. ⁴Being unable to get to Him because of the crowd, they re-moved the roof above Him; and when they had dug an open-ing, they let down the pallet on which the paralytic was lying. ⁵And Jesus seeing their faith said to the paralytic, "Son, your sins are forgiven." ⁶But some of the scribes were sit-ting there and reasoning in their hearts, ⁷"Why does this man speak that way? He is blaspheming; who can forgive sins but God alone?" ⁸Immediately Jesus, aware in His spirit that they were reasoning that way within themselves, said to them, "Why are you reasoning about these things in your hearts? ⁹Which is easier, to say to the paralytic, 'Your sins are forgiven'; or to say, 'Get up, and pick up your pallet and walk'? ¹⁰But so that you may know that the Son of Man has authority on earth to forgive sins"—He said to the paralytic,

[11]"I say to you, get up, pick up your pallet and go home." [12]And he got up and immediately picked up the pallet and went out in the sight of everyone, so that they were all amazed and were glorifying God, saying, "We have never seen anything like this."

Luke 5:17–26

[17]One day He was teaching; and there were some Pharisees and teachers of the law sitting there, who had come from every village of Galilee and Judea and from Jerusalem; and the power of the Lord was present for Him to perform healing. [18]And some men were carrying on a bed a man who was paralyzed; and they were trying to bring him in and to set him down in front of Him. [19]But not finding any way to bring him in because of the crowd, they went up on the roof and let him down through the tiles with his stretcher, into the middle of the crowd, in front of Jesus. [20]Seeing their faith, He said, "Friend, your sins are forgiven you." [21]The scribes and the Pharisees began to reason, saying, "Who is this man who speaks blasphemies? Who can forgive sins, but God alone?" [22]But Jesus, aware of their reasonings, answered and said to them, "Why are you reasoning in your hearts? [23]Which is easier, to say, 'Your sins have been forgiven you,' or to say, 'Get up and walk'? [24]But, so that you may know that the Son of Man has authority on earth to forgive sins,"—He said to the paralytic—"I say to you, get up, and pick up your stretcher and go home." [25]Immediately he got up before them, and picked up what he had been lying on, and went home glorifying God. [26]They were all struck with astonishment and began glorifying God; and they were filled with fear, saying, "We have seen remarkable things today."

At the close of the trip, Jesus returned to Capernaum—probably to Peter's house—to recuperate. He did not get much rest, however, for word quickly spread that He was back in town. The house where He was staying was soon packed with people.

Among those present were Pharisees and scribes (Mt. 9:3; Mk. 2:6; Lk. 5:17, 21). These men were the self-appointed guardians of the Law and the custodians of traditions.

Some of these had come from as far as Jerusalem (Lk. 5:17). Priests and Levites had come from Jerusalem to interrogate John the Baptizer when his popularity increased (Jn. 1:19). Now scribes and Pharisees came to check on Jesus.

While Jesus was preaching, four men tore up the roof and let down a friend who was paralyzed. Jesus' heart went out to the man, and He said, **"Son, your sins are forgiven"** (Mk. 2:5).

Christ's critics were shocked. They thought, **"Why does this man speak that way? He is blaspheming; who can forgive sins but God alone?"** (Mk. 2:7). The Greek word βλασφημέω (*blasphemeo*), translated "blaspheme," means "to speak against." It is often used to refer to slander. The same Greek word is used in Titus 3:2 and 2 Peter 2:2. The Jews also used the word to refer to any language that reflected on the nature or character of God. The reasoning of the scribes and the Pharisees went like this:

1. Only God can forgive sins.
2. This man is not God.
3. Therefore, He is guilty of blasphemy.

There was nothing wrong with their logic; the problem was that their second premise was incorrect. The reasoning of the visitors from Jerusalem *should* have gone like this:

1. Only God can forgive sin.
2. This Man *can* forgive sin.
3. Therefore He *is* God.

Unfortunately, they were too filled with prejudice, jealousy, and self-interest even to consider the claims of Jesus.

Immediately Jesus, aware in His spirit that they were reasoning that way within themselves, said to them, "Why are you reasoning about these things in your hearts? Which is easier, to say to the paralytic, 'Your sins are forgiven'; or to say, 'Get up, and pick up your pallet and walk'? But so that you may know that the Son of

Man has authority on earth to forgive sins,"—He said to the paralytic, "I say to you, get up, pick up your pallet and go home" (Mk. 2:8–11).

Jesus used His authority over disease to prove that He did have authority over sin.

When Christ told the paralytic to get up, **he got up and immediately picked up the pallet and went out in the sight of everyone; so that they were all amazed and were glorifying God, saying, "We have never seen anything like this"** (Mk. 2:12).

This was the beginning of the hostility which Jesus faced until He was crucified. It would not be long until spies would follow Him everywhere He went, trying to find some impropriety they could use to destroy Him.

NEAR CAPERNAUM: THE CALL OF MATTHEW (MT. 9:9; MK. 2:13, 14; LK. 5:27, 28)

Jesus had done several things to make His critics unhappy: He had touched an unclean leper. He had indicated that He could forgive sin. One more incident incited their anger: He called a tax collector to be one of His disciples.

Matthew 9:9

⁹As Jesus went on from there, He saw a man called Matthew, sitting in the tax collector's booth; and He said to him, "Follow Me!" And he got up and followed Him.

Mark 2:13, 14

¹³And He went out again by the seashore; and all the people were coming to Him, and He was teaching them. ¹⁴As He passed by, He saw Levi the son of Alphaeus sitting in the tax booth, and He said to him, "Follow Me!" And he got up and followed Him.

Luke 5:27, 28

²⁷After that He went out and noticed a tax collector named Levi sitting in the tax booth, and He said to him, "Follow Me."

[28]And he left everything behind, and got up and began to follow Him.

One of Christ's favorite spots in the vicinity of Capernaum was the seashore. When He went there again, multitudes followed Him and He taught them (Mk. 2:13).

Nearby was the toll booth of a **tax collector** (Lk. 5:27). The term for "tax collector" in the original language means "tax man." (The KJV has the term "publican," which can be confusing in some countries where a "publican" is a man who operates a "pub," a public bar where alcoholic beverages are sold.) The booth may have been by the lake to collect duty on goods and people being ferried across, or it may have been on a nearby road to collect taxes on produce that was brought into Capernaum. The tax collector's name was Matthew (Mt. 9:9). He was a son of Alphaeus and was also known as Levi (Mk. 2:14).

Tax collectors in general were hated by the Jews. A Jew who cooperated with the Romans was considered a traitor. Robert L. Thomas wrote,

> Tax-gatherers such as Matthew . . . estimated the worth of merchants' goods that were in transit and collected taxes on them for the Roman government. . . . Vague tariff rates allowed the tax-gatherer to levy higher fees so as to increase his own profit. Whether or not Matthew was among the dishonest majority of his occupation is not known, but merely belonging to a class that had been excommunicated by fellow Jews was enough to make him despised.[5]

Jesus had probably often passed Matthew's booth on His way to and from the Sea of Galilee. No doubt, the tax collector, sitting in his booth, had had many opportunities to listen to Christ as He preached. This day was different, however, for Jesus stopped and said to him, **"Follow Me!"** (Mk. 2:14). Like

---

[5]Robert L. Thomas, ed., and Stanley N. Gundry, assoc. ed., *A Harmony of the Gospels* (Chicago: Moody Press, 1978), 55.

the call to Peter, Andrew, James, and John, this was a call to full-time discipleship. Like the fishermen, Matthew **left everything behind, and got up and began to follow Him** (Lk. 5:28). Understand what Matthew's decision cost him. The fishermen who left their nets to follow Jesus could return to fishing (see Jn. 21:3); but once Matthew turned his back on his Roman "employers," he could not return to his work as a tax collector. Many harmonies place the feast of Matthew immediately following his call (Mt. 9:10–13; Mk. 2:15–17; Lk. 5:29–32), and it fits well here.

APPLICATION:
"THEY WERE ALL AMAZED, AND GLORIFIED GOD": THE HEALING MINISTRY OF JESUS

The Gospel Accounts indicate that an important part of Jesus' ministry was the healing that He did. For instance, in the synagogue at Capernaum, Jesus cast an unclean spirit out of a man (Mk. 1:21–28; Lk. 4:31–37). As a result, the people "were all amazed. . . . Immediately the news about Him spread everywhere into all the surrounding district of Galilee" (Mk. 1:27, 28).

From the synagogue, Jesus and His disciples went into the home of Peter and Andrew. There Jesus healed Peter's mother-in-law. That evening "they brought to Him many who were demon-possessed; and He cast out the spirits with a word, and healed all who were ill" (Mt. 8:16; see vv. 14–17; Mk. 1:29–34; Lk. 4:38–41).

The next morning, Jesus began a preaching tour through the province (Mt. 4:23–25; Mk. 1:35–39; Lk. 4:42–44).

> Jesus was going throughout all Galilee, teaching in their synagogues and proclaiming the gospel of the kingdom, and healing every kind of disease and every kind of sickness among the people. . . . Large crowds followed Him from Galilee and the Decapolis and Jerusalem and Judea and from beyond the Jordan (Mt. 4:23–25).

One miracle done on that preaching tour is recorded in detail: the healing of a leper (Mt. 8:2–4; Mk. 1:40–45; Lk. 5:12–

16). Jesus told the healed leper to tell no one, but he did. Jesus became so popular that He "could no longer publicly enter a city . . . and they were coming to Him from everywhere" (Mk. 1:45).

Jesus came back to Capernaum—probably to get some rest—but He was unable to rest because everyone gathered at the home where He was staying. That was the setting for Jesus' healing the man let down through the roof (Mt. 9:2–8; Mk. 2:1–12; Lk. 5:17–26). Jesus said to the man, "I say to you, get up, pick up your pallet and go home" (Mk. 2:11). According to Mark, the man "got up and immediately picked up the pallet and went out in the sight of everyone, so that they were all amazed and were glorifying God, saying, 'We have never seen anything like this'" (Mk. 2:12). The KJV says that "they were all amazed, and glorified God."

As we continue our study of the Gospel Accounts, we will constantly read about Jesus' miracles, including His miraculous healings. It may be worthwhile to spend some time on His miracles—and especially His healing of the sick.

The *Reasonableness* of Jesus' Miracles

Jesus really did miracles. They happened just as recorded in Matthew, Mark, Luke, and John. Those who do not want to believe in the Bible and in the deity of Jesus make fun of the miracles in the Bible. "Do you really believe a whale swallowed Jonah?" they ask. "Do you really think Jesus literally fed five thousand people with a few loaves and a few fishes?" Some who claim to be Christians have gone to great lengths to explain away the miracles—to find some rationalistic explanation: "Oh, those were just ignorant people back then who didn't have the knowledge we have. They called things miracles that really weren't miracles."

I repeat: *The miracles of Jesus actually happened just as they are recorded in Matthew, Mark, Luke, and John.* Here are a few of the many reasons for believing this statement to be true.

I believe this to be true because I believe in God. If one believes in God, he must also believe that "all things are possible with God" (Mk. 10:27).

I believe this to be true because I believe in the Bible. We have good cause for believing that the Bible is inspired of God (2 Tim. 3:16). Through the years, it has shown itself to be a trustworthy book, a book to which we can literally trust our lives. This God-inspired Bible tells us of the miracles of Jesus.

My next reason is closely related to the one just mentioned: I believe this to be true because the miracles of Jesus were recorded by trustworthy witnesses. The way they were recorded and the time they were recorded point to the fact that they were recorded by rational men, not by men unaware of what really happened—and certainly not by men intent on deception.

I believe this to be true because miracles are consistent with who Jesus was—or who He claimed to be. Jesus claimed to be the Son of God, the Messiah, the Light of the World, the Bread of Life, the One who could forgive sin. Those were extravagant claims. One who makes claims like that must either demonstrate the truth of those claims or be found a liar. Someone has said that Jesus was either a liar, a lunatic, or the Lord. Those are the only possibilities. If one is not willing to call Jesus a liar or a lunatic, then He must acknowledge Him as the Lord—and His ability to do miracles would be consistent with that position.

I believe this to be true because there is no way to explain Jesus and His influence apart from His miracles. When I was a student at Abilene Christian University, some theologians were conducting what they called "The Search for the Historical Jesus." They did not believe in miracles—in their minds, "miracles" were superstitious nonsense—so they were trying to get rid of the miraculous elements in the story of Jesus to find "the real Jesus" who walked on the earth. They ended up with an unknown, uneducated moral philosopher who lived in an obscure corner of the world. Someone said that if *that* "Jesus" could change the course of history, that would be a greater miracle than any ever attributed to Christ in the New Testament. One of my teachers, J. D. Thomas, compared what these scholars were attempting with trying to peel an onion to find its core. When one gets through peeling, there is nothing left. We cannot explain Jesus and His influence apart from His miracles.

I believe that Jesus' miracles really happened as they are recorded in the Gospel Accounts because not even Jesus' enemies could deny that He performed miracles. When Jesus healed the paralytic, His critics were present. Jesus gave them a challenge: "'But so that you may know that the Son of Man has authority on earth to forgive sins'—He said to the paralytic, 'I say to you, get up, pick up your pallet and go home'" (Mk. 2:10, 11). His critics could not deny that the man got up and walked.

In John 9, we read about the healing of a man born blind. Jesus' enemies were unhappy about it and tried to discredit Jesus, but one thing they did not do: They did not deny that a miracle had taken place (Jn. 9:16).

In John 11 we read about the raising of Lazarus. Notice what Jesus' enemies said: "What are we doing? For this man is performing many signs" (Jn. 11:47).

When Peter preached about Jesus to his fellow Jews on the Day of Pentecost, he said, "Jesus the Nazarene, a man attested to you by God with miracles and wonders and signs which God performed through Him in your midst, *just as you yourselves know*" (Acts 2:22; emphasis added). Nobody stopped him and shouted, "No, He didn't!"

It was not merely true in Bible times that people could not deny that Jesus did miracles. In the early days of Christianity, there arose men who wrote books in an attempt to destroy Christianity. Among them were Celsus, Hierocles, and Julian the Apostate. Almost without exception, one thing these men did not do was deny that Jesus had performed miracles.

Further, I believe that Jesus' miracles were authentic because even today we cannot explain them away. Occasionally, someone says, "Sure, they thought Jesus was doing miracles, but there were other men going around claiming to perform miracles, like Simon the sorcerer, and people thought *they* were miracle-workers. Jesus just deceived the people." This argument might have some weight if it were not for the facts: The very ones who were deceiving the people, who knew how to fool the people and use mob psychology, were themselves convinced by the miracles of Jesus and the apostles. Examine the story of Simon the Sorcerer in Acts 8. Also, consider Judas. Judas had inside knowledge of all that Jesus did. If Jesus had been duping the crowds, Judas would certainly have known it. When Judas decided to betray Jesus, however, he could not tell Jesus' enemies anything they could use in His trial. All he could do was tell them where to find Jesus so they could arrest Him.

Some have protested, "Even if these accounts are trustworthy, even if these things really happened, those who wrote about them didn't *understand* what was happening. They didn't know about psychosomatic disease. Today we know that 80 percent of the physical problems people have are related to some problem in the mind. *That's* how Jesus was able to heal."

While many illnesses are related to the mind, this cannot explain the healing of the man with leprosy. This cannot explain the restoration of shrunken limbs. This cannot explain the healing of the man born blind: That man was not one born with sight who later developed a psychosomatic blindness; he was *born* blind. What about Jesus' raising of Lazarus after Lazarus had been dead three days and was already stinking? (Jn. 11). Did Lazarus just *think* he had been dead three days?

Many of Jesus' miracles were done in public. They were done before unbelievers. They were done over a long period of time and involved great variety in the demonstration of power: power over nature, power over disease, power over demons, power involving supernatural knowledge, power involving creation, and power over death. There is no way to explain them away.

Jesus really did...

...heal a paralytic in the synagogue at Capernaum.

...heal Peter's mother-in-law.

...heal all who came to Him in Capernaum—and in Galilee.

...heal a man full of leprosy.

...heal the man let down through the roof at Capernaum.

The *Reality* of Jesus' Miracle

Let us now take a closer look at the miracles of Jesus—specifically His healings. We will encounter miracles like these again and again in our reading.

Jesus' Miracles Then

We use the term "miracle" loosely today: We speak of "the miracle of birth." We say, "If I pass my test, it will be a miracle" or "If I get through this year without an ulcer, it will be a miracle." Biblically, however, the word "miracle" has a special meaning. It was not something that happened every day. It was not something that resulted from natural law or human effort. It was supernatural, because for the moment natural laws were laid aside and the supernatural predominated—but it was more than that. It was the supernatural working in the natural world in a way that all could see and hear and acknowledge that a miracle had occurred.

To demonstrate what we are talking about, let us use several examples to learn certain facts about Jesus' healing.

First, notice that Jesus was not limited in His miracles. He had received the Spirit "without measure" or limit (Jn. 3:34).

He was not limited by the faith of others. Sometimes the person healed had faith, as was the case with the leper (Mt. 8:2). Sometimes, however, there was no indication that the person healed had faith. For instance, in the case of the healing of the man let down through the roof, Jesus saw the faith of the four friends, not the sick man's faith (Mt. 9:2; Mk. 2:5). Those Jesus raised from the dead certainly demonstrated no faith in His ability to perform miracles.

Jesus was not limited regarding the types of physical problems He could heal. He healed "*every kind* of disease and *every kind* of sickness among the people*" (Mt. 4:23; emphasis added). He healed something as "simple" as fever, and He also healed a man "*covered* with leprosy" (Lk. 5:12; emphasis added). When one has genuine power to heal, there are no limitations regarding whom he can heal and whom he cannot heal.

Neither was Jesus limited by the number of people who needed to be healed. He could heal them all. He experienced no failures.

> The news about Him spread throughout all Syria; and they brought to Him *all* who were ill, . . . *and He healed them* (Mt. 4:24; emphasis added).

He . . . healed *all* who were ill (Mt. 8:16; emphasis added).

> . . . all those who had any who were sick with various diseases brought them to Him; and laying His hands on *each one of them*, He was healing them (Lk. 4:40; emphasis added).

Second, Jesus' healings had certain distinctive characteristics:

(1) The healing was *immediate*. People did not get well gradually. Concerning the leper, we read, "And immediately his leprosy was cleansed" (Mt. 8:3c; see also Mk. 1:42; Lk. 5:13). Regarding the paralytic, Mark 2:12 says, "And he got up and immediately picked up the pallet and went out in the sight of everyone . . ." (see also Lk. 5:25).

(2) The healing was *complete*. People were not healed partially. The man in the synagogue was completely all right after Jesus cast out the demon. Peter's mother-in-law was completely well after Jesus healed her; she immediately returned to her normal activities. The leper did not just "get better"; he was cleansed. The paralyzed man on a pallet picked up his bed and walked out the door. As our study continues, we will see many other cases: The blind were made to see, withered limbs were restored, and people were raised from the dead.

(3) The healing was *convincing*. The miracles of Jesus were of such a nature that no one could deny that these miracles had taken place. Some tried to discredit Jesus, even saying that He did His miracles by the power of Beelzebul; but they could not deny that miracles were done.

One of the best examples is the case of the healing of the man let down through the roof. Even Jesus' enemies could not deny that a miracle had occurred on that occasion. As a result, the crowds began to grow and Jesus' popularity increased: "The news about Him spread. . . . Large crowds followed Him from Galilee and the Decapolis and Jerusalem and Judea and from beyond the Jordan" (Mt. 4:24, 25). After Christ healed the demoniac in the synagogue, we read,

> They were all amazed, so that they debated among them-

selves, saying, "What is this? . . . He commands even the unclean spirits, and they obey Him." Immediately the news about Him spread everywhere into all the surrounding district of Galilee (Mk. 1:27, 28).

After He healed the leper, "the news about Him was spreading even farther, and large crowds were gathering to hear Him and to be healed of their sicknesses" (Lk. 5:15).

Third, Jesus' aim was primarily spiritual. His purpose was to save souls, not just relieve suffering. Luke 4:43 says, "But He said to them, 'I must preach the kingdom of God to the other cities also, for I was sent *for this purpose*'" (emphasis added). He did not say that He was sent to heal, but rather that He was sent to preach so that people might be saved (see Lk. 19:10).

This does not mean that Jesus was unmoved by human suffering. When He saw the leper, He was "moved with compassion" (Mk. 1:41). It does mean that Jesus' first priority was not healing or performing other miracles. He was more concerned about men's souls, not their bodies. When the man was let down through the roof, the first thing Jesus did was forgive his sins (Mk. 2:5).

So-called Miracles Now

One reason people do not believe in the miracles of Jesus is that some today claim to have the same power that Jesus and the apostles had. When skeptics examine what these imposters do—and determine that it is not miraculous—they conclude that Jesus and the apostles could not do miracles either. However, let us notice some differences between Jesus' miracles and so-called miracles today.

As we saw, Jesus was not limited in His miracles—not by the faith of others, not by the kind of physical problem, not by the number of cases. In contrast, when men today cannot heal someone, they often say, "He didn't have enough faith." They say, in effect, "We are limited by the other man's faith." Further, we saw that Jesus could heal any and all diseases, while there are illnesses that so-called healers of today will not attempt to cure. Any time they conduct their "healing services," people go home from those services unhealed.

Let us especially make a contrast regarding three characteristics of Jesus' miracles: Jesus' miracles were, first, *immediate* and, second, *complete*. So-called healers often insist that the one "healed" is better and will continue to get better. If we were to attend a "healing service," we would not see withered limbs fill out; we would not see the dead raised. The third characteristic is devastating to those claiming to do the same miracles that Jesus did. Jesus' miracles were *convincing*: Jesus' miracles convinced His enemies; they convinced the skeptics; no one could deny that a miracle had taken place. I have been to a "healing service" and seen many more on television, but I have not seen a miracle yet. It is not hard to deny that miracles are occurring today.

Finally, there is a contrast in emphasis: Jesus' emphasis was never on the physical, the relief of suffering. Rather, His emphasis was on the spiritual man. In the "healing services" I have seen, the emphasis and the excitement centered on physical ailments.

Among the hindrances in convincing men today that Jesus did miracles are the sham miracles of today. Those guilty of such will have to give an account someday.

The *Result* of Jesus' Miracles

Our final consideration builds on a truth noticed earlier. Let us close with this thought because it is what the miracles of Jesus—whether healing, stilling a storm, or raising the dead—were all about: Jesus' miracles proved Him to be God's Son and our Savior.

The miracles of Jesus had a powerful impact on those who saw them. This can be illustrated by the case of the man let down through the roof. When all three accounts are put together, we can see how much this miracle impressed those present:

- They were amazed (Mk. 2:12).
- They were astonished (Lk. 5:26).
- They were filled with awe (Mt. 9:8).
- They glorified God (Mt. 9:8; Mk. 2:12; Lk. 5:25, 26).

Jesus stressed that the basic purpose of His miracles was to convince people that He was truly the Son of God. For instance, to prove that He had the authority to forgive sin (something only God can do), He healed the paralytic who was let down through the roof (Mt. 9:4–6). As our study continues, that truth will be illustrated again and again. When John the Baptizer wondered whether or not Jesus was the Messiah, rather than saying, "Yes," Jesus healed many people. Then He said, in effect, "Go and report to John what you have seen" (see Lk. 7:20–23).

John especially emphasized this fact. In John 2:11 Jesus' first miracle strengthened His disciples' faith in Him. In John 5:36 Christ said that the "works that I do—testify about Me, that the Father has sent Me." Jesus challenged His disciples to "believe because of the works themselves" (Jn. 14:11). Someone may say, "I wish I could have seen Jesus' miracles. Then I would believe." John covered that, too:

> Therefore many other signs Jesus also performed in the presence of the disciples, which are not written in this book; but these have been *written* so that you may believe that Jesus is the Christ, the Son of God; and that believing you may have life in His name (Jn. 20:30, 31; emphasis added).

Christ's miracles do not have to be repeated. We have the sure testimony of those who observed them. If we will not believe their testimony, we would not believe even if we saw the miracles with our own eyes (see Lk. 16:31).

Conclusion

The miracles of Jesus teach some important lessons. For instance, they demonstrate that Jesus is concerned about the problems of others. Christ is *still* moved with compassion when we have problems of any kind. More important, the miracles teach that Jesus is really the Son of God. We can therefore be saved from our sins—and someday go to be with Him throughout eternity.

PART V

CHRIST'S MINISTRY FROM THE SECOND PASSOVER TO THE THIRD

Includes a Harmony of

Mt. 5:1—8:1, 5–13, 18, 23–34; 9:1, 10–38; 10:1—14:36

Mk. 2:15—6:56

Lk. 4:16–30; 5:29—9:17; 11:14–36

Jn. 5:1—6:71

SECTION I
JESUS' HEALING

Includes a Harmony of

Mt. 10:2–4; 12:1–21

Mk. 2:23—3:19

Lk. 6:1–16

Jn. 5:1–47

Part V focuses on the events that occurred between the second Passover and the third of Christ's earthly ministry. Jesus' personal ministry is frequently stated to have lasted three and one-half years, which is an educated guess based on the belief that the Gospel of John mentions four Passovers. John definitely mentions three Passovers: 2:13; 6:4; 13:1. The fourth reference is to "a feast of the Jews" (Jn. 5:1), which may or may not have been a Passover. Various explanations have been given in favor of this being a Passover, including the fact that it would be hard to fit in all the events of Jesus' life if His ministry were less than three years. It is, of course, possible that there were additional Passovers during Jesus' ministry not mentioned by John—and that His ministry could have been four or more years.

The exact length of Jesus' personal ministry was not important enough for God to reveal. We cannot state categorically that "Jesus' ministry lasted three and one-half years" when the Scriptures do not say that. A. T. Robertson wrote, "All we can say is that we know that the ministry of Jesus was [at least] two and a half years in length with the probability of three and a half."[1]

As we continue our study of the Great Galilean Ministry, we should note that, from this point on, there are many, many differences in the various harmonies regarding the order of events. Not all variations are listed in this study, although other possibilities are occasionally mentioned. The exact sequence of events is not a matter of great importance; otherwise, the Holy Spirit would have been clearer on the order.

As Jesus continued His work in Galilee, His popularity increased. Crowds came to hear Him preach and to seek heal-

---

[1]A. T. Robertson, *A Harmony of the Gospels for Students of the Life of Christ* (New York: Harper & Row, 1950), 269–70.

ing. During the time covered in this section, Jesus selected His twelve apostles, setting the stage for the monumental Sermon on the Mount—which we will study in the next section.

Perhaps most significant during this time was the increasing hostility of the Jewish leaders. Spies followed Jesus everywhere, trying to discover some basis for accusing Him (Mt. 12:10; Mk. 3:2). When Christ escaped His enemies' traps, it filled them with rage (Lk. 6:11). Matthew wrote that "the Pharisees . . . conspired against Him, as to how they might destroy Him" (Mt. 12:14; see Mk. 3:6). John recorded that "the Jews were persecuting Jesus," and that they "were seeking all the more to kill Him" (Jn. 5:16, 18).

Why did the writers of the Gospel Accounts think it necessary to document the irrational hatred of the Jewish hierarchy? Perhaps they wanted to clarify their part in the crucifixion of Jesus. No greater shame existed in New Testament times than the disgrace of dying on a Roman cross (Heb. 6:6; see 12:2). Skeptics may be inclined to sneer, "If Jesus was really the perfect individual you say He was, why did He die as a condemned criminal?" Our texts help to answer that question.

The antagonism revolved around Sabbath regulations. The Gospel Accounts tell of six Sabbath controversies. We will study three of these in this section and then see what Jesus did to counter—to some extent—the effects of the opposition.

The word "Sabbath" basically means "rest." When God created the world, He rested on the seventh day (Gen. 2:1–3). Later, the seventh-day rest, called the Sabbath, was given as part of the Ten Commandments (Ex. 20:8–11). The Sabbath was a day of rest, a time to reflect on God, a time for rejoicing. To ensure that the Sabbath was observed, God imposed severe penalties for violating it (see Num. 15:32–36; Neh. 13:15–22; Jer. 17:19–27).

God's laws were sufficiently strict, but men were not willing to leave it at that. The regulations evolved to include such ludicrous traditions as these: A nailed shoe could not be worn on the Sabbath because that was a burden; one man could carry a loaf of bread, but two men could not carry the loaf between them. H. I. Hester wrote,

The observance of this day had developed into a very complicated and burdensome chore. The Mosaic restrictions had been elaborated and multiplied until they numbered into the hundreds. Many of these regulations were utterly ridiculous. For example, wearing false teeth on the Sabbath was considered carrying a burden, as was the plucking out of a grey hair, or picking a head of wheat, or even writing together two letters of the alphabet. These multiplied regulations had made the keeping of the Sabbath . . . practically impossible. . . . The whole system had destroyed the very spirit of the Sabbath.[2]

Warren W. Wiersbe observed, "They had taken the Sabbath—God's gift to man—and had transformed it into a prison house of regulations and restrictions."[3]

As the Jews attempted to entrap Jesus, their obscure and complicated Sabbath rules became "their favorite piece of legislation."[4] Since (for all practical purposes) no one could keep all of their Sabbath laws perfectly, they thought that they would have no trouble catching Jesus in a violation—and such a violation carried the death penalty (see Num. 15:32–36).

JESUS HEALED A CRIPPLED MAN ON THE SABBATH AND DEFENDED THE ACT (JN. 5:1–47)

[1]**After these things there was a feast of the Jews, and Jesus went up to Jerusalem.**

[2]**Now there is in Jerusalem by the sheep gate a pool, which is called in Hebrew Bethesda, having five porticoes. [3]In these lay a multitude of those who were sick, blind, lame, and with-**

---

[2]H. I. Hester, *The Heart of the New Testament* (Liberty, Mo.: Quality Press, 1963), 142.

[3]Warren W. Wiersbe, *The Bible Exposition Commentary*, vol. 1 (Wheaton, Ill.: Victor Books, 1989), 305.

[4]Adam Fahling, *The Life of Christ* (St. Louis, Mo.: Concordia Publishing House, 1936), 195.

ered, [waiting for the moving of the waters; ⁴for an angel of the Lord went down at certain seasons into the pool and stirred up the water; whoever then first, after the stirring up of the water, stepped in was made well from whatever disease with which he was afflicted.] ⁵A man was there who had been ill for thirty-eight years. ⁶When Jesus saw him lying there, and knew that he had already been a long time in that condition, He said to him, "Do you wish to get well?" ⁷The sick man answered Him, "Sir, I have no man to put me into the pool when the water is stirred up, but while I am coming, another steps down before me." ⁸Jesus said to him, "Get up, pick up your pallet and walk." ⁹Immediately the man became well, and picked up his pallet and began to walk.

Now it was the Sabbath on that day. ¹⁰So the Jews were saying to the man who was cured, "It is the Sabbath, and it is not permissible for you to carry your pallet." ¹¹But he answered them, "He who made me well was the one who said to me, 'Pick up your pallet and walk.'" ¹²They asked him, "Who is the man who said to you, 'Pick up your pallet and walk'?" ¹³But the man who was healed did not know who it was, for Jesus had slipped away while there was a crowd in that place. ¹⁴Afterward Jesus found him in the temple and said to him, "Behold, you have become well; do not sin anymore, so that nothing worse happens to you." ¹⁵The man went away, and told the Jews that it was Jesus who had made him well. ¹⁶For this reason the Jews were persecuting Jesus, because He was doing these things on the Sabbath. ¹⁷But He answered them, "My Father is working until now, and I Myself am working." ¹⁸For this reason therefore the Jews were seeking all the more to kill Him, because He not only was breaking the Sabbath, but also was calling God His own Father, making Himself equal with God.

¹⁹Therefore Jesus answered and was saying to them, "Truly, truly, I say to you, the Son can do nothing of Himself, unless it is something He sees the Father doing; for whatever the Father does, these things the Son also does in like manner. ²⁰For the Father loves the Son, and shows Him all things that He Himself is doing; and the Father will show Him greater

works than these, so that you will marvel. [21]For just as the Father raises the dead and gives them life, even so the Son also gives life to whom He wishes. [22]For not even the Father judges anyone, but He has given all judgment to the Son, [23]so that all will honor the Son even as they honor the Father. He who does not honor the Son does not honor the Father who sent Him.

[24]"Truly, truly, I say to you, he who hears My word, and believes Him who sent Me, has eternal life, and does not come into judgment, but has passed out of death into life. [25]Truly, truly, I say to you, an hour is coming and now is, when the dead will hear the voice of the Son of God, and those who hear will live. [26]For just as the Father has life in Himself, even so He gave to the Son also to have life in Himself; [27]and He gave Him authority to execute judgment, because He is the Son of Man. [28]Do not marvel at this; for an hour is coming, in which all who are in the tombs will hear His voice, [29]and will come forth; those who did the good deeds to a resurrection of life, those who committed the evil deeds to a resurrection of judgment.

[30]"I can do nothing on My own initiative. As I hear, I judge; and My judgment is just, because I do not seek My own will, but the will of Him who sent Me.

[31]"If I alone testify about Myself, My testimony is not true. [32]There is another who testifies of Me, and I know that the testimony which He gives about Me is true. [33]You have sent to John, and he has testified to the truth. [34]But the testimony which I receive is not from man, but I say these things so that you may be saved. [35]He was the lamp that was burning and was shining and you were willing to rejoice for a while in his light. [36]But the testimony which I have is greater than the testimony of John; for the works which the Father has given Me to accomplish—the very works that I do—testify about Me, that the Father has sent Me. [37]And the Father who sent Me, He has testified of Me. You have neither heard His voice at any time nor seen His form. [38]You do not have His word abiding in you, for you do not believe Him whom He sent. [39]You search the Scriptures because you think that in them

you have eternal life; it is these that testify about Me; [40]and you are unwilling to come to Me so that you may have life. [41]I do not receive glory from men; [42]but I know you, that you do not have the love of God in yourselves. [43]I have come in My Father's name, and you do not receive Me; if another comes in his own name, you will receive him. [44]How can you believe, when you receive glory from one another and you do not seek the glory that is from the one and only God? [45]Do not think that I will accuse you before the Father; the one who accuses you is Moses, in whom you have set your hope. [46]For if you believed Moses, you would believe Me, for he wrote about Me. [47]But if you do not believe his writings, how will you believe My words?"

Jesus had been busy in the Great Galilean Ministry, but now He took a break to go to Jerusalem for a religious feast (Jn. 5:1). The law of Moses required Jewish men to go to Jerusalem three times a year for the major feasts—Passover, Pentecost, and the Feast of Tabernacles—and Jesus always kept the Law (Mt. 5:17). While it is uncertain which feast this was, a good case can be made for this being the Passover.

During the previous Passover, Jesus had enraged the Jewish religious authorities by chasing the religious merchandisers from the temple. At this Passover, He infuriated them by healing a man at the pool of Bethesda. John recorded the miracle in these words: **Jesus said to him, "Get up, pick up your pallet and walk." Immediately the man became well, and picked up his pallet and began to walk** (Jn. 5:8, 9a). John then added this significant statement: **Now it was the *Sabbath* on that day** (Jn. 5:9b; emphasis added). According to Rabbinic tradition, it was lawful to carry a man on his mat on the Sabbath (in their reasoning, the mat was "incidental"), but it was unlawful just to carry a mat.

At first, the Jewish leaders assailed the man who was carrying the mat under his arm; but when they discovered that it was Jesus who had told him to pick up his bed, their attack turned on Him. Their assault prompted the first public sermon by Jesus recorded in detail, the first of several lengthy discourses in which

Jesus was forced to defend Himself.

Jesus' basic defense on this occasion was that if God could **work** on the Sabbath, so could He (Jn. 5:17). He gave examples of activities in which He and His Father were partners (Jn. 5:19–30). Jesus' aligning Himself with God horrified the Jews: He was **making Himself equal with God** (Jn. 5:18). Christ then produced a series of witnesses to prove that He was who He claimed to be: John the Baptizer, the miracles that He did, the Scriptures, and especially God Himself (Jn. 5:31–47). Burton Coffman said that Jesus' words to His enemies on this occasion "are among the most profound and instructive in holy writ."[5]

Apparently, Jesus left Jerusalem shortly after this encounter. At least, nothing else is recorded regarding this trip to Jerusalem.

APPLICATION:
"EQUAL WITH GOD" (JN. 5:16–47)

Early in His Great Galilean Ministry, Jesus made a trip to Jerusalem. While there, He healed a man beside the pool of Bethesda (Jn. 5:2–9a). In telling of this event, John added this terse comment: "Now it was the Sabbath on that day" (Jn. 5:9b).

Incriminating Charges (Jn. 5:16–18)

The result of the healing was a face-to-face confrontation with the Jewish authorities. The religious leaders accused Jesus of breaking the Sabbath.

Our Lord's reply was "My Father is working until now, and I Myself am working" (Jn. 5:17). In other words, "It is true that God rested on the seventh day, but this does not mean that God ceased to do good (Gen. 2:2). Even on the Sabbath, He sustains the universe (Heb. 1:3). Even on the Sabbath, He sends sunshine and rain (Mt. 5:45)." Jesus' argument was that since God helps people on the seventh day, it was all right for Him (that is, Jesus) to help people on that day.

Christ's words enraged the Jewish leaders, for they saw the implications of His argument. In the first place, He said, "*My*

---

[5]James Burton Coffman, *Commentary on John* (Austin, Tex.: Firm Foundation Publishing House, 1974), 158.

Father." Men normally spoke of "our Father" (Mt. 6:9; Rom. 1:7; 1 Cor. 1:3), but Jesus said, "My Father" (Mt. 7:21; 10:32; 11:27)—implying a special relationship. In the second place, Jesus pictured God and Himself as being involved in the same activity: "My Father is working . . . , and I Myself am working." As a result, "the Jews were seeking all the more to kill Him, because He . . . was calling God His own Father, *making Himself equal with God*" (Jn. 5:17, 18; emphasis added).

Liberal theologians read the Gospel Accounts and say that Jesus never claimed to be the Son of God, never claimed to be divine. The religious leaders in Christ's day had no trouble understanding the significance of His words.

If Jesus did *not* mean to imply that He was "equal with God," it would have been simple for Him to say, "Oh, no, you have misunderstood Me! That is *not* what I said." He did not deny their charge, but rather used their accusation as an opportunity to deliver a masterful discourse on His relationship with His Father. This is one of the great sermons in the Book of John.

Incredible Claims (Jn. 5:19–30)

Jesus' Premise

Jesus' basic premise was that He and His Father were *united* in what they did. The phrase "making Himself equal with God" might be taken to mean that Christ thought of Himself as God's competitor, but He emphasized that such was not the case. He stressed that "the Son can do nothing of Himself" (Jn. 5:19). Again, He said, "I can do nothing on My own initiative" (Jn. 5:30).

Examples

Jesus gave several examples of how He and His Father were united. In verses 21 through 30, three themes keep reappearing and overlapping: giving life, raising the dead, and judging mankind. The Jews thought it was *God's* prerogative (and His alone) to give life, raise the dead, and pronounce judgment—but Christ boldly claimed that He and God were coworkers in these functions (see Gen. 18:25; Deut. 32:39).

(1) *United in giving life.* Jesus first spoke of giving life: "For

just as the Father raises the dead and gives them life, even so the Son also gives life to whom He wishes" (Jn. 5:21). At this juncture of the discourse, the words probably referred to Jesus' giving spiritual life. Jesus also said, "Truly, truly, I say to you, he who hears My word, and believes Him who sent Me, has eternal life, and does not come into judgment, but has passed out of death into life" (Jn. 5:24).

(2) *United in raising the dead.* The claim of verse 21 could also include giving bodily life. Jesus predicted that the Jews would see Him perform even "greater works [miracles]" than they had seen so far, and that they would "marvel" (Jn. 5:20). This was probably a reference to the raising of the dead during Christ's personal ministry—especially the raising of Lazarus, which would cause such a stir in Jerusalem (Jn. 11:1–48; 12:1, 9–11).

Jesus' power went beyond the raising of a handful of people from death during His stay on earth, however. Anticipating the end of this age, He announced,

> . . . an hour is coming, in which all who are in the tombs will hear His voice [that is, the voice of the Son of Man; Jn. 5:27], and will come forth; those who did the good deeds to a resurrection of life, those who committed the evil deeds to a resurrection of judgment (Jn. 5:28, 29).

This is a clear and concise statement concerning the general resurrection of all mankind at the Second Coming.

(3) *United in judgment.* As verses 28 and 29 imply, the resurrection will be followed by the Judgment Day. In this work, too, Jesus will be united with His Father. He said, "For not even the Father judges anyone, but He has given all judgment to the Son" (Jn. 5:22). He insisted that God "gave Him authority to execute judgment, because He is the Son of Man" (Jn. 5:27). Again, He claimed, "I judge; and My judgment is just" (Jn. 5:30).

Since Jesus and His Father are united in giving life, raising the dead, and judgment, what should the response of His listeners have been? Christ said that all should "honor the Son even as they honor the Father" and added that "He who does not honor the Son does not honor the Father who sent Him" (Jn. 5:23).

Jesus made audacious claims. He would be forced either to offer proof that what He was saying was true or to retract His statements.

Impeccable Credentials (Jn. 5:31–47)

Jesus recognized that He and His claims were on trial. He called a progression of witnesses to testify on His behalf.

His introductory statement regarding witnesses sounds strange: "If I alone testify about Myself, My testimony is not true" (Jn. 5:31). The word "alone" has been added by the translators. Christ literally said, "If I bear witness of Myself, My testimony is not true." Jesus had been "testifying," or "bearing witness," concerning Himself (Jn. 5:19–30). Taken out of context, verse 31 could sound as if Jesus was saying that He had not been telling the truth.

Jesus' defense in John 5 should be compared with His defense in chapter 8. On that occasion, the Pharisees said to Christ, "You are testifying about Yourself; Your testimony is not true" (Jn. 8:13). Jesus replied, "Even if I testify about Myself, *My testimony is true*" (Jn. 5:14; emphasis added). Then He added, "Even in your law it has been written that the testimony of two men is true. I am He who testifies about Myself, and the Father who sent Me testifies about Me" (Jn. 5:17, 18).

Comparing the two statements makes clear that in John 5 Jesus was not confessing to a lie. Rather, He was acknowledging that, according to the law of Moses, the witness of one person was insufficient. The testimony of two or three witnesses was required (Num. 35:30; Deut. 17:6; 19:15; see Mt. 18:16). That is why the NASB translators added the word "alone" to verse 31: If Christ alone bore witness concerning Himself, this would not be accepted *in a Jewish court*.

Jesus therefore added a second Witness, the same Witness mentioned in chapter 8: His Father. Christ said, "There is another who testifies of Me, and I know that the testimony which He gives about Me is true" (Jn. 5:32). In context, this refers to God. Jesus emphasized, "And the Father who sent Me, He has testified of Me" (Jn. 5:37a). Several witnesses would be produced, but the testimony of each was, in effect, testimony from the one perfect Witness, God. These Jews had neither seen God nor heard His voice (Jn. 5:37b), but He had clearly spoken to them through His agents.

The Witness of John

The veracity of Jesus' claims did not rest on human testimony (Jn. 5:34a, 36a), but the first witness called was a man: John the Baptizer. John was called because he was God's special messenger (Mal. 3:1; Lk. 7:27) and because his testimony concerning the Messiah had never been refuted.

Christ said, "You have sent to John, and he has testified to the truth" (Jn. 5:33). This reference is to the time a delegation had been sent from Jerusalem to question John (Jn. 1:19–28). John had told them, ". . . among you stands One whom you do not know. It is He who comes after me, the thong of whose sandal I am not worthy to untie" (Jn. 1:26, 27). The next day, John had pointed to Jesus and said, "Behold, the Lamb of God who takes away the sin of the world!"; "I myself have seen, and have testified that this is the Son of God" (Jn. 5:29, 34).

John had a single purpose in life: to direct people to Jesus. "One of the great religious portraits of Europe is Grunewald's 'John the Baptist.' . . . The striking feature of the painting is its focus on the pointing index finger of John as he directs attention to Christ. . . ."[6]

Concerning the witness of John, Christ said, "He was the lamp that was burning and was shining and you were willing to rejoice for a while in his light" (Jn. 5:35). The key phrase in this sentence is "for a while." R. C. Foster wrote, "They had rejoiced in John's light for a time—until the light had been turned on their sins!"[7] After that, they had wanted nothing more to do with him.

If they *had* accepted John's testimony, they would also have accepted Jesus. Then they could have been saved (Jn. 5:34b).

---

[6]Bruce Milne, *The Message of John* (Downers Grove, Ill.: InterVarsity Press, 1993), 98.

[7]R. C. Foster, *Studies in the Life of Christ* (Grand Rapids, Mich.: Baker Book House, 1971), 451.

The Witness of Miracles

Christ next spoke of the witness of His miracles: "But the testimony which I have is greater than the testimony of John; for the works which the Father has given Me to accomplish—the very works that I do—testify about Me, that the Father has sent Me" (Jn. 5:36). The word "works" could be used to speak of the entirety of Jesus' life; certainly, all that He did testified to the fact that He was God's Son. Christ, however, had in mind the miracles that He did by the power of God.

Jesus had performed many miracles on a previous trip to Jerusalem (Jn. 2:23). Concerning those miraculous deeds, Nicodemus had said, " . . . we know that You have come from God …; for no one can do these signs that You do unless God is with him" (Jn. 3:2). Christ had also done at least one miracle on the present trip to Jerusalem. It is possible that the man He had healed by the pool was standing nearby as He spoke these words.

Jesus' critics could not deny that He did miracles, but still they refused to accept Him as the Messiah.

The Witness of the Scriptures

Jesus had called as witnesses a messenger from God and signs from God. Now He called upon the testimony of the Word of God: "You search the Scriptures because you think that in them you have eternal life; it is these that testify about Me" (Jn. 5:39). Hundreds of passages in the Old Testament pointed forward to Christ (Ps. 2; 22; Is. 53). Jesus later spoke of "all things which are written about Me in the Law of Moses and the Prophets and the Psalms" (Lk. 24:44).

In their own way, the Jewish leaders were devoted to the Scriptures. Rabbinic writings said, "He who has gained for himself words of the Law has gained for himself life in the world to come."[8] For this reason, they pored over the Scriptures. They counted the words; they counted the letters; they put every "jot" and "tittle" (Mt. 5:18; KJV) under their theological microscope. Still, they missed the purpose of the Scriptures, which were

---

[8]Aboth 2:8; quoted in Frank Pack, *The Gospel According to John, Part 1* (Austin, Tex.: Sweet Publishing Co., 1975), 95.

designed to bring people to Christ (Gal. 3:24).

They were like men carefully examining a sign post—measuring it, drawing sketches of it, writing descriptions of it—instead of traveling to the destination it indicated. Warren W. Wiersbe wrote that the Jews "sought to know the Word of God, but they did not know the God of the Word!"[9] Jesus perceived that they had the Word in their heads but not in their hearts. He told them, "You do not have His word abiding in you" (Jn. 5:38a).

Jesus, referring to the writings of Moses, made a striking statement of the fact that the Scriptures witnessed concerning Him:

> Do not think that I will accuse you before the Father; the one who accuses you is Moses, in whom you have set your hope. For if you believed Moses, you would believe Me, for he wrote about Me. But if you do not believe his writings, how will you believe My words? (Jn. 5:45–47).

Moses had written of the "Seed" that would come (Gen. 3:15; 22:18; see Gal. 3:16). He had prophesied that this promised One would come from the tribe of Judah (Gen. 49:10). He had spoken of a prophet that would arise like himself (Deut. 18:15–18). *All* of his writings were saturated with types and antitypes anticipating the Messiah. Therefore, Jesus said that Moses not only was a witness *for* Him, but also, in the end, would stand as a witness *against* those who rejected Him. He declared, "The one who accuses you is Moses" (Jn. 5:45b).

With this mass of evidence at their disposal, why did the Jewish leaders reject Jesus? Jesus said the problem was one of will and heart. The One who "knew what was in man" (Jn. 2:25) gave this indictment: "You are *unwilling* to come to Me. . . . You do *not have the love of God* in yourselves" (Jn. 5:40–42; emphasis added).

One problem was that they were seeking glory from men instead of "the glory that is from the one and only God" (Jn. 5:44).

---

[9]Wiersbe, 308.

Jesus told the leaders, in effect, that if one were to come claiming to be the Messiah but lacked heaven-sent credentials, they would receive him as long as he flattered them and furthered their agenda (Jn. 5:43b). In contrast, the Jews refused to accept Jesus, who came with heaven's approval (Jn. 5:43a), because He refused to give them the glory they thought they deserved.

The condition of the religious authorities in Jerusalem could be summarized by saying that they knew so much that was not true, about things that did not matter, that they were deaf, dumb, and blind to the truth (see Mt. 13:15).

Isn't it sobering to realize that it is possible to be a diligent student of the Word without ever coming to a saving knowledge of the truth? May God help us always to approach the Scriptures with the right attitude (a "love of the truth"; 2 Thess. 2:10) and with the right aim (to "know the Lord"; Heb. 8:11).

Conclusion

The Jewish leaders probably expected Jesus to be intimidated when they accused Him of breaking the Sabbath, but He was not. Instead, He met their challenge and made radical claims. Since the Jews were unable to refute His arguments, they should have accepted Him as the Son of God—but, sadly, they remained unwilling to do so.

John 5 was not written just to expose the hardness of the hearts of first-century Jews. Rather, it was written to lay bare our hearts in the twenty-first century. Jesus' claims allow none to remain neutral. C. S. Lewis wrote concerning those claims,

> In the mouth of any speaker who is not God, these words would imply what I can only regard as a silliness and conceit unrivalled by any character in history.
> ... You must make your choice. Either this man was, and is, the Son of God: or else a madman or something worse. You can shut Him up for a fool, you can spit at Him and kill Him as a demon; or you can fall at His feet and call Him Lord and God.[10]

---

[10]C. S. Lewis, *Mere Christianity* (New York: Macmillan Co., 1952), 55–56.

Jesus was on trial in John 5—and He is still on trial in the hearts of mankind. Today *we* are the jury. What is our verdict?

JESUS DEFENDED HIS DISCIPLES WHO PLUCKED GRAIN ON THE SABBATH (MT. 12:1–8; MK. 2:23–28; LK. 6:1–5)

Matthew 12:1–8

¹At that time Jesus went through the grainfields on the Sabbath, and His disciples became hungry and began to pick the heads of grain and eat. ²But when the Pharisees saw this, they said to Him, "Look, Your disciples do what is not lawful to do on a Sabbath." ³But He said to them, "Have you not read what David did when he became hungry, he and his companions, ⁴how he entered the house of God, and they ate the consecrated bread, which was not lawful for him to eat nor for those with him, but for the priests alone? ⁵Or have you not read in the Law, that on the Sabbath the priests in the temple break the Sabbath and are innocent? ⁶But I say to you that something greater than the temple is here. ⁷But if you had known what this means, 'I desire compassion, and not a sacrifice,' you would not have condemned the innocent. ⁸For the Son of Man is Lord of the Sabbath."

Mark 2:23–28

²³And it happened that He was passing through the grainfields on the Sabbath, and His disciples began to make their way along while picking the heads of grain. ²⁴The Pharisees were saying to Him, "Look, why are they doing what is not lawful on the Sabbath?" ²⁵And He said to them, "Have you never read what David did when he was in need and he and his companions became hungry; ²⁶how he entered the house of God in the time of Abiathar the high priest, and ate the consecrated bread, which is not lawful for anyone to eat except the priests, and he also gave it to those who were with him?" ²⁷Jesus said to them, "The Sabbath was made for man, and not man for the Sabbath. ²⁸So the Son of Man is Lord

even of the Sabbath."

Luke 6:1–5

¹Now it happened that He was passing through some grainfields on a Sabbath; and His disciples were picking the heads of grain, rubbing them in their hands, and eating the grain. ²But some of the Pharisees said, "Why do you do what is not lawful on the Sabbath?" ³And Jesus answering them said, "Have you not even read what David did when he was hungry, he and those who were with him, ⁴how he entered the house of God, and took and ate the consecrated bread which is not lawful for any to eat except the priests alone, and gave it to his companions?" ⁵And He was saying to them, "The Son of Man is Lord of the Sabbath."

After Christ returned to Galilee, one Sabbath He and His disciples were walking through a grainfield, **and His disciples became hungry and began to pick the heads of grain and eat** (Mt. 12:1). Luke added that the disciples were **rubbing** [the heads of grain] **in their hands** (Lk. 6:1). Grain on the stalk is covered with a husk which needs to be removed before the grain is eaten. Jesus' followers were rubbing the heads together in their hands to loosen the husks. They could then blow away the husks and toss the raw grain into their mouths.

As they were picking, rubbing, blowing, and chewing, a flock of Pharisees suddenly appeared and began to accuse them of breaking the Sabbath. According to Luke, the Pharisees confronted the *disciples*. According to Matthew and Mark, the Pharisees challenged *Jesus*. They probably did both. This scene has a humorous touch: Imagine the pompous Pharisees in their ornate robes, crouched down in a grain field, hiding and waiting to pounce on Jesus for the slightest infraction of their beloved traditions.

The accusation was not that they were stealing another man's grain. The Law allowed travelers to pick grain and eat it (Deut. 23:25). The accusation was that the Sabbath laws about labor had been violated. As far as the Pharisees were concerned, picking a few heads of grain was equivalent to harvesting, rubbing the grain was like threshing, blowing away the husks was winnowing, and eating the heads was grinding. (They would probably also add that the disciples had "prepared a meal," which was forbidden on the Sabbath.)

Jesus' defense on this occasion was different than that presented in Jerusalem. At the close, He said that the Pharisees were condemning **the innocent** (Mt. 12:7). In other words, Jesus pleaded "not guilty." He did so on five grounds:

(1) "Not guilty"—because David was not judged guilty when he ate of the sacred bread in the tabernacle to appease his hunger (Mt. 12:3, 4; Lk. 6:3, 4; see 1 Sam. 21:6; Lev. 24:5–9).

(2) "Not guilty"—because the priests were not judged guilty when they worked on the Sabbath (Mt. 12:5; see Num. 28:9, 18, 19). The Sabbath was the busiest day of the week for the priests.

(3) "Not guilty"—because the Sabbath was intended to be a blessing, not a burden: **The Sabbath was made for man, and not man for the Sabbath** (Mk. 2:27). To deny the disciples simple sustenance on the Sabbath placed an unreasonable burden on them.

(4) "Not guilty"—because relieving suffering (including hunger) was more important than fulfilling rituals (especially man-made rituals). Jesus reminded His accusers of the teaching of Hosea 6:6: **"I desire compassion, and not a sacrifice"** (Mt. 12:7).

(5) "Not guilty"— because the Messiah could not be subjected to men's traditions. Jesus made two statements that must have made the Pharisees livid: **"But I say to you that something** [or, Someone] **greater than the temple is here"** (Mt. 12:6); **"For the Son of Man is Lord of the Sabbath"** (Mt. 12:8; see Mk. 2:28; Lk. 6:5). Jesus was obviously referring to Himself. He, not they, had the authority to decide what could or could not be done within the framework of the Old Testament laws concerning the Sabbath.

None of these examples should be taken as proof that we can break God's laws with impunity. Jesus' point was that if the Jewish leaders did not condemn David or the priests, why did they condemn Him and His followers?

The Pharisees must have gone away consumed with anger,

muttering to themselves.

JESUS DEFENDED HEALING A WITHERED HAND ON THE SABBATH
(MT. 12:9–14; MK. 3:1–6; LK. 6:6–11)

Matthew 12:9–14

⁹Departing from there, He went into their synagogue.
¹⁰And a man was there whose hand was withered. And they
questioned Jesus, asking, "Is it lawful to heal on the Sabbath?"—so that they might accuse Him. ¹¹And He said to them,
"What man is there among you who has a sheep, and if it falls
into a pit on the Sabbath, will he not take hold of it and lift it
out? ¹²How much more valuable then is a man than a sheep!
So then, it is lawful to do good on the Sabbath." ¹³Then He said
to the man, "Stretch out your hand!" He stretched it out, and
it was restored to normal, like the other. ¹⁴But the Pharisees
went out and conspired against Him, as to how they might
destroy Him.

Mark 3:1–6

¹He entered again into a synagogue; and a man was there
whose hand was withered. ²They were watching Him to see if
He would heal him on the Sabbath, so that they might accuse
Him. ³He said to the man with the withered hand, "Get up
and come forward!" ⁴And He said to them, "Is it lawful to do
good or to do harm on the Sabbath, to save a life or to kill?"
But they kept silent. ⁵After looking around at them with anger,
grieved at their hardness of heart, He said to the man, "Stretch
out your hand." And he stretched it out, and his hand was
restored. ⁶The Pharisees went out and immediately began
conspiring with the Herodians against Him, as to how they
might destroy Him.

Luke 6:6–11

⁶On another Sabbath He entered the synagogue and was
teaching; and there was a man there whose right hand was

withered. [7]The scribes and the Pharisees were watching Him closely to see if He healed on the Sabbath, so that they might find reason to accuse Him. [8]But He knew what they were thinking, and He said to the man with the withered hand, "Get up and come forward!" And he got up and came forward. [9]And Jesus said to them, "I ask you, is it lawful to do good or to do harm on the Sabbath, to save a life or to destroy it?" [10]After looking around at them all, He said to him, "Stretch out your hand!" And he did so; and his hand was restored. [11]But they themselves were filled with rage, and discussed together what they might do to Jesus.

Shortly afterward, **on another Sabbath**, Jesus went into a synagogue where He was allowed to teach (Lk. 6:6). According to Matthew's account, **He went into *their* synagogue** (Mt. 12:9; emphasis added), referring to the Pharisees who had tried to indict Him in the grainfield.

Present in the assembly was **a man . . . whose hand was withered** (Mt. 12:10). Perhaps he was brought there by Christ's enemies to set a trap for Him. The Pharisees watched for a while **to see if [Jesus] would heal him on the Sabbath, so that they might accuse Him**. They desired to accuse Him before a Jewish council that could impose the death penalty (Mk. 3:2). Finally, they could stand it no longer and interrupted Christ's sermon, blurting out, **"Is it lawful to heal on the Sabbath?"** (Mt. 12:10).

Jesus was not intimidated. He told the man with the withered hand, **"Get up and come forward!"** (Mk. 3:3). With the man standing before the assembly, Christ asked His questioners, **"Is it lawful to do good or to do harm on the Sabbath, to save a life or to destroy it?"** (Lk. 6:9). Their own regulations permitted physicians and others to save life on the seventh day.[11] Jesus then used a simple illustration to which all could relate:

What man is there among you who has a sheep, and if

---

[11]Alfred Edersheim, *The Life and Times of Jesus the Messiah*, New Updated Version (Peabody, Mass.: Hendrickson Publishers, 1993), 515.

**it falls into a pit on the Sabbath, will he not take hold
of it and lift it out? How much more valuable then is
a man than a sheep! So then, it is lawful to do good on
the Sabbath** (Mt. 12:11, 12).

Heartbroken at His enemies' lack of compassion (Mk. 3:5),
Jesus told the man, **"Stretch óut your hand!"** (Mt. 12:13a). **He
stretched it out, and it was restored to normal, like the other**
(Mt. 12:13b). It was a miracle which all could see.

His enemies had been silenced (again), but they were not
prepared to admit defeat. They **went out and conspired against
Him, as to how they might destroy Him** (Mt. 12:14). Mark's
account adds this almost unbelievable detail: **The Pharisees
went out and immediately began conspiring with the Herodians against Him** (Mk. 3:6). The Pharisees *despised* the Herodians because they supported the pagan/Gentile innovations of
Herod the Great, but they evidently believed that they needed
their political influence to silence Christ. They hated the Herodians, but they hated Jesus more.

Before leaving this section on Sabbath controversy, notice
that Jesus never broke God's Sabbath laws, nor did He encourage anyone else to do so. Occasionally, however, He did violate
the man-made traditions that had proliferated through the
years—and this enraged His enemies. We have not quite reached
the halfway point in Jesus' public ministry, and already His
adversaries were working night and day to destroy Him and His
influence. J. W. McGarvey wrote, "From this point the blood red
line of conspiracy against the life of Jesus runs through [the]
Gospel."[12]

---

[12]J. W. McGarvey and Philip Y. Pendleton, *The Fourfold Gospel or A Harmony
of the Four Gospels* (Cincinnati: Standard Publishing Co., 1914), 198.

JESUS HEALED MULTITUDES BESIDE THE SEA OF GALILEE (MT. 12:15–21; MK. 3:7–12)

Matthew 12:15–21

¹⁵But Jesus, aware of this, withdrew from there. Many followed Him, and He healed them all, ¹⁶and warned them not to tell who He was. ¹⁷This was to fulfill what was spoken through Isaiah the prophet:

¹⁸"Behold, My Servant whom I have chosen;
My Beloved in whom My soul is well-pleased;
I will put My Spirit upon Him,
And He shall proclaim justice to the Gentiles.
¹⁹He will not quarrel, nor cry out;
Nor will anyone hear His voice in the streets.
²⁰A battered reed He will not break off,
And a smoldering wick He will not put out,
Until He leads justice to victory.
²¹And in His name the Gentiles will hope."

Mark 3:7–12

⁷Jesus withdrew to the sea with His disciples; and a great multitude from Galilee followed; and also from Judea, ⁸and from Jerusalem, and from Idumea, and beyond the Jordan, and the vicinity of Tyre and Sidon, a great number of people heard of all that He was doing and came to Him. ⁹And He told His disciples that a boat should stand ready for Him because of the crowd, so that they would not crowd Him; ¹⁰for He had healed many, with the result that all those who had afflictions pressed around Him in order to touch Him. ¹¹Whenever the unclean spirits saw Him, they would fall down before Him and shout, "You are the Son of God!" ¹²And He earnestly warned them not to tell who He was.

In response to the three Sabbath confrontations, Jesus took significant steps. The first thing He did was separate Himself from His enemies to avoid further conflict. After Matthew's account records that the Pharisees "conspired against Him, as to how they might destroy Him" (Mt. 12:14), it then says that **Jesus, aware of this, withdrew from there** (Mt. 12:15a). This was Christ's first withdrawal in an attempt to defuse the tension. There would be others.

Jesus withdrew to the sea [that is, the Sea of Galilee] **with His disciples** (Mk. 3:7a). Even there, people found Him: . . . **and a great multitude from Galilee followed; and also from Judea, and from Jerusalem, and from Idumea, and beyond the Jordan, and the vicinity of Tyre and Sidon** . . . (Mk. 3:7b, 8). Jesus taught the people, healed their sick, and cast out demons; but He urged everyone not to broadcast what He had done (Mt. 12:15, 16; see Mk. 3:11, 12). Additional publicity would further infuriate those who hated Him.

Matthew emphasized that everything that had happened was a fulfillment of prophecy (Mt. 12:17–21; see Is. 42:1–4). Jesus' withdrawal from the city and instructions to keep silence fulfilled the words **He will not quarrel, nor cry out; nor will anyone hear His voice in the streets** (Mt. 12:19). His healing of the sick and infirm showed His concern for those who were like **a battered reed** or like a wick almost extinguished (Mt. 12:20). The coming of people from outside Palestine (from Idumea, Tyre, and Sidon) stressed the significance of Jesus' ministry for the Gentiles (Mt. 12:18, 21).

Jesus was continuing to teach and heal, but He was also going out of His way to avoid an immediate showdown with the Jewish leaders.

AFTER PRAYER, JESUS SELECTED TWELVE APOSTLES (MT. 10:2–4; MK. 3:13–19; LK. 6:12–16)

Matthew 10:2–4
²**Now the names of the twelve apostles are these: The first, Simon, who is called Peter, and Andrew his brother; and James the son of Zebedee, and John his brother; ³Philip and Bartholomew; Thomas and Matthew the tax collector; James the son**

of Alphaeus, and Thaddaeus; [4]Simon the Zealot, and Judas
Iscariot, the one who betrayed Him.

Mark 3:13–19

[13]And He went up on the mountain and summoned those
whom He Himself wanted, and they came to Him. [14]And He
appointed twelve, so that they would be with Him and that
He could send them out to preach, [15]and to have authority to
cast out the demons. [16]And He appointed the twelve: Simon (to
whom He gave the name Peter), [17]and James, the son of Zebedee,
and John the brother of James (to them He gave the name
Boanerges, which means, "Sons of Thunder"); [18]and Andrew,
and Philip, and Bartholomew, and Matthew, and Thomas, and
James the son of Alphaeus, and Thaddaeus, and Simon the
Zealot; [19]and Judas Iscariot, who betrayed Him.

Luke 6:12–16

[12]It was at this time that He went off to the mountain to
pray, and He spent the whole night in prayer to God. [13]And
when day came, He called His disciples to Him and chose
twelve of them, whom He also named as apostles: [14]Simon,
whom He also named Peter, and Andrew his brother; and
James and John; and Philip and Bartholomew; [15]and Matthew
and Thomas; James the son of Alphaeus, and Simon who was
called the Zealot; [16]Judas the son of James, and Judas Iscariot,
who became a traitor.

Jesus' next response to increasing hostility was to select
twelve men to carry on His work when He was gone. His days
were obviously numbered, and it was imperative that special
men be trained before His death. Mark explained that these
were selected **that they would be with Him and that He could
send them out to preach** (Mk. 3:14). They would travel with
Him and learn from His teaching and His example. He would
also send them on special missions so they might gain experience. Thus they would be taught and trained. From this time,
much of Christ's effort was directed toward the preparation of
the apostles.

The choosing of the Twelve was not done without consulting God. Before Jesus made His decisions, He **went off to the mountain to pray, and He spent the whole night in prayer to God** (Lk. 6:12). All decisions should be preceded by prayer.

Jesus had gathered around Himself a number of full-time disciples. After the night of prayer, He summoned these **and chose twelve of them** (Lk. 6:13a). He called the ones selected **apostles** (Lk. 6:13b; see Mt. 10:2). The word "apostle" means "one sent." The word can be used in a general way to refer to anyone sent on a special mission. Jesus Himself was called an apostle because He was sent by God (Heb. 3:1). For other examples of the term "apostle" being used in a general sense, see Acts 14:14; Romans 16:7; 2 Corinthians 8:23; Philippians 2:25. (The Greek word ἀπόστολος [apostolos] is translated as "messenger" in some places.) However, the word has an added importance regarding the twelve who would be commissioned by Jesus Himself.

The fact that *twelve* were chosen is significant: The number "twelve" had special meaning to the Jews; in Hebrew thought, it suggested religious completeness. There had been twelve patriarchs and twelve tribes of Israel; now Jesus selected twelve apostles.

Mark's list of the apostles reads like this:

> . . . **Simon (to whom He gave the name Peter), and James, the son of Zebedee, and John the brother of James (to them He gave the name Boanerges, which means, "Sons of Thunder"); and Andrew, and Philip, and Bartholomew, and Matthew, and Thomas, and James the son of Alphaeus, and Thaddaeus, and Simon the Zealot; and Judas Iscariot, who betrayed Him** (Mk. 3:16–19).

Here is Luke's list:

> **Simon, whom He also named Peter, and Andrew his brother; and James and John; and Philip and Bartholomew; and Matthew and Thomas; James the son of**

Alphaeus, and Simon who was called the Zealot; Judas the son of James, and Judas Iscariot, who became a traitor (Lk. 6:14–16).

Matthew did not give his list until a later occasion (when Jesus sent the Twelve on a training mission). However, that list should be included for the purpose of comparison:

Now the names of the twelve apostles are these: The first, Simon, who is called Peter, and Andrew his brother; and James the son of Zebedee, and John his brother; Philip and Bartholomew; Thomas and Matthew the tax collector; James the son of Alphaeus, and Thaddaeus; Simon the Zealot, and Judas Iscariot, the one who betrayed Him (Mt. 10:2–4).

A fourth and final list is found in Acts 1, prior to the time when Judas was replaced:

. . . Peter and John and James and Andrew, Philip and Thomas, Bartholomew and Matthew, James the son of Alphaeus, and Simon the Zealot, and Judas the son of James (Acts 1:13).

There is value in comparing the four lists. Notice, for example, that Peter heads each list. This does not prove that Peter was "the first pope," but it does suggest that his impetuosity and considerable talent made him a natural leader among the apostles. We also see that the name of Judas concludes the first three lists. His act of infamy qualified him for that dubious distinction.

Other details could be pointed out. For instance, there are several sets of brothers (Thaddaeus was apparently also known as "Judas the son of James"). Perhaps most significant is that each list in the Gospel Accounts can be broken into three sets of four—and the same individual heads each set in each list. Peter heads the first group, Philip heads the second group, while James the son of Alphaeus heads the third. Since there is considerable variation in the arrangement of names within each group, the uniform placement of these three names seems deliberate. Peter, Philip, and James the son of Alphaeus may have been "group leaders" regarding training missions and other special projects.

We have already met several of the selected men: Peter and Andrew (Jn. 1:40, 41; Mt. 4:18), James and John (Mt. 4:21), Philip and perhaps Bartholomew (Jn. 1:43, 45), and Matthew (Mt. 9:9). Little is said concerning the others in the New Testament, but we know three key details concerning them. First, they would all have been called as Peter, Andrew, James, John, and Matthew were called. Second, like Peter and the others, they were evidently chosen because of their potential, not because of previous spiritual attainments. Third, they would all be empowered by Jesus to teach and cast out demons (see Mt. 10:1). Each of these details would even apply to Judas Iscariot.

SECTION II

THE SERMON ON THE MOUNT

Includes a Harmony of

Mt. 5:1—7:29

Lk. 6:17–49

John Stott wrote,

> The Sermon on the Mount is probably the best-known part of the teaching of Jesus, though arguably it is the least understood, and certainly it is the least obeyed. It is the nearest thing to a manifesto that he ever uttered, for it is his own description of what he wanted his followers to be and to do.[1]

E. Stanley Jones said, "The greatest need of modern Christianity is the rediscovery of the sermon on the Mount as the only practical way to live."[2] Harvey Scott called Matthew 5—7 "the constitution of Christianity."[3]

The Sermon on the Mount abounds in contrasts. The first half features contrasts between what the Jews had been taught and what Jesus taught. The second half is characterized by contrasts between the two ways a man can choose to go. Christ urged His listeners, "Enter through the narrow gate; for the gate is wide and the way is broad that leads to destruction, and there are many who enter through it. For the gate is small and the way is narrow that leads to life, and there are few who find it" (Mt. 7:13, 14). (The KJV has the word "strait" twice in these verses. "Strait" means "narrow," but many, when they hear the word, think of "straight"—the shortest distance between two points.) Matthew 6:19—7:27 is filled with examples of the two pathways we can

---

[1]John R. W. Stott, *The Message of the Sermon on the Mount* (Downers Grove, Ill.: Inter-Varsity Press, 1978), 15.

[2]E. Stanley Jones, *The Christ of the Mount* (Nashville: Abingdon Press, 1931), 14.

[3]Harvey Scott, *The Sermon on the Mount* (Texarkana, Tex.: The Christian Helper, 1947), 3.

travel. This text confronts us with choices we must make: choices that will lead to life or to destruction.

INTRODUCTORY STATEMENTS
(MT. 5:1, 2; LK. 6:17–20)

Matthew 5:1, 2
¹When Jesus saw the crowds, He went up on the mountain; and after He sat down, His disciples came to Him. ²He opened His mouth and began to teach them, saying.

Luke 6:17–20
¹⁷Jesus came down with them and stood on a level place; and there was a large crowd of His disciples, and a great throng of people from all Judea and Jerusalem and the coastal region of Tyre and Sidon, ¹⁸who had come to hear Him and to be healed of their diseases; and those who were troubled with unclean spirits were being cured. ¹⁹And all the people were trying to touch Him, for power was coming from Him and healing them all.

²⁰And turning His gaze toward His disciples, He began to say, "Blessed are you who are poor, for yours is the kingdom of God."

Jesus had chosen men to carry on His work after His death. His initial act of preparing them was to deliver a comprehensive discourse on what would be expected of citizens in the Messianic kingdom. This we know as "The Sermon on the Mount."

Many were privileged to hear this masterful presentation (Mt. 5:1; 7:28; Lk. 6:17; 7:1), but it was specifically directed to Jesus' disciples (Mt. 5:1, 2; Lk. 6:20). We may think of it as an orientation session for the newly appointed apostles.

The discourse touches on the attitude necessary to *become* a citizen of the kingdom (see Mt. 5:3–6; 6:33; 7:21, 24–27). Primarily, though, it deals with how one who is *already* a follower of Jesus should conduct himself.

Jesus was addressing a Jewish audience during the Jewish Dispensation. He thus referred to the Jewish supreme court (the Sanhedrin) (Mt. 5:22), to sacrifices at the altar (Mt. 5:23), and to Jerusalem as "the city of [God]" (Mt. 5:35). However, these words have been preserved as part of the New Testament of Jesus; so, in making application, we need to adapt the terminology to Christian concepts. For instance, "if you are presenting your offering at the altar" (Mt. 5:23) suggests the idea "if you come to worship God."

The better known version of this sermon is found in Matthew 5—7, but a shorter version appears in Luke 6:20–49. There are differences in the two accounts. For instance, Matthew has 107 verses while Luke has 30 verses, and the wording is different. These particular differences should not cause concern. Each writer presented the portion of the sermon suited to his inspired purposes. All but six verses of Matthew's account of the sermon are found elsewhere in the Book of Luke—and slightly different wording is to be expected from independent witnesses. Most agree that both Matthew and Luke give a summary of what Jesus said, not every word that was spoken.

According to Matthew, Jesus **went up on the mountain** and **sat down** (Mt. 5:1) before He taught. In contrast, Luke wrote that, prior to Jesus' teaching, He **stood on a level place** (Lk. 6:17). It is not impossible, however, to reconcile the two. Jesus could first have healed the multitudes as He stood on a level place at the foot of the mountain (Lk. 6:12, 17–19), and then He could have withdrawn a short distance up the mountainside and sat down to teach His disciples—with the multitudes remaining within hearing distance. According to Jerome, an early Christian writer, in his day it was commonly thought that the sermon was preached on the mountain called the Horns of Hattin, which has a level place where a crowd could assemble.

The fact that the sermons in Matthew and Luke begin in a similar way (Mt. 5:3–12; Lk. 6:20–23), end in a similar way (Mt. 7:24–27; Lk. 6:47–49), and follow the same general order in the middle seems to indicate that the two sermons are the same. Whether they are or not is not a matter of great importance. If they are not the same sermon, they are similar sermons preached during approximately the same period of time to the same basic audience. (Compare Mt. 5:1; 8:1, 5 with Lk. 6:17, 20; 7:1.) For this reason, they can be studied together. Since Matthew's account is better known and more comprehensive, his version will be our primary source, and Luke's account will serve as a supplementary source.

THE BEATITUDES: PROMISES TO THE MESSIAH'S SUBJECTS (MT. 5:3–12; LK. 6:20–26)

Matthew 5:3–12

[3]"Blessed are the poor in spirit, for theirs is the kingdom of heaven.

[4]"Blessed are those who mourn, for they shall be comforted.

[5]"Blessed are the gentle, for they shall inherit the earth.

[6]"Blessed are those who hunger and thirst for righteousness, for they shall be satisfied.

[7]"Blessed are the merciful, for they shall receive mercy.

[8]"Blessed are the pure in heart, for they shall see God.

[9]"Blessed are the peacemakers, for they shall be called sons of God.

[10]"Blessed are those who have been persecuted for the sake of righteousness, for theirs is the kingdom of heaven.

[11]"Blessed are you when people insult you and persecute you, and falsely say all kinds of evil against you because of Me. [12]Rejoice and be glad, for your reward in heaven is great; for in the same way they persecuted the prophets who were before you."

Luke 6:20–26

[20]And turning His gaze toward His disciples, He began to say, "Blessed are you who are poor, for yours is the kingdom of God. [21]Blessed are you who hunger now, for you shall be satisfied. Blessed are you who weep now, for you shall laugh. [22]Blessed are you when men hate you, and ostracize you, and insult you, and scorn your name as evil, for the sake of the Son

of Man. ²³Be glad in that day and leap for joy, for behold, your reward is great in heaven. For in the same way their fathers used to treat the prophets. ²⁴But woe to you who are rich, for you are receiving your comfort in full. ²⁵Woe to you who are well-fed now, for you shall be hungry. Woe to you who laugh now, for you shall mourn and weep. ²⁶Woe to you when all men speak well of you, for their fathers used to treat the false prophets in the same way."

The sermon starts with a series of statements, each of which begins with the word **blessed**. These are called "the Beatitudes." This designation comes from the Latin version of the Bible, where the first word in each sentence is *beati*, the Latin word for "blessed" or "happy."

To anyone who reads the Sermon on the Mount, it is obvious that following Jesus is not easy (Mt. 5:10–12). Christ therefore began with words of encouragement, enumerating how people would be blessed if they heard His words and acted on them (see 7:24, 25). To some extent, faithful disciples enjoy these blessings in this life, but their full realization will be in the life to come. Luke's account includes *woes* that will fall upon those who are unwilling to submit to Jesus (Lk. 6:24–26).

INFLUENCE (AND RESPONSIBILITIES) OF THE MESSIAH'S SUBJECTS (MT. 5:13–16)

¹³"You are the salt of the earth; but if the salt has become tasteless, how can it be made salty again? It is no longer good for anything, except to be thrown out and trampled under foot by men.

¹⁴"You are the light of the world. A city set on a hill cannot be hidden; ¹⁵nor does anyone light a lamp and put it under a basket, but on the lampstand, and it gives light to all who are in the house. ¹⁶Let your light shine before men in such a way that they may see your good works, and glorify your Father who is in heaven."

The Beatitudes established that following Jesus would bring

blessings to the followers. Christ next declared that doing His will would also bless others—as He spoke of His disciples being **the salt of the earth** and **the light of the world**. Many passages in the Bible teach on the power and importance of influence (for example, Prov. 27:17; Hos. 4:9; 1 Cor. 5:6; 15:33; Phil. 2:15; 1 Pet. 2:12), but none is more challenging and thought-provoking than Matthew 5:13–16.

APPLICATION:
YOU ARE MORE VALUABLE
THAN YOU THINK (MT. 5:13)

Salt and light are two of the most common elements on the earth. Go anywhere in the world, and you will find salt and light. These were just as common in Jesus' day. As a boy, Jesus would have seen His mother salting the meat, and each evening He would have seen her lighting her tiny lamps. As ordinary as they were, however, Jesus used salt and light to give Christians one of their greatest compliments—and to set forth some of their greatest challenges:

> You are the salt of the earth; but if the salt has become tasteless, how can it be made salty again? It is no longer good for anything, except to be thrown out and trampled under foot by men.
> You are the light of the world. A city set on a hill cannot be hidden; nor does anyone light a lamp and put it under a basket, but on the lampstand, and it gives light to all who are in the house. Let your light shine before men in such a way that they may see your good works, and glorify your Father who is in heaven (Mt. 5:13–16).

These words are the second main section in the Sermon on the Mount. Christ had just given the Beatitudes, outlining the type of character required to be His disciple. Next, He told of the *effect* of that character, as He said, "You are the salt of the earth"; "You are the light of the world." This is perhaps the greatest passage in the Bible on the power of Christian influence.

Salt and light were and still are tremendously important. Life cannot be sustained without salt and light. The physical body requires salt to function, and physical life cannot exist without light. If the sun were suddenly extinguished, in a matter of hours our planet would be covered with ice. When Jesus said that we as Christians are salt and light, He was saying that we are extremely important—and that His purposes cannot be accomplished without us.

In this study, we will discuss being the salt of the earth. In the next, we will talk about being the light of the world.

A Compliment

When Jesus said, "You are the salt of the earth," His words were, first of all, a compliment. This is where we get the expression "He's the salt of the earth."

Jesus did not address this tribute to Jewish religious leaders or Roman senators or Athenian philosophers, but to His listeners: farmers, fishermen, merchants, and their wives and children. He praised what the world calls "ordinary people."

The statement "You are the salt of the earth" says something about the earth, and it says something about followers of Christ. To appreciate the importance of the words, we must understand the role of salt in Bible times.

Salt Was Valuable

Salt was valued in Jesus' day. It was often used as a medium of exchange or to pay wages. This is the source of the expression "He's worth his salt."

Jesus said, "You are the salt of the earth"—and salt has value. What does this say about the earth? It says that this earth has no real value. What does this say about Christians? It says that Christians do have worth—and that the only importance that this world has comes from the presence of Christians.

If you are a Christian, you are valuable in God's eyes. Do not sell yourself short.

Salt Gave Flavor

In those days, as today, one of the uses of salt was to add to the flavor of food. Job asked, "Can something tasteless be eaten without salt, or is there any taste in the white of an egg?" (Job 6:6). The patriarch then pronounced unsalted food "loathsome" (Job 6:7).

The following story is an illustration of the great worth of salt:

> A king asked his three daughters how much they loved him. Two of them replied that they loved him better than all the gold and silver in the world. The youngest one said she loved him better than salt. The king was not pleased with her answer, as he thought that salt was not very palatable. But the cook, overhearing the remark, put no salt in anything for breakfast [the] next morning, and the meal was so insipid that the king could not enjoy it. He then saw the force of his daughter's remarks. She loved him so well that nothing was good without him.[4]

Those who have to live on "salt-free" diets struggle with how to improve the flavor of food without adding salt. Salt substitutes help, but none is as effective as "adding a dash of salt."

"You are the salt of the earth"—and salt adds flavor. What does this say about the earth? It says that this earth is insipid, that in the long run everything this world has to offer ends up tasteless. What does it say about you as a Christian? It says that you are what gives zest to life. Do not sell yourself short.

Salt Had Multiple Uses

Much more could be said about the value of salt. For instance, salt can create thirst. You have probably heard the expression "You can lead a horse to water, but you can't make him drink." That statement needs an addendum: ". . . but you can feed him salt." When I was a boy, I occasionally did this when showing animals at fairs. If one of my show animals looked gaunt, I put a little salt

---

[4]A. C. Dixon, quoted in Leslie G. Thomas, *The Sermon on the Mount: A Series of Studies in the Moral and Religious Teaching of Jesus* (Nashville: Gospel Advocate Co., 1958), 22.

in his feed. This made him drink more water and fill out. This can apply to us: As Christians, we can create a thirst for the Water of Life (Jn. 4:10–15) by the lives we lead.

Also, salt was sometimes used as a symbol of purity in Jesus' day. Further, it was added to Jewish sacrifices (Lev. 2:13). All of this says something about the value of Christians.

Salt Was a Preservative

Probably the most important use of salt in Bible times, and that which gave it its greatest value, was its use as a preservative. In those days, you could not go to the city and buy a refrigerator or freezer in which to keep meat cold and fresh. Fresh meat spoiled quickly; that is the nature of meat.

When I was growing up, my family took one real vacation that I remember. For this trip, we got in the car and headed eastward, traveling through eastern Oklahoma and parts of Arkansas. While we were gone, the gas company turned off the gas to work on the gas lines—and we had a gas refrigerator. When we got home, we had a refrigerator full of rotten meat. Mother did everything she could to get the smell out of the refrigerator. It stood with its door open in our back yard for weeks as she waited for the smell to abate. As long as we had that appliance, it had a peculiar, pungent aroma.

What did people do in Bible times to preserve meat? They rubbed salt into it. Fishermen packed their fish in salt. It was not that people loved the taste of salt that much; rather, it was that they had to salt their meat if they did not want it to spoil. Some of you may have done your own butchering, curing hams with salt or making salt pork to prevent spoilage.

"You are the salt of the earth"—and salt preserves. What does this say about the earth? It says that this earth is decaying, putrefying, rotting. This is basic to our understanding of the world. No matter how glamorous it may appear, it is actually dying and disintegrating before our eyes. This world puts on a beautiful face; but if you look closely, it is all paint and powder. Beneath the brilliant colors is a faded, wrinkled reality.

This truth is readily apparent to anyone with even a limited knowledge of biblical teaching. Statistics are unnecessary. You can look at the declining moral standards of the world, the shortage of honesty and integrity, and the lack of interest in spiritual matters. Nothing about this world can attract the one who sees beneath the surface.

In contrast, what does this say about Christians? It says that Christians are the preserving power of the earth.

In recent decades, various factors have been hailed as this earth's hope and salvation: science, education, psychology and psychiatry, technology, better living conditions, legislation, social reform, and military might. Mankind has made progress in all of these areas—significant progress in some—yet the world seems to get increasingly worse. Jesus said that the only real hope for the world is faithful Christians.

As a small amount of salt can preserve a large piece of meat, so a few dedicated Christians can preserve society. Do you remember the story of Abraham and the destruction of Sodom and Gomorrah (Gen. 18)? Ten—as few as ten—righteous people would have preserved those cities (Gen. 18:32). Imagine someone going to the Chamber of Commerce in Sodom and Gomorrah and saying, "Much of what you have accomplished is impressive; but if you want these great cities to see another day, you had better move in ten folk like old Abraham who lives up there on the hill." How would they have responded? Regardless of what their response might have been, ten people like Abraham *would* have preserved those cities.

Let us pause to anticipate a contrast. Light influences by what it *does*, while salt influences by what it *is*. As faithful children of God, we do not flaunt our Christianity, but people know who we are and what we stand for. When we walk into a room, it is not uncommon for the language and the jokes to be cleaned up. People may try to embarrass us: "We can't tell that story. What's-his-name is here now!" Our presence—just the *fact* of our presence—makes a difference. Salt influences by what it *is*.

Jesus spoke these words to what the world considers "ordinary" people. In the original language, the word "you" is emphasized: Jesus said, *"You* are the salt of the earth." His statement is inclusive and exclusive: It includes all His followers and excludes everyone other than His followers. Jesus did not say this to the religious, financial, social, or political leaders of His day, but rather to the "ordinary" salt-of-the-earth people willing to follow Him.

A Challenge

When Jesus said, "You are the salt of the earth," this was not only a compliment, but also a challenge. Salt has value and has the capacity to be a preservative *because it has a distinctive quality*. As Christians, we, too, need a distinctive quality. One way of expressing this quality is to say that we must be *different* from the world.

> And do not be conformed to this world, but be transformed by the renewing of your mind . . . (Rom. 12:2).

> . . . do you not know that friendship with the world is hostility toward God? Therefore whoever wishes to be a friend of the world makes himself an enemy of God (Jas. 4:4).

> Do not love the world nor the things in the world. If anyone loves the world, the love of the Father is not in him (1 Jn. 2:15).

If salt had the same composition as meat, it could not preserve the meat. If we are like the world, we have no preserving quality. This does not mean that we are to be odd, but it does mean that we are to be distinctive.

Can people look at us and see that we are Christians—by what we do, by the way we talk, by the topics we discuss, by the way we dress, by the way we meet difficulties? Being a Christian should affect how we treat our families, how we talk to shopkeepers, how we play our games.

Jesus did not say, "You are the salt of *the church*," but rather, "You are the salt of *the earth*." Polls indicate that most church activities take place in church buildings. We need to be "salt" where other people are: in the marketplace, in the schoolroom, in the office. Jesus was the friend of sinners (Mt. 11:19). A book called

Out of the Salt Shaker & into the World[5] urges Christians to get into society, where they can have a positive influence on others.

Wherever you go, wherever you are, you are commissioned to be God's preserving power. You probably visit homes, go places, and make contacts unique to you as a child of God. That is God's special place for you, your special place of influence. Never forget the challenge of being "the salt of the earth."

In the last part of verse 13, Jesus emphasized the seriousness of this challenge: ". . . but if the salt has become tasteless, how can it be made salty again? It is no longer good for anything, except to be thrown out and trampled under foot by men." The KJV speaks of the salt losing its "savour." The NIV has "If the salt loses its saltiness, how can it be made salty again?"

Many of us have difficulty understanding how salt can lose its taste and saltiness, since we buy pure white salt in a box. That salt is always going to be salty. Even if only one grain is left, that grain will be salty. Salt in Bible times, however, was the result of the evaporation of sea water. That salt naturally contained impurities. If the salt was scraped off the ground, some sand or dirt was invariably mixed with the salt. If the resulting salty mass was exposed to the elements, much of the sodium chloride could leach out. What was left was a substance with enough salt to sterilize the earth, but not enough to be of value. That "salt" had lost its distinctive quality.

Good land was at a premium in the land of Palestine. They used every available inch for the production of crops. Crisscrossing the fields were narrow paths used by the farmers. People did not dare throw salt that had "lost its saltiness" on a field, because that would destroy the fertility of the soil. Instead, they threw the salty mass on the paths, where it could do no damage. There it was "trampled under foot by men."

This illustration is Jesus' sad commentary on the Christian who makes no attempt to realize his potential as "the salt of the earth." His stark conclusion is that such a person is "good for nothing."

---

[5]Rebecca Manley Pippert, *Out of the Salt Shaker & into the World* (Downers Grove, Ill.: InterVarsity Press, 1979).

Conclusion

Salt is an ordinary item used by Jesus to teach invaluable lessons. All of us are impressed with the words "You are the salt of the earth." Jesus paid us a great compliment when He spoke those words. We are special to the Lord; we have value. Let us never sell ourselves short.

He also gave us a great challenge. No greater insult can be spoken against a man than to say that he is "good for nothing." We do not want to be "good for nothing" spiritually. Let us determine to live a distinctive life, different from the world. God help us all to be "the salt of the earth."

APPLICATION:
"LET YOUR LIGHT SHINE" (MT. 5:14–16)

Focus your attention on Matthew 5:14–16:

> "You are the light of the world. A city set on a hill cannot be hidden; nor does anyone light a lamp and put it under a basket, but on the lampstand, and it gives light to all who are in the house. Let your light shine before men in such a way that they may see your good works, and glorify your Father who is in heaven."

A Compliment

"You are the light of the world." These words tell us that, as Christians, we not only participate in God's plans and purposes but, to some extent, we also share in the *characteristics* of God and Jesus. John said, "God is Light" (1 Jn. 1:5). Jesus said, "I am the Light of the world" (Jn. 8:12). Through these verses, Jesus points to His followers and says, *"You* are the light of the world."

What did Jesus mean by the expression "You are the light of the world"? Consider a contrast between salt and light. The primary purpose of salt in those days was largely *negative*: to prevent decay. The primary purpose of light is *positive*: to dispel darkness.

Jesus' imagery tells us something about the world and something about Christians. This world is in *darkness*. Those in the world do not like to admit this. Sometimes when people reject the Bible, they say, "We live in an *enlightened* age." You may have heard the expression "New evidence has come to *light*." The fact, however, is that this world is shrouded in the darkness of sin. Every intellect not illuminated by God's holy Word is a darkened intellect.

The world actually prefers darkness. Light exposes "the hidden things of darkness" (1 Cor. 4:5; KJV). Jesus said that the people of His day "loved the darkness rather than the Light, for their deeds were evil" (Jn. 3:19). My wife and I once owned some rental property. After one family moved out, we went over the next evening to inspect the house. They had left it in a terrible condition, full of filth. When we turned on the light, thousands of roaches scampered in every direction. Roaches do not like the light—and neither does a sinful world. Nevertheless, light is precisely what the world *needs*.

Our text not only declares that the world is in darkness, but it also says that Christians are the *light* of this world. *Christians* are the ones who have the light. If you know Jesus and the Bible, then you know more about marriage, parenting, how to deal with problems, and what life is all about than any PhD who is not a Christian.

As Jesus' followers, we are to let our light *shine*. We let it shine by leading the right kind of life. We let it shine by teaching God's Word.

I do not like the moral and spiritual darkness in the world. I must confess that the darkness discourages me. Sometimes the darkness grows so thick that I feel like giving up. At times like that, I have to remind myself that light has no purpose if there is no darkness. The purpose of light is to dispel darkness. That is why God put me at this place at this time.

A pertinent passage is Philippians 2:15, 16. Paul challenged his readers "to be blameless and innocent, children of God above reproach *in the midst of a crooked and perverse generation, among whom you appear as lights* in the world. . . ." (Emphasis added.)

The blacker the darkness is, the more brilliant the light appears. An appliance in my bedroom has a little green bulb that burns all the time. In the daytime, the light is not even noticeable. At night, however, after my eyes adjust to the darkness, I can see everything in the room in the soft, green glow. Even a tiny light has value when everything else is dark.

We are not "light" because of some inherent illuminating power within us. Rather, we are "light" because of our connection with the sources of light: God and Jesus. Christians are comparable to the moon as it reflects the light of the sun. We may also be compared to light bulbs that shine because of an external power source. Nevertheless, Jesus has greatly honored us with the words "You are the light of the world."

A Challenge

Christ's words are not just a compliment, but also a challenge: We must let our light *shine*.

Jesus said, "A city set on a hill cannot be hidden" (Mt. 5:14b). In those days, cities were built on hills or mountains for at least two reasons. The first was a practical reason: This would not waste valuable farming land. The second was a protection reason: From the top of a hill, the inhabitants of the city could see their enemies approaching below. Cities "set on a hill" were generally easier to defend. As a traveler went through the land, he could always tell when he was coming to a city: There it was, sitting on a hill. Jesus' point was that, even as men did not hide their cities, so we should not hide our light (our influence). That application is clear in the words that follow.

Jesus continued, "Nor does anyone light a lamp and put it under a basket" (Mt. 5:15a). The KJV has "Neither do men . . . put it under a bushel." This confused me when I was a child, because the bushel baskets we used were porous. If I had placed a candle or lamp under one of those baskets, light would have streamed through the cracks. The 1995 edition of the NASB has "a peck-measure." This was a large earthen bowl capable of holding about a peck, which is the equivalent of eight quarts (one-fourth of a bushel), or 8.81 liters. Placing a lamp under one of those solid containers would effectively nullify its light. It would also eventually *extinguish* the light when the oxygen ran out—but Jesus' primary emphasis was on *hiding* the light.

The illustration of putting our light under a peck-measure has the same basic meaning as the illustration of salt losing its saltiness in the application "You Are More Valuable Than You Think." Unsalty "salt" has no value; neither does a hidden light. Even as it was possible for a salty mass to lose its saltiness, it is possible for light to lose its power to dispel darkness. How can that happen? The light can be hidden. Unfortunately, many who have claimed to follow Jesus have hidden their light under "the bushel" of ignorance, the "bushel" of worldliness, or the "bushel" of halfheartedness. Regarding the last category, God said, "I hate those who are double-minded" (Ps. 119:113a)—that is, those with a divided allegiance. Moffatt translated this verse, "I hate men who are half and half."[6]

In Jesus' day, people did not put lamps under bowls; rather, they put their lamps on lampstands (Mt. 5:15b). These stands were high on the walls. Sometimes the stand was a niche in the wall; often it was a small shelf of wood or metal. Placed on such a stand, a lamp could give "light to all who are in the house" (Mt. 5:15c). Even so, Jesus said, "Let *your* light shine before men" (Mt. 5:16a; emphasis added).

How do we do that? Jesus said, "Let your light shine before men in such a way *that they may see your good works*" (Mt. 5:16a, b; emphasis added). As we do "good works"—by living as we should and helping others—we are letting our light shine.

I anticipate a protest from those familiar with the Sermon on the Mount. In the next chapter, Jesus warned against praying and fasting to be "seen by men" (Mt. 6:5; see 6:16). What is the difference between doing something *to be* seen and doing something that *is* seen? The answer is "attitude and purpose." There is a vast difference between doing good works to be seen of men so that others might praise *us*, and allowing others to see our good works so that they will glorify *God*.

If our light is to do any good, men must *see* it. Someone has said that, ultimately, there is no such thing as secret discipleship. Either the secrecy will destroy the discipleship or the disciple-

---

[6]James Moffatt, *The Bible: A New Translation* (New York: Harper & Brothers, 1954), 685.

ship will destroy the secrecy.

Why are we to let our light shine? We are not to seek personal aggrandizement; rather, we should seek to glorify God. The purpose of light is not to call attention to itself, but to illuminate that on which its beams are shed. Our purpose in leading the godly Christian life is not to call attention to ourselves, but rather (as Jesus said) to "glorify [our] Father who is in heaven" (Mt. 5:16c).

Conclusion

Salt and light are important. We think we need many things, but only a handful are essential. Among the essentials are salt and light; we would not want to be without them. Jesus said, "You are the salt of the earth"; "You are the light of the world." We should appreciate the compliment imbedded in those sentences.

How is the church known? When people mention the church, what do they say? Do their words indicate that it *stands for* something (that it is "salt") and that it is *doing* something for the Lord (that it is "light")?

Often we cry about the sinful world that surrounds us. We ask, *"Why?* Why is it getting so bad?" Perhaps we should ask, *"Where?* Where are the salt and the light?" May God help each of us to be "the salt of the earth" and "the light of the world."

THE RELATIONSHIP OF MESSIANIC TEACHING TO THE OLD TESTAMENT AND TO MAN-MADE TRADITIONS CONCERNING OLD TESTAMENT TEACHING (MT. 5:17–48; LK. 6:27–30, 32–36)

The longest segment of the Sermon on the Mount is Matthew 5:17–48, which contrasts the law of Moses—and related man-made traditions—with Jesus' teaching. It was essential that Christ's disciples have a clear understanding of His relationship to the Law and also His attitude toward the many traditions that men had tacked onto the Law.

The introductory statement is significant. Jesus began,

Do not think that I came to abolish the Law or the Prophets; I did not come to abolish but to fulfill. For truly I say to you, until heaven and earth pass away, not the smallest letter or stroke shall pass from the Law until all is accomplished (Mt. 5:17, 18).

The fact that Jesus came not "to abolish but to fulfill" the Law has led some to believe that we are still under the Old Testament today. This interpretation of Christ's words would make Him contradict the plain teaching of His inspired apostles. Paul wrote of Jesus' "abolishing in His flesh . . . the Law of commandments contained in ordinances, so that in Himself He might make the two [Jew and Gentile] into one new man" (Eph. 2:15). The apostle further said, concerning the "decrees" of the Law, that Jesus had taken that set of ordinances out of the way, "having nailed it to the cross" (Col. 2:14, 16).

Christ's words in Matthew 5:17, 18 can be understood by considering that the Old Testament was a covenant, an agreement between God and the Jews (see Deut. 4:13; 5:2, 3). Think of the Old Testament as a *contract* between God and Israel. Jesus did not come to "abolish" that contract (toss it aside or destroy it) but to "fulfill" it. This He did in His life, death, and resurrection. Will Ed Warren wrote, "He fulfilled its prophecies, He kept the demands of the Law, and accomplished the Law's purposes (Gal. 3:19; 5:14)."[7]

A fulfilled covenant/contract is no longer a binding covenant/contract. For instance, consider what happens when a person signs a contract concerning the purchase of a piece of property. Once he has fulfilled that contract by meeting all the conditions (including making all the payments), it becomes a *fulfilled* contract; it is no longer binding. Even so, when Jesus fulfilled the Law, it ceased to be binding on God's people (see Gal. 3:16, 19, 24, 25).

---

[7]Will Ed Warren, Class Syllabus, *The Life of Christ: The Synoptic Gospels*, (Searcy, Ark: Harding University, 1991), 26.

At the time Jesus preached on the mount, however, the Law was still in force. As long as that was the case, Christ taught His disciples to honor its demands (Mt. 5:19, 20). His objection was not to the Law, but to Jewish misinterpretations of the Law.

In the verses that follow, Jesus expanded several commandments of the Law to include the attitude of heart essential to keeping the commandments. He also contrasted His way with the way that the people had been taught by the scribes and the Pharisees.

Murder—and Anger (Mt. 5:21–26)

[21]"You have heard that the ancients were told, 'You shall not commit murder' and 'Whoever commits murder shall be liable to the court.' [22]But I say to you that everyone who is angry with his brother shall be guilty before the court; and whoever says to his brother, 'You good-for-nothing,' shall be guilty before the supreme court; and whoever says, 'You fool,' shall be guilty enough to go into the fiery hell. [23]Therefore if you are presenting your offering at the altar, and there remember that your brother has something against you, [24]leave your offering there before the altar and go; first be reconciled to your brother, and then come and present your offering. [25]Make friends quickly with your opponent at law while you are with him on the way, so that your opponent may not hand you over to the judge, and the judge to the officer, and you be thrown into prison. [26]Truly I say to you, you will not come out of there until you have paid up the last cent."

In the Ten Commandments, commandment six said, "You shall not murder" (Ex. 20:13; Deut. 5:17). This basic requirement has been incorporated into the new covenant (Rom. 13:9), but Jesus expanded the original commandment to include a warning against the *motive* for murder and the circumstances that can lead to murder (Mt. 5:22). He entreated all who have strong disagreements with others to work out their differences—at once (Mt. 5:23–26).

235

Adultery—and Lust (Mt. 5:27–30)

²⁷"You have heard that it was said, 'You shall not commit adultery'; ²⁸but I say to you that everyone who looks at a woman with lust for her has already committed adultery with her in his heart. ²⁹If your right eye makes you stumble, tear it out and throw it from you; for it is better for you to lose one of the parts of your body, than for your whole body to be thrown into hell. ³⁰If your right hand makes you stumble, cut it off and throw it from you; for it is better for you to lose one of the parts of your body, than for your whole body to go into hell."

Commandment seven of the Decalogue declared, "You shall not commit adultery" (Ex. 20:14; Deut. 5:18). This precept is also part of Jesus' New Testament (Rom. 13:9), but again Christ expanded the command to include that which produces it: in this case, **lust** (Mt. 5:28). He told His followers to **tear ... out** anything in their lives that would encourage forbidden desire (Mt. 5:29, 30). Jesus was not encouraging mutilation of the body in Matthew 5:29, 30; such an act would violate biblical teaching on treating the body as the temple of God (1 Cor. 6:19; 3:17). Amputation of parts of the body would not change the condition of the heart (Mt. 15:19). Jesus was using hyperbole (exaggeration) to make His point.

Divorce—and Reason (Mt. 5:31, 32)

³¹"It was said, 'Whoever sends his wife away, let him give her a certificate of divorce'; ³²but I say to you that everyone who divorces his wife, except for the reason of unchastity, makes her commit adultery; and whoever marries a divorced woman commits adultery."

Jesus had more to say about adultery, in connection with the subject of divorce. He quoted from Deuteronomy 24:1–4, a commandment concerning giving **"a certificate of divorce"**— a commandment that has *not* been brought into the New Testament. Some scribes had interpreted Deuteronomy 24:1–4 to justify divorce "for any reason at all" (Mt. 19:3), but Jesus said that the only scriptural reason for divorce is sexual unfaithfulness on the part of one of the marriage partners (Mt. 5:32). This subject is expanded in Matthew 19:3–9.

Vows—and Integrity (Mt. 5:33–37)

³³**"Again, you have heard that the ancients were told, 'You shall not make false vows, but shall fulfill your vows to the Lord.' ³⁴But I say to you, make no oath at all, either by heaven, for it is the throne of God, ³⁵or by the earth, for it is the footstool of His feet, or by Jerusalem, for it is the city of the great King. ³⁶Nor shall you make an oath by your head, for you cannot make one hair white or black. ³⁷But let your statement be, 'Yes, yes' or 'No, no'; anything beyond these is of evil."**

The next contrast concerned the making of solemn vows. Jesus' quotation in verse 33 is how Jewish teachers summarized passages such as Leviticus 19:12; Numbers 30:2; and Deuteronomy 23:21, 23. The Jews allowed some oaths and forbade others, but Jesus said simply, **"Make no oath at all"** (Mt. 5:34; see Jas. 5:12). Christ's disciples should be so consistent in telling the truth that it is unnecessary to resort to oaths to convince others to accept their word. Note that this did not forbid civil oaths. When being tried by the Sanhedrin, Jesus answered under oath (Mt. 26:63, 64).

Retaliation—and Nonresistance (Mt. 5:38–42; Lk. 6:29, 30, 34)

Matthew 5:38–42
³⁸**"You have heard that it was said, 'An eye for an eye, and a tooth for a tooth.' ³⁹But I say to you, do not resist an evil person; but whoever slaps you on your right cheek, turn the other to him also. ⁴⁰If anyone wants to sue you and take your shirt, let him have your coat also. ⁴¹Whoever forces you to go one mile, go with him two. ⁴²Give to him who asks of you, and do not turn away from him who wants to borrow from you."**

Luke 6:29, 30, 34

²⁹"Whoever hits you on the cheek, offer him the other also; and whoever takes away your coat, do not withhold your shirt from him either. ³⁰Give to everyone who asks of you, and whoever takes away what is yours, do not demand it back."

³⁴"If you lend to those from whom you expect to receive, what credit is that to you? Even sinners lend to sinners in order to receive back the same amount."

What Jesus had said thus far must have made some of His listeners wonder if they were hearing Him correctly. If so, His last two contrasts would have staggered them.

The next contrast had to do with the principle of **"an eye for an eye, and a tooth for a tooth"** (Mt. 5:38), found in Exodus 21:24, Leviticus 24:20, and Deuteronomy 19:21. This Old Testament instruction had been primarily directed to those responsible for official judgments; one purpose had been to limit the punishment meted out. Unfortunately, the Jews had appropriated the teaching as justification for private vengeance. Some individuals still try to use this Old Testament teaching as justification for private vengeance today.

Jesus taught against retaliation and personal revenge. He commanded His followers to "go the second mile" (see Mt. 5:41) in getting along with others, even being willing to suffer mistreatment if necessary (Mt. 5:39–42; see 1 Cor. 6:7).

Verses 39 through 42 are among the most challenging in the Sermon on the Mount. Jesus' being put on trial for His life is the best illustration of the principle involved. Of course, some qualification is needed. Total nonresistance to evil would encourage wrongdoing. However, we must not qualify the passage so as to soften the radical nature of its teaching.

Enemies—and Love (Mt. 5:43–48; Lk. 6:27, 28, 33, 34, 36)

Matthew 5:43–48

⁴³"You have heard that it was said, 'You shall love your neighbor and hate your enemy.' ⁴⁴But I say to you, love your enemies

and pray for those who persecute you, [45]so that you may be sons of your Father who is in heaven; for He causes His sun to rise on the evil and the good, and sends rain on the righteous and the unrighteous. [46]For if you love those who love you, what reward do you have? Do not even the tax collectors do the same? [47]If you greet only your brothers, what more are you doing than others? Do not even the Gentiles do the same? [48]Therefore you are to be perfect, as your heavenly Father is perfect."

Luke 6:27, 28, 33, 34, 36

[27]"But I say to you who hear, love your enemies, do good to those who hate you, [28]bless those who curse you, pray for those who mistreat you."

[33]"If you do good to those who do good to you, what credit is that to you? For even sinners do the same. [34]If you lend to those from whom you expect to receive, what credit is that to you? Even sinners lend to sinners in order to receive back the same amount."

[36]"Be merciful, just as your Father is merciful."

Next, Jesus spoke about the treatment of enemies. There is a close relationship between this contrast and the previous one.

The Law commanded, "Love your neighbor" (Lev. 19:18). Jewish teachers had interpreted that to mean that as long as one loved his **"neighbor,"** it was all right to hate an enemy (Mt. 5:43)—an injunction *not* found in the Old Testament. The Old Testament did command punishment of Israel's enemies for their treatment of God's people (for instance, see Deut. 23:3–6), but it did not teach that the Jews were to hate their enemies. They were to "hate evil" (Ps. 97:10; Prov. 8:13), but not people.

Jesus heartily endorsed the principle of loving one's neighbor and made this part of His new covenant (Mt. 22:39; Rom. 13:8–10; Gal. 5:14; Jas. 2:8). However, He vehemently disagreed with the policy of hating enemies. He taught His disciples to love and pray for their enemies, to be concerned about the needs of all people, even as God is (Mt. 5:44–48).

The challenge to **be perfect** as God **is perfect** (Mt. 5:48) has concerned many, since none of us can be perfect in the sense of being sinless (Rom. 3:23). Luke's account instructs us to **be merciful** as God **is merciful** (Lk. 6:36). The teaching is that in the matter of *mercy* we are to "be perfect" as God is—*in that* we show mercy both to the righteous and to the unrighteous (Mt. 5:45).

RELIGIOUS ACTS TO BE FROM THE HEART, NOT FOR SHOW (MT. 6:1–18)

Jesus had admonished His listeners to let their righteousness surpass that "of the scribes and Pharisees" (Mt. 5:20). One shortcoming of many scribes and Pharisees was that their acts of piety were done to receive the praise of men rather than the praise of God. Jesus thus emphasized the importance of proper motivation in obeying God: **"Beware of practicing your righteousness before men to be noticed by them; otherwise you have no reward with your Father who is in heaven"** (Mt. 6:1). Jesus then gave three illustrations of what He meant.

Alms-giving (Mt. 6:2–4)

²**"So when you give to the poor, do not sound a trumpet before you, as the hypocrites do in the synagogues and in the streets, so that they may be honored by men. Truly I say to you, they have their reward in full. ³But when you give to the poor, do not let your left hand know what your right hand is doing, ⁴so that your giving will be in secret; and your Father who sees what is done in secret will reward you."**

Jesus first of all spoke of the Jewish practice of giving alms. The Greek word ἐλεημοσύνη (*eleemosune*) is translated **give to the poor**. The Old Testament taught that giving to the poor was a sacred duty (Deut. 15:11), but some Jews made a production of their giving (Mt. 6:2). Jesus urged His followers to share quietly, not calling attention to what they gave (Mt. 6:3, 4).

Some have taken Jesus' teaching about the **right hand** and **left hand** (Mt. 6:3), plus the word **secret** (Mt. 6:4), to mean that Christians must make certain that no one knows how much they give. This view of the passage would seem to contradict Jesus' previous teaching about "letting our lights shine" before others so they can *see* our good works (see Mt. 5:16). This can be reconciled by noting that there is a difference in doing that which is seen (Mt. 5:16) and in doing something *to be* seen (see Mt. 6:2, 5, 16). J. W. McGarvey was right when he wrote, "The command does not forbid publicity, but that spirit which *desires* publicity."[8]

Praying (Mt. 6:7–15)

[7]"And when you are praying, do not use meaningless repetition as the Gentiles do, for they suppose that they will be heard for their many words. [8]So do not be like them; for your Father knows what you need before you ask Him.
[9]"Pray, then, in this way:
'Our Father who is in heaven,
Hallowed be Your name.
[10]Your kingdom come.
Your will be done,
On earth as it is in heaven.
[11]Give us this day our daily bread.
[12]And forgive us our debts, as we also have forgiven our debtors.
[13]And do not lead us into temptation, but deliver us from evil. [For Yours is the kingdom and the power and the glory forever. Amen.]'
[14]For if you forgive others for their transgressions, your heavenly Father will also forgive you. [15]But if you do not forgive others, then your Father will not forgive your transgressions."

Jesus' second illustration was about praying. He condemned the public show of the hypocrites regarding their prayers, and He urged His disciples to cultivate the practice of private, personal prayers (Mt. 6:5, 6).

---

[8]J. W. McGarvey and Philip Y. Pendleton, *The Fourfold Gospel or A Harmony of the Four Gospels* (Cincinnati: Standard Publishing Co., 1914), 251.

While Jesus was on the subject of prayer, He added other observations: He condemned the practice of **meaningless repetition** (Mt. 6:7), and He shared a model prayer with His listeners (Mt. 6:9–13). The sample prayer included a line about forgiveness, which prompted Christ to speak thought-provoking words about the necessity of forgiving others (Mt. 6:14, 15).

This prayer is generally called "The Lord's Prayer" in spite of the fact that, as far as we know, Jesus never actually prayed the prayer. A better term for the prayer is "The Model Prayer." It has also been called "The Disciples' Prayer." Much of the prayer was repeated on another occasion (Lk. 11:2–4). On neither occasion was it given by Jesus as a prayer to be repeated by rote in public services. Reciting the prayer could violate Jesus' teaching regarding "meaningless repetition" (Mt. 6:7). If the prayer is used in any setting today, one phrase in it must be changed. We cannot pray, **"Your kingdom come"** (Mt. 6:10), since the kingdom/church has already come. (Notice Jesus' promise in Mk. 9:1 and Acts 1:8 and its fulfillment in Acts 2:1–4.) The model prayer will be addressed in more detail later.

Fasting (Mt. 6:16–18)

[16]**"Whenever you fast, do not put on a gloomy face as the hypocrites do, for they neglect their appearance so that they will be noticed by men when they are fasting. Truly I say to you, they have their reward in full.** [17]**But you, when you fast, anoint your head and wash your face** [18]**so that your fasting will not be noticed by men, but by your Father who is in secret; and your Father who sees what is done in secret will reward you."**

The third illustration concerned fasting. The Old Testament had no specific command to fast, but in the Law Jews were told to "humble" their souls on the Day of Atonement (Lev. 16:29, 31), and fasting was one way to do this (Ps. 35:13). At a later time, fasts were established to commemorate national disasters (Zech. 8:19). By Jesus' time, the Pharisees fasted twice a week (Lk. 18:12). On those days, they made sure everyone knew they had "afflicted" themselves. Jesus told His listeners, in effect, "If and when you fast, keep it to yourself" (Mt. 6:16–18).

THE SECURITY OF HEAVENLY TREASURES CONTRASTED WITH EARTHLY ANXIETIES (MT. 6:19–34)

The first part of Matthew 6:19–34 contains several contrasts. In verses 19 through 21, there is a contrast between laying up treasures on earth and storing up treasures in heaven. In verses 22 and 23, we see the difference between being filled with light and being filled with darkness. Verse 24 tells of two possible masters: God and wealth. All three contrasts relate to a single theme: Are our affections focused on this earth, or are they centered in heaven? Then, the segment that follows is one of the most practical (and most universally needed) in the entire sermon. It is on the sin of worry.

Treasures (Mt. 6:19–21; see Lk. 12:33, 34)

[19]"**Do not store up for yourselves treasures on earth, where moth and rust destroy, and where thieves break in and steal.** [20]**But store up for yourselves treasures in heaven, where neither moth nor rust destroys, and where thieves do not break in or steal;** [21]**for where your treasure is, there your heart will be also.**"

Jesus challenged His disciples not to lay up treasures on earth, but rather to store them in heaven. Inspiration tells us how to lay up treasures in heaven in 1 Timothy 6:18, 19. Banks, as we know them, were nonexistent in those days, so people often hid their treasures in their houses or buried them in the ground—where they could be ravished by nature (Jas. 5:2, 3a) or by thieves. Christ emphasized that earthly treasures are fleeting—that only heavenly treasures last (Mt. 6:19, 20).

Christ was not outlawing reasonable provision for the future, but He condemned the amassing of possessions as an end within itself. His primary concern was with a person's priorities:

. . . **where your treasure is, there your heart will be also** (Mt. 6:21). It is also true that where your heart is, there your treasure will be also.

Eyes (Mt. 6:22, 23; see Lk. 11:34–36)

²²**"The eye is the lamp of the body; so then if your eye is clear, your whole body will be full of light. ²³But if your eye is bad, your whole body will be full of darkness. If then the light that is in you is darkness, how great is the darkness!"**

Jesus illustrated the importance of right priorities by using an analogy familiar to the people of that day: the use of the eye to stand for one's disposition of heart. As the eye is to the body, so the heart is to the soul. The Old Testament taught that "he who is generous [literally, "has a good eye"] will be blessed" (Prov. 22:9a), while "a man with an evil eye hastens after wealth" (Prov. 28:22a). We do not employ the same figure of speech today, but we use a similar one to speak of the way we "look" at life.

Christ's illustration is simple: If a man's physical eyes are good, he is **filled with light**; but if he is blind, he is **filled with darkness**. Even so, if a man's heart is good (in context, centered on heaven), he is filled with spiritual light; but if his heart is evil (that is, centered on this world), he is filled with spiritual darkness.

Masters (Mt. 6:24; see Lk. 16:13)

²⁴**"No one can serve two masters; for either he will hate the one and love the other, or he will be devoted to one and despise the other. You cannot serve God and wealth."**

Each of us must decide which is more important in our lives. We can serve God, or we can become a slave to this world—but we cannot do both (see Rom. 6:16–18). We must make the choice between God and wealth. The word used in the KJV, "mammon," was a common Chaldean word for material riches.

Worry or Faith (Mt. 6:25–34)

[25]"For this reason I say to you, do not be worried about your life, as to what you will eat or what you will drink; nor for your body, as to what you will put on. Is not life more than food, and the body more than clothing? [26]Look at the birds of the air, that they do not sow, nor reap nor gather into barns, and yet your heavenly Father feeds them. Are you not worth much more than they? [27]And who of you by being worried can add a single hour to his life? [28]And why are you worried about clothing? Observe how the lilies of the field grow; they do not toil nor do they spin, [29]yet I say to you that not even Solomon in all his glory clothed himself like one of these. [30]But if God so clothes the grass of the field, which is alive today and tomorrow is thrown into the furnace, will He not much more clothe you? You of little faith! [31]Do not worry then, saying, 'What will we eat?' or 'What will we drink?' or 'What will we wear for clothing?' [32]For the Gentiles eagerly seek all these things; for your heavenly Father knows that you need all these things. [33]But seek first His kingdom and His righteousness, and all these things will be added to you.

[34]"So do not worry about tomorrow; for tomorrow will care for itself. Each day has enough trouble of its own."

These verses tie closely with the previous ones. If our affections are centered on this earth, we will worry. If they are focused on heaven, there is no need to worry. John Franklin Carter summarized the passage by saying that worry is . . .

1. Unnecessary, because . . . since God supplies food for fowls and raiment for flowers, He will certainly supply the needs of His servants (Mt. 6:26, 28–30).
2. Unavailing, because just as being anxious will not add . . . to one's stature, it will not produce any other needful benefits (Mt. 6:27).
3. Unseemly [inappropriate], because to the Christian, life should mean more than food, and the body more than . . . adornment. Moreover, by being anxious about these mat-

ters the Christian puts himself in a class with the . . . heathen . . . (Mt. 6:25, 32).[9]

The secret to conquering worry is hinted at in Jesus' characterization of the anxious: **"You of little faith!"** (Mt. 6:30b; emphasis added). The key to overcoming anxiety is faith: faith in God who knows our needs (Mt. 6:32) and who will give us the necessities of life *if* we **seek first His kingdom and His righteousness** (Mt. 6:33). To "seek first His kingdom and His righteousness" is to acknowledge God's kingship and to strive to obey His royal commands. Since Jesus used the terms "kingdom" and "church" interchangeably in Matthew 16:18, 19, we can also make application to putting the interests of the Lord's church above our own. Since God is God, He knows; since He is our Father, He cares.

Jesus was not teaching against concern for the future, but there is a difference between legitimate concern and the mindless fretting that saps our energy and renders us less capable of meeting future challenges. Jesus was not opposed to planning ahead. Jesus was preparing for the future even as He spoke these words. He was preparing His apostles for the time when He would leave this world. In the Old Testament, ants were put forth as an approved example of preparing for the future (Prov. 30:25). Other passages, such as Proverbs 21:5; 25:8; and 2 Corinthians 8:20, 21, also advocate thinking ahead (as opposed to functioning with little or no thought). The principle of stewardship motivates us to prepare for tomorrow as best we can. We are stewards of everything that God has put in our hands, including our possessions and our time. We must be faithful to our stewardship (see 1 Cor. 4:2). However, once we have done that, we should leave matters in the hands of God—and not worry.

APPLICATION:
THE MODEL PRAYER (MT. 6:9–15; LK. 11:1–4)

Children have a million questions—many of which start with

---

[9]John Franklin Carter, *A Layman's Harmony of the Gospels* (Nashville: Broadman Press, 1961), 110.

"Why?" Teen-agers are concerned about what they will do for a living—and how to tell if they are in love. Adults want to know how to prosper in life. However, Jesus' disciples wanted to know *how to pray*: "It happened that while Jesus was praying in a certain place, after He had finished, one of His disciples said to Him, 'Lord, teach us to pray just as John also taught his disciples'" (Lk. 11:1). Christ's answer has been called "The Lord's Prayer."

> "When you pray, say: 'Father, hallowed be Your name. Your kingdom come. Give us each day our daily bread. And forgive us our sins, for we ourselves also forgive everyone who is indebted to us. And lead us not into temptation'" (Lk. 11:2–4).

The more familiar version of this prayer is found in Matthew 6, in the Sermon on the Mount:

> "Pray, then, in this way: 'Our Father who is in heaven, hallowed be Your name. Your kingdom come. Your will be done, on earth as it is in heaven. Give us this day our daily bread. And forgive us our debts, as we also have forgiven our debtors. And do not lead us into temptation, but deliver us from evil. [For Yours is the kingdom and the power and the glory forever. Amen]'" (Mt. 6:9–13).

This passage is one of the best known in all the Bible. Perhaps only Psalm 23 is more familiar. Unfortunately, many have committed this prayer to memory but have not taken it to heart. What does this prayer really teach? What kind of challenge does it extend to each of us?

Let us begin with a few negatives. First, the prayer in Matthew 6:9–13 and Luke 11:1–4 was not intended to be a ritualistic prayer. In the verses immediately preceding Matthew 6:9–13, Jesus warned against "meaningless repetition" (Mt. 6:7). Further, the Lord said, "Pray, then, in this way" (Mt. 6:9a) or "After this manner" (KJV), *not* "use these exact words." When Jesus later repeated the prayer (Lk. 11:1–4), even He did not use exactly the same words: He used 68 words in Matthew (in the NASB translation, including the last of verse 13; the KJV has 66 words; and the Greek text uses 57 words, without the last part of verse 13). In Luke's account, the prayer contains only 37 words (in the NASB translation; the KJV has 58 words, while the Greek text has 38 words).

Second, the familiar title "The Lord's Prayer" is inaccurate. The prayer was given that designation by some nameless scholar in the Dark Ages, and the name has stayed with it. However, if Jesus Himself ever prayed this prayer, there is no record of it. Some have said that the *true* "Lord's Prayer" is in John 17. His words in Matthew 6:9–15 and Luke 11:1–4 can be called "The *Model* Prayer." It is a model in many ways. It is a model in scope: It contains an acknowledgment of the greatness of God. It expresses concern for the kingdom plus all those who are in the world. It even touches on personal needs. It is also a model in brevity and simplicity. It is covered in five verses in Matthew and three verses in Luke. It takes only about twenty seconds to read the longest version aloud.

Christ's prayer is a model in other ways. Matthew 6 will be used as the primary text because it is longer (and therefore more complete) and because it is better known—while occasional references to Luke 11 will be made.

A Model in Its Direction

This prayer is a model in its direction. In the first place, it is directed to *God*: "*Our Father* who is in heaven" (Mt. 6:9b; emphasis added). We are to pray to God—not to Mary or to some saint, but to God. Paul said that we are always to give "thanks for all things in the name of our Lord Jesus Christ *to God,* even the Father" (Eph. 5:20; emphasis added). Again, we are to pray to God, our *Father*. Jehovah is not an impersonal God, but a Father who cares and provides. Further, we are to pray to God, who is *our* Father. This is not the prayer of a hermit; it is not the prayer of an only child. The phrase "our Father" acknowledges our common brotherhood. When we pray "our Father," we indicate that we have come together to discuss family matters.

The prayer is also a model in its direction because it is directed *heavenward*: "Our Father *who is in heaven*" (Mt. 6:9b; emphasis added). This world is God's creation and possession, but it is not His home. Our religion is a heaven-centered religion. Jesus came from heaven, and He returned to heaven. He is now at the right hand of God in heaven, interceding for us. He will someday come from heaven to gather His own, who will spend an eternity in heaven with Him. Paul wrote that "our citizenship is in heaven" (Phil. 3:20). Jesus told His disciples to "rejoice that your names are recorded in heaven" (Lk. 10:20). He challenges all of us to "store up for [ourselves] treasures in heaven" (Mt. 6:20).

A Model in Its Reverence

The prayer is also a model in its reverence. God is not a casual friend; He is our *Father*—and His name is *holy*. The prayer continues, "Hallowed be Your name" (Mt. 6:9c; see Lk. 11:2b). The word translated "hallowed" comes from the Greek word for "holy" and means to "regard or reverence as holy."[110] In the Old Testament, the psalmist said, "Holy and awesome is His name" (Ps. 111:9c). Moses commanded, "You shall not take the name of the Lord your God in vain" (Ex. 20:7a). Jesus' model prayer lets us know that, even under the new covenant, we are to approach God with a profound sense of awe.

A Model in Its Emphasis

The reverence just mentioned sets the tone as we come to the petitions in the prayer. The initial concern expressed is not for self, but for God's plans and purposes: "Your kingdom come" (Mt. 6:10a; see Lk. 11:2c).

What was the "kingdom" they were anticipating? It was *the church*. Let us review some key passages on the Messianic kingdom:

- *Daniel 2:44*. Daniel promised that the Messianic kingdom would come in the days of the fourth kingdom, the Roman Empire.

---

[10]*The Analytical Greek Lexicon* (London: Samuel Bagster & Sons Ltd., 1971), 3.

- *Matthew 3:2; 4:17.* While the Romans ruled the world, John the Baptizer and then Jesus came preaching, "The kingdom of heaven is at hand."
- *Matthew 16:18, 19.* At Caesarea Philippi, Jesus spoke of establishing His kingdom; He called it His "church."
- *Mark 9:1.* Christ told His disciples that the kingdom would come in their lifetime and that it would "come with power." He later said that the power would come when the Holy Spirit came (Acts 1:6–8).
- *Acts 2:1–4.* The Holy Spirit came on the first Pentecost after the death, burial, and resurrection of Jesus. At that time the power came and the kingdom/church was established.
- *Acts 2:47.* From that point on, the kingdom/church is spoken of as being in existence. When people were saved, God added them to His church (KJV), rescuing them from "the domain of darkness" and transferring them "to the kingdom of His beloved Son" (Col. 1:13). Christians are in an unshakable kingdom (Heb. 12:28)—the church which the gates of Hades cannot destroy (Mt. 16:18).

When Jesus had the disciples pray, "Your kingdom come," they were, in effect, praying, "Your church be established." The Lord was asking His disciples to be participants in God's grand, eternal design which included the church (see Eph. 3:10, 11).

Should we pray this part of the prayer today? Since the kingdom/church has already been established, it is best not to use those exact words. We could qualify the petition by saying, "Your kingdom come *into all the world*" or "Your kingdom come *into the hearts of all men.*" If we use the words without qualification, we give credence to premillennialists who believe that Christ's kingdom has not yet been established.

Even though we need to adapt the words, the prayer does teach that we should be *concerned* about the kingdom/church— and that we should include its welfare in our prayers. We should pray for the church that meets locally and for the church around the world. By doing so, we can *still* be participants in God's great plan to make known His wisdom "through the church" according to His "eternal purpose which He carried out in Christ Jesus our Lord" (Ephesians 3:10, 11).

A Model in Its Concern

The next petition continues the emphasis on the spiritual, but the emphasis shifts from the church/kingdom to all the earth: "Your will be done, on earth as it is in heaven" (Mt. 6:10b, c). The desire is expressed that everyone on earth obey the will of God. Even to contemplate such a possibility staggers the mind. Think about how His will is done in heaven. Picture the angels and the archangels standing before the throne of God. See them eager to hear His commands and prompt to obey them. It would be marvelous if the will of God were obeyed this way in all the earth.

For this part of the prayer to be answered, since God's will is revealed in His Word, we must take that Word to all the earth (Mt. 28:18–20; Mk. 16:15, 16). We must encourage people everywhere to obey the Lord's commands.

The principal value of this part of the prayer, however, is that it forces us to examine our own *attitudes* toward His will. Frankly, many of us are not always happy with God's will for our lives. Someone has said that "men don't like the parts handed out to them by the King of heaven." Some have been, in effect, praying, "*My* will be done on the earth." The purpose of prayer is not to get God to submit to our will, but to learn to subject our will to His.

A Model in Its Restraint

We are halfway through the prayer, and there has not been a personal request—but our hearts should now be prepared for one. We next read, "Give us this day our daily bread" (Mt. 6:11). Luke's account has "Give us *each* day our daily bread" (Lk. 11:3; emphasis added). Notice the restraint in this prayer. This is not a request for *cake* (or other luxuries), but for *bread*. It is not a request for *a month's supply* of bread, but enough for that *day*.

One of the lessons in this part of the prayer is that we should be content with the *necessities* of life. Food is one of the few things we *must* have. It is not wrong to ask for other blessings, but our happiness should not be dependent upon the accumulation of things. Paul wrote, "If we have food and covering, with these we shall be content" (1 Tim. 6:8).

Other lessons are found in this section of the prayer. For instance, we are reminded that *God* is the source of all our blessings. We are to pray to Him for something as simple and basic as our daily bread. We are not to say, "Look what *I* did," but rather "Look what *God* has done for me." Everything we have, we have "picked up" along the way; but the One who put those blessings there to be "picked up" is God. We are to work for our daily bread (see 2 Thess. 3:11, 12), but we must still recognize that God is the ultimate Source of every blessing. An old verse serves as a reminder of this truth:

> Back of the loaf is the flour,
>   And back of the flour the mill;
> And back of the mill is the wheat
>   That waveth on yonder hill;
> And back of the hill is the sun
>   And the rain and the Father's will.[11]

Jesus' prayer further implies the need to be unselfish. We are not to pray for *"my* daily bread," but for *"our* daily bread." Throughout the prayer, there is an emphasis on the community of Christians. Read the prayer again. The personal pronoun "I" is not found. The prayer is saturated with concern for others.

A Model in Its Humility

Another personal request comes next in the prayer: "And forgive us our debts" (Mt. 6:12a). The Greek word translated "debts" refers to that which is owed, but the reference is to a spiritual debt, not a financial one. In the New Testament, the Greek word in the singular is used to refer to an offense, fault, or sin.[12] Luke's account has "And forgive us our sins" (Lk. 11:4a).

---

[11]This anonymous translation and adaptation is based on Peter Christian Lukin, "Back of the Bread," *Chansons de Notre Chalet*, 1944.

[12]*Analytical Greek Lexicon*, 296.

He used the words translated "sins" and "debts" interchangeably. A version of this prayer used by many people has the word "trespasses" (another word that can mean "sins"): "Forgive us our trespasses as we forgive those who trespass against us." Standing before a holy God, we admit we are sinners and ask God to forgive us. This strikes at the heart of our pride.

The next part of this request strikes even more sharply at our pride: "As we also have forgiven our debtors" (Mt. 6:12b). It is so hard to forgive. When someone hurts us, our ego and pride are wounded. We may be inclined to think, "I could *never* forgive him [or her]!" We must learn to say, in effect, "This is not so important; I must let it go."

Attempts have been made to get around the strong teaching of Matthew 6:12 (see Mt. 6:14, 15). Some ask, "Can I really forgive a person who does not repent and ask for forgiveness?" Some point to Luke 17:3 and the fact that God does not forgive us until we repent. However, we are not talking about the restoration of fellowship, but about *the attitude* in our hearts. On the cross, Jesus prayed, "Father, forgive them; for they do not know what they are doing" (Lk. 23:34a). Even though He uttered that prayer, the guilt of their sins remained on their souls until they repented (see Acts 2:36–38). Nevertheless (and here is what we must learn to do), Jesus had forgiven them in *His* heart. If someone does you harm, your relationship with that person will probably remain strained until that individual admits he did wrong; but your greatest concern must be to make sure that *your* heart holds no animosity. You must take care that "no root of bitterness" springs up (Heb. 12:15), filling your heart and choking out the love you should have for others.

Luke's account of this part of the prayer has this positive note: "For we ourselves also forgive everyone who is indebted to us" (Lk. 11:4b). What if we are not willing to forgive? It has been said that the man who is unwilling to forgive destroys the bridge over which he himself must pass. Consider the thought-provoking words of Jesus immediately following the model prayer: "For if you forgive others for their transgressions, your heavenly Father will also forgive you. But if you do not forgive others, then your Father will not forgive your transgressions" (Mt. 6:14, 15).

A Model in Its Insight

The prayer continues: "And do not lead us into temptation, but deliver us from evil" (Mt. 6:13a; see Lk. 11:4c). The Greek word translated "temptation" can have a variety of meanings, but in this verse, it is used interchangeably with "evil." In this context, it refers to "the temptation to do evil." The model prayer is a model in its insight because it is concerned not only with the forgiveness of sins, but also with staying away from that which leads to sin.

Regarding the word "evil," the Greek text has a definite article before it: "*the* evil." The meaning could be "the evil [thing]" (that is, anything that is evil) or "the evil [one]" (that is, the devil). Since the second (the devil) is responsible for the first (all that is evil), either rendering conveys the same basic thought.

This part of the prayer teaches us to ask God's help in staying away from temptation, for help in meeting temptations that come our way, and for help in defeating Satan. Since God tempts no one (Jas. 1:13), the phrase "Lead us not into temptation" must mean something like "Help us not to be led into temptation." These words also place responsibility on us. Too frequently, we want God to get us out of trouble after we have walked into a tempting circumstance with our eyes wide open. We cannot consistently pray, "Lead us not into temptation" and then deliberately and knowingly go into situations in which we know we will be tempted.

A Model in Its Praise

The final words of the familiar "Lord's prayer" are in brackets in the NASB: "[For Yours is the kingdom and the power and the glory forever. Amen]" (Mt. 6:13b). This ending is not found in the earlier manuscripts. There is evidence, however, that these words were used in the early centuries of the church, and they are found somewhere in most translations—in the footnotes or margin notes, if nowhere else. They are a fitting way to close the prayer. They return to the source of all that is good, God Himself:

- His is "the kingdom." The kingdom belongs to Him, and

He is over all. We must acknowledge that truth.

- His is "the power." Whatever power men may possess is puny compared to the power of God. We must recognize that fact also.
- His is "the glory," and we should proclaim it.
- All this will be true "forever." "Amen."

Conclusion

That is the model prayer. Does it teach *everything* we need to know about prayer? No. For instance, it is not in the name of Jesus. The model prayer was spoken while the law of Moses was still in effect and today could be prayed by any conscientious Jew. Paul taught that, under the New Covenant, we are to give "thanks for all things *in the name of our Lord Jesus Christ* to God, even the Father" (Eph. 5:20; emphasis added). The familiar phrase "in the name of Jesus" is not just something we say; it is an acknowledgment of our understanding that Jesus is now our Mediator (1 Tim. 2:5).

Further, the requests in the model prayer are general in nature. When we pray, we are to be specific. We need to give thanks for specific blessings, confess specific sins, and pray for specific people.

Nevertheless, there is much we can learn from the model prayer. It is a model in its direction, reverence, emphasis, concern, restraint, humility, insight, and praise.

TEACHING ON JUDGING
(MT. 7:1–6; LK. 6:37–42)

Matthew 7:1–6

[1]"Do not judge so that you will not be judged. [2]For in the way you judge, you will be judged; and by your standard of measure, it will be measured to you. [3]Why do you look at the speck that is in your brother's eye, but do not notice the log that is in your own eye? [4]Or how can you say to your brother, 'Let me take the speck out of your eye,' and behold, the log is in your own eye? [5]You hypocrite, first take the log out of your own eye, and then you will see clearly to take the speck out of

your brother's eye.

⁶"Do not give what is holy to dogs, and do not throw your pearls before swine, or they will trample them under their feet, and turn and tear you to pieces.

Luke 6:37–42

³⁷"Do not judge, and you will not be judged; and do not condemn, and you will not be condemned; pardon, and you will be pardoned. ³⁸Give, and it will be given to you. They will pour into your lap a good measure—pressed down, shaken together, and running over. For by your standard of measure it will be measured to you in return."

³⁹And He also spoke a parable to them: "A blind man cannot guide a blind man, can he? Will they not both fall into a pit? ⁴⁰A pupil is not above his teacher; but everyone, after he has been fully trained, will be like his teacher. ⁴¹Why do you look at the speck that is in your brother's eye, but do not notice the log that is in your own eye? ⁴²Or how can you say to your brother, 'Brother, let me take out the speck that is in your eye,' when you yourself do not see the log that is in your own eye? You hypocrite, first take the log out of your own eye, and then you will see clearly to take out the speck that is in your brother's eye."

Jesus turned from a disciple's attitude toward material possessions to his attitude toward others. Matthew 7:1–5 condemns having a judgmental spirit. Some think that the passage forbids any judgments, but Jesus Himself said to "judge with righteous judgment" (Jn. 7:24). The Greek word translated **judge** is κρίνω (*krino*), the word from which we get the English word "criticize." We generally think of the word "criticize" in a negative sense—pointing out flaws in another—but the word "criticize" just means "to evaluate." That evaluation can be negative or positive; it can be bad, or it can be good; it can be destructive, or it can be constructive. The necessity of making judgments is highlighted in one of our texts: Matthew 7:6 says not to **give what is holy to dogs** or to **throw . . . pearls before swine**, which involves using good judgment regarding those whom we teach. When verses

1 through 6 are taken as a whole, it is apparent that Jesus was not prohibiting all judgment, but rather was denouncing a harsh, unkind, unsympathetic spirit.

In Luke's account of the sermon, Jesus added a comment on blind leaders of the blind—and their disciples (Lk. 6:39). Jesus later referred to the Pharisees as "blind guides of the blind" (Mt. 15:12, 14). Christ was rebuking the Pharisees and anyone with a Pharisaical spirit toward others. One should also notice that Luke 6:39 says Jesus **also spoke a parable to them**. This is the first time in our study that the word "parable" has been used.

TEACHING ON PRAYER (MT. 7:7–11)

[7]**"Ask, and it will be given to you; seek, and you will find; knock, and it will be opened to you.** [8]**For everyone who asks receives, and he who seeks finds, and to him who knocks it will be opened.** [9]**Or what man is there among you who, when his son asks for a loaf, will give him a stone?** [10]**Or if he asks for a fish, he will not give him a snake, will he?** [11]**If you then, being evil, know how to give good gifts to your children, how much more will your Father who is in heaven give what is good to those who ask Him!"**

Before Jesus concluded the sermon (with instruction on obedience), He included two generic segments that would enable His listeners to meet the challenges He had placed before them. The contrasts in these passages are not stated, but they are implied. The first (Mt. 7:7–11) is on the power of persistent prayer. It could be thought of as a follow-up to the section on worry. If disciples are not to worry about tomorrow, what should they do? They should pray. Verses 7 through 11 come between two passages on human relationships (Mt. 7:1–6 and 7:12). The passage thus lets us know that prayer is essential to getting along with people.

The key words in verses 7 and 8 are **ask**, **seek**, and **knock**. The sequence of the words suggests an increasing intensity in our prayers. Also, the original text uses the present tense, which implies continuation: Continue to ask; continue to seek; continue to knock. Jesus was emphasizing the need to be persistent in prayer (see Lk. 18:1). By an interesting coincidence, the first letters of "ask," "seek," and "knock" are "a," "s," and "k," which spell "ask." James wrote, ". . . you do not have because you do not ask" (Jas. 4:2).

Why should we be persistent in prayer? Because we have a God who loves us and who will answer our prayers (see Jas. 5:16b–18). Christ stressed this with an illustration about earthly fathers providing for their children (Mt. 7:9, 10). Even so, our heavenly Father will provide for us (Mt. 7:11).

Other comparisons are made in the Scriptures of our Father in heaven treating us in a way similar to how our fathers on earth treat us. (See, for instance, Heb. 12:4–13.) We must, however, be careful not to conclude that in *every* respect our heavenly Father is like our earthly fathers. Every earthly father has made mistakes in dealing with his children, but God does not make mistakes. Some have tried to make passages like Matthew 7:7–11 teach that God would never send anyone to hell, because (they say) no earthly father would ever do that to his children. To interpret the passage this way is to make it contradict plain passages on the Judgment (such as Mt. 25:31–46).

Whatever challenge life may bring, Jesus would have us "ask of God, who gives to all generously ..." (Jas. 1:5).

THE GOLDEN RULE (MT. 7:12; LK. 6:31)

Matthew 7:12
[12]"In everything, therefore, treat people the same way you want them to treat you, for this is the Law and the Prophets."

Luke 6:31
[31]"Treat others the same way you want them to treat you."

The next section is only one verse. Although this thought could be included with the next part of the sermon, it is important enough to be listed alone. The verse enunciates the principle commonly called The Golden Rule: **In everything, ... treat people the same way you want them to treat you** (Mt. 7:12a).

The contrast here is implied rather than stated—but it is easy to recognize. In dealing with others, we are often concerned about what *we* want: "*I need* this or that in our relationship," we say. The Golden Rule moves us from selfishness to self-forgetfulness. It challenges us first to consider what the other person may need. All this is implicit in the Lord's words "Do to others as you would have them do to you" (Lk. 6:31; NIV).

Jesus said that **this is the Law and the Prophets** (Mt. 7:12b). If the teachings of the Law and the Prophets, regarding their precepts on how to get along with other people, could be compressed down to capsule size, this is what would be left: "However you want people to treat you, treat them that way."

THE TWO WAYS—AND FALSE PROPHETS
(MT. 7:13–23; LK. 6:43–45)

Destruction or Life (Mt. 7:13, 14)

13"Enter through the narrow gate; for the gate is wide and the way is broad that leads to destruction, and there are many who enter through it. 14For the gate is small and the way is narrow that leads to life, and there are few who find it."

Jesus began to wrap up His sermon with the words of Matthew 7:13. The concluding verses of the sermon include a warning against false teachers (Mt. 7:15–20), but primarily they are concerned with Christ's disciples *living* the principles that He had taught. Jesus did not intend that His sermon should be engraved on a plaque and admired. He rather desired that it should radiate from the lives of His followers.

The contrast of verses 13 and 14 is obvious. There are two ways—and only two ways—that each of us can go: The narrow way leads to life, and the broad way leads to destruction (see Lk. 13:23, 24). The narrow way is the difficult pathway, and only a **few** are willing to make the sacrifices necessary to travel on it. The broad way is the easy way, the popular way, chosen by **many**. Most do not like to face this unpleasant truth, but if Jesus' words mean anything, they teach that more will be lost than will be saved.

How can we get on the narrow way? Jesus answered that question in the verses that follow: by obeying what He tells us (Mt. 7:21–27). Just as important, how can we *stay* on the narrow way? The New Testament does not teach that it is impossible for one who is on the narrow way to leave (see 1 Cor. 10:12; Jas. 5:19, 20). Sadly, more than one traveler on the narrow way has tired of its restrictions and has abandoned it for the broad, easy way. How can we stay on the narrow way? By *continuing* to obey Christ's commands. (Review Mt. 7:24–27.)

What difference does it make which road we travel? One leads to *life*—eternal life with God (Rom. 2:7). The other leads to *destruction*—everlasting destruction, away from the presence of the Lord (2 Thess. 1:9). In simple terms, one is the highway to heaven while the other is the low road to hell.

Bad Fruit or Good (Mt. 7:15–20; Lk. 6:43–45)

Matthew 7:15–20

[15]**"Beware of the false prophets, who come to you in sheep's clothing, but inwardly are ravenous wolves.** [16]**You will know them by their fruits. Grapes are not gathered from thorn bushes nor figs from thistles, are they?** [17]**So every good tree bears good fruit, but the bad tree bears bad fruit.** [18]**A good tree cannot produce bad fruit, nor can a bad tree produce good fruit.** [19]**Every tree that does not bear good fruit is cut down and thrown into the fire.** [20]**So then, you will know them by their fruits."**

Luke 6:43–45

[43]**"For there is no good tree which produces bad fruit, nor, on the other hand, a bad tree which produces good fruit.** [44]**For each tree is known by its own fruit. For men do not gather figs from thorns, nor do they pick grapes from a briar bush.** [45]**The good man out of the good treasure of his heart brings forth what is good; and the evil man out of the evil treasure brings forth what is evil; for his mouth speaks from that which fills his heart."**

It makes a world of difference which road is traveled. Actually, it makes an *eternity* of difference which road is traveled. The devil does not want mankind to understand that. He leads people to think that it makes no difference which road they are on (that is, how they live), or else that the broad way is actually the narrow way. To accomplish this, he uses false teachers.

A prophet was one who spoke for God; a false prophet was one who claimed to speak for God but did not. Jesus called false prophets **wolves in sheep's clothing** (see Mt. 7:15). They appeared to be something that they were not. They spread a thin layer of truth over their ungodly error and covered their evil with a mantle of good works (see Mt. 7:22, 23).

Christ may have been especially warning His listeners concerning the teachings of the scribes and the Pharisees, but false teachers have plagued the church from its beginning until now (Mt. 24:11, 24; Acts 20:29, 30; 2 Pet. 2:1). It is imperative that false prophets are identified. We can know them by the **fruit** they bear: the fruit of their lives and the fruit of their teaching (Mt. 7:16–20; see Rom. 16:17). Both their lives and their teaching need to be compared with God's Word (1 Jn. 4:1; Acts 17:11).

Luke's account adds that what a man teaches reveals something about his heart, **for his mouth speaks from that which fills his heart** (Lk. 6:45). This verse can have general application concerning our speech: What we say reveals our hearts. In context, however, the words are especially applied to those who claim to speak for God. Jesus' admonition is as timely today as when He first spoke the words **"Beware of the false prophets"** (Mt. 7:15a). A word of caution must be added here: Do not interpret this verse in such a way that it contradicts Jesus' teaching against judging in Matthew 7:1. Put the best construction possible on the speech of another.

Saying and Doing (Mt. 7:21–23)

[21]"Not everyone who says to Me, 'Lord, Lord,' will enter the kingdom of heaven, but he who does the will of My Father who is in heaven will enter. [22]Many will say to Me on that day, 'Lord, Lord, did we not prophesy in Your name, and in Your name cast out demons, and in Your name perform many mira-

cles?' [23]**And then I will declare to them, 'I never knew you; depart from Me, you who practice lawlessness.'"**

Do all false prophets know that they are false prophets? Does everyone on the broad way know that he is on the road to destruction? Evidently not. Jesus' words in Matthew 7:21–23 suggest that it is possible to be self-deceived.

That day refers to the Day of Judgment (Acts 17:31). In this illustration, had the protestors on the Judgment Day actually done everything they claimed to have done? Jesus did not deny their claims—but even if they had performed good works, they also were workers of evil, for Christ accused them of practicing lawlessness. Their precise deeds are relatively unimportant. The most important (and saddest) words are **"I never knew you."**

In the Bible, the word "know" can mean "to have a close relationship." This word describes a number of different relationships. It includes marital relationships. The Bible says that Adam "knew" his wife (Gen. 4:1; see KJV). The NASB has this margin note: "[Literally], *knew*." The word is also used to describe the relationship between God and man (1 Cor. 1:21; Gal. 4:9; Phil. 3:10). Paul wrote, "The Lord knows those who are His" (2 Tim. 2:19). When Jesus said, "I never knew you," He was asserting that the accused had never had a saved relationship with Him. They had not followed Him and His teachings, but had refused to commit their lives to Him as Master and Lord. Whatever their good works, they had not been done "in Christ" (2 Cor. 5:17; Eph. 2:13; 3:21; Rom. 16:3, 9), but rather outside of Christ.

If we want to be sure that Jesus knows us, we will do what the Lord tells us to do to become Christians (Rom. 6:3–7, 11, 17, 18, 23; Gal. 3:26, 27), and then we will obey Him to the best of our ability. J. W. McGarvey put it this way: "... obedience to the extent of our possibility amid the weaknesses of the flesh, accompanied by daily compliance with the conditions of pardon for our daily sin, has ever secured the favor of God."[13]

---

[13]McGarvey and Pendleton, 268.

CONCLUSION AND APPLICATION (THE TWO BUILDERS) (MT. 7:24–29; LK. 6:46–49)

Matthew 7:24–29

[24]"Therefore everyone who hears these words of Mine and acts on them, may be compared to a wise man who built his house on the rock. [25]And the rain fell, and the floods came, and the winds blew and slammed against that house; and yet it did not fall, for it had been founded on the rock. [26]Everyone who hears these words of Mine and does not act on them, will be like a foolish man who built his house on the sand. [27]The rain fell, and the floods came, and the winds blew and slammed against that house; and it fell—and great was its fall."

[28]When Jesus had finished these words, the crowds were amazed at His teaching; [29]for He was teaching them as one having authority, and not as their scribes.

Luke 6:46–49

[46]"Why do you call Me, 'Lord, Lord,' and do not do what I say? [47]Everyone who comes to Me and hears My words and acts on them, I will show you whom he is like: [48]he is like a man building a house, who dug deep and laid a foundation on the rock; and when a flood occurred, the torrent burst against that house and could not shake it, because it had been well built. [49]But the one who has heard and has not acted accordingly, is like a man who built a house on the ground without any foundation; and the torrent burst against it and immediately it collapsed, and the ruin of that house was great."

The final words of the Sermon on the Mount stress the necessity of obeying Christ. Jesus closed with the now familiar illustration of the two builders: the wise man who built on the rock and the foolish man who built on the sand. The first, Jesus said, could be compared with the individual who heard His words and acted on them, while the second was like the person who heard but did nothing.

The world makes many distinctions between individuals: the rich and the poor, the beautiful and the plain, the skilled and the unskilled, the successful and the failures. In the end, only one distinction will matter: whether we are on the narrow way that leads to everlasting life or the broad way that leads to eternal destruction (Mt. 25:46; Jn. 3:16; Rom. 2:7, 8; 6:23).

Luke's account expands the illustration by saying that the first man **dug deep and laid a foundation on the rock** (Lk. 6:48), while the second built **on the ground without any foundation** (Lk. 6:49). As a carpenter (see Mk. 6:3), Christ understood the importance of laying a solid foundation, but even those with little or no experience at construction can appreciate that a house needs a foundation. Every life needs a foundation.

One of the tragedies of our age is that so many lives are built on the shifting sands of earthly opinion. Our lives need the firm foundation of Jesus and His Word (see 1 Cor. 3:11; Eph. 2:20). We can have that stability if (and only if) we do Christ's will.

Jesus' words in Luke's account still challenge would-be disciples: **"Why do you call Me, 'Lord, Lord,' and do not do what I say?"** (Lk. 6:46).

When Jesus had finished these words, the crowds were amazed at His teaching; for He was teaching them as one having authority, and not as their scribes (Mt. 7:28, 29). The scribes did not speak on their own authority. Instead, they quoted endless authorities who had spoken on the subject under discussion.

The Sermon on the Mount is still a challenge today, but we cannot comprehend the impact the words would have had on those who first heard them. By any definition of the term, the sermon was revolutionary. Most, if not all, of it went contrary to the teaching Jesus' listeners had heard all of their lives. Jesus' teaching *still* goes contrary to concepts held dear by the world.

These teachings were especially directed to those who were Jesus' disciples at that time (Mt. 5:1, 2)—plus the multitude that was present (Mt. 7:28)—but they have been preserved for each of us. Christ said, **"Therefore *everyone* who hears these words of Mine and acts on them, may be compared to a wise man who built his house on the rock"** (Mt. 7:24; emphasis added). We should not only "hear" His words, but also act on them. Even after almost two thousand years, the Sermon on the Mount is still amazing. Read it; study it; but, above all, make every effort to practice it.

APPLICATION:
HOW TO GET ALONG WITH OTHERS
(MT. 7:1–12)

One of the challenges we have in living the Christian life is getting along with people. Jesus understood this, so He said much in the Sermon on the Mount regarding relationships. He said to be merciful to others and to be a peacemaker (Mt. 5:7, 9). He encouraged each of the listeners to be a good influence (Mt. 5:13–16). He said not to be angry with a brother, but to be reconciled to him (Mt. 5:21–26). Christ even spoke on how we should relate to those who would try to hurt us (that is, our enemies) (Mt. 5:38–48). However, one entire section of Jesus' teaching on this topic: Matthew 7:1–12. These verses have much to say about how to get along with others.

Before we examine these verses in detail, perhaps I should tell you why the entire passage is included in a study on getting along with others. It is more or less obvious that verses 1 through 6 deal with relationships as they speak of judging and not giving that which is holy to the dogs. Next, however, in verses 7 through 11, Jesus taught concerning prayer and its efficacy. We might think that He had left the subject of relationships—except that verse 12 says, ". . . therefore" and then gives the ultimate instruction on how to live in harmony with others: the Golden Rule. The word "therefore" indicates that Jesus was wrapping up His subject. Thus, *in some way*, verses 7 through 11 relate to the overall theme.

Six truths can be drawn from our text: six essentials for getting along with others.

Essential One: Forego Judging (Mt. 7:1, 2)

What Jesus Commanded (Mt. 7:1a)

If we want to get along with others, Jesus first said that *we must stop being judgmental*. The passage begins, "Do not judge" (Mt. 7:1a). In the original text, the form used indicates that His listeners needed to *stop* being judgmental. Williams' translation has "Stop criticizing others."[14]

At first thought, this seems a negative way to start a section on relationships, a section that closes with the beautiful Golden Rule. Jesus may have begun like this for several reasons.

Christ may have commenced with a warning about judging because He was *meeting a universal need*. All of His listeners needed this admonition, and *we* need this admonition. Probably, no twenty-four-hour period goes by without each of us violating Jesus' command in Matthew 7:1. Nothing destroys a relationship more quickly than a failure to obey this one command.

Another possibility is that Jesus began with the subject of judging *to offset a bad influence*. The scribes and the Pharisees were never far from His mind. They were already following Him everywhere He went, trying to find some fault to use in accusing him (Lk. 6:1–7). His enemies (which included the Pharisees) were already making plans to kill Him (Jn. 5:18).

Thus, in the Sermon on the Mount, Jesus made many references to them, directly and indirectly. In Matthew 5:20 He said, ". . . unless your righteousness surpasses that of the scribes and Pharisees, you will not enter the kingdom of heaven." In the latter part of chapter 5, Christ contrasted His teaching with traditions about the Law; these traditions were perpetuated by the Pharisees. In the first part of chapter 6, Jesus spoke of hypocrites who sounded trumpets as they gave alms, who prayed on street corners with endless repetition, who wanted everyone to know when they fasted. Everyone would have recognized the Pharisees in His descriptions. Luke's account includes a reference to teachers who were blind leaders of the blind (Lk. 6:39, 40), an obvious

---

[14]Charles B. Williams, *The New Testament: A Translation in the Language of the People* (Chicago: Moody Press, 1949), 23.

reference to the scribes and the Pharisees (Mt. 15:12–14).

The scribes and the Pharisees were guilty of the kind of judgment Jesus was denouncing. They condemned large segments of society: tax collectors (Lk. 18:9–14), the Samaritans, and Gentiles. Further, they considered themselves superior to everyone else. They looked down on others and had little compassion for them. If we would get along with others, our righteousness must surpass that of the scribes and the Pharisees.

Jesus may also have started as He did *to eliminate the negative aspect* of relationships before getting to the positive. Before we plant flowers, we sometimes have to pull weeds.

For whatever reason, this is where Christ started: "Do not judge so that you will not be judged."

What Jesus Did Not Mean (Mt. 7:1a)

The worldly-minded and biblically illiterate know a handful of passages, and this is one of them. Especially, they are familiar with the KJV phrasing: "Judge not, that ye be not judged."

In my own experience, I have most often heard these words on the lips of the guilty or those who sympathized with them: "Judge not, that ye be not judged." These individuals would interpret the words to mean that we are never to say that anyone else is wrong or that we are never to imply that dire consequences await the sinner who does not repent and change his ways. *Is* that what Jesus intended to teach? It is clear that those who condemn others for judging actions as "wrong" stand self-condemned by their own words.

Before noting what the word "judge" *does* mean in Matthew 7:1, let us look at what it does *not* mean.

Since the Bible does not contradict itself, Jesus' words do *not* mean that we should do away with civil judgment (that is, judgments by the courts of the land). God gave civil government the right to judge (see 1 Pet. 2:13, 14; Tit. 3:1; Rom. 13:1).

Some will respond, "*Of course*, the passage is not concerned with civil judgments. It is condemning a congregation or its elders for judging any of its members, for saying that they are wrong and should be disciplined." Not only do the unchurched feel this way, but some church members do too. An elder of a certain congregation said to me, "We never withdraw fellowship from anyone where I am an elder. After all, Jesus said, 'Judge not, that ye be not judged.'"

We know that the Bible does not contradict itself. Therefore, Matthew 7:1 does *not* teach that we should never exercise church discipline. Jesus, who said "Judge not," also taught us to exercise church discipline (Mt. 18:15–17). When He sent the Holy Spirit to guide the apostles into all truth (Jn. 16:13), He inspired Paul and others to reveal powerful passages on the necessity of church discipline (1 Cor. 5:5, 9; 2 Thess. 3:6, 14, 15; Tit. 3:9–11).

Another may respond, "Maybe the passage isn't talking about church discipline, but at least it is teaching that, as individual Christians, we never have the right to say that someone else is wrong morally or doctrinally."

Since the Bible does not contradict itself, Matthew 7:1 does *not* teach that we are never to make judgments about other people. Verse 6 says, "Do not give what is holy to dogs, and do not throw your pearls before swine. . . ." We cannot obey that command without making a judgment regarding who are "dogs" and who are "pigs." Matthew 7:15–20 warns against false prophets and says that we can know false prophets by the "fruit" of their labors: "You will know them by their fruits" (Mt. 7:16a). Preachers sometimes say, "We are not judges; we are fruit-inspectors." If space permitted, we could look at other passages which indicate that we are required to make judgments about others (Rom. 16:17; Gal. 1:8, 9; Phil. 3:2; 1 Jn. 4:1).

What Jesus Meant (Mt. 7:1a)

Having stressed what the word "judge" does not mean in our text, we still need to answer the question "What *does* it mean?"

Jesus' words teach that there is *a certain type* of judging that we must avoid. Let me suggest several aspects of the judgment that Jesus condemns.

(1) A common shortcoming is to allow our background, prejudices, and preferences to color our judgment. It is hard to avoid this. The ancient Greeks sometimes held important trials in the dark so that they would be swayed only by the facts. Sociologists say that one reason many are judgmental is that they suf-

fer from "low self-esteem." When one has low self-esteem, he can either lift himself up, or he can pull others down—and many find it easier to pull others down.

(2) We often judge hastily, without having all of the facts or knowing all of the circumstances. We may not have complete information about what really happened. We may not understand the background of the accused. We may not know whether this was the rule or the exception in his life. When Jesus told the multitude to "judge with righteous judgment," He first said, "Do not judge according to appearance" (Jn. 7:24a).

(3) Too often when we judge someone, we attempt to make a judgment concerning his *motivation*. Since we are not Jesus, who "knew what was in man" (Jn. 2:25), there is no way we can be sure of the motives of another. We can say, "He did this or that," but we cannot say with certainty, "He did this or that *because*...." Paul asked, "For what person perceives (knows and understands) what passes through a man's thoughts except the man's own spirit within him?" (1 Cor. 2:11a; AB).

(4) Jesus was also condemning putting the worst possible construction on what people do instead of the best. Moffatt's translation of 1 Corinthians 13:7b says that love is "always eager to believe the best."[15] It is true that we can know a person by what he does, but often his actions are subject to at least two different interpretations: one good and one bad. When that is the case, which interpretation do we generally put on what that person has done?

(5) As a result of the negative approaches to judgment just enumerated, we are sometimes harsh, bitter, and hypercritical in our judgments, when we should temper our judgments with mercy and love. Peter said, "Above all, keep fervent in your love for one another, because love covers a multitude of sins" (1 Pet. 4:8). Getting along with others is largely a matter of *spirit*. On one side, there is a loving, sympathetic spirit that believes the best and tries to lift up and help. On the other side, there is a harsh, unsympathetic, judgmental spirit that rejoices in seeing someone "get what he deserves."

---

[15]Moffatt, 217.

What Jesus Promised (Mt. 7:1b, 2)

Keeping all this in mind, let us study the rest of the passage: the end of verse 1 plus verse 2: ". . . that you will not be judged. For in the way you judge, you will be judged; and by your standard of measure, it will be measured to you."

As we read His promise, *we see our need for mercy.* Life is a mirror; we are generally treated as we treat others. A principle woven into the fabric of the universe is that, sooner or later, we reap what we sow (Gal. 6:7). Haman was hanged on the gallows he had prepared for Mordecai (Esther 7). Ecclesiastes 10:8a states that "he who digs a pit may fall into it."

Matthew 7:1, 2 is especially applicable to God's *eternal* judgment (see Mt. 7:21–27). Someday each one of us will stand before the Lord and "give an account of himself to God" (Rom. 14:12). In the end, this is the Judgment that matters. Imagine yourself before the great white throne (Rev. 20:11), being judged the way you judged others, being measured by the standard by which you have measured others. If you were judged in this fashion, would you go to the right or to the left (Mt. 25:31–33)? Consider these chilling words from the Book of James: "For judgment will be merciless to one who has shown no mercy" (2:13a).

Second, *we should see our need for common sense.* Regarding the admonitions found in Matthew 7:1–12, some common sense must be used. Jesus was not saying in verses 1 and 2 that the only factor of divine judgment will be whether or not we have been judgmental. He was not teaching that if we think everyone is all right regardless of how he lives, God will also say that we are spiritually acceptable. Even if we had only the Sermon on the Mount, we would recognize such an interpretation of 7:1, 2 to be untrue: At the end of the sermon, Jesus said that the one who hears His sayings and does them (not neglecting any of them) is like a wise man who built his house on a rock (Mt. 7:24, 25).

Third, *we see our need for humility.* In the first two verses of chapter 7, Jesus *was* emphasizing that, although we constantly have to make judgments—to protect ourselves and to help others—we must realize that we are not God. Since we are not God, our judgments will naturally be flawed. In our relationships with others, we must remember that ultimately both we and they will stand before God—and it is *God* who will make the final judgments. Let us therefore be merciful, kind, and patient in our dealings with others.

Essential Two: Make Needed Changes (Mt. 7:3–5)

When it comes to the need for change, we invariably prefer to look at others instead of ourselves. Jesus understood this. He said,

> Why do you look at the speck that is in your brother's eye, but do not notice the log that is in your own eye? Or how can you say to your brother, "Let me take the speck out of your eye," and behold, the log is in your own eye? You hypocrite, first take the log out of your own eye, and then you will see clearly to take the speck out of your brother's eye (Mt. 7:3–5).

This passage has a touch of humor. Jesus did not tell jokes, but He did use humor. Try to imagine a man with a massive log protruding from his eye as he struggles to position himself to see a speck that is in another man's eye. Can you see that huge log swinging first this way and then that, as those nearby have to duck to keep from being hit in the head? Jesus would have us understand that it is *ridiculous* to try to be judges when we may be in a worse condition than those we are judging.

Christ may have been thinking of the hypocrisy of the scribes and the Pharisees, but the truths of this passage convict us too. It is easy to see the faults of others while ignoring our own. Do you remember the story of King David, who committed adultery with Bathsheba and then had her husband killed (2 Sam. 11)? Nathan told David the tale of the rich man who killed the poor man's lamb. David was ready to "hang" the offender until Nathan said, "You are the man!" (2 Sam. 12:1–7). Then, instead of a hanging, David was ready for a prayer meeting (2 Sam. 12:13; Ps. 51; 32).

In the matter of getting along with others, Jesus wants us first to examine *ourselves* to see what changes *we* need to make.

Incidentally, the first part of verse 3 can add another item to the list of judgmental practices condemned by Christ. The Greek word βλέπω (*blepo*), translated "look," means "to scrutinize, to examine closely."[16] This term indicates that one looks with "a more intent, earnest contemplation." A speck is not easy to see. When someone tells you, "I have a speck in my eye," you probably cannot see it unless the light is exactly right and you get very close. We could add this far-too-prevalent characteristic to the list of bad judgmental habits: looking for the worst in people instead of the best and painstakingly scrutinizing every word and action in an attempt to find some fault to criticize. That was precisely how the scribes and the Pharisees were treating Jesus.

Many commentators and some translators think that Christ used the figures of a "speck" and a "log" because these items have the same composition. One is very small and the other very large, but both may be composed of wood. The NIV has "speck of sawdust" and "plank."

The possibility of the speck and the log being made of the same substance provokes some interesting thoughts. It is a fact of human nature that we are often overly sensitive regarding faults in others that we have in our own lives. Psychologists call this "projection": projecting into the lives of others what we see in our own lives. Further, it is a fact that our sins generally do not look as bad to us as the same sins look to us when we see them in others' lives. Bertrand Russell illustrated this with the way we view situations: "I am firm; you are obstinate; he is pig-headed. I have reconsidered; you have changed your mind; he has gone back on his word."

If Christ deliberately used an illustration with two items made of wood, then we have the absurd situation of a man with a log-sized sin acting superior to another who has the same sin, speck-sized. Paul wrote of this kind of inconsistency in Romans 2:1–3:

---

[16]W. E. Vine, *The Expanded Vine's Expository Dictionary of New Testament Words*, ed. John R. Kohlenberger III with James A. Swanson (Minneapolis: Bethany House Publishers, 1984), 106.

Therefore you have no excuse, everyone of you who passes judgment, for in that which you judge another, you condemn yourself; for you who judge practice the same things. And we know that the judgment of God rightly falls upon those who practice such things. But do you suppose this, O man, when you pass judgment on those who practice such things and do the same yourself, that you will escape the judgment of God?

How did Jesus characterize those who acted this way? Jesus minced no words; in the first part of Matthew 7:5, He said, "You *hypocrite*"! Being *hypercritical* makes us *hypocritical*. If we constantly criticize others, we are implying that our record is clear, that our lives are right—otherwise we would not be qualified to judge. At the same time, we have these huge telephone poles sticking out of our eye sockets.

Again, we say that, regarding judgment, we must start with self. Jesus said, *"First* take the log out of your own eye." It is easy to confess the sins of others; it is hard to confess our own sins. Paul mentioned self-examination in a variety of contexts: "Test yourselves . . . ; examine yourselves!" (2 Cor. 13:5a); "But a man must examine himself. . . ."; "But if we judged ourselves rightly, we would not be judged" (1 Cor. 11:28, 31). Romans 14:13 is especially applicable. Phillips' translation renders this verse, "Let us therefore stop turning critical eyes on one another. If we must be critical, *let us be critical of our own conduct* and see that we do nothing to make a brother stumble or fall."[17] (Emphasis added.)

What sin/log should be removed? Any sin should be removed—but in this context, we are especially talking about the sin of being judgmental.

Even in the matter of self-examination, some common sense is in order. We are not talking about a morbid obsession with personal failures and shortcomings, what someone has called "a perpetual autopsy." Nevertheless, if we would get along with others, our *first* concern must be to make needed changes in our

---

[17]J. B. Phillips, *The New Testament in Modern English* (New York: Macmillan Co., 1958), 344.

own lives. If we start with self, we will be less disposed toward being judgmental of others.

We could now leave verses 3 through 5, for we have covered the primary emphasis of the verses—but a beautiful truth at the end of verse 5 needs to be stressed.

Essential Three: Help Others Humbly (Mt. 7:5b)

If we really love someone and see sin in his life, we will try to help him remove that sin. This is implicit in the latter part of verse 5, After Jesus charged each one first to take the log from his own eye, He said, "And *then* you will see clearly to take the speck out of your brother's eye." (Emphasis added.) Jesus said that our first priority is to work on our own sins, but He did *not* discourage helping a brother with his sins once our own lives are in order (see Mt. 5:23, 24).

Many passages teach on the need to help a brother remove sin from his heart and life:

> Brethren, even if anyone is caught in any trespass, you who are spiritual, restore such a one in a spirit of gentleness; each one looking to yourself, so that you too will not be tempted. Bear one another's burdens, and thereby fulfill the law of Christ (Gal. 6:1, 2).

> My brethren, if any among you strays from the truth and one turns him back, let him know that he who turns a sinner from the error of his way will save his soul from death and will cover a multitude of sins (Jas. 5:19, 20).

Jesus' illustration of the speck in the eye highlights the need for help: The eye is sensitive. Even a tiny speck in the eye is no laughing matter. If you have children, you have probably heard the anguish in the voice when one of them has cried, "I have something in my eye!"

The illustration also indicates the approach that needs to be taken by the one helping. If I have something in my eye and a friend volunteers to help get it out, I want him to be ever so careful and sympathetic. We need to be that sensitive in dealing with others. Paul said to "restore such a one *in a spirit of gentleness*" (Gal. 6:1; emphasis added).

We are all sinners in the presence of a holy God before whom we shall someday stand in judgment. Everyone needs help spiritually, so let us help each other—but, as we do so, let us render that help with care and compassion.

Essential Four: Deal with Differences And Difficulties (Mt. 7:6)

We have come to the verse on "dogs" and "swine" (Mt. 7:6). Here is a puzzle: This verse seems to go against the spirit of what Jesus had been saying. Should we go around calling others "dogs" and "swine"? I think Christ put this sentence in for balance: We are not to be hypocritical, faultfinding, self-appointed "inspectors of warts," but neither are we to be gullible. God gave us common sense, and He expects us to use it in dealing with people. We are not to be callous and censorious, but neither are we to be careless and credulous.

If Jesus had only given us verses 1 through 5, He might have left us vulnerable, afraid of making any judgment lest we make a wrong judgment that would come down upon our heads. In verse 6, however, He indicated that there are *some* judgment calls that we must make regarding others. He illustrated this fact with a reference to dogs and pigs: "Do not give what is holy to dogs, and do not throw your pearls before swine, or they will trample them under their feet, and turn and tear you to pieces."

Before discussing the meaning of Christ's words, we need to understand the nature of dogs and swine, especially in that day. Both were ceremonially unclean animals under the law of Moses. The pig was specifically designated "unclean" (Lev. 11:7); the dog was "unclean" because it did not have split hoofs and did not chew the cud (Lev. 11:3, 4). When you think of dogs in Matthew 7:6, do not think of the pampered pets owned by some, but rather think of vicious, savage, filthy scavengers running in packs. The term "dog" was sometimes used in the Bible as a metaphor for those who were sinful (Mt. 15:26; Phil. 3:2; Rev. 22:15).

The pig was the epitome of uncleanness in the Jewish mind.

This being the case, most, if not all, pigs in Palestine would have been running wild. That fact is missed by many commentators. As they struggle with verse 6, they say that "turn and tear you to pieces" must be talking about the dogs instead of the pigs. They thus show their ignorance of these animals. They have never been around a mother sow who will try to tear a person's leg off if she thinks he is too close to her new babies. They are unaware of the viciousness of wild pigs who, pound for pound, are among the most dangerous of creatures.

Keeping in mind the disposition of dogs and pigs, look again at verse 6. Jesus once more presented scenes of the ridiculous. He first spoke of giving "what is holy to dogs." There is no way a mongrel can appreciate that which is holy or sacred. Some think the passage refers to the unthinkable circumstance of a priest taking meat from the altar of sacrifice and tossing it to a pack of dogs. This would never, never, never be done. Any part of the carcass left would be burned (Lev. 6:24–30; 7:17).

Then Jesus made reference to throwing "pearls before swine." Even as dogs cannot appreciate that which is holy, so pigs will never appreciate pearls. As soon as they discovered that the pearls were not food (perhaps by breaking a tooth in an attempt to eat the gems), they would indeed be inclined to "turn and tear you to pieces." My mind goes back to long-ago days when I rose before daybreak to feed the hogs. As soon as the pigs heard me mixing their food in an old metal bucket, they would go berserk. As I approached their pen, they would be squealing and climbing all over each other. I had a hard time pouring the food into the feeding trough, which was invariably occupied by at least three or four hungry hogs. If I had poured pearls into the trough instead of a mixture of ground grain and milk, as soon as the pigs discovered that was the case, I would have been praying for the fence to remain strong.

Now we must ask, "Who are the 'dogs' and the 'swine' to whom Jesus referred?" That question is best answered by first asking, "What is the 'holy' and what are the 'pearls'?" Jesus referred to the kingdom (church) as the *"pearl* of great value" (Mt. 13:45, 46). The message about the kingdom (church) is called the good news (gospel) (see Mt. 4:23; 9:35; 24:14). God's Word is *holy* (Rom. 1:2; 2 Pet. 2:21), and this holy message is spoken of as a "treasure" (2 Cor. 4:7).

All this being true, most commentators believe that Christ was warning against giving the Word to individuals who lack appreciation of the spiritual: those who continually reject the truth, the kind of people spoken of in Titus 1:15 "who are defiled and unbelieving," having "both their mind and their conscience . . . defiled." Jesus may have had in mind the scribes and the Pharisees who refused to accept His words.

Some commentators take exception to this interpretation of verse 6, but I believe that this is the simplest explanation of the passage and that it accords with other passages of Scripture. In giving "the limited commission," Jesus told His disciples that when they were rejected they were to shake the dust off their sandals and move on (Mt. 10:13, 14). Each time Paul's message was rejected by the Jews, he would turn to the Gentiles (Acts 13:44–51; 18:5, 6; 19:9; 28:17–28).

This is a hard judgment to make. We do not have the right to decide in advance that someone is a "dog" or a "pig." Love always believes the best, and we should give everyone the opportunity to hear the gospel (Mt. 28:18–20; Mk. 16:15, 16). On the other hand, if we continually try to teach someone and are constantly rejected, at some point, common sense (and the principle of being good stewards of our time; Eph. 5:16) will say, "Stop casting your pearls before swine and find someone else to teach."

Jesus' illustrations in 7:1–12 made clear that we will have to relate to many different kinds of people, and that we have to learn how to treat each kind. There are hurting people with specks in their eyes, individuals who deserve our love and attention. There are also hogs and dogs whom we will never be able to help. They will resist every effort on our part to get close to them. Their only interest in us will be in determining how to tear us to pieces. The best we can do with these individuals is to leave them alone.

Think of Jesus' tenderness with the woman who washed His feet with her tears (Lk. 7:36–50) and with the woman taken in adultery (Jn. 8:2–11). Contrast this with His scathing denunciation of the hardhearted scribes and Pharisees in Matthew 23. Again and again, He said, "Woe to you, scribes and Pharisees, *hypocrites*" (Mt. 23:13–15, 23, 25, 27, 29; emphasis added).

Christ did not say to shoot the dogs or the pigs. He just said to leave them alone: Do not throw them holy things; do not give them pearls. Paul's admonition is appropriate here: "If possible, *so far as it depends on you*, be at peace with all men" (Rom. 12:18; emphasis added).

Essential Five: Rely on God (Mt. 7:7–11)

This brings us to the great passage on the power of prayer, verses 7 through 11. I will not deal with these verses in detail. My purpose, rather, is to suggest how this passage fits into the context of the subject we have been discussing: how to get along with people.

We have learned that we are not to be judgmental, that we are to be merciful and kind. At the same time, it has been stressed that we are not to be gullible; we need to know when to shake the dust off our feet. These judgments are difficult to make. How can we keep from being tough when we should be tender, or tender when we should be tough? Verses 7 through 11 give us the answer. We must rely on God:

> Ask, and it will be given to you; seek, and you will find; knock, and it will be opened to you. For everyone who asks receives, and he who seeks finds, and to him who knocks it will be opened. Or what man is there among you who, when his son asks for a loaf, will give him a stone? Or if he asks for a fish, he will not give him a snake, will he? If you then, being evil, know how to give good gifts to your children, how much more will your Father who is in heaven give what is good to those who ask Him!

These are great verses. God answers prayer. Even as a loving father responds to the needs and requests of his children, so God responds to us.

This passage relates to our subject in several ways. For

instance, God shows mercy to us, and this implies that we should show mercy to others. It emphasizes that we can go to God with our needs—in this case, the need to know how to treat others. In this regard, the message is similar to that of James 1:5a: "But if any of you lacks wisdom, let him ask of God."

Verse 11 says that God will "give what is *good* to those who ask Him!" Someone may say, "A bigger house would be good . . . or better transportation . . . or a better-paying job"—but what is really "good"? Are not spiritual gifts the best? Among these would be a discerning spirit: the ability to know how to deal with all kinds of people. If you really want to get along with people, if relationships are important to you, then you will spend much time in prayer.

Essential Six: Apply the Golden Rule (Mt. 7:12)

Verse 12 has been called the high point of the Sermon on the Mount. Certainly, it climaxes the discussion on how to get along with others. The passage begins, "In everything, therefore. . . ." In a sense, it summarizes all that has been said in the sermon regarding human relationships—whether with brother or enemy, whether with friend or foe. Specifically, it sums up everything that we have learned in 7:1–11 about getting along with others: "In everything, therefore, treat people the same way you want them to treat you, for this is the Law and the Prophets." We generally put it this way: "Do unto others as you would have them do unto you." This is probably the universally best-known statement of Jesus. Almost everyone admires these words; even those who do not live by the precept admire the principle.

Prior to Jesus, many had worded the principle of verse 12 in the negative: "Do *not* do unto others what you would *not* want them to do to you." Among those who expressed this were Socrates, Aristotle, Hillel (the noted Jewish teacher), Confucius, and Buddha. Jesus, however, was the first to express it positively: "*Do* unto others. . . ."

There is a world of difference between the negative and the positive approaches—much more than merely the inclusion or exclusion of the word "not." The negative statement was largely a matter of self-protection, while the positive is a matter of self-forgetfulness. Further, it is possible to fulfill the negative by doing nothing. On the basis of the negative expression, the "goats" condemned in Matthew 25 could have been saved. They had not necessarily done evil, but they had neglected to do good (see Mt. 25:31, 32, 41, 42). One can only fulfill the positive expression by doing good. Again, one does not even have to be religious to embrace the negative philosophy, for that is a naturalistic way of looking at life—but the second is the basis of pure religion (Mt. 7:12b). Phillips' translation has "this is the essence of all true religion."[18]

This passage comes at the end of the discussion because it summarizes what came before, but it is also here because it enunciates a principle that will cover a thousand and one other situations that arise in relationships. Imagine that you had a book that dealt with every possible relationship problem. Try to visualize how large such a volume would be. Then imagine that you are interacting with someone and a crisis arises. You start frantically leafing through the book to find how to deal with it. After an hour or so, you find the answer you need—but the other person is gone. Instead of giving you such a volume, Jesus said, in effect, "Here's how to handle *any* crisis: Ask yourself, 'What if the situation were reversed? How would I want to be treated?' Then treat the other person like that."

This is simple, yet so profound. Just imagine how the world would be if all of life were conducted on this basis. What if every business were so conducted? What if every employee treated others as he would like to be treated? What if every organization honored this principle? What if the people in every home, every school, every nation, every congregation always treated others the way they would want to be treated?

Most of us understand what the Golden Rule is talking about. The passage has reference to general truths that apply to all people. We all want to be treated with tenderness and compassion, so we need to treat others that way. We like to be appreciated, so we should express appreciation for others. We want others to

---

[18]Ibid., 14.

believe the best of us, to put the best construction on what we do, so we should do the same for them. The list can be extended: We want others to try to understand us, to cover our lapses into stupidity with the mantle of kindness, to forgive us—so let us "do unto others" as we would have them do unto us.

Wouldn't it be wonderful if we lived in a world where everyone treated everyone else like that? Wouldn't it be wonderful if *we* treated everyone like that?

Conclusion

Mahatma Gandhi (1869–1948), the influential leader in India, is said to have been greatly impressed with Christianity. He was especially impressed with the great teachings found in the Sermon on the Mount, including the Golden Rule. When asked why he was not a Christian, he replied sadly that he had not seen any Christian *living* by those principles. Do we live by the principles we have studied?

Matthew 7:1–12 is followed by these familiar words:

> Enter through the narrow gate; for the gate is wide and the way is broad that leads to destruction, and there are many who enter through it. For the gate is small and the way is narrow that leads to life, and there are few who find it (Mt. 7:13, 14).

Would I be too bold to suggest that the gate is so narrow that it will only allow entrance to . . .

- those who are not judgmental?
- those whose first concern is in making needed changes in their own lives?
- those who help others humbly and sensitively?
- those who have learned how to deal with differences and difficulties?
- those who have determined to rely on God?
- those who live by the Golden Rule?

While Matthew 7:13, 14 must be applied to more than just

human relationships, surely the passage includes this. It is so important to learn to get along with other people.

SECTION III

JESUS' TEACHING AND HEALING

Includes a Harmony of

Mt. 8:1, 5–13; 11:2–30; 12:22–50

Mk. 3:20–35

Lk. 7:1—8:3, 19–21; 11:14–36

A CENTURION'S SERVANT HEALED
(MT. 8:1, 5–13; LK. 7:1–10)

Matthew 8:1, 5–13

[1]When Jesus came down from the mountain, large crowds followed Him.

[5]And when Jesus entered Capernaum, a centurion came to Him, imploring Him, [6]and saying, "Lord, my servant is lying paralyzed at home, fearfully tormented." [7]Jesus said to him, "I will come and heal him." [8]But the centurion said, "Lord, I am not worthy for You to come under my roof, but just say the word, and my servant will be healed. [9]For I also am a man under authority, with soldiers under me; and I say to this one, 'Go!' and he goes, and to another, 'Come!' and he comes, and to my slave, 'Do this!' and he does it." [10]Now when Jesus heard this, He marveled and said to those who were following, "Truly I say to you, I have not found such great faith with anyone in Israel. [11]I say to you that many will come from east and west, and recline at the table with Abraham, Isaac and Jacob in the kingdom of heaven; [12]but the sons of the kingdom will be cast out into the outer darkness; in that place there will be weeping and gnashing of teeth." [13]And Jesus said to the centurion, "Go; it shall be done for you as you have believed." And the servant was healed that very moment.

Luke 7:1–10

[1]When He had completed all His discourse in the hearing of the people, He went to Capernaum.

[2]And a centurion's slave, who was highly regarded by him,

was sick and about to die. ³When he heard about Jesus, he sent some Jewish elders asking Him to come and save the life of his slave. ⁴When they came to Jesus, they earnestly implored Him, saying, "He is worthy for You to grant this to him; ⁵for he loves our nation and it was he who built us our synagogue." ⁶Now Jesus started on His way with them; and when He was not far from the house, the centurion sent friends, saying to Him, "Lord, do not trouble Yourself further, for I am not worthy for You to come under my roof; ⁷for this reason I did not even consider myself worthy to come to You, but just say the word, and my servant will be healed. ⁸For I also am a man placed under authority, with soldiers under me; and I say to this one, 'Go!' and he goes, and to another, 'Come!' and he comes, and to my slave, 'Do this!' and he does it." ⁹Now when Jesus heard this, He marveled at him, and turned and said to the crowd that was following Him, "I say to you, not even in Israel have I found such great faith." ¹⁰When those who had been sent returned to the house, they found the slave in good health.

After the Sermon on the Mount, **when Jesus came down from the mountain, large crowds followed Him** (Mt. 8:1). From that time forward, Christ would be surrounded by crowds everywhere He traveled (see Lk. 7:9, 11). Jesus did not see those around Him simply as a mass of people. He saw them as individuals with needs. A phrase found in Luke 7:13 expresses Christ's attitude: "When the Lord saw her, *He felt compassion....*" (Emphasis added.)

We will be looking at four vivid examples of Jesus' care and compassion for those around Him. Since all four incidents are in the Book of Luke, it is the primary source used. Two of the incidents are also in the Book of Matthew, which makes a good supplementary source.

After completing His discourse on the mountain, Jesus returned to Capernaum (Lk. 7:1). While there, a **centurion** sent a Jewish delegation to beg Christ to heal his servant (Lk. 7:2–5). Perhaps he had heard of Jesus' healing a fellow-townsman's son earlier (Jn. 4:46–54). Matthew's account indicates that the centurion spoke directly to Jesus, while in Luke's account, the officer sent people to speak to Christ. Perhaps both were true, or perhaps the centurion, who had a feeling of unworthiness, only spoke to Christ *through* those he sent.

A "centurion" was a Roman officer over one hundred soldiers (as his title indicates). This particular centurion was on good terms with the Jewish community. He had furnished funds for the building of their synagogue.

The centurion's concern was for one of his slaves. The **servant** was **lying paralyzed** at the officer's home—in great pain and **about to die** (Mt. 8:6; Lk. 7:2). Luke's account records that the servant **was highly regarded** by the centurion (Lk. 7:2). The KJV has "was dear unto him." We have all had someone we counted "dear" who was seriously ill and can understand the centurion's uneasiness.

Jesus responded by starting to the soldier's house, but the man sent word that he was not worthy for Christ to enter his home. He acknowledged Jesus' spiritual authority (Lk. 7:6–8). **Now when Jesus heard this, He marveled and said to those who were following, "Truly I say to you, I have not found such great faith with anyone in Israel"** (Mt. 8:10). The faith of the centurion prompted a prediction that many Gentiles (those **from east and west**) would be part of Christ's kingdom while many Jews (**the sons of the kingdom**) would not (Mt. 8:11, 12). **And the servant was healed that very moment** (Mt. 8:13b).

Jesus is not still walking the earth, and His time for performing miracles has passed; but He still cares when sickness invades our homes.

A WIDOW'S SON RAISED
(LK. 7:11–17)

[11]**Soon afterwards He went to a city called Nain; and His disciples were going along with Him, accompanied by a large crowd.** [12]**Now as He approached the gate of the city, a dead man was being carried out, the only son of his mother, and she was a widow; and a sizeable crowd from the city was with her.** [13]**When the Lord saw her, He felt compassion for her, and said**

to her, "Do not weep." ¹⁴And He came up and touched the coffin; and the bearers came to a halt. And He said, "Young man, I say to you, arise!" ¹⁵The dead man sat up and began to speak. And Jesus gave him back to his mother. ¹⁶Fear gripped them all, and they began glorifying God, saying, "A great prophet has arisen among us!" and, "God has visited His people!" ¹⁷This report concerning Him went out all over Judea and in all the surrounding district.

Soon afterwards (some manuscripts have "the next day"; the KJV has "the day after"), Christ traveled to the city of **Nain** (Lk. 7:11), which was twenty or so miles south-southwest of Capernaum. (See the map "Palestine During the Life of Christ" in the appendix.) As Jesus, His disciples, and the ever-present multitude **approached the gate of the city, a dead man was being carried out, the only son of his mother, and she was a widow** (Lk. 7:12).

In those days, a widow was considered destitute. When this woman's husband had died, she at least still had a son on whom she could depend. Then a second tragedy had struck: Her only son had died. She faced a future with little hope.

Verse 13 says that when the Lord saw the widow of Nain, **He felt compassion for her**. He also feels compassion for us when sorrow fills our eyes with tears (Jas. 5:11b).

Christ told the woman not to weep (Lk. 7:13b). Then He touched the open **coffin**. The Greek word σορός (*soros*), translated "coffin," could also refer to a wooden stretcher on which the body was carried (a "bier"; KJV). Some believe that the Jews seldom used coffins. As Christ touched the coffin or bier, He spoke to the son: **"Young man, I say to you, arise!"** (Lk. 7:14). **The dead man sat up** [showing that his body had been healed] **and began to speak** [demonstrating that his mind had also been restored] (Lk. 7:15a).

This is the first recorded raising of the dead during Jesus' ministry, but it was only an extension of what He had been doing: healing the sick. Both kinds of miracles reversed destructive forces that devastated the physical body. Anyone who claims to be able to heal the body should also be able to raise the dead.

The consistency of this argument is seen in the abilities of the Apostle Peter. Peter could heal the sick and also raise the dead (Acts 9:32–43).

And Jesus gave him back to his mother (Lk. 7:15b). Surely there was tenderness on Christ's face as He put the young man's hand in the hand of his mother. The fact that we no longer live in the age of miracles does not mean that Jesus does not care when death tears us apart. He gives us strength for the day (Jer. 16:19a)—and we look forward to that great day when He will raise the dead and we will be reunited with those we love (1 Thess. 4:13–18).

When the young man sat up, all those present were stunned. **. . . they began glorifying God, saying, "A great prophet has arisen among us!" and, "God has visited His people!"** (Lk. 7:16).

JOHN THE BAPTIZER ANSWERED
(MT. 11:2–30; LK. 7:18–35)

Matthew 11:2–30
2Now when John, while imprisoned, heard of the works of Christ, he sent word by his disciples 3and said to Him, "Are You the Expected One, or shall we look for someone else?" 4Jesus answered and said to them, "Go and report to John what you hear and see: 5the blind receive sight and the lame walk, the lepers are cleansed and the deaf hear, the dead are raised up, and the poor have the gospel preached to them. 6And blessed is he who does not take offense at Me."

7As these men were going away, Jesus began to speak to the crowds about John, "What did you go out into the wilderness to see? A reed shaken by the wind? 8But what did you go out to see? A man dressed in soft clothing? Those who wear soft clothing are in kings' palaces! 9But what did you go out to see? A prophet? Yes, I tell you, and one who is more than a prophet. 10This is the one about whom it is written,

'Behold, I send My messenger ahead of You,
Who will prepare Your way before You.'
11Truly I say to you, among those born of women there has not arisen anyone greater than John the Baptist! Yet the one who

is least in the kingdom of heaven is greater than he. [12]From the days of John the Baptist until now the kingdom of heaven suffers violence, and violent men take it by force. [13]For all the prophets and the Law prophesied until John. [14]And if you are willing to accept it, John himself is Elijah who was to come. [15]He who has ears to hear, let him hear.

[16]"But to what shall I compare this generation? It is like children sitting in the market places, who call out to the other children, [17]and say, 'We played the flute for you, and you did not dance; we sang a dirge, and you did not mourn.' [18]For John came neither eating nor drinking, and they say, 'He has a demon!' [19]The Son of Man came eating and drinking, and they say, 'Behold, a gluttonous man and a drunkard, a friend of tax collectors and sinners!' Yet wisdom is vindicated by her deeds."

[20]Then He began to denounce the cities in which most of His miracles were done, because they did not repent. [21]"Woe to you, Chorazin! Woe to you, Bethsaida! For if the miracles had occurred in Tyre and Sidon which occurred in you, they would have repented long ago in sackcloth and ashes. [22]Nevertheless I say to you, it will be more tolerable for Tyre and Sidon in the day of judgment than for you. [23]And you, Capernaum, will not be exalted to heaven, will you? You will descend to Hades; for if the miracles had occurred in Sodom which occurred in you, it would have remained to this day. [24]Nevertheless I say to you that it will be more tolerable for the land of Sodom in the day of judgment, than for you."

[25]At that time Jesus said, "I praise You, Father, Lord of heaven and earth, that You have hidden these things from the wise and intelligent and have revealed them to infants. [26]Yes, Father, for this way was well-pleasing in Your sight. [27]All things have been handed over to Me by My Father; and no one knows the Son except the Father; nor does anyone know the Father except the Son, and anyone to whom the Son wills to reveal Him.

[28]"Come to Me, all who are weary and heavy-laden, and I will give you rest. [29]Take My yoke upon you and learn from Me, for I am gentle and humble in heart, and you will find

rest for your souls. [30]For My yoke is easy and My burden is light."

Luke 7:18–35

[18]The disciples of John reported to him about all these things. [19]Summoning two of his disciples, John sent them to the Lord, saying, "Are You the Expected One, or do we look for someone else?" [20]When the men came to Him, they said, "John the Baptist has sent us to You, to ask, 'Are You the Expected One, or do we look for someone else?'" [21]At that very time He cured many people of diseases and afflictions and evil spirits; and He gave sight to many who were blind. [22]And He answered and said to them, "Go and report to John what you have seen and heard: the blind receive sight, the lame walk, the lepers are cleansed, and the deaf hear, the dead are raised up, the poor have the gospel preached to them. [23]Blessed is he who does not take offense at Me."

[24]When the messengers of John had left, He began to speak to the crowds about John, "What did you go out into the wilderness to see? A reed shaken by the wind? [25]But what did you go out to see? A man dressed in soft clothing? Those who are splendidly clothed and live in luxury are found in royal palaces! [26]But what did you go out to see? A prophet? Yes, I say to you, and one who is more than a prophet. [27]This is the one about whom it is written,

'Behold, I send My messenger ahead of You,

Who will prepare Your way before You.'

[28]I say to you, among those born of women there is no one greater than John; yet he who is least in the kingdom of God is greater than he." [29]When all the people and the tax collectors heard this, they acknowledged God's justice, having been baptized with the baptism of John. [30]But the Pharisees and the lawyers rejected God's purpose for themselves, not having been baptized by John.

[31]"To what then shall I compare the men of this generation, and what are they like? [32]They are like children who sit in the market place and call to one another, and they say, 'We played the flute for you, and you did not dance; we sang a

dirge, and you did not weep.' ³³For John the Baptist has come eating no bread and drinking no wine, and you say, 'He has a demon!' ³⁴The Son of Man has come eating and drinking, and you say, 'Behold, a gluttonous man and a drunkard, a friend of tax collectors and sinners!' ³⁵Yet wisdom is vindicated by all her children."

The news of Jesus' raising the dead spread through the country, even to the southern province of Judea (Lk. 7:17), where John had been imprisoned by Herod. According to Josephus, the Baptizer was being held captive at Herod's palace at Machaerus in Perea, on the eastern shore of the Dead Sea. (See the map "Palestine During the Life of Christ" in the appendix.)

When John's disciples reported to him about Christ's activities, he sent two of them to the Lord asking, **"Are You the Expected One, or do we look for someone else?"** (Lk. 7:19b). The Greek word ἔρχομαι (*erchomai*), translated "Expected One," literally means "Coming One" (see KJV). John had used the same word earlier when he had spoken of the One "who is *coming* after me" (Mt. 3:11; emphasis added).

Since John had not hesitated to declare that Jesus was the Messiah (the One who was to come) (Jn. 1:29–36; 3:23–30), some commentators are unwilling to admit the possibility that the Baptizer had a momentary doubt. The Bible does not, however, represent its heroes as free from imperfections. If we take the text in its most natural sense, in the dark cell beneath the Black Castle, John struggled with his faith.

It is not difficult to understand how this could have happened. In the first place, this vigorous man of the wilderness had been forced into inactivity. He had been imprisoned for months. This had to prey on his mind. It would have been harder and harder to keep corrosive thoughts at bay.

Further, Jesus was probably not carrying out the agenda that John had expected. The Baptizer had portrayed the Messiah as vigorously wielding an axe, as One thoroughly cleansing the threshing floor (Mt. 3:10, 12). John probably had the same materialistic concept of the kingdom as every other Jew (including the apostles; Acts 1:6). He may have expected the Lord to raise an army, to defeat Rome, to run the ungodly Jewish leaders out of town. He may even have expected Christ to free him and to visit punishment on Herod. Instead, Jesus was "just" going about the country, teaching and helping people.

John, knowing Herod and Herodias, probably anticipated that his death was imminent. It is not surprising, therefore, that he would desire reassurance: "Did I fulfill my God-given mission, or were my labors in vain?" Thus he sent his disciples to Jesus with the question, "Art thou he that should come? or look we for another?" (Lk. 7:19; KJV).

Most of us, at some time or another, have had questions about our faith. Some have suffered the dark torment of doubt. Understand that as long as we do not shut the door on God, He does not shut the door on us. As long as we have honest hearts that continue to search the Word, the Lord is as patient with us as with children (Lk. 8:15; 1 Pet. 2:2; 1 Tim. 1:16). When doubt tortures our minds, Jesus cares.

John's disciples found Christ during one of His busy healing sessions. When He heard the question, He did not charge the men to tell their teacher, "Shame on you for asking such questions!" Rather, He told them, **"Go and report to John what you have seen and heard: the blind receive sight, the lame walk, the lepers are cleansed, and the deaf hear, the dead are raised up, the poor have the gospel preached to them"** (Lk. 7:22). This answer alluded to familiar Messianic quotations from Isaiah 35:5 and 61:1. Jesus wanted to assure the Baptizer that even though He might not be carrying out the program *men* had envisioned for the Messiah, He was fulfilling *God's* agenda.

He added, **"Blessed is he who does not take offense at Me"** (Lk. 7:23). Others were offended at Jesus' claims (Mt. 13:57), but Christ did not want John to be among them. This was His way of encouraging the Baptizer to "keep the faith." One paraphrase has "Happy is the one who does not lose his faith in me."[1]

---

[1]Kenneth N. Taylor, *The Living Gospels* (Wheaton, Ill.: Tyndale House, 1966).

As far as we know, this was the last communication between Jesus and John. We are not told John's response to Jesus' message; but the fact that, several years later, Matthew and Luke recorded Christ's glowing commendation of John is sufficient evidence that, with the Lord's help, John was able to put his doubt to rest. J. W. McGarvey penned this encouraging thought: "One act does not make a character, one doubt does not unmake it."[2]

John's question prompted two discourses by Jesus. The first was a vindication of John (Lk. 7:24–30). Christ emphasized that John was the messenger described in Malachi's prophecy (Lk. 7:27; Mal. 3:1; see Mt. 11:10; Mk. 1:2)—the **Elijah who was to come** (Mt. 11:14; Mal. 4:5). He said that **among those born of women there is no one greater than John** (Lk. 7:28a).

Jesus then added these amazing words: **"Yet he who is least in the kingdom of God is greater than he"** (Lk. 7:28b). After what Jesus had just said about John, the only way this statement could be true is if the Baptizer was never in the kingdom. There is an "old legal maxim which says, 'The least of the greatest is greater than the greatest of the least,' which is as much to say that the smallest diamond is of more precious substance than the largest flint [rock]."[3] John prepared the way for the kingdom/church, but Christians today have the more exalted privilege of being a vital part of it.

The people rejoiced at Christ's commendation of John because they had been baptized by him (Lk. 7:29). This reminded Jesus that the Jewish leaders had *not* responded to the Baptizer's teaching: **But the Pharisees and the lawyers rejected God's purpose for themselves, not having been baptized by John** (Lk. 7:30).

This prompted Christ's second discourse—on the kind of unbelief that amazed and saddened Him. He chided the Pharisees for being like children who stubbornly refused to be satisfied: They had criticized John for his asceticism, and now they con-

---

[2]J. W. McGarvey and Philip Y. Pendleton, *The Fourfold Gospel or A Harmony of the Four Gospels* (Cincinnati: Standard Publishing Co., 1914), 282.
[3]Ibid., 283.

demned Jesus for His sociability (Lk. 7:31–34). He also rebuked the cities that had enjoyed the benefit of His miracles, cities whose citizens still spurned Him (Mt. 11:20–24; see the map "Palestine During the Life of Christ" in the appendix).

Christ's burdened heart turned to His Father. A prayer came from His lips, including thanks to God that He had **hidden these things from the wise and intelligent** [men like the Pharisees who considered themselves wise (Jn. 9:40)] **and . . . revealed them to infants** [those humble enough to acknowledge their need (Mt. 5:3; 18:3)] (Mt. 11:25). Jesus then turned to the crowd and extended what is often called the Great Invitation:

> **Come to Me, all who are weary and heavy-laden, and I will give you rest. Take My yoke upon you and learn from Me, for I am gentle and humble in heart, and you will find rest for your souls. For My yoke is easy and My burden is light** (Mt. 11:28–30).

A "yoke" was a crossbar with two U-shaped pieces that "yoked" together two animals working as a team. Some parts of the world still use yokes; others use some system of harness. The term was generally used in the Scriptures to refer to an undesired burden (Is. 9:4; Jer. 27:12; Acts 15:10; Gal. 5:1; 1 Tim. 6:1). In Jesus' illustration, however, the point is that the believer is "yoked" *with Christ*—and Christ Himself will carry the major portion of the weight, if we will let Him. Thus He said that His yoke was "easy" and His burden was "light."

Many people are struggling through life with heavy burdens. Even those who are burdened with doubt, as John was, should rejoice that Jesus cares.

JESUS' FEET ANOINTED
(LK. 7:36–50)

³⁶Now one of the Pharisees was requesting Him to dine with him, and He entered the Pharisee's house and reclined at

the table. ³⁷And there was a woman in the city who was a sinner; and when she learned that He was reclining at the table in the Pharisee's house, she brought an alabaster vial of perfume, ³⁸and standing behind Him at His feet, weeping, she began to wet His feet with her tears, and kept wiping them with the hair of her head, and kissing His feet and anointing them with the perfume. ³⁹Now when the Pharisee who had invited Him saw this, he said to himself, "If this man were a prophet He would know who and what sort of person this woman is who is touching Him, that she is a sinner." ⁴⁰And Jesus answered him, "Simon, I have something to say to you." And he replied, "Say it, Teacher." ⁴¹"A money-lender had two debtors: one owed five hundred denarii, and the other fifty. ⁴²When they were unable to repay, he graciously forgave them both. So which of them will love him more?" ⁴³Simon answered and said, "I suppose the one whom he forgave more." And He said to him, "You have judged correctly." ⁴⁴Turning toward the woman, He said to Simon, "Do you see this woman? I entered your house; you gave Me no water for My feet, but she has wet My feet with her tears and wiped them with her hair. ⁴⁵You gave Me no kiss; but she, since the time I came in, has not ceased to kiss My feet. ⁴⁶You did not anoint My head with oil, but she anointed My feet with perfume. ⁴⁷For this reason I say to you, her sins, which are many, have been forgiven, for she loved much; but he who is forgiven little, loves little." ⁴⁸Then He said to her, "Your sins have been forgiven." ⁴⁹Those who were reclining at the table with Him began to say to themselves, "Who is this man who even forgives sins?" ⁵⁰And He said to the woman, "Your faith has saved you; go in peace."

Luke 7:36 comes almost as a surprise. Immediately after Jesus' castigation of the Pharisees (Lk. 7:30–35), we read, **Now one of the Pharisees was requesting Him to dine with him** (Lk. 7:36a). We do not know where this incident took place. Luke 7:37 mentions **the city**, but we do not know what city that was. The Pharisee's name was **Simon** (Lk. 7:40). The story of what happened when Christ accepted his invitation has been called "one of the most touching incidents of Jesus' whole ministry."[4]

Regarding this incident, we should note that this is not the anointing that occurred near the end of Christ's life (Mt. 26:6–13; Mk. 14:3–9; Jn. 12:3–8). The place, time, occasion, participants, and results were different. Both feasts were at the home of a man named Simon; but one Simon was a Pharisee, while the other was a (cleansed) leper. (Simon was a common name. Nine Simons are mentioned in the New Testament; there were probably thousands in Palestine.) In both cases, Jesus was anointed with perfume, but by different women with different results.

We should also note that no Scripture supports the popular idea that the sinful woman in the Luke 7 story was Mary Magdalene. She is mentioned shortly after this incident (Lk. 8:2), but she is introduced as part of a group that has not been mentioned before. Also, Mary Magdalene had been demon-possessed (Lk. 8:2), but McGarvey observed that "there is no connection between sin and demon-possession. The former implies a disregard for the accepted rules of religious conduct, while the latter implies no sinfulness. This affliction was never spoken of as a reproach, but only as a misfortune."[5]

Back to the story: We are not sure why Simon wanted Jesus to come to his house. Whatever his reason, he was blatantly inhospitable (Lk. 7:44–46). In contrast to the host's disrespect, the story tells of the affection of a sinful woman who forced her way into the banquet, uninvited. Standing behind Him, **she began to wet His feet with her tears, and kept wiping them with the hair of her head, and kissing His feet and anointing them with . . . perfume** (Lk. 7:38).

Simon was shocked. He said to himself, **"If this man were a prophet He would know who and what sort of person this woman is who is touching Him, that she is a sinner"** (Lk. 7:39). The Pharisee thought he was making a judgment regarding

---

[4]B. S. Dean, "The Great Galilean Ministry," *Truth for Today* (March 1992): 18.

[5]McGarvey and Pendleton, 291.

who Jesus was; he really was making a judgment concerning his own spiritual condition.

Knowing Simon's thoughts, Christ told the brief but beautiful parable of the two debtors. Jesus taught that one who is unconscious of his spiritual needs, as was the Pharisee, **loves little**. In contrast, the woman who had sinned much realized that she was incapable of paying the debt of her sin. Thus, when she was forgiven, she **loved much** (Lk. 7:47).

In this section, we have had four illustrations of the fact that Jesus cares: Jesus cares when sickness invades our homes; Jesus cares when death breaks our hearts; Jesus cares when doubt clouds our minds; Jesus cares when sin overwhelms our lives. Peter wrote, "Therefore humble yourselves under the mighty hand of God, that He may exalt you at the proper time, casting all your anxiety on Him, *because He cares for you*" (1 Pet. 5:6, 7; emphasis added).

Those who realize how much Jesus cares, and how much He has done for them, will love Him much—and will *show* their appreciation. Since the Lord has showered His blessings upon us, we should love Him and ought to *express* that love.

APPLICATION:
LOVE, TEARS, AND FORGIVENESS
(LK. 7:36–50)

Jesus loved to eat with others. He ate with His disciples (Mk. 14:14; Lk. 22:15). He ate with His friends (Lk. 10:38–42; Jn. 12:1, 2). He ate with tax collectors and sinners (Lk. 5:29, 30). He even ate with Pharisees (Lk. 11:37–54; 14:1–6). As far as we know, Christ never turned down an invitation to dinner.

Luke 7:36–50 tells about the first time Jesus was invited to eat with a Pharisee. A surprising turn of events gave rise to one of Jesus' most touching messages on love and forgiveness.

A Remarkable Request (Lk. 7:36a)

The story begins, "Now one of the Pharisees was requesting Him to dine with him" (Lk. 7:36a). The Pharisee's name was Simon (Lk. 7:40, 43, 44). In the original language, the word translated "was requesting" suggests urgency. Simon invited Jesus (Lk. 7:39) again and again until He accepted the invitation.

Why was Simon anxious for Christ to eat with him? Various suggestions have been given.

Maybe the Pharisee liked Jesus. Not every Pharisee hated Christ (Jn. 7:45–52; Lk. 13:31). As a rule, we invite people into our homes because we enjoy their company. However, in view of subsequent events, this hardly seems to have been Simon's motivation.

His purpose might have been that of other Pharisees: Perhaps he was trying to trap Jesus or discover some fault he could use in accusing Him. This is possible, but nothing in the narrative indicates a deliberate attempt on the part of Simon to ensnare Christ.

Simon's motivation seems to be somewhere between the first two suggestions. He had surely heard what his fellow Pharisees were saying about the Lord. At the same time, he was probably aware of the popular opinion of Christ. Shortly before this, Jesus had been at Nain, where the people had exclaimed, "A great prophet has arisen among us!" (Lk. 7:16). Simon's use of the word "prophet" (Lk. 7:39) may indicate that he had heard of the words used at Nain. The question on Simon's mind seems to have been "Who is this Man, really?"

Other reasons for the invitation have been proposed, but whatever Simon's purpose, Jesus would have been aware of it (Jn. 2:25). This prompts another question: Why would Christ accept such a dubious invitation? Again, several possibilities come to mind.

Jesus surely knew that Simon was uncertain who and what He was. Thus He may have gone to help Simon. Others would be present during the meal (see Lk. 7:49); maybe Christ went to teach them. Further, Jesus likely knew what would happen during the meal. Even though He forfeited some divine attributes when He became flesh (Phil. 2:6, 7; see Mk. 13:32), Jesus could still read minds (Jn. 2:25) and had some supernatural knowledge about others (Jn. 1:48; 4:17, 18). To some extent, He could foresee the future (Jn. 6:71; Mk. 8:31). He *may* have foreseen that the woman would be at the feast. He could have gone to encourage the woman who would "crash the party." Finally, Jesus enjoyed eating with, talking with, and having fellowship with people—all kinds of people, even those who opposed Him. He had taught His disciples to love their enemies (Mt. 5:44); maybe He was giving a practical demonstration of such love.

The correct answer to why Jesus went to Simon's house is probably "All of the above." The important fact is that Jesus *did* accept the invitation—and went to eat with a Pharisee.

An Inhospitable Individual (Lk. 7:36b, 44–46)

Verse 36b says, "And He entered the Pharisee's house and reclined at the table." We learn later that much happened (or, rather, did *not* happen) between Jesus' entering the house and His reclining at the table.

In those days, social customs and circumstances dictated that certain courtesies be extended to a guest who entered a home. First, the host gave the visitor a kiss of welcome (Mt. 26:49; Acts 20:37; Rom. 16:16). Ordinarily, this was a kiss on the cheek.

Then someone provided a basin of water and a towel so that the visitor might wash his feet (Jn. 13:4, 5; 1 Tim. 5:10). This menial task was often performed by servants. The procedure was practical, because men wore sandals as they walked along the filthy pathways. The ritual provided comfort for the visitor and also protected the rugs and cushions in the home of the host.

A third courtesy, though not as common, was often extended to an honored guest: the provision of oil or ointment for the head and/or face (Ps. 45:7; Eccles. 9:8; Amos 6:6). If the visitor had spent hours under the grueling sun, this expression of kindness was both welcome and refreshing.

When Jesus arrived at Simon's house, not one of these amenities was extended to him. He later told His host, "I entered your house; you gave Me no water for My feet. . . . You gave Me no kiss. . . . You did not anoint My head with oil . . ." (Lk. 7:44–46). There is no indication that the other guests (Lk. 7:49) were also neglected. The words "Me" and "My" in verses 44 through 46 imply that only Christ received this triple insult.

A Weeping Woman (Lk. 7:36–39, 44–46)

Before we continue with the story, some explanations are needed. What is meant by the statement that Jesus "reclined at the table" (Lk. 7:36)? How was an uninvited guest able to make her way into the feast with seemingly little difficulty (Lk. 7:37)? When she arrived, why did she find herself at Jesus' feet (Lk. 7:38) instead of His head? We need to set the scene.

First, picture the guests around the table. The usual position for dining was reclining on one's left side, supported by the left elbow. This allowed the right hand to pick up food. The head was toward the food, while the feet pointed away. Two other details should be mentioned: The feet were bare, the sandals having been left by the door, and none but men were present. Women were allowed at feasts only to serve or to entertain (see Mt. 14:6).

Next, envision the general commotion of an Eastern feast. There was talking and laughter. There were servants coming and going—filling cups, removing one course and bringing the next. There were probably also curious onlookers around the wall of the room or courtyard where the feast was held. Privacy, as we know it in the western world, was relatively unknown in the East at that time. Spectators often intruded on a banquet, especially if they learned that a renowned personality was present. It would therefore have been easy for an uninvited sinner to show up suddenly, in the middle of Simon's dinner party.

With these facts in mind, let us continue with the text: "And there was a woman in the city who was a sinner; and when she learned that He was reclining at the table in the Pharisee's house, she brought an alabaster vial of perfume" (Lk. 7:37).

This woman is called "a sinner." One edition of the NASB has this margin note: "i.e., an immoral woman." Jesus later said that her sins were "many" (Lk. 7:47). Whatever her sins, they were well-known; she had a bad reputation (Lk. 7:39). Most commentators conclude that the word "sinner" in verse 37 is a euphemism for "prostitute." All of us are sinners (Rom. 3:23), but this woman's sins do not seem to be of the ordinary variety that plague most of us. Her sins were of such a nature that they had made her notorious.

This notorious sinner knew who Jesus was and that her life had been turned around by Him. Jesus' parable of the two debtors teaches that one who is *forgiven* much *loves* much (Lk. 7:47). Since the woman expressed her love for Jesus from the moment she entered the room, she must have been forgiven prior to entering the room. The two may never have had a face-to-face encounter before, but she could have had many opportunities to hear Him speak. She had seen His love for sinners and the outcast (see Mt. 11:5, 19). She may have heard His tender invitation found in Matthew 11:28–30.

Her strong desire to see Jesus, the courage it would have taken to break into an all-male occasion, the tears she shed (Lk. 7:37, 38)—these are evidence of the powerful emotions filling this woman's heart. Try to understand her hopelessness before she learned of Christ: the dread of each new day, her aversion to others, the self-loathing. Then she had heard Jesus, and the light of truth had driven away the darkness in her mind. Faith (Lk. 7:50) had replaced skepticism; godly sorrow (Lk. 7:38) had replaced the sorrow of the world (2 Cor. 7:10). Her life had been changed.

She apparently lacked one thing: an opportunity to express her appreciation. When she learned that Jesus was in the area, she hurried to the home of Simon, clutching a flask of perfume—perhaps once a tool of her trade, but now a medium to express her love and gratitude.

Upon reaching the Pharisee's house, it had not been hard, in the hustle and bustle of the feast, for her to make her way through the crowd until she spotted Jesus. She walked around the table to where He was. When she stood close to her Savior, her emotions overflowed and her tears fell like rain.

As her teardrops fell on Jesus' travel-stained feet, they would have mixed with the dust from the trail. She unbound her hair and began wiping at the muddied spots with her tresses. It was considered a disgrace for a full-grown Jewish woman to wear her hair unbound in public. A Jewish girl bound up her hair the day she was married and never again appeared in public with her hair down. Oblivious to any gasps, the woman continued to rub at Jesus' feet.

Then she began to kiss His feet. When you read that she kissed the Lord's feet, do not think of the soft, manicured feet of a pampered prince. Think of the rough, cracked feet of this restless Preacher who walked everywhere He traveled—feet, on this occasion, still caked with the dust and debris of the Galilean pathways. According to verse 45, she kissed those rugged feet again and again. Finally, she picked up her flask, opened it, and began pouring perfumed oil on His feet.

We can imagine the effect this was having on Simon's banquet. Keep in mind that Pharisees had nothing to do with women in public. Remember the sinister reputation of this woman in this community. Add to this the outlandish behavior of the woman in her weeping, wiping, and pouring—not to mention her scandalous behavior in letting down her hair. Conversation had dried up, no doubt, and every eye was on this woman and Jesus.

How did the details of this situation affect Christ? Did He see the woman before He felt the tears splashing on His feet? What was His immediate response to her extravagant and unorthodox expressions of gratitude?

We cannot be sure of Christ's initial reaction, but we are told of the effect on Simon. The Pharisee was probably embarrassed by what he considered an inappropriate display in his house—but he was also filled with a certain satisfaction. If he had any questions about what kind of person Jesus was, those questions had been answered. "He said to himself, 'If this man were a prophet He would know who and what sort of person this woman is who is touching Him, that she is a sinner'" (Lk. 7:39).

As far as Simon was concerned, the facts only permitted two possible conclusions: Either Jesus did not know what kind of person the woman was and therefore was not a prophet, or else He knew who she was and did not care. In the latter case, He would not be a good man. According to rabbinic (uninspired) traditions, to be touched by a sinful woman made one ceremonially unclean. What Simon did not realize is that Jesus *did* know who she was and what she had been. He also knew who and what Simon was—and was about to expose him to everyone present.

A Simple Story (Lk. 7:40–50)

Knowing His host's thoughts, "Jesus answered him, 'Simon, I have something to say to you'" (Lk. 7:40a). As far as the Pharisee was concerned, the drama was over, the riddle had been solved. You can almost hear the irony in his voice as he replied, "Say it, Teacher" (Lk. 7:40b). "Teacher" is a literal translation of the Greek. This is an honorary title that Simon used for Jesus—probably spoken in irony, since the Pharisee had decided that Christ was *not* a spokesman for God (that is, a prophet).

Jesus then told a simple little story, an anecdote just two sentences long. It has three characters, with a minimum of plot: "A moneylender had two debtors: one owed five hundred denarii, and the other fifty. When they were unable to repay, he graciously forgave them both" (Lk. 7:41, 42a). A denarius was a day's wages for a common laborer (see Mt. 20:2). Thus one debtor owed almost two months' wages to a moneylender, while the other owed everything he could make in almost two years.

When you read "moneylender," do not think of your friendly neighborhood banker. Rather, think of an individual often characterized as money-gouging, hardhearted, and flinty-faced: the kind of person who preys on the poor, who charges an outrageous rate of interest, and who is not lenient to those unable to pay on time.

Christ followed the story by asking, "So which of them [the two debtors] will love him [the moneylender] more?" (Lk. 7:42b). Most moneylenders then and now would snort and say, "I don't want love. I want *money!*"

Being unable to pay a debt has always been serious business. Matthew 18:23–35 tells of men being thrown into prison and tortured because they could not pay their debts. Jesus' simple story therefore took an unexpected turn when He said that the moneylender forgave the debts of the two men. Moneylenders have been known to break legs or crack ribs, but they seldom say, "Don't worry about what you owe me. Forget it!" However, the moneylender in Christ's parable did just that.

Jesus then turned to Simon and asked, "So which of them [the two forgiven debtors] will love him [the forgiving moneylender] more?" (Lk. 7:42b). The Pharisee was probably bored. In his mind, the story was undoubtedly stupid and the question absurdly simple. You can almost hear the condescension in his voice as he answered, "I suppose the one whom he forgave more" (Lk. 7:43a).

Jesus said to him, "You have judged correctly" (Lk. 7:43b). Underline the word "judged." Simon had not merely given an answer; he had announced a judgment—a judgment on himself. His own words would convict him.

Turning to the woman, Christ said to the Pharisee, "Do you see this woman?" (Lk. 7:44a). I can imagine Simon thinking, "What a ridiculous question! How could I not see her? She has ruined my dinner party and embarrassed me! I would have had her thrown out at once if I had not wanted to see Jesus' reaction. Certainly, I see her!" However, he had not really seen her, had he? His eyes had been so full of what she *had been* that he could not see her for what she *was*. The poet Tennyson wrote these sad words: "The world will not believe a man repents."[6]

Looking at the woman, but speaking to Simon, Jesus continued,

> I entered your house; you gave Me no water for My feet, but she has wet My feet with her tears and wiped them with her hair. You gave Me no kiss; but she, since the time I came in, has not ceased to kiss My feet. You did not anoint My head with oil, but she anointed My feet with perfume (Lk. 7:44b–46).

Jesus then applied the story He had told: "For this reason I say to you, her sins, which are many, have been forgiven, for she loved much; but he who is forgiven little, loves little" (Lk. 7:47).

Look back at the parable in verses 41 and 42. Burton Coffman[7] suggested this application:

---

[6]Alfred, Lord Tennyson, *Geraint and Enid*; quoted in W. Emery Barnes, *The Forgiveness of Jesus Christ* (New York: Macmillan Co., 1936), 53.

[7]Adapted from James Burton Coffman, *Commentary on Luke* (Abilene, Tex.: ACU Press, 1975), 147.

The lender = Jesus Christ our Lord.

The one who owed 500 denarii = the sinful woman.

The one who owed 50 denarii = the Pharisee.

Their both being unable to pay = the fact that no mortal can
   atone for even the most insignificant of his sins.

His freely forgiving both = the unmerited favor of God in
   providing a means of forgiveness for all.

One must use caution in finding significance in each detail
of a parable. In this case, for example, the Lord does not have
the characteristics of an unsavory moneychanger. Another non-
parallel is that one should not take the parable to teach that
Simon (the fifty-denarii debtor?) was forgiven. Details of a parable are not to be pressed. Nevertheless, the suggested parallels
are interesting.

If Coffman's application is accurate, the 450-denarii difference in debts would have been *in the estimation of Simon*. The
Pharisee surely would have considered himself ten times
better than the sinful woman—if not a hundred times, or a thousand. Was he really better? The woman was guilty of sins of
the flesh, while he was guilty of sins of the spirit. She was
guilty of the sin of commission, while he was guilty of the sin
of omission. She was probably noted for one sin, while the
Pharisee had multiplied his sins: He was guilty of pride, self-
centeredness, self-righteousness, prejudice, spiritual blindness,
and hypocrisy.

The specific amounts mentioned in the parable are, of course,
unimportant. What is significant is that both debtors were
"unable to repay" (Lk. 7:42). All of us are sinners (Rom. 3:23),
and none of us can do enough good works to offset his debt of
sin (Rom. 6:23a). Each of us stands empty-handed in the presence of the One who has given us so much.

What hope do we have? Our only hope is in the gracious-
ness of the Lord. As a rule, moneylenders are not merciful—
but God is. As Paul said, "Grace, mercy and peace" is "from
God the Father and Christ Jesus our Lord" (1 Tim. 1:2; 2 Tim.
1:2).

"The parable does not deal with the *amount* of sin in a person's life but the *awareness* of that sin in his heart."[8] The woman was deeply aware of the enormity of her sin. This was evidenced by her tears. Her love for Christ overflowed. In contrast, Simon, having no awareness of personal sin, felt no guilt, no obligation to express love. Someone has said that "the greatest of sins is to be conscious of no sin."[9]

How did Jesus' host respond to His accusations? The Pharisee was perhaps speechless. At least, there is no record of any response.

Christ then spoke directly to the woman for the first time: "Your sins have been forgiven" (Lk. 7:48). He did not say, "Your sins *are* forgiven," but "Your sins *have been* forgiven." As already suggested, her sins had been forgiven in the past, but Jesus assured her of that forgiveness. The Jerusalem Bible quotes Jesus as saying, ". . . her sins, her many sins must have been forgiven her, or she would not have shown such great love" (Lk. 7:47).

Love is an important part of our attaining forgiveness (Jn. 14:15; 1 Jn. 5:3), but the emphasis in this story is that an appreciation of being forgiven will *produce* love: He who is aware of being forgiven much loves much, "but he who is forgiven little, loves little" (Lk. 7:47b).

When Jesus told the woman her sins had been forgiven, the other guests were scandalized. They murmured, "Who is this man who even forgives sins?" (Lk. 7:49b). In their minds, forgiving sins was God's prerogative alone, and Jesus was once again claiming equality with God (see Mk. 2:5–12).

Ignoring the others, Jesus said to the woman, "Your faith has saved you" (Lk. 7:50a). Her faith would have come from seeing and hearing Jesus (Rom. 10:17). Now that faith had been expressed. She had demonstrated the principle of Galatians 5:6: That which "counts is faith expressing itself through love" (NIV).

Jesus then told her to "go in peace" (Lk. 7:50b). The Greek preposition translated "in" in verse 50 is εἰς (*eis*), which means

---

[8]Warren W. Wiersbe, *The Bible Exposition Commentary*, vol. 1 (Wheaton, Ill.: Victor Books, 1989), 198.

[9]William Barclay, *The Gospel of Luke*, rev. ed., The Daily Study Bible Series (Philadelphia: Westminster Press, 1975), 95.

"into." Literally, He was saying, "Go *into* peace." Peace of heart and mind had been missing from her life in the past, but now she was given a fresh start (2 Cor. 5:17; Rom. 5:1).

Christ did not gloss over the woman's sins. He called them "many" (Lk. 7:47). Instead of dismissing her sins as trivial, He gave her motivation to quit sinning. On a later occasion, when Jesus was confronted with another sinful woman, as He told her goodbye, He said, "From now on sin no more" (Jn. 8:11b). On this occasion, that same admonition was implied.

Lessons on Love

Did Jesus' rebuke have any effect on Simon? Did the woman live a godly life from that moment on? We hope so, but the text does not say. The Bible was not written to satisfy our curiosity; neither was this story written to condemn or commend the original participants. Rather, it was recorded to cause us to examine our own hearts and lives. Let us ask ourselves the following questions:

(1) *"Am I aware of the enormity of my sin?"* Simon was encumbered with respectability. Do not misunderstand me: Respectability is to be desired, but it is a poor substitute for righteousness. It is infinitely harder to reach the heart of a respectable sinner than it is to reach the heart of the ungodly individual willing to acknowledge his sin. Let each of us say, "My debt is great, O Lord!"

(2) *"Am I aware of the wonder of being forgiven of my sins?"* Jesus did so many wonderful deeds. He healed a nobleman's servant; He raised the dead; He performed many miracles—but the most wonderful thing He did was help a poor woman to find the peace of forgiveness.

Remember that the parable of the two debtors is not perfectly parallel with reality. Here is another example: A money-lender could just *say,* "The debt is forgiven" and take the loss. God could not do that. Rather, the debt of our sin had to be *paid*—paid by His Son's death on the cross (Jn. 3:16; 2 Cor. 5:21; Col. 2:14). Let each of us say, "Thanks be to God for His indescribable gift!" (2 Cor. 9:15).

(3) *"Having been forgiven much, do I love much?"* If the story

of the cross has become commonplace, our hearts will never be filled with a consuming passion. Let us understand that Jesus loved us (Rom. 8:37) and continues to love us (Rev. 1:5). Let our affection for Him be renewed day by day.

(4) *"Has my love found expression?"* The woman's immoderate gestures of appreciation would have been puzzling and embarrassing to many who were present at Simon's house. Some probably wondered about her sanity. True love, however, does not count the cost. It finds expression in extravagance. Let each of us say, "Help me *show* my love, O Lord!"

Conclusion

As far as we know, Jesus never turned down an invitation to dinner. This serves as a reminder of Christ's wondrous invitation in Revelation 3:20: "Behold, I stand at the door and knock; if anyone hears My voice and opens the door, I will come in to him and will dine with him, and he with Me." Jesus wants to dine with us, but first we must invite Him into our lives.

SECOND GALILEAN TOUR
(LK. 8:1–3)

[1]Soon afterwards, He began going around from one city and village to another, proclaiming and preaching the kingdom of God. The twelve were with Him, [2]and also some women who had been healed of evil spirits and sicknesses: Mary who was called Magdalene, from whom seven demons had gone out, [3]and Joanna the wife of Chuza, Herod's steward, and Susanna, and many others who were contributing to their support out of their private means.

Only a few days in Christ's ministry are reported in detail. One is known as "A Busy Day."[10]

This day came at the end (or near the end) of Jesus' second tour of Galilee. Christ had previously traveled from Capernaum

---

[10]A. T. Robertson, *A Harmony of the Gospels for Students of the Life of Christ* (New York: Harper & Row, 1950), 61.

to Nain (Lk. 7:1, 11) and then to undisclosed locations (Lk. 7:20, 21, 36, 37). Luke recorded that **soon afterwards, He began going around from one city and village to another, proclaiming and preaching the kingdom of God. The twelve were with Him** (Lk. 8:1). Only Luke recorded this tour, although Matthew and Mark gave hints about the trips away from Capernaum.

On the first tour of Galilee, four disciples had traveled with Jesus. On this trip, the Twelve were with Him as part of their apprenticeship. Jesus would also have been accompanied by the ever-present crowd.

Luke reported that certain women, who had been helped by Jesus, likewise traveled with Him and the apostles. These **were contributing** to help the Lord **out of their private means** (Lk. 8:3b). It was not uncommon for Jewish women to support their teachers. If Jesus and the apostles were not fed by the citizens in a given city, the women probably bought food and prepared it. We should not suppose that this support was lavish since Jesus is always portrayed as among the poorest of men (Lk. 9:48; 2 Cor. 8:9; see Mt. 17:24–26). Some of the women are named: **Mary who was called Magdalene, from whom seven demons had gone out, and Joanna the wife of Chuza, Herod's steward, and Susanna** (Lk. 8:2b, 3a).

Mary was called "Magdalene" because she was from the little village of Magdala, on the western coast of the Sea of Galilee (see the map "Palestine During the Life of Christ" in the appendix). We will meet her again (Mk. 15:47; 16:1, 9; Jn. 19:25; 20:1–18).

Joanna was identified by her husband, Chuza, who was Herod's steward. The usual word for "steward" is not used in the Greek text. Rather, the word used, ἐπίτροπος (*epitropos*), means "administrator, superintendent or governor."[11] The LB paraphrase has "Chuza was King Herod's business manager and was in charge of his palace and domestic affairs." The message of Jesus had reached even into Herod's household. We will meet Joanna later (Lk. 24:10).

We do not read of Susanna elsewhere. McGarvey wrote that

---

[11]McGarvey and Pendleton, 297.

"of Susanna there is no other record, this being enough to immortalize her."[12]

Regarding Jesus' tour, we read that one day He "came home, and the crowd gathered again" (Mk. 3:20a). This could just mean that Christ entered the house of a host during the tour. Since the subsequent activities are followed by Jesus' teaching "by the sea" (Mk. 4:1), it is more likely that He returned to Capernaum at the end of the trip—and that "home" was His usual place to stay in that city.

Whatever the city, the incidents that occurred there led to a "busy day." On the same day, Jesus probably spoke the parables recorded in Matthew 13, Mark 4, and Luke 8 (see Mt. 12:50—13:3). The day probably closed with the stilling of a storm on the Sea of Galilee and the healing of the Gerasene demoniacs (Mk. 4:33—5:19).

BLASPHEMOUS ACCUSATIONS
(MT. 12:22–37; MK. 3:20–30; LK. 11:14–23)

Matthew 12:22–37

[22]**Then a demon-possessed man who was blind and mute was brought to Jesus, and He healed him, so that the mute man spoke and saw.** [23]**All the crowds were amazed, and were saying, "This man cannot be the Son of David, can he?"** [24]**But when the Pharisees heard this, they said, "This man casts out demons only by Beelzebul the ruler of the demons."**

[25]**And knowing their thoughts Jesus said to them, "Any kingdom divided against itself is laid waste; and any city or house divided against itself will not stand.** [26]**If Satan casts out Satan, he is divided against himself; how then will his kingdom stand?** [27]**If I by Beelzebul cast out demons, by whom do your sons cast them out? For this reason they will be your judges.** [28]**But if I cast out demons by the Spirit of God, then the kingdom of God has come upon you.** [29]**Or how can anyone enter the strong man's house and carry off his property, unless he first binds the strong man? And then he will plunder his house.**

---

[12]Ibid.

³⁰He who is not with Me is against Me; and he who does not gather with Me scatters.

³¹"Therefore I say to you, any sin and blasphemy shall be forgiven people, but blasphemy against the Spirit shall not be forgiven. ³²Whoever speaks a word against the Son of Man, it shall be forgiven him; but whoever speaks against the Holy Spirit, it shall not be forgiven him, either in this age or in the age to come.

³³"Either make the tree good and its fruit good, or make the tree bad and its fruit bad; for the tree is known by its fruit. ³⁴You brood of vipers, how can you, being evil, speak what is good? For the mouth speaks out of that which fills the heart. ³⁵The good man brings out of his good treasure what is good; and the evil man brings out of his evil treasure what is evil. ³⁶But I tell you that every careless word that people speak, they shall give an accounting for it in the day of judgment. ³⁷For by your words you will be justified, and by your words you will be condemned."

Mark 3:20–30

²⁰And He came home, and the crowd gathered again, to such an extent that they could not even eat a meal. ²¹When His own people heard of this, they went out to take custody of Him; for they were saying, "He has lost His senses." ²²The scribes who came down from Jerusalem were saying, "He is possessed by Beelzebul," and "He casts out the demons by the ruler of the demons." ²³And He called them to Himself and began speaking to them in parables, "How can Satan cast out Satan? ²⁴If a kingdom is divided against itself, that kingdom cannot stand. ²⁵If a house is divided against itself, that house will not be able to stand. ²⁶If Satan has risen up against himself and is divided, he cannot stand, but he is finished! ²⁷But no one can enter the strong man's house and plunder his property unless he first binds the strong man, and then he will plunder his house.

²⁸"Truly I say to you, all sins shall be forgiven the sons of men, and whatever blasphemies they utter; ²⁹but whoever blasphemes against the Holy Spirit never has forgiveness, but is

guilty of an eternal sin"— [30]because they were saying, "He has an unclean spirit."

Luke 11:14–23

[14]And He was casting out a demon, and it was mute; when the demon had gone out, the mute man spoke; and the crowds were amazed. [15]But some of them said, "He casts out demons by Beelzebul, the ruler of the demons." [16]Others, to test Him, were demanding of Him a sign from heaven. [17]But He knew their thoughts and said to them, "Any kingdom divided against itself is laid waste; and a house divided against itself falls. [18]If Satan also is divided against himself, how will his kingdom stand? For you say that I cast demons out by Beelzebul. [19]And if I by Beelzebul cast out demons, by whom do your sons cast them out? So they will be your judges. [20]But if I cast out demons by the finger of God, then the kingdom of God has come upon you. [21]When a strong man, fully armed, guards his own house, his possessions are undisturbed. [22]But when someone stronger than he attacks him and overpowers him, he takes away from him all his armor on which he had relied and distributes his plunder. [23]He who is not with Me is against Me; and he who does not gather with Me, scatters."

Jesus' practice was to go out early to an isolated place to pray (Mk. 1:35). At the beginning of this busy day, Christ was returning to the place He was staying, perhaps to eat His morning meal. When He arrived, the house was packed with people eager to listen or to be healed (see Mk. 2:1, 2). Mark 3:20 says that **He came home, and the crowd gathered again, to such an extent that they** [Jesus and His disciples] **could not even eat a meal** (compare with Mk. 6:31). Undisturbed, Christ began to help them.

One specific miracle is reported, a triple miracle of restoring sanity, sight, and speech: Jesus cast a demon out of a man who was blind and unable to speak (Mt. 12:22). (The inability to speak usually also indicated an inability to hear, so this may actually have been a quadruple miracle.) The people were amazed and said, **"This man cannot be the Son of David, can he?"** (Mt.

12:23b). The form of the sentence in the original indicates a cautious acknowledgment that Jesus might indeed be "the Son of David" (that is, the Messiah).

Somehow, word of Christ's hectic schedule reached the ears of some of His friends and family: **When His own people heard of this, they went out to take custody of Him; for they were saying, "He has lost His senses"** (Mk. 3:21). The Greek text translated "His own people" literally means "the ones with him." These had some relationship with Jesus—probably a family relationship. The Greek word κρατέω (*krateo*), translated "to take custody," literally means "to seize." It is sometimes used in the New Testament to refer to arresting someone (Mt. 14:3; Acts 24:6). The word indicates that they planned to force Him to go with them whether He wanted to or not. Most sympathize when sacrifice is necessary to reach an earthly goal; they understand when long hours are required on a secular job. However, most people do not comprehend why anyone would be willing to exhaust himself for the kingdom of God. Family members thought the Lord had "lost His senses."

While Jesus was teaching and healing, the Pharisees and the scribes (Mt. 12:24; Mk. 3:22) were present as usual. Some had even come **from Jerusalem** (Mk. 3:22) to harass Him. The admission of the crowd that He might be "the Son of David" (Mt. 12:23) apparently intensified their hatred. They soon launched a new attack. Unable to deny that Christ was performing miracles, they accused Him of being in league with Satan. They said, **"He is possessed by Beelzebul"** (Mk. 3:22a). "Beelzebul" (or Beelzebub or Baal-zebub) was the name of a pagan god (2 Kings 1:2). The name literally means "the lord of the flies." In this context, the name is used to refer to Satan (Mk. 3:22, 23). They also said, **"He casts out the demons by the ruler of the demons"** (Mk. 3:22b).

Jesus answered their accusation with three arguments. Mark calls these arguments **parables** (Mk. 3:23). The Lord first said that their accusation was *illogical.* **"Any kingdom divided against itself is laid waste; and any city or house divided against itself will not stand. If Satan casts out Satan, he is divided against himself; how then will his kingdom stand?"**

(Mt. 12:25, 26).

Second, He said that their accusation was *inconsistent*. They believed that their own **sons** (that is, disciples) were able to cast out demons (Mt. 12:27), but they did not believe that their followers exorcised demons by the power of Satan. Any accusation leveled against Christ could and should also have been leveled against their own countrymen.

Third, He said that their accusation was *impossible*. To plunder a strong man's house, it would first be necessary to bind the strong man (that is, Satan) (Mt. 12:29).[13] By casting out demons, Jesus was defeating Satan, not abetting him.

Jesus then turned from the defensive to the offensive: **"I say to you, any sin and blasphemy shall be forgiven people, but blasphemy against the** [Holy] **Spirit shall not be forgiven"** (Mt. 12:31). The word "blaspheme" means "to speak against." The scribes and the Pharisees were guilty of blaspheming against the Holy Spirit because they were attributing the work of the Spirit (Mt. 12:28) to Satan. Christ said, **"Whoever speaks against the Holy Spirit, it shall not be forgiven him"** (Mt. 12:32).

Understand that Jesus did not condemn His enemies for an inadvertent slip of the tongue. Rather, He denounced them for their obstinate hardness of heart. He emphasized that **the mouth speaks out of that which fills** *the heart* (Mt. 12:34b; emphasis added). They had developed such a state of mind that they called "evil good, and good evil" (Is. 5:20). How had the scribes and the Pharisees reached such a deplorable condition? By constantly and consistently refusing to consider the Spirit-engendered evidence that proved Jesus to be the Messiah, their hearts had become rock-hard (Jn. 12:40).

Sometimes people wonder if they have committed "the sin against the Holy Spirit." A wise old preacher said, "If you're worried that you've committed it, you haven't." He meant that such concern is evidence that one's heart is not irreversibly hard-

---

[13]For a full discussion on the "binding" of the devil, see David L. Roper, *Revelation 12 — 22*, Truth for Today Commentary: An Exegesis & Application of the Holy Scriptures (Searcy, Ark.: Resource Publications, 2002), 303–309.

ened. Actually, since Jesus is not still walking the earth, performing miracles by the power of the Spirit, people today cannot be guilty of the *exact* sin the Pharisees committed. Still, a *similar* sin is possible: People can allow their hearts to become so hardened that "it is impossible to renew them again to repentance" (Heb. 6:6; see vv. 4–6).

SIGN-SEEKERS
(MT. 12:38–45; LK. 11:16, 24–26, 29–36)

Matthew 12:38–45

[38]Then some of the scribes and Pharisees said to Him, "Teacher, we want to see a sign from You." [39]But He answered and said to them, "An evil and adulterous generation craves for a sign; and yet no sign will be given to it but the sign of Jonah the prophet; [40]for just as Jonah was three days and three nights in the belly of the sea monster, so will the Son of Man be three days and three nights in the heart of the earth. [41]The men of Nineveh will stand up with this generation at the judgment, and will condemn it because they repented at the preaching of Jonah; and behold, something greater than Jonah is here. [42]The Queen of the South will rise up with this generation at the judgment and will condemn it, because she came from the ends of the earth to hear the wisdom of Solomon; and behold, something greater than Solomon is here.

[43]"Now when the unclean spirit goes out of a man, it passes through waterless places seeking rest, and does not find it. [44]Then it says, 'I will return to my house from which I came'; and when it comes, it finds it unoccupied, swept, and put in order. [45]Then it goes and takes along with it seven other spirits more wicked than itself, and they go in and live there; and the last state of that man becomes worse than the first. That is the way it will also be with this evil generation."

Luke 11:16, 24–26, 29–36

[16]Others, to test Him, were demanding of Him a sign from heaven.

²⁴"When the unclean spirit goes out of a man, it passes through waterless places seeking rest, and not finding any, it says, 'I will return to my house from which I came.' ²⁵And when it comes, it finds it swept and put in order. ²⁶Then it goes and takes along seven other spirits more evil than itself, and they go in and live there; and the last state of that man becomes worse than the first."

²⁹As the crowds were increasing, He began to say, "This generation is a wicked generation; it seeks for a sign, and yet no sign will be given to it but the sign of Jonah. ³⁰For just as Jonah became a sign to the Ninevites, so will the Son of Man be to this generation. ³¹The Queen of the South will rise up with the men of this generation at the judgment and condemn them, because she came from the ends of the earth to hear the wisdom of Solomon; and behold, something greater than Solomon is here. ³²The men of Nineveh will stand up with this generation at the judgment and condemn it, because they repented at the preaching of Jonah; and behold, something greater than Jonah is here.

³³"No one, after lighting a lamp, puts it away in a cellar nor under a basket, but on the lampstand, so that those who enter may see the light. ³⁴The eye is the lamp of your body; when your eye is clear, your whole body also is full of light; but when it is bad, your body also is full of darkness. ³⁵Then watch out that the light in you is not darkness. ³⁶If therefore your whole body is full of light, with no dark part in it, it will be wholly illumined, as when the lamp illumines you with its rays."

Unable to fault Jesus' logic and stinging from His rebuke, His enemies tried another strategy: **Then some of the scribes and Pharisees said to Him, "Teacher . . ."** (Mt. 12:38a). Hypocrisy was involved in their giving Jesus the honorary title of "Teacher" (see Lk. 7:40). Next, they said, **". . . we want to see a sign from You"** (Mt. 12:38b). As they had dogged Christ's footsteps, they had seen miracle after miracle. On that very day, they had seen a triple miracle performed. What more did they want? Luke said they **were demanding of Him a sign** *from heaven* (Lk. 11:16; emphasis added). Maybe they were challenging Jesus to produce a portent from the skies, like Elijah's fire from heaven (1 Kings 18:36–38; 2 Kings 1:10).

Christ did not do "miracles on demand" (Mt. 4:3, 4; Lk. 23:8, 9). He never did miracles as a vulgar display ("for show"). Further, He knew that no miracle—from heaven, earth, or under the earth—would convince these hardhearted critics. He replied,

> **An evil and adulterous generation craves for a sign; and yet no sign will be given to it but the sign of Jonah the prophet; for just as Jonah was three days and three nights in the belly of the sea monster, so will the Son of Man be three days and three nights in the heart of the earth** (Mt. 12:39, 40).

This was a veiled reference to the resurrection of Jesus: On the third day after His death and burial, He would rise again (Mt. 16:21; 17:23; 20:19). Christ's enemies did not understand His words; nor did His disciples. (This was spoken before Jesus had announced His impending death to His apostles.) Nevertheless, the Resurrection was and is the ultimate "sign" that Christ is the Son of God (Rom. 1:4).

As far as we can tell, "Jesus was one full day, two full nights, and parts of two other days in the grave."[14] Why, then, did He say that He would be "three days and three nights" in the grave? J. W. McGarvey gave this explanation:

> . . . as the Jews reckoned a part of a day as a whole day when it occurred at the beginning or end of a series, [Jesus] was correctly spoken of as being three days in the grave. The Jews had three phrases . . . : "on the third day," "after three days," and "three days and three nights," which all meant the same thing; that is, three days, two of which might be fractional days. With them three full days and nights would be counted as four days unless

---

[14]McGarvey and Pendleton, 306.

the count began at sundown, the exact beginning of a day [Acts 10:1–30]. For instances of Jewish computation of days see [1 Kings 12:25, 12; Esther 4:1, 16; Matthew 27:63, 64].[15]

Jesus resumed rebuking the scribes and the Pharisees (and those influenced by them). He said that ungodly Nineveh was not as obstinate as they, and that the pagan Queen of Sheba (**the Queen of the South**) was more open-minded (Mt. 12:41, 42; Lk. 11:31, 32). He combined two of His favorite figures of speech to teach that if His critics would open their hearts, their lives would be filled with **light** (Lk. 11:33–36).

One of Christ's more striking illustrations told of an **unclean spirit** or demon that left a man and then returned with seven **other spirits** worse than he (Mt. 12:43–45; Lk. 11:24–26). This little parable can have general application; but, in context, it referred to the Jewish spiritual leaders. After the Babylonian Captivity, they had cast out the "demon" of idolatry—but they had not replaced that "demon" with positive faith in God and obedience to His will. As a result, they were now inhabited with "seven demons" worse than the first: "demons" such as ignorance, prejudice, self-righteousness, hypocrisy, unbelief, rebellion, and misplaced values. Notice the *parallel* of this *parable*—the parallel between a man filled with demons and the Jewish leaders who were filled with sin. These leaders were not necessarily demon-possessed, but they definitely had been influenced by the devil and his demons.

JESUS' FAMILY
(MT. 12:46–50; MK. 3:31–35; LK. 8:19–21; 11:27, 28)

Matthew 12:46–50

⁴⁶While He was still speaking to the crowds, behold, His mother and brothers were standing outside, seeking to speak to Him. ⁴⁷Someone said to Him, "Behold, Your mother and Your brothers are standing outside seeking to speak to You." ⁴⁸But

---

[15]Ibid.

Jesus answered the one who was telling Him and said, "Who is My mother and who are My brothers?" [49]And stretching out His hand toward His disciples, He said, "Behold My mother and My brothers! [50]For whoever does the will of My Father who is in heaven, he is My brother and sister and mother."

Mark 3:31–35

[31]Then His mother and His brothers arrived, and standing outside they sent word to Him and called Him. [32]A crowd was sitting around Him, and they said to Him, "Behold, Your mother and Your brothers are outside looking for You." [33]Answering them, He said, "Who are My mother and My brothers?" [34]Looking about at those who were sitting around Him, He said, "Behold My mother and My brothers! [35]For whoever does the will of God, he is My brother and sister and mother."

Luke 8:19–21; 11:27, 28

[19]And His mother and brothers came to Him, and they were unable to get to Him because of the crowd. [20]And it was reported to Him, "Your mother and Your brothers are standing outside, wishing to see You." [21]But He answered and said to them, "My mother and My brothers are these who hear the word of God and do it."

[27]While Jesus was saying these things, one of the women in the crowd raised her voice and said to Him, "Blessed is the womb that bore You and the breasts at which You nursed." [28]But He said, "On the contrary, blessed are those who hear the word of God and observe it."

The story of Jesus' family is in Luke 8, illustrating the need to hear and obey. At the spot where Matthew and Mark have the story, Luke includes the episode of the woman saying that Christ's mother was "blessed" (Lk. 11:27, 28). Since all these episodes teach basically the same lesson, they are grouped together.

As Jesus spoke forcefully, a woman in the crowd cried out, "Blessed is the womb that bore You and the breasts at which

You nursed" (Lk. 11:27b). This is the only recorded fulfillment of Mary's prediction (Lk. 1:48). Christ answered, "On the contrary, blessed are those who hear the word of God and observe it" (Lk. 11:28). Jesus' words here and in Matthew 12:48–50 are a strong indictment against the erroneous worship of Mary.

Jesus was not depreciating His mother, whom He loved. This was evidenced by the fact that one of His last concerns before He died was for His mother (Jn. 19:26, 27). Rather, He was emphasizing that being an obedient son of God is more important than being the mother of Christ. Only one could be the Lord's physical mother, but all of us can be His disciples.

This important truth was re-emphasized a short time later. As Christ continued to teach the multitudes (Mt. 12:46), **His mother and His brothers arrived** (Mk. 3:31a). Unable to get to Him for the crowd, they sent word that they wanted to see Him (Mk. 3:31b, 32). We are not sure why they were looking for Jesus. Mark 3:21 and 3:31 seem to tie together; perhaps the family came to take Him home for some enforced rest. Whatever their reason, the words **Your mother and Your brothers are . . . looking for You** (Mk. 3:32) constituted an interruption in Jesus' presentation.

Ever the Master Teacher, Christ turned the interruption into a teaching opportunity by asking, **"Who is My mother and who are My brothers?"** (Mt. 12:48). Pointing to His disciples who were seated nearby, He said, **"Behold My mother and My brothers! For whoever does the will of My Father who is in heaven, he is My brother and sister and mother"** (Mt. 12:49b, 50). Luke expressed Jesus' declaration in these words: **"My mother and My brothers are these who hear the word of God and do it"** (Lk. 8:21).

Christ was not belittling family ties. Family responsibilities were of utmost importance to Him (Mt. 15:4–6; Jn. 19:26, 27; see 1 Tim. 5:8). Once more, however, He was emphasizing that there is a relationship higher and greater than that of the physical family: our spiritual ties with Him and with His Father. It is wonderful to realize that if we "hear the word of God and do it" (Lk. 8:21; see Mt. 7:21–27), we can have a relationship with

Jesus closer than that which He enjoyed with His mother and His physical brothers.

These were encouraging words to Christ's disciples (as they are to us), but also view them in the context of this day when the Lord had been so bitterly attacked. He needed to gather about Him a group of committed disciples who would serve as seed for the church after He was gone. It was imperative that these new relationships, lasting relationships, be established.

The "busy day" was far from over. Much teaching remained to be done, along with a number of notable miracles.

APPLICATION:
OUR TWO FAMILIES
(MT. 12:46–50; MK. 3:20, 21, 31–35; LK. 8:19–21)

At the end of Jesus' second tour of Galilee, He had a very busy day. The day started with the healing of a demoniac who was blind and unable to speak (Mt. 12:22, 23). This triggered the accusation that Christ cast out demons by the power of the devil (Mt. 12:23–30). After Jesus answered that allegation, His enemies demanded to see "a sign from heaven" (Lk. 11:16). In a day filled with conflict, an odd little incident occurred. (Read Mark's account, given in Mark 3:31–35.)

As we read this section, many questions come to mind: "What purpose did the gospel writers have in telling us about this?"; "Why didn't Jesus acknowledge His family—especially His mother?"; "What lesson or lessons does God intend for us to learn from this incident?" These and other questions will be answered in this study.

Jesus' Two Families

Let us begin with Jesus' two families.

Jesus' Physical Family

Most are aware that Jesus was born into a physical family. His legal father was Joseph (Mt. 1:16; Lk. 3:23; Jn. 1:45; 6:42), and His mother was Mary (Mt. 1:18; 2:11; 13:55; Lk. 2:34). Mary was a virgin when Christ was born; but after His birth, Joseph and

Mary lived together as man and wife. They had four sons, half-brothers to Jesus: "James and Joseph and Simon and Judas" (Mt. 13:55; see Mk. 6:3). They also had at least two daughters (Mt.13:56; see Mk. 6:3). Christ thus grew up in a household of at least nine people. From every indication, it was a happy home.

When Jesus left home to begin His public ministry, however, His family relationships changed. There may have been some jealousy and resentment on the part of His younger brothers. John reported that they were unwilling to accept Him as the Messiah and even spoke to Him on occasion with sarcasm (Jn. 7:3–5). Christ's mother, Mary, had a clearer idea of who He was (see Lk. 2:19, 51), but even she did not totally understand His mission (see Jn. 2:3, 4).

This brings us to the episode of Mark 3. Let us begin with verses 20 and 21 in order to get some background:

> And He came home, and the crowd gathered again, to such an extent that they could not even eat a meal. When His own people heard of this, they went out to take custody of Him; for they were saying, "He has lost His senses."

Instead of "His own people," the NIV has "his family." The phrase "to take custody" indicates that they intended to take Jesus home with them whether He wanted to go or not.

The fact that Jesus did not take time to eat was probably not the only reason His friends and family thought He had "lost His senses." William Barclay listed several factors that may have caused them to reach that conclusion:[16]

(1) Jesus had thrown away *security*. What sensible man would give up a business which was bringing in money every week, in order to become a vagrant who had no place to lay His head?

(2) He was evidently not concerned about *safety*. What rational man would take on the whole Jewish establishment, a battle that He was doomed to lose?

---

[16]William Barclay, *The Gospel of Mark*, rev. ed., The Daily Study Bible Series (Philadelphia: Westminster Press, 1975), 76–77. The paragraphs that follow are a summary of Barclay's points.

(3) He was more and more isolating Himself from the mainstream of *society*. What reasonable man would hope to succeed with an odd assortment of uneducated men, most having hands with calluses and some having dubious reputations?

Burton Coffman wrote,

> Zeal in the service of God has never been intelligible to carnal and [unregenerate] men. Zeal for business, war, science, pleasure, politics, or nearly any earthly pursuit, is admired, complimented, and emulated; but let a man devote himself fully to the service of holy religion, and the neighbors begin to shake their heads and say, "He's getting carried away with it!"[17]

We cannot be certain that Jesus' "own people" in verse 21 are the same as "His mother and His brothers" in verse 31, but there is a natural progression: In verse 21 Christ's "people" decided that they needed to take Him into custody, so they *"went out"* (emphasis added)—traveling to where He was. After some time elapsed (Mk. 3:22–29), "His mother and His brothers *arrived*" at the place where He was (Mk. 3:31; emphasis added). It certainly appears that the people in verses 21 and 31 are the same.

If there is a connection between verses 21 and 31, and if Mary and Jesus' brothers had come to help Him "in spite of Himself," this question arises: "Why would Christ's mother go along with such a plan?" After all, she had greater insight into who Jesus was than did His siblings. That is true, but keep in mind two facts: (1) Although she had some knowledge of who Jesus was, her understanding was incomplete; and (2) she was still a mother with a mother's concern. What mother is not concerned when her boy does not eat properly? She was probably not one of those distressed about her Son's sanity, but she could easily have worried about His safety. Mary's cousin's son (John the Baptizer, son of Elizabeth) had already been arrested, and his death appeared imminent. What mother would not have been concerned?

---

[17]James Burton Coffman, *Commentary on Mark* (Austin, Tex.: Firm Foundation Publishing House, 1975), 63.

Charity dictates that we put the best possible construction on the aims of Mary and Jesus' brothers. Even if their motives were misguided, they probably believed that their intervention would be "for His own good."

That brings us to Mark 3:31: "Then His mother and His brothers arrived" where Jesus was. "A crowd was sitting around Him" (Mk. 3:32a), and Christ "was still speaking" to them (Mt. 12:46). People were pressed so tightly around Jesus that Mary and the brothers were "unable to get to Him because of the crowd" (Lk. 8:19; compare with Mk. 2:1, 2).

According to Matthew, "His mother and brothers were standing outside, seeking to speak to Him" (Mt. 12:46). They probably tried to get Jesus' attention, but either He did not hear them or He ignored them. They then sent word that they wanted to talk to Him. They may have whispered to someone at the edge of the crowd and then that person whispering to the one in front of him and so forth: "Pass it on. Jesus' mother and brothers are here! They want to see Him!" At last, the message reached those on the front row, and several interrupted Christ: "Behold, Your mother and Your brothers are outside looking for You" (Mk. 3:32).

Whether their motives were good, bad, or in-between, there was an audaciousness in Jesus' family's unwillingness to wait until He finished teaching. They were, in effect, saying, "We are *family*. You should stop and see us *now*. What *we* want is more important than what *You* are doing!"

Jesus' Spiritual Family

The impertinent request put Christ "in one of the most painful situations, one of the most delicate dilemmas of his earthly ministry."[18] He would have been reluctant to rebuff His family, but He needed to convey to them and to the others present the nature and the importance of His work.

What did the Master Teacher do when faced with this situation? He turned the untimely interruption into timely instruction. He asked, "Who is My mother and who are My brothers?"

---

[18]Charles R. Erdman, *The Gospel of Mark* (Philadelphia: Westminster Press, 1967), 74.

(Mt. 12:48). Then He answered, ". . . whoever does the will of My Father who is in heaven, he is My brother and sister and mother" (Mt. 12:50).

Christ was not depreciating the family when He spoke those words. Some sects insist that their disciples break their ties with their natural families, but Jesus did not teach any such principle, nor did He encourage it. Family was important to Him. He castigated the scribes and the Pharisees for failing to honor and care for their parents (Mt. 15:1–8). One of His last acts before He died was to make sure His mother was cared for (Jn. 19:26, 27). William Arnot wrote,

> He loved his mother and his brethren with the true affection of a son and a brother. The bosom on which he slept when he was an infant, he never tore when he became a youth and a man. The woman who cherished him from his birth was dear to his heart till death.[19]

At the same time, the Lord wanted to make clear that there is a relationship deeper, more precious, and more abiding than any earthly tie.

To get this point across, Christ looked "about at those who were sitting around Him," and said, "Behold My mother and My brothers!" (Mk. 3:34). According to Matthew's account, He stretched "out His hand toward His disciples" as He said, "Behold My mother and My brothers! For whoever does the will of My Father who is in heaven, he is My brother and sister and mother" (Mt. 12:49, 50). Observe that Jesus did not include "Father" in that list, for that role is reserved for God alone (Mt. 23:9).

Do not concern yourself with which disciples qualify as Jesus' "brothers," which as His "sisters," or which as His "mother." He was not putting Christians into three different categories. Rather, this was His striking way of saying, "Whoever does the will of My Father is My *family*, My *spiritual* fam-

---

[19]William Arnot, *Lesser Parables of Our Lord* (Grand Rapids, Mich.: Kregel Publications, 1884), 115.

ily." To use Luke's terminology, He emphasized that His family consists of those "who hear the word of God and do it" (Lk. 8:21).

In Matthew and Mark, Christ spoke of doing "the *will*" of the Father, while, in Luke, the phrase used is "the *word* of God." There is no contradiction. The only way we can know the *will* of God is through His *Word*.

If we would be part of the family of the Lord, we must *hear* the Word of God—and then we must *do* it (see Mt. 7:21–27). The only way we can know God's will is through Jesus (Mt. 11:27). Therefore, to hear and do God's will, we must hear and do what *Christ* taught. What is involved in "doing"? To "do" the Word is to believe all that it teaches, to obey all that it commands, and to hope for all that it promises.

The Jews of Christ's day needed this lesson. They thought they would always be part of God's family by right of physical descent from Abraham (see Lk. 3:7–9; Jn. 8:39). They needed to understand that fleshly kinship did not guarantee a place in God's household (see Rom. 9:6, 7). Descent from Abraham was not as important as the decision to follow Jesus. What counted was not pedigree, but performance. If they desired a continuing relationship with the Father, they had to *hear* and *do*.

We also need this lesson. It is important to hear the Word (Rom. 10:17). It is admirable to read the Bible daily (Acts 17:11) and to attend every Bible class and worship service possible (Heb. 10:25). A preacher is thrilled to see his listeners open their Bibles and take notes as he is preaching (see Ps. 119:16). Nevertheless, as commendable as these activities are, they "profit nothing" if one simply hears the Word and then does nothing about what he hears. (See Gal. 5:2; KJV.) Jesus' half-brother James wrote, "But prove yourselves doers of the word, and not merely hearers who delude themselves" (Jas. 1:22).

We have seen, then, that Jesus had two families—the first, physical, and the second, spiritual. He taught that one becomes part of the second through obedience to the Lord. He stressed that, as important as the physical family is, the spiritual family is infinitely more important.

The Christian's Two Families

Now let us turn to the two families to which we can belong.

Physical Families

I was blessed with two Christian parents, Dave H. and Lillian Roper, and one brother, Coy. The Lord further blessed my life by giving me a Christian wife, Jo; three daughters, Cindy, Debbie, and Angi; two sons-in-law, Richard Honaker and Dan Lovejoy; and two grandchildren, Seth David and Rachel. These and others in my family mean more than life to me.

You, too, were born into a physical family. I hope it was a Christian family; but even if it was not, you probably had people who cared for you and supplied your needs. Perhaps, like me, you are married and have children—or maybe not. Whatever your situation, I hope you appreciate the basic value of the family. It was God's first institution (Gen. 2:18, 21–24; 4:1) and is still the cornerstone of society.

Unfortunately, some today have not grasped how significant the family is. Some abandon their families, while others neglect them. Some parents do not care for their children, and some children do not care for their aged parents. Paul wrote that "if anyone does not provide for his own, and especially for those of his household, he has denied the faith and is worse than an unbeliever" (1 Tim. 5:8). Again, he said that children and grandchildren "must first learn to practice piety in regard to their own family" (1 Tim. 5:4).

The Spiritual Family

If we understand how important the physical family is, then this statement takes on added meaning: There is a family far more important—the spiritual family, God's family. Paul wrote to the Christians in Ephesus, "So then you are no longer strangers and aliens, but you are fellow citizens with the saints, *and are of God's household*" (Eph. 2:19; emphasis added). The word "household" is another way of saying "family." The NCV renders the last part of the verse, "You belong to God's family." In Galatians 6:10 this family is called "the household of the faith." In 1 Peter 4:17 it is called "the household of God" (see Eph. 3:15).

What is this spiritual family? Paul said that it is the church. He told Timothy, "I write so that you will know how one ought to conduct himself in *the household of God*, which is *the church of the living God*, the pillar and support of the truth" (1 Tim. 3:15; emphasis added).

In this family, God is our Father (Mt. 6:9; Rom. 1:7), and we are His children (Jn. 1:12, 13; Rom. 8:14, 15; Eph. 5:1; Phil. 2:15; 1 Jn. 3:1, 2). Paul wrote, "The Spirit Himself testifies . . . that we are children of God, and if children, heirs also, heirs of God and fellow heirs with Christ" (Rom. 8:16, 17). He quoted these words from God: "'And I will be a father to you, and you shall be sons and daughters to Me,' says the Lord Almighty" (2 Cor. 6:18). In this spiritual household, other members of the church are our brothers and sisters (Acts 6:3; Rom. 16:1; 1 Cor. 7:15; Philem. 1, 2; Jas. 2:15).

How do we become part of this family? In our texts, Jesus said that we become part of His family when we hear and do the Word. John wrote that we become God's children through "a new birth" (see Jn. 1:11–13; 3:3, 5). Luke recorded that people became part of God's family, the church, when they believed in Christ, repented of their sins, and were baptized (immersed in water) for the remission of their sins (Acts 2:36–38, 41, 47; see 1 Cor. 12:13). This does not mean that there are three ways to become part of God's family; rather, Jesus, John, and Luke were referring to the same process. What is that process?

We hear the Word, which produces faith (Rom. 10:17). Then we must "do" that Word—by repenting of our sins (Lk. 13:3), confessing our faith in Jesus (Mt. 10:32), and being baptized (immersed in water) (Mk. 16:16; Acts 22:16). When we do that, we are "born of water and the Spirit" (Jn. 3:5) into God's family. Peter wrote, " . . . you have in obedience to the truth purified your souls . . . , for you have been born again not of seed which is perishable but imperishable, that is, through the living and enduring word of God" (1 Pet. 1:22, 23). In this way, we become members of God's family.

I thank God for the physical family. I thank God more for His spiritual family, the church. Here is a brief comparison of the two: Both the physical family and the spiritual family are God's institutions. The first is natural; the second is supernatural. The first is entered by a physical birth, while the second is entered by a spiritual birth. The first is for the purpose of generation, while the second is for the purpose of regeneration (Tit. 3:5). The first is for time (Mt. 22:30), while the second is for both time and eternity (Heb. 12:23). The first is important; the second is essential. The first is good; the second is better. I should also add that entrance into both is made possible by suffering: the first, the suffering of our mothers; and the second, the suffering of Jesus on the cross for our sins. (See Acts 20:28; Eph. 5:23, 25.)

William Barclay wrote that true kinship lies in having a common experience, a common interest, a common obedience, and a common goal.[20] All these we find in God's family, the church. I cannot count the times I have heard a member of the church say that he felt closer to his brothers and sisters in Christ than to his fleshly brothers and sisters.

I lack the words to convey how wonderful it is to be in God's family. It would be an honor to be a member of the royal family in a country that had a king. There would be innumerable advantages in having a father who was a multimillionaire. None of these compare, however, with being part of the Lord's family, with God as your Father. The late C. R. Nichols was once told that he walked as if he "owned the world." The venerable old preacher replied, "My Father does!"

Since the spiritual family is so important, Jesus taught that our loyalty to this family is to transcend all other loyalties (see Lk. 9:59–62). In Luke 14:26, He spoke these startling words: "If anyone comes to Me, and does not hate his own father and mother and wife and children and brothers and sisters, yes, and even his own life, he cannot be My disciple." Gordon Powell once invited members of his radio audience to submit topics for a series of sermons on "Difficult Sayings of Jesus." He received more requests to preach on Luke 14:26 than any other text.[21]

------

[20]Barclay, 82–83.
[21]Gordon Powell, *Difficult Sayings of Jesus* (N.p.: Fleming H. Revell Co., 1962), 21.

You may already realize that the word "hate" in Luke 14:26 does not mean what we usually mean by "hate." Otherwise, Jesus contradicted Himself. In the Sermon on the Mount, He taught people to love their enemies (Mt. 5:44). Surely, He would not tell us to love our enemies and at the same time tell us to hate our own household.

The apparent discrepancy disappears when we discover that the word "hate" is sometimes used in the Bible to mean "love less" (see Deut. 21:15; KJV). That this is the meaning of "hate" in Luke 14:26 is apparent when we compare that statement with a similar statement in Matthew 10:37: "He who loves father or mother *more than* Me is not worthy of Me; and he who loves son or daughter *more than* Me is not worthy of Me." (Emphasis added.) Christ was thus saying in Luke 14:26 that we are to love our physical families *less than* we love Him and God.

We must take care, however, that we do not dilute the radical words of Luke 14 to such an extent that they lose their impact. Our love for God and His family should be so great that, *by comparison*, our love for our physical families could be called *hatred*.

Again, I stress that this does not mean that we are to neglect our natural families. Most of those who put the church/kingdom first (Mt. 6:33) find that the relationships in their physical families are enhanced (see Eph. 5:25, 28, 33; 6:1–4). William Hendriksen said that "observing this rule [to be loyal first to our spiritual family] is . . . the best service we can render to our earthly family."[22]

Your Two Families

We have talked about Jesus' two families and the Christian's two families. Now let us look more closely at your two families.

The Two in Harmony

You have "the best of both worlds" when your two families blend.

---

[22]William Hendriksen, *New Testament Commentary: The Gospel of Luke* (Grand Rapids, Mich.: Baker Book House, 1978), 437.

Let us return to the story with which we started. As usual, having recorded the incident, the writers apparently had no interest in telling us the sequel. After Jesus' rebuke, did His mother and brothers stay nearby? After Jesus finished teaching the multitude, did He visit with His family? We are not told. Of one thing we can be sure: Jesus did not let them or anyone else deter Him from His mission. No one would be dragging Him home for enforced "R and R." We can also be reasonably certain that Jesus did not ignore his family when He had a break from His work. Both His mother and His brothers will appear again in the account of His life, and there is no indication that Christ had broken ties with them (Jn. 7:2–10; 19:25–27).

Ultimately, this story had a happy ending. Eventually, His brothers came to believe in Him. One of His resurrection appearances was to His half-brother James (1 Cor. 15:7). His mother and His brothers were with the apostles as they waited in Jerusalem for the coming of the Holy Spirit (Acts 1:14). James became one of the leaders in the church in Jerusalem (Acts 12:17; 15:13; 21:18; Gal. 1:19) and wrote the Book of James (Jas. 1:1). Another half-brother, Judas (or Jude), wrote the Book of Jude (Jude 1). The church historian Eusebius said that the other brothers also served as leaders in various congregations (see 1 Cor. 9:5).

In other words, Jesus' physical family finally became part of His spiritual family. You should be thankful if the members of your physical family are also Christians.

The Two in Conflict

Unfortunately, the two families may not always blend. Sometimes serious conflict occurs. Jesus anticipated this. He said,

> Do not think that I came to bring peace on the earth; I did not come to bring peace, but a sword. For I came to set a man against his father, and a daughter against her mother, and a daughter-in-law against her mother-in-law; and a man's enemies will be the members of his household (Mt. 10:34–36).

He told His disciples, "But you will be betrayed even by parents and brothers and relatives and friends, and they will put some of you to death" (Lk. 21:16). These two passages do not mean that Christ desired discord in families. Rather, He knew that the nature of the gospel and the commitment it requires would not be understood by the worldly-minded, and that strife would therefore be inevitable at times.

Do not go out of your way to stir up trouble in your household or your circle of friends. Paul wrote, "If possible, so far as it depends on you, be at peace with all men" (Rom. 12:18). If, in spite of your best efforts to get along with others, your family still abandons you, find peace in the knowledge that the Lord will not abandon you (Heb. 13:5). He has promised:

> Truly I say to you, there is no one who has left house or brothers or sisters or mother or father or children or farms, for My sake and for the gospel's sake, but that he will receive a hundred times as much now in the present age, houses and brothers and sisters and mothers and children and farms, along with persecutions; and in the age to come, eternal life (Mk. 10:29, 30).

Conclusion

If your two families do not overlap, make every effort to bring those you love into God's family, the church. Even if you are unsuccessful, there will be comfort in knowing that you did what you could.

SECTION IV

THE FIRST GREAT
GROUP OF PARABLES

Includes a Harmony of

Mt. 13:1–53

Mk. 4:1–34

Lk. 8:4–18

THE OCCASION AND SETTING
(MT. 13:1–3; MK. 4:1, 2; LK. 8:4)

A key event on what has been called the "Busy Day" was the Pharisees' accusation that Jesus was casting out demons by the power of Satan. The confrontation that followed marked a turning point in the ministry of Christ. One result was that Jesus changed His preaching style: More and more of His public teaching was done through parables (Mt. 13:34, 35; Mk. 4:33, 34). Another consequence was Christ's first recorded withdrawal across the Sea of Galilee (Mk. 4:33, 35).

Before His withdrawal, the Lord addressed a crowd, using His "first great group of parables." He presented three "great groups" of parables in all. The second group is found in Luke 15:1—16:31. The third group is found in Matthew 21:23—22:14 and related passages in Mark and Luke.

Matthew 13:1–3

¹That day Jesus went out of the house and was sitting by the sea. ²And large crowds gathered to Him, so He got into a boat and sat down, and the whole crowd was standing on the beach.

³And He spoke many things to them in parables. . . .

Mark 4:1, 2

¹He began to teach again by the sea. And such a very large crowd gathered to Him that He got into a boat in the sea and sat down; and the whole crowd was by the sea on the land. ²And He was teaching them many things in parables. . . .

Luke 8:4

⁴When a large crowd was coming together, and those from

**the various cities were journeying to Him, He spoke by way
of a parable.**

After the incident with His mother and brothers, Christ left
the house where He had been teaching and went to one of His
favorite spots: the shore of the Sea of Galilee (Mt. 13:1; Mk. 4:1).
As usual, people came from everywhere to hear Him (Lk. 8:4),
and once more He was forced to speak from a boat while the
crowd stood on the shore. The situation may have been familiar, but His sermon was not: It consisted of a series of stories—
all of them short, some very short. **And He spoke many things
to them in parables** (Mt. 13:3a; see Mk. 4:2a; Lk. 8:4).

Jesus had used parables before. In Luke's account of the Sermon on the Mount, it is said that Christ "spoke a parable" about
the blind leading the blind (Lk. 6:39). When Jesus ate with Simon
the Pharisee, He told the story of the two debtors (Lk. 7:41, 42).
Most agree that the story is a parable even though it is not designated as one in the text. Many classify His illustration of the
seven demons as a parable (Lk. 11:24–26). What was different
about this occasion was Christ's extensive and exclusive use of
parables. Matthew wrote, "All these things Jesus spoke to the
crowds in parables, and He did not speak to them without a
parable" (Mt. 13:34; see Mk. 4:33, 34). The primary thrust of the
statement "He did not speak to them without a parable" was
in reference to Jesus' teaching at this time by the Sea of Galilee.
Following that period of teaching, Christ did speak to the multitudes using methods other than parables. Nevertheless, from
that time on, parables played a much larger role in His teaching. Instead of using parables to illustrate His teaching, parables
became an instrument of His teaching.

Jesus was not the only preacher who used parables. Parables were part of the repertoire of Old Testament speakers (Ps.
78:2; Ezek. 17:2; 20:49; 24:3; Hos. 12:10). Still, Christ is "the only
teacher in history distinguished in any marked degree by the use
of parables."[1] Whenever parables are mentioned, we invariably

---

[1]J. W. McGarvey and Philip Y. Pendleton, *The Fourfold Gospel or A Harmony
of the Four Gospels* (Cincinnati: Standard Publishing Co., 1914), 338.

think of Him. F. LaGard Smith wrote, "As the Great Teacher, Jesus uses numerous methods of instructing his disciples. . . . Of all his methods, however, perhaps the most interesting and distinctive mode of teaching is his use of parables."[2] H. I. Hester said, "The parables of Jesus are unexcelled for literary beauty: 'They are the finest literary art in the world, combining simplicity, profundity, elementary emotion and spiritual intensity.'"[33]

Since parables figure so prominently in the rest of Jesus' ministry, we need to look at parables in general. Then we will survey the ten or so parables spoken by Christ on "The Busy Day."

Parables: What?

The word "parable" comes from a compound Greek word (παραβολή, *parabole*) which combines the Greek preposition meaning "alongside" (παρά, *para*) with the noun form of the word meaning "to throw" (βάλλω, *ballo*). It literally means "that which is thrown alongside." It is related to the word "parallel," which can be illustrated by drawing two parallel lines.

In a parable, a statement or story (spoken) was "thrown alongside" a spiritual truth (usually unspoken). The statement or story was generally deceptively simple, but its purpose was to teach a significant, profound truth. The parallelism can be illustrated as follows:

spoken statement or story
unspoken spiritual truth

As the parables sought to communicate divine truth, the more or less familiar situation was first generally stated, while the unfamiliar spiritual truth was generally unstated but implied.

---

[2] F. LaGard Smith, *The Narrated Bible in Chronological Order* (Eugene, Oreg.: Harvest House Publishers, 1984), 1394.

[3] H. I. Hester, *The Heart of the New Testament* (Liberty, Mo.: Quality Press, 1963), 147. Hester quoted William Sanday (1843–1920), an English preacher, author, and professor at Cambridge.

In some books on "hermeneutics" (the study of how to interpret the Scriptures), the technical definition of parable is "an extended simile." A simile is a figure of speech that makes a comparison, generally employing the word "like" or "as." "Sly like a fox" and "red as a beet" are similes. Some parables fit this definition; but in the New Testament, the term is not restricted in this way. Some parables are introduced with "like," "as," or something similar (Mt. 13:31, 33, 44, 45), but not all (Mt. 13:3; see Lk. 7:41, 42). Further, sometimes the parable is not "extended" in any sense of the word, but is strikingly brief (Lk. 6:39).

The parable has also been called "an earthly story with a heavenly meaning." This fits some of the better known parables, such as the parable of the good Samaritan (Lk. 10:30–37) and the parable of the lost son (Lk. 15:11–32), but it would be hard to classify some parables as stories (see Lk. 6:39; 8:16).

Check different listings of Jesus' parables, and you will find passages that could be classified as similes, metaphors, allegories, or other comparative figures of speech. Sometimes the parables are what we usually call illustrations. In Luke 4:23 Christ referred to a proverb as a parable. Because the term "parable" has such a broad use in the New Testament, it is hard to find two listings of Jesus' parables that totally agree. It is best, therefore, to think of a New Testament parable simply as a comparison drawn between a more or less familiar situation and an unfamiliar spiritual truth.

As a rule, the parables of our Lord are about everyday events, situations encountered by His listeners in their families and businesses. At times, He used the less familiar—such as the world of demons (Lk. 11:24–26) or the state of the dead (Lk. 16:19–31)—but none of the parables should be viewed as "fairy tales." All of them were based in *reality*.

Parables: Why?

Jesus' extensive use of parables on this occasion surprised His disciples. After He finished, they came to Him privately and asked, "Why do You speak to them in parables?" (Mt. 13:10). Why *did* Christ use parables?

First, He used parables to reveal truth to the open-minded. As a rule, when we consider the purpose of parables, we first think of their positive value:

- Parables capture our attention: Almost everyone likes a story.
- Parables stimulate our thinking: They make us ask, "What does this mean?"
- Parables enlighten our understanding: They illustrate abstract principles.
- Parables facilitate our retention: They are easy to remember.

Parables aid our understanding and appreciation of spiritual concepts. No doubt, they also helped Jesus' disciples. Christ compared the wise teacher to a man "who brings out of his treasure things new and old" (Mt. 13:52). Parables were a new way of teaching old truths.

Second, He used parables to conceal truth from the closed-minded. When Jesus' disciples asked Him why He was teaching with parables, He did not focus on the positive, but on the negative. He said, "Therefore I speak to them in parables; because while seeing they do not see, and while hearing they do not hear, nor do they understand" (Mt. 13:13). He quoted Isaiah: "For the heart of this people has become dull, with their ears they scarcely hear, and they have closed their eyes . . ." (Mt. 13:15; see Is. 6:10).

As you read these words, keep in mind the context: By accusing Jesus of casting out demons by the power of Beelzebul, the Pharisees had demonstrated that their hearts were hardened beyond repair. It was obvious that they did not listen to Jesus to learn truth, but rather to find some way to trap Him. In this hostile environment, Jesus started telling "stories"—stories that probably seemed like nonsense to those unwilling to learn, but stories that enlightened the hearts of those willing to take the time to discover their meaning (Mt. 13:16, 17).

Parables thus separated honest hearts from hardened hearts. In a sense, they were a judgment on the closed-minded.

Parables: How?

Since parables will play a greater and greater part in our study of Christ's teaching ministry, we should say a few words about how to interpret them.

The general procedure for interpreting biblical figures of speech has three steps: (1) understand the figure; (2) ascertain the biblical truth to which it relates; (3) determine what the two have in common. These steps may be adapted for the study of parables: (1) Find out all you can about the background of the story or statement that Jesus made. The settings may have been familiar to His first hearers, but some settings are unfamiliar to us today. (2) Try to determine the basic truth being taught. Occasionally, Jesus explained the parable in detail (Mt. 13:18–23, 36–43). At times He followed the parable with an application (Lk. 7:42b–47; 10:29, 36, 37; 12:40). The context often provides a clue as to the message of the parable (Lk. 15:1–3; 18:1). Sometimes the only help you will have is a general knowledge of Christ's kingdom truths. (3) Finally, place the parable and the truth side by side to see how the parable sheds light on the basic truth.

In connection with the third step, it should be understood that, as a rule, *one central truth* is emphasized in each parable. There are exceptions to this, but we must be careful not to over-interpret a parable and try to make every detail mean something. For instance, in the parable of a man who bought a field in order to obtain the treasure buried in it (Mt. 13:44), the point is that the kingdom is valuable, not that we should imitate the man's actions (which, at best, were suspect). The earlier parable of the two debtors did not associate God with the unscrupulous moneylenders of that day. In the same way, if we attempted to make every detail "fit," Jesus' words in Luke 12:39, 40 would suggest that He is a thief, and the parable in Luke 18:1–6 would label God an unrighteous judge.

A few more general principles of interpreting parables should be understood. (1) Most parables are "kingdom" parables (see Mt. 13:24, 31, 33, 44, 45, 47). Their purpose was to reveal some aspect of the kingdom, including how citizens of the kingdom/church should conduct themselves. (2) When two parables have similar details, the details do not necessarily have the identical meaning in both parables. For instance, in the parable of the sower, "the seed is the word of God" (Lk. 8:11), while in the parable of the tares, the seeds are "the sons of the kingdom" (Mt. 13:38). (3) Since parables are figures of speech, they basically illustrate truth rather than revealing new truth. One should therefore "hesitate to prove a religious doctrine just by the interpretation of a single parable."[4]

The record of the parables spoken on the "Busy Day" may be incomplete (see Mk. 4:2), but Matthew reported at least nine. Mark has several of the same parables as Matthew, plus one that Matthew did not record. Only one of the parables is found in Luke: the parable of the sower.

THE PARABLE OF THE SOWER—
AND EXPLANATION
(MT. 13:3–23; MK. 4:3–25; LK. 8:5–18)

The parable of the sower is found in all three synoptic Gospel Accounts because of its importance. Jesus told His disciples that if they did not understand this parable, they could not understand any of the parables (Mk. 4:13). It provided a key to all parables. It was a key to understanding why parables were necessary. Many, if not most, of those who came to hear Jesus had hardened, shallow, or divided hearts. This particular parable also provided a key to understanding parables in general. Learning how to interpret this story would help Christ's followers to interpret other parables.

Matthew 13:3–23

³**And He spoke many things to them in parables, saying, "Behold, the sower went out to sow; ⁴and as he sowed, some seeds fell beside the road, and the birds came and ate them up. ⁵Others fell on the rocky places, where they did not have much soil; and immediately they sprang up, because they had no depth of soil. ⁶But when the sun had risen, they were scorched;**

---

[4]John Franklin Carter, *A Layman's Harmony of the Gospels* (Nashville: Broadman Press, 1961), 89.

and because they had no root, they withered away. ⁷Others fell among the thorns, and the thorns came up and choked them out. ⁸And others fell on the good soil and yielded a crop, some a hundredfold, some sixty, and some thirty. ⁹He who has ears, let him hear."

¹⁰And the disciples came and said to Him, "Why do You speak to them in parables?" ¹¹Jesus answered them, "To you it has been granted to know the mysteries of the kingdom of heaven, but to them it has not been granted. ¹²For whoever has, to him more shall be given, and he will have an abundance; but whoever does not have, even what he has shall be taken away from him. ¹³Therefore I speak to them in parables; because while seeing they do not see, and while hearing they do not hear, nor do they understand. ¹⁴In their case the prophecy of Isaiah is being fulfilled, which says,

'You will keep on hearing, but will not understand;
You will keep on seeing, but will not perceive;
¹⁵For the heart of this people has become dull,
With their ears they scarcely hear,
And they have closed their eyes,
Otherwise they would see with their eyes,
Hear with their ears,
And understand with their heart and return,
And I would heal them.'

¹⁶But blessed are your eyes, because they see; and your ears, because they hear. ¹⁷For truly I say to you that many prophets and righteous men desired to see what you see, and did not see it, and to hear what you hear, and did not hear it.

¹⁸"Hear then the parable of the sower. ¹⁹When anyone hears the word of the kingdom and does not understand it, the evil one comes and snatches away what has been sown in his heart. This is the one on whom seed was sown beside the road. ²⁰The one on whom seed was sown on the rocky places, this is the man who hears the word and immediately receives it with joy; ²¹yet he has no firm root in himself, but is only temporary, and when affliction or persecution arises because of the word, immediately he falls away. ²²And the one on whom seed was sown among the thorns, this is the man who hears the word,

and the worry of the world and the deceitfulness of wealth choke the word, and it becomes unfruitful. [23]And the one on whom seed was sown on the good soil, this is the man who hears the word and understands it; who indeed bears fruit and brings forth, some a hundredfold, some sixty, and some thirty."

Mark 4:3–25

[3]"Listen to this! Behold, the sower went out to sow; [4]as he was sowing, some seed fell beside the road, and the birds came and ate it up. [5]Other seed fell on the rocky ground where it did not have much soil; and immediately it sprang up because it had no depth of soil. [6]And after the sun had risen, it was scorched; and because it had no root, it withered away. [7]Other seed fell among the thorns, and the thorns came up and choked it, and it yielded no crop. [8]Other seeds fell into the good soil, and as they grew up and increased, they yielded a crop and produced thirty, sixty, and a hundredfold." [9]And He was saying, "He who has ears to hear, let him hear."

[10]As soon as He was alone, His followers, along with the twelve, began asking Him about the parables. [11]And He was saying to them, "To you has been given the mystery of the kingdom of God, but those who are outside get everything in parables, [12]so that while seeing, they may see and not perceive, and while hearing, they may hear and not understand, otherwise they might return and be forgiven."

[13]And He said to them, "Do you not understand this parable? How will you understand all the parables? [14]The sower sows the word. [15]These are the ones who are beside the road where the word is sown; and when they hear, immediately Satan comes and takes away the word which has been sown in them. [16]In a similar way these are the ones on whom seed was sown on the rocky places, who, when they hear the word, immediately receive it with joy; [17]and they have no firm root in themselves, but are only temporary; then, when affliction or persecution arises because of the word, immediately they fall away. [18]And others are the ones on whom seed was sown among the thorns; these are the ones who have heard the word, [19]but

345

the worries of the world, and the deceitfulness of riches, and the desires for other things enter in and choke the word, and it becomes unfruitful. [20]And those are the ones on whom seed was sown on the good soil; and they hear the word and accept it and bear fruit, thirty, sixty, and a hundredfold."

[21]And He was saying to them, "A lamp is not brought to be put under a basket, is it, or under a bed? Is it not brought to be put on the lampstand? [22]For nothing is hidden, except to be revealed; nor has anything been secret, but that it would come to light. [23]If anyone has ears to hear, let him hear." [24]And He was saying to them, "Take care what you listen to. By your standard of measure it will be measured to you; and more will be given you besides. [25]For whoever has, to him more shall be given; and whoever does not have, even what he has shall be taken away from him."

Luke 8:5–18

[5]"The sower went out to sow his seed; and as he sowed, some fell beside the road, and it was trampled under foot and the birds of the air ate it up. [6]Other seed fell on rocky soil, and as soon as it grew up, it withered away, because it had no moisture. [7]Other seed fell among the thorns; and the thorns grew up with it and choked it out. [8]Other seed fell into the good soil, and grew up, and produced a crop a hundred times as great." As He said these things, He would call out, "He who has ears to hear, let him hear."

[9]His disciples began questioning Him as to what this parable meant. [10]And He said, "To you it has been granted to know the mysteries of the kingdom of God, but to the rest it is in parables, so that seeing they may not see, and hearing they may not understand.

[11]"Now the parable is this: the seed is the word of God. [12]Those beside the road are those who have heard; then the devil comes and takes away the word from their heart, so that they will not believe and be saved. [13]Those on the rocky soil are those who, when they hear, receive the word with joy; and these have no firm root; they believe for a while, and in time of temptation fall away. [14]The seed which fell among the

thorns, these are the ones who have heard, and as they go on their way they are choked with worries and riches and pleasures of this life, and bring no fruit to maturity. [15]But the seed in the good soil, these are the ones who have heard the word in an honest and good heart, and hold it fast, and bear fruit with perseverance.

[16]"Now no one after lighting a lamp covers it over with a container, or puts it under a bed; but he puts it on a lampstand, so that those who come in may see the light. [17]For nothing is hidden that will not become evident, nor anything secret that will not be known and come to light. [18]So take care how you listen; for whoever has, to him more shall be given; and whoever does not have, even what he thinks he has shall be taken away from him."

Jesus started His teaching by the sea by telling about four kinds of soils: way-side soil, rocky soil, thorny soil, and good soil. After He finished telling the story, as soon as He was alone with His disciples, they asked Him what the parable meant (Mk. 4:10; Lk. 8:9). At that time, He apparently explained the parable of the sower and the parable of the tares—and then added a few parables intended for the disciples only.

The Lord explained that each of the soils represented a condition of the heart affecting how that heart would receive the Word. Many, if not most, of those who came to hear Jesus had hardened, shallow, or divided hearts. Only those with **honest and good** hearts could and would live spiritually fruitful lives (Lk. 8:15).

Every day, Jesus was surrounded by all four heart-types. The hardhearted Pharisees were trying to trap Christ. The shallow-minded multitude was caught up in the excitement of Christ's ministry and miracles, but they failed to grasp the real nature of His mission. There were even divided hearts present—typified by Judas, who was struggling with his love for money (see Jn. 12:6). There were also the few honest-and-good hearts around Him who made His effort worthwhile.

This parable served a practical purpose with Jesus' disciples in explaining why He had been rejected by the Jewish leaders.

It would also serve a practical purpose in the days ahead when they began their own preaching: It would explain why some would accept the gospel and why others would not. The message of this parable is still vitally needed by all who teach and preach the Word today.

THE PARABLE OF SILENT GROWTH
(MK. 4:26–29)

[26]And He was saying, "The kingdom of God is like a man who casts seed upon the soil; [27]and he goes to bed at night and gets up by day, and the seed sprouts and grows—how, he himself does not know. [28]The soil produces crops by itself; first the blade, then the head, then the mature grain in the head. [29]But when the crop permits, he immediately puts in the sickle, because the harvest has come."

According to Mark, immediately after Jesus told the parable of the sower, He told of a seed that grew by itself until harvest time. This parable is sometimes called "The Parable of the Seed Growing by Itself." It is a simple story whose details are familiar to any who have planted a crop that did not require cultivation. As a grain field, it would not be cultivated between the planting and the harvesting. Such may have been watered and fertilized, but any attempt at cultivation would uproot the plants. As in the previous parable, we should probably think of the soil as the human heart and the seed as the gospel. The parable was most likely told to encourage the disciples:

- The gospel has its effect in the hearts of listeners, whether we are aware of it or not.
- It takes time for the seed to germinate and grow, so we need to be patient.
- If we remain faithful to the task of sowing, God will ultimately give the increase (1 Cor. 3:6).

THE PARABLE OF THE TARES— AND EXPLANATION (MT. 13:24–30, 36–43)

[24]Jesus presented another parable to them, saying, "The kingdom of heaven may be compared to a man who sowed good seed in his field. [25]But while his men were sleeping, his enemy came and sowed tares among the wheat, and went away. [26]But when the wheat sprouted and bore grain, then the tares became evident also. [27]The slaves of the landowner came and said to him, 'Sir, did you not sow good seed in your field? How then does it have tares?' [28]And he said to them, 'An enemy has done this!' The slaves said to him, 'Do you want us, then, to go and gather them up?' [29]But he said, 'No; for while you are gathering up the tares, you may uproot the wheat with them. [30]Allow both to grow together until the harvest; and in the time of the harvest I will say to the reapers, "First gather up the tares and bind them in bundles to burn them up; but gather the wheat into my barn."'"

[36]Then He left the crowds and went into the house. And His disciples came to Him and said, "Explain to us the parable of the tares of the field." [37]And He said, "The one who sows the good seed is the Son of Man, [38]and the field is the world; and as for the good seed, these are the sons of the kingdom; and the tares are the sons of the evil one; [39]and the enemy who sowed them is the devil, and the harvest is the end of the age; and the reapers are angels. [40]So just as the tares are gathered up and burned with fire, so shall it be at the end of the age. [41]The Son of Man will send forth His angels, and they will gather out of His kingdom all stumbling blocks, and those who commit lawlessness, [42]and will throw them into the furnace of fire; in that place there will be weeping and gnashing of teeth. [43]Then the righteous will shine forth as the sun in the kingdom of their Father. He who has ears, let him hear. "

Jesus spoke another parable about seed growing: He told

about an enemy who sowed tares in a field shortly after wheat had been sown. Tares were weeds that resembled wheat, especially in the early stages of growth. When the destructive deed was discovered, the servants came to their master and asked if they should pull up the tares. Since the roots of the young plants would have been intertwined, the master said, **"No; for while you are gathering up the tares, you may uproot the wheat with them"** (Mt. 13:29). He instructed them to let the plants grow together until harvest and then, at that point, to divide the desired crop from the undesired (Mt. 13:30).

The disciples later asked Christ to explain the parable (Mt. 13:36). He said that the enemy was the devil, and that the harvest was at the end of the age (Mt. 13:39). In this series of parables, there are two relating to the final Day of Judgment; this is one of them. The second parable is the story of the dragnet. Verses 39 through 43 give a vivid picture of the Second Coming and the Judgment that will follow.

Some have tried to make this parable apply to church discipline, saying that it teaches us not to make any effort to exclude workers of evil from our fellowship. Such an interpretation would make Jesus contradict Himself (Mt. 18:15–18; see also 1 Cor. 5:4, 5, 11, 13b). J. W. McGarvey wrote, "This parable and its explanation are sometimes urged as an argument against church discipline, but such a use of them is clearly erroneous. The field is not the church, but the world, and the teaching of the parable is that we are not to attempt to exterminate evil men."[5] John Carter agreed: ". . . 'the children of the Kingdom' and 'the children of the wicked one' are to live together in the world until the end of the age. Very clearly [the parable] is not . . . an injunction on a church to retain in its membership those that live disorderly or those who are manifestly unbelievers."[6]

Perhaps this parable was given to help the disciples understand why so many were unreceptive: Their enemy, the devil, was at work. It would also have given them a clearer vision of the long-range nature of their work.

---

[5]McGarvey and Pendleton, 339.
[6]Carter, 132.

THE PARABLES OF THE MUSTARD SEED
AND THE LEAVEN
(MT. 13:31–35; MK. 4:30–34)

Matthew 13:31–35

³¹He presented another parable to them, saying, "The kingdom of heaven is like a mustard seed, which a man took and sowed in his field; ³²and this is smaller than all other seeds, but when it is full grown, it is larger than the garden plants and becomes a tree, so that the birds of the air come and nest in its branches."

³³He spoke another parable to them, "The kingdom of heaven is like leaven, which a woman took and hid in three pecks of flour until it was all leavened."

³⁴All these things Jesus spoke to the crowds in parables, and He did not speak to them without a parable. ³⁵This was to fulfill what was spoken through the prophet:

"I will open My mouth in parables;
I will utter things hidden since the foundation of the world."

Mark 4:30–34

³⁰And He said, "How shall we picture the kingdom of God, or by what parable shall we present it? ³¹It is like a mustard seed, which, when sown upon the soil, though it is smaller than all the seeds that are upon the soil, ³²yet when it is sown, it grows up and becomes larger than all the garden plants and forms large branches; so that the birds of the air can nest under its shade."

³³With many such parables He was speaking the word to them, so far as they were able to hear it; ³⁴and He did not speak to them without a parable; but He was explaining everything privately to His own disciples.

Several pairs in this series of parables fit together; this is one of the pairs. As far as the record goes, the rest of the parables spoken that day were very short and were given without explanation. The first of these continued the theme of growing seed:

the parable of the mustard seed. Here the emphasis was on the size of the seed as compared with the resultant plant. The mustard seed was tiny, but it produced a huge plant. (It is important to think of the mustard plant in that time and place, not necessarily the way mustard is grown now.) This parable was probably spoken to encourage the disciples. Although Christ's movement had a small beginning, it would spread and succeed beyond their wildest dreams if they remained faithful to the task of sowing.

In the next parable, the parable of the leaven, the setting changed from a farmer sowing in his field to a woman making bread for her household. A word of explanation is in order for those unfamiliar with bread-making prior to prepackaged yeast: When a woman made bread, she pinched off a small piece of the dough and kept this wrapped in a warm place. The next time she made bread, she worked the small piece into her dough and set the dough aside. The leaven would spread through all the dough, causing it to rise. She would then pinch off a small piece of that dough to use the next time she baked. Over time, a tiny amount of leaven would leaven hundreds, even thousands, of loaves of bread.

Though the imagery is different, the message seems to be basically the same as that of the parable of the mustard seed. The Word has built-in power that enables it to spread and grow. As a rule, "leaven" is used in the New Testament in a bad sense, to illustrate an undesirable influence (Mt. 16:6; 1 Cor. 5:6–8; Gal. 5:9). Both the parable of the mustard seed and the parable of the leaven may have been warning the disciples against the insidious influence of evil. In the context, though, a positive view of both parables seems to be intended.

THE PARABLES OF THE TREASURE AND THE PEARL (MT. 13:44–46)

⁴⁴"The kingdom of heaven is like a treasure hidden in the field, which a man found and hid again; and from joy over it he goes and sells all that he has and buys that field.

⁴⁵"Again, the kingdom of heaven is like a merchant seek-

ing fine pearls, [46]and upon finding one pearl of great value, he went and sold all that he had and bought it."

The rest of the parables in Matthew 13 may have been spoken privately to the disciples (Mt. 13:36). The first of these go together: Both are about men who located something of great value. The first unearthed a treasure accidentally (Mt. 13:44), while the second found a long-sought gem (Mt. 13:45, 46). In each case, the man recognized the worth of what he had discovered and paid the price to acquire it. These parables teach that the treasure of salvation in the Gospel can be found. Some find the gospel "treasure" accidentally, while some find it because they are searching for it. Perhaps the most common way that people find the truth when they really are not looking for it is through their association with a friend or a mate.

Many lessons could be drawn from these parables, but one purpose was surely to encourage Jesus' followers. The challenge placed before them was worth every sacrifice it would take to meet it.

THE PARABLE OF THE DRAGNET
(MT. 13:47–53)

[47]"Again, the kingdom of heaven is like a dragnet cast into the sea, and gathering fish of every kind; [48]and when it was filled, they drew it up on the beach; and they sat down and gathered the good fish into containers, but the bad they threw away. [49]So it will be at the end of the age; the angels will come forth and take out the wicked from among the righteous, [50]and will throw them into the furnace of fire; in that place there will be weeping and gnashing of teeth.

[51]"Have you understood all these things?" They said to Him, "Yes." [52]And Jesus said to them, "Therefore every scribe who has become a disciple of the kingdom of heaven is like a head of a household, who brings out of his treasure things new and old."

[53]When Jesus had finished these parables, He departed from there.

The series of parables closed with a story about fishing on the Sea of Galilee with a dragnet that collected both good fish and bad. When a Jew heard about **good** and **bad** fish, he would probably think "clean" and "unclean." The Law allowed him to eat only fish with fins and scales (Lev. 11:9–12). Since the dragnet caught both clean and unclean fish, it was necessary for the fishermen to sort out what was edible and what was not. Jesus compared this sorting process to the final Judgment. In this sense, this parable is like the parable of the tares. There also may have been an additional lesson for the disciples. Jesus had said, "I will make you fishers of men" (Mt. 4:19). Now, perhaps He was telling them not to be surprised at "the catch" that their teaching would "drag in."

After Jesus had spoken the parables, He asked His followers a question: **"Have you understood all these things?"** and they replied, **"Yes"** (Mt. 13:51). They may have partially understood, but subsequent events indicate that their understanding was limited. In order to profit from these Scriptures, we must heed two instructions from the Lord: "Take care *what* you listen to" (Mk. 4:24; emphasis added), and "take care *how* you listen" (Lk. 8:18; emphasis added). "He who has ears to hear, let him hear" (Mk. 4:9; see v. 23).

APPLICATION:
"HEAR THE PARABLE OF THE SOWER"
(MT. 13:3–10, 18–23; MK. 4:2–10, 13–20; LK. 8:4–9, 11–15)

The longer I preach, the more convinced I become that, to a great extent, the audience determines the effectiveness of any sermon. I can preach a sermon in one place and people pronounce it outstanding; I can preach the same sermon in another place and some listeners consider it mediocre or even bad. In one place, a sermon may touch many hearts; in another, the same sermon may have no visible response. Although I must grant that my presentation can vary to some extent, the major difference seems to be with the audience. Jesus once taught a parable that emphasized the part that listeners play in the success of the gospel.[7]

The Parable (Mt. 13:3–9; Mk. 4:2–9; Lk. 8:4–8)

Jesus began, "Behold, the sower went out to sow" (Mt. 13:3b).

Way-Side Soil: Hardened

"And as he sowed, some seeds fell beside the road" (Mt. 13:4a). There were no fences between fields in Palestine at that time, and paths ran through the fields. These pathways would be packed and hardened by the feet of those who passed through the fields. The seed could not penetrate this soil, so it lay on the surface. As a result, "it was trampled under foot and the birds of the air ate it up" (Lk. 8:5b).

Rocky Soil: Shallow

"Others [that is, other seeds] fell on the rocky places, where they did not have much soil" (Mt. 13:5a). This was ground where underlying rock was barely covered by soil. Such spots would be common in the fields of Palestine, as in all mountainous countries. This ground was as hard as the way-side soil, but it gave the appearance of being good soil.

When the seed fell on this type ground, it could penetrate the earth a short distance and begin to grow. However, the soil was so shallow that the plants could not develop a deep root system. "And immediately they sprang up, because they had no depth of soil" (Mt. 13:5b). The result was that ". . . when the sun had risen, they were scorched; and because they had no root [and "no moisture"; Lk. 8:6], they withered away" (Mt. 13:6).

Thorny Soil: Divided

"[Other seeds] fell among the thorns" (Mt. 13:7a). This was good, rich soil, but ground already inhabited by thorns. J. W. McGarvey wrote that there are sixteen varieties of thorns in Pal-

---

[7]Since my notes go back many years, some sources for this application may have been overlooked. McGarvey and Pendleton's *The Fourfold Gospel* was a major source.

estine and that in places they grow so thick that a man on horse-back cannot ride through them.[8]

It is possible that this soil had the look of good earth because the tops of the thorns had been cut off—but the roots remained beneath the surface. When I was a boy and Dad told me to hoe the garden, I confess that sometimes I scraped the weeds off at ground level. That way the garden *looked* free of weeds, and the job did not take nearly as long. Of course, the end result was that I had to hoe the garden again much sooner.

The seed was able to grow in this soil and was even able to develop a root system, but "the thorns grew up with it" (Lk. 8:7). As a result, "the thorns came up and choked them [the young plants] out" (Mt. 13:7b). I once jotted down this truth from a long-forgotten source: "The soil can only support a certain amount of vegetation, and every living weed means a choked blade of corn." The thorns did not kill the plants, as was the case with the rocky soil. The plants grew, but they were stunted. They developed heads, but those heads were empty—so the plants "yielded no crop" (Mk. 4:7).

Good Soil: Soft, Deep, and Clean

"And others fell on the good soil" (Mt. 13:8a). This was the good, fertile soil, prepared and ready to receive the seed. It was the opposite of the other soils. The way-side soil was hard, but this was soft. The rocky soil was shallow, while this was deep. The thorny soil was full of weeds, but this was clean. Here the seed could penetrate and grow without interference. What was the result? The soil "yielded a crop, some a hundredfold, some sixty, and some thirty" (Mt. 13:8b).

After Jesus told the parable, He said, "He who has ears, let him hear" (Mt. 13:9). He emphasized that this was not a story to be heard and forgotten. He was challenging His listeners to grasp its meaning.

The Application (Mt. 13:10, 18–23; Mk. 4:10, 13–20; Lk. 8:9, 11–15)

Jesus' disciples came to Him, asking why He spoke in para-

---

[8]McGarvey and Pendleton, 334.

bles (Mt. 13:10) and what this parable meant (Lk. 8:9). Then Christ explained it. He began, "Hear then the parable of the sower" (Mt. 13:18).

Before we get to His explanation of the soils, we need to look at the significance of the seed, the sower, and the field. First, we can consider the *seed*: Jesus said, "Now the parable is this: the seed is the word of God" (Lk. 8:11). Again, He said that "the sower sows the word" (Mk. 4:14). The seed is the "imperishable . . . word of God" (1 Pet. 1:23), and the *sower* is the one who sows or spreads the Word—the teacher or preacher. Paul, speaking of his preaching, said, "I planted" (1 Cor. 3:6a). What about the *field*? This is the heart or mind of man. It is the mind that has the capacity to grasp the Word. Jesus explained "the good soil" as "the ones who have heard the word in an honest and good heart" (Lk. 8:15).

Here is the thrust of the parable: The sower and the seed were the same in every case; the difference was in the soils. It is true that the soil (the heart) needs to be prepared by the sower (the teacher) and kept clean, but in this parable only the condition of the soil (the heart) is considered. Each was in a different condition to receive the seed, so the outcome was different in each case. This parable should cause each one of us to ask himself or herself, "What is the condition of my heart? How do I receive the Word?"

Let us now look at Jesus' explanation of the four different kinds of heart soil.

Way-Side Soil: The Hardened Heart

The soil by the side of the pathway represents *the hardened heart*—trampled down by indifference or prejudice and "hardened by the deceitfulness of sin" (Heb. 3:13). When we teach people, we often meet those who have no interest in the gospel. Paul spoke of this type person in 1 Corinthians 2:14: "But a natural man does not accept the things of the Spirit of God, for they are foolishness to him; and he cannot understand them, because they are spiritually appraised." These lack a "love of the truth" (2 Thess. 2:10). The seed of the Word cannot penetrate their hearts.

Jesus thus said, "When anyone hears the word of the kingdom and does not understand it, the evil one comes and snatches away what has been sown in his heart. This is the one on whom seed was sown beside the road" (Mt. 13:19). Even as birds pick up seeds from the roadside, so the devil plucks away the Word from the man with a hardened heart. How? The simplest and most common way is by immediately filling his mind with a thousand other thoughts. Why does Satan do this? ". . . so that they will not believe and be saved" (Lk. 8:12). Faith comes from the Word of God (Rom. 10:17), and the devil does not want people to hear the Word and believe it. He wants as many as possible to be with him in hell.

Is it possible that any who read these words have this kind of heart? Is it possible that any have hardened their hearts against receiving the Word? The Bible pleads, "Today if you hear His voice, do not harden your hearts" (Heb. 4:7b). Rather, "in humility receive the word implanted, which is able to save your souls" (Jas. 1:21). Remember: To lose the seed is to lose life . . . for spiritual life is in the seed.

Rocky Soil: The Shallow Heart

Jesus then explained the meaning of the rocky soil: "The one on whom seed was sown on the rocky places, this is the man who hears the word and immediately receives it with joy" (Mt. 13:20). The rocky soil depicts shallow-minded, superficial individuals. Maybe you have encountered this kind of person: He seems to receive the truth with joy. He quickly obeys the gospel, and each of us rejoices: "Isn't it wonderful that it took him such a short time to become a Christian!" Then, just as quickly, his interest dies, and our hearts are broken. This person is like the plant that quickly sprang up because it had no depth of earth. For whatever reason, this individual has not become grounded in the truth (see Col. 1:23; KJV). He has failed to comprehend the true significance of Christianity.

According to Jesus' description, such an individual "has no firm root in himself, but is only temporary" (Mt. 13:21a). The KJV says that he endures "for a while." He presents a better appearance than the first type of soil, but he does not endure "to the end" (Mt. 10:22). The end result, then, is the same: ". . . and when affliction or persecution arises because of the word, immediately he falls away" (Mt. 13:21). As a shallow-rooted plant withers before the sun, so this individual withers before tribulation and persecution. Even as the sun strengthens the plant that is firmly rooted and withers the one with shallow roots, so persecution will strengthen the Christian deeply rooted (see Col. 2:7) in Christ and wither the superficial disciple.[9]

Note the repetition of the word "immediately" in the parable: He *immediately . . . with joy*" received the Word, but when he discovered that with the Word came persecution, he "*immediately*" fell away. When he found that the cross must come before the crown, he denounced the crown to avoid the cross.

One of the best ways to see how "deeply rooted" we are is to check how we react to persecution. The shallow Christian often looks as "healthy" as any other Christian until being a follower of Jesus gets hard, until it becomes easier to disobey God than to obey Him:

- Until it is easier to stay in bed than it is to go to Bible study.
- Until it is easier to go fishing than to go to worship services.
- Until it is easier to remain quiet than to share the gospel.
- Until it is easier to go along with the world than to be "the light of the world."
- Until it is easier to let error go unheeded than to stand up for the truth.

How do *we* react "when affliction or persecution arises because of the word"?

Thorny Soil: The Divided Heart

We come next to the thorny soil. Jesus gave the following explanation of this type of soil: "And the one on whom seed was

---

[9]Adapted from McGarvey and Pendleton, 334.

sown among the thorns, this is the man who hears the word, and the worry of the world and the deceitfulness of wealth choke the word, and it becomes unfruitful" (Mt. 13:22).

This is, to me, the saddest of the conditions described in this parable. Even as the soil depicted was rich and loamy, so this is a person who shows much promise. He is not hardened, nor is he shallow; he has richness of character and depth of personality. He has the potential to become a fruitful child of God. Unfortunately, his heart is full of worldly "thorns." Maybe, like my hoeing when I was a boy, he has "scraped them off" so they do not show on the surface—but his tie with the world is still there in his heart.

When this individual becomes a Christian, there is every indication of true conversion. However, instead of putting Christ in first place in his heart (Mt. 6:33), he is filled with the cares of this world (Mt. 13:22; KJV), "the deceitfulness of wealth" (Mt. 13:22), the "pleasures of this life" (Lk. 8:14), and "the lusts of other things" (Mk. 4:19; KJV). Even as the soil can only support so much vegetation, so is the heart with one's affections: "You cannot serve [both] God and wealth" (Mt. 6:24b)—or God and pleasure, or God and anything else.

Because of the nature of his heart, the Word within him is choked. It is not killed or destroyed, but it is choked. As thorns sap the vitality of plants among them, so this man is drained of his spiritual zest. With his capabilities, he could have been a great Christian, but his only desire is to be a great businessman or a great politician or a great something else.

The result is that he is unfruitful in the service of the Lord. Christ said that this individual brings "no fruit to maturity" (Lk. 8:14). Even as the empty head of grain has the appearance of having fruit, so this individual exhibits the outward forms of Christianity, but in reality his life is an empty shell. He bears no fruit for Christ. In the end, he will find that he has gained the world but lost his soul (Mk. 8:36).

Again, it is time for self-examination. Have we let any of these problems sap our spiritual vitality?

(1) *The cares and worries of the world.* Do we let insignificant matters distract us from giving ourselves wholeheartedly to the

Lord? Like Martha, are we "worried and bothered about so many things" (Lk. 10:41) that we have forgotten what is really "necessary" (Lk. 10:41, 42)?

(2) *Deceitful riches.* Have we let riches deceive us into thinking that accumulating possessions is all that matters? We need little—and we need that but for a short while. Let us never neglect the important things in life in our mad rush to "get ahead."

(3) *Pleasures and lusts.* Is it possible that worldliness could be sapping our spiritual life? Is the world residing in our hearts? Do we spend more time and energy on "having fun" than we do in service to God and man?

Too many of us fall into the category of the divided heart. We have talent and potential that could be used for God, but we allow other interests to crowd out our love for Him. Let us strive to keep our hearts focused on the Lord. Jesus said, "Blessed are the pure in heart" (Mt. 5:8a). Paul wrote, "Therefore if you have been raised up with Christ, keep seeking the things above, where Christ is, seated at the right hand of God. Set your mind on the things above, not on the things that are on earth" (Col. 3:1, 2).

Good Soil: The Honest and Good Heart

At last we come to "the good soil," which Jesus identified as those with "honest and good" hearts (Lk. 8:15). Their hearts are not hardened, shallow, or divided. They "hear the word and accept it" (Mk. 4:20). They put forth the effort necessary to "understand" the Word (Mt. 13:23). Once they have received the Word, they "hold it fast" (Lk. 8:15). They are like the man described by the psalmist: Their "delight is in the law of the Lord" (Ps. 1:2).

In such a heart, the Word can germinate, grow, and ultimately produce fruit. Jesus said that "this is the man who hears the word and understands it; who indeed bears fruit and brings forth, some a hundredfold, some sixty, and some thirty" (Mt. 13:23). Different soils have different potential, so the percentage of increase varies, but all of these—a hundredfold, sixtyfold, thirtyfold—are good returns. Here, at last, is the desired result from sowing the seed: a mature Christian bearing spiritual fruit in his life.

Once more, let each of us look at himself or herself. Let each one ask, "Do I have an honest and good heart? Do I eagerly receive the Word of God? Do I have a desire to obey Him in every way?"

One way to answer those questions is to take "the fruit test." Jesus said, "You will know them by their fruits" (Mt. 7:16a). Have we borne fruit in our lives? Have we been children of God long enough that God can rightfully expect to find fruit in our lives? Christ said, "My Father is glorified by this, that you bear much fruit, and so prove to be My disciples" (Jn. 15:8). Paul wrote that we have been joined to Christ "in order that we might bear fruit for God" (Rom. 7:4). He urged us to "walk in a manner worthy of the Lord, to please Him in all respects, bearing fruit in every good work and increasing in the knowledge of God" (Col. 1:10).

What does it mean to "bear fruit"? The word "fruit" can mean "result; outcome."[10] To "bear fruit" for the Lord means that the Word has the desired *outcome* in our lives, that people can see the practical *result* of the Word in how we live. We are "bearing fruit" as our behavior reflects the character of Jesus. We are "bearing fruit" as we treat people with greater kindness and as we help others. We are "bearing fruit" as our love for spiritual things becomes apparent in our faithful worship and increased service. We are "bearing fruit" as we share the gospel and bring others closer to the Lord.

We repeat the words of Christ: "He who has ears, let him hear" (Mt. 13:9). This can serve not only as a call to understand, but also as a summary of our texts: Let us hear and accept Christ's words, and we will be blessed.

Conclusion

May we receive the Word with the attitude of heart prescribed by James:

Therefore, putting aside all filthiness and all that remains of wickedness, in humility receive the word implanted,

---

[10]*American Heritage Dictionary*, 4th ed. (2001), s.v. "fruit."

which is able to save your souls. But prove yourselves doers of the word, and not merely hearers who delude themselves (Jas. 1:21, 22).

SECTION V

THROUGHOUT GALILEE

Includes a Harmony of

**Mt. 8:18, 23–34; 9:1, 10–38;
10:1—11:1; 13:54—14:36**

Mk. 2:15–22; 4:35—6:56

**Lk. 4:16–30; 5:29–39;
8:22–56; 9:1–17**

Jn. 6:1–17

STILLING THE STORM
(MT. 8:18, 23–27; MK. 4:35–41; LK. 8:22–25)

The following passages complete the biblical account of the "Busy Day"—that day which began with the Pharisees' blasphemous accusations and which ended with Jesus' withdrawal to the east side of the Sea of Galilee. An important theme is found in the disciples' words when Christ stilled the storm: **"Who then is this, that even the wind and the sea obey Him?"** (Mk. 4:41; see Lk. 8:25; Mt. 8:27). The question "Who is this?" echoed throughout Jesus' ministry—indicating how difficult it was for people to comprehend who He really was. When Christ healed the man let down through the roof, the Pharisees asked, "Who is this man who speaks blasphemies?" (Lk. 5:21). When Jesus forgave the woman who had washed His feet with her tears, the other guests asked, "Who is this man who even forgives sins?" (Lk. 7:49). When a report of Christ's activities reached King Herod, he asked, "Who is this man about whom I hear such things?" (Lk. 9:9). When Jesus made His triumphal entry into Jerusalem, "all the city was stirred, saying, 'Who is this?'" (Mt. 21:10).

Matthew 8:18, 23–27

^18^**Now when Jesus saw a crowd around Him, He gave orders to depart to the other side of the sea.**

^23^**When He got into the boat, His disciples followed Him.** ^24^**And behold, there arose a great storm on the sea, so that the boat was being covered with the waves; but Jesus Himself was asleep.** ^25^**And they came to Him and woke Him, saying, "Save us, Lord; we are perishing!"** ^26^**He said to them, "Why are you afraid, you men of little faith?" Then He got up and rebuked** the winds and the sea, and it became perfectly calm. ²⁷The men were amazed, and said, "What kind of a man is this, that even the winds and the sea obey Him?"

Mark 4:35–41

³⁵On that day, when evening came, He said to them, "Let us go over to the other side." ³⁶Leaving the crowd, they took Him along with them in the boat, just as He was; and other boats were with Him. ³⁷And there arose a fierce gale of wind, and the waves were breaking over the boat so much that the boat was already filling up. ³⁸Jesus Himself was in the stern, asleep on the cushion; and they woke Him and said to Him, "Teacher, do You not care that we are perishing?" ³⁹And He got up and rebuked the wind and said to the sea, "Hush, be still." And the wind died down and it became perfectly calm. ⁴⁰And He said to them, "Why are you afraid? How is it that you have no faith?" ⁴¹They became very much afraid and said to one another, "Who then is this, that even the wind and the sea obey Him?"

Luke 8:22–25

²²Now on one of those days Jesus and His disciples got into a boat, and He said to them, "Let us go over to the other side of the lake." So they launched out. ²³But as they were sailing along He fell asleep; and a fierce gale of wind descended on the lake, and they began to be swamped and to be in danger. ²⁴They came to Jesus and woke Him up, saying, "Master, Master, we are perishing!" And He got up and rebuked the wind and the surging waves, and they stopped, and it became calm. ²⁵And He said to them, "Where is your faith?" They were fearful and amazed, saying to one another, "Who then is this, that He commands even the winds and the water, and they obey Him?"

In the previous section, we read that "when Jesus had finished these parables, He departed from there" (Mt. 13:53). Matthew then told about would-be disciples (Mt. 8:19–22), the same or similar event recorded much later in Luke 9:57–

62.[1] In this harmony, we will go to Christ's first withdrawal from Galilee.

Mark reported that Christ departed to the eastern shore of the Sea of Galilee: **On that day** [the day He spoke in many parables (Mk. 4:34)], **when evening came, He said to them, "Let us go over to the other side"** (Mk. 4:35). "Evening" is a flexible term. It could have been early in the evening or late in the evening. When at last they reached the other shore, one of the demoniacs was able to see them from a distance (Mk. 5:6). Maybe they left early in the evening and it was not yet dark when they reached the other side. Maybe they left late in the evening, and because of the storm they took all night to get there, arriving early the next morning. The first possibility is more likely.

This was the first of four recorded trips that Christ made to the east side of the sea. Mark wrote, **Leaving the crowd, they took Him along with them in the boat, just as He was** (Mk. 4:36a)—that is, they left immediately, without preparation and without provisions. Mark added, **And other boats were with Him** (Mk. 4:36b). These boats could have been drawn alongside the boat Jesus was in (Mk. 4:1) to allow more people to hear Him. Perhaps this detail was inserted to show that there were other witnesses to the storm that quickly arose and then quickly ceased.

Christ's reason for the trip was to give Him a break from the crowd (see Mt. 8:18; Mk. 4:36). Though He was fully God, He was also fully man, and the "Busy Day" had left Him exhausted. He soon fell asleep (Lk. 8:23). Mark observed that **Jesus Himself was in the stern, asleep on the cushion . . .** (Mk. 4:38). The stern was at the rear of the boat, where there was more room. "The cushion" was probably a seat cover, perhaps a fleece that could be rolled up to serve as a pillow. J. W. Shepard wrote,

Faintness, weariness and exhaustion dominated the phy-

---

[1]Matthew 8:19–22 is included in a study of Luke 9:57–62 in volume 2 of David Roper, *The Life of Christ*.

sique of the human Jesus, and he lay immersed in profound slumber, fanned by the breeze of the lake and
soothed by the gentle rhythmic motion of the boat. . . .
Near him, his disciples converse[d] in subdued tones
about the happenings of the day, while others quietly
manage[d] the sails and guide[d] the gliding craft over
the placid waters.[2]

The distance across the water from Capernaum to the
country of the Gerasenes was only a few miles. Under favorable circumstances, the journey could be made in two or three
hours.

This trip was not under favorable circumstances. Before long,
a storm broke: **. . . there arose a great storm on the sea as a fierce
gale of wind descended on the lake** (Mt. 8:24; Lk. 8:23a). The
waves were **breaking over the boat so much that the boat was
. . . filling up** (Mk. 4:37). They **began to be swamped and to be
in danger** (Lk. 8:23).

The Sea of Galilee is subject to sudden storms. It is seven
hundred feet below sea level and is surrounded by mountainous terrain. When cool air pours down the mountainsides onto
the lake, in a matter of moments the calm surface can be turned
into a turbulent mass of frothing waves. Some in the boat were
fishermen and had no doubt seen many storms on this sea. The
fact that even these were frightened indicates that this was no
ordinary tempest.

As the boat was tossed by the waves, Jesus continued to sleep.
We could ask, "Who is this who can sleep through a storm?" Our
first answer might be "a Man who is completely exhausted." A
more complete answer would be "an exhausted Man who trusts
in His God."

Jesus was not disturbed by the storm, but His disciples
were. It is also possible that they just wanted Jesus to be as worried as they were. Most of us like company when we worry. The

---

[2]J. W. Shepard, *The Christ of the Gospels* (Nashville: Parthenon Press, 1939),
232; quoted in H. I. Hester, *The Heart of the New Testament* (Liberty, Mo.: Quality Press, 1963), 148.

synoptic writers recorded "a babble of confused voices"[3]: **They came to Jesus and woke Him up, saying, "Master, Master, we are perishing!"** (Lk. 8:24); **And they came to Him . . . , saying, "Save us, Lord; we are perishing!"** (Mt. 8:25); **. . . and they . . . said to Him, "Teacher, do You not care that we are perishing?"** (Mk. 4:38).

We are not sure what they expected Jesus to do. They had never seen Him calm a storm before, and they apparently were surprised when He stilled this one (Mt. 8:27; Mk. 4:41; Lk. 8:25). Perhaps they were like the frightened child who cries out to his parent, "Do something!"—Though he has no idea what that "something" might be.

The disciples were terrified, but Christ was not. He first rebuked the disciples: **"Why are you afraid, you men of little faith?"** (Mt. 8:26a). Mark and Luke recorded the rebuke (or a second rebuke) after the storm was stilled (Mk. 4:40; Lk. 8:25). Then He **rebuked the wind and the surging waves**, saying, **"Hush, be still"** (Lk. 8:24b; Mk. 4:39a). The waves **stopped**, and **the wind died down and it became perfectly calm** (Lk. 8:24; Mk. 4:39b). The instantaneous calming of both the winds and the waves was a double miracle, for ordinarily the surface of the water would remain rough for a time even after the wind ceased.

Jesus' disciples had seen storms come and go on the Sea of Galilee, but they had never seen anything like this. The profound impact on them is seen as they were overwhelmed and cried out, **"What kind of a man is this . . . ?"** (Mt. 8:27); **"Who . . . is this, that He commands even the winds and the water, and they obey Him?"** (Lk. 8:25b). The answer to their question is "a Man of power" (see Lk. 4:14; 5:17; 6:19; 8:46; 1 Cor. 5:4; 2 Cor. 12:9).

---

[3]J. W. McGarvey and Philip Y. Pendleton, *The Fourfold Gospel or A Harmony of the Four Gospels* (Cincinnati: Standard Publishing Co., 1914), 343.

HEALING TWO DEMONIACS
(MT. 8:28–34; 9:1; MK. 5:1–21; LK. 8:26–40)

Matthew 8:28–34

[28]When He came to the other side into the country of the Gadarenes, two men who were demon-possessed met Him as they were coming out of the tombs. They were so extremely violent that no one could pass by that way. [29]And they cried out, saying, "What business do we have with each other, Son of God? Have You come here to torment us before the time?" [30]Now there was a herd of many swine feeding at a distance from them. [31]The demons began to entreat Him, saying, "If You are going to cast us out, send us into the herd of swine." [32]And He said to them, "Go!" And they came out and went into the swine, and the whole herd rushed down the steep bank into the sea and perished in the waters. [33]The herdsmen ran away, and went to the city and reported everything, including what had happened to the demoniacs. [34]And behold, the whole city came out to meet Jesus; and when they saw Him, they implored Him to leave their region.

Mark 5:1–21

[1]They came to the other side of the sea, into the country of the Gerasenes. [2]When He got out of the boat, immediately a man from the tombs with an unclean spirit met Him, [3]and he had his dwelling among the tombs. And no one was able to bind him anymore, even with a chain; [4]because he had often been bound with shackles and chains, and the chains had been torn apart by him and the shackles broken in pieces, and no one was strong enough to subdue him. [5]Constantly, night and day, he was screaming among the tombs and in the mountains, and gashing himself with stones. [6]Seeing Jesus from a distance, he ran up and bowed down before Him; [7]and shouting with a loud voice, he said, "What business do we have with each other, Jesus, Son of the Most High God? I implore You by God, do not torment me!" [8]For He had been saying to him, "Come out of the man, you unclean spirit!" [9]And He was asking him, "What is your name?" And he said to Him, "My name

is Legion; for we are many." [10]And he began to implore Him earnestly not to send them out of the country. [11]Now there was a large herd of swine feeding nearby on the mountain. [12]The demons implored Him, saying, "Send us into the swine so that we may enter them." [13]Jesus gave them permission. And coming out, the unclean spirits entered the swine; and the herd rushed down the steep bank into the sea, about two thousand of them; and they were drowned in the sea.

[14]Their herdsmen ran away and reported it in the city and in the country. And the people came to see what it was that had happened. [15]They came to Jesus and observed the man who had been demon-possessed sitting down, clothed and in his right mind, the very man who had had the "legion"; and they became frightened. [16]Those who had seen it described to them how it had happened to the demon-possessed man, and all about the swine. [17]And they began to implore Him to leave their region. [18]As He was getting into the boat, the man who had been demon-possessed was imploring Him that he might accompany Him. [19]And He did not let him, but He said to him, "Go home to your people and report to them what great things the Lord has done for you, and how He had mercy on you." [20]And he went away and began to proclaim in Decapolis what great things Jesus had done for him; and everyone was amazed.

[21]When Jesus had crossed over again in the boat to the other side, a large crowd gathered around Him; and so He stayed by the seashore.

Luke 8:26–40

[26]Then they sailed to the country of the Gerasenes, which is opposite Galilee. [27]And when He came out onto the land, He was met by a man from the city who was possessed with demons; and who had not put on any clothing for a long time, and was not living in a house, but in the tombs. [28]Seeing Jesus, he cried out and fell before Him, and said in a loud voice, "What business do we have with each other, Jesus, Son of the Most High God? I beg You, do not torment me." [29]For He had commanded the unclean spirit to come out of the man. For it had

373

seized him many times; and he was bound with chains and shackles and kept under guard, and yet he would break his bonds and be driven by the demon into the desert. ³⁰And Jesus asked him, "What is your name?" And he said, "Legion"; for many demons had entered him. ³¹They were imploring Him not to command them to go away into the abyss.

³²Now there was a herd of many swine feeding there on the mountain; and the demons implored Him to permit them to enter the swine. And He gave them permission. ³³And the demons came out of the man and entered the swine; and the herd rushed down the steep bank into the lake and was drowned.

³⁴When the herdsmen saw what had happened, they ran away and reported it in the city and out in the country. ³⁵The people went out to see what had happened; and they came to Jesus, and found the man from whom the demons had gone out, sitting down at the feet of Jesus, clothed and in his right mind; and they became frightened. ³⁶Those who had seen it reported to them how the man who was demon-possessed had been made well. ³⁷And all the people of the country of the Gerasenes and the surrounding district asked Him to leave them, for they were gripped with great fear; and He got into a boat and returned. ³⁸But the man from whom the demons had gone out was begging Him that he might accompany Him; but He sent him away, saying, ³⁹"Return to your house and describe what great things God has done for you." So he went away, proclaiming throughout the whole city what great things Jesus had done for him.

⁴⁰And as Jesus returned, the people welcomed Him, for they had all been waiting for Him.

At last, Jesus and the disciples reached their destination on the east side of the sea. Matthew said they arrived at **the country of the Gadarenes** (Mt. 8:28), while Mark and Luke called the area **the country of the Gerasenes** (Mk. 5:1; Lk. 8:26). Gerasa (also known as Gergesa) was a village on the east shore. The entire area was ruled by the city of Gadara, some miles to the southeast. It was therefore known both as "the country of the

Gerasenes" and as "the country of the Gadarenes." Critics of the Bible called this "a contradiction" until the ruins of "Kherasa" (that is, Gerasa) were found.

If Jesus had hoped to relax in that isolated spot, rest was denied Him, for He was greeted by a strange welcoming committee. When He came to the other side into the country of the Gadarenes, **two men who were demon-possessed met Him as they were coming out of the tombs** (Mt. 8:28a). Matthew told of two demoniacs, while Mark and Luke concentrated on the one who was the more notorious of the two.

When Jesus started to cast out the evil spirits from the men, the demons asked to be allowed to enter a herd of pigs rooting on a hill nearby. When the demons entered the hogs, the herd went crazy, rushed down the hill into the sea, and were drowned.

Years ago, John S. Sweeney was debating a denominational preacher on the mode of baptism: whether the New Testament teaches that baptism should be by immersion or by sprinkling. The denominational preacher took the extreme position that there were no examples of immersion in the New Testament. In an attempt at humor, he said, "Well, yes, there was one case of immersion in the New Testament"—and he referred to the story of the two thousand pigs that drowned in the sea. When brother Sweeney took the platform, he replied, "Yes, that was a case of immersion—and because the devil lost his bacon in the deal, he's been trying to change the mode ever since!"[4]

When the people of the area learned what had happened, they begged Christ to leave. (They were fearful of losing more livestock, I suppose.) As Jesus prepared to comply with their request, one of the healed men asked to go with Him (Mk. 5:18). Jesus replied, **"Go home to your people and report to them what great things the Lord has done for you, and how He had**

---

[4]This story was adapted from my notes on brother J. W. Roberts' class on the Life of Christ, 68. Earl West listed brother Sweeney among the better-known debaters of his day (Earl I. West, *The Search for the Ancient Order*, vol. 4, *A History of The Restoration Movement 1919–1950* [Germantown, Tenn.: Religious Book Service, 1987], 214).

mercy on you" (Mk. 5:19).

We may wonder why Jesus told this man to share what had happened, when He had instructed others not to tell (Mk. 1:43, 44). One reason may be that this healing occurred beyond the sphere of influence of the Pharisees and the scribes. Publicity in this area would be less likely to stir up animosity with His enemies. Another possible reason is that, since Jesus was forced to leave before He could preach, He wanted to leave a witness in this place.

The man did what the Lord asked him to do: **And he went away and began to proclaim in Decapolis** [the area of ten cities] **what great things Jesus had done for him; and everyone was amazed** (Mk. 5:20). As a result, the next time Christ came to that region, He had a more favorable reception (Mk. 7:31–37).

EATING WITH SINNERS
(AND A DISCOURSE ON FASTING)
(MT. 9:10–17; MK. 2:15–22; LK. 5:29–39)

When the people of Gerasene asked Him to leave, "getting into a boat, Jesus crossed over the sea and came to His own city" (Mt. 9:1). That is, He returned to Capernaum. There large crowds met Him (see Mk. 5:21; Lk. 8:40). Precisely what happened next is hard to say. Not long after He returned, He raised Jairus' daughter from the dead (Mt. 9:18–26; Mk. 5:22–43; Lk. 8:41–56). However, Matthew inserted another story before that. After recording his call to discipleship, Matthew told of a banquet he gave in Christ's honor. All the writers of the synoptic Gospels told of this event, a gathering which resulted in much criticism of the Guest of honor.

Many harmonies have the story of Jairus' daughter immediately after Jesus returned to the west side of the sea. Others insert the story of Matthew's feast before the story of Jairus, on the basis of Matthew 9:18, which indicates that Christ's discourse at Matthew's feast was interrupted by Jairus. John Broadus, who followed the latter approach, inserted this note: "The question of the position [of the story of Matthew's feast]

cannot be settled, and it makes no difference as to understanding the content of the section."[5]

Matthew 9:10–17

[10]Then it happened that as Jesus was reclining at the table
in the house, behold, many tax collectors and sinners came and
were dining with Jesus and His disciples. [11]When the Pharisees saw this, they said to His disciples, "Why is your Teacher
eating with the tax collectors and sinners?" [12]But when Jesus
heard this, He said, "It is not those who are healthy who need
a physician, but those who are sick. [13]But go and learn what
this means: 'I desire compassion, and not sacrifice,' for I did
not come to call the righteous, but sinners."

[14]Then the disciples of John came to Him, asking, "Why
do we and the Pharisees fast, but Your disciples do not fast?"
[15]And Jesus said to them, "The attendants of the bridegroom
cannot mourn as long as the bridegroom is with them, can
they? But the days will come when the bridegroom is taken
away from them, and then they will fast. [16]But no one puts a
patch of unshrunk cloth on an old garment; for the patch pulls
away from the garment, and a worse tear results. [17]Nor do
people put new wine into old wineskins; otherwise the wineskins burst, and the wine pours out and the wineskins are
ruined; but they put new wine into fresh wineskins, and both
are preserved."

Mark 2:15–22

[15]And it happened that He was reclining at the table in his
house, and many tax collectors and sinners were dining with
Jesus and His disciples; for there were many of them, and
they were following Him. [16]When the scribes of the Pharisees saw that He was eating with the sinners and tax collectors, they said to His disciples, "Why is He eating and drinking with tax collectors and sinners?" [17]And hearing this, Jesus

---

[5]John A. Broadus, *Harmony of the Gospels in the Revised Edition* (New York:
A. C. Armstrong & Son, 1906), 36; quoted in John Franklin Carter, *A Layman's
Harmony of the Gospels* (Nashville: Broadman Press, 1961), 138.

said to them, "It is not those who are healthy who need a physician, but those who are sick; I did not come to call the righteous, but sinners."

[18]John's disciples and the Pharisees were fasting; and they came and said to Him, "Why do John's disciples and the disciples of the Pharisees fast, but Your disciples do not fast?" [19]And Jesus said to them, "While the bridegroom is with them, the attendants of the bridegroom cannot fast, can they? So long as they have the bridegroom with them, they cannot fast. [20]But the days will come when the bridegroom is taken away from them, and then they will fast in that day.

[21]"No one sews a patch of unshrunk cloth on an old garment; otherwise the patch pulls away from it, the new from the old, and a worse tear results. [22]No one puts new wine into old wineskins; otherwise the wine will burst the skins, and the wine is lost and the skins as well; but one puts new wine into fresh wineskins."

Luke 5:29–39

[29]And Levi gave a big reception for Him in his house; and there was a great crowd of tax collectors and other people who were reclining at the table with them. [30]The Pharisees and their scribes began grumbling at His disciples, saying, "Why do you eat and drink with the tax collectors and sinners?" [31]And Jesus answered and said to them, "It is not those who are well who need a physician, but those who are sick. [32]I have not come to call the righteous but sinners to repentance."

[33]And they said to Him, "The disciples of John often fast and offer prayers, the disciples of the Pharisees also do the same, but Yours eat and drink." [34]And Jesus said to them, "You cannot make the attendants of the bridegroom fast while the bridegroom is with them, can you? [35]But the days will come; and when the bridegroom is taken away from them, then they will fast in those days." [36]And He was also telling them a parable: "No one tears a piece of cloth from a new garment and puts it on an old garment; otherwise he will both tear the new, and the piece from the new will not match the old. [37]And no one

puts new wine into old wineskins; otherwise the new wine will burst the skins and it will be spilled out, and the skins will be ruined. ³⁸But new wine must be put into fresh wineskins. ³⁹And no one, after drinking old wine wishes for new; for he says, 'The old is good enough.'"

Levi [that is, Matthew] gave a big reception for Him [that is, Jesus] in his house (Lk. 5:29a). Naturally, Matthew invited his old friends and former associates. Soon his house was filled with tax gatherers and other outcasts of society: . . . many tax collectors and sinners were dining with Jesus and His disciples; for there were many of them, and they were following Him (Mk. 2:15). J. W. McGarvey stressed that Jesus' actions and arguments in this situation "do not justify us in keeping company with bad people for any other purpose than to do them good—that is, as their soul's physician."[6]

The Pharisees, who dogged the Lord constantly, began to grumble (Lk. 5:30a). They asked His disciples, "Why is your Teacher eating with the tax collectors and sinners?" (Mt. 9:11). Christ's reply is a classic: "It is not those who are well who need a physician, but those who are sick. I have not come to call the righteous but sinners to repentance" (Lk. 5:31, 32). In this context, "the righteous" refers to those who *thought* they were righteous and did not need repentance—in other words, Jesus meant the scribes and the Pharisees.

Matthew's account of Jesus' reply (Mt. 9:12, 13) includes a quotation from Hosea 6:6. Christ used the quotation in another context to stress that allowing men to satisfy hunger is showing mercy (Mt. 12:7). In Matthew 9, His point is that encouraging sinners to come to repentance is showing mercy.

Undeterred, the Pharisees launched a second criticism, perhaps prompted by the fact that Jesus and His disciples were enjoying themselves at Matthew's feast: "Why do John's disciples and the disciples of the Pharisees fast, but Your disciples do not fast?" (Mk. 2:18). Some of John's disciples were present, and their voices chimed in, asking, "Why?" (Mt. 9:14). It is

---

[6]McGarvey and Pendleton, 350.

sad to see John's disciples aligned with the Pharisees on this question.

The essence of their question was "Why are you not continuing the traditions that our fathers started long ago?" Christ replied, in effect, that the coming of the Messiah ushered in a new era, one not always compatible with past traditions. Jesus' answer had two parts. The first was that the tradition of fasting was inappropriate for His disciples. He compared the coming of the Messiah to a wedding celebration (Mt. 9:15; Mk. 2:19, 20; Lk. 5:34, 35): Such celebrations were times for rejoicing, not for mourning. Fasting, to the Jews, was a symbol of penitence and affliction.

The second part of His answer was that incorporating man-made traditions would be disastrous to the Messiah's regime. To tack the Pharisees' traditions onto His teaching would be like sewing new cloth onto old (Lk. 5:36). When the new cloth shrank, it would tear the old cloth. Again, to attempt to combine the old traditions with His new way would be like putting new wine into old wine skins. Animal skins were used in those days to make containers to hold liquids. This is still the practice in some parts of the world. As time went by, these skins became dry, brittle, and fragile. The dregs in the bottom of the old skins would cause the new wine to ferment and expand, which would crack the old, brittle skins (Lk. 5:37).

Jesus knew that the Pharisees would be unwilling to accept His new way. Sadly, He spoke of those who would not even consider change, who would always say, "The old is good enough" (Lk. 5:39). Christ was not speaking of those unwilling to change from old uninspired traditions to new uninspired traditions. Rather, He was referring to Pharisees who were unwilling to give up their man-made traditions so that they could embrace Christ's way.

APPLICATION:
REACHING OUT TO THE UNLOVABLE
(MK. 5:1–20)

Several years ago, a telephone company had an effective television advertising slogan: "Reach out and touch someone." The idea was that someone was waiting for a phone call from the viewer, someone who would be overjoyed by such a call.[7]

The idea of reaching out to others is not new. The greatest "Reacher-Outer" who ever lived was Jesus Christ. He reached out to people wherever He went—the sick, the blind, the lame, the grieving, the sinful—and those He touched were never the same again. In the church, we are to be followers of Jesus (1 Pet. 2:21). He is our Head (Eph. 1:21, 22), and we are to be His hands, His feet, His lips. We are to be *members* (parts) of His body (Rom. 12:5). According to the Great Commission (Mt. 28:18–20), we fail to act as the Lord's church if we do not reach out to people with our lives and with the gospel.

Mark 5 presents a story about Jesus reaching out and touching a man—a man who was unlovely and unlovable. Matthew's account of the incident tells of two demoniacs, while Mark and Luke tell only of the principal one. Like Mark, we will concentrate on the more notorious of the two. There are important lessons in this story for us.

The Reality (Mk. 5:1–5)

Real Problems
    Our text begins:

> They came to the other side of the sea, into the country of the Gerasenes. When He got out of the boat, immediately a man from the tombs with an unclean spirit met Him, and he had his dwelling among the tombs. And no one was able to bind him anymore, even with a chain; because he had often been bound with shackles and chains, and the chains had been torn apart by him and the shackles broken in pieces, and no one was strong enough to subdue him. Constantly, night and day, he was scream-

---

[7]The idea for this study came from a sermon by Prentice Meador, Jr., found in *Sermons for Today*, vol. 2 (Abilene, Tex.: Biblical Research Press, 1981), 134–41.

ing among the tombs and in the mountains, and gashing himself with stones (Mk. 5:1–5).

After a long, hectic day, evening had finally come (Mk. 4:35a). Christ said to His disciples, "Let us go over to the other side" (Mk. 4:35b)—that is, to the other side of the Sea of Galilee (see Mk. 4:36; 5:1). He occasionally did this to get away from the crowds. As they started their journey, Jesus, who was exhausted, fell asleep (Mk. 4:38). During the trip, there arose a violent storm, which Christ stilled (Mk. 4:36–41). As our story opens, the Lord and His disciples had at last covered the five or so miles—and arrived at the country of the Gerasenes (Mk. 5:1), on the east side of the sea.

If Jesus had gone to this sparsely populated area for rest, He did not get it. Our text says that "when He got out of the boat, *immediately* a man from the tombs with an unclean spirit met Him" (Mk. 5:2; emphasis added). Joe Schubert wrote:

> They were at a part of the lakeside where there were many caves in the limestone rock of the cliffs that over-looked the Sea of Galilee. In these caves were many tombs in which the bodies of the dead had been placed. At the best of times, this would be an eerie place. But at night, it must have been grim indeed. Out of those tombs there came a demon-possessed man. . . .[8]

Why did the man live in the tombs? Because he had been cast out of society. The people of the area had tried to bind him with chains and shackles, but no restraint would hold him. At last, they had apparently forced him to leave.

Do you have the picture of verses 1 through 5 in your mind? The moment Jesus stepped out of the boat, a crazed man appeared out of the gloom. He was naked and filthy. His body was covered with running sores caused by self-mutilation. His hair was tangled; his eyes were wild. *This* was the one who needed Jesus

---

[8]Joe Schubert, "Overcoming Fear," *Preacher's Periodical* (December 1983): 27.

to reach out to him. *This* was the test of Christ's willingness to reach out.

Imagined Excuses

Think about how Christ could have responded to this need.

(1) He might have said, "I'm too tired. It's late. I've had a long, hard day!" Jesus had experienced such a day. We understand what it feels like to be exhausted. Many are trying to "keep up" with others near us. Some are working long hours just to pay the bills. In many families, the mother works away from the home. As a result, when the day's work is done, time and energy are gone. Little is left for reaching out to others; church work does not fit into busy, tiring schedules.

(2) He might have said, "This is not *My* responsibility." This man had family in the area (Mk. 5:19; see Lk. 8:39), so Jesus might have said, "He is *their* responsibility. After all, I have been working hard in Galilee, and I've come here for a short vacation. Let someone else take care of him!" One of the great needs of our society is a feeling of personal responsibility. One of the great needs of the church is a feeling of personal responsibility.[9]

(3) He might have said, "This is *not* a good 'prospect' for conversion." Suppose that we decided to go from house to house in our community to find people interested in the gospel. Then suppose that, while two of the workers were going down the street, a wild man similar to the demoniac in Mark 5 sprang from the darkness. I can assure you that the two workers would *not* come back and report this man as "a good prospect" for teaching. Many of us want to find individuals who are more or less like ourselves and who are eager to learn the truth. Many of us do *not* want to study with someone as loaded down with problems as was this man.

(4) He might have said, "Don't you know that there's a risk involved? If I try to help him, it probably won't do any good, and I could just end up making people unhappy with Me." One of the risks of reaching out to another is that you can get your

---

[9]Meador, 138.

hand slapped. Isn't it true that we sometimes hesitate to talk to our friends and neighbors about the Word of God for fear that they will cease to be our friends, will cease to love us? As we shall see, most of those in the country of the Gerasenes did *not* appreciate the fact that Christ had reached out to the demoniac, and they begged Him to leave (Mk. 5:17).

Real Concern

Jesus could have given every excuse that I have mentioned—but He did not. What enabled Him to overcome the natural barriers that this man represented? *His love for people.* Christ was people-oriented; He cared for people. Here was someone who needed Him. Yes, the man was unloved and unlovable. He was disoriented; his life was out of control. He was self-destructive, maybe even suicidal. Nevertheless, he was a person with needs. Thus, in spite of the fact that Jesus was tired, in spite of the fact that this man was unattractive, in spite of the fact that others were perhaps not fulfilling their responsibilities, Christ took the risk and reached out to him.

The Response (Mk. 5:6–16)

Jesus' Might

Our reading continues: "Seeing Jesus from a distance, he [the demoniac] ran up and bowed down before Him; and shouting with a loud voice, he said, 'What business do we have with each other, Jesus, Son of the Most High God?'" (Mk. 5:6, 7a). James 2:19 stresses that "demons . . . believe, and shudder."

These words came from the man's mouth: "I implore You by God, do not torment me!" (Mk. 5:7b). This statement seems strange since Jesus came to heal the man, not to torment him—but this was surely the demons speaking through the man.

According to Matthew's account, they asked, "Have You come here to torment us before the time?" (Mt. 8:29). The time is coming when the devil's forces will be judged and cast into the lake of fire, along with their master, to be tormented forever (see 2 Pet. 2:4; Rev. 19:20; 20:10). Verse 8 tells why the demons were worried about their fate: "For He had been saying to him,

'Come out of the man, you unclean spirit!'"

Jesus asked, "What is your name?" The man replied, "My name is Legion; for we are many" (Mk. 5:9). A legion was a Roman regiment of approximately six thousand soldiers. The man did not necessarily have six thousand demons inside him, but the term indicates that he was filled with innumerable demons. (Shortly, they would go into *two thousand* pigs [Mk. 5:13].)

Notice that the man first used the singular: *"My* name is Legion." Then he used the plural: "for *we* are many." It is difficult to imagine the confusion that existed in one whose body and mind was controlled by demonic forces. It would have to drive a man mad. Mark 5:15 observes that the man was "in his right mind" *after* the demons left him.

The demons began to beg Christ "earnestly not to send them out of the country" (Mk. 5:10). Luke wrote that "they were imploring Him not to command them to go away into the abyss" (Lk. 8:31). (The KJV has the phrase "the deep," but the Greek has ἄβυσσον [*abusson*]; in other words, "abyss.") "The abyss" was the usual habitat of demons, but they did not want the Lord to force them back to that place—not yet, anyway. They wanted to continue their activity for a while.

It happened that "there was a large herd of swine feeding nearby on the mountain" (Mk. 5:11). The demons pleaded with Christ, "Send us into the swine so that we may enter them" (Mk. 5:12). Why did they make this strange request? Perhaps the only way demons could function outside the abyss was in a living host. At any rate, "Jesus gave them permission. And coming out, the unclean spirits entered the swine" (Mk. 5:13a).

If the legion of demons had made their request in order to continue their demonic activity, they were doomed to disappointment; because as soon as they entered their new hosts, the hogs went crazy. "And the herd rushed down the steep bank into the sea, about two thousand of them; and they were drowned in the sea" (Mk. 5:13b). Two thousand squealing hogs must have made quite a sight and sound as they thundered down the mountainside and splashed into the water.

Among those who observed this eerie sight were pig herders who had been tending the pigs for nearby city-dwellers. Immediately, the "herdsmen ran away and reported it in the city and in the country" (Mk. 5:14a). They "described to them how it had happened to the demon-possessed man, and all about the swine" (Mk. 5:16).

> And the people came to see what it was that had happened. They came to Jesus and observed the man who had been demon-possessed sitting down, clothed and in his right mind, the very man who had had the "legion" (Mk. 5:14b, 15a).

They saw the formerly frenzied man now "sitting" quietly. No longer was he naked, but "clothed." No longer was he maniacal, but "in his right mind." Jesus had reached out to an unlovable individual—and his life had been totally changed.

Jesus' Motivation

How was Jesus able to reach out to the unlovable? While we know He did it because He loved people, we can add other thoughts:

(1) He was sensitive to people's needs. He was always looking for an opportunity to help. The demoniac did not look like much, but he was a soul in need, so this was an opportunity.

(2) He was willing to start where the needy person was, not where He would have wished him to be. He might have told the wild man, "Let me clean you up and find you some clothes, and then we'll talk about your demon problem." Instead, He ignored the man's appearance and cast out the demons. Then, the text says, the man was clothed. Sometimes, as we reach out to people, we first have to help them get their lives turned around and then help them come to an understanding of the will of the Lord. We have to start where people are, not where we wish they were.

(3) He was willing to talk to the man—and listen to his problems. He even listened to several thousand demons. Listening demonstrates a desire to understand. Listening is almost a lost art, but nothing says "I love you" more than listening, really listening.

(4) He was willing to rely on God's power. The man's life

was not changed by human psychology, but by divine power. We do not have the miraculous power that Jesus possessed, but God has still endued us with power. We have the power of the Word (Rom. 1:16) and God's power working in our lives (Eph. 3:20). Let us learn to depend on Him instead of on our own limited resources.

The Results (Mk. 5:15–20)

What was the outcome of Jesus' reaching out to the unlovable?

A Man Changed

We have already seen some of the results. A life was completely turned around. It would be hard to imagine a greater contrast than that of this man before and after he met Jesus.

Men Untouched

Some were not happy about all that had occurred. Instead of being excited that a fellow human being had been salvaged, "they became frightened" (Mk. 5:15b). Apparently, they were afraid they might lose more swine. The people "began to implore Him to leave their region" (Mk. 5:17). They did not beg Jesus to stay and help reclaim any other citizens who were oppressed by the devil. Rather, they said, in effect, "Get out!"

Jesus did what they asked. They could not have made a more tragic request, but Christ complied with it. He never stayed where He was unwanted, and He never forced God's way on anyone. Neither can we. We are to share what we can of the Word; then, if people say, "Leave!" we should leave.

An Area Taught

A final result needs to be mentioned: Reaching out begets reaching out. Listen to the rest of the story:

As He was getting into the boat, the man who had been demon-possessed was imploring Him that he might accompany Him. And He did not let him, but He said to him, "Go home to your people and report to them what

great things the Lord has done for you, and how He had
mercy on you." And he went away and began to proclaim
in Decapolis what great things Jesus had done for him;
and everyone was amazed (Mk. 5:18–20).

Jesus would also say to *us*, "Go home to your people—to
your friends, family, and neighbors—and tell them what great
things the Lord has done for you, and how He had mercy on
you." A few may protest, "But I don't have any close friends who
are not members of the church." Then find some. Be a friend in
your neighborhood. Be a friend where you work. Be a friend at
school. Then you can share. Someone has said that evangelism
is just one beggar telling another beggar where they can both get
bread. Our text declares that evangelism is just one sufferer telling another sufferer where they can both find relief.

Conclusion
Charles Hodge sometimes takes an eighteen-inch ruler into
the pulpit. He holds it up, notes its length, and says, "This is how
far some Christians will miss heaven." Then, holding one end
of the ruler by his head and the other end by his chest, he says,
"That's the distance from the head to the heart." The "heart" spoken of in the Bible is not in the chest—but the illustration still
makes a valid point.
It is possible that many of us know in our heads (intellectu-
ally) that we should reach out to others—even to the unlovable—
to help them in their needs and to share the gospel with them. At
the same time, it is possible that the message has never reached
our hearts. Perhaps we have not been motivated to do whatever
it takes to reach: to rearrange our schedules, to overcome our
fears, or whatever else has been preventing us from doing what
we should do. It is indeed possible that some of us could "miss
heaven by eighteen inches."

RAISING JAIRUS' DAUGHTER
(AND HEALING AN INVALID)
(MT. 9:18–26; MK. 5:22–43; LK. 8:41–56)

When Jesus returned to the western shore of the Sea of Galilee, a crowd awaited Him (Mk. 5:21; Lk. 8:40). At that time, He
performed several notable miracles, including the raising of Jairus' daughter from the dead. Shortly afterward, He made a third
tour of Galilee, starting at His hometown of Nazareth.

A key word in this sequence of events is "belief," or "faith."
(The same Greek word, πίστις [*pistis*], is sometimes translated
"belief" and sometimes "faith.") When Christ healed a woman,
He said, **". . . your faith has made you well"** (Mt. 9:22). He said
to a synagogue official, **"Do not be afraid . . . , only believe"**
(Mk. 5:36). He asked two blind men if they believed that He
could heal them. When they answered, "Yes, Lord," He said,
"It shall be done to you according to your faith" (Mt. 9:28, 29).
When He was rejected at Nazareth, "He wondered at their unbelief" (Mk. 6:6).

Some who claim to have miraculous powers attempt to use
these verses to teach that even Jesus could not do miracles unless
people first believed. They then excuse their failures by saying
that those not healed "didn't have enough faith." It is true that
faith is emphasized in these passages, but it is not true that Jesus'
ability to perform miracles was dependent on the faith of those
He helped. In our studies so far, we have seen a number of cases
where faith was not present or was even impossible. In this section, we will see a dead girl raised, and she certainly had no faith
prior to her resurrection.

Why, then, was faith emphasized during these incidents?
Jesus had reached a crucial point in His ministry. He had done
many miracles prior to that time, and one purpose of those miracles was to produce faith (Jn. 20:30, 31). He knew that, in a matter of months, He would leave this earth. When He did so, He
needed to leave behind a strong core of believers. Thus, more
and more, He urged people to believe.

Matthew 9:18–26

[18]While He was saying these things to them, a synagogue official came and bowed down before Him, and said, "My daughter has just died; but come and lay Your hand on her, and she will live." [19]Jesus got up and began to follow him, and so did His disciples.

[20]And a woman who had been suffering from a hemorrhage for twelve years, came up behind Him and touched the fringe of His cloak; [21]for she was saying to herself, "If I only touch His garment, I will get well." [22]But Jesus turning and seeing her said, "Daughter, take courage; your faith has made you well." At once the woman was made well.

[23]When Jesus came into the official's house, and saw the flute-players and the crowd in noisy disorder, [24]He said, "Leave; for the girl has not died, but is asleep." And they began laughing at Him. [25]But when the crowd had been sent out, He entered and took her by the hand, and the girl got up. [26]This news spread throughout all that land.

Mark 5:22–43

[22]One of the synagogue officials named Jairus came up, and on seeing Him, fell at His feet [23]and implored Him earnestly, saying, "My little daughter is at the point of death; please come and lay Your hands on her, so that she will get well and live." [24]And He went off with him; and a large crowd was following Him and pressing in on Him.

[25]A woman who had had a hemorrhage for twelve years, [26]and had endured much at the hands of many physicians, and had spent all that she had and was not helped at all, but rather had grown worse— [27]after hearing about Jesus, she came up in the crowd behind Him and touched His cloak. [28]For she thought, "If I just touch His garments, I will get well." [29]Immediately the flow of her blood was dried up; and she felt in her body that she was healed of her affliction. [30]Immediately Jesus, perceiving in Himself that the power proceeding from Him had gone forth, turned around in the crowd and said, "Who touched My garments?" [31]And His disciples said to Him, "You see the crowd pressing in on You, and You say, 'Who

touched Me?'" [32]And He looked around to see the woman who had done this. [33]But the woman fearing and trembling, aware of what had happened to her, came and fell down before Him and told Him the whole truth. [34]And He said to her, "Daughter, your faith has made you well; go in peace and be healed of your affliction."

[35]While He was still speaking, they came from the house of the synagogue official, saying, "Your daughter has died; why trouble the Teacher anymore?" [36]But Jesus, overhearing what was being spoken, said to the synagogue official, "Do not be afraid any longer, only believe." [37]And He allowed no one to accompany Him, except Peter and James and John the brother of James. [38]They came to the house of the synagogue official; and He saw a commotion, and people loudly weeping and wailing. [39]And entering in, He said to them, "Why make a commotion and weep? The child has not died, but is asleep." [40]They began laughing at Him. But putting them all out, He took along the child's father and mother and His own companions, and entered the room where the child was. [41]Taking the child by the hand, He said to her, "Talitha kum!" (which translated means, "Little girl, I say to you, get up!"). [42]Immediately the girl got up and began to walk, for she was twelve years old. And immediately they were completely astounded. [43]And He gave them strict orders that no one should know about this, and He said that something should be given her to eat.

Luke 8:41–56

[41]And there came a man named Jairus, and he was an official of the synagogue; and he fell at Jesus' feet, and began to implore Him to come to his house; [42]for he had an only daughter, about twelve years old, and she was dying. But as He went, the crowds were pressing against Him.

[43]And a woman who had a hemorrhage for twelve years, and could not be healed by anyone, [44]came up behind Him and touched the fringe of His cloak, and immediately her hemorrhage stopped. [45]And Jesus said, "Who is the one who touched Me?" And while they were all denying it, Peter said, "Master,

the people are crowding and pressing in on You." ⁴⁶But Jesus said, "Someone did touch Me, for I was aware that power had gone out of Me." ⁴⁷When the woman saw that she had not escaped notice, she came trembling and fell down before Him, and declared in the presence of all the people the reason why she had touched Him, and how she had been immediately healed. ⁴⁸And He said to her, "Daughter, your faith has made you well; go in peace."

⁴⁹While He was still speaking, someone came from the house of the synagogue official, saying, "Your daughter has died; do not trouble the Teacher anymore." ⁵⁰But when Jesus heard this, He answered him, "Do not be afraid any longer; only believe, and she will be made well." ⁵¹When He came to the house, He did not allow anyone to enter with Him, except Peter and John and James, and the girl's father and mother. ⁵²Now they were all weeping and lamenting for her; but He said, "Stop weeping, for she has not died, but is asleep." ⁵³And they began laughing at Him, knowing that she had died. ⁵⁴He, however, took her by the hand and called, saying, "Child, arise!" ⁵⁵And her spirit returned, and she got up immediately; and He gave orders for something to be given her to eat. ⁵⁶Her parents were amazed; but He instructed them to tell no one what had happened.

A man named Jairus came to Jesus. The NASB calls this man **one of the synagogue officials** (Mk. 5:22; see Lk. 8:41). The KJV refers to him as "one of the rulers of the synagogue." "Synagogue officials" is translated from ἀρχισυνάγωγος (*archisunagogos*), a compound Greek word that literally means "those over (the) synagogue." The "ruler" or "head" of the synagogue was part of the board of "elders" (see Lk. 7:3), who were responsible for the synagogue.

In the Jewish hierarchy, synagogue elders ranked below the scribes. The term "elder" in the Gospel Accounts sometimes means "ancestor" (Mt. 15:2), but it usually refers to someone then living. The term was used to refer to religious leaders in general. Jesus often referred to being rejected by "the elders and chief priests and scribes" (Mt. 16:21; see 21:23). The Sanhedrin was sometimes called "the Council of elders" (Lk. 22:66).

The "ruler" of the synagogue had charge of the services, including maintaining order (see Lk. 13:14) and inviting men to read or speak (see Acts 13:15). A synagogue ruler in a Jewish city was a highly respected individual. (A subordinate synagogue official was called "the attendant" [see Lk. 4:20].)

When Jairus approached Christ, he **fell at His feet**, bowing **down before Him**, asking Him to come and heal his twelve-year-old daughter, who was **at the point of death** (Mk. 5:22; Mt. 9:18; Mk. 5:23). In Matthew's account, Jairus said that his daughter had **just died** (Mt. 9:18). This was probably a grieving father's way of saying, "She was almost dead when I left and might already be dead, so we need to hurry!" Dr. Luke stressed that **she was dying** (Lk. 8:42).

The official may have heard that Jesus had healed a royal officer's son in Capernaum (Jn. 4:46–53) and that He had also healed a centurion's servant in that city (Lk. 7:1–10). Casting dignity aside, he threw himself at the Lord's feet, begging Him to help his "only daughter" (Lk. 8:42). As J. W. McGarvey observed, "his needs were greater than his pride."[10]

Jesus did not hesitate. Following the ruler, He started toward his home. Their pace was slow; the LB says that they had to push their way "through the crowds" (Lk. 8:42; see also Mk. 5:24, 31).

On the way to Jairus' house, an unusual incident occurred. It has been called "The Parenthetical Miracle," because it is a miraculous incident tucked inside the account of another miraculous incident.

As Jesus made His way through the crowd, a determined invalid forced her way through the packed bodies until she reached Christ. Dr. Luke said that she had suffered with **a hemorrhage for twelve years, and could not be healed by anyone** (Lk. 8:43). According to the law of Moses, she would have been perpetually "unclean" (see Lev. 15:19, 26). Mark's summary was not as kind to Luke's fellow practitioners: He said that the woman **had endured much at the hands of many physicians, and had**

---

[10]McGarvey and Pendleton, 352.

spent all that she had and was not helped at all, but rather had grown worse (Mk. 5:26). In those days, most doctors mixed "a thimbleful" of elementary physiology with "a cupful" of herbal medicine and "a tubful" of superstitious ritualism.

We can only imagine what this woman had suffered. She was probably pale, emaciated, doubled over with pain. However, when she heard that the Lord was coming that way, she found hidden strength. She forced her way through the crowd until she was directly behind Him, near enough to reach out and touch Him.

She thought to herself, **"If I only touch His garment, I will get well"** (Mt. 9:21; see Mk. 5:28). It was commonly believed that items that had come in contact with the person of a miracle-worker held miraculous power (see Mt. 14:36; Acts 19:11, 12). Perhaps the woman thought that it would be audacious to bother Jesus and decided simply to touch His clothing. Whatever her reasoning, the woman had faith in Christ's power.

She reached out **and touched the fringe of His cloak** (Mt. 9:20). "The fringe" may have been one of the tassels required to remind the people of the Law (Deut. 22:12). The KJV has "the hem of his garment," which has become a colloquial phrase.

When she touched His garment, **immediately the flow of her blood was dried up; and she felt in her body that she was healed of her affliction** (Mk. 5:29). We speak of "feeling bad" when we are sick, and "feeling good" when the sickness is gone. This woman went instantly from "feeling bad" to "feeling good." I can see her body straightening, color coming back into her cheeks, and a smile spreading across her face.

Jesus was immediately aware that power had gone forth from His person (Mk. 5:30a; Lk. 8:46). As finite humans, we cannot understand divine power, but the detail is fascinating. The words suggest that it cost Christ something to perform miracles. Perhaps every miracle He performed drained Him in some way, yet He never counted the cost; He never hesitated to reach out to others.

When Jesus felt that power had left Him, He stopped and asked, **"Who touched My garments?"** (Mk. 5:30b). This surprised His disciples. They responded, **"You see the crowd press-**

ing in on You, and You say, 'Who touched Me?'" (Mk. 5:31). It also perplexes us a little. Does this mean that Christ had no idea who the woman was? Matthew's and Mark's accounts seem to imply that Jesus did know who the woman was, what she had done, and why she had done it. They indicate that, with little or no hesitation, Jesus turned and looked at the woman (Mt. 9:22; Mk. 5:32).

Often the purpose of Christ's questions was not to gain information for Himself but rather to impress truths on others (see Jn. 6:5, 6). That may have been the case on this occasion. Perhaps He wanted those around Him to know of the woman's faith—and how her faith had resulted in her life being blessed. Maybe He wanted the woman to have a clearer idea of what had happened and why it had happened. Luke wrote,

> **When the woman saw that she had not escaped notice, she came trembling and fell down before Him, and declared in the presence of all the people the reason why she had touched Him, and how she had been immediately healed. And He said to her, "Daughter, your faith has made you well; go in peace"** (Lk. 8:47, 48).

The benediction "Go in peace" provided assurance that the cure was permanent, that her malady would not return.

Picture the woman leaving—and then shift your gaze to Jairus. He had been trying to rush Jesus to his home, where his little daughter lingered at death's door. As he pushed through the crowd, he must have silently said this prayer again and again: "Lord, help us not to be too late. God, help us to get there before she dies!" Now, he was forced to stand and wait while Christ dealt with an invalid woman. Jairus might have been tempted to cry out, "Jesus, help her later! She has been sick for twelve years. Another day or two is not going to matter. My little girl needs You *now*!"

If the ruler was frustrated by the delay, the frustration turned to despair, for word came to him: **"Your daughter has died; do not trouble the Teacher anymore"** (Lk. 8:49b). The father's heart must have died within him.

Christ would have been aware of Jairus' despondency. He said to him tenderly, **"Do not be afraid any longer; only believe, and she will be made well"** (Lk. 8:50; see Mk. 5:36).

The expression "be made well" is what would be expected if the girl had "only" been sick. The miracle of raising the dead was in the same category as the miracle of healing the sick. Those who claim to be able to heal miraculously should be ready to back up their claim by raising the dead.

Jesus continued with Jairus to his home. When they arrived, even though the daughter had been dead only a short while, funeral proceedings were already underway. In that time and place, burial normally occurred the same day.

A family's social position was indicated by the number of professional mourners they could afford to hire and the amount of noise the mourners could make. Even the poor were expected to have at least one wailing woman. Thus, upon entering the official's house, Christ **saw a commotion, the crowd in noisy disorder** (Mk. 5:38; Mt. 9:23). There was the plaintive sound of **flute-players** and the piercing cries of **people loudly weeping and wailing** (Mt. 9:23; Mk. 5:38).

One of Jesus' hardest tasks that day was probably to quiet that noisy bunch enough so that they could hear Him. When He had their attention, He told them to **stop weeping** and to **leave**. He said, **"The child has not died, but is asleep"** (Lk. 8:52; Mt. 9:24; Mk. 5:39). "Sleep" is a common euphemism for death (see Jn. 11:11–14). When He said that, the house that had been filled with wailing shook with laughter (Mt. 9:24; Mk. 5:40). Luke said, **And they began laughing at Him, knowing that she had died** (Lk. 8:53). The laughter would have been mocking and scoffing. Part of the reaction to Jesus' statement may have been fear on the part of professional mourners that they would not be paid.

After showing the scoffers and unbelievers to the door (Mk. 5:40a), Christ took Jairus and his wife, along with three of His disciples—Peter, James, and John (Mk. 5:37)—into the room where the child's body had been laid.

Peter, James, and John have been called "the inner circle" of the apostles. This is the first of three recorded occasions when Jesus singled them out for special attention. The other two occasions were during the Transfiguration and in the Garden of Geth-semane (Mt. 17:1; Mk. 14:33). Why these three were special to Jesus, we do not know. Maybe it was because of their future roles: Peter was a leader in the early church; James was the first martyr; as far as we know, John continued his work longer than any of the other apostles. These three were, of course, among those who had first believed in Jesus.

Picture the dramatic scene in your mind: Christ walked to the girl's lifeless body and took her hand, already cold in death. He spoke softly, **"Talitha kum!"**—Aramaic words which meant, **"Little girl, I say to you, get up!"** (Mk. 5:41). The words were simple, words such as one might use to wake a child in the morning.[11]

Immediately, the child's **spirit returned** (Lk. 8:55). Can you see her eyes flutter open? Can you hear the gasps from her parents? Mk. 5:42 says that she **got up and began to walk.** Can you see her running into the arms of her mother and father? Can you picture Jesus smiling and telling the flustered mother to prepare a meal for her daughter (Mk. 5:43; Lk. 8:55)?

This was the second recorded raising of the dead by Jesus. The first was the raising of the son of the widow of Nain (Lk. 7). The third will be the raising of Lazarus (Jn. 11). Because of the growing animosity of the Pharisees, Jesus wanted this to be a private affair. He gave Mr. and Mrs. Jairus **strict orders that no one should know about this** (Mk. 5:43; see Lk. 8:56)—but, as usual, it was not long until word of the incident **spread throughout all that land** (Mt. 9:26).

The scene is a memorable one: that of a deliriously happy mother urging her daughter to eat while a beaming father looked on. If anyone had asked that man, "Do you believe, Jairus?" the answer would have been a resounding "Yes!"

HEALING BLIND MEN AND A DEMONIAC (AND BEING CRITICIZED) (MT. 9:27–34)

[27]As Jesus went on from there, two blind men followed

---

[11]Adapted from McGarvey and Pendleton, 356.

Him, crying out, "Have mercy on us, Son of David!" ²⁸When He entered the house, the blind men came up to Him, and Jesus said to them, "Do you believe that I am able to do this?" They said to Him, "Yes, Lord." ²⁹Then He touched their eyes, saying, "It shall be done to you according to your faith." ³⁰And their eyes were opened. And Jesus sternly warned them: "See that no one knows about this!" ³¹But they went out and spread the news about Him throughout all that land.

³²As they were going out, a mute, demon-possessed man was brought to Him. ³³After the demon was cast out, the mute man spoke; and the crowds were amazed, and were saying, "Nothing like this has ever been seen in Israel." ³⁴But the Pharisees were saying, "He casts out the demons by the ruler of the demons."

According to Matthew, as Jesus left Jairus' house, two blind men followed Him, crying, **"Have mercy on us, Son of David!"** "Son of David" was a Messianic title used by the Jews, based on 2 Samuel 7:12 (Mt. 9:27). They even followed Him into the house where He was staying (Mt. 9:28a). Finally, Christ turned to them and asked, **"Do you believe that I am able to do this?" They said to Him, "Yes, Lord." Then He touched their eyes, saying, "It shall be done to you according to your faith." And their eyes were opened** (Mt. 9:28b–30a). Sometimes Jesus touched those He healed and sometimes He did not. The power was not in the procedure, but in His person. Once more, Jesus told them to tell no one (Mt. 9:30b)—and once more the news spread everywhere (Mt. 9:31).

When Christ came out of the house, He was immediately surrounded by the multitudes, and He resumed His ministry of teaching and healing. A demon-possessed man, unable to speak, was brought to Him (Mt. 9:32). The man may have had a physical malady (deafness, resulting in the inability to speak) along with demon-possession, but probably his muteness was a result of the demon-possession (see Mk. 9:17). When Jesus cast out the demon, the man began to talk. **The crowds were amazed, and were saying, "Nothing like this has ever been seen in Israel"** (Mt. 9:33).

As usual, the Lord's critics were also present. They repeated their blasphemous accusation: **"He casts out the demons by the ruler of the demons"** (Mt. 9:34). Prejudice had closed their ears and blinded their hearts (see Mt. 13:15). No matter what Christ did, they refused to believe.

VISITING NAZARETH
(AND BEING REJECTED)
(MT. 13:54–58; MK. 6:1–6a; LK. 4:16–31)

Luke wrote of Christ's rejection at Nazareth earlier in His account, apparently to explain why Capernaum, and not Nazareth, served as His headquarters during the Galilean ministry (see Lk. 4:16–31). Many writers are therefore convinced that Jesus was rejected twice at Nazareth: early in His Galilean ministry and near the end of that ministry. That may be the case, but it seems that Matthew's and Mark's accounts complement Luke's account: In each, Jesus went into the synagogue and began to teach (Mt. 13:54; Mk. 6:2; Lk. 4:16–21). In each, the people were first impressed by His words (Mt. 13:54; Mk. 6:2; Lk. 4:22) and then offended because He was (to paraphrase) just "a hometown boy" (see Mt. 13:55–57; Mk. 6:3, 4; Lk. 4:22). It is true that Matthew and Mark give details that Luke does not, while Luke provides information not found in Matthew and Mark; but this data is not contradictory—just supplementary. We will therefore study the accounts together.

Matthew 13:54–58

[54]**He came to His hometown and began teaching them in their synagogue, so that they were astonished, and said, "Where did this man get this wisdom and these miraculous powers?** [55]**Is not this the carpenter's son? Is not His mother called Mary, and His brothers, James and Joseph and Simon and Judas?** [56]**And His sisters, are they not all with us? Where then did this man get all these things?"** [57]**And they took offense at Him. But Jesus said to them, "A prophet is not without honor except in his hometown and in his own household."** [58]**And He did not do many miracles there because of their unbelief.**

Mark 6:1–6a

¹Jesus went out from there and came into His hometown; and His disciples followed Him. ²When the Sabbath came, He began to teach in the synagogue; and the many listeners were astonished, saying, "Where did this man get these things, and what is this wisdom given to Him, and such miracles as these performed by His hands? ³Is not this the carpenter, the son of Mary, and brother of James and Joses and Judas and Simon? Are not His sisters here with us?" And they took offense at Him. ⁴Jesus said to them, "A prophet is not without honor except in his hometown and among his own relatives and in his own household." ⁵And He could do no miracle there except that He laid His hands on a few sick people and healed them. ⁶And He wondered at their unbelief.

Luke 4:16–31

¹⁶And He came to Nazareth, where He had been brought up; and as was His custom, He entered the synagogue on the Sabbath, and stood up to read. ¹⁷And the book of the prophet Isaiah was handed to Him. And He opened the book and found the place where it was written,

¹⁸"The Spirit of the Lord is upon Me,
Because He anointed Me to preach the gospel to the poor.
He has sent Me to proclaim release to the captives,
And recovery of sight to the blind,
To set free those who are oppressed,
¹⁹To proclaim the favorable year of the Lord."

²⁰And He closed the book, gave it back to the attendant and sat down; and the eyes of all in the synagogue were fixed on Him. ²¹And He began to say to them, "Today this Scripture has been fulfilled in your hearing." ²²And all were speaking well of Him, and wondering at the gracious words which were falling from His lips; and they were saying, "Is this not Joseph's son?" ²³And He said to them, "No doubt you will quote this proverb to Me, 'Physician, heal yourself! Whatever we heard was done at Capernaum, do here in your hometown as well.'" ²⁴And He said, "Truly I say to you, no prophet is welcome in his hometown. ²⁵But I say to you in truth, there were many

widows in Israel in the days of Elijah, when the sky was shut up for three years and six months, when a great famine came over all the land; ²⁶and yet Elijah was sent to none of them, but only to Zarephath, in the land of Sidon, to a woman who was a widow. ²⁷And there were many lepers in Israel in the time of Elisha the prophet; and none of them was cleansed, but only Naaman the Syrian." ²⁸And all the people in the synagogue were filled with rage as they heard these things; ²⁹and they got up and drove Him out of the city, and led Him to the brow of the hill on which their city had been built, in order to throw Him down the cliff. ³⁰But passing through their midst, He went His way.

³¹And He came down to Capernaum, a city of Galilee, and He was teaching them on the Sabbath.

Shortly after Jesus healed Jairus' daughter (Mk. 5:37–43), He went to His **hometown** of Nazareth (Mt. 13:54; Mk. 6:1). This was probably His first stop on His third tour of Galilee (Mk. 6:6; see Mt. 9:35).

Luke begins, **And He came to Nazareth, where He had been brought up** (Lk. 4:16a). Nazareth was the little town where Jesus had grown up. It was north of Jerusalem in the province of Galilee, about halfway between the Jordan River and the Mediterranean Sea.

. . . and as was His custom, He entered the synagogue on the Sabbath (Lk. 4:16b). It was Christ's custom or habit to attend synagogue services every Sabbath. The NCV has "he went to the synagogue, as he always did." Attending worship faithfully should not be *just* a habit, but it is a good habit to have.

Something of synagogue services can be learned from later rabbinical writings. The service began with everyone reciting together the Shema (from Deut. 6:4–9). *Shema* (שְׁמַע) is a Hebrew word meaning "hear," referring, in its most narrow sense, to Deuteronomy 6:4. When recited in the daily prayers, the Shema includes Deuteronomy 6:4–9 and 11:13–21, Numbers 15:37–41, and additional benedictions. After several prayers, a portion of the Law was read. Next was a reading from the

Prophets. Jesus either volunteered or was asked to do that part of the service.

He stood up to read. And the book of the prophet Isaiah was handed to Him (Lk. 4:16c, 17a). It would have been handed to Him by **the attendant** (Lk. 4:20). The KJV has "minister"; the NCV has "assistant." The Greek word ὑπηρετης (*huperetes*), translated "attendant," "minister," and "assistant," literally means "under-rower." It originally referred to the rowers who labored below the decks in large oar-powered ships. It had come to refer to one who did a difficult, unappreciated job. The "attendant" was a paid employee who had charge of the building and its contents, including the copies of the Scriptures. This man was not a "ruler of the synagogue" (Lk. 8:41; KJV); that is a different position. Men with this position helped with the services and often helped in the Sabbath schools. In some ways, they were similar to our deacons.

The attendant would have taken the scroll of Isaiah from a cabinet called "the ark." The scrolls were large; their rollers were three feet or more in length. The Book of Isaiah, which is a long book, was normally on a scroll by itself. The man handed the scroll to Jesus.

And He opened the book and found the place where it was written (Lk. 4:17b, c). He spread out the scroll to the place of the previous reading, checked where He was, and started rolling to the right or to the left to find the text He wanted to read. In those days, they had no chapter or verse divisions. Have you considered how familiar with the Book of Isaiah the Lord had to be in order to locate the desired text? He found what He was looking for—the passage identified today as Isaiah 61:1, 2—and read:

**"The Spirit of the Lord is upon Me,
Because He anointed Me to preach the gospel to the poor.
He has sent Me to proclaim release to the captives,
And recovery of sight to the blind,
To set free those who are oppressed,
To proclaim the favorable year of the Lord"** (Lk. 4:18, 19).

There was some disagreement as to whether or not certain portions of Isaiah referred to the Messiah, but there was no controversy about this passage. Every rabbi believed that these words were speaking of the Messiah: When the Messiah came, God's Spirit would be upon Him. He would preach the gospel to the poor. He would bring deliverance to "the captives." The word for "captives" is the word used to describe those who had been taken captive in war. He would restore sight to the blind.

As we read this list of the Messiah's work, we can first think of the terms in a literal sense—because Jesus literally helped men in the ways mentioned. Then we can think of them in a spiritual sense. The reference to the Messiah's bringing deliverance to "the captives" had special significance to those who were the captives of Satan. Likewise, Jesus not only healed the physically blind, but also healed the spiritually blind.

The next part of the text is interesting: The Messiah would "set free those who are oppressed." This phrase seems to come from Isaiah 58:6 instead of 61:1, 2. It is possible that Jesus paused, rolled the scroll back to this reference, read it, and then rolled forward again to the part we know as chapter 61. Again, this indicates how familiar Jesus was with the Book of Isaiah.

The passage in Isaiah 61 concluded with the promise that the Messiah would "proclaim the favorable year of the Lord" (Lk. 4:19). The phrase "the favorable year of the Lord" did not refer to a calendar year, but rather to a time when everything would be made right.

The idea of "the favorable year of the Lord" may have been based on the Old Testament teaching concerning the Year of Jubilee (see Lev. 25; 27). The Jews were supposed to operate on cycles of seven years. Every seventh year, the land was to lie fallow. After seven cycles of seven years—in other words, after forty-nine years—the next year, the fiftieth year, was to be the Year of Jubilee. On that year, debts were to be cancelled, slaves were to be set free, and land was to be restored to the families to which it had originally been allotted. The Year of Jubilee was to be the year when people got to start over again. We do not know how well the Jews carried out the instructions about the seven-year cycles and the Year of Jubilee, but we do know that they looked forward to "the year" when the Messiah would make every-thing right.

When Jesus finished reading from Isaiah, **He closed the book** (Lk. 4:20a); in other words, He rolled up the scroll. He gave it back to the attendant, who would have reverently put it away; then the Lord **sat down** (Lk. 4:20b). (Men stood up to read and sat down to teach.) Christ was ready to explain the passage just read. **And the eyes of all in the synagogue were fixed on Him** (Lk. 4:20c). Something about His person, something about the way He read, had heightened their anticipation. There was an air of expectancy. Every eye was on Jesus.

And He began to say to them, "Today this Scripture has been fulfilled in your hearing" (Lk. 4:21). In effect, He said, "This is not speaking of what has happened in the past or what will occur in the future. The application is not to an event in Jeru-salem or some other location. It refers to right here, right now. *Today* this Scripture has been fulfilled in *your* hearing." In simple terms, Jesus was saying that what He had been doing was the fulfillment of the passage—that *He* was the Messiah.

The synagogue was filled with people with whom Christ had associated for almost thirty years of His life. He had grown up with many of them. He had learned to love them. This was their opportunity to accept Him as the Messiah and to receive the blessings about which Isaiah had written.

How did they respond? At first, **all were speaking well of Him, and wondering at the gracious words which were falling from His lips; and they were saying, "Is this not Joseph's son?"** (Lk. 4:22). I can imagine their amazement as they talked about the Boy and the young Man they had known: "I have a chest in my house that He made!"; "I have a plow that He repaired!"; "Didn't He do a good job today! How did He learn to speak so well?" They asked, **"Is not this the carpenter . . . ?"** (Mk. 6:3). Not only was Jesus' legal father a carpenter, but He Himself had learned the trade. Then, doubt crept into their minds. Matthew gives an extended account of this part of the story:

> **. . . they were astonished, and said, "Where did this man get this wisdom and these miraculous powers? Is not**

this the carpenter's son? Is not His mother called Mary, and His brothers, James and Joseph and Simon and Judas? And His sisters, are they not all with us? Where then did this man get all these things?" And they took offense at Him (Mt. 13:54b–57a; see Mk. 6:3).

The mundane details of Jesus' earlier life kept them from seeing who He really was. He had built their furniture and repaired their equipment. They were amazed that He could speak so well, but He was still just "a hometown boy." They were "offended," insulted, upset. Matthew and Mark tell us that their problem was **unbelief** (Mt. 13:58; Mk. 6:6). They had their opportunity to follow the Lord, but they refused to believe.

Jesus probably heard their comments. Besides, He could read their thoughts (Jn. 2:25). He responded, **"No doubt you will quote this proverb to Me, 'Physician, heal yourself!'"** (Lk. 4:23a). That proverb normally meant "Take care of your own problems before you try to solve ours." It was used in a slightly different sense here. Christ continued by echoing their thoughts: **"'Whatever we heard was done at Capernaum, do here in your hometown as well'"** (Lk. 4:23b). The "physician" proverb was being used to mean *"Prove* that you are a physician by doing miracles here as You have in Capernaum."

Those in the synagogue knew what Jesus had done at Capernaum, less than twenty miles away. They had probably heard of His other miracles (see Lk. 7:17). They would have had numerous opportunities to see and hear Christ as He traveled about the province (see Lk. 8:1). None of this was enough. They were asking for a special sign, a spectacular miracle just for them. This was not an expression of faith, but of unbelief.

Christ did perform some miracles at Nazareth (Mk. 6:5)—but **He did not do many miracles there because of their unbelief** (Mt. 13:58). Mark's account says that Jesus *could* **do no miracle there except that He laid His hands on a few sick people and healed them** (Mk. 6:5; emphasis added). Anytime the Bible says that God (or Jesus) cannot do something, understand that it means "doing it would not be *consistent with* His will and purpose." It must have broken Christ's heart that they refused to believe in Him. The NASB says that **He wondered at their un-belief** (Mk. 6:6). One paraphrase says, "He could hardly accept the fact that they wouldn't believe in him" (LB).

Jesus said to them, **"Truly I say to you, no prophet is welcome in his hometown"** (Lk. 4:24). According to Mark, He said, **"A prophet is not without honor except in his hometown and among his own relatives and in his own household"** (Mk. 6:4). This proverb is not always true, but it is generally true. Often, when we have known individuals all our lives, it is difficult for us to recognize and appreciate their accomplishments.

Christ continued,

> **But I say to you in truth, there were many widows in Israel in the days of Elijah, when the sky was shut up for three years and six months, when a great famine came over all the land; and yet Elijah was sent to none of them, but only to Zarephath, in the land of Sidon, to a woman who was a widow** (Lk. 4:25, 26).

He was, in effect, saying, "I have come in the spirit of the prophets. In the days of Elijah, God sent the prophet outside the land. Elijah could have helped Jewish widows, but instead God had him help a Gentile widow in Zarephath."

Christ gave another illustration: **"And there were many lepers in Israel in the time of Elisha the prophet; and none of them was cleansed, but only Naaman the Syrian"** (Lk. 4:27). Elisha was Elijah's successor. He could have healed many Jewish lepers; instead, in the providence of God, he healed a Gentile leper. Jesus' illustrations show God's concern for Gentiles, implying that the Messiah had come not only for the Jews, but also for the Gentiles. In Jesus' day, if you wanted to make a Jew angry, all you had to do was imply that God was also concerned about the Gentiles.

How did the people react to Christ's examples? Does the Bible say, "And all the people in the synagogue were filled with *faith* as they heard these things"? No. **And all the people in the synagogue were filled with *rage* as they heard these things** (Lk. 4:28; emphasis added).

Abandoning the normal decorum of a synagogue service, they turned into a mindless mob (compare with Acts 7:54, 57–59a). **And they got up and drove Him out of the city, and led Him to the brow of the hill on which their city had been built** (Lk. 4:29a). Nazareth was build on the Lebanon Ridge, which extended south in Galilee. Many high spots in the area would have served their deadly purpose.

They took Jesus there **to throw Him down the cliff** (Lk. 4:29b). Since He had implied that He was the Messiah, they perhaps judged Him guilty of blasphemy, a sin that carried the penalty of death by stoning (Lev. 24:16). Generally stoning was carried out by picking up stones and pelting the guilty. Sometimes, however, the victim was dropped into a crevice and boulders were rolled on top of him. The latter was probably what the citizens of Nazareth had in mind.

Whatever they intended, Luke 4:30 says that **passing through their midst, He went His way.** Did He let the full impact of His personality be seen, so that the spectators were overwhelmed and unable to act (as the moneychangers apparently were when He cleansed the temple), or did He perform a miracle? We will never know—at least, not in this life. Since His "hour" had not yet come (see Jn. 7:30; 8:20), whatever was necessary, He did it. He then left Nazareth. As far as we know, that was His last visit there. They had rejected Him; now He rejected them.

APPLICATION:
HOW JESUS DEALT WITH REJECTION
(LK. 4:16–31)

Jesus was rejected in His own hometown. How did Jesus deal with this? What enabled Him to meet and conquer rejection? How can we handle rejection when it comes our way? Here are seven suggestions related to our text:

1. *He was able to deal with rejection because He anticipated it* (see Mk. 8:31; Lk. 17:25). It was part of His mission. The only way to avoid rejection is not to venture anything. If you never put your hand out, you will never get it cut off—but neither

will you ever reach anything. Anticipation of rejection prepared Jesus mentally.

2. *He was able to handle rejection because He had a special relationship with God.* That relationship was implicit in the prophecy of Isaiah: "The Spirit of the Lord is upon Me, because He anointed Me to preach the gospel" (Lk. 4:18; see Acts 10:38). That anointing took place at Jesus' baptism, when the Spirit came upon Him (Lk. 3:22). From that moment on, Luke shows that Christ was always "full of the Holy Spirit" (Lk. 4:1; see v. 14). He renewed that relationship constantly through His prayer life (Lk. 5:16; 6:12; 9:28; 11:1). He always knew that even if He was rejected by men, He had not been rejected by God (see 2 Tim. 4:16, 17).

3. *He was able to handle rejection because He attended synagogue services regularly.* It was Christ's custom or habit to go to the synagogue. If anyone could ever have truthfully said, "I don't *need* the public worship services," it would have been Jesus. Nevertheless, when God's people met to study or worship, He *wanted* to be with them.

What about God's people at that time? As a whole, were the Israelites godly? Were they people of integrity? Were they filled with faith and love for God, or were they at a low ebb spiritually? Jesus could easily have said, "I'm not going to the synagogue because it is filled with hypocrites." He could honestly have said, "I'm better than they are!"—but He did not. Christ did not go to the synagogue because the worshipers had a perfect relationship with God; rather, He went because He wanted to enhance His own relationship with God.

Today, we worship with the church, not in a synagogue— but we still need the attitude of the Lord (1 Pet. 2:21). We are to meet together regularly to encourage one another (Heb. 10:24, 25). The support of our brothers and sisters in Christ can help us when we are rejected by the world.

4. *He was able to handle rejection because He knew the Scriptures.* Picture Him rolling and unrolling the scroll, turning to the passages He wanted to read. Do you see where these suggestions are leading? God has given us *many* resources to strengthen us. He has given us prayer, an essential part of our relationship with Him. He has given us the Bible to read so we can hear His com-

forting voice. He has given us the opportunity to meet together and encourage one another. Unfortunately, many of us do not utilize these heavenly resources. Then we wonder why we crumble when we are rejected.

5. *He was able to handle rejection because He knew who He was and understood His place in God's plan.* He could read Isaiah 61 and say, in effect, "That is talking about *Me*. I am doing what God wants Me to do." Often, we cannot handle rejection because of personal insecurity. We cannot always see how we fit into God's plan. We do not realize that we are special, that we are God's people. If you are a Christian, you are God's man or God's woman, and God has a plan for your life.

6. *He was able to handle rejection because He was committed to doing right even though He might be rejected.* When He spoke to the people of Nazareth, He had to be aware of the distinct possibility that they would not accept what He had to say—but He said it anyway. If and when we are rejected, there is comfort in the knowledge that we have done what God wanted us to do.

7. *He was able to handle rejection because He never allowed rejection to discourage Him to the point of quitting.* Many unfaithful Christians could benefit from this lesson.

In our text, Jesus was not rejected by the world, but by men and women who claimed to be God's people. He was not rejected in the marketplace, but in a building dedicated to the worship of God. Today many Christians once were faithful in their worship and work for the Lord. Then they "got their feelings hurt" by other Christians. As a result, they "left the church." They have vowed never to have anything more to do with the Lord's people. Jesus was not only rejected by God's people, but they even tried to kill Him. How many unfaithful Christians have had their lives threatened by other members of the church? The Lord did not let the weakness of humans affect His commitment to doing what was right.

Let us determine that no one will ever keep us from being what we should be and doing what we should do. With that kind of commitment to the Lord, we can handle whatever rejection life may bring.

JESUS' THIRD TOUR OF GALILEE
(AND INSTRUCTIONS TO THE TWELVE)
(MT. 9:35–38; 10:1–42; 11:1; MK. 6:6b–13; LK. 9:1–6)

Near the end of the Great Galilean Ministry, Jesus and His disciples made a final tour of Galilee. The tour was a success, but that success brought danger—because it brought Christ to the attention of the despot Herod, who ruled the region. King Herod had recently beheaded John the Baptizer, and tension filled the air. After Jesus' disciples returned from traveling through the province, they would withdraw from the king's domain—to the eastern shore of the Sea of Galilee. There Jesus would feed over five thousand individuals (Mt. 14:21). This would be the high point of His popularity.

Matthew 9:35–38; 10:1–42; 11:1

³⁵Jesus was going through all the cities and villages, teaching in their synagogues and proclaiming the gospel of the kingdom, and healing every kind of disease and every kind of sickness.

³⁶Seeing the people, He felt compassion for them, because they were distressed and dispirited like sheep without a shepherd. ³⁷Then He said to His disciples, "The harvest is plentiful, but the workers are few. ³⁸Therefore beseech the Lord of the harvest to send out workers into His harvest."

¹Jesus summoned His twelve disciples and gave them authority over unclean spirits, to cast them out, and to heal every kind of disease and every kind of sickness.

²Now the names of the twelve apostles are these: The first, Simon, who is called Peter, and Andrew his brother; and James the son of Zebedee, and John his brother; ³Philip and Bartholomew; Thomas and Matthew the tax collector; James the son of Alphaeus, and Thaddaeus; ⁴Simon the Zealot, and Judas Iscariot, the one who betrayed Him.

⁵These twelve Jesus sent out after instructing them: "Do not go in the way of the Gentiles, and do not enter any city of the Samaritans; ⁶but rather go to the lost sheep of the house of Israel. ⁷And as you go, preach, saying, 'The kingdom of heaven

is at hand.' [8]Heal the sick, raise the dead, cleanse the lepers, cast out demons. Freely you received, freely give. [9]Do not acquire gold, or silver, or copper for your money belts, [10]or a bag for your journey, or even two coats, or sandals, or a staff; for the worker is worthy of his support. [11]And whatever city or village you enter, inquire who is worthy in it, and stay at his house until you leave that city. [12]As you enter the house, give it your greeting. [13]If the house is worthy, give it your blessing of peace. But if it is not worthy, take back your blessing of peace. [14]Whoever does not receive you, nor heed your words, as you go out of that house or that city, shake the dust off your feet. [15]Truly I say to you, it will be more tolerable for the land of Sodom and Gomorrah in the day of judgment than for that city.

[16]"Behold, I send you out as sheep in the midst of wolves; so be shrewd as serpents and innocent as doves. [17]But beware of men, for they will hand you over to the courts and scourge you in their synagogues; [18]and you will even be brought before governors and kings for My sake, as a testimony to them and to the Gentiles. [19]But when they hand you over, do not worry about how or what you are to say; for it will be given you in that hour what you are to say. [20]For it is not you who speak, but it is the Spirit of your Father who speaks in you.

[21]"Brother will betray brother to death, and a father his child; and children will rise up against parents and cause them to be put to death. [22]You will be hated by all because of My name, but it is the one who has endured to the end who will be saved.

[23]"But whenever they persecute you in one city, flee to the next; for truly I say to you, you will not finish going through the cities of Israel until the Son of Man comes.

[24]"A disciple is not above his teacher, nor a slave above his master. [25]It is enough for the disciple that he become like his teacher, and the slave like his master. If they have called the head of the house Beelzebul, how much more will they malign the members of his household!

[26]"Therefore do not fear them, for there is nothing concealed that will not be revealed, or hidden that will not be known.

²⁷What I tell you in the darkness, speak in the light; and what you hear whispered in your ear, proclaim upon the housetops. ²⁸Do not fear those who kill the body but are unable to kill the soul; but rather fear Him who is able to destroy both soul and body in hell. ²⁹Are not two sparrows sold for a cent? And yet not one of them will fall to the ground apart from your Father. ³⁰But the very hairs of your head are all numbered. ³¹So do not fear; you are more valuable than many sparrows.

³²"Therefore everyone who confesses Me before men, I will also confess him before My Father who is in heaven. ³³But whoever denies Me before men, I will also deny him before My Father who is in heaven.

³⁴"Do not think that I came to bring peace on the earth; I did not come to bring peace, but a sword. ³⁵For I came to set a man against his father, and a daughter against her mother, and a daughter-in-law against her mother-in-law; ³⁶and a man's enemies will be the members of his household.

³⁷"He who loves father or mother more than Me is not worthy of Me; and he who loves son or daughter more than Me is not worthy of Me. ³⁸And he who does not take his cross and follow after Me is not worthy of Me. ³⁹He who has found his life will lose it, and he who has lost his life for My sake will find it.

⁴⁰"He who receives you receives Me, and he who receives Me receives Him who sent Me. ⁴¹He who receives a prophet in the name of a prophet shall receive a prophet's reward; and he who receives a righteous man in the name of a righteous man shall receive a righteous man's reward. ⁴²And whoever in the name of a disciple gives to one of these little ones even a cup of cold water to drink, truly I say to you, he shall not lose his reward."

¹When Jesus had finished giving instructions to His twelve disciples, He departed from there to teach and preach in their cities.

Mark 6:6b–13

⁶ᵇAnd He was going around the villages teaching.

⁷And He summoned the twelve and began to send them out in pairs, and gave them authority over the unclean spirits; ⁸and He instructed them that they should take nothing for their journey, except a mere staff—no bread, no bag, no money in their belt— ⁹but to wear sandals; and He added, "Do not put on two tunics." ¹⁰And He said to them, "Wherever you enter a house, stay there until you leave town. ¹¹Any place that does not receive you or listen to you, as you go out from there, shake the dust off the soles of your feet for a testimony against them." ¹²They went out and preached that men should repent. ¹³And they were casting out many demons and were anointing with oil many sick people and healing them.

Luke 9:1–6

¹And He called the twelve together, and gave them power and authority over all the demons and to heal diseases. ²And He sent them out to proclaim the kingdom of God and to perform healing. ³And He said to them, "Take nothing for your journey, neither a staff, nor a bag, nor bread, nor money; and do not even have two tunics apiece. ⁴Whatever house you enter, stay there until you leave that city. ⁵And as for those who do not receive you, as you go out from that city, shake the dust off your feet as a testimony against them." ⁶Departing, they began going throughout the villages, preaching the gospel and healing everywhere.

Knowing that His time was growing short, Jesus wanted to make one more tour of Galilee, to give each inhabitant the opportunity to follow Him. Mark 6:6b says simply, **And He was going around the villages teaching.** Matthew's account gives a more comprehensive summary: **Jesus was going through all the cities and villages, teaching in their synagogues and proclaiming the gospel of the kingdom, and healing every kind of disease and every kind of sickness** (Mt. 9:35).

As Christ looked on those who came to hear Him, **He felt compassion for them, because they were distressed and dispirited like sheep without a shepherd** (Mt. 9:36). The phrase "sheep without a shepherd" is a graphic figure indicating their great spiritual need. Sheep without a shepherd are without guidance, nourishment, and protection. Similar language had been used in the Old Testament when God's people suffered because of a lack of spiritual leadership (Num. 27:17; 1 Kings 22:17; Ezek. 34:5).

Earlier, Jesus had told His disciples, concerning the Samaritans, ". . . lift up your eyes and look on the fields, that they are white for harvest" (Jn. 4:35b). Here He used corresponding imagery regarding the Galileans—**"The harvest is plentiful"**—with the addition of this sad note: **"but the workers are few"** (Mt. 9:37). He said, **"Therefore beseech the Lord of the harvest to send out workers into His harvest"** (Mt. 9:38). Christ needed help to reach His fellow countrymen.

Jesus' solution to the shortage of harvesters was to send His twelve apostles to the cities of the region. This served two purposes. First, it guaranteed that all in the area had the opportunity to hear "the gospel of the kingdom" (Mt. 9:35). Second, it provided valuable training for the Twelve—experience they needed for the time when Christ would no longer be with them. On Jesus' first tour of Galilee, He had been accompanied by a handful of disciples. On the second, the Twelve had been with Him, to observe how He taught and ministered. The time had come to send them out on their own.

Preparation is essential to success. Christ did not fail to prepare His workers for their important work:

(1) *To prepare the apostles, He organized them.* He divided them into teams of two, according to Mark 6:7. The list of apostles in Matthew 10:2–4 shows that they were grouped in pairs. This may indicate how Jesus sent them out. Sending them forth in twos gave weight to their message (Deut. 17:6; 19:15; Mt. 18:16; Jn. 8:17; 2 Cor. 13:1; 1 Tim. 5:19). It also provided mutual strength (see Eccles. 4:12). The two could supplement each other's work and encourage one other.

Christ may also have made assignments regarding where each team was to go. Matthew 11:1 says that Jesus Himself went to preach in **their cities,** which could refer to cities that had been assigned to them (compare with Lk. 10:1). It is possible that the phrase refers to the hometowns of the disciples. There would have been some kind of agreement regarding how long the tour was to last and where the apostles were to go when it was over (see Mk. 6:30; Lk. 9:10).

(2) *To prepare the apostles, He instructed them.* (Compare the instruction here with the instruction Jesus gave when He sent out the Seventy in Lk. 10:1–16.) Jesus' comprehensive instruction was the most important part of the preparation.

He told them what to do. They were to go only to the Jews (Mt. 10:5, 6). Later, they would be concerned about the "other sheep" (the Gentiles; see Jn. 10:16). On this journey, however, they were to concentrate on the "sheep without a shepherd" (Mt. 9:36)— that is **the lost sheep of the house of Israel** (Mt. 10:6). Because of this limitation, Matthew 10 has been called the "Limited Commission" in contrast with Matthew 28:18–20, which gives the "Great Commission" (to *all*).

When the Twelve went to the Jews, they were to teach. They were to preach the good news that the kingdom was **"at hand"** (Mt. 10:7). They were to command people to **repent** (Mk. 6:12; see Mt. 4:17). They were to tell people about Jesus. This is implied by the fact that their preaching made the name of Jesus well known throughout all the area (see Mt. 14:1; Mk. 6:13, 14).

Further, as they traveled and taught, they were to do miracles (see Lk. 9:6). Jesus told them, **"Heal the sick, raise the dead, cleanse the lepers, cast out demons"** (Mt. 10:8a). (More about this later.)

He told them what to take. They were to take bare essentials and depend on the hospitality of the receptive wherever they went. He said that **the worker is worthy of his support** (Mt. 10:10b).

When the three accounts of the instructions are compared, they seem to indicate that Christ allowed the disciples to take one each of what was needed in the way of clothing, but no replacements. They were not to take any money or provisions: **"Do not acquire gold, or silver, or copper for your money belts, or a bag for your journey"** (Mt. 10:9, 10a). The phrase "money belt" is translated from the Greek word for "girdle," the leather or cloth band that circled the waist. Sometimes money was secreted in these bands (see Mk. 6:8), so "money belts" conveys the idea. The "bag" was the shoulder bag that held provisions for trips. This might be compared to an overnight case or backpack. Since the apostles were to take no provisions, they would not need bags such as these. These prohibitions were not applicable to all preaching tours (note Lk. 22:35, 36), but this journey was probably a short tour of only a few weeks and that they were going to people who practiced hospitality.

Christ was emphasizing the urgency of their task. He was also teaching His followers to trust in the Lord for the necessities of life (see Lk. 22:35; Mt. 6:33).

He told them what to expect. Some would accept their message (Mt. 10:11, 13a), but many would reject it (Mt. 10:13b, 14, 16, 17, 21, 22, 24, 25). **As you enter the house, give it your greeting. If the house is worthy, give it your blessing of peace. But if it is not worthy, take back your blessing of peace** (Mt. 10:12, 13). The normal greeting upon entering a home was "Peace to this house." If, however, the inhabitants of the house rejected the apostles' message, they would not receive the "peace" offered in the greeting (see Mt. 10:14, 15).

He told them how to react. There were some things they were *not* to do. They were *not* to waste time on those who rejected them and their message. Jesus said, **"Whoever does not receive you, nor heed your words, as you go out of that house or that city, shake the dust off your feet"** (Mt. 10:14; see Mk. 6:11; Lk. 9:5). In that day, shaking the dust off their feet was a symbolic gesture of rejection. For instance, the Jews believed that anything touched by unbelieving Gentiles was "unclean." Therefore, upon returning to Palestine after they had been in a Gentile country, they shook the defiled Gentile dust off their feet. The symbolic act commanded by Jesus indicated that unbelieving Jews were no better than unbelieving Gentiles. It indicated that when people rejected God's message, God rejected them.

They were *not* to be intimidated by rejection. **Therefore do not fear them** [those who persecute you], **for there is nothing concealed that will not be revealed, or hidden that will not be known** (Mt. 10:26). Regarding the persecution they would receive, Jesus said, **. . . beware of men, for they will . . . scourge**

you in their synagogues (Mt. 10:17). An extreme form of discipline administered in the synagogues was scourging (beating, whipping). This was administered by "the attendant." When Christ spoke of that which was "concealed" and "hidden" in Matthew 10:26, He was probably referring to the schemes of His enemies to destroy Him, His apostles, and their work. The LB paraphrase has "their secret plots will become public information." This promise was fulfilled; today we read about those devilish plans in the pages of the New Testament.

Christ challenged the apostles to speak boldly of their faith (Mt. 10:27) and promised, **"Therefore everyone who confesses Me before men, I will also confess him before My Father who is in heaven. But whoever denies Me before men, I will also deny him before My Father who is in heaven"** (Mt. 10:32, 33). These promises apply to any confession (or denial) of the Lord; but, in this context, they have special application to the day-to-day acknowledgment (or rejection) of Him before others. These verses are sometimes used in connection with the confession of faith that is made before baptism. The promise of the verses applies to that confession, but we should understand that our confession of Jesus does not end with that one public affirmation of faith.

There were also things the Twelve *were* to do in response to rejection. They needed to learn that, though they were rejected by men, they were not rejected by God. He would still care for them (Mt. 10:29–31). They were to understand that rejecting them was equivalent to rejecting the One who sent them (see Mt. 10:40).

> **"He who receives a prophet in the name of a prophet shall receive a prophet's reward; and he who receives a righteous man in the name of a righteous man shall receive a righteous man's reward. And whoever in the name of a disciple gives to one of these little ones even a cup of cold water to drink, truly I say to you, he shall not lose his reward"** (Mt. 10:41, 42).

In context, "these little ones" probably refers to the apostles.

Earlier, Jesus had promised that those who rejected the apostles would be cursed (Mt. 10:14, 15); here He promised that those who accepted them and their message would be blessed. Note that only *one* factor of salvation is considered here: acceptance of the apostles as manifested in giving a cup of cold water. The teaching is not that any one act (such as offering a drink of water) ensures salvation. Rather, *everything else being equal,* those who received the disciples would be the ones who would be saved.

(3) *To prepare the apostles, Jesus did not just organize them and instruct them; He also empowered them.* He gave them what they needed to fulfill their task. Up to the time of the Limited Commission, only Jesus had performed miracles; but now He enabled the Twelve to do similar works: He **gave them authority over unclean spirits, to cast them out, and to heal every kind of disease and every kind of sickness** (Mt. 10:1; see Mk. 6:7; Lk. 9:1). Luke wrote that Christ **gave them power and authority over all the demons** (Lk. 9:1). Further, He promised them inspiration as needed:

> But when they hand you over, do not worry about how or what you are to say; for it will be given you in that hour what you are to say. For it is not you who speak, but it is the Spirit of your Father who speaks in you (Mt. 10:19, 20).

Matthew 10:23 is considered the most difficult verse in Matthew 10: **. . . you will not finish going through the cities of Israel until the Son of Man comes**. We are not sure of the significance of the word "comes." The word could refer to the Lord's coming in judgment against the Jews when Jerusalem was destroyed in A.D. 70; this would make the passage tie in with verse 15. It is possible that the passage simply means that Jesus would be coming along behind the Twelve—to the same cities (see Mt. 11:1).

As we consider how Jesus prepared the apostles, it is obvious that He had in mind more than the upcoming two-or-three-week tour of the province of Galilee. The references to **gover-**

nors and kings and **Gentiles** (Mt. 10:18), as well as many of the persecution predictions (Mt. 10:17, 18, 21–23, 34–39), point to the work and treatment of the apostles following the establishment of the church.

When Christ gave the Limited Commission in Matthew 10, He gave detailed instructions. When He gave the Great Commission in Matthew 28:18–20 (and Mk. 16:15, 16; also alluded to in Lk. 24:46, 47), He said, in effect, "Just do it!" Perhaps that was because He had previously told His disciples what to do and what to expect when they preached—in passages such as Matthew 10.

Some of the special provisions of Matthew 10 do not apply to us today. We are not to go only to the Jews (Mt. 28:19; Mk. 16:15). We have not been miraculously empowered as were the apostles, and we are not miraculously inspired when we speak. We are not required to take little or nothing with us when we travel elsewhere to preach. Nevertheless, many of the principles of Matthew 10 are still valid in the twenty-first century.

We, too, need planning and organization before we take the gospel to the world. Jesus' organizing was not elaborate. In the same way, ours should be as simple as possible. Organization should be kept to the minimum needed to do the job. It is possible to devote so much time to "getting organized" that we never do any work. Common sense is the order of the day. Consider the words of wisdom in Matthew 10:16.

One detail of Christ's organizational instruction that should be seriously considered is His sending the apostles by twos. As a rule, there is value in sending missionaries out in teams.

We still need preparation before we take the gospel to others. Jesus sent out the Twelve *after* **instructing them** (Mt. 10:5; emphasis added; see also 11:1). Do not make the assumption that everyone knows what to do and how to do it. Never skimp on instruction. Further, we still need to realize that God is watching over us as we take the gospel (Mt. 10:28–31), and we still need to be encouraged to endure to the end (Mt. 10:22).

After Jesus finished His instructions, the apostles left in six teams of two. **They went out and preached that men should repent. And they were casting out many demons and were**

419

anointing with oil many sick people and healing them (Mk. 6:12, 13).

The "anointing with oil" in connection with healing (see Jas. 5:14) is something of a mystery. There were three basic reasons to anoint someone with oil. (1) It had a ceremonial purpose—as part of a setting-apart ceremony (see Ex. 30:25, 26, 30; 1 Sam. 9:16; 15:1; 16:13). (2) It had a practical purpose—as part of personal grooming (see Ruth 3:3; 2 Sam. 14:2). In this connection, to anoint another's head with oil was to bring refreshment to his person (see Lk. 7:46; Heb. 1:9). (3) It had a medical purpose—as part of the treatment of wounds (see Is. 1:6; Lk. 10:34); oil soothed and protected the wound. Since there is no record that Jesus ever anointed anyone with oil in connection with His healing, this was probably not an essential part of the process. Christ sometimes engaged in symbolic acts in connection with His healing—touching the afflicted, anointing eyes with mud, and the like—which had little or nothing to do with the final results. The apostles' anointing with oil was probably in the same category.

After the disciples left, Christ resumed His own tour of the area (Mt. 11:1). Now, instead of one team journeying through the province of Galilee, preaching and healing, there were seven.

APPLICATION:
THE KING AND HIS AMBASSADORS (MT. 10)

The emphasis in the Book of Matthew is on the King and His kingdom. Through chapter 9, Matthew has stressed the King's credentials, providing a record of fulfilled prophecy and mighty miracles.

At the end of Matthew 9, however, King Jesus had a need. He had been "going through all the cities and the villages, teaching in their synagogues and proclaiming the gospel of the kingdom, and healing every kind of disease and every kind of sickness" (Mt. 9:35). His heart had gone out to the multitudes (Mt. 9:36); but even though the harvest was plentiful, the workers were few (Mt. 9:37). Christ could not do the task alone; He needed assistance. To help spread the news, He chose twelve special emissaries (Mt. 10:2–4).

Matthew 10 is the account of Jesus sending the apostles to preach in Galilee. It basically consists of the instructions Jesus gave them (see Mt. 10:5; 11:1). Most of the directions relate to that specific tour. For instance, the Twelve were told to go only to Jews, not to Gentiles or Samaritans (Mt. 10:5, 6).

As we look more closely, we see that the Lord was also preparing them for a later time, after He returned to heaven, when they would be His representatives on the earth. Jesus spoke of them being brought "before governors and kings" for His sake, "as a testimony to them and to the Gentiles" (Mt. 10:18). That did not occur on this tour, which excluded the Gentiles. Rather, that prophetic statement was fulfilled during the events recorded in the Book of Acts (for instance, see chaps. 23 through 26). In other words, Jesus' instructions for the apostles went beyond their immediate challenge.

Chapter 10 also has lessons for us. While the whole chapter cannot be covered, I do want to pull from it thoughts on ambassadors past and ambassadors present.

The term "ambassador" is drawn from Ephesians 6:20 where Paul spoke of himself as "an ambassador in chains." The word "ambassador" is from a form of the word for "old" or "older." As a rule, secular ambassadors of that day were older men. Many commentators think that the word "aged" in Philemon 9 should be translated "ambassador." If Paul was "an ambassador," so were the other apostles. Matthew 10 stresses that the apostles *represented* Jesus. The primary task of an ambassador is to represent the one who sends him.

Ambassadors Past

Let us start with ambassadors past: Christ's special one-time ambassadors. These men were called "apostles" (Mt. 10:2). The word "apostle" is a transliterated Greek word that literally means "one sent." The word was sometimes used in a general sense to refer to anyone sent forth—especially one sent by the Lord (2 Cor. 8:23; Phil. 2:25), but these twelve men were special. They had to meet unique qualifications (see Acts 1:21, 22; 1 Cor. 9:1; Eph. 4:11). This was not a position that could be passed on to succeeding generations. These special ambassadors are listed in Mt. 10:2–4:

> Now the names of the twelve apostles are these: The first, Simon, who is called Peter, and Andrew his brother; and James the son of Zebedee, and John his brother; Philip and Bartholomew; Thomas and Matthew the tax collector; James the son of Alphaeus, and Thaddaeus; Simon the Zealot, and Judas Iscariot, the one who betrayed Him.

As we read this list, two facts strike us. (1) Viewed from the standpoint of the world, these were ordinary men. They had no elevated social status, no special training, no unique talents. They were ordinary men called to an extraordinary task. The Lord can use anyone and everyone. (2) Viewed from any standpoint, it was a strange mixture. For instance, there was Matthew, who had been a tax collector for the Romans, working alongside Simon the Zealot. The Zealots were a fanatical nationalist group that specialized in terrorism. Before they met Jesus, Simon might have stuck a dagger into Matthew—but the Lord can help all people live in peace.

Matthew 10 tells of several aspects of these men and their task.

Their Special Credentials (Mt. 10:1, 8)

The apostles were given special credentials (see Acts 2:43; 2 Cor. 12:12; Heb. 2:1–4). They were given power to cast out demons, to heal sickness, and to raise the dead (Mt. 10:1, 8). For the first time, Jesus shared His miraculous powers. When God commissions someone, He bestows whatever is needed to carry out that commission.

We have not been given the same powers the Twelve had, but the principle is the same: The Lord will give us what we need to carry out His commission to us.

Their Special Commission (Mt. 10:5–7)

The apostles were given a special commission, one we generally call the Limited Commission. It was limited in scope: As already noted, they were to go to the Jews only, not to the Gentiles or the Samaritans (Mt. 10:5, 6). It was also limited in its message: They were to preach, "The kingdom of heaven is at hand" (Mt. 10:7). They urged men to repent in order to prepare for the coming kingdom (Mk. 6:12; see Mt. 3:2; 4:17).

Our commission is different; we call it the Great Commission (Mt. 28:18–20; Mk. 16:15, 16; see Lk. 24:46, 47). It is unlimited in its scope: We are to go into all the world. The Great Commission is also unlimited in its message: We are to preach the gospel in its fullness to all men. We are to tell everyone that King Jesus has come, that His kingdom/church has been established, and that anyone can come into it.

Their Special Instructions (Mt. 10:9–16)

The apostles were given special instructions: They were to travel light (Mt. 10:9, 10) and stay in the homes of the receptive (Mt. 10:11–13a). They were not to waste time on the unreceptive, but to move on when they were rejected (Mt. 10:13b–15). They were to use wisdom in their teaching (Mt. 10:16b).

These instructions were given specifically for them, but we need similar lessons. We must learn to trust the Lord to provide for us. We should be filled with a sense of urgency. We need to use wisdom and discernment in making decisions concerning the Lord's work.

Their Special Encouragement (Mt. 10:19, 20, 40–42)

Finally, the apostles were given special encouragement: They were encouraged by being told that when they were arrested, the Holy Spirit would tell them what to say (Mt. 10:19, 20). Burton Coffman said, "This is one of the strongest statements in the New Testament of that inspiration which guided the apostles into all truth."[12] In contrast with this, we have to study to be able to "give an answer" to others (1 Pet. 3:15; KJV).

They were also encouraged by Christ's assurance that, as His special ambassadors, they were representing Him. He told

---

[12]James Burton Coffman, *Commentary on Matthew* (Austin, Tex.: Firm Foundation Publishing House, 1968), 137.

them that anyone who received them was also receiving Him (Mt. 10:40–42; see also John 13:20). To be commissioned by the king or the president of a nation would be a great honor. The honor of being commissioned by the "King of kings, and Lord of lords" (Rev. 19:16) is far greater.

Some teach that what Jesus said in the New Testament is weightier than what the apostles wrote or said. Matthew 10:42 and John 13:20 suggest that we are to receive the teaching of the apostles for what it is: the teaching of Jesus. If we accept the apostles, we are accepting Christ. On the other hand, if we reject them (and their teaching), we are rejecting Christ.

The apostles were Jesus' *special* ambassadors. Distinctive instructions to them (such as giving no thought to what they would say) do not apply to us. However, there are also lessons in this chapter for us—so let us turn to ambassadors present: Jesus' everyday ambassadors.

Ambassadors Present

We are not ambassadors in the special sense that the apostles were, but we still represent the Lord on earth today. Paul wrote to the Corinthians:

> Therefore if anyone is in Christ, he is a new creature; the old things passed away; behold, new things have come. Now all these things are from God, who reconciled us to Himself through Christ and gave us the ministry of reconciliation, namely, that God was in Christ reconciling the world to Himself, not counting their trespasses against them, and He has committed to us the word of reconciliation.
>
> Therefore, we are ambassadors for Christ, as though God were making an appeal through us; we beg you on behalf of Christ, be reconciled to God (2 Cor. 5:17–20).

Paul's words had primary reference to his own ministry, but they seem to imply that the church has a similar ministry—that every Christian has the responsibility of reconciling men to God and that, when we do so, we speak "on behalf of Christ."

Many passages emphasize that faithful Christians are Jesus' representatives on earth today; the New Testament teaches that it is impossible to separate Christ and His faithful followers. When someone gives a cup of cold water to one of Jesus' disciples, it is as though he were doing this service to Jesus Himself (Mt. 10:42; see 25:35, 40). When Saul persecuted members of the church (Acts 8:3), he was actually persecuting Christ (Acts 9:4).

We have been baptized into His body (1 Cor. 12:13), the church, which is spoken of as His "fullness" (Eph. 1:22, 23). When we are baptized, we "clothe ourselves" with the Lord (see Gal. 3:27). We are in Jesus, and He is in us (Rom. 8:1; Col. 1:27). Each of us can say, ". . . it is no longer I who live, but Christ lives in me" (Gal. 2:20).

William Barclay wrote, "The Christian is Jesus Christ's ambassador to men. He goes forth from the presence of Christ, bearing with him the word and the beauty of his Master."[13] As previously noted, we have our commission: to go into all the world as the Lord's representatives and to take His message to all men (Mt. 28:18–20; Mk. 16:15, 16). Keeping this in mind, let us return to our text and pull from it general truths that apply to all of Christ's present-day ambassadors.

A Life to Live (Mt. 10:28, 32, 33, 37–39)

As Christ's ambassadors, we should live a special kind of life. Remember, we are representing the King.

This should be a life characterized by *godly fear.* Jesus said, "Do not fear those who kill the body but are unable to kill the soul; but rather fear Him who is able to destroy both soul and body in hell" (Mt. 10:28).

This should be a life characterized by *boldness in proclaiming the Lord.* Christ said, "Therefore everyone who confesses Me before men, I will also confess him before My Father who is in

---

[13]William Barclay, *The Gospel of Matthew,* vol. 1, rev. ed., The Daily Study Bible Series (Philadelphia: Westminster Press, 1975), 361.

heaven. But whoever denies Me before men, I will also deny him before My Father who is in heaven" (Mt. 10:32, 33). We are to acknowledge Him in word. Barclay suggested that "far more people deny Jesus Christ by cowardly silence than by deliberate words."[14] We should also acknowledge Him in deed (see Tit. 1:16). The President of the US may have his Secret Service, but Jesus does not. We should openly acknowledge that we are servants of our King.

This should be a life characterized by *right priorities.* God, Jesus, and the kingdom must be placed above all else. They are more important than our families. Jesus said, "He who loves father or mother more than Me is not worthy of Me; and he who loves son or daughter more than Me is not worthy of Me" (Mt. 10:37). The Lord's kingdom is more important than our very lives. Again, Christ said that "he who has lost his life for My sake will find it" (Mt. 10:39b). This promise comforted early Christians as they faced Roman persecution.

This should be a life characterized by *self-denial.* Jesus said, "And he who does not take his cross and follow after Me is not worthy of Me" (Mt. 10:38). This is the first mention of the cross in the Book of Matthew. Jesus later "took up His cross"—literally. We are to be willing to follow Him.

Persecution to Endure (Mt. 10:16–18, 21, 22, 34–36)
As Christ's "ambassadors," we can expect persecution. Jesus told His disciples, "I send you out as sheep in the midst of wolves" (Mt. 10:16a). That may sound strange since Christ is King of kings, but history is a record of rebellion against authority. If they persecuted Him (Mt. 10:25), why would they not persecute His followers (Mt. 10:24)?

The chapter mentions three types of persecution. First is persecution from the organized religion of that day: "But beware of men, for they will hand you over to the courts and scourge you in their synagogues" (Mt. 10:17). Christians in some parts of the world today understand what it is like to be persecuted by organized religion.

[14]Ibid., 392.

Second is persecution from governmental authorities: "And you will . . . be brought before governors and kings for My sake" (Mt. 10:18a). Immediately, we think of Paul's persecution, and of the first martyrs. Again, some of our brethren today have undergone, and are undergoing, this type of persecution.

The third type of persecution is from an unexpected source: the family.

"Brother will betray brother to death, and a father his child; and children will rise up against parents and cause them to be put to death" (Mt. 10:21).

"Do not think that I came to bring peace on the earth; I did not come to bring peace, but a sword. For I came to set a man against his father, and a daughter against her mother, and a daughter-in-law against her mother-in-law; and a man's enemies will be the members of his household" (Mt. 10:34–36).

Jesus frankly told His followers: "You will be hated by all because of My name" (Mt. 10:22a). He was starkly honest with them. He gave the job description and then, in effect, asked, "Do you want the job?"

Why do we say so little about persecution when the New Testament says so much about it? (See Rom. 8:14–17; Phil. 1:27–30; 1 Pet. 2:18–21; 5:8, 9; 2 Tim. 3:10–12.) When the early church met, they talked about dangers they had to face for the Lord. Some of us are more likely to complain about being too busy, too tired, too hot, or too cold. They endured persecution while we do not like inconvenience. "Must Jesus bear the cross alone?"

Resources to Expect (Mt. 10:26–31)

Christ's words in Matthew 10 were not all negative. There was another side to the coin. As Jesus' "ambassadors," we have the power and resources of the King at our disposal.

Three times in the chapter, the Lord told His disciples not to fear. Do not fear when you are maligned because, in the end, the truth will triumph: "Therefore do not fear them, for there is nothing concealed that will not be revealed, or hidden that will not be known" (Mt. 10:26). The gospel would be proclaimed "upon the housetops" (Mt. 10:27).

Do not fear when your life is threatened, because all that men can do is kill the body: "Do not fear those who kill the body but are unable to kill the soul; but rather fear Him who is able to destroy both soul and body in hell" (Mt. 10:28). Someone has written, "Fear Him, ye saints, and you will then have nothing else to fear." It was said of John Knox, as they buried his body, "Here lies one who feared God so much that he never feared the face of any man."[15]

Do not fear, because the all-powerful God is on your side.

"Are not two sparrows sold for a cent? And yet not one of them will fall to the ground apart from your Father. But the very hairs of your head are all numbered. So do not fear; you are more valuable than many sparrows" (Mt. 10:29–31).

Conclusion

The challenge that Jesus gave His apostles—and the challenge He gives us—is summarized in verse 39: "He who has found his life will lose it, and he who has lost his life for My sake will find it." Early writers tell us that the first martyrs faced the flames or the wild beasts with this verse on their lips: "He who . . . has lost his life for My sake will find it."

Matthew 10:39 is not just a passage for martyrs. It is for each of us. It contains the most frequently recorded saying of the Lord in the New Testament. This saying is found six times in the Gospel Accounts. (The other five are in Mt. 16:25; Mk. 8:35; Lk. 9:24; 17:33; Jn. 12:25.) Jesus wanted us to learn the importance of losing our lives in His service. "He who has found his life will lose it, and he who has lost his life for My sake will find it."

---

[15]Ibid., 386.

HEROD'S INTEREST IN JESUS
(AND ACCOUNT OF THE DEATH
OF JOHN THE BAPTIZER)
(MT. 14:1–12a; MK. 6:14–29; LK. 9:7–9)

Matthew 14:1–12a

[1]At that time Herod the tetrarch heard the news about Jesus, [2]and said to his servants, "This is John the Baptist; he has risen from the dead, and that is why miraculous powers are at work in him."

[3]For when Herod had John arrested, he bound him and put him in prison because of Herodias, the wife of his brother Philip. [4]For John had been saying to him, "It is not lawful for you to have her." [5]Although Herod wanted to put him to death, he feared the crowd, because they regarded John as a prophet.

[6]But when Herod's birthday came, the daughter of Herodias danced before them and pleased Herod, [7]so much that he promised with an oath to give her whatever she asked. [8]Having been prompted by her mother, she said, "Give me here on a platter the head of John the Baptist." [9]Although he was grieved, the king commanded it to be given because of his oaths, and because of his dinner guests. [10]He sent and had John beheaded in the prison. [11]And his head was brought on a platter and given to the girl, and she brought it to her mother. [12a]His disciples came and took away the body and buried it.

Mark 6:14–29

[14]And King Herod heard of it, for His name had become well known; and people were saying, "John the Baptist has risen from the dead, and that is why these miraculous powers are at work in Him." [15]But others were saying, "He is Elijah." And others were saying, "He is a prophet, like one of the prophets of old." [16]But when Herod heard of it, he kept saying, "John, whom I beheaded, has risen!"

[17]For Herod himself had sent and had John arrested and bound in prison on account of Herodias, the wife of his brother Philip, because he had married her. [18]For John had been say-

ing to Herod, "It is not lawful for you to have your brother's wife." [19]Herodias had a grudge against him and wanted to put him to death and could not do so; [20]for Herod was afraid of John, knowing that he was a righteous and holy man, and he kept him safe. And when he heard him, he was very perplexed; but he used to enjoy listening to him. [21]A strategic day came when Herod on his birthday gave a banquet for his lords and military commanders and the leading men of Galilee; [22]and when the daughter of Herodias herself came in and danced, she pleased Herod and his dinner guests; and the king said to the girl, "Ask me for whatever you want and I will give it to you." [23]And he swore to her, "Whatever you ask of me, I will give it to you; up to half of my kingdom." [24]And she went out and said to her mother, "What shall I ask for?" And she said, "The head of John the Baptist." [25]Immediately she came in a hurry to the king and asked, saying, "I want you to give me at once the head of John the Baptist on a platter." [26]And although the king was very sorry, yet because of his oaths and because of his dinner guests, he was unwilling to refuse her. [27]Immediately the king sent an executioner and commanded him to bring back his head. And he went and had him beheaded in the prison, [28]and brought his head on a platter, and gave it to the girl; and the girl gave it to her mother. [29]When his disciples heard about this, they came and took away his body and laid it in a tomb.

Luke 9:7–9

[7]Now Herod the tetrarch heard of all that was happening; and he was greatly perplexed, because it was said by some that John had risen from the dead, [8]and by some that Elijah had appeared, and by others that one of the prophets of old had risen again. [9]Herod said, "I myself had John beheaded; but who is this man about whom I hear such things?" And he kept trying to see Him.

As previously noted, Galilee was ruled by King Herod. This was Herod Antipas, a son of the infamous Herod the Great. Prior to Christ's sending out the Twelve, the king had evidently paid little or no attention to the work of Jesus. As a rule, as long as "peasant reformers" did not stir the masses to rebellion, the government was unconcerned about them. Now, as seven teams of evangelists crisscrossed his territory, Herod could no longer ignore this new movement.

Matthew's account says, **At that time Herod the tetrarch heard the news about Jesus** (Mt. 14:1). In Mark's account, after a summary of the work of the Twelve (Mk. 6:13), he wrote, **And King Herod heard of it, for His name** [that is, the name of Jesus] **had become well known** (Mk. 6:14a). Luke wrote of the success of the apostles (Lk. 9:6) and then said, **Now Herod the tetrarch heard of all that was happening; and he was greatly perplexed . . .** (Lk. 9:7a).

Word reached Herod's ears regarding what people were saying about Jesus: Some said that He was Elijah; others believed that some other prophet had arisen from the dead (Lk. 9:8; Mk. 6:15; compare with Mt. 16:13, 14). The Jews did not think of Jesus as the Messiah, because they expected the Messiah to come "with pomp and circumstance"; but they were willing to concede that He could be a prophet. Through the years, men have consistently fallen short in their estimation of Jesus.

What made the king nervous, however, was that some were saying, **"John the Baptist has risen from the dead, and that is why these miraculous powers are at work in Him"** (Mk. 6:14b; see Lk. 9:7b). Evidently, these did not know that Jesus and John had had ministries at the same time. Ignorance has never hindered men in their speculation. This talk made the tetrarch nervous because he had beheaded John not long before. (Matthew 14:13 says that when Jesus heard of John's death, He withdrew across the Sea of Galilee, where He fed the five thousand. Mark 6:30–32 says that shortly after the disciples returned from their tour of Galilee, they withdrew to the other side of the sea. A comparison of the accounts indicates that John was killed while Jesus and His disciples were making the third tour of Galilee, and that word reached Christ at the end of the tour.)

Herod had imprisoned John the Baptizer a year or so earlier to appease his wife, Herodias. The king had lured Herodias, his half-brother Philip's wife, away from Philip and had married her (Mt. 14:3). Herodias herself was a descendant of Herod the Great; she was Herod Antipas' half-niece. Her marriage to Herod Antipas had broken a number of Levitical laws. The Law condemned marriage to a near relative (see Lev. 18:1–18; 20:11–21). It also prohibited a man from marrying his brother's wife when that brother was still living (Lev. 18:16; Deut. 25:5–10). John had thus told Herod, **"It is not lawful for you to have her"** (Mt. 14:4)—which had infuriated Herodias (Mk. 6:19). We do not know exactly when and how John delivered that bold message, but we do know its result.

In spite of Herodias' desire to have John put to death (Mk. 6:19), Herod had been reluctant to go that far—fearing that the death of the prophet might result in an uprising (see Mt. 14:5). Also, he had held a grudging respect for John. Mark wrote that **Herod was afraid of John, knowing that he was a righteous and holy man, and he kept him safe** (Mk. 6:20a). Then Mark added this strange note: **And when he heard him, he was very perplexed; but he used to enjoy listening to him** (Mk. 6:20b). John, in his rough clothing, would have been quite a sight when he appeared before Herod, who was accustomed to royal finery. Still, a troubled look must have crossed the king's face as the prophet shook a finger in his direction. The LB paraphrase has "Herod was disturbed whenever he talked with John, but even so he liked to listen to him."

Herod had managed to protect John from Herodias—until a fateful day when the king decided to give himself a birthday party (Mt. 14:6; Mk. 6:21). General accounts of pagan banquets in that day, plus a knowledge of the moral standards of the Herods, leave no doubt as to what kind of banquet this was. At the height of the orgy, Herodias' daughter came into the banquet room to dance (Mt. 14:6; Mk. 6:22). Josephus said that the girl's name was Salome. Modesty forbids my being explicit regarding the nature of her performance.

Mark 6:21 says that **a strategic day came.** This refers to *Herodias'* strategy. Her daughter's dance was part of that strategy. Herodias knew her lustful husband well. The fact that Herodias would use her daughter in this way to further her fiendish plans, plus the fact that the king would allow his step-daughter to exhibit herself in such a manner before his drunken companions, reveals much about the character of the Herod family.

The text says that Salome's dance **pleased Herod and his dinner guests** (Mk. 6:22a). The king told the girl, **"Ask me for whatever you want and I will give it to you"** (Mk. 6:22b). He swore with an oath, **"Whatever you ask of me, I will give it to you; up to half of my kingdom"** (Mk. 6:23; see Mt. 14:7). Such extravagant offers were typical of eastern rulers (see Esther 5:3, 6; 7:2)—but the rulers did not look kindly on those who took advantage of such offers.

Salome did not hesitate. **Having been prompted by her mother**, she asked for the head of John the Baptizer **on a platter** (Mt. 14:8). Herodias did not want a report of his death; that might be faked. She did not want to see his body; a death scene could be staged. Only when she saw his detached head, his lifeblood draining from his severed veins, would she be satisfied. Further, she wanted the prophet's head **at once** (Mk. 6:25)—before Herod had a chance to change his mind.

Matthew's account leaves the impression that Herodias had previously rehearsed Salome regarding what to ask for, while Mark's account indicates that Salome had to go ask her mother after the offer was made (Mk. 6:24). The exact order of events is unimportant. It is possible that Salome's asking her mother was a bit of play-acting to avoid the appearance that this was prearranged.

When the request was made, the king was immediately sorry; but rather than "lose face" with those who had witnessed his vow, he ordered that John be beheaded. The deed was quickly done:

Immediately the king sent an executioner and commanded him to bring back his head. And he went and had him beheaded in the prison, and brought his head on a platter, and gave it to the girl; and the girl gave it to her mother (Mk. 6:27, 28).

The act may have made Herodias happy, but it brought Herod

TRUTH FOR TODAY COMMENTARY

no peace of mind. He was **grieved** by what he had done (Mt. 14:9). Herod did not exhibit much of a conscience, but at least he was exceedingly uneasy. Thus, when he heard the super-stitious speculation of the masses, he was filled with a sense of foreboding. Mark recorded that **he kept saying, "John, whom I beheaded, has risen!"** (Mk. 6:16; see Mt. 14:2).

Herod decided that he needed to see Jesus to satisfy his mind regarding whether or not He really was John (Lk. 9:9a). Luke wrote that **he kept trying to see Him** (Lk. 9:9b). Herod had abundant resources at his disposal in Galilee. One with a public ministry like Christ's would ordinarily not be hard for the king to find.

We later learn that Herod's quest to see Jesus did not wane. During the last week of Christ's earthly ministry, we read that the king "had wanted to see Him for a long time, because he had been hearing about Him and was hoping to see some sign per-formed by Him" (Lk. 23:8). After interrogating Jesus, if Herod had decided that Christ posed a threat, he certainly would have ordered His death (see Lk. 13:31–33). Consider how his father, Herod the Great, had reacted upon learning of the birth of Jesus (Mt. 21:3, 13). The king's interest in Christ's work was a real and imminent threat.

JESUS' WITHDRAWAL FROM HEROD'S TERRITORY (AND RETURN)

Return of the Twelve and Retirement to the East Coast Of the Sea of Galilee (Mt. 14:12b, 13; Mk. 6:30–32; Lk. 9:10; Jn. 6:1)

Matthew 14:12b–13
¹²ᵇ**And they went and reported to Jesus.**

¹³**Now when Jesus heard about John, He withdrew from there in a boat to a secluded place by Himself; and when the people heard of this, they followed Him on foot from the cities.**

Mark 6:30–32
³⁰**The apostles gathered together with Jesus; and they**

reported to Him all that they had done and taught. ³¹And He said to them, "Come away by yourselves to a secluded place and rest a while." (For there were many people coming and going, and they did not even have time to eat.) ³²They went away in the boat to a secluded place by themselves.

Luke 9:10
¹⁰When the apostles returned, they gave an account to Him of all that they had done. Taking them with Him, He withdrew by Himself to a city called Bethsaida.

John 6:1
¹After these things Jesus went away to the other side of the Sea of Galilee (or Tiberias).

Jesus completed His tour, and He and His disciples regrouped. They probably returned to Capernaum, the center of Jesus' activities and the usual termination point of His journeys. **When the apostles returned,** they **gathered together with Jesus; and they reported to Him all that they had done and taught** (Lk. 9:10a; Mk. 6:30; see Mt. 14:12b). This "debriefing" was crucial to their training. They needed to talk about what they had done, what had "worked" and what had not. They needed to admit their mistakes and ask, "What should we have done?" They must have had dozens of questions to ask.

Even as Christ attempted to help His disciples, they were again thronged by tenacious crowds. There were **many people coming and going, and they did not even have time to eat** (Mk. 6:31b; compare with Mk. 3:20)—much less wrap up their first preaching tour.

Then disturbing news came about the death of John. His sorrowing disciples had been allowed to take his body and place it in a tomb (Mk. 6:29; see Mt. 14:12a). They then went to tell Jesus, arriving about the same time as His apostles (Mt. 14:12b).

Now when Jesus heard about John (Mt. 14:13a), He proposed to His disciples that they go to a secluded location (Mk. 6:31). Matthew's account says that Jesus **withdrew . . . by Himself** (Mt. 14:13), while Mark's account says, **They** [Christ and the

435

apostles] **went away . . . to a secluded place** (Mk. 6:32). Luke's account combines the two thoughts: **Taking them** [the Twelve] **with Him, He withdrew by Himself** (Lk. 9:10).

This withdrawal served at least two purposes. First, it would remove Christ and His followers from Herod's territory. From this point on, Jesus would spend little time in Galilee. He would return from time to time for brief visits, but the bulk of His work in that province was now complete. Second, the withdrawal should give Christ needed time alone with His disciples. All of them had just returned from an arduous journey, and their bodies cried out for rest (Mk. 6:31a). Furthermore, time with the Lord would help them deal with all that had happened on their first preaching tour.

Once more, they headed east across the Sea of Galilee. Matthew and Mark said that they went **to a secluded place** (Mt. 14:13a; Mk. 6:31a), while Luke indicated that they traveled to **a city called Bethsaida** (Lk. 9:10b).

There were at least two cities named Bethsaida near the sea. Jesus and the disciples traveled to a Bethsaida on the east side of the sea; but after they had been there for a while, Christ sent His disciples *back* to a Bethsaida on the other side of the sea, near Capernaum (Mk. 6:45). Philip (who became an apostle) was from this Bethsaida (Jn. 1:44; 12:21), which was called "the city of Andrew and Peter" (Jn. 1:44). The other, toward which Jesus and the Twelve now traveled, was a village on the northeast side of the sea. Its full name was Bethsaida-Julias. Evidently, their destination was a deserted area on the seashore, not far from the town.

APPLICATION:
"A VOICE CRYING IN THE WILDERNESS":
THE MINISTRY OF JOHN

The time was about A.D. 26; the place, Bethany beyond the Jordan. A preacher, about thirty years old, had been stirring up the people on both sides of the Dead Sea. A committee of priests and Levites came to him and asked, "Who are you?" (Jn. 1:19b). Understanding the reason for their question, he answered, "I am not the Christ" (Jn. 1:20b). They persisted in their interrogation:

> They asked him, "What then? Are you Elijah?" And he said, "I am not." "Are you the Prophet?" And he answered, "No." Then they said to him, "Who are you, so that we may give an answer to those who sent us? What do you say about yourself?" (Jn. 1:21, 22).

Back came this cryptic answer: "I am a voice of one crying in the wilderness" (Jn. 1:23a).

The young man who called himself "a voice . . . crying in the wilderness" was John the Baptizer. His terminology came from Isaiah 40, which told of the forerunner of the Messiah:

> A voice is calling, "Clear the way for the Lord in the wilderness; make smooth in the desert a highway for our God. Let every valley be lifted up, and every mountain and hill be made low; and let the rough ground become a plain, and the rugged terrain a broad valley" (Is. 40:3, 4).

Heralds or harbingers not only announced the coming of a king, but also prepared for his coming—laying up provisions and (as emphasized in this text) making a road on which he could travel.

The phrase "a voice . . . crying in the wilderness" in John 1:23 summarizes the phenomenon that was John: First and foremost, he was *a voice*; he was a man with a message. That message was to be presented in a unique setting: *in the wilderness*. John literally preached in a physical wilderness, but "the wilderness" referred to in Isaiah 40 and John 1 was more than rocks, sand, and scorpions. John also preached in a wilderness of sin. He dared to be a voice where other voices had been silenced.

We will look briefly at John's life—to appreciate the man he was and the message he had for his day and ours.[16]

---

[16]My notes on this study about John the Baptizer were made years ago, and they were not properly documented. I apologize in advance for any instance when I may fail to give credit to whom credit is due.

A Voice Crying "Deny Yourself"
In a Wilderness of Self-indulgence

John might be pictured as a man with wind-blown hair and sunburned skin. His rough clothing was made of camel's hair. Around his waist was a wide leather belt. He lived off the land, subsisting on a diet of locusts (insects like grasshoppers) and wild honey. He was the epitome of self-denial and self-discipline.

What produced a man like this? One factor was *godly parents*. His father was a priest named Zacharias; his mother was Elizabeth (Lk. 1:5). Luke 1:6 summarizes their lives: "They were both righteous in the sight of God, walking blamelessly in all the commandments and requirements of the Lord." The most striking part of that verse is the word "both." Some have had a godly mother but not a godly father. A few have had a godly father but not a godly mother. *Both* of John's parents loved the Lord and lived according to His precepts. A man cannot have a greater heritage than that.

Another factor was *a godly purpose*. You may remember the story of Zacharias and Elizabeth: how they longed for a child, how an angel appeared to Zacharias, and how John was finally born to Elizabeth. Let us focus on the words of the angel to the old priest in the temple:

> Do not be afraid, Zacharias, for your petition has been heard, and your wife Elizabeth will bear you a son, and you will give him the name John. You will have joy and gladness, and many will rejoice at his birth. For he will be great in the sight of the Lord; and he will drink no wine or liquor, and he will be filled with the Holy Spirit while yet in his mother's womb. And he will turn many of the sons of Israel back to the Lord their God. It is he who will go as a forerunner before Him in the spirit and power of Elijah, to turn the hearts of the fathers back to the children, and the disobedient to the attitude of the righteous, so as to make ready a people prepared for the Lord (Lk. 1:13–17).

From the beginning of John's life, there was no question regarding who he was and what his purpose in life was to be. Every child needs to be told by his parents that God has a purpose for his or her life.

The third factor was *godly training*. We are told little about that training, although it is not difficult to imagine Zacharias and Elizabeth sharing with the boy what the angel had said and encouraging him to love and obey the Lord. As far as the text is concerned, we are given these sparse details regarding his early life: "And the child continued to grow and to become strong in spirit, and he lived in the deserts [or wilderness; the Greek word ἔρημος (*eremos*), translated "deserts" in Lk. 1:80, is the same basic word as that translated "wilderness" in Jn. 1:23] until the day of his public appearance to Israel" (Lk. 1:80). We do not know when or why John went into the desolate area around the Dead Sea. Some have suggested that his parents died while he was still young and that was the occasion for his move to the desert/wilderness—but that is speculation. Regardless, in God's wisdom, the wilderness was chosen as his training camp. From that base, he could see where the proud cities of Sodom and Gomorrah once stood, perfect examples of the consequences of self-indulgence.

Parents want a good environment for their children. Many of us think that a "good environment" requires a healthy and harmonious setting. John's early environment was the rugged terrain in eastern Judea. There he learned self-discipline. From that locale, a voice emerged crying "self-denial" in a wilderness of self-indulgence.

Can we hear that voice today? We live in a world of self-indulgence, and we desperately need John's message. After all, Jesus said, "If anyone wishes to come after Me, he must deny himself, and take up his cross and follow Me" (Mt. 16:24).

Because of his austere lifestyle (Lk. 7:33), some thought John had a demon. Hear this word of warning: The world will think that we, too, are demented if our concern is for others rather than for self. Jesus, however, stressed the greatness of such a life. Speaking of the Baptizer, He asked His listeners, "But what did you go out to see? A man dressed in soft clothing? Those who are splendidly clothed and live in luxury are found in royal palaces!" (Lk. 7:25). John was not interested in the easy life; let the kings in their castles keep their luxuries. Jesus also made this amazing statement: "I say to you, among those born of women there is no one greater than John" (Lk. 7:28a).

Let each of us compare our lives with John's and ask, "Am *I* living a life of self-discipline and self-denial?"

A Voice Crying "Change Your Ways"
In a Wilderness of Complacency

In "the fullness of the time" (Gal. 4:4), "the word of God came to John, the son of Zacharias, in the wilderness" (Lk. 3:2). In John's life, the Word of God was like the "bang!" of the starting pistol to a sprinter, like the gong of the bell to a fighter, like "Sic'im" to a bulldog.

John immediately began preaching, "Now in those days John the Baptist came, preaching in the wilderness of Judea, saying, 'Repent, for the kingdom of heaven is at hand'" (Mt. 3:1, 2). His task was that of preparing people for the coming of the Messiah and His kingdom. The preacher minced no words as he told his listeners that they needed to mend their lives:

> So he began saying to the crowds who were going out to be baptized by him, "You brood of vipers [you snakes!], who warned you to flee from the wrath to come? Therefore bear fruits in keeping with repentance, and do not begin to say to yourselves, 'We have Abraham for our father,' for I say to you that from these stones God is able to raise up children to Abraham" (Lk. 3:7, 8).

For too long, the people had thought that God would accept them simply because they were Jews. John's message was an alarm-clock message—designed to wake them up. He told them, in effect, that if they did not make major changes in their lives, they were not "fit for the kingdom of God" (see Lk. 9:62).

And the crowds were questioning him, saying, "Then what shall we do?" And he would answer and say to them, "The man who has two tunics is to share with him who has none; and he who has food is to do likewise." And some tax collectors also came to be baptized, and they said to him, "Teacher, what shall we do?" And he said to them, "Collect no more than what you have been ordered to." Some soldiers were questioning him, saying, "And what about us, what shall we do?" And he said to them, "Do not take money from anyone by force, or accuse anyone falsely, and be content with your wages" (Lk. 3:10–14).

We still need straightforward preaching today. We need preaching that will wake us up and prepare us for heaven. It is possible to condemn sin in such general terms that no sinner is ever convicted of his sin. John's preaching was pointed and practical.

Luke 3:18 says that "with many other exhortations [John] preached the gospel to the people." The word "gospel" means "good news." In what sense was telling people not to be selfish, not to be dishonest, and not to abuse their authority "good news"? It was "good news" because it demolished their complacency, forced them to reexamine their lives, and encouraged them to be the kind of people upon whom God could shower His grace.

Do we appreciate those who speak "the truth [the whole truth] in love" (Eph. 4:15; see Gal. 4:16)? We should no more want a timid preacher than we would desire a timid surgeon. Further, we should be willing to be voices crying, "Change your ways!" where that message is needed (see Gal. 6:1; Jas. 5:19, 20).

A Voice Crying "Believe" in a Wilderness of Doubt

One day, as John was preaching beside the Jordan, Jesus came to him to be baptized. John did not want to baptize Christ, but He persuaded him; and after Jesus' baptism, God spoke from heaven and the Holy Spirit descended as a dove (Mt. 3:13–17).

These manifestations confirmed in John's mind that Jesus was indeed the Messiah for whom he had been preparing the way. From that moment on, John's favorite message was "Behold, the Lamb of God!" (Jn. 1:29, 35, 36). John did not preach that Jesus was just a good man and a great teacher; he proclaimed Him to be the sacrifice for our sins, the One through whom we could be saved.

In a world of unbelief and skepticism, the clarion call of John still needs to be heard. Jesus is the Son of God. He is man's only hope. Let us preach this with the same conviction that John had.

A Voice Crying "Be Humble" in a Wilderness of Pride

The baptism of Jesus was the climax of John's ministry. At that point, his work was basically done, and from that time, his ministry declined. As a forerunner of the Messiah, John basically had three responsibilities: to clear the way for the Messiah, to prepare the way for the Messiah, and then to get out of the way of the Messiah.[17] That was fine with John; he was ready to fulfill whatever role God had planned for him.

Go with me to John 3, a passage that is a key to John's true greatness. When Christ's popularity began to soar, John's disciples came to him and said, "Rabbi, He who was with you beyond the Jordan, to whom you have testified, behold, He is baptizing and all are coming to Him" (Jn. 3:26). Can you hear the jealousy in their words? In effect, they were saying, "Once everyone came to us, but now they are coming to *Him*. Once we were center stage, but now the spotlight is on *Him*. *You* baptized Him; don't they know that makes *you* greater than He?"

Battles have been lost because of jealousy among generals. If the envy of his disciples had been encouraged by John, think of the damage it might have done to Jesus' embryonic movement. Listen to—and marvel at—the Baptizer's response to their complaint. He first said that Christ's success was God's will: "A man can receive nothing unless it has been given him from heaven" (Jn. 3:27). Then he emphasized that what was happening made him happy:

> You yourselves are my witnesses that I said, "I am not the Christ," but, "I have been sent ahead of Him." He

---

[17]This sentence was adapted from Charles R. Swindoll, *John the Baptizer* (Anaheim, Calif.: Insight for Living, 1991), 3.

who has the bride is the bridegroom; but the friend of the bridegroom, who stands and hears him, rejoices greatly because of the bridegroom's voice. So this joy of mine has been made full (Jn. 3:28, 29).

Finally, he spoke these remarkable words: "He must increase, but I must decrease" (Jn. 3:30). It takes a big, big man to speak words like these and mean them.

Most successful preachers I know struggle with John's dilemma. They enjoy the acclaim—whether they admit it or not. As a rule, however, when respected preachers grow older, they get fewer calls to preach and the spotlight shifts to younger preachers. It is hard for us to say, "That's good. They must increase and we must decrease. May God be with them!"

Preachers are not the only ones who struggle with their egos. What if others get the praise we thought we should have? What if others get the better jobs or promotions? Can we honestly say that we are happy for them? Can we sincerely say, "They must increase and we must decrease"?

For some of us, there is no bigger challenge than this. Remember that "God is opposed to the proud, but gives grace to the humble" (Jas. 4:6b). May God help us to be more like John, who cried "Be humble!" in a world of pride.

A Voice Crying "Be Brave"
In a Wilderness of Cowardice

Other incidents in the life of John could be studied, but we will close with the final scene of his life. We stated earlier that his preaching was pointed and practical. It was also intensely personal. No better illustration of this could be given than his indictment of King Herod.

... Herod the tetrarch was reprimanded by him because of Herodias, his brother's wife, and because of all the wicked things which Herod had done (Lk. 3:19).

... Herod had John arrested, ... and put him in prison because of Herodias, the wife of his brother Philip. For

John had been saying to him, "It is not lawful for you to have her" (Mt. 14:3, 4).

Exactly how the confrontation between John and Herod came about, we do not know. Did Herod come to hear John preach? It is later stated that Herod liked to listen to John (Mk. 6:20), so this is not outside the realm of possibility. Did John make a trip to one of Herod's castles? We are not given the details, but the Greek text indicates that John *continually* said to him that his marriage to Herodias was not lawful.

This took courage, massive courage. It took courage because Herod was an important man, a man with influence. It took courage because John was making a personal rebuke. It is one thing to condemn sin in general from the safety of the pulpit and another to tell someone, "You are wrong." It took courage because John was saying what Herod and Herodias needed to hear, not what they wanted to hear. Many "gospel messages" offend no one, but John blurted out, "It is not lawful for you to have her"— and that disturbed his hearers. It took courage because the prophet had to know that his words could cost him his life. One cannot aggravate a Herod with a wife like Herodias without suffering the consequences. They have been called the Ahab and Jezebel of the New Testament. Jesus said that John was no "reed shaken by the wind" (Mt. 11:7). Rather, he was God's steadfast and courageous voice speaking out against sin.

You may know the details of the sequel: how John was arrested and how he finally lost his life as the result of a drunken feast, a dancing girl, and a vengeful wife. According to human tradition, when the head of John was brought to Herodias, she stuck a long pin through the prophet's tongue and screamed, "You'll never again say, 'It is not lawful for you to have her'!"

Herodias may have thought that she had silenced John, but she had not. The voice of a man of courage cannot be stilled. The death of the Baptizer preyed on the mind of Herod, and when he heard of Jesus' work, he was haunted by the possibility that Jesus was John risen from the dead (Mk. 6:14). Even after John had been dead for some time, his influence was so great that

Jesus used his work to answer His questioners (Mt. 21:23–27; Lk. 20:2–8).

May God give us the courage of John: the courage to speak out against sin, whether in high or low places; the courage to go to people personally concerning their sin; the courage to speak that which people need, not necessarily what they want; the courage to stand for right, regardless of the possible consequences. Jesus still challenges each of us: ". . . be faithful, even if you have to die, and I will give you the crown of life" (Rev. 2:10; NCV).

Conclusion
John was "a voice . . . crying in the wilderness":

... a voice crying "deny yourself" in a wilderness of self-indulgence.
... a voice crying "change your ways" in a wilderness of complacency.
... a voice crying "believe" in a wilderness of doubt.
... a voice crying "be humble" in a wilderness of pride.
... a voice crying "be brave" in a wilderness of cowardice.

How was John able to be such a voice? What was his secret? He was committed to the Lord and to doing His will. He thus dared to be different. He was willing to speak where other voices had been silenced.

Feeding Five Thousand Men
(Mt. 14:13–21; Mk. 6:33–44; Lk. 9:11–17; Jn. 6:2–14)

Matthew 14:13–21
¹³**Now when Jesus heard about John, He withdrew from there in a boat to a secluded place by Himself; and when the people heard of this, they followed Him on foot from the cities.** ¹⁴**When He went ashore, He saw a large crowd, and felt compassion for them and healed their sick.**

¹⁵**When it was evening, the disciples came to Him and said, "This place is desolate and the hour is already late; so send the**

crowds away, that they may go into the villages and buy food for themselves." [16]But Jesus said to them, "They do not need to go away; you give them something to eat!" [17]They said to Him, "We have here only five loaves and two fish." [18]And He said, "Bring them here to Me." [19]Ordering the people to sit down on the grass, He took the five loaves and the two fish, and looking up toward heaven, He blessed the food, and breaking the loaves He gave them to the disciples, and the disciples gave them to the crowds, [20]and they all ate and were satisfied. They picked up what was left over of the broken pieces, twelve full baskets. [21]There were about five thousand men who ate, besides women and children.

Mark 6:33–44

[33]The people saw them going, and many recognized them and ran there together on foot from all the cities, and got there ahead of them. [34]When Jesus went ashore, He saw a large crowd, and He felt compassion for them because they were like sheep without a shepherd; and He began to teach them many things. [35]When it was already quite late, His disciples came to Him and said, "This place is desolate and it is already quite late; [36]send them away so that they may go into the surrounding countryside and villages and buy themselves something to eat." [37]But He answered them, "You give them something to eat!" And they said to Him, "Shall we go and spend two hundred denarii on bread and give them something to eat?" [38]And He said to them, "How many loaves do you have? Go look!" And when they found out, they said, "Five, and two fish." [39]And He commanded them all to sit down by groups on the green grass. [40]They sat down in groups of hundreds and of fifties. [41]And He took the five loaves and the two fish, and looking up toward heaven, He blessed the food and broke the loaves and He kept giving them to the disciples to set before them; and He divided up the two fish among them all. [42]They all ate and were satisfied, [43]and they picked up twelve full baskets of the broken pieces, and also of the fish. [44]There were five thousand men who ate the loaves.

Luke 9:11–17

[11]But the crowds were aware of this and followed Him; and welcoming them, He began speaking to them about the kingdom of God and curing those who had need of healing.

[12]Now the day was ending, and the twelve came and said to Him, "Send the crowd away, that they may go into the surrounding villages and countryside and find lodging and get something to eat; for here we are in a desolate place." [13]But He said to them, "You give them something to eat!" And they said, "We have no more than five loaves and two fish, unless perhaps we go and buy food for all these people." [14](For there were about five thousand men.) And He said to His disciples, "Have them sit down to eat in groups of about fifty each." [15]They did so, and had them all sit down. [16]Then He took the five loaves and the two fish, and looking up to heaven, He blessed them, and broke them, and kept giving them to the disciples to set before the people. [17]And they all ate and were satisfied; and the broken pieces which they had left over were picked up, twelve baskets full.

John 6:2–14

[2]A large crowd followed Him, because they saw the signs which He was performing on those who were sick. [3]Then Jesus went up on the mountain, and there He sat down with His disciples. [4]Now the Passover, the feast of the Jews, was near. [5]Therefore Jesus, lifting up His eyes and seeing that a large crowd was coming to Him, said to Philip, "Where are we to buy bread, so that these may eat?" [6]This He was saying to test him, for He Himself knew what He was intending to do. [7]Philip answered Him, "Two hundred denarii worth of bread is not sufficient for them, for everyone to receive a little." [8]One of His disciples, Andrew, Simon Peter's brother, said to Him, [9]"There is a lad here who has five barley loaves and two fish, but what are these for so many people?" [10]Jesus said, "Have the people sit down." Now there was much grass in the place. So the men sat down, in number about five thousand. [11]Jesus then took the loaves, and having given thanks, He distributed to those who were seated; likewise also of the fish as much as they wanted.

¹²**When they were filled, He said to His disciples, "Gather up the leftover fragments so that nothing will be lost." ¹³So they gathered them up, and filled twelve baskets with fragments from the five barley loaves which were left over by those who had eaten. ¹⁴Therefore when the people saw the sign which He had performed, they said, "This is truly the Prophet who is to come into the world."**

As already noted, Jesus had proposed that He and the apostles travel by boat to the eastern shore of the Sea of Galilee (Mk. 6:30–32; see Mt. 14:13; Jn. 6:1). Their destination was a deserted area somewhere near a village named Bethsaida-Julias (Lk. 9:10).

As they approached the shore, a multitude gathered—hundreds of people, with more arriving every minute. Christ graciously **felt compassion for them**. In His usual manner, He began to teach them and heal their sick (Mt. 14:14; Mk. 6:34; Lk. 9:11). While the day wore on, the crowd continued to swell until it numbered in the thousands (Lk. 9:14).

> **Therefore Jesus, lifting up His eyes and seeing that a large crowd was coming to Him, said to Philip, "Where are we to buy bread, so that these may eat?" This He was saying to test him, for He Himself knew what He was intending to do** (Jn. 6:5, 6).

Philip saw Christ's words as a test of his ability to calculate. He answered, **"Two hundred denarii worth of bread is not sufficient for them, for everyone to receive a little"** (Jn. 6:7). It was not, however, a mathematical test, but a test of faith. Soon afterward, the same basic test was given to the rest of the apostles:

> **When it was evening, the disciples came to Him and said, "This place is desolate and the hour is already late; so send the crowds away, that they may go into the villages and buy food for themselves." But Jesus said to them, "They do not need to go away; you give them**

something to eat!" (Mt. 14:15, 16).

The Twelve saw Christ's command to give the crowd "something to eat" as a test of their competence in checking resources. It is implied that they had no provisions themselves. If they had brought any food, they would surely have listed it in their report to Jesus on what was available. The fact that they did not is probably an indication of the urgency involved in their leaving Herod's territory. They had probably planned to buy food in a nearby town (see Jn. 4:8).

A poll of the crowd only produced a boy's snack (Mt. 14:17). The disciples had seen the Lord do many miracles, including stilling a storm and raising the dead. On this occasion, they had seen Him heal the sick. Further, Jesus had recently empowered them to perform miracles (Mt. 10:1). Nevertheless, they had a hard time understanding that if Christ could do one miracle, He could do any miracle, including feeding five thousand men plus women and children with a handful of bread and fish.

Taking the meager rations in hand, Jesus told the crowd to sit down on the grass (Mt. 14:19) for a meal—with only five small loaves and two tiny fish in evidence. In a sense, the test of faith was extended to everyone present. To their credit, the disciples and the multitude at least had enough faith to do as Christ commanded.

When we take a test, we are generally anxious to learn of the test results. In this case, the faith of those present was rewarded: A snack for one boy became an all-you-can-eat buffet for thousands of hungry people: **And they all ate and were satisfied. They picked up what was left over of the broken pieces, twelve full baskets. There were about five thousand men who ate, besides women and children** (Mt. 14:20, 21; see also Mk. 6:41– 44; Lk. 9:16; Jn. 6:12).

The diners were delighted (John 6:26 depicts their enthusiasm)—but they failed to realize that the meal itself was an added test: a test of how they perceived Jesus and His mission. Excited, they said to one another, **"This is truly the Prophet who is to come into the world"** (Jn. 6:14). This was the One they had been looking for. The people apparently had in mind Moses' statement that God would raise up a prophet like himself (Deut. 18:15). Jesus' sermon the next day indicates that the people were comparing Him to Moses (see Jn. 6:31, 32, 49, 58). Near the end of Jesus' ministry, similar excitement gripped the crowd when Christ made His triumphal entry into Jerusalem (see Mt. 21:1–11, 14–17; Mk. 11:1–11; Lk. 19:29–44; Jn. 12:12–19). Before long, plans were being formed "to come and take Him by force to make Him king" (Jn. 6:15).

APPLICATION:
WHEN PEOPLE REALLY NEED HELP
(MT. 14:13–21; MK. 6:33–44; LK. 9:11–17; JN. 6:2–14)

One of Christ's most significant miracles is the one commonly referred to as "the feeding of the five thousand." Other than the Resurrection, this is the only miracle recorded in all four Gospel Accounts. The repetition takes on added significance when you consider that, out of the thousands of miracles that Jesus did, John chose only seven—and that John normally deliberately avoided duplicating what the synoptic Gospel Accounts had recorded. Why was this particular miraculous event held in such high regard? Perhaps the reason is that it was one of the few "creative" miracles of the Lord. (A "creative" miracle is one in which Christ "created" something. Another example is His turning water to wine.) Maybe it is because no other single miracle was witnessed by such a large number of people under circumstances that precluded deception. Whatever the reason, the story of Jesus' feeding the multitude was important to early Christians. The motif of the loaves and fishes is common in early Christian art. The incident still has special meaning to Christians today. When polls are taken of favorite Bible stories, invariably this story is near the top of the list.

The feeding of the five thousand can be approached from various standpoints, but I want to use it as an example of how Jesus helped people—and how we can do the same. If the New Testament teaches anything, it teaches that, as followers of Christ, we should be sensitive to the needs of others and try to help them.

So then, while we have opportunity, let us do good to all people, and especially to those who are of the household of the faith (Gal. 6:10).

Pure and undefiled religion in the sight of our God and Father is this: to visit orphans and widows in their distress, and to keep oneself unstained by the world (Jas. 1:27).

But whoever has the world's goods, and sees his brother in need and closes his heart against him, how does the love of God abide in him? (1 Jn. 3:17).

The story of the feeding of the five thousand contains important principles on how to fulfill these commands—including *how to* and *how not to* help those who have genuine needs.

People Do Have Needs

The first part of the story highlights the fact that some people do indeed have legitimate needs. According to Paul's teaching in 2 Thessalonians 3, there are some we should *not* help because to do so would encourage laziness on their part. Real/genuine/legitimate needs are those needs that can be addressed scripturally. Let us begin with a review and some background information.

Jesus and His apostles had been traveling around Galilee. At the end of that tour, they learned that King Herod had beheaded John the Baptizer—and was now dangerously interested in their work. Christ proposed to the Twelve that they go to the east side of the Sea of Galilee. Their destination was a deserted area near Bethsaida-Julias, seven or eight miles across the north end of the Sea of Galilee (see the map "Palestine During the Life of Christ" in the appendix). Their boat trip across the sea was probably a leisurely affair. Christ—and perhaps a few of the disciples—could even have taken a nap on the journey (see Mt. 8:24).

People with Needs Then

In the meantime, the crowd at Capernaum somehow found out about Jesus' plans and "followed Him on foot from the cities" (Mt. 14:13). Mark wrote that they "ran there together on foot . . . , and got there ahead of them" (Mk. 6:33). Those familiar with that area assure us that this would have presented no special problems. Those traveling on foot had to cross the Jordan, but there was a ford a short distance north of where the river emptied into the Sea of Galilee. The young and fit likely raced along the shore while the old and infirm came at a slower pace. Among those hurrying as best they could were those bringing their sick for Jesus to heal (Mt. 14:13, 14). Everyone probably started out together, but soon a long procession was strung out around the north end of the sea.

When Jesus' boat approached the shore, a crowd was already there, eagerly awaiting His arrival (Mk. 6:33; Mt. 14:14). Did the disciples groan when they saw the crowd? Perhaps they did. When Jesus spoke of feeding the crowd, the disciples' response was to send them away (Mk. 6:36). They were tired and hungry (Mk. 6:31); they needed time with Christ.

The multitude was ever-present and demanding, but Jesus' response was unlike that of His apostles. He "felt compassion for [the people] because they were like sheep without a shepherd" (Mk. 6:34a; see Mt. 14:14). Luke wrote that He welcomed them (Lk. 9:11a). He did not endure them; He did not tolerate them; He *welcomed* them.

John said that they had "followed Him, because they saw the signs which He was performing on those who were sick" (Jn. 6:2). Christ immediately began "curing those who had need of healing" (Lk. 9:11c). Since He never missed an opportunity to preach, He also "began to teach them many things" (Mk. 6:34b), "speaking to them about the kingdom of God" (Lk. 9:11b).

It was another long day in the life of Jesus. He occasionally took a break on the side of a mountain in the area (see Jn. 6:4, 15). For the most part, however, He was busy teaching and healing. Meanwhile, the number in the multitude continued to grow (Jn. 6:5). John explained that "the Passover, the feast of the Jews, was near" (Jn. 6:4). It has been suggested that this was written to explain how the crowd grew, as pilgrims on their way to Jerusalem stopped to see what the excitement was about. The problem with this is that these would be likely to have ample supplies with them, but when the crowd was surveyed at the end of the day, no supplies were in evidence. Perhaps this detail was given to stress the time of the year, to explain why "much grass" was growing in that area (Jn. 6:10).

The crowd was later said to be "about five thousand men . . . , besides women and children" (Mt. 14:21). Estimates of the women and children vary, but there could have been between ten and fifteen thousand present. Some think that few women and children would have made that long run, while others say, "Nonsense!"

Throughout the day, Jesus nourished the people spiritually; but as evening drew near, the need for physical nourishment became critical. The thousands crowded on the plain—including Christ and His disciples—had gone the whole day without food. The Lord's sudden departure from Capernaum and the crowd's impulsive response would not have allowed time to prepare for the journey.

The need for physical food may seem commonplace in a day packed with exciting miracles and life-changing teaching, but God has made us in such a way that our bodies must be replenished from time to time. We are not to "live on bread alone" (Mt. 4:4), but an occasional biscuit or piece of cornbread is necessary to keep us going.

Jesus did not hesitate to call that need to the attention of His disciples. He pointed to the multitude and asked Philip, "Where are we to buy bread, so that these may eat?" (Jn. 6:5). Later He told the apostles to "give them something to eat" (Mt. 14:16). The crowd had needs, both physical and spiritual.

People with Needs Now

People still have needs, real needs, today. Their most important needs are spiritual. Jesus emphasized this when He asked, "For what will it profit a man if he gains the whole world and forfeits his soul? Or what will a man give in exchange for his soul?" (Mt. 16:26). However, people also have other needs,

needs which must not be ignored.

Certain needs, we have recognized for years—such as the needs for food and clothing. James 2:15 speaks of those who are "without clothing and in need of daily food." Depictions of early church buildings of the fourth and fifth centuries indicate that one or more rooms would typically be set aside to store food and clothing for the needy. Church buildings today often have similar rooms set aside for benevolence.

Another need that is widely understood is the necessity to care for widows and orphans. James wrote, "Pure and undefiled religion in the sight of our God and Father is this: to visit orphans and widows in their distress . . ." (Jas. 1:27). Many congregations have programs to ensure that their widows are not neglected (see Acts 6:1). Some Christians have adopted homeless children. Other arrangements to care for those in need have included children's homes and nursing homes. We have not always agreed on the best way to care for widows and orphans, but we agree that we must be concerned about them.

Other commonly recognized needs could be mentioned, such as the necessity to care for the sick. Jesus was concerned about the sick. He commended benevolent followers with these words: "I was sick, and you visited Me" (Mt. 25:36a). Most congregations try to help the sick, including taking meals as needed. In some countries, Christians have even built hospitals to help alleviate suffering.

Serving others as we currently do is good, but we should be sensitive to the fact that additional needs are always arising—or, at least, new expressions of old needs. Galatians 6:10 speaks of doing "good" in a general way; 1 Thessalonians 5:14 also indicates that we need to help people with whatever their needs may be. Homes are being torn apart by divorce. Children are neglected or abused. Alcoholism and drug addiction continue to rise. Sexual promiscuity is rampant, and the AIDS epidemic shows little sign of abating. Men and women struggle with serious emotional problems. The number of homeless "street people" in our cities is increasing. The list could go on.

There are no easy solutions to these problems. Developing elaborate programs to address these challenges may not be possible or practical for many congregations. Nevertheless, needs do exist—all kinds of needs, real needs, legitimate needs that we as individual Christians can help to meet.

We must keep our priorities straight and not be deterred from our goal of bringing people to a saving knowledge of Jesus Christ. At the same time, to ignore the pressing needs of those around us is to be something less than God intended for us to be. While the first great command is to "love the Lord your God with all your heart," the second is to "love your neighbor as yourself" (Mt. 22:37, 39). John wrote,

> But whoever has the world's goods, and sees his brother in need and closes his heart against him, how does the love of God abide in him? (1 Jn. 3:17).

> . . . the one who does not love his brother whom he has seen, cannot love God whom he has not seen. And this commandment we have from Him, that the one who loves God should love his brother also (1 Jn. 4:20, 21).

How Some Avoid Helping

As noted, Jesus was aware of the needs of the crowd, and He told His apostles to help them. The responses of the disciples are similar to the responses we sometimes give when asked for help.

"We Don't Have the Resources"

Apparently, Christ first challenged Philip:

> Therefore Jesus, lifting up His eyes and seeing that a large crowd was coming to Him, said to Philip, "Where are we to buy bread, so that these may eat?" This He was saying to test him, for He Himself knew what He was intending to do (Jn. 6:5, 6).

We are not sure why the Lord singled out Philip. Perhaps Philip was from that area and would have been the one most likely to know what resources were available. Philip was from Bethsaida (Jn. 1:44; 12:21). This was probably the Bethsaida that was a suburb of Capernaum, but it is possible that it was the Bethsaida on the east side of the sea, where the feeding of the five thousand took place (Lk. 9:10). Whatever the reason, Philip was asked; and the apostle's response was typical of how we often respond to challenges. In effect, he said, "Let us check whether or not *we* have the resources." Quickly, he estimated the number present. We do not know Philip's exact thinking; but in order to arrive at the figure mentioned, he had to go through a process similar to the following: He figured the minimum amount of bread needed for each person and multiplied that times the number of people. Then he calculated the current price of bread and multiplied that times the amount of bread needed. Then he gave Jesus the bottom line: "Two hundred denarii worth of bread is not sufficient for them, for everyone to receive a little" (Jn. 6:7; see Mk. 6:37). A denarius represented a day's wages for a common laborer (Mt. 20:2). It would take a worker more than half a year to earn two hundred denarii. The disciples' money bag surely would have contained only a fraction of that amount.

Isn't it true that we sometimes think that the answer to every problem is money, that our first response to a need is often to check the amount of money we have? If it is an individual challenge, perhaps we respond, "We just don't have the money." If it is a congregational challenge, maybe we say, "We have nothing allotted for this in the budget." A common failing, when we are confronted with a formidable task, is to see only our own resources instead of relying on God, who has limitless resources.

It has been said that, concerning the work of the Lord, Christians sometimes suffer from the "paralysis of analysis." Some apparently think that their ministry is to point out why this plan or that will *not* work.

"This Is Not Our Problem"

Later, all the apostles were confronted with the needs of the masses—and again we can see ourselves in their response: "Now the day was ending, and the twelve came and said to Him, 'Send the crowd away, that they may go into the surrounding villages and countryside and find lodging and get something to eat; for here we are in a desolate place'" (Lk. 9:12). The fact that the apostles mentioned "lodging" is proof that the majority of the thousands present on the plain were not from that area.

Their "solution" was something less than practical. Imagine the confusion that would result from ten to fifteen thousand people scattering to the little towns and villages in that area. Chaos would ensue if several thousand hungry people suddenly showed up in a small town, looking for food. Why did the disciples make this suggestion? Probably, being tired and hungry themselves, they did not want to deal with the problem.

Unfortunately, this is sometimes also our "solution" when confronted with people with needs: "Go away. Take care of yourselves. This is not my responsibility. I can't be bothered." We do not like to be disturbed. We do not want to shoulder the problems of others.

"They Don't Deserve It"

The apostles could have given additional reasons for not helping the crowd. For instance, they could have said, "They don't deserve our help. They really are not interested in spiritual matters. They are just here for free medical aid and free food." Subsequent events would have proved such an analysis correct; Jesus later indicated that the multitude was superficial and that its priorities were wrong (Jn. 6:26).

Christ would have been aware of the thoughts and motives of the people (Jn. 2:25), but He did not use this as an excuse not to help them. We are not to encourage laziness and sloth (2 Thess. 3:10); but if a need is legitimate, we must try to help—not because of who the recipient is, but because of who we are, or better yet, because of *whose* we are.

The Lord did not accept His disciples' excuses for not helping. Instead, He said, "You give them something to eat!" (Mk. 6:37). Did His eyes flash a bit when He spoke those words? He still will not accept excuses for His followers failing to "do good to all people, and especially to those who are of the household of the faith" (Gal. 6:10).

How We Can Help

That is the negative part of the story. Now let us look at the positive: How *can* we meet the challenge to help people when they have legitimate needs?

Imbibe the Spirit of Jesus

Probably the most important suggestion is that we must imbibe the spirit of Jesus. Christ had *compassion* on the multitude and *welcomed* them. The apostles may have seen nuisances, but He saw needs.

A lack of sensitivity to the needs of others is a widespread failing. We should learn to be sensitive to the needs of those around us. The person who expresses genuine concern and finds a way to help has a very special gift.

To take on the spirit of Jesus is the most important suggestion that can be given on helping others. If we develop Christ's attitude toward the needy, this will overcome our reluctance to help and will remove any obstacle. Nevertheless, a few specific suggestions may also be helpful. Let us continue with the story.

Use the Resources We Do Have

Philip and the other disciples had concentrated on what they did *not* have, but Jesus encouraged them to be aware of what resources *were* available. He said, "How many loaves do you have? Go look!" (Mk. 6:38a). The disciples' "solution" had been "Go buy" (see Mt. 14:15; Mk. 6:37), but Jesus' was "Go look: See what you *do* have."

Apparently, they checked with everyone present. Jesus and His apostles had left in such a hurry that they had brought no supplies with them, and the same was true of the crowd in general. The apostles made an extended search. Still, the only food they could find was a boy's snack. Andrew told the Master, "There is a lad here who has five barley loaves and two fish, but what are these for so many people?" (Jn. 6:9).

When you read "loaves," do not think of large bakery loaves

that might be put on the table to feed a family. These were small, flat cakes, not much bigger than a cracker. The loaves were made of barley; barley was a poor man's food. The fish would have been the tiny pickled fish for which the area was noted; think of sardines. "Five barley loaves and two fish": There would have been one small cake to be divided among a thousand men and one miniature fish for every 2,500 men. It was a snack that one hungry boy could consume and still remain hungry. Andrew's words were quite an understatement: "What are these for so many people?"

Think of this boy being willing to give up his food. Knowing how boys love to eat, someone once joked, "This was a greater miracle than the multiplying of the loaves!" Seriously, the contribution this lad made is remarkable. I can only conclude that, though he was young, he was nevertheless impressed with the Lord and had faith in Him.

Jesus wanted His followers to understand that, though they did not have much, they did have something. Most of us are better at cataloging what we do *not* have and are *not* able to do than we are at listing what we *do* have and *are* able to do. Rather than being embarrassed that our assets and talents are so meager, we should dedicate them to God anyway. He may use them to achieve surprising results.

Rely on the Lord's Resources, Not Our Own

When we use our resources in God's service, we become coworkers with the One who owns heaven and earth (Gen. 14:22)! Further, when you dedicate the little we have to His work, He can accomplish marvelous things with that little. A little in the hands of the Lord is always much. There is no better illustration of this than the incident we are studying.

Jesus told the apostles, "Have the people sit down" (Jn. 6:10). John added, "Now there was much grass in the place," a detail of an eyewitness explaining why the people would be willing to sit on the ground. (See also Mt. 14:19; Mk. 6:39.) "He commanded them ... to sit down by groups," and "they sat down in groups of hundreds and of fifties" (Mk. 6:39, 40). There are probably several reasons why Jesus had them sit that way. Such an arrangement would facilitate the work of feeding them. In addition, this would ensure that no one was left out. It is also possible that this helped in getting a count of the crowd—and helped to authenticate the miracle.

Do What the Lord Says, Whether We Understand It or Not
Did the Twelve feel a bit foolish as they organized the multitude? Did those present have a puzzled look as they were asked to sit down for a meal when only five loaves and two fish were available? To their credit, the crowd did what the Lord told them to do. It has been said that the first step to success in any venture is not to measure our resources but to determine God's will— and then to do it.

When everyone was ready, Christ "took the five loaves and the two fish, and looking up toward heaven," the source of all blessings (Jas. 1:17), "He blessed the food" (Mt. 14:19a) by giving thanks for it (see Jn. 6:11, 23). Jesus' example on this occasion teaches us that we should give thanks for our food—even when the fare is meager. The Jews had a saying: "He who enjoys anything without thanksgiving is as though he robbed God."[18] The Jewish prayer before meals was simple: "Blessed art thou, Jehovah our God, King of the universe, who bringest forth bread from the earth."[19] Perhaps Jesus used words similar to these.

Then came the mind-boggling part: Christ "broke the loaves and He kept giving them to the disciples to set before them [the people; Lk. 9:16]; and He divided up the two fish among them all" (Mk. 6:41). I want to cry out, "Wait a minute! Tell me more! Tell me exactly what this looked like! Give me details of what happened!" Once more, we have proof that the Bible was not written to satisfy our curiosity.

Regarding what happened, the miracle must have occurred exclusively in the hands of Jesus. Some think that Jesus gave

---

[18]William Barclay, *The Gospel of Luke*, rev. ed., The Daily Study Bible Series (Philadelphia: Westminster Press, 1975), 118.

[19]William Barclay, *The Gospel of Matthew*, vol. 2, rev. ed., The Daily Study Bible Series (Philadelphia: Westminster Press, 1975), 100.

each apostle a basketful and that the food continued to expand in their baskets as they distributed it. The text emphasizes, however, that "He *kept* giving [the bread] to the disciples to set before [the people]" (Mk. 6:41; the NASB correctly reflects the action of the verb used in the Greek text). In other words, the disciples had to keep coming back to fill up their baskets. Someone has said that Jesus was the chef and the disciples were just the waiters. Someone else described Christ as the manufacturer and the apostles as distributors.

Where did the baskets used by the apostles come from? We know from secular history that the Jews carried small baskets in the same way that people in my part of the world carry wallets or purses. It is the custom in most places in the world to carry a small container in which to place items that might be needed in the course of a day. Either the baskets were the disciples' own, or they could have borrowed them from people in the crowd.

The miracle seems similar to that of the inexhaustible bowl of meal and jar of oil in the days of Elijah (1 Kings 17:14–16)— that Jesus kept reaching into the bag or basket where the boy had stored his snack and kept pulling out more and more bread and fish. The smile on Christ's face surely widened as the eyes of all present grew larger and larger. It is not important to know the precise details. It is enough to know that a *miracle* took place.

According to Matthew, Mark, and Luke, the people ate until they "were satisfied" (Mt. 14:20a; Mk. 6:42; Lk. 9:17a). John emphasized that they had "as much as they wanted" and that they "were filled" (Jn. 6:11, 12). Since the crowd came looking for more of the same the next day (Jn. 6:26, 27, 34), Jesus may even have improved the quality of the repast—so that the dry, rough barley bread and the salty fish tasted like a royal banquet.

When everyone was full, Christ told His disciples, "Gather up the leftover fragments so that nothing will be lost" (Jn. 6:12), "and they picked up twelve full baskets of the broken pieces, and also of the fish" (Mk. 6:43).

What happened to the leftover food? Since it is an unimportant detail, the accounts do not say. If the twelve baskets belonged to the apostles, maybe this was their ration for the next week. If they had borrowed the baskets, maybe those who

461

allowed their baskets to be used got the leftovers. Surely, the little boy got a generous portion of what was left. Warren W. Wiersbe wrote, "I wonder how many of the pieces the lad took home with him? Imagine his mother's amazement when the boy told her the story!"[20] This part of the story has been used to show that the Lord does not believe in wasting resources—and that is a legitimate application. The primary purpose of the detail, though, is to stress the extravagant nature of the miracle. Not only were ten to fifteen thousand people fed from a meager supply, but there was vastly more food at the end than at the beginning.

Unfortunately, there are those who deny that an actual physical miracle occurred. Skeptics ridicule the idea that the people would have made this trip without provisions, but the biblical account affirms that to have been precisely the state of affairs. Some authors have popularized the idea that many present had stashed food under their robes and finally shared that food with others after the little boy unselfishly gave up his loaves and fishes. Even on the surface, this "explanation" makes no sense. If all Jesus did was shame the people into sharing their food, it is impossible to explain their exuberant desire to crown Him King (Jn. 6:15). If no food was produced that did not already exist, there would have been no reason for them to seek Him the next day, looking for more bread. Any attempt to "explain" what happened denies the plain teaching of John that Jesus performed a *"sign"*—that is, a miracle (Jn. 6:14; emphasis added). The biblical account is clear: Jesus took a boy's snack and multiplied it to feed thousands!

Discard Excuses for Failing to Help Others

Little in the hands of the Lord is much. Let us stop complaining about what we do not have and cannot do. Rather, let us use what we have and do what we can to help others—and then be prepared to be amazed at how He can multiply our resources and results.

[20]Warren W. Wiersbe, *The Bible Exposition Commentary*, vol. 1 (Wheaton, Ill.: Victor Books, 1989), 51.

Conclusion

Jesus intended for His apostles to learn from this experience—to learn that He could help them meet *any* challenge in life (see Mk. 6:52). They had trouble grasping that truth, but we should be more receptive. If we will stop giving excuses and start doing what we can, God will bless our efforts and will also bless the lives of others.

Walking on the Water
(Mt. 14:22–36; Mk. 6:45–56; Jn. 6:15–21a)

Matthew 14:22–36

²²Immediately He made the disciples get into the boat and go ahead of Him to the other side, while He sent the crowds away. ²³After He had sent the crowds away, He went up on the mountain by Himself to pray; and when it was evening, He was there alone. ²⁴But the boat was already a long distance from the land, battered by the waves; for the wind was contrary. ²⁵And in the fourth watch of the night He came to them, walking on the sea. ²⁶When the disciples saw Him walking on the sea, they were terrified, and said, "It is a ghost!" And they cried out in fear. ²⁷But immediately Jesus spoke to them, saying, "Take courage, it is I; do not be afraid."

²⁸Peter said to Him, "Lord, if it is You, command me to come to You on the water." ²⁹And He said, "Come!" And Peter got out of the boat, and walked on the water and came toward Jesus. ³⁰But seeing the wind, he became frightened, and beginning to sink, he cried out, "Lord, save me!" ³¹Immediately Jesus stretched out His hand and took hold of him, and said to him, "You of little faith, why did you doubt?" ³²When they got into the boat, the wind stopped. ³³And those who were in the boat worshiped Him, saying, "You are certainly God's Son!"

³⁴When they had crossed over, they came to land at Gennesaret. ³⁵And when the men of that place recognized Him, they sent word into all that surrounding district and brought to Him all who were sick; ³⁶and they implored Him that they might just touch the fringe of His cloak; and as many as touched it were cured.

Mark 6:45–56

⁴⁵Immediately Jesus made His disciples get into the boat and go ahead of Him to the other side to Bethsaida, while He Himself was sending the crowd away. ⁴⁶After bidding them farewell, He left for the mountain to pray.

⁴⁷When it was evening, the boat was in the middle of the sea, and He was alone on the land. ⁴⁸Seeing them straining at the oars, for the wind was against them, at about the fourth watch of the night He came to them, walking on the sea; and He intended to pass by them. ⁴⁹But when they saw Him walking on the sea, they supposed that it was a ghost, and cried out; ⁵⁰for they all saw Him and were terrified. But immediately He spoke with them and said to them, "Take courage; it is I, do not be afraid." ⁵¹Then He got into the boat with them, and the wind stopped; and they were utterly astonished, ⁵²for they had not gained any insight from the incident of the loaves, but their heart was hardened.

⁵³When they had crossed over they came to land at Gennesaret, and moored to the shore. ⁵⁴When they got out of the boat, immediately the people recognized Him, ⁵⁵and ran about that whole country and began to carry here and there on their pallets those who were sick, to the place they heard He was. ⁵⁶Wherever He entered villages, or cities, or countryside, they were laying the sick in the market places, and imploring Him that they might just touch the fringe of His cloak; and as many as touched it were being cured.

John 6:15–21a

¹⁵So Jesus, perceiving that they were intending to come and take Him by force to make Him king, withdrew again to the mountain by Himself alone.

¹⁶Now when evening came, His disciples went down to the sea, ¹⁷and after getting into a boat, they started to cross the sea to Capernaum. It had already become dark, and Jesus had not yet come to them. ¹⁸The sea began to be stirred up because a strong wind was blowing. ¹⁹Then, when they had rowed about three or four miles, they saw Jesus walking on the sea and drawing near to the boat; and they were frightened. ²⁰But He

said to them, "It is I; do not be afraid." ²¹ᵃSo they were willing to receive Him into the boat.

The crowd of five thousand-plus was so excited about being fed that they decided to **take [Jesus] by force to make Him king** (Jn. 6:15). The idea that they thought they could "make" Christ king indicates the shallowness of their thinking. Jesus had been *born* King (Mt. 2:2). There is a sense in which He was not crowned King until He ascended back to the Father. However, since Christ Himself acknowledged being "King of the Jews" (Mt. 27:11), we should view the statement of the Wise Men as being accurate. However, the people did not understand the kind of King He was. They had in mind the popular Jewish concept of an earthly king: one who could lead them in triumph against their enemies. Jesus' latest miracle had ignited their imaginations: He could serve not only as general over the army, but also as its quartermaster—supplying the troops with their daily rations. They failed to realize that accepting Him as an earthly king equaled a rejection of Him as their spiritual King.

Knowing their intentions, Christ first frustrated their plans by sending away His disciples. He told them to go to Bethsaida, which was near Capernaum (Mk. 6:45; Jn. 6:17). We are not told why Jesus sent His disciples away. Maybe He wanted their compliance with His command to influence the crowd also to leave. Maybe He did not want them caught up in the misguided zeal of the crowd. After all, they also struggled with materialistic misconceptions concerning the kingdom. Then Christ frustrated the plans of the crowd by dismissing them. Many stayed in the general vicinity (Jn. 6:22), but at least Jesus cooled the excitement by dispersing them. Finally, saddened, He climbed a nearby mountain (Jn. 6:3) to be alone and to pray (Mt. 14:22, 23; Mk. 6:45, 46; Jn. 6:15–17a). (Jesus had probably sat on the side of the mountain to teach the multitude, and then had come down onto the plain to feed the people.) He had many reasons to be sad. In addition to the general misunderstanding exhibited on that occasion by His apostles and the crowd, He had not yet had an opportunity to mourn the passing of His cousin, John the Baptizer.

465

When Jesus had told His apostles to get into the boat and go to Capernaum, they had apparently expected Him to join them after He finished with the crowd (see Jn. 6:17). Maybe they lingered near the shore; perhaps they rowed out a distance and waited. When the Lord did not come, they eventually started to cross the sea.

A few miles across the sea, they were hit by one of the sudden storms to which that body of water is subject. The NASB says they had gone **three or four miles** (Jn. 6:19), and the KJV has "five and twenty or thirty furlongs." The Greek has twenty-five or thirty *stadia*. *Stadia* is the plural of *stadion* (στάδιον), a Roman measurement of about 607 feet. At that point, **the sea began to be stirred up because a strong wind was blowing** (Jn. 6:18). Matthew added that they were **battered by the waves** (Mt. 14:24). The wind was blowing from the west, the direction they were trying to go (Mt. 14:24; Mk. 6:48), so they furled their sails and began to row (Mk. 6:48). They rowed for hours, making no headway in the tossing water.

They had left sometime in the evening when it became dark (see Jn. 6:16, 17), but Jesus did not come to them until **the fourth watch** (Mt. 14:25; Mk. 6:48), which was between 3:00 and 6:00 a.m. We can only imagine their exhaustion and despair. Once more, their faith was tested. Jesus did not send the storm, but every crisis in life tests our faith in Him. Jesus had rescued them before by stilling a storm, but on this occasion He was not with them. This time, He was far away.

Although Christ was separated from them by miles, He was keenly aware of their predicament. Mark wrote,

> **When it was evening, the boat was in the middle of the sea, and He was alone on the land.** *Seeing them straining at the oars*, **for the wind was against them, at about the fourth watch of the night He came to them, walking on the sea . . .** (Mk. 6:47, 48; emphasis added).

Walking on the water is one of Jesus' better-known miracles. When you picture it in your mind, do not envision Him treading a calm, smooth surface, as is generally depicted. Rather, see

Him bobbing up and down—first on top of a crest and then in a valley between the waves—as He marched over a storm-tossed sea.

As Christ neared the boat, the disciples caught a glimpse of Him—perhaps in a flash of lightning. His unexpected appearance frightened them more than the storm. Mark's account says that **He intended to pass by them** (Mk. 6:48; see also the KJV). Some have suggested that He "intended to pass by them" to avoid frightening them, and that may have been the case. The other accounts, however, indicate that Jesus was going **to them** (Mt. 14:25; Jn. 6:19). The Greek word translated "pass by" in Mark 6 could be translated "go alongside," and that is possibly the meaning here.

When the disciples saw Him walking on the sea, they were terrified, and said, "It is a ghost!" And they cried out in fear (Mt. 14:26; see Mk. 6:49, 50a). Why they thought He was a ghost, we are not told; but superstition reigned in the hearts of men in those days. Jesus quieted their fears, calling out to them, **"Take courage, it is I; do not be afraid"** (Mt. 14:27; see Mk. 6:50b; Jn. 6:20).

We then have the remarkable story of Peter walking on the water. He called out to Christ, **"Lord, if it is You, command me to come to You on the water"** (Mt. 14:28). **And He said, "Come!" And Peter got out of the boat, and walked on the water and came toward Jesus** (Mt. 14:29). I have often heard the comment that as long as the apostle kept his eyes on Jesus, he stayed afloat—but when he turned his gaze to the wind-tossed sea, **he became frightened** and began to sink (Mt. 14:30a). He cried out, **"Lord, save me!"** (Mt. 14:30b). **Immediately Jesus stretched out His hand and took hold of him, and said to him, "You of little faith, why did you doubt?"** (Mt. 14:31). Like some of us, Peter had enough faith to start the walk, but not enough to finish it.

The disciples helped Jesus and Peter into the boat (see Jn. 6:21a; Mt. 14:32a). Immediately, **the wind stopped; and they were utterly astonished** (Mk. 6:51). Then **those who were in the boat worshiped Him, saying, "You are certainly God's Son!"** (Mt. 14:33).

It seems like a story with a happy ending, but Mark's account indicates that, in reality, the apostles had failed a crucial test. He recorded that they were utterly astonished, **for they had not gained any insight from the incident of the loaves** (Mk. 6:51b, 52a). In addition to expressing His concern, every miracle Christ performed had theological implications. What "insight" should the disciples have gained "from the incident of the loaves"? They should have learned that if He had the power to feed them on the plain, He also had the power to protect them on the sea.

According to Mark, their problem was that **their heart was hardened** (Mk. 6:52b). They had some understanding and appreciation of Jesus, a measure of faith, but it was difficult for them to surrender their lives and hearts fully to Him. That particular problem did not originate with, or cease with, the Twelve.

JESUS' DISCOURSE ON THE BREAD OF LIFE (AND PETER'S CONFESSION) (JN. 6:21b–71)

[21b]**And immediately the boat was at the land to which they were going.**

[22]**The next day the crowd that stood on the other side of the sea saw that there was no other small boat there, except one, and that Jesus had not entered with His disciples into the boat, but that His disciples had gone away alone. [23]There came other small boats from Tiberias near to the place where they ate the bread after the Lord had given thanks. [24]So when the crowd saw that Jesus was not there, nor His disciples, they themselves got into the small boats, and came to Capernaum seeking Jesus. [25]When they found Him on the other side of the sea, they said to Him, "Rabbi, when did You get here?"**

[26]**Jesus answered them and said, "Truly, truly, I say to you, you seek Me, not because you saw signs, but because you ate of the loaves and were filled. [27]Do not work for the food which perishes, but for the food which endures to eternal life, which the Son of Man will give to you, for on Him the Father, God,**

has set His seal." ²⁸Therefore they said to Him, "What shall we do, so that we may work the works of God?" ²⁹Jesus answered and said to them, "This is the work of God, that you believe in Him whom He has sent." ³⁰So they said to Him, "What then do You do for a sign, so that we may see, and believe You? What work do You perform? ³¹Our fathers ate the manna in the wilderness; as it is written, 'He gave them bread out of heaven to eat.'" ³²Jesus then said to them, "Truly, truly, I say to you, it is not Moses who has given you the bread out of heaven, but it is My Father who gives you the true bread out of heaven. ³³For the bread of God is that which comes down out of heaven, and gives life to the world." ³⁴Then they said to Him, "Lord, always give us this bread."

³⁵Jesus said to them, "I am the bread of life; he who comes to Me will not hunger, and he who believes in Me will never thirst. ³⁶But I said to you that you have seen Me, and yet do not believe. ³⁷All that the Father gives Me will come to Me, and the one who comes to Me I will certainly not cast out. ³⁸For I have come down from heaven, not to do My own will, but the will of Him who sent Me. ³⁹This is the will of Him who sent Me, that of all that He has given Me I lose nothing, but raise it up on the last day. ⁴⁰For this is the will of My Father, that everyone who beholds the Son and believes in Him will have eternal life, and I Myself will raise him up on the last day."

⁴¹Therefore the Jews were grumbling about Him, because He said, "I am the bread that came down out of heaven." ⁴²They were saying, "Is not this Jesus, the son of Joseph, whose father and mother we know? How does He now say, 'I have come down out of heaven'?" ⁴³Jesus answered and said to them, "Do not grumble among yourselves. ⁴⁴No one can come to Me unless the Father who sent Me draws him; and I will raise him up on the last day. ⁴⁵It is written in the prophets, 'And they shall all be taught of God.' Everyone who has heard and learned from the Father, comes to Me. ⁴⁶Not that anyone has seen the Father, except the One who is from God; He has seen the Father. ⁴⁷Truly, truly, I say to you, he who believes has eternal life. ⁴⁸I am the bread of life. ⁴⁹Your fathers ate the manna in the wil-

derness, and they died. [50]This is the bread which comes down out of heaven, so that one may eat of it and not die. [51]I am the living bread that came down out of heaven; if anyone eats of this bread, he will live forever; and the bread also which I will give for the life of the world is My flesh."

[52]Then the Jews began to argue with one another, saying, "How can this man give us His flesh to eat?" [53]So Jesus said to them, "Truly, truly, I say to you, unless you eat the flesh of the Son of Man and drink His blood, you have no life in yourselves. [54]He who eats My flesh and drinks My blood has eternal life, and I will raise him up on the last day. [55]For My flesh is true food, and My blood is true drink. [56]He who eats My flesh and drinks My blood abides in Me, and I in him. [57]As the living Father sent Me, and I live because of the Father, so he who eats Me, he also will live because of Me. [58]This is the bread which came down out of heaven; not as the fathers ate and died; he who eats this bread will live forever." [59]These things He said in the synagogue as He taught in Capernaum.

[60]Therefore many of His disciples, when they heard this said, "This is a difficult statement; who can listen to it?" [61]But Jesus, conscious that His disciples grumbled at this, said to them, "Does this cause you to stumble? [62]What then if you see the Son of Man ascending to where He was before? [63]It is the Spirit who gives life; the flesh profits nothing; the words that I have spoken to you are spirit and are life. [64]But there are some of you who do not believe." For Jesus knew from the beginning who they were who did not believe, and who it was that would betray Him. [65]And He was saying, "For this reason I have said to you, that no one can come to Me unless it has been granted him from the Father."

[66]As a result of this many of His disciples withdrew and were not walking with Him anymore. [67]So Jesus said to the twelve, "You do not want to go away also, do you?" [68]Simon Peter answered Him, "Lord, to whom shall we go? You have words of eternal life. [69]We have believed and have come to know that You are the Holy One of God." [70]Jesus answered them, "Did I Myself not choose you, the twelve, and yet

**one of you is a devil?" ⁷¹Now He meant Judas the son of
Simon Iscariot, for he, one of the twelve, was going to betray
Him.**

John recorded one more miracle performed on that stormy
night. He wrote that as soon as Jesus and Peter got in the boat,
immediately the boat was at the land to which they were going
(Jn. 6:21b). They came ashore at the plain of Gennesaret, a fertile area south of Capernaum (Mt. 14:34; Mk. 6:53). Jesus headed
north for Capernaum, healing people as He went (Mt. 14:35, 36;
Mk. 6:54–56).

In the meantime, the crowd on the eastern side of the sea discovered that Jesus was no longer there (Jn. 6:22, 24). Boats from
the western shore showed up. The boats were from Tiberias on
the western shore. The boatmen may have seen the crowd and
landed at the spot in hopes of making money by taking people where they wanted to go. Those in the crowd made arrangements to be taken across to Capernaum, where they expected
Jesus to be (Jn. 6:23, 24). Earlier, they had traveled by foot from
Capernaum, but being ferried back to Capernaum would have
been an easier way to travel.

Those who were seeking Christ found Him teaching in the
synagogue (Jn. 6:59). Perplexed as to how He had left without
their knowledge (Jn. 6:22), they asked, **"Rabbi, when did You
get here?"** (Jn. 6:25b). This was the first of many questions asked
of the Lord that day. His questioners thought they were testing
Him; in reality, it was the inquirers who were put to the test. It
was time to expose their faith—or their lack of faith. Actually,
a series of tests ensued, starting with the crowd and narrowing
to the apostles. Jesus wanted everyone present to ask, *"What
attracts me to this Man? Why do I follow Him? Who do I really
think He is?"*

(1) *The crowd tested.* Instead of answering the question regarding His arrival in Capernaum, Jesus began His discourse on the
theme of the Bread of Life. He accused the crowd of following
Him for the wrong reason:

. . . Truly, truly, I say to you, you seek Me, not

because you saw signs [that is, the miracles which proved He was the Messiah], **but because you ate of the loaves and were filled. Do not work for the food which perishes, but for the food which endures to eternal life** (Jn. 6:26, 27a).

Christ was trying to get His listeners to examine their motives and priorities—but what they heard was that if they would *work*, they could have *nonperishable food*. They asked, **"What shall we do, so that we may work the works of God?"** (Jn. 6:28). This gave Jesus an opportunity to introduce the theme of His presentation: **"This is the work of God, that you *believe* in Him whom He has sent"** (Jn. 6:29; emphasis added).

The crowd did not like the direction the discussion was heading. Taking their cue from the Pharisees (see Mt. 12:38), they asked for a sign: **"What then do You do for a sign, so that we may see, and believe You?"** (Jn. 6:30). The day before, Christ had given them signs of healing and miraculous feeding, but that was insufficient. To those with hardened hearts, no sign would ever be enough.

What they really wanted was another free meal. After all, they had acknowledged that Jesus was the Prophet like Moses, and Moses had given their fathers bread in the wilderness—not just once, but every day (Jn. 6:31; see Ex. 16). Jesus replied that it was God rather than Moses who had given them bread (Jn. 6:32a). Further, God could now give them **the true bread out of heaven** that **gives life to the world** (Jn. 6:32b, 33b).

Bread that "gives life"—that was exactly what they wanted. They said, **"Lord, always give us this bread"** (Jn. 6:34). Compare this to the Samaritan woman's request in John 4:15. Many parallels exist between Jesus' discussion with the woman in John 4 and His sermon in John 6. Christ used the figure of water in John 4 because water was on the woman's mind, and He used the figure of bread in John 6 because the crowd's concern was food. The main point is the same. However, the John 4 discussion resulted in acceptance, while the John 6 discourse ended in rejection.

Once more Jesus' response took an unexpected—and unwelcome—turn. From His lips came this startling affirmation: **"*I* am the bread of life"** (Jn. 6:35a; emphasis added). This is the first of seven "I am" statements of Christ found in the Book of John (see also vv. 48 and 51). The other "I am" statements are in 8:12, 58; 10:11; 11:25; 14:6; and 15:1. Each has its distinctive significance, but each was also an affirmation of His deity; for only God can truthfully say, in any day and age, "I am" (in other words, "I am the ever-existent One"; see Ex. 3:13–15).

Jesus continued His staggering statement: **"He who comes to Me will not hunger, and he who believes in Me will never thirst"** (Jn. 6:35b). There was that persistent word "believe" again. (See also Jn. 6:40, 47.) He sadly added, **"But . . . you have seen Me, and yet do not believe"** (Jn. 6:36). J. W. McGarvey wrote,

> The personality of Jesus was the great proof of his divinity, but the Jews . . . refused to consider it, and kept clamoring for a sign. . . . If one refuses to believe in the sun when he sees its light, feels its heat and witnesses its life-giving power, by what sign will you demonstrate to him the existence of the sun?[21]

(2) *"The Jews" tested.* At that point, **the Jews** began grumbling **because He said, "I am the bread that came down out of heaven"** (Jn. 6:41). John often used the phrase "the Jews" to refer to the Jewish leaders (Jn. 1:19; 5:10, 15, 16, 18), and perhaps that is the meaning here.

In spite of the grumbling of the Jews, Jesus refused to back down on His claim. Rather, He made it stronger:

> **I am the bread of life. Your fathers ate the manna in the wilderness, and they died. This is the bread which comes down out of heaven, so that one may eat of it and not die. I am the living bread that came down out of heaven; if anyone eats of this bread, he will live forever; and the bread also which I will give for the life**

---

[21]McGarvey and Pendleton, 385.

of the world is My flesh (Jn. 6:48–51).

Jesus had become flesh (Jn. 1:14) in order to bring spiritual life (Jn. 10:10). Further, in a matter of months, He would voluntarily "give" His flesh to be nailed to a cross "for the life of the world." Such lofty concepts were beyond the grasp of the closed-minded Jews. Instead of humbly asking Christ to explain, they **began to argue . . . , saying, "How can this man give us His flesh to eat?"** (Jn. 6:52). Jesus' response was even more surprising and puzzling: **"I say to you, unless you eat the flesh of the Son of Man and drink His blood, you have no life in yourselves"** (Jn. 6:53).

The Jews were familiar with the figure of "eating bread" in a religious sense. David Smith pointed out, "Such language would sound less strange in Jewish than in modern ears, since in the Scriptures and in rabbinical literature alike, instruction is called *bread* and those who absorb it are said to eat it."[22] Even so, the thought of eating flesh and drinking blood must have been repulsive to them. The Law condemned the eating or drinking of blood (Lev. 17:10–14).

Jesus, of course, was not talking about the cannibalistic consumption of His literal flesh and blood. This is one of the passages used by Catholics to justify their mass, during which they claim that the bread and wine turn into the literal flesh and blood of Jesus. When Christ instituted the Lord's Supper, however, He made clear that it was a *memorial* feast (Lk. 22:19; 1 Cor. 11:24, 25). Jesus was talking about accepting Him as the Messiah "in the flesh." In fact, He had already told the skeptics how to "eat His flesh," but they had not been listening:

. . . . "This is the work of God, that you *believe* in Him whom He has sent" (Jn. 6:29; emphasis added).

---

[22]David Smith, *The Days of His Flesh: The Earthly Life of Our Lord and Saviour Jesus Christ*, 8th ed. (London: Hodder and Stoughton, 1910), 241; quoted in Robert Duncan Culver, *The Life of Christ* (Grand Rapids, Mich.: Baker Book House, 1976), 147n.

. . . "he who *believes* in Me will never thirst" (Jn. 6:35; emphasis added).

. . . "you have seen Me, and yet do not *believe*" (Jn. 6:36; emphasis added).

"For this is the will of My Father, that everyone who beholds the Son and *believes* in Him will have eternal life . . ." (Jn. 6:40; emphasis added).

"Truly, truly, I say to you, he who *believes* has eternal life" (Jn. 6:47; emphasis added).

Consider this: Jesus said that **he who believes *has eternal life*** (Jn. 6:47; emphasis added; see also v. 40). Shortly afterward, He said, **"He who eats My flesh and drinks My blood *has eternal life*"** (Jn. 6:54a; emphasis added). Unless there are two ways to life (and there is only one; Jn. 14:6), "eating His flesh and drinking His blood" equals "believing in Him."

Our faith comes from learning about Him and then accepting what we learn. Christ said, **"It is written in the prophets, 'And they shall all be taught of God'** [see Is. 54:13; Jer. 31:33, 34]. **Everyone who has heard and learned from the Father, comes to Me"** (Jn. 6:45). He also said, **"The words that I have spoken to you are spirit and are life"** (Jn. 6:63b).

Even as we assimilate food by eating, we assimilate Jesus by learning of Him, accepting Him, believing in Him, and obeying Him. Even as the food we eat becomes part of our bodies, so Christ's thoughts and character should become part of our souls. Johnny Ramsey wrote, "He is exhorting, 'Imbibe my spirit, imitate my thinking, follow my lead; yes, deepen in the ways of heaven!'"[23] We are challenged to "become partakers of the divine nature" (2 Pet. 1:4), to let Christ be "formed in" us (Gal. 4:19), until we can say with Paul, ". . . it is no longer I who live, but Christ lives in me" (Gal. 2:20).

---

[23]Johnny Ramsey, "Eat My Flesh; Drink My Blood," *Gospel Minutes* (27 July 1979): 3.

When Jesus spoke of eating His flesh and drinking His blood in John 6, He did not have in mind the Lord's Supper. It is natural that those of us familiar with the symbolism of the Supper should be reminded of it by Christ's terminology in verses 53 through 56. The context is clear, however, that Christ was not concerned about Christians partaking of communion, but rather about Jews accepting Him as the Messiah. Faith—or a lack of it—is the issue of the Sermon on the Bread of Life.

(3) *The disciples tested.* The tension continued to build: . . . **many of His disciples, when they heard this** [Jesus' words about being the Bread of Life] **said, "This is a difficult statement; who can listen to it?"** (Jn. 6:60). Keep in mind that this latest group of grumblers (Jn. 6:61a) were not His enemies or representatives of the shallow, bread-seeking crowd. Rather, they were His *disciples*, some of whom had been following Him for a long time. The term "disciples" included the Twelve (Jn. 6:64), plus the rest of His more-or-less full-time disciples (Lk. 6:13).

Why did Jesus' teaching disturb His followers? It contradicted their preconceptions of a political, sword-waving Messiah. Sadly, Christ asked them, **"Does this cause you to stumble? What then if you see the Son of Man ascending to where He was before?"** (Jn. 6:61b, 62). In other words, "If you have a hard time accepting Me as the Messiah because I focus on the spiritual instead of the physical, how are you going to handle My leaving this earth without setting up the kind of kingdom you are looking for?" Jesus' ascension to heaven did result in the kingdom/church being established—on the first Pentecost after His death, burial, and resurrection—but His followers were anticipating a different kind of kingdom.

Jesus again emphasized that spiritual matters were of far greater importance than fleshly ones (Jn. 6:63); but once more He had to conclude, **". . . there are some of you who do not believe"** (Jn. 6:64a). As mentioned earlier, Christ's discourse triggered one of the lowest points of His ministry. Here is that low point: **As a result of this** [His teaching on that occasion] **many of His disciples withdrew and were not walking with Him anymore** (Jn. 6:66). From this point on in John's account, he used the word "disciple" only in the sense of *"true* disciple."

Jesus' faith test produced grumbling, arguing, and finally withdrawal and rejection. The majority of His "class" failed the test.

(4) *The apostles tested.* The most crucial test remained. Christ turned to the Twelve and asked, **"You do not want to go away also, do you?"** (Jn. 6:67). Certainly, we perceive sadness and even concern in those words.

Peter's reply must have cheered His heart. Speaking for the apostles, He said, **"Lord, to whom shall we go? You have words of eternal life. We have believed and have come to know that You are the Holy One of God"** (Jn. 6:68, 69). In context, the key words are "We have *believed*." Was their faith perfect? No. Did they understand fully who Christ was? No. Was the true nature of the kingdom clear in their minds? No. Still, they were convinced that Jesus was the Messiah, and they were committed to Him. Their faith was growing. They had passed the test.

That is, *most* of them had passed the test. Peter was unaware of it, but he spoke for only eleven of the apostles. Up to the end, the rest of the apostles were not aware of Judas' unbelief (see Jn. 13:21, 22). Our text indicates that the incidents surrounding the sermon on the Bread of Life were a prime factor in Judas' ultimate rejection of Jesus (Jn. 6:64, 70, 71). Judas did not physically depart at this time, as did so many others, but his heart was no longer with the Lord. Disappointment must have flooded his soul when Christ refused the earthly throne with its attendant benefits (Jn. 6:15). (We are later told that Judas was preoccupied with money; see Jn. 12:6.) Disbelief must have overwhelmed him when Jesus' words drove away the masses; that was no way to build an empire. The Twelve, as a group, had received a passing score on the test, but Judas failed miserably.

There would be other tests for the apostles (see Mt. 16:13), but no other time of testing had such a broad effect on those who claimed to follow Jesus.

PART VI

CHRIST'S MINISTRY FROM THE
THIRD PASSOVER UNTIL HIS
ARRIVAL AT BETHANY

Includes a Harmony of

Mt. 15:1—20:34

Mk. 7:1—10:52

Lk. 9:18—19:27

Jn. 7:1—11:54

SECTION I
IN GALILEE

Includes a Harmony of

Mt. 15:1—18:35

Mk. 7:1—9:50

Lk. 9:18–50

After the sermon on the Bread of Life, "many of his disciples went back, and walked no more with him" (Jn. 6:66; KJV). From that moment, Christ concentrated more of His efforts on the preparation of the Twelve for the time when He would no longer be with them.

As we read through the Gospels, we will find the Lord withdrawing again and again from Galilee. One reason was to avoid conflict with His enemies, but another reason was to spend time with His apostles. However, Jesus was constantly hindered in that purpose. He was interrupted by both friend and foe. We will see how He managed to turn bothersome interruptions into beneficial interludes.

THE THIRD PASSOVER (SEE JN. 6:4; 7:1)

When John told of the feeding of the five thousand, he wrote, "Now the Passover, the feast of the Jews, was near" (Jn. 6:4). If the "feast of the Jews" in John 5:1 was a Passover, the one mentioned in 6:4 is the third Passover in the Book of John.

Many writers (perhaps most) believe that Jesus did not attend the "Passover" of John 6:4, mainly because of John 7:1, which says, "After these things Jesus was walking in Galilee, for He was unwilling to walk in Judea because the Jews were seeking to kill Him." If Jesus *did* attend the feast, He did so quietly and anonymously (compare with Jn. 7:10). We have no record of any events occurring in Jerusalem related to that Passover.

The main purpose of the Passover reference in John 6:4 is to help us with the chronology of the life of Christ. From the time of that Passover until about six months later, we have the final stage of the Great Galilean Ministry, a stage characterized by a series of withdrawals from that province.

REPROACHED FOR DISREGARDING TRADITION (MT. 15:1–20; MK. 7:1–23)

Matthew 15:1–20

¹Then some Pharisees and scribes came to Jesus from Jerusalem and said, ²"Why do Your disciples break the tradition of the elders? For they do not wash their hands when they eat bread." ³And He answered and said to them, "Why do you yourselves transgress the commandment of God for the sake of your tradition? ⁴For God said, 'Honor your father and mother,' and, 'He who speaks evil of father or mother is to be put to death.' ⁵But you say, 'Whoever says to his father or mother, "Whatever I have that would help you has been given to God," ⁶he is not to honor his father or his mother.' And by this you invalidated the word of God for the sake of your tradition. ⁷You hypocrites, rightly did Isaiah prophesy of you:

⁸'This people honors Me with their lips,
But their heart is far away from Me.
⁹But in vain do they worship Me,
Teaching as doctrines the precepts of men.'"

¹⁰After Jesus called the crowd to Him, He said to them, "Hear and understand. ¹¹It is not what enters into the mouth that defiles the man, but what proceeds out of the mouth, this defiles the man."

¹²Then the disciples came and said to Him, "Do You know that the Pharisees were offended when they heard this statement?" ¹³But He answered and said, "Every plant which My heavenly Father did not plant shall be uprooted. ¹⁴Let them alone; they are blind guides of the blind. And if a blind man guides a blind man, both will fall into a pit."

¹⁵Peter said to Him, "Explain the parable to us." ¹⁶Jesus said, "Are you still lacking in understanding also? ¹⁷Do you not understand that everything that goes into the mouth passes into the stomach, and is eliminated? ¹⁸But the things that proceed out of the mouth come from the heart, and those defile the man. ¹⁹For out of the heart come evil thoughts, murders, adulteries, fornications, thefts, false witness, slanders. ²⁰These are the things which defile the man; but to eat with unwashed

hands does not defile the man."

Mark 7:1–23

[1]The Pharisees and some of the scribes gathered around Him when they had come from Jerusalem, [2]and had seen that some of His disciples were eating their bread with impure hands, that is, unwashed. [3](For the Pharisees and all the Jews do not eat unless they carefully wash their hands, thus observing the traditions of the elders; [4]and when they come from the market place, they do not eat unless they cleanse themselves; and there are many other things which they have received in order to observe, such as the washing of cups and pitchers and copper pots.) [5]The Pharisees and the scribes asked Him, "Why do Your disciples not walk according to the tradition of the elders, but eat their bread with impure hands?" [6]And He said to them, "Rightly did Isaiah prophesy of you hypocrites, as it is written:

'This people honors Me with their lips,

But their heart is far away from Me.

[7]But in vain do they worship Me,

Teaching as doctrines the precepts of men.'

[8]Neglecting the commandment of God, you hold to the tradition of men."

[9]He was also saying to them, "You are experts at setting aside the commandment of God in order to keep your tradition. [10]For Moses said, 'Honor your father and your mother'; and, 'He who speaks evil of father or mother, is to be put to death'; [11]but you say, 'If a man says to his father or his mother, whatever I have that would help you is Corban (that is to say, given to God),' [12]you no longer permit him to do anything for his father or his mother; [13]thus invalidating the word of God by your tradition which you have handed down; and you do many things such as that."

[14]After He called the crowd to Him again, He began saying to them, "Listen to Me, all of you, and understand: [15]there is nothing outside the man which can defile him if it goes into him; but the things which proceed out of the man are what defile the man. [16]["If anyone has ears to hear, let him hear."]

485

[17]When he had left the crowd and entered the house, His disciples questioned Him about the parable. [18]And He said to them, "Are you so lacking in understanding also? Do you not understand that whatever goes into the man from outside cannot defile him, [19]because it does not go into his heart, but into his stomach, and is eliminated?" (Thus He declared all foods clean.) [20]And He was saying, "That which proceeds out of the man, that is what defiles the man. [21]For from within, out of the heart of men, proceed the evil thoughts, fornications, thefts, murders, adulteries, [22]deeds of coveting and wickedness, as well as deceit, sensuality, envy, slander, pride and foolishness. [23]All these evil things proceed from within and defile the man."

Jesus was teaching in Galilee when a committee of Pharisees and scribes arrived from Jerusalem. They did not hesitate to interrupt Christ. Mark 7:1 says that they **gathered around Him**. Imagine them shouldering their way through the crowd until they had Jesus surrounded, and then shouting in His face. This time, they had a new allegation: His disciples were eating with unwashed hands, thereby breaking an ancient tradition. The Pharisees considered those traditions as sacred as the law of Moses itself.

Christ turned the bothersome interruption into a beneficial interlude by using it as an opportunity to teach needed lessons on man-made traditions. He first addressed the accusers, giving stern warnings concerning the dangers of uninspired traditions. He emphasized that such traditions were **the precepts of men** (Mk. 7:7), not God. He accused the Pharisees of transgressing **the commandment of God for the sake of** [their] **tradition** (Mt. 15:3). He illustrated this with an ancient man-made tradition that allowed men to **dedicate to God** (see Mk. 7:11; Mt. 15:5) all or part of their money, and then to tell their aged, needy parents, "We're sorry, but we aren't allowed to use these funds to help you." As far as we know, the Pharisees never again used this particular accusation against Jesus and His disciples. Certainly, it was not brought up at His trial.

He then turned to the crowd. He said, in effect, that, as old and hallowed as the tradition about washing of hands was, its basic tenet was flawed: **It is not what enters into the mouth that defiles the man** [that is, makes him ceremonially unclean], **but what proceeds out of the mouth** [that is, a man's words], **this defiles the man** (Mt. 15:11). Understand that the issue was not hygiene, but rather ceremonial defilement. Peter later asked for an explanation, and Christ answered,

> **Do you not understand that everything that goes into the mouth passes into the stomach, and is eliminated? But the things that proceed out of the mouth come from the heart, and those defile the man. For out of the heart come evil thoughts, murders, adulteries, fornications, thefts, false witness, slanders. These are the things which defile the man; but to eat with unwashed hands does not defile the man** (Mt. 15:17–20).

When Jesus was at last alone with His disciples, He taught them. He warned them regarding the Pharisees themselves. He compared the teachings of the Pharisees to weeds that would be pulled up by God (Mt. 15:13). He referred to these religious leaders as blind guides leading the blind (those who followed their teachings without question). Jesus had used this analogy earlier (Lk. 6:39), and He would use it again (Mt. 23:16, 24). Jesus' warnings to His disciples concerning the Pharisees would continue (see Mt. 15:39—16:12; Mk. 8:10–21). These were needed lessons—lessons prompted by an interruption.

APPLICATION:
A GOOD IDEA GONE BAD
(MT. 15:1–6; MK. 7:1–5, 9–13)

In the play *Fiddler on the Roof*, when the Jewish father is shocked by how little the younger generation seems to care for the old ways, he sings a song about "Tradition, tradition!" Each time I watch the scene, I feel sympathy for everyone involved: the young people who are frustrated by customs that make no sense to them, as well as the older man who is devastated to see his familiar world slipping away.

If the father in the drama was baffled by the challenge to a few traditions in his day, think of how he would feel today. Never before have so many time-honored traditions been cast aside in so short a period—with little of permanent worth replacing them. It is a time of confusion as people search for meaning to life, trying to discover "who they are" apart from discarded values. This is true not only in society, but also in religion. Some automatically shun anything "traditional," while others try desperately to hold on to the past. Is there a safe and sane middle ground? If so, what is it? When are traditions good, and when are they bad? Few questions are more crucial in our chaotic world.

The longest discussion of traditions in the Bible is found in Matthew 15 and Mark 7—when Jesus had to defend His disciples against the charge that they were violating "the tradition of the elders." These two passages could be approached in a variety of ways, but we will use them to try to find answers to the questions just proposed.

It is not always easy to know when we should tenaciously cling to a tradition and when we should be willing to let it go. It is difficult for us to find a position that avoids extremes—and even more difficult to stay there. It is easier to apply the principles to others than to ourselves. None of us is exempt from the kind of traditionalism condemned by Jesus. Teachings of this kind cry out for self-examination and scrutiny.

A Tradition Can Be Bad (Mt. 15:1, 2; Mk. 7:1–5)

One day, as Jesus was teaching in Capernaum, He was accosted by a group of Pharisees (see Jn. 6:17, 59). These were not the common-variety Pharisees that had been following Him everywhere; these were go-for-the-throat debaters sent from Jerusalem to hasten Jesus' destruction. This is a deduction based on the facts that (1) the Pharisees were seeking an excuse to kill Him (see Jn. 5:18; 7:1) and (2) these Pharisees came all the way from Jerusalem to accuse Him. R. C. Foster called them "shock troops from the capital."[1]

---

[1]R. C. Foster, *Studies in the Life of Christ* (Grand Rapids, Mich.: Baker Book House, 1971), 664.

Since the accusation that Christ was breaking the Sabbath had proved counterproductive, the Pharisees tried a new charge. They asked, "Why do Your disciples break the tradition of the elders? For they do not wash their hands when they eat bread" (Mt. 15:2).

"The Tradition" Defined

To understand the allegation, one must know what "the tradition of the elders" was and why it was so important to the Pharisees. The word "tradition" is translated from a compound Greek word that basically means "that which has been handed down." The compound Greek word is παράδοσις (*paradosis*). *Para* (παρά) is a preposition that usually means "alongside," while *dosis* (δόσις) basically means "to give (or transfer)." According to Greek scholars, the combination of *para* and *dosis* denotes "that which has been passed (handed) on to others."[2] In Mark 7:13 both the noun form and the verb form of the word are used. The NASB translates this section of the verse "your *tradition* which you have *handed down.*" (Emphasis added.) In Matthew 15:2 Goodspeed translated the word as "rules handed down."[3]

The word is occasionally used in the Bible to refer to teaching that had been "handed down" from *God* (that is, inspired teaching; 1 Cor. 11:2; 2 Thess. 2:15; 3:6). More often, it refers to regulations handed down from *men* (Mt. 15:2, 3, 6; Mk. 7:3, 5, 8, 9, 13; Gal. 1:14; Col. 2:8). Phrases we could use to indicate this type of tradition include "man-made tradition" and "uninspired tradition." In this study, most of the time the word "tradition" will be used in its more common meaning of traditions originating with men.

The Pharisees spoke of "the tradition *of the elders.*" The term "elders" does not pertain to synagogue officials (Lk. 7:3), but rather to men of the past who were considered experts on the

---

[2]An explanation is given in W. E. Vine, *The Expanded Vine's Expository Dictionary of New Testament Words*, ed. John R. Kohlenberger III with James A. Swanson (Minneapolis: Bethany House Publishers, 1984), 1159–60.

[3]Edgar J. Goodspeed and J. M. Powis Smith, *The Short Bible: An American Translation* (New York: Modern Library, 1933), 347.

Law. For centuries, respected Jewish teachers had been rendering interpretations of, and decisions regarding, the law of Moses. Those teachings had grown into a sizeable body known as "the oral law" or "the tradition." These traditions were gathered together in the third century A.D. into a work known as the *Mishna* (or *Mishnah*). By the end of the third century, this had been enlarged with other material into a voluminous volume called the *Talmud*.

The Pharisees taught that Moses himself had given "the oral law" along with the written Law, and that this "oral law" had been handed down by the great teachers. This was untrue, of course. (Various religious groups today make a similar claim, trying to justify their man-made laws by alleging that they were taught by the apostles and were handed down orally through the centuries "by the church.") The Pharisees considered "the tradition" as binding as, or more binding than, the Law itself. Warren W. Wiersbe showed the emphasis placed on tradition:

> Rabbi Eleazar said, "He who expounds the Scriptures in opposition to the tradition has no share in the world to come." The *Mishna*, a collection of Jewish traditions in the *Talmud*, records, "It is a greater offense to teach anything contrary to the voice of the Rabbis than to contradict Scripture itself."[4]

The regulations of "the tradition" were thought of as "a hedge" around the Law itself. The idea was that if one never violated "the tradition," he would never violate the Law. It had not been a bad idea originally, but the rules had multiplied into the thousands and had mutated until they had become grotesque. It was a good idea gone bad.

"The Tradition" Demanded

"The tradition" regarding washing hands before eating is a good example. The Old Testament has much to say about cere-

---

[4]Warren W. Wiersbe, *The Bible Exposition Commentary*, vol. 1 (Wheaton, Ill.: Victor Books, 1989), 134.

monial uncleanness. (Read Lev. 11—15 and Num. 19.) As a rule, this "uncleanness" had little to do with hygiene, but much to do with a man's eligibility to approach God. Some of the rites to remove ritual uncleanness included washing. The original laws were complicated enough, but through the centuries, men had added to them until the regulations about ceremonial uncleanness and ceremonial washings had become too numerous to count.

The Pharisees' list of items, circumstances, and situations considered "unclean" was almost endless. Further, the "uncleanness" was transferable or infectious. For instance, if an unclean creature (such as a mouse) touched a bowl, that bowl was "unclean." Whatever was put in the bowl became "unclean." If anyone ate the contents of the bowl, he became "unclean." If anyone touched the "unclean" person, he became "unclean." On and on, the "unclean" cycle continued.

Thus Mark emphasized that "the Pharisees and all the Jews do not eat unless they carefully wash their hands" (Mk. 7:3a). The influence of the Pharisees was such that this tradition had become part of the daily ritual of the Jewish people as a whole. The literal meaning of the Greek word πυγμή (*pugme*), translated "carefully," is "with the fist."[5] Alfred Edersheim, in *The Life and Times of Jesus the Messiah*, described the elaborate washing ceremonies. Here are a few of the details:

> As the purifications were so frequent, and care had to be taken that the water had not been used for other purposes, . . . large vessels or jars were generally kept for the purpose. . . . It was the practice to draw water out of these . . . a measure equal to one and a half "egg-shells." . . . The water was poured on both hands. . . . The hands were lifted up, so as to make the water run to the wrist, in order to ensure that the whole hand was washed, and that the water polluted by the hand did not again run down the fingers. Similarly, each hand was rubbed with

---

[5]This definition is given in the center column of my copy of the NASB.

the other (the fist), provided the hand that rubbed had been [washed].[6]

Mark further noted that when the Pharisees "come from the market place, they do not eat unless they cleanse themselves" (Mk. 7:4a). *Many* things in the marketplace might have defiled them. They might even have come in contact with an unclean Gentile—or particles of unclean dust that had been touched by an unclean Gentile might have gotten on them. When they came home from the marketplace, they did not simply wash their hands; they washed their whole bodies. In other words, they took a bath before they would eat.

Mark added, "And there are *many other things* which they have received in order to observe, such as the washing of cups and pitchers and copper pots" (Mk. 7:4b; emphasis added). The Greek word βαπτισμός (*baptismos*), translated "washing," literally means "baptizing" or "immersing." Remember that the purpose of this washing was not sanitation, but ritual cleanliness. The regulations were innumerable and unbelievably complicated.

"The Tradition" Disregarded

Keeping all this in mind, imagine how appalled the Pharisees were at the rough-and-ready lifestyle of Jesus' apostles. The disciples did not even have time to eat (Mk. 6:31), much less go through the elaborate ritual washings prescribed in "the tradition of the elders." The apostles had even been known to pluck grain from the field and pop it into their mouths (Mt. 12:1–8). When the Pharisees saw "that some of His disciples were eating their bread with impure hands, that is, unwashed" (Mk. 7:2), they asked Jesus, "Why do Your disciples not walk according to the tradition of the elders, but eat their bread with impure hands?" (Mk. 7:5).

When a Tradition Is Bad (Mt. 15:3–6; Mk. 7:9–13)

Jesus was losing His patience with the self-righteous and

---

[6]Alfred Edersheim, *The Life and Times of Jesus the Messiah*, New Updated Version [Peabody, Mass.: Hendrickson Publishers, 1993], 482.

self-serving Pharisees. He did not bother to deny their charge or even answer it directly. Instead, He leveled an accusation at *them*:

> Why do you yourselves transgress the commandment of God for the sake of your tradition? For God said, "Honor your father and mother," and, "He who speaks evil of father or mother is to be put to death." But you say, "Whoever says to his father or mother, 'Whatever I have that would help you has been given to God,' he is not to honor his father or his mother." And by this you invalidated the word of God for the sake of your tradition (Mt. 15:3–6).

Originally, the purpose of the traditions was to place a hedge around the law of Moses, to help ensure that the Law was not violated. As time went by, however, as new rules multiplied, they related less and less to the original precepts—until finally they even went contrary to those commandments.

A Tradition That Was Bad

Christ could have given many examples of this (Mk. 7:13b), but He confined Himself to one: "For God said, 'Honor your father and mother,' and, 'He who speaks evil of father or mother is to be put to death'" (Mt. 15:4). Mark wrote, "For *Moses* said…" (Mk. 7:10), which is another proof that Jesus believed that Moses spoke by inspiration *from God* when he gave the Law.

The first of the commands listed by Jesus was one of the original Ten Commandments (Ex. 20:12; Deut. 5:16). The second was included in the laws that expanded and applied the Ten Commandments (Ex. 21:17; Lev. 20:9). These two commandments covered the positive and negative aspects of an individual's relationship with his parents. He *was* to respect and appreciate his father and mother. This included caring for their needs when they were old (see Prov. 23:22; 1 Tim. 5:8). He was *not* to do anything that would indicate disrespect.

Unfortunately, a man-made tradition had evolved, nullifying those commandments. Jesus' eyes must have flashed as He indicted His accusers:

> . . . You are experts at setting aside the commandment
> of God in order to keep your tradition. For Moses said,
> "Honor your father and your mother" . . . ; but you say,
> "If a man says to his father or his mother, whatever I
> have that would help you is Corban (that is to say, given
> to God)," you no longer permit him to do anything for
> his father or his mother; thus invalidating the word of
> God by your tradition which you have handed down"
> (Mk. 7:9–13a).

"Corban" is an Aramaic word meaning "offering" or "gift."
A Jew could make a vow that a certain portion of what he owned
was "Corban," "a gift" dedicated to God. Those resources might
remain in his possession until his death—at which time they
became the property of the temple—but as long as he lived, those
assets were considered untouchable. Some speculate that, even
though the assets technically belonged to God, the individual
himself might continue to make personal use of them as long as
he lived. According to Jesus, if a man made such a vow, the Pharisees would "no longer *permit* [or allow] him to do anything for
his father or his mother." The rabbis had a saying: "It is hard for
the parents, but the law is clear, vows must be kept."[7] The Old
Testament rule was that vows were to be kept (see Num. 30), but
to apply the laws regarding vows in such a way that the fundamental principles of the Ten Commandments were set aside was
ridiculous.

Picture this in your mind: A man and a woman approach the
house of their son. The woman has been crying. The man looks
grim. They knock on the door. When their son answers their
knock, they say, sadly, "We have lost everything we owned. You
are our last hope. If you cannot help us, we must beg or starve."
The young man looks at them with disdain, his parents who
brought him into the world, who nurtured and cared for him
through childhood. He says to them, "Sorry, I can't help you! I

---

[7]Quoted in Vine, 232.

did have some money saved up for your old age, but a Phari-see came by the other day and pointed out the financial advan-tages of declaring those funds to be Corban. So, goodbye! Find a way to provide for yourselves, and don't come around here any more asking for handouts!" With that, he slams the door in their faces.

Apparently, sad episodes similar to this occurred in the Lord's day. Jesus thus concluded this part of His indictment, "And by this you invalidated the word of God for the sake of your tradi-tion" (Mt. 15:6b). According to Mark, He added, "And you do *many* things such as that" (Mk. 7:13b; emphasis added).

Traditions That Are Good

Let us pause to note that traditions are not necessarily wrong within themselves—not even man-made traditions. There are biblical examples of God's people engaging in man-made tradi-tional ceremonies with the Lord's approval. Think of Jesus' involvement in the lives of the Jewish people—in their tradi-tional weddings, funerals, and the like. Consider Christ's atten-dance at the Feast of Dedication (Jn. 10:22), a Jewish feast that originated during the time between the Old Testament and the New Testament.

Tradition plays an important part in our lives. It gives continu-ity to our lives and adds a flavor and dimension to life that other-wise would be missing. In recent years, sociologists have stressed that having "roots" is important to the psychological well-being of an individual. Nothing is wrong with a group of people, even a congregation, having traditional ways of doing certain things— as long as the will of God is not thereby violated.

Traditions That Are Undeniably Bad

This brings us back to the question "When *is* a tradition wrong?" Jesus' first answer could be phrased like this: "When that tradition violates an express command of God." Christ said that the Pharisees *transgressed* the commandment of God for the sake of their tradition (Mt. 15:3), that they *set aside* the command-ment to keep their tradition (Mk. 7:9), that they thus *invalidated* the Word of God by their tradition (Mt. 15:6; Mk. 7:13). The Lord called the Pharisees "hypocrites" (Mt. 15:7; Mk. 7:6) because, while they were accusing the disciples of not keeping "the tradition of the *elders*," they themselves were disobeying "the commandment of *God*"!

Religiously, I was taught to think for myself. Further, I grew up in a part of the US where, in general, independent thought has been encouraged. Therefore, I did not fully appreciate Jesus' words to the Pharisees until I lived for ten years in Australia, where the dominant churches were (and are) almost totally bound by traditions. These denominations follow traditions about ecclesiastical authority which weaken biblical authority (read 2 Tim. 3:16, 17); traditions about "infant baptism" that void biblical teaching on baptism (Mk. 16:15, 16); traditions about "special days" that, for all practical purposes, nullify the instruction not to forsake the Christian assembly (Heb. 10:25); and so on. J. W. McGarvey wrote, "There is probably not one . . . addition or amendment [to God's revealed will] which does not to a greater or less degree make some commandment void."[8]

Conclusion

Most of us would probably agree that any man-made tradition that causes one to disobey a command of God is wrong. However, Jesus was not through with His indictment. The next study will become even more personal as we look at two more criteria that Christ gave to determine whether a tradition is good or bad.

APPLICATION:
WHEN IS A TRADITION BAD?
(MT. 15:7–20; MK. 7:6–8, 14–23)

A Tradition Is Bad When It Is Bound on Others
(Mt. 15:7–9; Mk. 7:6–8)

While Christ was speaking to the Pharisees, His words be-

---

[8]J. W. McGarvey and Philip Y. Pendleton, *The Fourfold Gospel or A Harmony of the Four Gospels* (Cincinnati: Standard Publishing Co., 1914), 396.

came very pointed: "You hypocrites, rightly did Isaiah prophesy of you: 'This people honors Me with their lips, but their heart is far away from Me. But in vain do they worship Me, teaching as doctrines the precepts of men'" (Mt. 15:7–9). The quotation is from Isaiah 29:13. In that passage, the prophet was condemning the hypocrites of his day. Jesus said that the inspired words applied as aptly to the religious leaders of His day.

A variety of important lessons can be drawn from Isaiah's words. "Lip service" is not enough; our obedience to the Lord must come from the heart (Mt. 22:37; Rom. 6:17; Eph. 6:6; Col. 3:16; 2 Cor. 9:7). We have seen that our worship is "vain" (empty) if it is not heart-motivated and heaven-authorized. In the present discussion, however, let us concentrate on the final part of the quotation: They were "teaching as doctrines the precepts of men." The context makes clear that they were teaching their "precepts of men" as though they were "doctrines" *of God.* As important as the traditions were to the Pharisees, Jesus wanted it understood that they were the dogmas of *men,* not of the Lord.

Binding Traditions as Though They Were Commandments

Did Christ condemn the Pharisees for going through their elaborate ablutions before each meal? No, if they wanted to waste time with absurd rituals, that was their business. Jesus' condemnation of the Pharisees was not because of their practice, but because they were trying to bind their practice on others. They had elevated their traditions to the status of divine commands. They taught that men *had* to keep their traditions. They condemned all who failed to keep them. Let us phrase the second criterion like this: *A tradition is bad when it is bound on others.*

Everyone can see that such a practice is wrong, at least in principle. Through the years, my family has developed its own unique (peculiar?) traditions regarding holidays and other celebrations. We enjoy these, and they help to define who we are. Of course, we make no effort to bind them on others. To condemn other households for not keeping our family traditions would be ridiculous, to say the least.

Jesus clearly taught that it is wrong to bind our religious traditions on others. It is when we attempt to *apply* this principle that controversy arises. People are naturally more comfortable with "the way it has always been done," and we are inclined to think that is the way it *should* be done. Nevertheless, we must strive to make a distinction between what cannot be changed (the revealed will of God) and what can be (the methods used to carry out His will).

Illustrations come to mind from the sphere of worship: Most congregations where I have preached have song books. Should we therefore condemn a congregation that projects the songs onto a screen? Wherever I have worshiped, it has been customary to have a sermon as part of the Sunday morning service. Would it be wrong to have a Sunday morning service primarily consisting of songs, prayers, and Scripture readings centered on the observance of the Lord's Supper? Congregations with which I have been associated have Sunday night services at the church building. If another congregation decided to have Sunday evening service in homes, would that be unscriptural? Some may question the *wisdom* of having the Sunday night service in homes, but that is a question of expediency, not one of scripturality. I am not asking, "Is it practical?" I am just asking, "Is it unscriptural?"

The New Testament gives us a basic pattern for worship, but many of the details are left to our judgment. Through the years, congregations tend to develop approaches that suit them for fulfilling the requirements of the Scriptures. Nothing is wrong with this, but we must take care that we make a distinction between what has been handed down from *God* (the divine pattern) and that which has been handed down from *men* (our procedures for carrying out the divine pattern). One factor in this discussion is the responsibility of the elders regarding the congregation which they oversee. In fulfilling their responsibility, they make decisions that affect that congregation. They must realize, however, that other congregations are not required to abide by their decisions. (That is the principle of local autonomy.)

When my family worked with the West Side church of Christ in Muskogee, Oklahoma, we had a song leader named Charles Kelly who sometimes varied the order of the worship service. For instance, we might have communion at the first of the service or at the last. Occasionally, he would even schedule the contribution at a different time than the Lord's Supper rather than having it immediately after the communion as was customary. His reasoning on this was that, even though it is convenient to take up the collection right after communion, people need to realize that the contribution is not part of the Lord's Supper. One Sunday morning when the collection was not taken up after the Lord's Supper, one visitor sprang up and hurried from the service. As she left the building, she exclaimed to a man in the foyer, "What kind of group have I gotten myself into?" Apparently, she believed that there is "a scriptural order of service," and that any deviation from that was "unscriptural."

It is essential that the distinction be made between God's commands and man's traditions; it is wrong to bind our man-made traditions on others. Assuming that we agree thus far, the crucial question is "How do we distinguish between the commands of God and the traditions of men?"

Distinguishing Between Traditions and Commandments
More and more, the word "traditional" is applied to anything that has been around for a while—with the implication that it is therefore old and outdated, of little or no importance, and can be cast aside with impunity. For instance, the phrase "the traditional family" (that is, a family consisting of a father, a mother, and their children) has recently been used in a derogatory fashion. "The traditional family" is under attack by those advocating "same-sex marriages" and other deviations from God's Word (such as "living together" arrangements vs. getting married). However, the arrangement of "the traditional family" is from God and has been around since the early chapters of Genesis. To those who believe in the Bible, the important question is not "How long has this arrangement been in existence?" but rather "Is it from heaven or from men?" (Mt. 21:25).

I become distressed when I hear faithful congregations of the Lord's church despairingly referred to as "traditional churches," and what they believe and practice dismissed as "the traditional position." Those who apply these labels tend to brand *everything* these churches do as "traditional"—making little distinction between what they do as a matter of faith and what is done as a matter of judgment.

Lecturers sometimes lump together every issue that has plagued the church in the past, indicating that *all* were merely matters of opinion and of no significance. Looking back, I agree that some of the conflicts seem unnecessary, but is it fair to dismiss every question with which the church has struggled? How would the inspired writers have reacted if Christians had thus minimized the issues of Judaism and Gnosticism that threatened the early church?

Let us agree on this: A man-made tradition is bad when it is bound on others. Let us also agree that we should not automatically classify any belief or practice as "traditional" simply because we think it creaks with age.

Earlier I said that the crucial question regards how to distinguish between the commands of God and the traditions of men. You know the answer to that question, and it has already been hinted at several times: Everything we believe, teach, and do must be scrutinized *in light of what the Scriptures teach.* The question is not "How have we always done it?" The question is certainly not "How would we *like* to do it?" The question is "What does God teach in His revealed will?" (see Acts 17:11). Let us borrow Jesus' phraseology (Mt. 21:25): If a doctrine or practice is "from heaven," it is bound upon every Christian. If it is "from men," we must not be guilty of binding it on others.

In giving this answer, have I settled every dispute regarding what is "traditional" and what is not? Have I answered every question that can be asked? No and no. My purpose has been to plead with Christians to avoid extremes. Let us not condemn others for not keeping our traditions, as cherished as they may be. At the same time, let us never dismiss a religious teaching or practice as "traditional" simply because it has been around for years. After all, the New Testament has been in existence for centuries. Let us determine to make the teaching of *God's Word* our standard for accepting or rejecting any religious teaching or practice.

Long ago, Joshua gave the people of God this message from Him: "Only be strong and very courageous; be careful to do according to all the law which Moses My servant commanded you; do not turn from it to the right or to the left, so that you may have success wherever you go" (Josh. 1:7; see also 23:6). We might think of turning "to the right" as binding that which God has not bound (man-made traditions) and turning "to the left" as loosing what God has bound (His revealed will). Let us set our hearts to avoid either extreme. Let us determine to "do according to all" the teaching of the New Testament of Jesus.

We could close on that thought—but Christ was not finished with His discussion. He had at least one more point to make regarding human traditions. This truth is not as clear but is nonetheless important. It requires as much soul-searching as the previous two criteria—perhaps even more.

A Tradition Is Bad When It Takes on Undue Significance (Mt. 15:10–20; Mk. 7:14–23)

The exchange between Jesus and the Pharisees was not private. Christ had no interest in defending Himself and His disciples before the hardhearted leaders, but He thought that those who had been listening deserved an explanation. Mark condensed to a single verse the sermon He preached on the fundamental issue that had been raised:

> After He called the crowd to Him again, He began saying to them, "Listen to Me, all of you, and understand: there is nothing outside the man which can defile him if it goes into him; but the things which proceed out of the man are what defile the man" (Mk. 7:14, 15).

Among other things, Jesus was teaching that the man-made regulation concerning washing before each meal was illogical. In truth, it is not what goes into a person, including food eaten with unwashed hands, that defiles him (Mt. 15:20b). Rather, one can be defiled by what comes out of him—that is, the individual's words and actions.

Christ's statement had implications beyond the immediate question of ritual washings. Mark mentioned one conclusion from what Jesus said: "Thus He declared all foods clean" (Mk.

7:19b). Mark's words do not mean that, at the time, the disciples understood this to be the case. Mark was writing thirty or so years later. Looking back, inspired men saw that this truth was an inescapable conclusion from what Christ had said. It is hard for those of us familiar with New Testament teaching to appreciate how radical the Lord's words would have sounded to His audience. The instruction of the Law regarding what Jews could and could not eat (Lev. 11) had been impressed upon them from birth (see Acts 10:14). Christ's words were so startling that, when He was alone with His disciples, Peter asked Him to "explain the parable to us" (Mt. 15:15). The use of the word "parable" indicates that Peter thought that the statement surely could not be taken literally.

Jesus probably shook His head as He said, "Are you so lacking in understanding also?" (Mk. 7:18a). He was not surprised that the crowd failed to understand, but apparently He had hoped that His apostles would have greater insight. Nevertheless, He patiently explained, "Do you not understand that whatever goes into the man from outside cannot defile him, because it does not go into his heart, but into his stomach, and is eliminated?" (Mk. 7:18b, 19a). In other words, eating and elimination is part of a natural process that has nothing to do with a man's moral worth.

A word of caution is in order. R. C. Foster wrote, "It would be utterly perverse to attempt to apply this principle to things which are self-destructive, such as intoxicating liquor or any sort of poison."[9] Some substances that can enter the mouth *can* do harm. How often parents say to small children, "Take that out of your mouth!" The body is "the temple of God" (1 Cor. 3:16, 17; 6:19); anything that harms that temple should be avoided. However, Christ did not have in mind that which was potentially harmful; His concern was with nourishing, healthful food which Jews considered "unclean."

He continued His explanation:

---

[9]Foster, 669.

That which proceeds out of the man, that is what defiles the man. For from within, out of the heart of men, proceed the evil thoughts, fornications, thefts, murders, adulteries, deeds of coveting and wickedness, as well as deceit, sensuality, envy, slander, pride and foolishness. All these evil things proceed from within and defile the man (Mk. 7:20–23).

A Heart Problem Then

Much could be said about the "evil things" listed, but I want to concentrate on the word "heart." Throughout this story, Jesus emphasized that the Pharisees' primary problem was a *heart* problem. Earlier, He had made such a statement because they were not worshiping God from *the heart* (Mt. 15:8; Mk. 7:6). Here, He said, in effect, that their focus was on the outside, that which goes into a man, when they should have been concentrating on the inside—*the heart*, the source of both good and evil.

This suggests a third criterion for determining whether or not a tradition is bad. *A tradition is bad when it takes on undue significance*—when it gives us a warped spiritual emphasis or becomes so important to us that the determination to observe it overshadows our concern for obeying God's commands. Christ said that the Pharisees' obsession with their traditions caused them to *neglect* the commandment of God (Mk. 7:8).

A Heart Problem Now?

As stated earlier, the concern of giving undue significance to traditions is more subtle than the other criteria for determining whether or not a tradition is bad. The test is more subjective than objective; nevertheless, it is important. This third danger may ensnare as many, or more, than the other two we have discussed. We may not have substituted our traditions for God's commandments. We may not condemn others for not keeping our traditions. It is still possible, however, that our traditions have become so important to us that we become more agitated when people ignore them than we do when people disobey the Lord.

Are you thinking, "I know people just like that"? A word of warning: This is not a principle to apply to *others*. It is a principle to apply to *self*. I cannot know another man's heart. I may *think* that a man's traditions are overly important to him, but I cannot *know* that. Two individuals could observe exactly the same traditions, one with a proper perspective and the other with a warped perspective. Let us not be guilty of judging others in this matter (Mt. 7:1, 2; Rom. 2:1); let each of us judge himself.

Conclusion

As we wrap up our discussion of Jesus' teaching on tradition, an uninspired slogan from the past comes to mind: "In matters of faith, unity; in matters of opinion, liberty; in all things, charity (or love)." The three parts of this motto suggest three questions we need to ask regarding what we do or teach religiously.

"In matters of faith, unity." A "matter of faith" is that concerning which God has spoken in His Word (Rom. 10:17). In such matters, we need to be united (1 Cor. 1:10). This suggests the first question we should ask: *"Do I have biblical authority for what I do and teach?"* The important question concerning any practice is not "How long has it been done this way?" but "Where did it originate?"

"In matters of opinion, liberty." A "matter of opinion" is that concerning which God has not spoken in His Word. It involves personal judgment. In such matters, we are not to bind our opinions on others. "Liberty" is the watchword. The Bible teaches us not to use our liberty in such a way that we hurt the church and other Christians (see 1 Cor. 8:9). This calls for constant heart-searching: *"Has an expedient way of carrying out a command, by reason of time, taken on the same significance in my mind as the command itself?"*

"In all things, charity [or love]." When fellow Christians disagree with us in matters of judgment, we should still love them (Jn. 13:35; Rom. 12:10). Brethren have been alienated and congregations divided because this basic principle was ignored. Each needs to ask this question: *"Do I have the spirit of Christ concerning harmless traditions that violate no Scripture and that are not*

504

bound as law?" It is foolish to insist on doing something a certain way just because "we've always done it that way." It is equally foolish to insist on doing things another way just to be different. Some individuals and congregations have apparently determined to be as different as they can—not because they have clear-cut evidence that their way is better, but because they are revolting against what they conceive of as "the traditional church." This is spiritual "adolescent behavior." There is no value in being different just for the sake of being different. When there is disagreement on a matter of opinion, love, consideration, and sensitivity are the order of the day.

The subject of traditions is complex. The basic principles are not hard to state, but applying them is difficult. This does not mean that the subject is therefore unimportant or that we need not strive to understand and obey the principles taught by Jesus in Matthew 15 and Mark 7. Rather, it means that none should be so bold as to claim to have all the answers. It means that we must be prepared to study, re-study, and then study further on every "issue" that arises. It means that we need to be patient with one another (Eph. 4:2).

WITHDRAWAL FROM HEROD'S TERRITORY (MT. 15:21; MK. 7:24)

Matthew 15:21
²¹Jesus went away from there, and withdrew into the district of Tyre and Sidon.

Mark 7:24
²⁴Jesus got up and went away from there to the region of Tyre. And when He had entered a house, He wanted no one to know of it; yet He could not escape notice.

After this clash with His enemies, Jesus **withdrew into the district of Tyre and Sidon** (Mt. 15:21). We have already suggested that one reason for the withdrawal was probably to get away from the Pharisees, but Christ's primary purpose was evidently to be alone with the Twelve. Some writers suggest that

Jesus went to Phoenicia for evangelistic purposes, but Mark 7:24 and Matthew 15:24 indicate that this was not the case. The increasing hostility of His foes made it even more imperative that He prepare His apostles for the day when His adversaries would kill Him.

As far as we know, this was the first time Jesus set foot on foreign soil. Tyre and Sidon were coastal cities of the ancient land of Phoenicia. Tyre and Phoenicia had played a part in the ancient history of the Jewish people—both positively and negatively. Phoenicia was a narrow strip of land situated on the northeastern corner of the Mediterranean Sea, to the northwest of Galilee. In the days of Christ, it was part of the Roman province of Syria.

HEALING OF THE DAUGHTER OF A PHOENICIAN (OR CANAANITE) WOMAN (MT. 15:21–28; MK. 7:24–30)

Matthew 15:21–28

²¹Jesus went away from there, and withdrew into the district of Tyre and Sidon. ²²And a Canaanite woman from that region came out and began to cry out, saying, "Have mercy on me, Lord, Son of David; my daughter is cruelly demon-possessed." ²³But He did not answer her a word. And His disciples came and implored Him, saying, "Send her away, because she keeps shouting at us." ²⁴But He answered and said, "I was sent only to the lost sheep of the house of Israel." ²⁵But she came and began to bow down before Him, saying, "Lord, help me!" ²⁶And He answered and said, "It is not good to take the children's bread and throw it to the dogs." ²⁷But she said, "Yes, Lord; but even the dogs feed on the crumbs which fall from their masters' table." ²⁸Then Jesus said to her, "O woman, your faith is great; it shall be done for you as you wish." And her daughter was healed at once.

Mark 7:24–30

²⁴Jesus got up and went away from there to the region of Tyre. And when He had entered a house, He wanted no one to

know of it; yet He could not escape notice. [25]But after hearing of Him, a woman whose little daughter had an unclean spirit immediately came and fell at His feet. [26]Now the woman was a Gentile, of the Syrophoenician race. And she kept asking Him to cast the demon out of her daughter. [27]And He was saying to her, "Let the children be satisfied first, for it is not good to take the children's bread and throw it to the dogs." [28]But she answered and said to Him, "Yes, Lord, but even the dogs under the table feed on the children's crumbs." [29]And He said to her, "Because of this answer go; the demon has gone out of your daughter." [30]And going back to her home, she found the child lying on the bed, the demon having left.

When Jesus arrived in the region of Tyre, He **entered a house**, desiring to keep His presence secret, but **He could not escape notice** (Mk. 7:24). We read earlier that news of Christ's ministry had reached even to "the vicinity of Tyre and Sidon" (Mk. 3:8). It was not long, therefore, before the Lord was interrupted by someone seeking His help: **But after hearing of Him, a woman whose little daughter had an unclean spirit immediately came and fell at His feet. Now the woman was a Gentile, of the Syrophoenician race** (Mk. 7:25, 26a). Instead of "Gentile," the original text has "Greek" (see the KJV). The term "Greek" is often used in the New Testament to refer to Gentiles in general. The term "Syrophoenician" distinguished Phoenicians from other citizens of the Syrian province.

The woman cried out, **"Have mercy on me, Lord, Son of David"** (Mt. 15:22a). "Son of David" was an Israelite Messianic term. The Jewish hope had filtered to the nations around them. (Compare this phrase with the Samaritan woman's use of the word "Messiah" in Jn. 4:25.) She told Jesus, **"My daughter is cruelly demon-possessed"** (Mt. 15:22b). Mark emphasized that she *kept* **asking Him to cast the demon out of her daughter** (Mk. 7:26b; emphasis added). According to Matthew, she kept shouting (Mt. 15:23). This was a persistent, *noisy* mother. Her little girl needed help, and she wanted everyone to know about it.

The interchange that ensued between Jesus and the woman is

one of the most dramatic and puzzling in the Gospel Accounts. On the surface, it appears that Christ deliberately insulted her.

Initially, He ignored her, and His disciples tried to get rid of her (Mt. 15:23). This was their "all-purpose solution" to pesky problems (see Mt. 14:15). In light of Matthew 15:24, they might have been suggesting that Jesus give her what she wanted so she would go away and leave them alone. When He finally spoke to her, He said, **"I was sent only to the lost sheep of the house of Israel"** (Mt. 15:24).

Nothing deterred this desperate mother. She continued to beg, **"Lord, help me!"** (Mt. 15:25). Jesus responded, **"Let the children be satisfied first, for it is not good to take the children's bread and throw it to the dogs"** (Mk. 7:27). "The children" in this sentence are obviously the Jews—which would make Gentiles "the dogs." The word "first" indicates that *later* the Gentiles *would* have their opportunity—which, of course, was the case.Instead of becoming angry, the mother cleverly answered, **"Yes, Lord, but even the dogs under the table feed on the children's crumbs which fall from [the] masters' table"** (Mk. 7:28; Mt. 15:27).

A smile must have spread across Jesus' face as He replied, **"O woman, your faith is great. Because of this answer, go. It shall be done for you as you wish. The demon has gone out of your daughter"** (Mt. 15:28a; Mk. 7:29). Matthew wrote that **her daughter was healed at once** (Mt. 15:28b). Mark recorded that when she got back home, **she found the child lying on the bed** [no doubt exhausted from the traumatic experience], **the demon having left** (Mk. 7:30).

As dramatic and fascinating as the story is, it is still perplexing. Commentators struggle to reconcile the words used by Jesus with what we know of His character and purpose. Some point out that Christ's words can be taken at face value. He really had been sent "to the lost sheep of the house of Israel" (Mt. 10:6). Later, "other sheep . . . not of this fold [that is, the Gentiles]" would be called so that both Jew and Gentile might "become one flock" under the care of the Good Shepherd (Jn. 10:16). This occurred when Christ gave the Great Commission to take the gospel to all people (Mt. 28:18–20; Mk. 16:15, 16). In the meantime (these commentators stress), Jesus was determined not to be deterred from His primary purpose (Mt. 10:5). Jesus could easily have been swamped by requests for help in Phoenicia, thwarting what He hoped to accomplish there. His focus on that purpose was no doubt a factor in Christ's initial response, but that surely is not the complete explanation. Jesus had previously responded positively to a Gentile's cry for help (Mt. 8:5–13). Further, after He left the area of Tyre, He would heal many Gentiles. As we consider why Christ spoke the way He did, we must rule out prejudice against Gentiles. Jesus was *not* afflicted with the usual Jewish bias against other races (see Lk. 2:32; Mt. 8:10–12; 12:18, 21). Every time Jesus helped a Gentile, He was planting the thought that God is also interested in non-Jews.

Others stress the fact that we do not know *how* Christ spoke the words directed to the woman. They remind us that, as a rule, Jesus adapted His approach to the character of the one to whom He spoke. (Contrast His approach to the Jewish leader in John 3 with His approach to the Samaritan woman in John 4.) They suggest, therefore, that this was an intentional lively interchange between the Lord and a woman with a quick mind and a sense of humor. Jesus likely spoke with a twinkle in His eye and had a smile on His face at the end of the conversation. This may be true, but there is still more to the story than this.

Here is another possibility for Christ's response to the woman's request. Since, at the end of the story, Jesus healed the young girl, this was His intention all along. Further, the purpose of His words seems to relate to His commendation of the mother's faith at the close of the story: "O woman, your faith is great" (Mt. 15:28a). B. S. Dean wrote, "Her faith, so humble, so unconquerable, must have brought refreshment after the hypocrisy of the Pharisees and the fickleness of the Galileans."[10] Only twice did Christ thus commend the faith of individuals—and both of those individuals were Gentiles: this Syrophoenician woman and a Roman centurion (Mt. 8:10; Lk. 7:9). In other words, one purpose of Jesus' seemingly harsh words may have been to demon-

---

[10]B. S. Dean, "The Great Galilean Ministry," *Truth for Today* (March 1992): 20.

strate to His disciples the depth of the woman's faith. Keep in mind that the Lord knew her heart (Jn. 2:25) and therefore her faith. Consider, then, this possibility: Jesus turned a bothersome interruption into a beneficial interlude by using the occasion as an object lesson for the apostles regarding the kind of faith they would need in the future. He knew the troubles that lay ahead for the Twelve (Mt. 10:17, 18, 21, 22, 24, 25). The only way they could be victorious was to have the kind of faith the woman had: a faith that refused to be discouraged or deterred (1 Jn. 5:4). Each of us needs this lesson.

AVOIDING HEROD'S TERRITORY
(MT. 15:29; MK. 7:31)

Matthew 15:29
²⁹**Departing from there, Jesus went along by the Sea of Galilee, and having gone up on the mountain, He was sitting there.**

Mark 7:31
³¹**Again He went out from the region of Tyre, and came through Sidon to the Sea of Galilee, within the region of Decapolis.**

When Jesus and His disciples finally left the region of Tyre, they did not immediately return to Galilee. Instead, still avoiding Herod's territory, they moved north to Sidon, then east across the mountains and the headwaters of the Jordan River, and finally south along the eastern coast of the Sea of Galilee until they reached a desolate spot (Mk. 8:4) in "the region of Decapolis" (Mk. 7:31; see the map "Palestine During the Life of Christ" in the appendix).

Some harmonies call this Jesus' "second withdrawal from Galilee" and others refer to it as His "third withdrawal from Galilee," in spite of the fact that He did not go from Galilee to Decapolis, and thus did not "withdraw." It is unimportant whether or not it was a "withdrawal"—and, if so, what number it was. It is sufficient to know that, during this period, Christ was avoiding Herod's territory.

HEALING OF MANY, INCLUDING A DEAF MAN (MT. 15:30, 31; MK. 7:32–37)

Matthew 15:30, 31

[30]**And large crowds came to Him, bringing with them those who were lame, crippled, blind, mute, and many others, and they laid them down at His feet; and He healed them.** [31]**So the crowd marveled as they saw the mute speaking, the crippled restored, and the lame walking, and the blind seeing; and they glorified the God of Israel.**

Mark 7:32–37

[32]**They brought to Him one who was deaf and spoke with difficulty, and they implored Him to lay His hand on him.** [33]**Jesus took him aside from the crowd, by himself, and put His fingers into his ears, and after spitting, He touched his tongue with the saliva;** [34]**and looking up to heaven with a deep sigh, He said to him, "Ephphatha!" that is, "Be opened!"** [35]**And his ears were opened, and the impediment of his tongue was removed, and he began speaking plainly.** [36]**And He gave them orders not to tell anyone; but the more He ordered them, the more widely they continued to proclaim it.** [37]**They were utterly astonished, saying, "He has done all things well; He makes even the deaf to hear and the mute to speak."**

When the Lord reached His destination, He climbed the side of a mountain and sat down (Mt. 15:29), no doubt to teach His disciples. Sitting was the position assumed for teaching in those days (Mt. 5:1, 2). Once more He was interrupted: **And large crowds came to Him, bringing with them those who were lame, crippled, blind, mute, and many others, and they laid them down at His feet** (Mt. 15:30a). The original text says that they "cast . . . down" those who were sick (compare the KJV and the ASV). We should not suppose that they mistreated these invalids, but the words do indicate their haste and concern.

This was the same general area where Jesus had healed two demoniacs and had been asked to leave the country (Mk. 5:17). Christ had instructed one of the healed men to share how the Lord had shown mercy to him (Mk. 5:19). Immediately, the man had begun "to proclaim in Decapolis what great things Jesus had done for him," and everyone who heard him had been amazed (Mk. 5:20). The effectiveness of the man's message is seen in the thousands (Mk. 8:9) that now came seeking help from all over the region (Mk. 8:3). Earlier, men from that region had said, "Get out!" Now people were begging, "Help us!"

If Christ became frustrated at these continual interruptions, He did not show it. On this occasion, He turned the interruption into an opportunity to point the hearts of a largely Gentile audience to the true and living God. This crowd had a different composition than the previous crowd on the eastern side of the sea (the five thousand). That crowd had followed Jesus from Capernaum and would have been largely Jewish. This crowd had come from the region and would have been primarily Gentile. **So the crowd marveled as they saw the mute speaking, the crippled restored, and the lame walking, and the blind seeing; and they glorified the God of Israel** (Mt. 15:30b, 31). The original text says that the "maimed" were made "whole" (see the KJV). The LB reflects the thought with this paraphrase: "those with missing arms and legs had new ones." The phrase "the God of Israel" is further proof that this was largely a Gentile audience.

Mark recorded one specific incident: the healing of **one who was deaf and spoke with difficulty** (Mk. 7:32). Apparently, the man's difficulty in speaking was not merely a result of being unable to hear. Mark 7:35 says that he had an "impediment of his tongue."

Jesus took him aside from the crowd, by himself, and put His fingers into his ears, and after spitting, He touched his tongue with the saliva; and looking up to heaven with a deep sigh, He said to him, "Ephphatha!" [an Aramaic word] that is, "Be opened!" (Mk. 7:33, 34).

The words "with the saliva" in the NASB are in italics, indicating that they were added by translators. The Greek text literally has "spitting, He touched his tongue." The original text does not indicate *where* Christ spit, nor does it say what (if anything) He did with the saliva. Why did Jesus put His fingers in the man's ears? Why did He spit? We are not told. Since these actions were not repeated in similar healings, they were incidental to what He did.

On the other hand, the "deep sigh" sent heavenward is significant. It lets us know that the Lord did not heal mechanically, without feeling; His heart was touched by every person who struggled with physical or spiritual maladies. One writer said that Christ may have sighed "because he thought of the millions there were of deaf and dumb who in this world would never hear and never speak."[11]

After Jesus said, "Be opened!" the man's **ears were opened, and the impediment of his tongue was removed, and he began speaking plainly** (Mk. 7:35). The people were **utterly astonished, saying, "He has done all things well"** (Mk. 7:37).

When Jesus eventually left that area, He left people whose hearts were ready to receive the gospel. When the church was scattered from Jerusalem (Acts 8:1–4), Christians went throughout the area around Palestine (Acts 8:2, 5; 11:19). The hearts of many of these were receptive because of the earlier work done by John the Baptizer, Jesus, and the apostles. If we react in the right way to interruptions, we will be exhibiting the spirit of the Lord—and this may open the door to teaching the gospel to those who interrupt us.

FEEDING FOUR THOUSAND MEN
(MT. 15:32–39; MK. 8:1–9)

Matthew 15:32–39
[32]And Jesus called His disciples to Him, and said, "I feel compassion for the people, because they have remained with

---

[11]McGarvey and Pendleton, 403. McGarvey's reference was to Frederic W. Farrar, *The Life of Christ* (New York: Cassell & Co., 1885), 229–30.

Me now three days and have nothing to eat; and I do not want to send them away hungry, for they might faint on the way." ³³The disciples said to Him, "Where would we get so many loaves in this desolate place to satisfy such a large crowd?" ³⁴And Jesus said to them, "How many loaves do you have?" And they said, "Seven, and a few small fish." ³⁵And He directed the people to sit down on the ground; ³⁶and He took the seven loaves and the fish; and giving thanks, He broke them and started giving them to the disciples, and the disciples gave them to the people. ³⁷And they all ate and were satisfied, and they picked up what was left over of the broken pieces, seven large baskets full. ³⁸And those who ate were four thousand men, besides women and children.

³⁹And sending away the crowds, Jesus got into the boat and came to the region of Magadan.

Mark 8:1–9

¹In those days, when there was again a large crowd and they had nothing to eat, Jesus called His disciples and said to them, ²"I feel compassion for the people because they have remained with Me now three days and have nothing to eat. ³If I send them away hungry to their homes, they will faint on the way; and some of them have come from a great distance." ⁴And His disciples answered Him, "Where will anyone be able to find enough bread here in this desolate place to satisfy these people?" ⁵And He was asking them, "How many loaves do you have?" And they said, "Seven." ⁶And He directed the people to sit down on the ground; and taking the seven loaves, He gave thanks and broke them, and started giving them to His disciples to serve to them, and they served them to the people. ⁷They also had a few small fish; and after He had blessed them, He ordered these to be served as well. ⁸And they ate and were satisfied; and they picked up seven large baskets full of what was left over of the broken pieces. ⁹About four thousand were there; and He sent them away.

Earlier, Jesus had instructed a healed man in the area to tell everyone what had happened to him (Mk. 5:19). This time, He gave His hearers "orders *not* to tell anyone" (Mk. 7:36a; emphasis added)—because His purpose had changed. He now needed time alone with His disciples.

As usual, His request was not heeded, and His fame spread through the region (see Mk. 7:36b). The numbers grew until **there was again a large crowd** (Mk. 8:1a): about **four thousand men, besides women and children** (Mt. 15:38). Probably between eight and twelve thousand were present, some of whom had come **from a great distance** (Mk. 8:3).

Once again, Jesus was gracious when interrupted—even when the interruption continued for three days (Mt. 15:32; Mk. 8:2). We are not given details concerning those three days, but no doubt He continued to teach and heal. (Compare with what He earlier did with the five thousand; see Mk. 6:34; Mt. 14:14.)

Unlike those who had earlier followed Christ from Capernaum (see Mt. 14:13, 14; Mk. 6:32–34; Lk. 9:10, 11), those in this crowd would have come prepared with provisions—but, after three days, they ran out of supplies. At that point, the nature of the interruption changed: They desperately needed food.

In keeping with His nature, the Lord again turned a bothersome interruption into a beneficial interlude. To reinforce an earlier lesson, He first presented the problem to His disciples (Mt. 15:32; Mk. 8:1–3). They said, in effect, "We have no idea how to handle this dilemma" (Mt. 15:33; Mk. 8:4).

Some commentators find it difficult to believe that the apostles could have so quickly forgotten the feeding of the five thousand. They conclude that the account of the feeding of the five thousand and the feeding of the four thousand are just variations of the same event. There is, however, no justification for such a conclusion.

First, Matthew and Mark recorded *both* events—and they were not writing down stories passed down over decades. Matthew wrote as an eyewitness since he was one of the apostles. Mark's account was based on eyewitness testimony (that of Peter, one of the apostles).

Second, Jesus later referred to *both* events during an admonition to His disciples (Mt. 16:9, 10; Mk. 8:19, 20).

Third, although there are similarities between the two events, there are also differences:

(1) The place was different. The location of the first miraculous feeding was near the northern end of the Sea of the Galilee; the second was near the southern end.

(2) The crowd was different. The first was largely Jewish; the second was largely Gentile.

(3) The size of the crowd was different—five thousand men vs. four thousand.

(4) The time involved was different. The first crowd had been there one day; the second crowd had been there three days.

(5) The reason for the need for food was different. The first crowd had not brought food; the second crowd had run out of food.

(6) The available resources were different. Five loaves and two fish were available the first time; seven loaves and a few fish were involved the second time.

(7) The tools used were different. Twelve small baskets were used in the first incident; seven large baskets were used in the second. A different Greek word for **basket** (σπυρίς, *spuris*) is used in connection with the second feeding. The word for "basket" in the feeding of the four thousand means "a *large* basket." These baskets were sometimes large enough to hold a man.

Other differences could be noted: The first crowd sat on the grass (Mt. 14:19; Mk. 6:39), while the second sat on the ground (Mt. 15:35; Mk. 8:6). The first crowd tried to make Jesus king; there was no similar response from the second crowd. Anyone who believes that the Bible is inspired must conclude that these are two separate incidents. That being the case, how can we explain the apostles' response?

The fact is, it generally took more than one time for the disciples to grasp a new truth. J. W. McGarvey wrote that "the failure to expect a miracle, despite previous experience, was a common occurrence in the history of Israel and of the twelve [see Num. 11:21–23; Ps. 78:19, 20]."[12] Consider also that hunger was not unknown to Christ and His apostles; as a rule, Jesus did not alleviate hunger with a miracle (see Jn. 4:6, 8, 31). Further, the

---

[12]Ibid., 405.

Twelve may have taken the Lord's strong rebuke following the feeding of the five thousand (Jn. 6:26, 27) as an indication that He would not again perform such a miracle. Taking all of these factors into consideration, their response was not as strange as it first appears to us.

Once again, Jesus miraculously fed the masses (Mt. 15:34–38; Mk. 8:5–9). Keep in mind that He did not do this merely to alleviate hunger, but also to teach the Twelve a needed lesson.

Jesus did not give up on His desire to be alone with His disciples. Having fed the people, He sent them away and traveled by boat to the west side of the sea (Mt. 15:39; Mk. 8:9, 10). More interruptions would come (Mt. 16:1; Mk. 8:11), and Christ would always turn those bothersome interruptions into beneficial interludes.

ANOTHER WITHDRAWAL FROM HEROD'S TERRITORY

We have seen Jesus in a series of withdrawals from Galilee: to the east side of the Sea of Galilee and also to the region of Tyre and Sidon in Phoenicia. We will again see Christ retreating from Galilee—this time far to the north, to the mountainous region of Caesarea Philippi.

Each withdrawal has had its highpoints. For instance, during one of them, the Lord fed five thousand and then walked on the water. However, none of the others included as many momentous events as this withdrawal. In the space of a week, all these events occurred: the good confession; the unveiling of Christ's plan to build His church; the first clear, unambiguous announcements concerning Jesus' death, resurrection, and second coming; and the Transfiguration. Most commentators agree that this was an extraordinary time for the Lord—a climactic period, a turning point in His ministry.

This must have been a time of extreme emotions for Jesus (see Mk. 8:12a). As One who was fully man, Christ was made like us "in all things" (Heb. 2:17). He could be happy (Lk. 10:21), and He could be sad (Lk. 19:41; Jn. 11:35). During the events covered in this part of our study, Jesus went from heartbreaking valleys to exhilarating mountain peaks, then back to the valleys.

In Galilee: Another Attack by Jesus' Enemies—Followed by
Another Withdrawal (Mt. 15:39—16:12; Mk. 8:10–21)

Matthew 15:39—16:12

³⁹And sending away the crowds, Jesus got into the boat and
came to the region of Magadan.

¹The Pharisees and Sadducees came up, and testing Jesus,
they asked Him to show them a sign from heaven. ²But He
replied to them, "When it is evening, you say, 'It will be fair
weather, for the sky is red.' ³And in the morning, 'There will
be a storm today, for the sky is red and threatening.' Do you
know how to discern the appearance of the sky, but cannot
discern the signs of the times? ⁴An evil and adulterous generation seeks after a sign; and a sign will not be given it, except
the sign of Jonah." And He left them and went away.

⁵And the disciples came to the other side of the sea, but
they had forgotten to bring any bread. ⁶And Jesus said to them,
"Watch out and beware of the leaven of the Pharisees and Sadducees." ⁷They began to discuss this among themselves, saying, "He said that because we did not bring any bread." ⁸But
Jesus, aware of this, said, "You men of little faith, why do you
discuss among yourselves that you have no bread? ⁹Do you not
yet understand or remember the five loaves of the five thousand, and how many baskets full you picked up? ¹⁰Or the seven
loaves of the four thousand, and how many large baskets full
you picked up? ¹¹How is it that you do not understand that I did
not speak to you concerning bread? But beware of the leaven of
the Pharisees and Sadducees." ¹²Then they understood that He
did not say to beware of the leaven of bread, but of the teaching of the Pharisees and Sadducees.

Mark 8:10–21

¹⁰And immediately He entered the boat with His disciples and
came to the district of Dalmanutha.

¹¹The Pharisees came out and began to argue with Him,
seeking from Him a sign from heaven, to test Him. ¹²Sighing
deeply in His spirit, He said, "Why does this generation seek
for a sign? Truly I say to you, no sign will be given to this gen-

eration." [13]Leaving them, He again embarked and went away to the other side.

[14]And they had forgotten to take bread, and did not have more than one loaf in the boat with them. [15]And He was giving orders to them, saying, "Watch out! Beware of the leaven of the Pharisees and the leaven of Herod." [16]They began to discuss with one another the fact that they had no bread. [17]And Jesus, aware of this, said to them, "Why do you discuss the fact that you have no bread? Do you not yet see or understand? Do you have a hardened heart? [18]Having eyes, do you not see? And having ears, do you not hear? And do you not remember, [19]when I broke the five loaves for the five thousand, how many baskets full of broken pieces you picked up?" They said to Him, "Twelve." [20]"When I broke the seven for the four thousand, how many large baskets full of broken pieces did you pick up?" And they said to Him, "Seven." [21]And He was saying to them, "Do you not yet understand?"

We last saw Jesus and His disciples on the east side of the Sea of Galilee. They got into a boat and crossed over to the west side of the sea—to **the region of Magadan** and **Dalmanutha** (Mt. 15:39; Mk. 8:10). This place may have been near the village of Magdala, which was four miles or so north of Tiberias (see the map "Palestine During the Life of Christ" in the appendix).

When Christ arrived, His old adversaries, the Pharisees, showed up **and began to argue with Him** (Mk. 8:11a). Strangely, they were accompanied by the Sadducees (Mt. 16:1). We referred to the Sadducees earlier in this volume, but this is the first time they have been mentioned in the Gospel Accounts. Normally, the Pharisees and the Sadducees were mortal enemies; but since both regarded Jesus as a threat, they had made an alliance to destroy Him. Like politics, hatred can "make strange bedfellows."

On this occasion, the Pharisees repeated a challenge that had been issued before. They asked Christ for **a sign from heaven, to test Him** (Mk. 8:11b; see Mt. 12:38–42; 16:1; Jn. 2:18). Since the Lord had done hundreds of miracles, including raising the dead, it would be hard to say exactly what they wanted. Perhaps there is significance in the words "from heaven." The original Greek text literally means "out of the heaven." This could mean "out of the sky," instead of "from God." The Greek word for "heaven" (οὐρανός, *ouranos*) is used in Matthew 16:2, 3 to mean "sky." Maybe the Pharisees were challenging Jesus to stop the sun and moon as Joshua had (Josh. 10:12, 13), to call fire from the skies as Elijah had (1 Kings 18:38), or something similar.

According to Mark, the confrontation of the Pharisees and the Sadducees caused Christ to sigh **deeply in His spirit** (Mk. 8:12). He knew that no miracle, no matter how spectacular, would satisfy them. They were like a blind man saying, "Show me the color purple and *then* I will believe there is such a color." Their eyes were closed; their hearts were hardened; there was no way they could be convinced.

Jesus gave them a short answer. He said that they were able to look at the sky and predict what the weather would be. There is an old saying: "A red sky at night is the shepherd's delight; a red sky in the morning is the shepherd's warning."[13] However, because of their prejudiced hearts, they were incapable of seeing Jesus and His ministry and understanding who He was (Mt. 16:2, 3). Note that the phrase **the signs of the times** refers to "the signs" (miracles) that Jesus was performing that proved that "the times" had come for which the Jews had been looking for centuries: the arrival of the Messiah and His kingdom. It does *not* refer to "the signs" of Christ's second coming, as some suggest.

Jesus concluded, **"An evil and adulterous generation seeks after a sign; and a sign will not be given it, except the sign of Jonah"** (Mt. 16:4a). This was a veiled reference to the ultimate proof of His deity, His resurrection (see Rom. 1:4). As Jonah was three days in the great fish, so Christ would be three days in the grave (Mt. 12:40).

If Jesus had planned to spend time in Galilee, the prompt arrival of His enemies rendered that impossible. Abruptly, **He**

---

[13]William Barclay, *The Gospel of Matthew*, vol. 2, rev. ed., The Daily Study Bible Series (Philadelphia: Westminster Press, 1975), 129.

left them and went away (Mt. 16:4b). Getting in a ship with His disciples, once more He headed for the eastern side of the Sea of Galilee (Mk. 8:13)—this time to the general vicinity of Bethsaida (see the map "Palestine During the Life of Christ" in the appendix).

During the trip, Christ gave His disciples a warning: **"Watch out and beware of the leaven of the Pharisees and Sadducees"** (Mt. 16:6). He also said, **"Beware of . . . the leaven of Herod"** (Mk. 8:15)—probably referring to the Herodians who were already working with the Pharisees to destroy Jesus (Mk. 3:6).

The figure of "leaven" is often used in the Scriptures to refer to influence, especially negative influence. Jesus probably had in mind biased notions taught by these groups that kept them from accepting Him as the Messiah. Even the disciples struggled with their own preconceived ideas about the Messiah and His kingdom. The Lord's warning might be phrased, "Beware of being influenced by preconceived ideas that can prevent you from seeing the truth."

The apostles had no idea what Christ was talking about. The reference to "leaven" made them think of bread. Jesus' departure had been so sudden that they had only brought one loaf of bread with them (Mk. 8:14). They decided that their Master's words were a reprimand for not making proper provision for the trip (Mt. 16:7; Mk. 8:16).

Jesus was disturbed by their lack of understanding, calling them **men of little faith** (Mt. 16:8). They were near the spot where He had recently fed five thousand men (Lk. 9:10–17), and not far from the place where He had fed the four thousand (Mk. 7:31; 8:1–9; see the map "Palestine During the Life of Christ" in the appendix). If He had fed thousands with meager supplies (Mt. 16:9, 10), they should have understood that He would have no trouble feeding their tiny group with one loaf, if necessary— and that He did not, therefore, have physical bread in mind. The apostles finally **understood that He did not say to beware of the leaven of bread, but of the *teaching* of the Pharisees and Sadducees** (Mt. 16:12; emphasis added).

In Bethsaida: A Blind Man Healed (Mk. 8:22–26)

Mark 8:22–26

²²**And they came to Bethsaida. And they brought a blind man to Jesus and implored Him to touch him.** ²³**Taking the blind man by the hand, He brought him out of the village; and after spitting on his eyes and laying His hands on him, He asked him, "Do you see anything?"** ²⁴**And he looked up and said, "I see men, for I see them like trees, walking around."** ²⁵**Then again He laid His hands on his eyes; and he looked intently and was restored, and began to see everything clearly.** ²⁶**And He sent him to his home, saying, "Do not even enter the village."**

As was generally the case, Christ had multiple purposes for withdrawing from Galilee. He wanted to distance Himself from His enemies (see Mt. 16:4b; Mk. 8:13), but He also wanted to spend time alone with His disciples. That latter purpose became increasingly important as the time of His death approached (Mk. 8:31). He decided to head far north, to the area of Caesarea Philippi, where there should be a minimum of distractions.

They started in that direction and **came to Bethsaida** (Mk. 8:22a). This was Bethsaida-Julias, on the northeastern shore of the sea (see the map "Palestine During the Life of Christ" in the appendix). When they reached the town, the people **brought a blind man to Jesus** to be healed (Mk. 8:22b). Christ did not refuse their request. As always, He had compassion—but He was determined to avoid gathering a crowd, since a large following would have delayed them on their trip. He led the man out of the town before healing him (Mk. 8:23a) and afterward told him, in effect, to go straight home without telling anyone (Mk. 8:26).

Only Mark tells of Jesus' miraculous healing of this blind man. This is one of the two miracles unique to Mark. (The other is the healing of the deaf man in Mk. 7:31–37.) This case of healing had several unusual features. Jesus only occasionally touched the ones He healed. Just one other time did He use spittle in connection with healing (Mk. 7:33, 34). The most unusual aspect of this incident, however, was that this is the only miracle done in two stages. It is often stated that this miracle was "gradual," but to use that terminology can leave the wrong impression. At most, only a few minutes were involved. This is unlike so-called "gradual miracles" today that are said to require days, weeks, or months. It has been suggested that, since it is sandwiched between two stories of the disciples' struggling with their understanding and faith, it is an object lesson to teach that faith does not come all at once, but in stages. We really do not know what Jesus' purpose was.

We have seen that features such as touching, spitting, and even the unique two-stage aspect of this miracle were incidental. Christ used a variety of methods to impress that the power was not in the procedure, but in the Person.

Near Caesarea Philippi: The Good Confession
(Mt. 16:13–20; Mk. 8:27–30; Lk. 9:18–21)

Matthew 16:13–20

[13]Now when Jesus came into the district of Caesarea Philippi, He was asking His disciples, "Who do people say that the Son of Man is?" [14]And they said, "Some say John the Baptist; and others, Elijah; but still others, Jeremiah, or one of the prophets." [15]He said to them, "But who do you say that I am?" [16]Simon Peter answered, "You are the Christ, the Son of the living God." [17]And Jesus said to him, "Blessed are you, Simon Barjona, because flesh and blood did not reveal this to you, but My Father who is in heaven. [18]I also say to you that you are Peter, and upon this rock I will build My church; and the gates of Hades will not overpower it. [19]I will give you the keys of the kingdom of heaven; and whatever you bind on earth shall have been bound in heaven, and whatever you loose on earth shall have been loosed in heaven." [20]Then He warned the disciples that they should tell no one that He was the Christ.

Mark 8:27–30

[27]Jesus went out, along with His disciples, to the villages

of Caesarea Philippi; and on the way He questioned His disciples, saying to them, "Who do people say that I am?" [28]They told Him, saying, "John the Baptist; and others say Elijah; but others, one of the prophets." [29]And He continued by questioning them, "But who do you say that I am?" Peter answered and said to Him, "You are the Christ." [30]And He warned them to tell no one about Him.

Luke 9:18–21

[18]And it happened that while He was praying alone, the disciples were with Him, and He questioned them, saying, "Who do the people say that I am?" [19]They answered and said, "John the Baptist, and others say Elijah; but others, that one of the prophets of old has risen again." [20]And He said to them, "But who do you say that I am?" And Peter answered and said, "The Christ of God." [21]But He warned them and instructed them not to tell this to anyone.

From Bethsaida-Julias, Christ and His followers continued their journey north until they finally arrived in the vicinity of Caesarea Philippi. Here Jesus would question His apostles to see if they really understood who He was. This was a crucial test for the disciples.

After Christ had prayed (Lk. 9:18), He called His disciples and asked, **"Who do people say that the Son of Man is?"** (Mt. 16:13). They answered, **"Some say John the Baptist; and others, Elijah; but still others, Jeremiah, or one of the prophets"** (Mt. 16:14; see Mk. 6:14–16; Lk. 9:7, 8). Each of the men named had been an outstanding servant of God. The words may sound like a compliment—but they were not. They were a rejection: a rejection of Jesus as the Messiah.

Then Jesus asked the all-important question: **"But who do you say that I am?"** (Mt. 16:15; emphasis added). His apostles had initially followed Him because they thought He was the promised Messiah (Jn. 1:41, 49)—but He had not fulfilled the national expectations regarding the Messiah. For a while, great crowds had followed Him, but then the tide of popular opinion had turned against Him (Jn. 6:66). In light of all this, did the disciples still believe in Him? Were they still sure, rock-solid sure, that He was the Messiah?

Peter spoke up, voicing what has become known as the Good Confession (see 1 Tim. 6:12, 13): **"You are the Christ, the Son of the living God"** (Mt. 16:16). "Christ" is the Greek form of "Messiah." Peter was affirming that he did indeed believe that Jesus was the One promised by the prophets, for whom the Jewish nation had been looking.

It is not hard to imagine elation in Jesus' voice as He said, **"Blessed are you, Simon Barjona** [Hebrew for "son of Jonah"], **because flesh and blood did not reveal this to you, but My Father who is in heaven. I also say to you that you are Peter, and upon this rock I will build My church"** (Mt. 16:17, 18a). This does not mean that Peter had received a special revelation that others had not received. Rather, it is an acknowledgment that the source of the truth about Jesus is God, not man. The *way* God had revealed this to Peter was through the life and teachings of Jesus.

Controversy has raged over the words "Peter" and "rock." Catholics contend that verse 18 teaches that the church was built on Peter. Matthew 16:18, 19 is their primary "proof" that Peter was the first pope. It is true that the Greek word Πετρος (*Petros*) translated "Peter" means "rock"—but Jesus used two different words for "rock" in verse 18. The word translated "Peter" is *petros*, while the word for "rock" is *petra* (πετρα). Not only are different words used, but also the first is in the masculine gender while the second is in the feminine gender. Further, the meanings of the words differ. W. E. Vine wrote, "*Petra* denotes a mass of rock, as distinct from *petros*, a detached stone or boulder, or a stone that might be thrown or easily moved."[14] It is sometimes contended that Jesus would have spoken in Aramaic, which does not have two separate words for "rock"—but that is just speculation. All we know for certain is that the inspired text which tells us about the incident is in Greek and uses two different words.

Christ was using a play on words. Perhaps He tossed a rock

---

[14]Vine, 974.

in His hands as He said, in effect, "You are Peter, a rock." Then
He no doubt gestured toward the ledge-rock foundation of Cae-
sarea Philippi, saying, "But upon a rock like *that*, I will build
My church."

What *was* the rock upon which the Lord was to build
His church? Most non-Catholic commentators agree that it was
the bedrock truth that Peter had just confessed. For instance,
J. W. McGarvey pointed out,

> . . . since Jesus himself occupies the position of builder in
> the metaphor, and Simon Peter the position of key-bearer,
> neither of them can properly be regarded as the founda-
> tion. The foundation must therefore be the confession
> which Peter has just spoken, since it is all that remains
> that is liable to such application.[15]

Some Protestant commentators point out that Ephesians 2:20
says that Christians are "built on the foundation of the apostles and prophets, Christ Jesus Himself being the corner stone."
From this passage they conclude that Christ *was* speaking of His
church being built on Peter in a sense—except it was not built
just on Peter, but rather on all the apostles. This interpretation
is not dangerous (it does answer the Catholic argument that the
church was build exclusively on Peter), but two comments are
in order: (1) The figures of Matthew 16 and Ephesians 2 are different and should not be confused. (2) Even in Ephesians 2:20,
the meaning would have to be that the church was built on the
teachings of the apostles and prophets—and their teachings were
centered in Jesus (see 1 Cor. 2:2; Gal. 6:14).

It is unfortunate that the Peter / rock controversy has obscured
the true significance of the occasion. Encouraged by Peter's confession, Jesus thought that His disciples were ready to have
the future unveiled. Thus He first made the startling statement
that He had come to establish a *church*, His church (see Eph. 1:22,
23; 2:16; 3:10, 11; 4:4; Col. 1:18). This statement is "startling" because it must have been completely unexpected. It did not accord

---

[15]McGarvey and Pendleton, 412.

with the Jewish concept of a material, physical kingdom.

In making this announcement, Christ did not totally abandon the Messianic/kingdom terminology with which His disciples were familiar (see Mt. 16:19); but He was, in effect, announcing that His kingdom would not be physical in nature, but rather spiritual. He had no interest in establishing a political institution; He was going to build His *church*.

This is the first use of the word "church" in the New Testament, but certainly not the last. The word "church" is found more than one hundred times in the New Testament. After Jesus' resurrection and the establishment of the kingdom/church, it became the predominant word for describing the followers of Christ as a group.

Let us return to Jesus' statement to Peter in Matthew 16:18, 19. Daniel had prophesied that the Messianic kingdom would be indestructible (Dan. 2:44a). Christ now declared that His church/kingdom would never be destroyed: **"And the gates of Hades will not overpower it"** (Mt. 16:18b). "Hades" is "the unseen world" of the dead, and for each individual, the "gate" to the Hadean world is death. The death of *Jesus* would not destroy the church: The devil apparently thought he was thwarting God's plans when he put Jesus on a cross, but that death was essential to the church's existence (Acts 20:28; Eph. 5:23, 25). Even the deaths of *church members* would not destroy it. If every member of the church were killed, this still would not destroy the church, because the **seed** of the church/kingdom is the Word (Lk. 8:11). Since the Word is indestructible (1 Pet. 1:23–25), the church will *always* exist, at least in seed form. Later, Satan would initiate persecution against Christians, but his tyranny would spread the church instead of destroying it (Acts 8:1–4).

Christ next rewarded the outspoken apostle with this promise: **"I will give you the keys of the kingdom of heaven; and whatever you bind on earth shall have been bound in heaven, and whatever you loose on earth shall have been loosed in heaven"** (Mt. 16:19).

The second part of that promise—the binding and loosing—was not Peter's exclusive prerogative; the promise was later extended to all the apostles (Mt. 18:18). Notice how the text reads:

"... whatever you bind on earth *shall have been bound* in heaven; and whatever you loose on earth *shall have been* loosed in heaven." (Emphasis added.) This reads somewhat awkwardly, but it is a literal translation. Because of the awkwardness, most translations do not attempt to translate the verse literally; they simply have "shall be" or "will be" bound or loosed (see the KJV and the NIV). Even the NASB was changed to say "shall be" in one revision, but the latest revision has returned to the literal translation. Jesus was emphasizing the importance of the inspired teaching of the apostles (it would both "bind" and "loose" men), but He was also stressing that they would not be the source of their doctrine: The "binding" and "loosing" would originate *in heaven,* and then (only then) would the apostles, by inspiration, "bind" and "loose" on earth.

Jesus did give Peter one special privilege—the first part of the promise: "I will give you the keys of the kingdom of heaven." The primary purpose of keys is to open and allow entrance. Peter was to be the first to tell both the Jews and the Gentiles how to be saved (Acts 2:14–43; 10:24–43, 47; 15:7), and thus how to enter the kingdom/church. Of course, telling people how to be saved was not a privilege enjoyed by Peter alone; all the apostles preached the saving gospel. Peter's special reward was to be *the first* to do so.

It had been an exciting day. The disciples still had much to learn, but their faith was intact. Jesus had to be pleased—but **He warned the disciples that they should tell no one that He was the Christ** (Mt. 16:20). The time would come for the bold proclamation of that truth (see Acts 2:36), but that time was not yet.

Near Caesarea Philippi: Jesus' Death Foretold
(Mt. 16:21–28; Mk. 8:31–38; Lk. 9:22–27)

Matthew 16:21–28

²¹From that time Jesus began to show His disciples that He must go to Jerusalem, and suffer many things from the elders and chief priests and scribes, and be killed, and be raised up on the third day. ²²Peter took Him aside and began to rebuke Him, saying, "God forbid it, Lord! This shall never happen to

You." [23]But He turned and said to Peter, "Get behind Me, Satan! You are a stumbling block to Me; for you are not setting your mind on God's interests, but man's."

[24]Then Jesus said to His disciples, "If anyone wishes to come after Me, he must deny himself, and take up his cross and follow Me. [25]For whoever wishes to save his life will lose it; but whoever loses his life for My sake will find it. [26]For what will it profit a man if he gains the whole world and forfeits his soul? Or what will a man give in exchange for his soul? [27]For the Son of Man is going to come in the glory of His Father with His angels, and will then repay every man according to his deeds.

[28]"Truly I say to you, there are some of those who are standing here who will not taste death until they see the Son of Man coming in His kingdom."

Mark 8:31–38

[31]And He began to teach them that the Son of Man must suffer many things and be rejected by the elders and the chief priests and the scribes, and be killed, and after three days rise again. [32]And He was stating the matter plainly. And Peter took Him aside and began to rebuke Him. [33]But turning around and seeing His disciples, He rebuked Peter and said, "Get behind Me, Satan; for you are not setting your mind on God's interests, but man's."

[34]And He summoned the crowd with His disciples, and said to them, "If anyone wishes to come after Me, he must deny himself, and take up his cross and follow Me. [35]For whoever wishes to save his life will lose it, but whoever loses his life for My sake and the gospel's will save it. [36]For what does it profit a man to gain the whole world, and forfeit his soul? [37]For what will a man give in exchange for his soul? [38]For whoever is ashamed of Me and My words in this adulterous and sinful generation, the Son of Man will also be ashamed of him when He comes in the glory of His Father with the holy angels."

Luke 9:22–27

[22]Saying, "The Son of Man must suffer many things and be

rejected by the elders and chief priests and scribes, and be killed and be raised up on the third day."

²³And He was saying to them all, "If anyone wishes to come after Me, he must deny himself, and take up his cross daily and follow Me. ²⁴For whoever wishes to save his life will lose it, but whoever loses his life for My sake, he is the one who will save it. ²⁵For what is a man profited if he gains the whole world, and loses or forfeits himself? ²⁶For whoever is ashamed of Me and My words, the Son of Man will be ashamed of him when He comes in His glory, and the glory of the Father and of the holy angels. ²⁷But I say to you truthfully, there are some of those standing here who will not taste death until they see the kingdom of God."

Because Jesus thought His disciples were ready to learn about the future, He had announced the establishment of His church. However, they would find it hard to accept the adjunct to that announcement. There could be no church without His death. The church would be the body of people saved by His blood (Eph. 5:23, 25; see Acts 20:28). The time had therefore come for Him to tell His apostles that He must die.

Christ had previously spoken in veiled terms regarding His impending death (Mt. 9:15; 10:38; 12:38–40; Jn. 2:19–22; 3:14, 15), but now He dropped the figurative language. Matthew wrote, **From that time Jesus began to show His disciples that He must go to Jerusalem, and suffer many things from the elders and chief priests and scribes, and be killed, and be raised up on the third day** (Mt. 16:21). The phrase "the elders and chief priests and scribes" was a synonym for the Sanhedrin, referring to three of its primary components. Underline the word "must" in your mind: Jesus was *committed* to fulfilling the plans and purposes of God (Jn. 6:38).

Mark's account says that Christ **began to teach them that the Son of Man must . . . be killed, and after three days rise again. And He was stating the matter** *plainly* (Mk. 8:31, 32a; emphasis added). The clarity of Jesus' statement did not make it easier for the disciples to understand and accept it. They had been taught their whole lives that the Messiah's kingdom would be political in nature. Therefore, Christ's words about dying made no sense to them at all. If you were reared in religious error but later came to understand the truth, you can appreciate their struggle.

Peter especially had problems with the Lord's announcement. After all, he had just confessed Jesus as the Christ, the Messiah. In his mind, he was also confessing that he had every confidence that Jesus would go ahead and set up His kingdom—a *physical* kingdom. As far as the apostle was concerned, the idea of a dead Messiah could not be reconciled with the concept of a reigning Messiah. Christ had added that "after three days" He would "rise again," but those words were also meaningless to the apostles (see Mk. 9:10). He therefore took it upon himself to correct Christ.

Not wishing to embarrass the Master before the others, **Peter took Him aside and began to rebuke Him, saying, "God forbid it, Lord! This shall never happen to You"** (Mt. 16:22). Peter's arrogance on this occasion is almost incomprehensible— but there have ever been people who profess to follow the Lord yet think they know more than He knows.

Jesus' rebuke was the most severe He ever gave the outspoken apostle: **He turned and said to Peter, "Get behind Me, Satan! You are a stumbling block to Me . . ."** (Mt. 16:23). A short time before, He had called him "Peter," His dependable "rock." Now He called him "Satan," His demonic adversary. (The literal meaning of the word "Satan" is "adversary.") Christ was saying that, in trying to deter Him from His destiny, Peter had become the devil's tool.

Peter's problem was that He was looking at the cross with human eyes instead of from the divine viewpoint. Jesus told him, **". . . you are not setting your mind on God's interests, but man's"** (Mt. 16:23).

The mind of the Lord was burdened by His coming death (Mt. 26:38, 39). Adding to that burden was the failure of His disciples to comprehend the true nature of His kingdom and reign. They were thinking in terms of diadems (a crown worn by a ruler) instead of death, crowns instead of crosses, praise instead of persecution.

Jesus called all the disciples and said to them,

> **If anyone wishes to come after Me, he must deny himself, and take up his cross and follow Me. For whoever wishes to save his life will lose it; but whoever loses his life for My sake will find it. For what will it profit a man if he gains the whole world and forfeits his soul? Or what will a man give in exchange for his soul?** (Mt. 16:24–26; see also Mk. 8:34–37; Lk. 9:23–25).

He added, **"For whoever is ashamed of Me and My words in this adulterous and sinful generation, the Son of Man will also be ashamed of him when He comes in the glory of His Father with the holy angels"** (Mk. 8:38). These words have general application, but keep in mind that Peter had just been "ashamed" of the words that Jesus had spoken regarding His death.

In His reprimand, Christ had mentioned coming "in the glory of His Father with the holy angels." He now assured His listeners, **"For the Son of Man *is* going to come in the glory of His Father with His angels, and will then repay every man according to his deeds"** (Mt. 16:27; emphasis added). This was the first clear prediction of the Second Coming. The apostles' minds must have been reeling from all this new revelation.

The Lord concluded by assuring His disciples that the prediction of His death did not mean that He had abandoned His plans to establish His kingdom: **"Truly I say to you, there are some of those who are standing here who will not taste death until they see the kingdom of God after it has come with power"** (Mk. 9:1; see also Mt. 16:28; Lk. 9:27). Pay close attention to the phrase "with *power*." Before Christ ascended to His Father, He would tell the apostles that they would "receive *power*" when the Holy Spirit came upon them (Acts 1:8; emphasis added) and that they should stay in Jerusalem until they were "clothed with *power* from on high" (Lk. 24:49; emphasis added). Ten days after the Ascension, on the Jewish feast of Pentecost, the power of the Holy Spirit came upon them (Acts 2:1–4) and Jesus fulfilled His promise to build His church/kingdom. (Read

Acts 5:11; 8:1; Col. 1:13; Rev. 1:6, 9.)

Those who believe that Jesus has not yet established His kingdom (such as premillennialists) struggle with Mark 9:1. One popular "dodge" is to say that this refers to the Transfiguration. J. W. McGarvey wrote, "Those who refer this expression to the transfiguration certainly err, for no visible kingdom was established at that time."[16]

Did the apostles understand what Christ meant about the kingdom coming with power during their lifetime? No, they no more understood this teaching than they did His announcements about the establishment of the church and His second coming—but the seed had been planted.

Near Caesarea Philippi (on Mount Hermon?):
The Transfiguration (Mt. 17:1–13; Mk. 9:2–13; Lk. 9:28–36)

Matthew 17:1–13
[1]Six days later Jesus took with Him Peter and James and John his brother, and led them up on a high mountain by themselves. [2]And He was transfigured before them; and His face shone like the sun, and His garments became as white as light. [3]And behold, Moses and Elijah appeared to them, talking with Him. [4]Peter said to Jesus, "Lord, it is good for us to be here; if You wish, I will make three tabernacles here, one for You, and one for Moses, and one for Elijah." [5]While he was still speaking, a bright cloud overshadowed them, and behold, a voice out of the cloud said, "This is My beloved Son, with whom I am well-pleased; listen to Him!" [6]When the disciples heard this, they fell face down to the ground and were terrified. [7]And Jesus came to them and touched them and said, "Get up, and do not be afraid." [8]And lifting up their eyes, they saw no one except Jesus Himself alone.

[9]As they were coming down from the mountain, Jesus commanded them, saying, "Tell the vision to no one until the Son of Man has risen from the dead." [10]And His disciples asked Him, "Why then do the scribes say that Elijah must come first?"

[16]Ibid., 417.

¹¹And He answered and said, "Elijah is coming and will restore all things; ¹²but I say to you that Elijah already came, and they did not recognize him, but did to him whatever they wished. So also the Son of Man is going to suffer at their hands." ¹³Then the disciples understood that He had spoken to them about John the Baptist.

Mark 9:2–13
²Six days later, Jesus took with Him Peter and James and John, and brought them up on a high mountain by themselves. And He was transfigured before them; ³and His garments became radiant and exceedingly white, as no launderer on earth can whiten them. ⁴Elijah appeared to them along with Moses; and they were talking with Jesus. ⁵Peter said to Jesus, "Rabbi, it is good for us to be here; let us make three tabernacles, one for You, and one for Moses, and one for Elijah." ⁶For he did not know what to answer; for they became terrified. ⁷Then a cloud formed, overshadowing them, and a voice came out of the cloud, "This is My beloved Son, listen to Him!" ⁸All at once they looked around and saw no one with them anymore, except Jesus alone.

⁹As they were coming down from the mountain, He gave them orders not to relate to anyone what they had seen, until the Son of Man rose from the dead. ¹⁰They seized upon that statement, discussing with one another what rising from the dead meant. ¹¹They asked Him, saying, "Why is it that the scribes say that Elijah must come first?" ¹²And He said to them, "Elijah does first come and restore all things. And yet how is it written of the Son of Man that He will suffer many things and be treated with contempt? ¹³But I say to you that Elijah has indeed come, and they did to him whatever they wished, just as it is written of him."

Luke 9:28–36
²⁸Some eight days after these sayings, He took along Peter and John and James, and went up on the mountain to pray. ²⁹And while He was praying, the appearance of His face became different, and His clothing became white and gleaming. ³⁰And

behold, two men were talking with Him; and they were Moses and Elijah, [31]who, appearing in glory, were speaking of His departure which He was about to accomplish at Jerusalem. [32]Now Peter and his companions had been overcome with sleep; but when they were fully awake, they saw His glory and the two men standing with Him. [33]And as these were leaving Him, Peter said to Jesus, "Master, it is good for us to be here; let us make three tabernacles: one for You, and one for Moses, and one for Elijah"—not realizing what he was saying. [34]While he was saying this, a cloud formed and began to overshadow them; and they were afraid as they entered the cloud. [35]Then a voice came out of the cloud, saying, "This is My Son, My Chosen One; listen to Him!" [36]And when the voice had spoken, Jesus was found alone. And they kept silent, and reported to no one in those days any of the things which they had seen.

The Gospel Accounts do not tell us what transpired over the next few days. We can only imagine the growing tension as the disciples struggled to reconcile Jesus' words with what they had been taught up to this point in their lives. At the end of that time, the Lord was probably ready for another mountaintop experience, and He got one—literally.

Six days later Jesus took with Him Peter and James and John his brother, and led them up on a high mountain by themselves. And He was transfigured before them; and His face shone like the sun, and His garments became as white as light. And behold, Moses and Elijah appeared to them, talking with Him (Mt. 17:1–3).

Luke recorded the topic of discussion between Moses, Elijah, and Christ: They **were speaking of His departure which He was about to accomplish at Jerusalem** (Lk. 9:31). In place of "departure," read "death." The disciples struggled with the idea of the Messiah dying, but these Old Testament heroes understood how essential His death was for the faithful of all ages (Heb. 9:15).

Overwhelmed by the experience and not knowing what to

say (Mk. 9:6), Peter blurted out, **"Lord, it is good for us to be here; if You wish, I will make three tabernacles here, one for You, and one for Moses, and one for Elijah"** (Mt. 17:4). Even as he spoke, **a bright cloud overshadowed them, and behold, a voice out of the cloud said, "This is My beloved Son, with whom I am well-pleased; listen to Him!"** (Mt. 17:5). After the voice had spoken, **they looked around and saw no one with them anymore, except Jesus alone** (Mk. 9:8).

This vision was for the benefit of the disciples: It confirmed the confession that Peter had made and confirmed the Lord's prediction of His impending death in Jerusalem. It stressed to the apostles that they should "listen to Him," *regardless* of what He should tell them.

This unprecedented event was also for the benefit of Jesus. The Twelve did not understand the importance of His death, but Moses and Elijah did. Men may have rejected Him, but God had not. The Lord had spoken from heaven at Christ's baptism, putting His stamp of approval on His thirty years of preparation. Now He gave His endorsement of Jesus' personal ministry. Thus heaven prepared Jesus for His coming ordeal.

As they were coming down from the mountain, Jesus commanded them, saying, "Tell the vision to no one until the Son of Man has risen from the dead" (Mt. 17:9). In His announcement concerning His death, Christ had mentioned His resurrection (Mt. 16:21); now He used that event as a time reference. Once more, His disciples were baffled; they discussed **what rising from the dead meant** (Mk. 9:10). Since the Lord often spoke in parables (Mt. 13:35), they evidently thought He was using figurative language.

They did not ask Jesus to explain what He meant by "rising from the dead," but they did ask about something else that bothered them. They had just seen Elijah, but the prophet had showed up well into Christ's ministry, not at the beginning. They thus asked, **"Why . . . do the scribes say that Elijah must come** *first*?" (Mt. 17:10; emphasis added).

Christ had earlier emphasized that the prophecies regarding the coming of Elijah had been fulfilled in the ministry of John the Baptizer (Mt. 11:14; Lk. 1:17), but the appearance of Elijah himself on the mount had confused the apostles. Jesus again explained that Elijah had already come (Mt. 17:12). **Then the disciples understood that He had spoken to them about John the Baptist** (Mt. 17:13).

APPLICATION:
"WE SAW HIS GLORY"
(MT. 17:1–8; MK. 9:2–8; LK. 9:28–36)

Think of being one of the apostles who walked with Jesus for three years. Consider all of the marvelous sights you would have seen: the feeding of the five thousand, Jesus' walking on water, the stilling of the storm, the raising of the dead. Now ask yourself, "Of all that I saw, what would have impressed me most?" I do not know how you would answer that question, but I do know a certain event that made an indelible impression on the apostles privileged to witness it: the Transfiguration. One of those present later said,

> . . . we were eyewitnesses of His majesty. For when He received honor and glory from God the Father, such an utterance as this was made to Him by the Majestic Glory, "This is My beloved Son with whom I am well-pleased"— and we ourselves heard this utterance made from heaven when we were with Him on the holy mountain (2 Pet. 1:16–18).

Another who was there wrote,

> In the beginning was the Word, and the Word was with God, and the Word was God (Jn. 1:1).

> And the Word became flesh, and dwelt among us, and we saw His glory, glory as of the only begotten from the Father, full of grace and truth (Jn. 1:14).

The writer probably had in mind more than the Transfiguration (see Jn. 2:11), but that memorable event was surely included in the statement "we saw His glory" (see Lk. 9:31, 32).

As we focus on the Transfiguration,[17] our primary text will be Matthew 17; but we will go to Mark 9 and Luke 9 for supplementary details. May this study help each of us to "see His glory."

The Important Incident
(Mt. 17:1, 2; Mk. 9:2, 3; Lk. 9:28, 29)

Our text begins, "*Six days later* Jesus took with Him Peter and James and John his brother, and led them up on a high mountain by themselves" (Mt. 17:1; emphasis added). Mark also has "*six* days later" (Mk. 9:2), but Luke has "some *eight* days after these sayings" (Lk. 9:28). Matthew and Mark counted the days between the two incidents, while Luke included those two days. Today, in my part of the world, we would say "a week later." What had happened six or so days before?

Almost a week earlier, Peter had made the Good Confession and Christ had promised to build His church (Mt. 16:16, 18). He had then revealed that He must die to fulfill that promise. "Jesus began to show His disciples that He must go to Jerusalem, and suffer many things from the elders and chief priests and scribes, and be killed . . ." (Mt. 16:21). Instead of going to Jerusalem to set up an earthly kingdom—as His disciples had in mind—He would be going to Jerusalem to die.

The disciples did not understand Christ's words; the death of the Messiah did not fit into their concept of the kingdom. "Peter took [Jesus] aside and began to rebuke Him, saying, 'God forbid it, Lord! This shall never happen to You'" (Mt. 16:22). Christ chided Peter and then all the apostles (Mt. 16:23–27; see Mk. 8:38; Lk. 9:26).

Imagine the tension that probably existed between Jesus and His followers—for six long days. There is no record of anything that transpired during those days. Finally, after six days, Jesus took three of the apostles, including the outspoken Peter, "up on a high mountain."

---

[17]The primary source for this study was G. Campbell Morgan, *The Crises of the Christ* (New York: Fleming H. Revell Co., 1936), 215–67. Morgan included three chapters on the Transfiguration.

We are not told why Jesus took those three, but on several occasions He separated them from the other apostles (Mk. 5:37; 9:2; 14:33). Maybe He did so because He anticipated needs they would have in the future. For instance, Peter needed to mature in his leadership, and James needed to be prepared for martyrdom (Acts 12:2). Perhaps He did so because He thought that He could best reach the other nine through these three. It is even possible that, like us, Jesus in His humanity needed special friends. John, who was among the three, is known as "the disciple whom Jesus loved" (Jn. 21:20; see 13:23; 19:26; 20:2).

Neither are we told what mountain they climbed. Peter just called it "the holy mountain" (2 Pet. 1:18). An uninspired tradition says that it was Mount Tabor in Galilee, but more likely it was Mount Hermon, not far from the place where Peter had made the Good Confession. Mount Hermon is the highest mountain in Palestine; its "snow-capped peaks" rise "nearly ten thousand feet above the floor of the valley."[18]

Jesus' reason for going up on the mountain was not to be transfigured, but rather to commune with His Father. Luke wrote, "He took along Peter and John and James, and went up on the mountain to pray" (Lk. 9:28). He may have wanted to help the apostles to improve their prayer lives—but, as was often the case, they went to sleep during the prayer service (Lk. 9:32; see Mt. 26:40, 43, 45).

Then, suddenly, "while He was praying," "He was transfigured before them" (Lk. 9:29a; Mt. 17:2a). The Greek word μεταμορφόω (metamorphoo), translated "transfigured," is the word from which we get "metamorphosis," a word indicating radical change. Words cannot express the magnificence of the transformation. The writers of the Gospel Accounts tried to describe the effect by using comparative terms.

And He was transfigured before them; and His face shone like the sun, and His garments became as white as light (Mt. 17:2).

---

[18]Gordon Powell, *Difficult Sayings of Jesus* (N.p.: Fleming H. Revell Co., 1962), 63.

. . . and His garments became radiant and exceedingly white, as no launderer on earth can whiten them (Mk. 9:3).

And . . . the appearance of His face became different, and His clothing became white and gleaming (Lk. 9:29).

Here is a possible way to reflect on what occurred. Jesus was the God-Man (Mt. 1:23), but as He walked upon the earth, most people saw only His humanity. On this special occasion, however, His God-ness was allowed to shine through His man-ness. Peter, James, and John had a glimpse of His deity afforded to few.

The Impressive Intention
(Mt. 17:3–8; Mk. 9:4–8; Lk. 9:30–36)

As our study progresses, we want to ask, "What was the purpose of the Transfiguration?" Let me suggest four possible reasons that this unique incident occurred.

Humanity Crowned

From time to time in the life of Christ, dramatic events crowned the past and prepared the way for the future. His baptism was such an event. At that time, God announced His approval of Jesus' thirty years of preparation and the Holy Spirit came upon Christ to prepare Him for His three years of public ministry (Mt. 3:16, 17). The Transfiguration was another climatic moment. On that occasion, God placed His "stamp of approval" not only on Jesus' years of preparation, but also on His years of ministry (Mt. 17:5).

Christ was what God had desired for mankind to be when He placed man on the earth. People had sinned (Gen. 3:5; Rom. 3:23), but Jesus had not (Heb. 4:15). At the time of the Transfiguration, Christ could have gone back into the presence of a holy God exactly as He was—if there had been no other reason for His coming. Of course, there was another reason, one which leads to a second purpose for the Transfiguration.

"Exodus" Confirmed

Luke wrote, "Now Peter and his companions had been overcome with sleep; but when they were fully awake, they saw His glory . . ." (Lk. 9:32). The writer wanted us to understand that Peter, James, and John did not have a dream; they were wide awake when they were dazzled by Jesus' appearance.

They soon had more to amaze them: "And behold, two men were talking with Him [Christ]; and they were Moses and Elijah" (Lk. 9:30; the KJV has "Elias," the Greek form of the Hebrew "Elijah"). Moses and Elijah were two of the greatest heroes of the Jewish faith (Heb. 11:23–29; Jas. 5:17). Peter, James, and John would have heard stories about them on their fathers' knees. They would have heard their names extolled by the rabbis. Moses was the great lawgiver; Elijah called men back to the Law.

We are not told why these two were privileged to stand with the Lord on the Mount of Transfiguration. Perhaps it was because both were linked with the Messiah in Old Testament prophecy (Deut. 18:15; Mal. 4:5, 6). Many assume that the reason these two were chosen is that Moses represented the Law, while Elijah represented the Prophets—two of the great witnesses to Jesus' deity (Jn. 1:45; see Lk. 24:44). Other possible ties with the life of Jesus have been suggested: All three had significant mountaintop experiences; the ending of all three lives was unusual (concerning Moses, see Deut. 34:6; concerning Elijah, see 2 Kings 2:11).

Jesus, Moses, and Elijah had much in common; there were many topics they might have discussed. Moses had not been permitted to enter the Promised Land (Num. 20:12), and it had been centuries since Elijah had walked the grassy plains of Galilee; they probably would have enjoyed talking with Jesus about His travels through the land. All three had known the trials of leadership; they could have discussed how exhausting it is to try to communicate even the most basic truths. If such a conversation had taken place, it might have gone like this: "Jesus said, 'Let Me tell you about My slow-to-learn disciples.' Moses said, 'Let me tell you about the stubborn Israelites!' And Elijah said, 'That's nothing! Let me tell you about Ahab and Jezebel!'" Their conversation was not, however, about these or similar matters.

According to Luke, they were "speaking of His departure which He [Christ] was about to accomplish at Jerusalem" (Lk. 9:31). The Greek word translated "departure" (ἔξοδον, *exodon*) is the word from which we get "exodus." "Exodus" is a compound word, combining the Greek word for "road" or "way" (ὁδός, *odos*) with the preposition for "out" (ἐξ, *ek* or *ex*); it literally means "the way out." Think of "Exit" signs over doors. Think of the Exodus from Egypt, the children of Israel leaving that country to go to the Promised Land. In Luke 9 the word "exodus" encompasses the death, resurrection, and ascension of the Lord. It graphically speaks of Christ's departure from this life and ultimately from this world.

Why did the topic of Jesus' impending crucifixion occupy the minds of Moses and Elijah? Their reason might have been *professional*: Their years of labor had pointed forward to this event. The purpose of the Law given by Moses was to bring men to Christ (Gal. 3:16, 19, 24, 25). Elijah had been one of the prophets laboring to prepare a people through whom the Messiah could come. According to the prophets, when the Christ/Messiah came, He was to die for the people (Is. 53:4–6).

More likely, however, Moses and Elijah had a *personal* reason for their interest in Jesus' death. They could not go to heaven unless He died for their sins. The Old Testament speaks of people being forgiven, but it was a provisional forgiveness, anticipating the ultimate sacrifice of Christ.

An illustration sometimes used is that of the Good Samaritan who gave the innkeeper money and said, "Take care of [the wounded man]; and whatever more you spend, when I return I will repay you" (Lk. 10:35). When the wounded man recovered and was ready to leave, if he had asked about the debt, the innkeeper would have said something like "Don't worry about it. It's taken care of." The debt, however, had only been settled *in anticipation of* the Samaritan's return to finish paying it.

The writer of the Book of Hebrews said that Jesus "is the mediator of a new covenant [the New Testament], so that, since *a death has taken place for the redemption of the transgressions that were committed under the first covenant [the Old Testament]*, those who have been called may receive the promise of the eternal inheritance" (Heb. 9:15; emphasis added). Pioneer preachers liked to say that "the blood of Jesus flowed both backward and forward."

Moses and Elijah thus had a vested interest in Christ's death. We noted that Jesus could have returned to heaven exactly as He was—but, had He done so, He would have been the only One in heaven who had inhabited human flesh. He had to die before Moses could go to heaven. He had to die before Elijah could go to heaven. This discussion was therefore of the utmost interest to the two Old Testament worthies.

The exchange was also important to the Lord. His disciples had tried to discourage Him from going to the cross (Mt. 16:22). Moses and Elijah no doubt encouraged Him to let nothing deter Him from carrying through with God's plan for man's salvation. Thus the Transfiguration not only crowned the past, but it also helped to prepare Jesus for the future—for the Crucifixion.

Authority Defined

In addition to those two primary purposes for the Transfiguration, other reasons should be mentioned. A third reason is that the authority of Christ was defined on that occasion.

The disciples were alarmed by what they saw (Mk. 9:6)—but, fearful or not, Peter could always be counted on to say *something*. He spoke up: "Lord, it is good for us to be here; if You wish, I will make three tabernacles here, one for You, and one for Moses, and one for Elijah" (Mt. 17:4). Mark said that Peter "did not know what to answer" (Mk. 9:6), while Luke recorded that he did not realize "what he was saying" (Lk. 9:33). Peter did not know what to say; and, after he said it, he did not know what he had said.

Peter did not know what he was saying when he specified the locale: "Lord, it is good for us to be *here*; . . . I will make three tabernacles *here*." In effect, the apostle was saying to Jesus, "This is exactly how I envisioned You as the Messiah! So forget about going to Jerusalem, where death awaits. Let's stay *here* on the mountain, where glory surrounds You." He did not understand that if Christ had stayed there, He would not have died for our sins (1 Cor. 15:3) and we all would be lost (Heb. 9:22b).

Further, Peter did not know what he was saying when he proposed building crude shelters: "I will make *three tabernacles* . . . , one for You, and one for Moses, and one for Elijah." Since the time for the Feast of Tabernacles was not far away (Jn. 7:2), some writers think that Peter was proposing that they celebrate that feast on the mountainside rather than in Jerusalem. J. W. McGarvey suggested that Peter could not let Moses and Elijah "depart without an effort to detain them, though the best inducement that he could offer was to build three booths, or arbors, made of the branches of trees, for their and Christ's accommodation."[19] Consider how pointless this was. What possible use would spirit beings have for brush arbors?

Especially, Peter did not know what he was saying when he put Moses and Elijah on a par with the Lord: "I will make three tabernacles …, *one for You, and one for Moses, and one for Elijah*." Many today are making the same mistake. In their minds, Jesus is just one among many great spiritual teachers and leaders. They would be more than happy to build multiple tabernacles honoring Jesus, Mohammed, Buddha, and so on. They need to hear God's response to Peter's suggestion: "While he was still speaking, a bright cloud overshadowed them, and behold, a voice out of the cloud said, 'This is My beloved Son, with whom I am well-pleased; listen to Him!'" (Mt. 17:5).

God's words were a divine identification: "This is My beloved Son." They indicated divine approval: "with whom I am well-pleased." They contained a divine injunction: "listen to *Him*!" In other words, "Don't listen to Moses; don't give heed to Elijah; just hear *Jesus*!" Today, we could add, "Don't hear anyone else who claims to be God's special spokesman!"

Apostles Prepared

Fourth, God's words in Matthew 17:5 should have held special significance for the apostles. They had been resisting Christ's prediction of His impending death (Mt. 16:21, 22). In context, God's words to Peter signified, "Listen to Jesus even when you don't understand, even if you disagree. *He* knows best." The way that "*seems* right" to us may in reality be "the way of death" (Proverbs 14:12; 16:25; emphasis added). Our wisdom is always limited; we need to learn to rely on the "wisdom of God" (Eph. 3:10).

---

[19]McGarvey and Pendleton, 419.

When the Voice came from the cloud, the disciples "fell face down to the ground and were terrified" (Mt. 17:6). Jesus came to them, tenderly touched them, and said "Get up, and do not be afraid" (Mt. 17:7). When they lifted up their eyes, "they saw no one except Jesus Himself alone" (Mt. 17:8).

The apostles did not understand all the implications of what had occurred, but they had seen the deity of Jesus. They had heard Moses and Elijah confirm the fact that Jesus had to die in Jerusalem. The Holy Spirit would later bring all things to their remembrance (Jn. 14:26); then all the pieces of the puzzle would fit together. In the meantime, at least they were somewhat better prepared for what was to come.

Conclusion

Would it not have been exciting to see the glorified Lord on that mountain? We will never have that experience; but, if we are faithful to Him, we *will* someday see Him in His glory. "We know that when He appears, . . . we will see Him just as He is" (1 Jn. 3:2). We can even see Moses and Elijah someday—in heaven.

Healing a Demon-possessed Boy
(Mt. 17:14–21; Mk. 9:14–29; Lk. 9:37–43)

When Christ reached the foot of the mountain, He immediately found Himself in another emotional valley—triggered by the inability of His disciples to heal a demon-possessed young man (Mt. 17:14–16).

During the final days of His earthly ministry, Jesus focused on preparing His apostles for His departure. As He traveled, "He did not want anyone to know about it. For He was teaching His disciples . . ." (Mk. 9:30b, 31). The LB paraphrase says, "He tried to avoid all publicity, so that He could spend time with His disciples, teaching them." A recurring theme in this teaching might be expressed as "What it means to be My disciple."

Matthew 17:14–21

¹⁴When they came to the crowd, a man came up to Jesus, falling on his knees before Him and saying, ¹⁵"Lord, have mercy on my son, for he is a lunatic and is very ill; for he

often falls into the fire and often into the water. ¹⁶I brought him to Your disciples, and they could not cure him." ¹⁷And Jesus answered and said, "You unbelieving and perverted generation, how long shall I be with you? How long shall I put up with you? Bring him here to Me." ¹⁸And Jesus rebuked him, and the demon came out of him, and the boy was cured at once.

¹⁹Then the disciples came to Jesus privately and said, "Why could we not drive it out?" ²⁰And He said to them, "Because of the littleness of your faith; for truly I say to you, if you have faith the size of a mustard seed, you will say to this mountain, 'Move from here to there,' and it will move; and nothing will be impossible to you. ²¹[But this kind does not go out except by prayer and fasting."]

Mark 9:14–29

¹⁴When they came back to the disciples, they saw a large crowd around them, and some scribes arguing with them. ¹⁵Immediately, when the entire crowd saw Him, they were amazed and began running up to greet Him. ¹⁶And He asked them, "What are you discussing with them?" ¹⁷And one of the crowd answered Him, "Teacher, I brought You my son, possessed with a spirit which makes him mute; ¹⁸and whenever it seizes him, it slams him to the ground and he foams at the mouth, and grinds his teeth and stiffens out. I told Your disciples to cast it out, and they could not do it." ¹⁹And He answered them and said, "O unbelieving generation, how long shall I be with you? How long shall I put up with you? Bring him to Me!" ²⁰They brought the boy to Him. When he saw Him, immediately the spirit threw him into a convulsion, and falling to the ground, he began rolling around and foaming at the mouth. ²¹And He asked his father, "How long has this been happening to him?" And he said, "From childhood. ²²It has often thrown him both into the fire and into the water to destroy him. But if You can do anything, take pity on us and help us!" ²³And Jesus said to him, "'If You can?' All things are possible to him who believes." ²⁴Immediately the boy's father cried out and said, "I do believe; help my unbelief." ²⁵When Jesus saw that

a crowd was rapidly gathering, He rebuked the unclean spirit, saying to it, "You deaf and mute spirit, I command you, come out of him and do not enter him again." [26]After crying out and throwing him into terrible convulsions, it came out; and the boy became so much like a corpse that most of them said, "He is dead!" [27]But Jesus took him by the hand and raised him; and he got up. [28]When He came into the house, His disciples began questioning Him privately, "Why could we not drive it out?" [29]And He said to them, "This kind cannot come out by anything but prayer."

Luke 9:37–43

[37]On the next day, when they came down from the mountain, a large crowd met Him. [38]And a man from the crowd shouted, saying, "Teacher, I beg You to look at my son, for he is my only boy, [39]and a spirit seizes him, and he suddenly screams, and it throws him into a convulsion with foaming at the mouth; and only with difficulty does it leave him, mauling him as it leaves. [40]I begged Your disciples to cast it out, and they could not." [41]And Jesus answered and said, "You unbelieving and perverted generation, how long shall I be with you and put up with you? Bring your son here." [42]While he was still approaching, the demon slammed him to the ground and threw him into a convulsion. But Jesus rebuked the unclean spirit, and healed the boy and gave him back to his father. [43]And they were all amazed at the greatness of God.

But while everyone was marveling at all that He was doing, He said to His disciples.

Jesus, Peter, James, and John descended from "the holy mountain" (2 Pet. 1:18), where the Lord had been transfigured. When Moses came down from the mountain after receiving the Ten Commandments, he was greeted by the turmoil of disobedience (Ex. 32); when Christ came down from the mountain after being transfigured, He was greeted by the chaos of unbelief.

A man had brought his demon-possessed son to be healed by Jesus, but the Lord's disciples had been unable to cast out the demon. The ever-present and ever-critical scribes were taking advantage of the situation to malign Christ's ministry. The weakness of faith in all present (the scribes, the multitude, the father of the boy, even Jesus' disciples) broke Christ's heart (Mt. 17:17; Mk. 9:19; Lk. 9:41). Still, He showed Himself faithful in spite of their faithlessness, and He healed the lad (Mt. 17:18; Mk. 9:25, 26; Lk. 9:41; see 2 Tim. 2:13).

Later, when the Lord and His apostles were alone, they asked Him, **"Why could we not drive** [the demon] **out?"** (Mt. 17:19; Mk. 9:28). He answered, **"Because of the littleness of your faith; for truly I say to you, if you have faith the size of a mustard seed, you will say to this mountain, 'Move from here to there,' and it will move; and nothing will be impossible to you"** (Mt. 17:20). Mark's account adds, **"This kind cannot come out by anything but prayer"** (Mk. 9:29). Like the father in the story (Mk. 9:24), the disciples believed—yet they did not truly believe (Mt. 17:20). Like us, they struggled with their faith.

Many writers believe that the apostles had been unable to cast out the demon because they were trusting in their *own* exorcising abilities. Paul wrote that "we would not trust in ourselves, but in God" (2 Cor. 1:9). Long ago, David said, "Offer the sacrifices of righteousness, and *trust in the Lord*" (Ps. 4:5; emphasis added). The Wise Man echoed that sentiment: "Trust in the Lord with all your heart and do not lean on your own understanding" (Prov. 3:5).

A true disciple acknowledges his own shortcomings (Rom. 3:10). He trusts in the Lord for his strength (see 2 Sam. 22:31; Ps. 9:10; 37:3, 5; 40:3, 4; 115:10, 11; Is. 26:4; Phil. 2:24).

APPLICATION:
"HELP MY UNBELIEF"
(MT. 17:14–20; MK. 9:14–29; LK. 9:37–43)

Many in the Bible struggled in their walk with God. We may identify personally with some of them. Elijah became discouraged (1 Kings 19:10). Jeremiah wept and felt that his work had been fruitless (Jer. 9:1; 13:17). Peter often spoke before he thought (Lk. 9:33). We can share in the plea of the father who said to Jesus, "I . . . believe; help my unbelief" (Mk. 9:24). When the man asked the Lord to heal his son, Christ replied, "All things are possible to him who believes" (Mk. 9:23). That is when the man cried out, "I do believe; help my unbelief."

No topic is more central to Christianity than faith—and no need is more crucial than the strengthening of faith. Paul wrote,

> For I am not ashamed of the gospel, for it is the power of God for salvation to everyone who believes, to the Jew first and also to the Greek. For in it the righteousness of God is revealed *from faith to faith*; as it is written, "But the righteous man shall live by faith" (Rom. 1:16, 17; emphasis added).

The NIV has "a righteousness that is by faith from *first to last*." (Emphasis added.) The NCV says that God's righteousness "begins and ends with faith."

"Without faith it is impossible to please [God]" (Heb. 11:6a). "By grace" we are "saved through faith" (Eph. 2:8a). We walk the Christian pathway "by faith, not by sight" (2 Cor. 5:7). Faith is the shield that protects us from the devil (Eph. 6:16). Faith "is the victory that has overcome the world" (1 Jn. 5:4b). The ultimate "outcome" of faith will be "the salvation" of our souls (1 Pet. 1:9).

As we consider the importance of faith, we, too, may be tempted to cry, "We believe; help our unbelief!" In our study concerning the man who first made that request, we will consider factors that weaken faith. Above all, we want to learn how faith can be strengthened.

A Test of Faith (Mt. 17:14–18; Mk. 9:14–27; Lk. 9:37–43)

At the beginning of the story, Jesus, Peter, James, and John had just come down from the Mount of Transfiguration, from the mountaintop of peace to the valley of conflict. That is life, and that is how God has willed it. Like Peter, we may prefer to dwell on the mountaintop with the Lord (Mt. 17:4), but life must be lived where the people—and the problems—are.

When Christ and His small band reached the place where they

had left the other nine apostles, "they saw . . . some scribes arguing with them" (Mk. 9:14). The scribes were probably challenging Jesus' credentials and the legitimacy of His ministry. Watching the debate was a curious crowd, the kind of morbid sightseers that today flock to car crashes and other disasters.

Mark 9:15 says that "when the entire crowd saw Him [Jesus], they were amazed." We should probably not think that they were amazed because something about Christ's person revealed that He had been transfigured (such as Moses' face shining when he came down from the mount). What happened on the Mountain of Transfiguration was to remain a secret for the moment (Mk. 9:9). The people may have been amazed because they had not expected Jesus back so soon.

A Feeble Boy

Jesus asked what the problem was (Mk. 9:16). He knew the situation, but He desired to turn the attention from His humiliated disciples onto Himself. A man stepped from the crowd. Falling at Christ's feet, he cried, "Lord, have mercy on my son" (Mt. 17:15a).

The man's son—his only son (Lk. 9:38)—was terribly afflicted. The lad was unable to hear or speak (Mk. 9:17, 25). He was demon-possessed (Mt. 17:18; Lk. 9:39, 42). The demon would throw him to the ground, where he would lie writhing, grinding his teeth, and foaming at the mouth (Mk. 9:18; Lk. 9:39). Because of the demon, he would fall into fire or water (Mt. 17:15; Mk. 9:22). Most houses had fires in the middle of the floor, and most streams did not have bridges. It would have been simple for the demon to cast the young man into fires and water. The father said that the demon's intention was to destroy his son (Mk. 9:22). More likely, the evil spirit's purpose was to torture the boy. Demons apparently needed to inhabit a living host.

The father called his son "moonstruck" (Mt. 17:15; original text) because of an ancient superstition that, in some way, seizures were caused by the moon. A literal translation would be "lunatic" (see the KJV and the NASB) which comes from *luna*, the Latin word for "moon." Because the word "lunatic" is now used to refer to someone who is crazy, some translations have substituted the word "epileptic" (see the RSV and the ASV). Translators probably did this because many of the symptoms resemble that of a grand mal epileptic seizure. Understand, however, that the symptoms did not result from the "abnormal electrical activity in the brain" responsible for epileptic seizures,[20] but from demon possession (Mt. 17:18; Mk. 9:25; Lk. 9:42). A superstitious crowd may have misunderstood the exact nature of the boy's affliction, but inspired men said that the boy had a demon. That settles the question for all who believe in inspiration.

A Frustrated Teacher

The Lord was disturbed by the scene before Him: the bothersome crowd, the belligerent scribes, the baffled disciples, and the bewildered father. We are given a rare glimpse at the human side of Jesus as He exclaimed, "You unbelieving and perverted generation, how long shall I be with you? How long shall I put up with you?" (Mt. 17:17a; see Num. 14:27; Deut. 32:5, 20; Ps. 95:10). When we hear Him ask, "How long shall I be with you?" we share the burden of His flesh and His longing to return to God. When we hear Him ask, "How long shall I put up with you?" we feel His frustration at trying to communicate with flesh-bound and prejudice-blinded humanity.

Some identify the "unbelieving and perverted generation" as one segment of the group addressed by Christ. I see no reason to leave out any of those present: the scribes with no faith, the multitude with ambivalent faith, His disciples with faltering faith, and the father whose faith had been shaken. All were typical of *that* "unbelieving . . . generation," and they are typical of the world in which we live. The only one present who believed in Christ without question was the demon, but we are not talking about him yet.

Jesus responded to the father's request, not "according to the poverty of . . . man's faith, but according to the riches of His

---

[20]Charles B. Clayman, medical ed., *The American Medical Association Home Medical Encyclopedia*, vol. 1, s.v. "Epilepsy."

grace"[21] (see Eph. 1:7). He said to the father, "Bring your son here" (Lk. 9:41b; see also Mt. 17:17b; Mk. 9:19b).

A Faltering Father

While they were bringing the boy to Jesus, the demon threw the lad into a convulsion. The young man "began rolling around and foaming at the mouth" (Mk. 9:20). The Lord asked the father about the boy's condition (Mk. 9:21)—not because He needed to know, but because the father needed to understand his hopelessness without Christ. The father's answer concluded with the words "But if You can do anything, take pity on us and help us!" (Mk. 9:22b).

Surely, Christ's eyes flashed as He echoed the man's words: "If You can?" (Mk. 9:23a; 1977 NASB). The father had evidently come with faith, expecting the Lord to heal his son. However, the failure of the disciples, followed by the attack of the scribes, had diluted his faith. His request was now tainted by doubt: *"If You can. . . ."*

Jesus told him, "All things are possible to him who believes" (Mk. 9:23b). Two observations should be made about this forceful statement. On the one hand, most understand that this statement requires some qualification. It would be ridiculous to assert that men of faith have unlimited, unconditional powers. On the other hand, we should not minimize what a man of faith can accomplish. William Barclay wrote, "To approach anything in the spirit of hopelessness is to make it hopeless; to approach anything in the spirit of faith is to make it a possibility."[22] He suggested the need for "a sense of the possible."[23]

After Christ said, "All things are possible to him who believes," "immediately the boy's father cried out and said, 'I

[21]R. Alan Cole, *The Gospel According to Mark,* rev. ed., Tyndale New Testament Commentaries (Grand Rapids, Mich.: Wm. B. Eerdmans Publishing Co.), 216.

[22]William Barclay, *The Gospel of Mark,* rev. ed., The Daily Study Bible Series (Philadelphia: Westminster Press, 1975), 218.

[23]Ibid. Barclay quoted the Italian political leader Camillo Benso di Cavour (1810–61), who said that statesmen need that sense.

do believe; help my unbelief'" (Mk. 9:23b, 24). Implied in these words is a fervent request: "It is true that my faith is not what it should be, but do not penalize my son for that. Please, please help him!"

A Faith-Inspiring Demonstration

Jesus turned to the boy and "rebuked the unclean spirit, saying to it, 'You deaf and mute spirit, I command you, come out of him and do not enter him again'" (Mk. 9:25). This verse says that Jesus did this "when [He] saw that a crowd was rapidly gathering." This might indicate that He had taken the man and the boy to one side to avoid undue publicity. Some think the opposite: that Christ did the miracle to instill faith in the gathering multitude.

The demon did not leave quietly. He cried out and threw the young man "into terrible convulsions" (Mk. 9:26a). R. Alan Cole called this display "the impotent rage of [a] defeated enemy."[24] Finally, reluctantly, the demon "came out" (Mk. 9:26b). The added command "do not enter him again" must have been a comfort to the father. The tragedy would not be repeated.

The boy, abused and exhausted, lay motionless upon the earth. He looked "so much like a corpse that most of them said, 'He is dead!'" (Mk. 9:26c). "But Jesus took him by the hand and raised him; and he got up" (Mk. 9:27). Then came the poignant moment when Christ "gave him back to his father" (Lk. 9:42; compare with Lk. 7:15). Men had failed, but Jesus had not. Of this moment, Burton Coffman wrote,

> Here is a prophecy of all time to eternity. Generations may rise and reject the Lord; unbelievers may wax bold and arrogant; and even the Lord's disciples may, through their own neglect of spiritual things, find themselves powerless to cope with life's problems; nevertheless Christ and his holy faith are always successful. "The gates of Hades" shall not prevail. . . .[25]

---

[24]Cole, 216.
[25]James Burton Coffman, *Commentary on Luke* (Austin, Tex.: Firm Foundation Publishing House, 1975), 186.

Once more Christ had glorified His Father. The people marveled and "were all amazed at the greatness of God" (Lk. 9:43).

The Power of Faith (Mt. 17:19–21; Mk. 9:28, 29)

When Jesus and His disciples were alone, they asked Him, "Why could we not drive [the demon] out?" (Mt. 17:19; see Mk. 9:28). They had to be genuinely puzzled. Christ had given them "authority over unclean spirits, to cast them out," and had specifically instructed them to "cast out demons" (Mt. 10:1, 8; see Mk. 6:7). This they had done; Mark recorded that "they were casting out many demons" (Mk. 6:13a). When therefore the distraught father showed up, they had probably expected no problems. Perhaps they spoke confidently as they said, "Jesus is not here right now, but don't worry; we'll take care of it! Just bring us your son!" No doubt they grew embarrassed as they tried again and again to cast out the demon without success.

A Lack of Faith

Jesus explained why their efforts had been ineffective: "Because of the littleness of your faith" (Mt. 17:20a). The apostles had some faith, or they would not have attempted to heal the boy; but in some way their faith was lacking. The Lord continued, "For truly I say to you, if you have faith the size of a mustard seed, you will say to this mountain, 'Move from here to there,' and it will move; and nothing will be impossible to you" (Mt. 17:20b). Jesus had just come down from a mountain, and He probably pointed to it as He said "*this* mountain." (The KJV adds verse 21, which is not found in most of the older manuscripts: "Howbeit this kind goeth not out but by prayer and fasting." The NASB includes the verse in brackets.)

Christ's mountain illustration has fascinated and puzzled many. He would later use the same illustration to stress the importance of praying with faith (Mt. 21:21, 22; Mk. 11:22–24). Paul used a similar figure of speech in 1 Corinthians 13:2. I am reminded of the old woman who had to climb over a hill to get to the well where she drew her water. After reading these passages, she prayed, "God, I do believe! So please remove that hill!"

When she looked up from her prayer, she exclaimed, "Just as I expected! It's still there!" To state the obvious, her prayer was hardly a prayer of faith.

We probably do the passage an injustice, however, if we think in terms of literal, physical outcroppings from the earth. There is no indication that Jesus and His disciples ever attempted to move a physical mountain. There would be little purpose for such a miracle in the Lord's spiritual agenda.

Mountains were commonly used as figures of speech in Christ's day. A mountain was probably the largest object with which the people were familiar. We use similar symbolism when we speak of being "buried under a mountain of work" or "making mountains out of molehills."

Among the Jews, "removing a mountain" was a familiar figure for overcoming obstacles (see Is. 40:4; 49:11; 54:10). The rabbis used the phrase to refer to removing barriers that seemed insurmountable.[26] It is almost certainly used in that sense in Matthew 17. Disposing of mountains of dirt and rock is child's play compared with dispensing some of the "mountains" that life puts in our pathway. Give me enough earth-moving equipment, a crew to use the equipment, and no deadline, and I can move almost any physical mountain. I do not, however, have that same self-confidence regarding the multiplied mountains of difficulty on humanity's landscape.

The apostles would later face overwhelming mountains of pain and persecution (see Mt. 5:11; Acts 8:1, 3). They did not need assurance that they could get rid of stony masses thrusting from the earth. They *did* need to know that, with the Lord's help, they would be able to overcome Satan-motivated and man-made mountains built up to discourage them.

Christ was assuring His followers that they could be victorious over any difficulty *if*—if they had faith the size of a mustard seed. The mustard seed, one of the smallest of seeds, was frequently used by Jesus as a symbol of that which is exceedingly tiny (Mt. 13:31; Lk. 13:19; 17:5, 6). The contrast Matthew 17:20 was between one of the smallest things familiar

---

[26]A discussion of the phrase appears in Barclay, 167.

to His listeners (a mustard seed) and one of the largest (a mountain). Thus the Lord emphasized the remarkable power of faith.

However, Christ did not simply have size in mind when He used the mustard seed as an illustration. Though the NASB has "faith the size of a mustard seed," the word "size" is not in the original text. The Greek text has "faith *as* a mustard seed" (see the KJV; emphasis added). This seed has several qualities that relate to the faith we ought to have. For instance,

- The mustard seed is small but real.
- The mustard seed is small but alive, as our faith should be alive (see Jas. 2:26).
- The mustard seed is small, but it has great potential (see Lk. 13:19).
- The mustard seed is small and weak, but it willingly accepts the strength of the soil that surrounds it.

The fourth quality is the most crucial. The *size* of our faith is not nearly as important as the *focus* of our faith. Paul said, "I can do all things . . ." (Phil. 4:13a). That sounds much like "All things are possible to him who believes" (Mk. 9:23b). Pay attention, however, to the end of Paul's statement: "I can do all things *through Him who strengthens me*" (Phil. 4:13; emphasis added). It is not our faith that gives us strength as much as it is the One in whom we believe. Imagine that you are walking down the road and come to a bridge spanning a raging river. You will not cross that bridge unless you *believe* it will support you. However, as you walk across it, is it your faith in the bridge that supports you or the bridge itself? Let us not be as concerned about the size of our faith as we are about what (or whom) we believe in.

Jesus' statement that "all things are possible to him who believes" must be considered alongside His later declaration that "*with God* all things are possible" (Mt. 19:26; emphasis added). There is no power apart from the Source of power. Paul wrote, "I know whom I have believed and I am convinced that *He* is able . . ." (2 Tim. 1:12; emphasis added). Hugo McCord translated the first part of that verse, "I know *him* whom I have trusted...."[27]

A Lapse in Prayer

Keep all of this in mind as we consider Jesus' answer to the apostles, as recorded by Mark. When the disciples asked why they could not cast out the demon, the Lord replied, "This kind cannot come out by anything but prayer" (Mk. 9:29; the KJV adds "and fasting"). Some writers think that the phrase "this kind" indicates that some demons were stronger than others. One thing is for sure: The demon that possessed the boy did not leave as docilely as the ones in passages we have previously studied.

If we isolated Mark 9:29, it would leave the impression that the apostles could not cast out the evil spirit because they had failed to pray when they tried to do so. However, *Jesus* did not utter a prayer before He exorcised the demon. He *had* spent a night in communion with God on the mountain (see Lk. 9:28) before He commanded the spirit to leave the boy.

More likely, the reference to prayer indicates that the disciples had neglected their prayer lives in general. Prayer is not saying "magic words" that make wondrous things happen; prayer is an acknowledgment of our dependence on the Creator of the universe. Many writers are convinced that the reason the apostles failed is that their faith had shifted from God to their own ability to cast out demons. John Franklin Carter suggested that they were "overly self-confident rather than consciously God-confident."[28] Like Samson, they had gone out to battle, not knowing that their power had departed (Judg. 16:20).

This can easily happen to each of us. God gives us gifts and blesses our efforts, and it is not long until we come to believe

---

[27]Hugo McCord, *McCord's New Testament Translation of the Everlasting Gospel* (Henderson, Tenn.: Freed-Hardeman University, 1988), 207. (Emphasis added.)

[28]John Franklin Carter, *A Layman's Harmony of the Gospels* (Nashville: Broadman Press, 1961), 176.

in *our* power to reason, *our* wisdom to make decisions, and *our* ability to perform. When that happens, spiritual disaster is not far away.

If a fire is to keep blazing, it must be constantly fed. If a battery is to continue to supply power, it must be repeatedly recharged. If one's spiritual life is to remain strong, he must regularly renew his relationship with the Lord. James said, "Draw near to God and He will draw near to you" (Jas. 4:8a). The prophet Isaiah wrote that "those who wait for the Lord will gain new strength; they will mount up with wings like eagles, they will run and not get tired, they will walk and not become weary" (Is. 40:31).

The Source of Faith

Having surveyed the story, let us take a few moments for personal application.[29]

Sources of Doubt

The first thing that stands out in this story is that several involved in the situation struggled with their faith, including the father and the apostles. People struggle with their faith today. Some reasons why can be found in our texts.

The problem of evil. Probably the number one reason that people doubt is that they have seen bad things happen to good people. In this incident, we find no indication that the boy had done anything to deserve his terrible affliction. There is no quick answer to the question of why bad things happen to good people, but two aspects of our story are worth noting: In the end, everything turned out all right, and Jesus used the occasion to glorify His Father (Lk. 9:43).

The impotence of disciples. The apostles failed where they should have succeeded. People sometimes become disillusioned by the shortcomings of Christians and let this influence their faith in God. They need to understand that our trust should not be in

---

[29]Some of the material in this last section is based on Rick Atchley, "Down in the Valley," sermon preached at the Southern Hills church of Christ, Abilene, Texas, 11 September 1988.

men, who invariably disappoint us, but in Him who never forsakes those who seek Him (Ps. 9:10).

The attacks of the world. The father's faith was weakened not only by the disciples' failure, but also by the scribes' assault. For every pulpit that proclaims faith, Satan has a thousand ways to express doubt—and this adversely affects the masses. We must learn to shut our ears to messengers of skepticism and open them to evangelists of certainty.

The reality of self. Jesus' rebuke of the father forced self-examination, causing him to admit the weakness of his belief. If we are honest with ourselves, we will acknowledge that we are not what we should be. This reality hinders some of us more than do all the other factors put together. Discouragement can lead to despair, which can produce doubt. We have stressed that Jesus did not respond to the father according to the poverty of his faith, but according to the riches of His grace. Let us hold on to that truth when we are discouraged.

These and other factors take their toll on the faith of many. Maybe they have even affected us. Writer John Westerhoff described four styles of faith, which we might think of as levels of faith: (1) *Experienced faith* is the faith of children, faith they experience from their parents and others. (2) *Affiliated faith* is the faith of older children and many adults, the measure of faith that comes from affiliating with those who have faith. (3) *Searching faith* is faith asking questions, faith struggling to become a personal faith. (4) *Owned faith* is personal faith, faith that has developed successfully beyond level three. It has been suggested that 70 percent of individuals never pass level two. It has been further suggested that if a person does not progress beyond level two, at some point in that individual's life, something will happen to shake his faith and make him abandon his relationship with the Lord.[30]

Whether or not you concur with these conclusions, we can agree that faith must grow—and that many of us still have far

---

[30]John H. Westerhoff III, *Will Our Children Have Faith?* (New York: Harper-Collins Publishers, 1976), 89–99. His terms have been borrowed, but not his point of view.

to go. The words of the father still haunt us: "I believe; help my unbelief."

Sources of Faith

How can "unbelief" be helped? What will cause our faith to grow? The starting point is to acknowledge our need as the father did, but where do we go from there? Using our texts, let us search for sources of faith.

Learning. One reason Jesus cast out the demon was to counteract the unbelief that He faced. When the lad was made whole, the people "were all amazed at the greatness of God" (Lk. 9:43a). Christ is not walking among us today, performing miracles, but we still have the inspired record of His amazing deeds. John wrote,

> Therefore many other signs Jesus also performed in the presence of the disciples, which are not written in this book; but these have been *written so that you may believe* that Jesus is the Christ, the Son of God; and that believing you may have life in His name (Jn. 20:30, 31; emphasis added).

The definitive answer on how to build faith is "Study the Word, especially the word about Jesus." The night before His death, Christ prayed for the apostles and "for those also who believe in Me *through their word*" (Jn. 17:20; emphasis added). Paul wrote, "So faith comes from hearing, and hearing by the word of Christ" (Rom. 10:17). The phrase "word of Christ" can mean "message *about* Christ." The NCV has "tells them *about* Christ" (emphasis added). If we want our faith to grow, we should read and study God's Word daily (see Acts 17:11; 2 Tim. 2:15; KJV).

Living. It is insufficient, however, to have a head full of knowledge. If faith is to be real and alive, it must be active. James taught that faith is perfected through works (Jas. 2:22). He wrote that "faith without works is useless" (Jas. 2:20) and that "just as the body without the spirit is dead, so also faith without works is dead" (Jas. 2:26).

Beware of using a weak faith as an excuse to do nothing.

Though we are "unworthy" servants (Lk. 17:10), we still need to serve (Mt. 20:26). Though "we do not know how to pray as we should" (Rom. 8:26), we still need to pray (1 Thess. 5:17). Even so, though our faith is limited, it must still act. Muscles grow through exercise, and so does our faith.

Someone has suggested that when we face a challenge, we should ask, "What would faith do in this situation?" and then *do* it. Begin each day affirming, "Today I will live as a believer!"

Leaving and leaning. Other suggestions could be given: We need to avoid that which destroys faith and cultivate that which encourages faith. This includes encouraging faith-building relationships (see 1 Cor. 15:33; 2 Tim. 1:5) and filling our minds with faith-building information (Phil. 4:8). Again, we need to do all we can to draw closer to God (Jas. 4:8) and learn to rely on Him (Ps. 37:5). This will involve strengthening our prayer lives (Eph. 1:18; Jude 20). Our texts suggest the relationship between faith and prayer (Mt. 17:20; Mk. 9:29). We need to learn the ancient art of meditating on the Scriptures: We need to spend time thinking about the Word (Ps. 1:2) and about what God has done (Ps. 143:5) for us and for others. The list could go on.

Conclusion

Sooner or later, all of us come down from the mountaintop of order into the valley of chaos. We cannot wait until our lives are out of control to develop a strong personal faith. The time to build faith is *now.* Our prayer for one another should be the same as Christ's for Peter: "that your faith may not fail" (Lk. 22:32).

Returning to Galilee (Jesus' Death Again Foretold)
(Mt. 17:22, 23; Mk. 9:30–32; Lk. 9:43–45)

Matthew 17:22, 23

²²And while they were gathering together in Galilee, Jesus said to them, "The Son of Man is going to be delivered into the hands of men; ²³and they will kill Him, and He will be raised on the third day." And they were deeply grieved.

561

Mark 9:30–32

[30]From there they went out and began to go through Galilee, and He did not want anyone to know about it. [31]For He was teaching His disciples and telling them, "The Son of Man is to be delivered into the hands of men, and they will kill Him; and when He has been killed, He will rise three days later." [32]But they did not understand this statement, and they were afraid to ask Him.

Luke 9:43–45

[43]And they were all amazed at the greatness of God.

But while everyone was marveling at all that He was doing, He said to His disciples, [44]"Let these words sink into your ears; for the Son of Man is going to be delivered into the hands of men." [45]But they did not understand this statement, and it was concealed from them so that they would not perceive it; and they were afraid to ask Him about this statement.

Jesus and the Twelve returned from "the district of Caesarea Philippi" (Mt. 16:13; see Mk. 8:27) to **Galilee** (Mt. 17:22; Mk. 9:30a). Precisely when they returned to Galilee is unclear. Most commentators believe that the Transfiguration and the healing of the demon-possessed boy took place near Caesarea Philippi, and that, *after* these events, Jesus returned to Galilee. Some think that Jesus and the Twelve had already traveled to Galilee before the Transfiguration and the healing took place. A few commentators think that the trip to Galilee took place *between* the Transfiguration and the healing.

Unlike His approach during previous tours of Galilee, this time Christ avoided crowds while they traveled in that province. **He did not want anyone to know about it. For He was teaching His disciples . . .** (Mk. 9:30b, 31).

One topic to which He constantly returned was that of His impending death: . . . He was teaching His disciples **and telling them, "The Son of Man is to be delivered into the hands of men, and they will kill Him; and when He has been killed, He will rise three days later"** (Mk. 9:31; see Mt. 17:22, 23; Lk. 9:44b). Mark's account has "three days *later,*" while Matthew's has "*on*

the third day." To many of us, the two terms have different meanings—but they did not to the Jews. Keep this in mind when we
study Jesus' three days in the tomb.

According to Luke's account, He prefaced His announcement
by saying, **"Let these words sink into your ears"** (Lk. 9:44a). This
is a graphic way of saying, "Listen and think about it! Listen and
remember what I say! Listen and understand!" Hearing words
is not the same as listening. Anytime the Lord speaks, we need
to let His words *sink* into our ears and minds, so that they will
find expression in our lives.

The disciples were **deeply grieved** (Mt. 17:23) by Jesus'
words, but once more **they did not understand this statement**
(Mk. 9:32a). They did not understand the statement about His
death because the idea of the Messiah dying went contrary to
their Messianic hopes. They did not understand the statement
about His resurrection because that concept was contrary to their
experience (see Mk. 9:10).

The apostles still had in mind a physical, earthly, political
kingdom. Shortly after the announcement about Jesus' death,
the apostles started arguing about who would be greatest in the
kingdom (see Lk. 9:45, 46). For an example of how Jesus' teaching on His death confused other Jews who possessed the same
concepts as the apostles, see John 12:33, 34.

Though the Twelve did not understand Christ, **they were
afraid to ask Him** for additional explanation (Mk. 9:32b). Maybe
they were afraid because they thought their questions would
be perceived as unbelief. Maybe they were afraid of being reprimanded as Peter had been (Mt. 16:23). Maybe they were just
hesitant to expose their ignorance. The only way to gain new
knowledge is to acknowledge ignorance. Such an admission is
painful, but it is necessary.

Luke's account of this incident adds a puzzling detail: . . .
**they did not understand this statement, *and it was concealed
from them* so that they would not perceive it** . . . (Lk. 9:45;
emphasis added). Who or what concealed the meaning from
the disciples? The Lord may have concealed the meaning because Jesus' statement would have overwhelmed them if they
had fully comprehended it. Satan may have concealed it; after

563

all, he constantly tries to remove the Word from people's minds (Lk. 8:12). However, Burton Coffman was probably right when he said, "The concealment was not due to the design of God [I would add "or the devil"] but to the limitations of men."[31] Likely, the concealing agent was the apostles' preconception regarding the kingdom.

Whether or not that was the case, the disciples *did* have a hard time accepting what the Lord had to say about His approaching death, burial, and resurrection. An essential quality of discipleship is to accept what the Lord says, even if it disagrees with one's own ideas and reasoning. Paul stressed the futility of depending on human wisdom when he wrote,

> For the word of the cross is foolishness to those who are perishing, but to us who are being saved it is the power of God. For it is written, "I will destroy the wisdom of the wise, and the cleverness of the clever I will set aside." Where is the wise man? Where is the scribe? Where is the debater of this age? Has not God made foolish the wisdom of the world? For since in the wisdom of God the world through its wisdom did not come to know God, God was well-pleased through the foolishness of the message preached to save those who believe (1 Cor. 1:18–21).

A true disciple does not rely on human reasoning (Prov. 3:5), but on divine revelation (2 Tim. 3:16, 17).

QUESTION ABOUT THE TEMPLE TAX
(MT. 17:24–27)

[24]When they came to Capernaum, those who collected the two-drachma tax came to Peter and said, "Does your teacher not pay the two-drachma tax?" [25]He said, "Yes." And when he came into the house, Jesus spoke to him first, saying, "What do you think, Simon? From whom do the kings of the earth collect

---

[31]Coffman, 187.

customs or poll-tax, from their sons or from strangers?" ²⁶When
Peter said, "From strangers," Jesus said to him, "Then the sons
are exempt. ²⁷However, so that we do not offend them, go to
the sea and throw in a hook, and take the first fish that comes
up; and when you open its mouth, you will find a shekel. Take
that and give it to them for you and Me."

Only Matthew, the former tax collector, recorded the temple-
tax incident. As Jesus and His troupe traveled in Galilee, they came
to the city that had served as the Lord's headquarters during His
ministry in that province. **When they came to Capernaum, those
who collected the two-drachma tax came to Peter and said,
"Does your teacher not pay the two-drachma tax?"** (Mt. 17:24).
The drachma was a Greek coin roughly equivalent to the Roman
denarius we have encountered in our studies (see Lk. 7:41; Jn.
6:7)—a day's wages for a common laborer (see Mt. 20:2).

In the original text, the word "tax" is not found in verse 24,
but Jesus did use the term in verse 25. The tax in question was
the temple tax. The law of Moses required that every Jewish
male, twenty years or older, pay half a shekel for temple upkeep
and worship expenses (Ex. 30:11–16; see 2 Kings 12:12; 2 Chron.
24:5–9; Neh. 10:32). The shekel was roughly equivalent to four
denarii or four drachma, so half a shekel was two denarii or two
drachma.

The tax collectors in this passage would have been Jewish
temple officials rather than Roman tax collectors. The temple tax
was ordinarily paid in the spring, and it was now early fall; but
for months Christ had been absent from Capernaum (His "place
of residence"). Now the tax gatherers heard He was back in town
and came looking for Him. Maybe they had a quota to fill, but
they were probably more interested in collecting incriminating
evidence against Him.

Christ often stayed at Peter's house when He was in
Capernaum (see Mk. 1:29, 30; 2:1), so the officials went there to
find Him. Encountering Peter outside the house, they asked,
"Does your teacher not pay the two-drachma tax?" (Mt. 17:24b).
(Since Peter **came into the house** [Mt. 17:25] after talking to the
officials, he must have been outside the house during the con-

versation.) Never at a loss for words, the apostle said, **"Yes"** (Mt. 17:25a). Maybe he said "Yes" because the Lord had paid the tax in previous years. Maybe he gave that answer because he knew that Christ taught obedience to the Law. Perhaps, as was often the case with Peter, he just said the first thing that came to his mind.

Whatever Peter's reason, the Lord, who knew what had happened, saw this as an opportunity to teach a vital lesson. "When [the apostle] came into the house," before he had a chance to relate the incident, **Jesus spoke to him first, saying, "What do you think, Simon? From whom do the kings of the earth collect customs or poll-tax, from their sons or from strangers?"** (Mt. 17:25b). Peter had no trouble with that question. He answered, **"From strangers"** (Mt. 17:26a). Jesus replied, **"Then the sons are exempt"** (Mt. 17:26b). The obvious implication is that, as the Son of the King (God), Christ was exempt from the tax on His Father's house (the temple). Jesus was not necessarily saying that Peter was also exempt; but whether or not the apostle was exempt, Christ's conclusion was the same: The tax should still be paid. To put it another way, the Lord had *a right* not to pay the tax— but Peter needed to learn that a disciple does not insist on his rights if, by so doing, he hurts his Master's cause.

Jesus continued, **"However, so that we do not offend them, go to the sea and throw in a hook, and take the first fish that comes up; and when you open its mouth, you will find a shekel. Take that and give it to them for you and Me"** (Mt. 17:27). Being a commercial fisherman, Peter normally used a net (Mt. 4:18), but a net caught hundreds of fish. All that Peter needed on this occasion was one fish. The Greek word translated "shekel" is στατήρ (*stater*), a Greek coin worth four drachma— exactly enough to pay the temple tax for two men. This is the only place this four-drachma coin is mentioned in the New Testament. Richard Rogers wrote, "What a Paradox! A King too poverty-stricken to pay the annual temple tax at only a half-shekel."[32]

---

[32]Richard Rogers, *Behold Your King (Book of Matthew)* (Lubbock, Tex.: Sunset Study Series, n.d.), 22.

The miracle proposed by Christ was unique. It is the only one that involved money, it is the only one that benefited Him personally, it is the only miraculous incident of which we are not told the outcome, and it is without a doubt the strangest of the Lord's miracles. Surely, we see a touch of humor in Jesus' words as He told *a fisherman*—one who often opened his *mouth* without thinking—to find the solution to his problem in *a fish's mouth*.

We must not let the novelty of the miracle obscure the key words in Jesus' instructions: "So that we do not offend them." The Greek word σκανδαλίζω (*skandalizo*), translated "offend," is the word from which we get "scandalize." Christ was not concerned about offending the officials' sensibilities; He *was* concerned about doing anything that could cast an unfavorable light on His ministry. He wanted Peter to understand that doing what is right takes precedence over insisting on one's rights.

This thought is a "hard saying" (Jn. 6:60; KJV). It is natural to insist on our rights. We demand that we get what we deserve. We oppose any who would deprive us of that which is rightfully ours. Jesus calls us to rise above that natural impulse, to consider always how our actions will affect His cause. To use the terminology of our text, if insisting on our rights would create "a scandal" regarding Christ's cause, we should forgo our rights. Paul wrote two lengthy discussions on the need to give up one's rights under certain circumstances (Rom. 14; 1 Cor. 8—10).

Jesus did not merely teach this kind of self-forgetfulness; He lived it. We saw a demonstration of this at the beginning of His earthly ministry. He had a right not to be baptized by John because He was "without sin" (Heb. 4:15; see Mt. 3:14), but He gave up that right "to fulfill all righteousness" (Mt. 3:15). We will see a demonstration at the end of Christ's ministry. He had a right not to die because He had done nothing worthy of death (Lk. 23:4), but He gave up that right so that we might be saved (1 Cor. 15:3).

A true disciple is not so much concerned about his rights as he is concerned about seeing the Lord glorified and seeing His cause prosper.

TEACHING ON THE NECESSITY OF CHILDLIKENESS
(MT. 18:1–14; MK. 9:33–50; LK. 9:46–50)

Matthew 18:1–14

[1]At that time the disciples came to Jesus and said, "Who then is greatest in the kingdom of heaven?" [2]And He called a child to Himself and set him before them, [3]and said, "Truly I say to you, unless you are converted and become like children, you will not enter the kingdom of heaven. [4]Whoever then humbles himself as this child, he is the greatest in the kingdom of heaven. [5]And whoever receives one such child in My name receives Me; [6]but whoever causes one of these little ones who believe in Me to stumble, it would be better for him to have a heavy millstone hung around his neck, and to be drowned in the depth of the sea.

[7]"Woe to the world because of its stumbling blocks! For it is inevitable that stumbling blocks come; but woe to that man through whom the stumbling block comes!

[8]"If your hand or your foot causes you to stumble, cut it off and throw it from you; it is better for you to enter life crippled or lame, than to have two hands or two feet and be cast into the eternal fire. [9]If your eye causes you to stumble, pluck it out and throw it from you. It is better for you to enter life with one eye, than to have two eyes and be cast into the fiery hell.

[10]"See that you do not despise one of these little ones, for I say to you that their angels in heaven continually see the face of My Father who is in heaven. [11][For the Son of Man has come to save that which was lost.]

[12]"What do you think? If any man has a hundred sheep, and one of them has gone astray, does he not leave the ninety-nine on the mountains and go and search for the one that is straying? [13]If it turns out that he finds it, truly I say to you, he rejoices over it more than over the ninety-nine which have not gone astray. [14]So it is not the will of your Father who is in heaven that one of these little ones perish."

Mark 9:33–50

[33]They came to Capernaum; and when He was in the house, He began to question them, "What were you discussing on the way?" [34]But they kept silent, for on the way they had discussed with one another which of them was the greatest. [35]Sitting down, He called the twelve and said to them, "If anyone wants to be first, he shall be last of all and servant of all." [36]Taking a child, He set him before them, and taking him in His arms, He said to them, [37]"Whoever receives one child like this in My name receives Me; and whoever receives Me does not receive Me, but Him who sent Me."

[38]John said to Him, "Teacher, we saw someone casting out demons in Your name, and we tried to prevent him because he was not following us." [39]But Jesus said, "Do not hinder him, for there is no one who will perform a miracle in My name, and be able soon afterward to speak evil of Me. [40]For he who is not against us is for us. [41]For whoever gives you a cup of water to drink because of your name as followers of Christ, truly I say to you, he will not lose his reward.

[42]"Whoever causes one of these little ones who believe to stumble, it would be better for him if, with a heavy millstone hung around his neck, he had been cast into the sea. [43]If your hand causes you to stumble, cut it off; it is better for you to enter life crippled, than, having your two hands, to go into hell, into the unquenchable fire, [44][where their worm does not die, and the fire is not quenched.] [45]If your foot causes you to stumble, cut it off; it is better for you to enter life lame, than, having your two feet, to be cast into hell, [46][where their worm does not die, and the fire is not quenched.] [47]If your eye causes you to stumble, throw it out; it is better for you to enter the kingdom of God with one eye, than, having two eyes, to be cast into hell, [48]where their worm does not die, and the fire is not quenched.

[49]"For everyone will be salted with fire. [50]Salt is good; but if the salt becomes unsalty, with what will you make it salty again? Have salt in yourselves, and be at peace with one another."

Luke 9:46–50

⁴⁶**An argument started among them as to which of them might be the greatest.** ⁴⁷**But Jesus, knowing what they were thinking in their heart, took a child and stood him by His side,** ⁴⁸**and said to them, "Whoever receives this child in My name receives Me, and whoever receives Me receives Him who sent Me; for the one who is least among all of you, this is the one who is great."**

⁴⁹**John answered and said, "Master, we saw someone casting out demons in Your name; and we tried to prevent him because he does not follow along with us."** ⁵⁰**But Jesus said to him, "Do not hinder him; for he who is not against you is for you."**

Jesus had identified His Messianic kingdom as the church He would build (Mt. 16:18, 19). He constantly tried to impress on His followers that His kingdom would be spiritual—not earthly, fleshly, or political. It would be located in the hearts of men, not on a map. His disciples totally failed to comprehend this truth. Their lack of understanding is evident in the next recorded incident.

One day, as they traveled, the Twelve began to argue concerning **which of them might be the greatest "in the kingdom"** (Lk. 9:46; see Mt. 18:1; Mk. 9:34). Their argument might have been prompted by Jesus' promise to Peter (Mt. 16:19) or by the Lord's taking only Peter, James, and John up on the mountain with Him (Mt. 17:1). We are given no details, but we have no reason to exclude any of the apostles from the argument—even Peter, James, and John, who probably assumed that the Lord was considering them for top positions in an earthly kingdom. (Look ahead to Mt. 20:21; Mk. 10:37.)

When they reached their destination, Christ asked them, **"What were you discussing on the way?"** (Mk. 9:33). (They had evidently done more traveling around Galilee, after which they returned to Capernaum.) At first, the disciples did not answer (Mk. 9:34), likely because of embarrassment. However, when it became obvious that Jesus knew exactly what they had been discussing (Lk. 9:47), they asked, **"Who then *is* greatest in the kingdom of heaven?"** (Mt. 18:1; emphasis added).

J. W. McGarvey wrote, "Had Jesus wished to teach the primacy of Peter, no better opportunity could have been found."[33] Instead, Christ used the occasion to teach a most needed lesson: **"If anyone wants to be first, he shall be last of all and servant of all"; "for the one who is least among all of you, this is the one who is great"** (Mk. 9:35; Lk. 9:48b).

To get across this message, the Master Teacher used a living visual aid: **He called a child to Himself and set him before them** (Mt. 18:2). **Taking** [the child] **in His arms** (Mk. 9:36), He said to His disciples, **"Truly I say to you, unless you are converted and become like children, you will not enter the kingdom of heaven. Whoever then humbles himself as this child, he is the greatest in the kingdom of heaven"** (Mt. 18:3, 4).

Many truths can be drawn from Christ's words. For instance, they expose the error of the doctrine of Total Hereditary Depravity: the belief that a baby is born "totally depraved" because of Adam's sin. Jesus said that we must become *like* children to enter the kingdom. Again, the Lord's words show the fallacy of so-called infant baptism. A child is ready "as is" for the kingdom and requires no man-made ceremony to make him so.

Christ, however, was focusing on one truth in His illustration: the need for humility, a willingness to serve instead of being served. True humility is found in the quality discussed previously: self-forgetfulness. Generally speaking, small children do not classify themselves by meaningless terms such as "great" or "insignificant." In that day, children were near the bottom of the social scale. Today they are often the first to be served, but in that day, they were generally the last. The Lord was trying to get His disciples to see that in order to be of any value in His kingdom, they had to be ready to assume a humble role. He continued to do this in the days that followed. Jesus often warned the disciples against self-seeking ambition (see Mt. 23:8–12; Lk. 22:24–27).

The need for humility is taught throughout the New Testament. (See Lk. 14:11; 18:14; Acts 20:19; Eph. 4:2; Col. 3:12; Jas. 4:6; 1 Pet. 3:8.) Paul said, "Do nothing from selfishness . . . , but with

---

[33]McGarvey and Pendleton, 430–31.

humility of mind regard one another as more important than yourselves" (Phil. 2:3). Peter wrote,

> . . . all of you, clothe yourselves with humility toward one another, for God is opposed to the proud, but gives grace to the humble.
>
> Therefore humble yourselves under the mighty hand of God, that He may exalt you at the proper time (1 Pet. 5:5, 6).

To be first, we must be last. To be great, we must be least. These principles were hard for a first-century audience to understand, much less to accept. They are doubly hard today in today's prideful world of self-aggrandizement and self-promotion. Christ's words should prompt a prayer in our hearts: "God, help me to be more humble. Help me to be more childlike."

Jesus' visual demonstration introduced a discourse with a variety of teachings that related directly or indirectly to children (Mt. 18:5–14; especially note vv. 5, 6, 10, and 14). As the message progressed, the term "little ones" was expanded to include not only children, but also disciples with a childlike faith (perhaps with special emphasis on new converts). Matthew 18:6 speaks of little ones *who believe*. Mark 9:37 seems to equate welcoming a little one with giving *a disciple* a cup of cold water. The reference to the sheep *going astray* in Matthew 18:12, 13 seems to have special reference to **little ones** (Mt. 18:14). Most of the lessons are equally applicable to small children and to childlike disciples.

Christ began this part of His sermon by saying that "little ones" should be welcomed: **"Whoever receives one child like this in My name receives Me; and whoever receives Me does not receive Me, but Him who sent Me"** (Mk. 9:37). Jesus had previously used the same words to refer to people receiving His disciples (Mt. 10:40; see also Jn. 13:20).

Little children are special. The potential in each—for good or for ill—is great. We should never think of them as nuisances to be tolerated. We should love them, nurture them, and try to protect them. We should see them as opportunity personified.

We should do all we can to teach and train them in the right way (Prov. 22:6).

Jesus' words about "receiving" people and the use of the phrase "in My name" reminded John of a recent incident during which he had *not* received someone who was doing something in Christ's name. As students sometimes do, he interrupted his Teacher: **"Master, we saw someone casting out demons in Your name; and we tried to prevent him because he does not follow along with us"** (Lk. 9:49).

Who was the "someone" to whom John referred? The text does not say. Since that "someone" was evidently casting out demons, apparently he was not a fake—as were some who later tried to use Jesus' name in exorcism (Acts 19:13–16). Keep in mind that Jesus had disciples other than the Twelve (Lk. 6:13) and that the apostles were not the only ones to whom the Lord imparted miraculous powers during His earthly ministry (see Lk. 10:1, 17).

The key words in John's statement are probably these: ". . . he does not follow along *with us.*" In other words, he was not one of the twelve apostles who were traveling with the Lord at that time. Remember that the setting of this discussion was the jealous ambition of the apostles. The Twelve may have been envious of another disciple of Jesus who, though not an apostle, had the faith to do what they had been unable to do a short time before (Mt. 17:16, 19, 20).

Jesus answered John, **"Do not hinder him, for there is no one who will perform a miracle in My name, and be able soon afterward to speak evil of Me. For he who is not against us is for us"** (Mk. 9:39, 40). The Lord's main thought seems clear. He was saying, in effect, "We need all the friends we can get. So many are speaking evil of Me today that it is refreshing to know that at least one will not."

Unfortunately, some use verse 40—"For he who is not against us is for us"—to teach that Christ accepts anyone who claims to be "for" Him and does good deeds in His name. They insist, therefore, that we also should accept individuals like these—whether or not they obey Jesus' commandments. That interpretation would make the verse contradict Matthew 7:21–23:

Not everyone who says to Me, "Lord, Lord," will enter the kingdom of heaven, but he who does the will of My Father who is in heaven will enter. Many will say to Me on that day, "Lord, Lord, did we not prophesy in Your name, *and in Your name cast out demons,* and in Your name perform many miracles?" And then I will declare to them, "I never knew you; depart from Me, you who practice lawlessness." (Emphasis added.)

Mark 9:40 is the other side of a truth announced earlier by the Lord: "He who is not with Me is against Me; and he who does not gather with Me scatters" (Mt. 12:30). When the two passages are placed side by side, they declare the impossibility of being neutral about Jesus.

In Mark 9:41 Jesus returned to the theme of welcoming/receiving, except that He now applied the topic to His apostles: **"For whoever gives you a cup of water to drink because of your name as followers of Christ, truly I say to you, he will not lose his reward"** (Mk. 9:41). When the Lord made that statement, He was not packing all the requirements for salvation into a single verse and a single act. If He were, we could dispense with the invitation to believe and be baptized (Mk. 16:15, 16; Gal. 3:26, 27); we could just hand people cups of water and urge them to give the water to Christians. Jesus was simply stating that God is pleased when people encourage those who wear His name.

Christ then returned to the theme of the "little ones": **"But whoever causes one of these little ones who believe in Me to stumble, it would be better for him to have a heavy millstone hung around his neck, and to be drowned in the depth of the sea"** (Mt. 18:6; see Mk. 9:42). The Greek word μύλος (*mulos*), translated "millstone," referred to a millstone so huge that it had to be turned by a donkey. To be dragged under the sea by such a weight would be a tragedy, but not as great a tragedy as that which awaits those who cause "little ones" to stumble.

The teaching is the same whether we apply the term "little ones" to children, new converts, or Christians in general. We should strive never to do anything that would influence another to do wrong (see Rom. 14:13, 21). A **woe** is pronounced on the man through whom stumbling comes (Mt. 18:7).

Jesus' words call for self-examination: Are we harboring anything that would harm us and others? If so, it should be ripped from our lives:

> **If your hand causes you to stumble, cut it off; it is better for you to enter life crippled, than, having your two hands, to go into hell, into the unquenchable fire. . . . If your foot causes you to stumble, cut it off; it is better for you to enter life lame, than, having your two feet, to be cast into hell. . . . If your eye causes you to stumble, throw it out; it is better for you to enter the kingdom of God with one eye, than, having two eyes, to be cast into hell, where their worm does not die, and the fire is not quenched** (Mk. 9:43–48).

Jesus had used similar terminology earlier in the Sermon on the Mount (see Mt. 5:27–30). The Lord was not encouraging the crippling of the body, but the chastening of the soul. Anything that encourages evil in our lives—no matter how precious—must be ruthlessly expunged.

That Jesus used figurative language to describe hell, or Gehenna (Gk: γέενναν, *geennan*) is obvious. Literal worms do not live in literal fire. It is generally agreed that the figures of the worms (maggots) and fire are derived from the garbage dump south of Jerusalem called the valley of Hinnom, or Ben-hinnom (see 2 Chron. 28:3; 33:6; Neh. 11:30; Jer. 7:31, 32; 19:2, 6; 32:35). The figure of worms probably refers to the eternal gnawing of a guilty conscience (Lk. 16:25–28), while the figure of fire refers to the agony of being eternally separated from God's presence (2 Thess. 1:9).

In speaking of hell, Jesus added these unexpected words: **"For everyone will be salted with fire"** (Mk. 9:49). He had earlier used the figure of salt (Mt. 5:13) to refer to a *preserving* agent. The idea of preservation is probably also in view here. The ungodly shall be "preserved" in the fires of hell; that is, they shall never die. The assurance of being preserved in heaven is a glorious thought; the idea of being preserved in hell is a horror beyond compare.

In the next verse, Christ gave another twist to the salt imagery: **"Salt is good; but if the salt becomes unsalty, with what will you make it salty again? Have salt in yourselves, and be at peace with one another"** (Mk. 9:50). The Lord was repeating the point made in the Sermon on the Mount (Mt. 5:13), with the addition of this application: If they continued to argue among themselves (Lk. 9:46), they would lose their saltiness; they could not be "the salt of the earth." They needed to learn to "be at peace with one another," even as we need to be at peace with one another.

Jesus returned to His theme of "little ones": **"See that you do not despise one of these little ones, for I say to you that their angels in heaven continually see the face of My Father who is in heaven"** (Mt. 18:10). The Greek word καταφρονέω (*kataphroneo*), translated "despise," combines the words for "down" (κατά, *kata*) and "mind" (φρονέω, *phroneo*). It signifies what we mean by "looking down" on another individual. We should never look down on children . . . or a new convert . . . or any other child of God. Each is precious in God's sight.

The latter part of verse 10 is both fascinating and tantalizing: "their angels in heaven continually see the face of My Father who is in heaven." These few words have prompted the reams that have been written about "guardian angels." The Bible does teach that angels are "ministering spirits, sent out to render service for the sake of those who will inherit salvation" (Heb. 1:14). Further, to quote McGarvey, this verse suggests that "the ministration of angels is not only general but special, certain angels being entrusted with the care of certain individuals."[34] Anything beyond those general truths is speculation.

The fact that children die every day, sometimes in hideous ways, should be enough to convince us that "guardian angels" are not authorized to set aside God's natural laws. In fact, the general tenor of God's Word would suggest that their primary concern is not physical health, but spiritual well-being. We would

---

[34]Ibid., 434.

probably do well to consider Matthew 18:10 as simply another proof that God cares for those who are His and stop there (1 Pet. 5:7; see Ezek. 34:12).

The Lord concluded His teaching on "little ones" with an illustration familiar to most of us:

> **What do you think? If any man has a hundred sheep, and one of them has gone astray, does he not leave the ninety-nine on the mountains and go and search for the one that is straying? If it turns out that he finds it, truly I say to you, he rejoices over it more than over the ninety-nine which have not gone astray. So it is not the will of your Father who is in heaven that one of these little ones perish** (Mt. 18:12–14).

Jesus later coupled the figure of a lost sheep with the figures of a lost coin and a lost boy to produce one of the most memorable chapters in the Bible, Luke 15. His point here is the same as it is there: God is "not willing that any should perish, but that all should come to repentance" (2 Pet. 3:9; KJV).

Again, application can be made to a variety of "little ones." Little children grow up and go astray in the mountains of sin (Rom. 3:23); we need to bring them gently back to the Lord. A new convert—or an old convert—can "drift away" from the faith (Heb. 2:1); we need to "restore such a one in a spirit of gentleness" (Gal. 6:1; see Jas. 5:19, 20).

FINAL TEACHING IN GALILEE: PROBLEMS BETWEEN BRETHREN (MT. 18:15–35)

[15]"If your brother sins, go and show him his fault in private; if he listens to you, you have won your brother. [16]But if he does not listen to you, take one or two more with you, so that by the mouth of two or three witnesses every fact may be confirmed. [17]If he refuses to listen to them, tell it to the church; and if he refuses to listen even to the church, let him be to you as a Gentile and a tax collector. [18]Truly I say to you, whatever you bind

on earth shall have been bound in heaven; and whatever you loose on earth shall have been loosed in heaven.

[19]"Again I say to you, that if two of you agree on earth about anything that they may ask, it shall be done for them by My Father who is in heaven. [20]For where two or three have gathered together in My name, I am there in their midst."

[21]Then Peter came and said to Him, "Lord, how often shall my brother sin against me and I forgive him? Up to seven times?" [22]Jesus said to him, "I do not say to you, up to seven times, but up to seventy times seven.

[23]"For this reason the kingdom of heaven may be compared to a king who wished to settle accounts with his slaves. [24]When he had begun to settle them, one who owed him ten thousand talents was brought to him. [25]But since he did not have the means to repay, his lord commanded him to be sold, along with his wife and children and all that he had, and repayment to be made. [26]So the slave fell to the ground and prostrated himself before him, saying, 'Have patience with me and I will repay you everything.' [27]And the lord of that slave felt compassion and released him and forgave him the debt. [28]But that slave went out and found one of his fellow slaves who owed him a hundred denarii; and he seized him and began to choke him, saying, 'Pay back what you owe.' [29]So his fellow slave fell to the ground and began to plead with him, saying, 'Have patience with me and I will repay you.' [30]But he was unwilling and went and threw him in prison until he should pay back what was owed. [31]So when his fellow slaves saw what had happened, they were deeply grieved and came and reported to their lord all that had happened. [32]Then summoning him, his lord said to him, 'You wicked slave, I forgave you all that debt because you pleaded with me. [33]Should you not also have had mercy on your fellow slave, in the same way that I had mercy on you?' [34]And his lord, moved with anger, handed him over to the torturers until he should repay all that was owed him. [35]My heavenly Father will also do the same to you, if each of you does not forgive his brother from your heart."

Jesus' final discourse in Galilee was prompted by a heated

argument among the disciples concerning who would be great-est in the kingdom (Mt. 18:1; Lk. 9:46). The first part of Jesus' response (that we just studied) had to do with being childlike; the second part focused on getting along with others.

Jesus had talked about sinning against others (Mt. 18:6; Mk. 9:42). Now He was ready to explore the other side of the ques-tion: What if His hearers were sinned against? The key verse is Matthew 18:15: **"If your brother sins, go and show him his fault in private; if he listens to you, you have won your brother."**

The KJV has "if thy brother shall trespass *against thee*" (emphasis added). The last phrase, though not found in the bet-ter manuscripts, conveys the focus of this section. (A compara-ble phrase is found in v. 21.) Understand, however, that since the phrase is not found in verse 15, the passage has wider applica-tion than personal slight. Anytime a brother is enmeshed in sin that can damn his soul, each of us has a responsibility to go to him in love.

In the Sermon on the Mount, Jesus explained what a Chris-tian should do if he knows a brother has something against him: He is to go to him (Mt. 5:23, 24). Here Jesus was discussing what a Christian should do if he has something against a brother: He is to go to him. If both parties in a dispute act like Christians, they will both go . . . and will meet each other somewhere in the middle. However, if one of the parties does not do what he should, that does not excuse the other: Whether a person is the offended or the offender, he is to go to the other person and try to work it out.

Now underline the phrase "in private"; the original text has "between you and him alone" (see the KJV). When someone does something that hurts a Christian, he should not maximize it and publicize it; rather, he should minimize it and localize it. Gayle Oler[35] put it this way: "Before you complain to your husband or wife, your friends or relatives, the elders or the preacher, or even your dog, you should *first* go to that individual."

---

[35]Gayle Oler was the superintendent of Boles Children's Home in Quin-lan, Texas, for many years. This statement was made long ago at the Eastside church of Christ in Midwest City, Oklahoma.

We may object, "But that's hard!" Yes, it is, but it is also necessary. Obedience to this command will defuse most explosive situations. In contrast, if we ignore Christ's instructions—if we do not resolve the matter but share our unhappiness with everyone around us instead—people will begin to take sides. When that happens, great harm is done to the body of Christ.

If a Christian goes with the right attitude to a brother who has sinned against him (Gal. 6:1), he can generally work through the problem—but not always. When that is the case, follow Jesus' instruction on what to do next: **"But if he does not listen to you, take one or two more with you, so that by the mouth of two or three witnesses every fact may be confirmed"** (Mt. 18:16). The need for two or three witnesses is emphasized in both the Old and the New Testaments (Deut. 19:15; 2 Cor. 13:1). The others may add insight regarding what happened previously, they can perhaps facilitate reconciliation, and they can certainly testify later as to what transpired in the meeting. Verse 17 implies that they do not go simply to listen. **"If he refuses to listen to them"** implies that they do some talking and try to work out matters between the estranged parties.

What if taking others does not produce the desired result? Jesus said, "If he refuses to listen to them, **tell it to the church; and if he refuses to listen even to the church, let him be to you as a Gentile and a tax collector"** (Mt. 18:17). Christ's use of the word "church" here is noteworthy. Two chapters before, He promised to build His church (Mt. 16:18). Now He pictured the church as a body of people authorized by the Lord to include or exclude individuals from their fellowship. The word "church" is found in only these two passages in the Gospel Accounts. The first use of the word refers to the universal church. The second use of the word refers to a local congregation.

Jesus did not specify *how* we are to "tell it to the church." Sometimes it would be better to share such information in a special meeting of the members rather than during a public worship assembly. If a congregation has elders, they can determine the best way to handle matters like this.

Especially interesting to us is the phrase "if he refuses to listen even to the church." This could mean that the offender refuses to abide by a decision reached by the church (see 1 Cor. 5:12b). If we take "the church" in its basic meaning (those saved by the blood of Jesus), we would interpret the verse like this: "If he refuses to listen to all His brothers and sisters in Christ who come to him in love. . . ." What if, when a brother sinned, every member of the congregation came to him and begged him in tears to return to the Lord? What kind of impact would this have? An individual would have to be totally sin-hardened to resist a flood of loving entreaties.

What if even that does not bring the sinner back? Then, Jesus said that the church should withdraw its fellowship: "Let him be to you as a Gentile and a tax collector" (Mt. 18:17; see 2 Cor. 2:4–11; 2 Thess. 3:6, 14, 15; 1 Tim. 5:20; and Rom. 16:17). "As a Gentile and a tax collector" is a figurative way of saying "as though he were not a Christian." Other passages make clear that the purpose of this action is not primarily punitive, but rather to bring the individual to his senses and to restore him to the Lord (see 2 Thess. 3:14, 15). Discipline carried out in the right spirit is not an expression of hatred and spite, but of love and concern (see Heb. 12:6).

Disciplining a child is never pleasant, and disciplining a brother or sister in Christ is not a happy occasion. Jesus knew that; so, to encourage His listeners, He assured them that if a congregation carried out these instructions, God would be with them (Mt. 18:18–20).

He said, **"Again I say to you, that if two of you agree on earth about anything that they may ask, it shall be done for them by My Father who is in heaven"** (Mt. 18:19). The promise in this verse is the same as the one made earlier to Peter in the latter part of Matthew 16:19. Since Christ was speaking directly to the apostles in Matthew 18:19, most commentators consider this promise to be primarily to them. Since the context is the subject of church discipline, however, general application can be made to congregational action. If a congregation "binds" as heaven has "bound" (that is, does only what heaven has authorized), then their action is God-pleasing. (This verse should not be taken as an unqualified promise that two Christians can ask for anything they want and God will give it to them [1 Jn. 5:14].)

Verse 20 is a familiar passage: **For where two or three have gathered together in My name, I am there in their midst.** We can and do make general application of this promise, but keep in mind that, in context, Christ was referring to two or three coming together in His name to exercise church discipline.

Jesus' teaching about going to a sinful brother prompted Peter to wonder how often he should forgive such a brother. He asked, **"Lord, how often shall my brother sin against me and I forgive him? Up to seven times?"** (Mt. 18:21). Peter probably thought he was being generous; the rabbis only required three times. Surely he was surprised when Christ replied, **"I do not say to you, up to seven times, but up to seventy times seven"** (Mt. 18:22). In other words, forgiveness should have no limits.

The Lord then related the "parable of the unmerciful servant," in which a servant who, having been forgiven a great debt, refused to forgive a fellow servant a paltry sum (Mt. 18:23–35). The obvious application is that since God has forgiven us so much, we should be willing to forgive others.

The teachings of the Lord in Matthew 18:15–35 are desperately needed in our relationships with our brethren—or with anyone else, for that matter. He enumerated two principles for us to follow: (1) When one of us has something against another, instead of complaining to everyone else, he is to go to that person; and (2) we are not to hold grudges, but be ready to forgive.

We have begun a transition from the end of Christ's Great Galilean Ministry to the beginning of His Closing Ministry in All Parts of Palestine. The Closing Ministry lasted about six months, from the Feast of Tabernacles to the following Passover. **A key verse for this ministry is Luke 9:51: "When the days were approaching for His ascension [encompassing His death, burial, and resurrection], He was determined to go to Jerusalem." The Greek text literally means "as the days were fulfilled for His ascension, he set his face to go to Jerusalem" (see the KJV; emphasis added). We will see Jesus traveling in Judea and Perea, but always His thoughts were centered on His impending death in Jerusalem. The gathering cloud of evil did not deter Him; He marched resolutely toward that dark event.**

APPENDIX

CHARTS, LISTS, AND MAPS

THE FEASTS OF THE JEWS

NAME OF FEAST	HOW IT WAS DESIGNATED	MONTH OBSERVED	MONTH OF SACRED YEAR	MONTH OF CIVIL YEAR	ENGLISH MONTH NEARLY	DURATION OF FEAST	WHERE OBSERVED	MAIN FEATURE OF ITS OBSERVANCE	WHAT IT SIGNIFIED	OTHER NAMES
Passover	Greater Feast	Nisan or Abib	1st	7th	April	1 Week	Jerusalem	Eating paschal lamb	Passing over of death and departure from Egypt	Unleavened Bread
Pentecost	Greater Feast	Sivan	3rd	9th	June	1 Day	Jerusalem	Offering of two loaves, representing first fruits of wheat	Giving the Law at Mt. Sinai	Weeks; First Fruits; Wheat Harvest
Tabernacles	Greater Feast	Tisri or Ethanim	7th	1st	October	1 Week	Jerusalem	Living in booths	Life in the Wilderness	Ingathering

THE FEASTS OF THE JEWS (CONT.)

NAME OF FEAST	HOW IT WAS DESIGNATED	MONTH OBSERVED	MONTH OF SACRED YEAR	MONTH OF CIVIL YEAR	ENGLISH MONTH NEARLY	DURATION OF FEAST	WHERE OBSERVED	MAIN FEATURE OF ITS OBSERVANCE	WHAT IT SIGNIFIED	OTHER NAMES
Trumpets	Lesser Feast	Tisri or Ethanim	7th	1st	October	1 Day	Anywhere	Blowing of trumpets	New Year's Day	
Dedication	Lesser Feast	Chisleu	9th	3rd	December	8 Days	Anywhere	Rejoicing, singing, lighting of lamps and torches	Rededication of temple after re-capturing it from heathen	Lights
Purim	Lesser Feast	Adar	12th	6th	March	2 Days	Anywhere	Reading Book of Esther	Queen Esther's rescue of the Jews	

Reprinted from *Training for Service* by Orrin Root © 1964. Revised by Eleanor Daniel © 1983, Standard Publishing. Used by permission.

JESUS' LINEAGE

As Traced Through Joseph (Matthew 1:6–17)

As Traced Through Mary (Luke 3:23–31)

DAVID
begat
Solomon and Nathan

Solomon begat	Nathan begat
Rehoboam who begat	Mattatha who begat
	Menna who begat
Abijah who begat	Melea who begat
Asa who begat	Eliakim who begat
	Jonam who begat
Jehoshaphat who begat	Joseph who begat
Joram who begat	Judah who begat
	Simeon who begat
Uzziah who begat	Levi who begat
Jotham who begat	Matthat who begat
	Jorim who begat
Ahaz who begat	Eliezer who begat
Hezekiah who begat	Joshua who begat
	Er who begat
Manasseh who begat	Elmadam who begat
Amon who begat	Cosam who begat
	Addi who begat
Josiah who begat	Melchi who begat
Jeconiah who begat	Neri

Shealtiel who married a daughter of Neri and begat
Zerubbabel who begat
Abihud and Rhesa

Abihud begat	Rhesa begat
	Joanan who begat
Eliakim who begat	Joda who begat
	Josech who begat
Azor who begat	Semein who begat
	Mattathias who begat
Zadok who begat	Maath who begat
	Naggai who begat
Achim who begat	Hesli who begat
	Nahum who begat
Eliud who begat	Amos who begat
	Mattathias who begat
Eleazer who begat	Joseph who begat
	Jannai who begat
Matthan who begat	Melchi who begat
	Levi who begat
	Matthat who begat
Jacob who begat	Eli who begat Mary.

Joseph who married Mary (daughter of Eli)
of whom was born
JESUS CHRIST.

(Adapted from *The Divine Biography of Christ*, M. V. Showalter)

JESUS' LINEAGE FROM DAVID

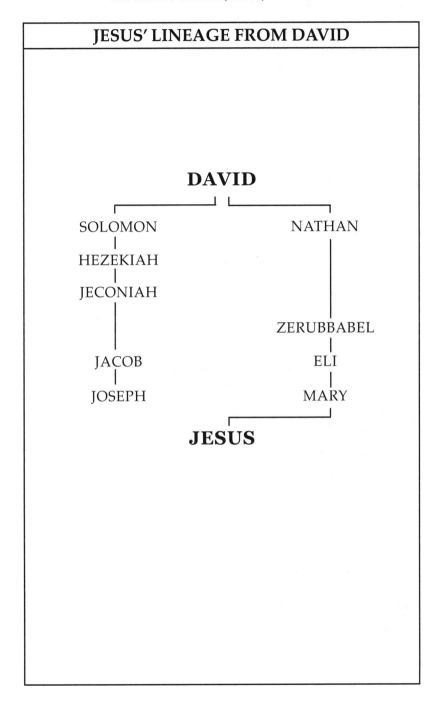

APOSTLES

◆ **Peter**—He was also known as Simon. His name was changed to Cephas, meaning "rock." He conducted his evangelistic work among the Jews and wrote the Books of 1 and 2 Peter. He may also have assisted in the writing of the Gospel of Mark.

◆ **Andrew**—He was Peter's brother and introduced Peter to Jesus (Jn. 1:40–42). These brothers were fishermen from Bethsaida.

◆ **James**—He was John's brother. Both were sons of Zebedee and Salome and worked with their father in Bethsaida. Sometimes called "the Greater," James preached in Jerusalem and Judea. He was beheaded by Herod in A.D. 44, becoming the first apostolic martyr.

◆ **John**—He was James' brother. Both were fishermen, along with their father (Mk. 1:19, 20). Jesus called the two brothers "Sons of Thunder" (Mk. 3:17). John labored among the churches of Asia Minor, especially Ephesus. In A.D. 95, he was exiled to Patmos, where he recorded the Revelation. His writings also include the Gospel of John and the Epistles of 1, 2, and 3 John.

◆ **Philip**—He was from Bethsaida. He told Nathanael about Jesus (Jn. 1:44–46).

◆ **Bartholomew**—He was probably the Nathanael of John's Gospel Account (Jn. 1:44–46). He was from Cana of Galilee.

The apostles were special messengers of the Lord, appointed by Him, who could give personal testimony regarding His life and resurrection. When Judas Iscariot was replaced, the new apostle was to be one who had been with Jesus and His followers throughout His earthly ministry (Acts 1:21). Later, Christ appeared to Paul to qualify him to become the apostle to the Gentiles (see 1 Cor. 15:8). Some information listed here was taken from Frank L. Cox, "The Glorious Company of the Apostles," *The Minister's Monthly* (February 1960): 254.

APOSTLES (cont.)

◆ **Thomas**—He was also called Didymus ("the twin") (Jn. 11:16; 20:24; 21:2). His home was Galilee. He is claimed by Christians in Syria as the founder of the church in that country; he may also have established churches in Persia and India.

◆ **Matthew**—He was also known as Levi, son of Alphaeus (Mt. 9:9; Mk. 2:14). He was from Capernaum and served as a tax collector for the Roman government.

◆ **James**—Sometimes called "the Less," this James was a son of Alphaeus and Mary (Mt. 10:3; 27:56). (Could James and Matthew have been brothers? We do not know.) He was from Galilee and was the writer of the Book of James.

◆ **Thaddaeus**—A son of James, this man was also called Judas or Jude (Mt. 10:3; Lk. 6:16). He was a Galilean.

◆ **Simon the Zealot**—He was also known as the Cananaean, another word for "zealot," transliterated from an Aramaic term. Simon was from Galilee.

◆ **Judas Iscariot**—"Iscariot" probably indicates that he was from the city of Kerioth in Judea. He betrayed Jesus and then committed suicide.

◆ **Matthias**—After Judas Iscariot's death, Matthias was chosen by lot to replace him (Acts 1:26). We know from Acts 1:22 that Matthias had been with Jesus and His disciples "beginning with the baptism of John until the day that He was taken up."

◆ **Paul**—Saul, later Paul, a persecutor of the church, was called to be a special apostle for the Gentiles (Rom. 11:13; 1 Cor. 1:1; 9:1; 15:9; 2 Cor. 12:12; Gal. 1:1; 1 Tim. 2:7). Jesus appeared to him on the road to Damascus. He wrote a vast amount of the New Testament.

THE APOSTLES AS LISTED IN THE SCRIPTURES*

Matthew 10:2–4	Mark 3:16–19	Luke 6:13–16	Acts 1:13
Simon Peter	Simon Peter	Simon Peter	Peter
Andrew	James	Andrew	John
James	John	James	James
John	Andrew	John	Andrew
Philip	Philip	Philip	Philip
Bartholomew	Bartholomew	Bartholomew	Thomas
Thomas	Matthew	Matthew	Bartholomew
Matthew	Thomas	Thomas	Matthew
James the son	James the son	James the son	James the son
of Alphaeus	of Alphaeus	of Alphaeus	of Alphaeus
Thaddaeus	Thaddaeus	Simon the Zealot	Simon the Zealot
Simon the Zealot**	Simon the Zealot	Judas the son	Judas the son
		of James	of James
Judas Iscariot	Judas Iscariot	Judas Iscariot	

*Dotted lines indicate the groupings discussed on pages 213 and 214.
**The Greek uses a different word instead of "Zealot" in Matthew and Mark (see the KJV), but it has the same meaning.

NEW TESTAMENT PROPHECIES THAT CAN BE CHECKED

Prophecy	Prophesied in	Fulfilled
An angel said that Jesus would be great and would be called the Son of God.	Luke 1:32–35	Though born to a poor young woman in a remote village, Jesus is known to many as the great Son of God.
Mary said all generations would call her blessed.	Luke 1:48	Mary is still being called blessed.
Jesus prophesied that few would enter the way that leads to life.	Matthew 7:13, 14	True believers continue to be few.
Jesus prophesied that He is greater than Solomon.	Matthew 12:42	History has proved this to be true.
Jesus prophesied that Hades would not prevail against the church.	Matthew 16:18	His church still exists.
Jesus said that where the gospel was preached the woman who anointed Him would be mentioned.	Matthew 26:13	She is still being mentioned where the gospel is preached.
Jesus said His words would never pass away.	Matthew 24:35	His Word continues throughout the ages.
Jesus said the gospel would be preached in all nations.	Mark 13:10; Luke 24:47	It is being preached in all nations.
Jesus said He would draw all men, meaning people of all nations, to Him.	John 12:32	People of all nations have been drawn to Jesus.

—compiled by Owen Olbricht

The Miracles of Jesus

	Matthew	Mark	Luke	John
Changing water to wine				2:1–11
Casting out a demon in Capernaum		1:23–26	4:33–35	
Healing Peter's mother-in-law	8:14–17	1:29–31	4:38, 39	
Providing a miraculous catch of fish			5:1–11	
Healing a leper	8:2–4	1:40–45	5:12–16	
Healing a paralytic	9:1–8	2:1–12	5:17–26	
Restoring a shriveled hand	12:10–13	3:1–5	6:6–11	
Healing a centurion's servant	8:5–13		7:1–10	
Raising a widow's son			7:11–17	
Stilling a storm	8:23–27	4:37–41	8:22–25	
Healing the Gadarene demoniacs	8:28–34	5:1–20	8:26–39	
Healing a bleeding woman & Jairus' daughter	9:18–26	5:21–43	8:40–56	
Healing two blind men	9:27–31			
Healing a mute man	9:32, 33			
Healing the official's son				4:46–54
Healing a crippled man				5:1–9
Feeding the five thousand	14:15–21	6:35–44	9:10–17	6:1–14

	Matthew	Mark	Luke	John
Walking on water	14:25–33	6:48–52		6:16–21
Feeding the four thousand	15:32–39	8:1–9		
Getting tax money from a fish's mouth	17:24–27			
Casting out a demon	12:22, 23		11:14	
Healing a Canaanite woman's daughter	15:21–28	7:24–30		
Healing a deaf man		7:31–37		
Healing a blind man		8:22–26		
Healing a demon-possessed boy	17:14–18	9:14–29	9:37–43	
Healing a crippled woman			13:11–17	
Healing a man with dropsy			14:1–6	
Healing ten lepers			17:11–19	
Healing a man born blind				9:1–7
Raising Lazarus				11:1–45
Healing two blind men	20:29–34	10:46–52	18:35–43	
Cursing a fig tree	21:18–22	11:12–14		
Restoring Malchus' ear			22:50, 51	
Providing a miraculous catch of fish				21:1–14

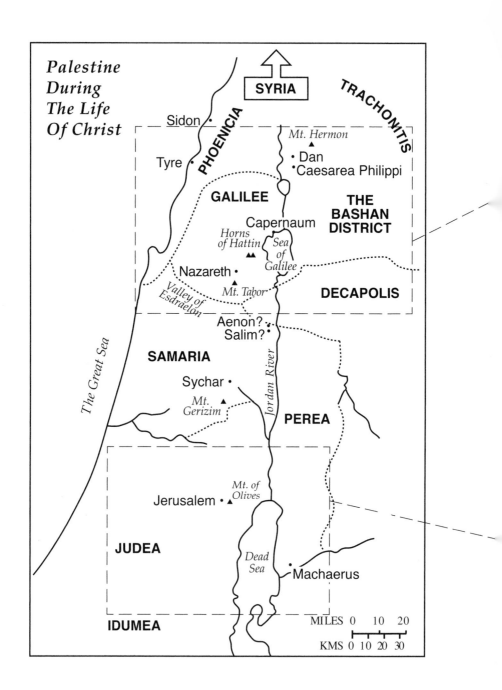

Palestine During The Life Of Christ

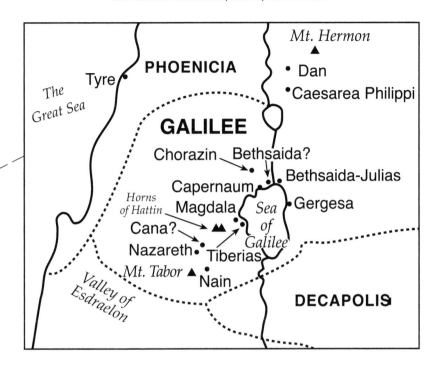

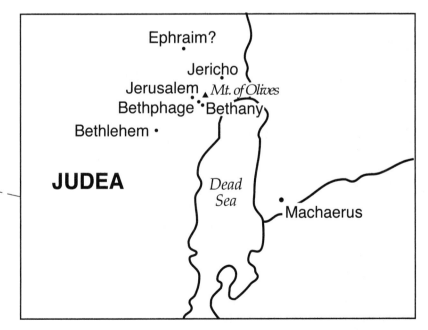

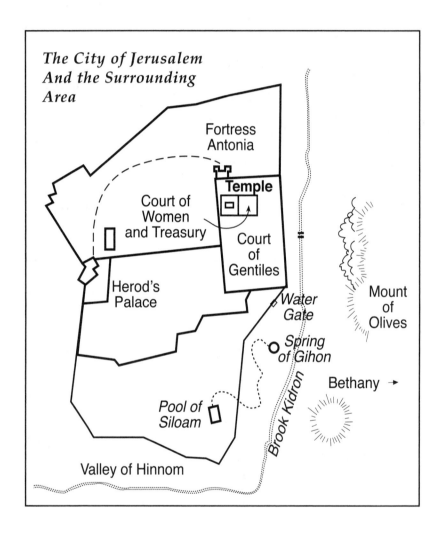

The City of Jerusalem
And the Surrounding
Area

Fortress
Antonia

Temple

Court of
Women
and Treasury

Court
of
Gentiles

Herod's
Palace

Water
Gate

Mount
of
Olives

Spring
of Gihon

Bethany →

Pool of
Siloam

Brook Kidron

Valley of Hinnom

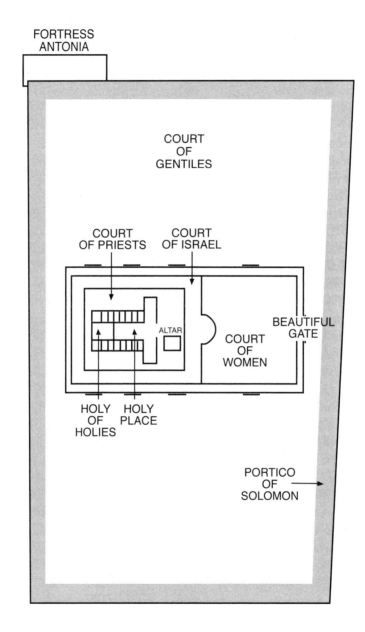

The Temple

FROM THE EDITOR
HAVE YOU HEARD . . .
ABOUT TRUTH FOR TODAY?

What are the big missionary needs of our time? Those who study missionary evangelism point to two paramount needs that are ever present in the mission field.

THE BIG NEEDS OF WORLD EVANGELISM

First, they tell us that educating and maturing the national Christian man so that he can preach to his own people in their own language is of supreme importance. Giving this type of assistance to the national man will help to make our missionary efforts more self-supporting and more enduring. We appreciate one of our own preaching to us, and so do other peoples of the world. When we consider the work "our work," we approach it with greater care and will sacrifice more for it. This principle holds true in all cultures.

Christianity can flourish in any nation and culture, in any time or circumstance, if we will let it. When it is established through national preachers, it is far more likely to grow and blossom in the lives of the national people and not become an effort that is totally dependent upon American support.

After the Restoration Movement began in America, it did not take the early preachers long to realize that they had to teach young men to preach if the movement was really to grow. Thus very early in the history of the Restoration Movement schools were established. Wisdom suggested that route.

Christians should be grateful for every mission effort that is going on, such as campaigns, medical missions, and television presentations. However, we must not overlook the surpassing value of providing educational opportunities overseas that will assist a man in becoming capable of preaching effectively to his own people. This approach is absolutely vital to the ongoing success of the overall missionary work of the church.

Second, those who have researched missionary evangelism tell us that we need to make available biblical literature that provides an understanding of the Bible on the level of the people. Those whom the missionary is seeking to teach need their own copies of the Bible and assistance in understanding the Scriptures. They require guidance so they can grow quickly and accurately in their comprehension of the Bible. (See Acts 8:30, 31.)

When Tex Williams, the former director of World Bible School, was on Harding University's campus sometime ago, he spoke to students about mission work. As a guest lecturer, he told one of the mission classes that the greatest need of Africa is Christian literature. "Without this literature," he said, "they simply cannot become Christians and grow into Christian maturity as they should." There is possibly one exception to this principle. The exception would be places where there is the presence of well-grounded men of faith continually teaching and preaching. This exception obviously applies to only a few places around the world. Even then, biblical literature is needed to support the teaching done.

Let us all consider carefully these two obvious missionary needs. Our efforts must be geared to meeting them. Not to address them is to ignore the clear results of the research that has been done in mission evangelism.

ADDRESSING THESE NEEDS

An effort is currently being made to address both of these big missionary needs. It has been designated the Truth for Today World Mission School (TFTWMS). Started in 1990 as a work under the oversight of the Champions church of Christ in Houston, Texas, it has proven to be a wonderful way to combine three methods of evangelism and thus minister to these supreme needs.

First, TFTWMS is a unique preacher school. An education in the Scriptures is mailed to the national preacher. The work started with 1,460 native preachers enrolled from 110 nations. Now literature is mailed to 37,000 people in 145 nations. These preachers were recommended to the school by World Bible School teachers, missionaries, campaigners, and the national preachers themselves. The school has enjoyed amazing growth.

Second, it is a printed preacher school. Every three months, the men enrolled receive the equivalent of 450 pages of expository studies on the Scriptures. It is believed that the expository type of study crosses cultures better than other types of study. The materials sent give a thorough treatment of the New Testament book or Old Testament book being studied. It is designed to keep the national preacher enrolled in the school until he receives a study of each of the New Testament and Old Testament books, as well as several important special studies.

Picture three normal-sized books that are 150 pages in length, and you have the equivalent of the amount of material that is sent to these men every three months. The entire curriculum calls for these men to receive books that are 150 pages in size, that cover the entire Bible, and that include special studies on leadership, building sermons and Bible lessons, and soul-winning.

Third, in addition to sending expository studies to these men, a flexible, on-site preacher school is sometimes used as a follow-up to the printed material. This on-site school is literally taken to where the men are. Preachers and teachers go into a country and study with the national preachers in that location for two or three weeks. Students are provided with food and a syllabus for the classes they attend. They stay at that location day and night for the entire length of the school. They thus enjoy fellowship with other preaching brethren and are given opportunities to ask questions and receive feedback on problems they are facing.

The printed preacher school and the on-site school answer the big need of giving the national man an opportunity to prepare himself to preach to his own people in their own language. Since this work is accomplished to some extent through the printed page, it also answers the need of providing Christian literature for these teachers and preachers who are in desperate need of it.

THE STRONG POINTS

This unique missionary effort has strong points that should be immediately recognized. First, it provides an education to national men inexpensively. Expository materials can be sent to each of these men every two months in a cost-efficient way. Money for missions is hard to find or raise; what missionary money we have should be used to the maximum. TFTWMS sends an education to hundreds of national men with a small amount of money.

Second, the thrust of this work is to educate national men in their own land. Bringing these men to the United States for an education is very expensive. Often, when the national man tastes of the blessings of America, he does not want to return to his land. It is almost essential that a way be found through which the national preacher can receive an education in his own country.

Third, this effort can reach out to hundreds of national men quickly. All of these men are in need of assistance now! How can we get it to them? This method is one of the most practical ways of immediately getting materials to them.

Fourth, it allows the national man to receive an education over a period of time. Because the education comes in the form of printed matter, they have access to the material for months and even years. These men need time to comprehend and assimilate the studies. The printed page offers them that opportunity. They can read and re-read it. They can easily store it. They can share it with others. It can be retained in their possession for as long as ten to fifteen years.

PICTURING THE EFFECTIVENESS

Picture 37,000 men (and thousands more as the work grows) in 145 nations of the world, going out to preach in their own languages to their own people. They are committed to Christ but have had little teaching upon which to build. Furthermore, these men will never have the opportunity to study in the United States to enable them to preach more accurately and faithfully. They have few books, if any. Picture yourself in this type of situation. What would you need?

Can you imagine how these men would be assisted if they received materials on every Old Testament and New Testament book? Can you imagine how encouraging it would be to them to be able to attend a two- to three-week preacher school in their community? Can you picture them in a school, taking several courses in Bible studies, having fellowship with other preachers, having opportunities to have their questions answered, and getting assistance regarding the problems they are facing? Can you not see how these opportunities would increase their effectiveness in leading souls to Christ and in edifying those who have become Christians?

HELPING THOSE WHO HAVE NOT HEARD

In order to help those who have never heard the gospel to become Christians, a special book was designed in 1998 by TFTWMS. It contains three hundred plus pages on how to become a Christian. The reader of the book is introduced to God, Christ, the Holy Spirit, the Bible, the earthly life of Jesus, the death, burial, and resurrection of Jesus, the establishment of the church, and how one can live for Christ today as a member of His church. Then, in the last two hundred pages of the book, there is a complete copy of the New Testament (NASB).

Thousands of these books have been sent to Africa, the Eastern European countries, India, Latin America, and other areas. The success rate has been very high—almost amazing. The book, 512 pages in length, can be printed and sent to someone in another country for $1.50. It is an attempt to bring together the very message that any Christian would want to provide for someone who has not heard the gospel.

In 2005 a ten-year plan was made to cover a large area of the earth each year with these books. Before printing, the book is culturally adapted for the specific area into which it is being sent and translated into the most prevalent languages of that area.

HOW CAN YOU HELP?

Your help is needed to maintain this missionary effort that has become one of the largest, most cost-effective and productive efforts. Here is a two-part challenge for every Christian:

First, would you challenge the church where you worship and with whom you work to give a one-time contribution to this work? Even a small contribution will go a long way in providing teaching materials and on-site training for these national preachers.

Second, could you give a one-time contribution to this work? This contribution, of course, would have to be above and beyond your regular contribution to the local congregation of which you are a part. We are not asking anyone to interrupt his commitment to the work of the local congregation. The church needs more works, not fewer works. This effort is designed to strengthen every missionary activity and does not seek to detract from any one of them.

You would be surprised how much can be done if we all do a little extra. No one person has a lot of light, but if we put our lights together, we can have a big light that will reach out into all of the world. Would you decide today to dig a little deeper and give a little extra for this wonderful method of world evangelization?

CONTRIBUTIONS NEEDED

Contributions should be made out to Truth for Today World Mission School and sent to 2209 S. Benton, Searcy, AR 72143. Will you assist us in providing study materials for national preachers? This work is under the oversight of the Champions church of Christ in Houston, Texas.

Eddie Cloer